PROGRAM FOR ATHLETIC COACHES' EDUCATION
3rd Edition

PACE

Editors

Vern Seefeldt, Ph.D.
Director and Professor Emeritus

Michael A. Clark, Ph.D.
Assistant Professor

Associate Editor

Eugene W. Brown, Ph.D.
Associate Professor

Institute for the Study of Youth Sports
Department of Kinesiology
Michigan State University
East Lansing, Michigan

COOPER
Publishing
Group

Library of Congress Cataloging in Publication Data:

Seefeldt, Vern, 1933
Clark, Michael A.
Eugene W. Brown

PROGRAM FOR ATHLETIC COACHES' EDUCATION (PACE)
3rd Edition

The Publisher gratefully acknowledges Merrill A. Ritter, M.D., and Marjorie J. Albohm, A.T.,C., for generously allowing the use of illustrations from their book, *Your Injury: A Common Sense Guide to Sports Injuries*, which have been reproduced in Figures 15-1, 15-2, 15-3, 15-4, 15-5, and 15-6.

ISBN: 1-884125-97-2

Printed in the United States of America by Cooper Publishing Group, LLC, P.O. Box 1129, Traverse City, MI 49685.

The Publisher and Author disclaim responsibility for any adverse effects or consequences from the misapplication or injudicious use of the information contained within this text.

Contents

Preface

The content in *Program for Athletic Coaches' Education (PACE)* grew out of a need for practical, relevant information that was appropriate for beginning level interscholastic coaches. In PACE, authors of the various chapters have combined their talents as academicians with their years of experience as coaches, officials, administrators, athletes, and parents of athletes to provide content that addresses the day-to-day problems of coaches.

The PACE manual is written in six sections devoted to the common problems faced by most coaches. Each chapter within a section is written so that its content will stand alone if the reader wishes to pursue a single topic. However, cross references also unify the content for readers who are interested in the comprehensive topic of coaches' education. All tables, illustrations, lists, forms, and references are provided within each chapter, thus eliminating the need to seek appended material elsewhere in the volume.

The PACE manual was field-tested for 13 years, in various settings within the state of Michigan. This formative evaluation included middle school, junior high, and high school coaches; athletic directors; and volunteer youth agency coaches. The suggestions of these clients for the revision of the manual's original content are reflected in this edition.

The content of PACE is generic, rather than sport-specific, in response to the need expressed by athletic directors and principals that their coaches would benefit most from a comprehensive education, in lieu of exposure to the technical information that is commonly associated with a specific sport. Although examples of specific sports are used as illustrations throughout PACE, they are included primarily to impress on coaches that the values and benefits of athletics and their potential negative effects transcend a single sport.

The temptation to provide in-depth information about any area has been avoided. Rather, the reader is informed of the basic principles and procedures associated with a topic and subsequently provided with examples of how this content may be used in a practical setting. Most chapters contain references and suggested readings for coaches who are interested in pursuing additional information on topics covered within the chapter.

The authors are aware that this introductory course in athletic coaching is not a substitute for a program of courses leading to a degree in physical education or coaching. Rather, we hope that an acquaintance with the breadth of information in PACE will stimulate coaches to seek additional opportunities for education through clinics, courses, and supplemental reading. Clearly, coaching young athletes offers endless possibilities for self-improvement. We hope that PACE is the inauguration to a long and enjoyable pattern of using knowledge to enhance the sports experiences of young athletes.

Vern Seefeldt and Michael A. Clark,
Editors

Acknowledgements

The development of the **Program of Athletic Coaches' Education (PACE)** in Michigan was enhanced by the contributions of many individuals. Class members who contributed to its present status by suggesting changes in its content could not be identified here; nevertheless, their insights are greatly appreciated.

Persons whose contributions were more tangible and easily identified are:

Bill Bupp, Assistant Director, Michigan High School Athletic Association, East Lansing, Michigan who provided the title and acronym for the program.

Dale Kutchey, Athletic Director, Waterford School System, Waterford, Michigan who developed the logo for PACE.

The PACE Steering Committee, comprised of the following former and current athletic directors, provided advice about the program content, conducted assessments of the presentations and contributed materials that were incorporated into the chapters:

   Jim Feldkamp, Troy, Michigan
   John Fundukian, Novi Community Schools, Novi, Michigan
   Bob Gershman, Berkley, Michigan
   Tom Healey, Clio Area High School, Clio, Michigan
   George Heitsch, West Bloomfield, Michigan
   Ron Holland, Farmington, Michigan
   Dale Kutchey, Waterford, Michigan
   Chuck Nurek, Auburn Hills, Michigan
   Eric Britner, Ann Arbor, Michigan
   Hugh Matson, Saginaw Michigan

The Executive Director of the Michigan High School Athletic Association, John Roberts, whose vision led to the promotion of educational programs for interscholastic coaches, and

Jerry Cvengros, Associate Director, MHSAA, who chaired the PACE Steering Committee and provided overall supervision and implementation of PACE, and

Nate Hampton and Gina Mazzolini, Assistant Directors, MHSAA, who, along with Jerry Cvengros, articulated the good will of the MHSAA throughout Michigan as a part of their presentations during the PACE courses, and

Sally Fisher, MHSAA, whose competence as secretary, accountant, records manager and registrar has resulted in the efficient implementation of PACE in Michigan.

Coaches Make the Difference

I'm the son of a coach. I was a coach. Every boss I've ever had was a coach. I owe almost everything I am to coaches—the overlooked, underpaid, high school and junior high school coach.

But more importantly, coaches have made athletics the most cost efficient and educationally accountable aspect of secondary school. Nowhere in education do you find it as often as you do in school athletics that teachers are teaching what they want to teach, to students who are learning what they want to learn, and both are willing to work hour after hour on their own time, **after** school, to make certain that everything that can be taught is taught and everything that can be learned is learned.

Coaches may not be the reason students come out for sports, but they're usually the reason students **stay** out for sports. Coaches don't give students ability, but they discover or develop it. Coaches make both the quantitative and qualitative difference.

Coaches are the reason some schools win more than others. Coaches are the reason some schools have better sportsmanship than others. Coaches are the reason some schools have a more educationally based program than others. Coaches make the difference between a program of excesses and a program of education.

Coaches are the critical link in the educational process of athletics. They are the critical link in the sportsmanship at contests, and they are the critical link in the traditions of success which some schools enjoy. It has always been so, and it always will be so.

No one higher up or lower down the organizational chart has more impact on athletes than do coaches. Coaches are the **delivery system** of educational athletics, and they have delivered **well**!

Coaches, nothing that is done in high school athletics in this state is more important than what you do with your athletes day-in and day-out during the season. Thank you for your essential contribution and, please, stay with your high calling. **You** make the difference.

Coach, this is **educational** athletics. Learning is more important than winning. But your attention to the information in this book and your cooperation with the administrators of your school will help your teams be successful.

It is important that you see yourself as the teacher of students more than the coach of a sport. Your support of coaches of other sports and your encouragement that "your athletes" participate in other sports and school activities will help these students receive a complete educational experience that will serve them better than any one-dimensional experience.

John E. Roberts
Executive Director
Michigan High School Athletic Association

Code of Conduct for Interscholastic Coaches

Marty Litherland, Ph.D.

As the subsequent chapters will attest, the coach has a number of responsibilities to a variety of groups. The following Code of Conduct reflects a summary of these responsibilities.

1. The coach shall strive to acquire and implement the most current knowledge of the rules, strategies, and teaching methods of the sport.

2. The coach shall structure a safe environment for the athlete during practices, games, travel, and other team functions.

3. The coach shall work closely with parents and community members to promote an understanding of the role of interscholastic athletics in the total educational experience.

4. The coach shall have the welfare of the athlete as the primary concern when making decisions that relate to the care of injuries, rehabilitation, and return to activity.

5. The coach shall promote effective communication with players, officials, fellow coaches, parents, school administrators, and community members.

6. The coach shall serve as a leader and model in the development of appropriate conduct for the athlete both within and beyond the sport setting.

7. The coach shall use strategies in practice and competition that reflect a standard of fairness to all competitors and that are designed to encourage play within the letter and spirit of the rules.

8. The coach shall keep the concepts of winning and losing in proper perspective.

9. The coach shall enforce team policies with fairness, consistency, and an appreciation for individual differences.

10. The coach shall be knowledgeable of the state association's policies pertaining to the sport and shall ensure that the regulations governing eligibility are upheld.

Contributors

Ray Allen
Department of Kinesiology
Michigan State University
Ray is an assistant professor teaching courses in curriculum and instruction. Ray has an extensive coaching background at all levels of competition. At the high school level, Ray was a head baseball coach for four seasons, winning three conference titles. At the collegiate level, his women's softball teams won one championship in three years, his baseball teams won three championships in five seasons, and his junior varsity women's basketball teams were undefeated in conference play over his three seasons as coach. Ray also served as an assistant football coach for fifteen years. Thirteen years were spent at the collegiate level, including stints as an offensive and defensive coordinator in two different programs. He also was a college assistant coach in a women's basketball program that made three consecutive appearances in the NCAA tournament. Ray is currently involved in his most challenging endeavor—coaching his daughters' basketball and softball teams.

Roderick (Todd) Bartee, Ph.D.
Division of Kinesiology
University of Wyoming
Todd received his doctorate in Health Behavior and Health Promotion from the University of Alabama where he served as a teaching and research assistant. His research focuses on the use of dietary supplements marketed to enhance performance, weight loss or both among adolescent and collegiate athletes at the competitive and recreational levels. Todd is most interested in determining why individuals take dietary supplements so health professionals can begin to develop, implement and evaluate theory based educational and behavior change prevention and intervention strategies.

Rebecca Battista, M.S.
Institute for the Study of Youth Sports
Michigan State University
Rebecca attended Lock Haven University, where she received a bachelor's degree in Health Science in 1992. While at Lock Haven she was a member of the women's lacrosse team. In 1995 she completed a second bachelor's degree from the University of Delaware in Physical Education. After a year spent working in the health and fitness field, she returned to academics and completed a master's degree in exercise physiology from Indiana University. With a research interest in the sport of swimming she became the Physiology Research Assistant for USA Swimming in 1998. Currently she is pursuing her doctorate at Michigan State University in growth and motor development. Throughout her career she has coached youth soccer and girls lacrosse. Her sports background is in field hockey and lacrosse.

Ronda Bokram, M.S., R.D.
Olin Health Center
Michigan State University
Ronda received a Bachelor of Science degree in clinical dietetics from Michigan State University and a Master of Science degree from the University of Wisconsin—Madison. Currently Ronda is on staff in the Health Education Department, Olin Health Center. Her areas of specialty include disordered eating and sports nutrition. She works individually with athletes and counsels athletic teams regarding nutrition. During her leisure time, Ronda has served as the outdoor and indoor soccer coach for her son's and daughter's teams.

Eugene W. Brown, Ph.D.
Institute for the Study of Youth Sports
Michigan State University
Gene Brown's athletic interests date back to high school, where he earned varsity letters in football and baseball. At the State University College at Cortland, New York, Gene participated in football, wrestling, and tennis, and received a bachelor's degree in 1968. He earned a master's degree at the University of Iowa, where he coached the University High School's wrestling and tennis teams. Gene taught at Hope College from 1970-73 and coached the college's soccer team to two Michigan Intercollegiate Athletic Association championships. In 1979, he received his Ph.D. with an emphasis in

biomechanics from the University of Oregon. From 1976-79, he was a member of the faculty of the Department of Physical Education and Athletics at California State University, Los Angeles. Since then, he has been a biomechanist on the faculty of the Department of Kinesiology and the Youth Sports Institute at Michigan State University.

Jody Brylinsky, Ph.D.
Sports Studies Program
Western Michigan University
Jody has been involved in physical education, health education and coaching since 1977. She is currently an associate professor of the graduate level Sports Studies Program at Western Michigan University in Kalamazoo. She has been a proponent of coaching education and accreditation, and most recently she helped author the standards and manual for the National Council for the Accreditation of Coaching Education. Jody has written and presented over 100 papers about coaching education, youth sport, sexual harassment, body image, sportsmanship, gender equity, athlete health and problem-solving skill development. She has served in a variety of leadership positions, most recently as president of the National Association of Physical Education and Sport and, previously to that Jody was vice president for Coaching Enhancement for the National Association of Girls and Women in Sport. In 1999 she was awarded the Midwest Association of College and University Physical Educators' Scholar Lecturer for the Midwest District of AAHPEPD. She also has been recognized as a Project Gold Participant by the United States Olympic Committee and been named as the Michigan Special Olympics Area 16 Volunteer of the Year. She has received numerous grants for research that advances the science of coaching education with various populations.

Mark D. Carlson, M.D.
Professor of Medicine and Vice Chairman for the Department of Medicine
University Hospitals of Cleveland and Case Western Reserve University.
Mark graduated from the Kansas University School of Medicine, received a Master of Arts Degree in Public Policy from Duke University, was a resident in Medicine at Case Western Reserve University, and a Cardiology and Cardiac Electrophysiology Fellow at the Massachusetts General Hospital and Harvard University. He is a practicing cardiac electrophysiologist, evaluating and managing patients with heart rhythm disorders and teaching medical students and post-graduate physician trainees these skills. He has published widely in the medical literature. His research interests include the mechanisms and management of heart rhythm disorders. A long-time sports enthusiast, Mark played organized baseball, football, basketball, and soccer in his youth. As an undergraduate student he served as Equipment Manager for the Kansas State University Wildcats.

Michael A. Clark, Ph.D.
Institute for the Study of Youth Sports
Michigan State University
Originally from Kansas, Mike received three degrees from Michigan State University. Although working briefly in Washington D.C. and the State University of New York system, he spent more than 20 years as a teacher, coach and athletic administrator in Michigan public schools. He joined the Institute for the Study of Youth Sports in 1992 and coordinates outreach programs for the Institute. Mike also has worked on various publications and research efforts—most notably the *PACE Manual, Youth Baseball: A Complete Handbook,* the *National Standards for Athletic Coaches* as well as a field-based study of how youth baseball is actually played. Mike continues his involvement in sports by serving as a basketball coach and track starter as well as by being official scorer for the Lansing Lugnuts—a Class A minor league baseball team. He enjoys running and golf when he has the chance.

James Patrick Corcoran, M.A.
Oak Park YMCA
Oak Park, Illinois
Born and raised in the Chicago suburbs, Jim Corcoran lettered as a high school varsity hockey player and was recruited to play for Saint Scholastica College in Minnesota. A severe injury forced him to limit collegiate competition to the Illinois State University Hockey Club. He also played for the Phoenix Whalers and the Greyhounds, all-star traveling hockey teams in Arizona. Jim has taught baseball in youth camps in Phoenix and has coached in the U.S.A. Hockey organization. Jim has worked as an alcohol and other drug educator in various capacities, including with Ohio State University. His hobbies include golf, tennis, softball, swimming, running, and hockey.

Sean P. Cumming Ph.D.
Institute for the Study of Youth Sports
Michigan State University
Born and raised in Scotland Sean competed in and coached track and field. Sean has recently completed a PhD in Kinesiology at Michigan State University where he worked for four years as a graduate assistant at the Institute. Prior to completing his Ph.D Sean earned an honors degree in Psychology from the University of Edinburgh and a Masters degree in Exercise and Sport Psychology from the University of Exeter. Sean's other interests include American football, exercise, cinema, music, and cooking.

Jerome S. Cvengros, M.S.
Adjunct Professor, Kinesiology Department
Michigan State University
Author of the popular *Youth Football: A Complete Handbook*, Jerry Cvengros participated in high school football, baseball, basketball and track. He attended the University of Wisconsin-Madison on a football scholarship. His 27 years of coaching, teaching, and administration experience include a 13-year term as athletic director at Escanaba High School, where he was principal from 1983 to 1988. Jerry was named Michigan Football Coach of the Year in 1979 and 1981; Upper Peninsula Coach of the Year in 1968, 1972, 1973, and 1979; and Upper Midwest States Football Coach of the Year in 1981. He joined the Michigan High School Athletic Association in 1988, where he is associate director. Jerry's professional accomplishments include service as chair of the National Federation Coaches' Association. He also has been a member of the Federation's rules committee for football. Jerry led the effort to develop the Program for Athletic Coaches' Education (*PACE*) program in Michigan high schools.

Gail M. Dummer, Ph.D.
Department of Kinesiology
Michigan State University
Gail teaches courses in adapted physical activity at Michigan State University and is the author of over 85 publications on adapted physical activity and sport. Her outreach contributions to the profession have focused on competitive swimming for athletes with disabilities. She has served in many capacities within USA Swimming and the United States Olympic Committee, including coach for the 1994 and 1998 USA teams that competed at the IPC World Swimming Championships, assistant announcer for the swimming competition at the 1996 Atlanta Paralympic Games, meet director for the 1996 and 2000 USA Paralympic Swimming Trials, meet director for several USA Swimming Disability Championships, director for training camps for elite swimmers with a disability, and chairperson of the Adapted Swimming Committee. She is a member of the editorial board of the Adapted Physical Activity Quarterly. Gail earned her bachelor's degree at the University of Minnesota in 1972 and her master's and doctoral degrees at the University of California-Berkeley in 1973 and 1978, respectively.

Joey C. Eisenman, Ph.D.
University of Wyoming
Joey Eisenmann is an assistant professor in the Division of Kinesiology and Health at the University of Wyoming. He received his doctorate in kinesiology from Michigan State University where he served as a research assistant at the Institute for the Study of Youth Sports. His research focuses on pediatric exercise physiology and epidemiology. From a physiological standpoint, he is interested in the growth and maturation of the oxygen transport system while his interests in pediatric exercise epidemiology are in the complex relationships between physical activity and cardiovascular disease risk factors during youth and subsequent adult health outcomes.

Martha (Marty) Ewing, Ph.D.
Institute for the Study of Youth Sports
Michigan State University
Marty Ewing grew up in Kansas and earned a bachelor's degree at Kansas State University. Heading north, she taught and coached volleyball at Iowa State University before moving to the Pacific Northwest to coach women's tennis, basketball and volleyball at Washington State University. Marty returned to the Midwest to coach volleyball and tennis at Purdue University and receive a doctorate in sports psychology from the University of Illinois. She joined the faculty of Michigan State University in 1983, where she serves as sports psychologist on the MSU Sports Medicine team.

James Feldkamp, Ed.S.
Director of Athletics
Troy (Michigan) Public Schools
A native of Ohio, Jim Feldkamp has spent most of his life in Michigan, where he played high school basketball, football, and baseball, and ran cross-country. At Eastern Michigan University—where he earned both his bachelor's and master's degrees—Jim played basketball and baseball. He received his specialist's degree at Wayne State University. His coaching experience includes 14 years as a head basketball coach and several years as a baseball and football coach. For more than two decades he has been an athletic director. Jim's hobbies include traveling, golf, and reading.

Deborah Feltz, Ph.D.
Chair, Department of Kinesiology
Michigan State University
New York State native Deborah Feltz pursued undergraduate studies at the State University of New York at Buffalo, then taught physical education to elementary through high school students and coached softball, volleyball and field hockey. She also worked at Plymouth State College in New Hampshire. Moving to Pennsylvania State University, Deborah earned her master's and Ph.D., with specialization in sport psychology. She joined the Department of Health and Physical Education and the Institute for the Study of Youth Sports at Michigan State in 1980. She became chair of the Department of Kinesiology at Michigan State in 1989. A consultant to the United States Olympic Committee's sport psychology program, Deborah enjoys skiing, soccer, softball, and running.

Jeremy Flynn, M.A.
Institute for the Study of Youth Sports
Michigan State University
Jeremy is a recent addition to the Institute for the Study of Youth Sports. He obtained a bachelor's degree in sports management from Taylor University where participated on football team. He is currently finishing his master's degree in sports administration at Michigan State University. His career aspirations are in the field of student-athlete support services and coaching.

Lori Gano-Overway, Ph.D.
Department of Kinesiology
Michigan State University
A Michigan native, Lori Gano-Overway attended college at Hope College where she pursued a degree in Psychology and Business Administration as well as competed in swimming. Following a short period in the business world, Lori returned to sports and academics earning her master's degree with a specialty in sport psychology from Purdue University in 1995. While in Indiana, she also returned to coaching swimming at the youth level. Lori continued her education at Michigan State University where she recently completed her doctorate in sport psychology. Her hobbies include swimming, hiking, and walking her dogs.

John Haubenstricker, Ph.D.
Director, Institute for the Study of Youth Sports
Michigan State University
A native of Michigan, John Haubenstricker lettered in high school football, basketball, baseball and track. He attended Concordia College in River Forest, Illinois where he played football and baseball, officiated basketball, and received his bachelor's degree in 1961. Following a year of graduate study, John returned to Concordia, where he coached football, baseball and wrestling and directed the intramural program for men. He received a master's degree in physical education and child development from the University of Minnesota in 1965 and a doctorate from Michigan State University in 1971, with a specialty in motor development. John joined the MSU faculty in 1973, and served as Coordinator of the Motor Performance Study from 1978-1999. He was appointed Director of the Institute for the Study of Youth Sports in 2000.

Rich Kimball, M.A.
Athletic Director
Northwest (Jackson, Michigan) Public Schools
Rich grew up in Massachusetts, where he lettered in high school football, ice hockey and lacrosse. He continued to play ice hockey and lacrosse at the varsity level as a college student in Boudoin, Maine. After seven years of teaching and

coaching several high school sports, he entered Michigan State University, where he earned a master's degree with a specialty in exercise physiology in 1983. For more than a decade, Rich served as MSU's men's lacrosse coach. He currently directs the comprehensive athletic program of Northwest Public Schools. Rich's hobbies include back-packing and reading.

Wade Lillegard, M.D.
Duluth (Minnesota) Clinic
Born and raised in Montana, Wade Lillegard wrestled and played football in high school, then received his bachelor's degree in Helena. He attended medical school at the Uniform Services Academy of the Health Sciences in Bethesda, Maryland, graduating in 1983. Post-graduate work has included family medicine training at Fort Benning, Georgia and a sports medicine fellowship at Michigan State University. Wade is a sports medicine physician in Duluth, Minnesota. Hobbies include running, weight training, and golf.

Cathy D. Lirgg, A.T.C., Ph.D.
University of Arkansas
Cathy was raised in Ohio, where she graduated from Muskingham College in 1968, after competing in field hockey, volleyball, basketball and softball. She taught and coached for four years at the high school level before completing her master's in physical education with a specialty in athletic training at Indiana State University. Certified by the National Athletic Trainers Association (N.A.T.A.), Cathy worked at Carthage and Albion colleges before she completed her doctoral program in sport psychology at Michigan State. She is currently an associate professor in the Department of Health, Physical Education and Recreation at the University of Arkansas (Fayetteville). Cathy enjoys officiating softball and basketball games and playing golf and soccer.

Martha Litherland, Ph.D.
Grand Valley State University
Longtime physical educator and coach Marty Litherland received a master's degree, with a specialty in athletic administration and coaching, from Bowling Green State University in 1980. She received her doctorate (from Michigan State in 1995) in the psycho-social aspects of sport with an emphasis in coaches' education. At Defiance College in Ohio Marty led the basketball program to four consecutive 20 plus winning seasons and earned "Coach of the Year" distinctions three times. A former All-American softball player, Marty is currently coordinator of Northern Michigan programming for Grand Valley State University. She is located in Traverse City where she enjoys cycling, kayaking and cross-country skiing.

Thomas J. Mackowiak, A.T.C.
Department of Intercollegiate Athletics
Michigan State University
Tom Mackowiak has been a member of the Michigan State University athletic training staff since 1987. He current serves as staff athletic trainer working with the Spartan Men's Basketball program. He received his bachelor's degree in 1979 from Ball State University with a major in Special Education and a minor in Athletic Training. He completed his master's degree from Michigan State in 1981. Tom served as the first head athletic trainer for East Lansing High School in 1980-81. He was the Director of Sports Medicine at the University of Detroit from 1981-1987. A former Michigan Athletic Trainers Society membership chairperson and an active member of the National Strength and Conditioning Association, Tom also is an instructor in the Department of Kinesiology. Tom is currently pursuing his Doctorate in the Department of Kinesiology in Program Design and Curriculum Evaluation.

B. Patrick Maloy, J.D., M.S.A.
Department of Kinesiology
University of Michigan
Pat Maloy competed in high school football and baseball before playing semi-pro baseball during his college years. He earned his bachelor's from Wheeling Jesuit University, his law degree at the University of Notre Dame, and a master's degree in sports administration from Ohio University in 1985. He had a law practice for 11 years and worked in corporate management for three years prior to joining the faculty of the University of Michigan. He teaches courses in the legal aspects and management of sport, recreation and facility management. He received a State of Michigan Teaching Excellence Award in 1991. He has written extensively on sports management and coaching obligations.

Christopher McGrew, M.D.
School of Medicine
Department of Orthopaedics and Rehabilitation
University of New Mexico
Chris McGrew was born and raised in Louisiana, where he lettered in cross country and track and ran on two-time state champion cross-country teams. After earning a bachelor's degree in zoology at Louisiana State University in 1980, he went on for his M.D. at LSU-Shreveport, followed by a residency in family practice. Chris completed a sports medicine fellowship at Michigan State University, where he served as one of the team physicians for MSU's athletic program. He is now at the University of New Mexico, where he is on the faculty of the School of Medicine and a team physician for the Intercollegiate Athletic Program. His hobbies include long distance running, swimming, cycling, backpacking and fly fishing.

Anthony (Tony) Moreno, M. S., C.S.C.S.
Institute for the Study of Youth Sports
Michigan State University
From 1989 to 1992, Tony served as a graduate assistant strength and conditioning coach at Long Beach State and as assistant strength coach at Cal State Fullerton. In 1992 he started operations of a profitable fitness facility in Mammoth Lakes, California. In addition to providing community wellness, he operated a variety of sport conditioning camps for young athletes from the southern California area. In 1996 he sold his business to further his academic interests, receiving his master's degree from the University of Nevada in 1998. He is currently a doctoral student in sport biomechanics at Michigan State University. Among his research interests are youth sport injuries, resistance training, and American football. He is a certified strength coach through the National Strength and Conditioning Association and is a USA Weightlifting Level I coach.

Sally Nogle, A.T.C., Ph.D.
Associate Head Athletic Trainer
Department of Intercollegiate Athletics
Michigan State University
Sally Nogle has served as a member of the Michigan State University athletic training staff since October, 1983. Sally is the associate staff athletic trainer working with Spartan Football. She brings International and Olympic experience to the MSU staff. In 1984, Sally worked with the U.S. Volleyball Team at the Summer Olympics in Los Angeles and in 1985 and 1986, she worked at the U.S. Olympic Sports Festival in Baton Rouge and Houston. Sally has also worked with the U.S. Rowing Team at the Summer Olympics in Seoul, South Korea in 1988 and was a member of the 1996 athletic training staff at the 1996 Olympic Games in Atlanta. She earned a bachelor's degree in physical education in 1979 and a master's degree in 1983, both from San Diego State University. She recently completed her doctorate at Michigan State. Sally coordinates MSU's athletic rehabilitation programs, and serving as an instructor in the Department of Kinesiology. She was honored by the Michigan Athletic Trainers Society in 1999 with the Distinguished Athletic Trainers Award. Sally includes softball, basketball, and golf on her list of interests.

John E. (Jack) Roberts
Executive Director
Michigan High School Athletic Association
A Wisconsin native, Jack Roberts was a very successful high school athlete, playing football, basketball and baseball. He went on to play collegiate football at Dartmouth, where he received a bachelor's degree. After teaching high school in Wisconsin and Colorado, Jack joined the staff of the National Federation of State High School Associations, eventually serving as Assistant Director. While with the Federation, he developed rules programs in several sports and worked closely with the governing bodies of collegiate sport. Since becoming Executive Director of the Michigan High School Athletic Association, Jack has been a strong advocate for both coaching education and scholastic sports. Under his direction, *PACE* programs have prepared more than 10,000 coaches. Moreover, Jack has made Michigan a leader in the effort to maintain the educational integrity of high school sport.

Lionel W. (Lonnie) Rosen
Department of Psychiatry
Michigan State University

Lonnie Rosen received his bachelor's degree in pharmacy and a master's in physiology. However, during his medical studies at Jefferson Medical College, he became interested in psychiatry. After serving his residency in psychiatry, he made eating disorders and sports psychiatry his specialties. Lonnie not only conducts research in these areas, he also does clinical work with athletes. Much of his work focuses on efforts to deal with the consequences of sport, body image and disordered eating. He has published in such diverse areas as pathogenic weight-control in female athletes and seasonal mood disturbances in collegiate hockey players.

Thomas Sawyer, Ed.D.
Director, The Center for Coaching Education
Indiana State University

A professor of recreation and sport management at Indiana State, Tom has coached collegiate sports for more than 10 years in baseball, soccer, and track and field and interscholastic soccer for 10 years. He has officiated in baseball, basketball, football, soccer, swimming and diving, track and field, and wrestling at both the high school and collegiate levels. Tom was a collegiate HPER-A administrator for more than 19 years. He currently teaches undergraduate and graduate courses in sports management and legal issues and has been instrumental in developing the delivery system for the *PACE* program.

Vern Seefeldt, Ph.D.
Professor and Director Emeritus, Institute for the Study of Youth Sports
Michigan State University

Vern Seefeldt was born in Wisconsin, where he participated in high school baseball, football, basketball and track. After graduating from the University of Wisconsin at LaCrosse with a bachelor's degrees in biological science and physical education, he was a high school teacher and coached football, basketball and baseball. Vern earned his doctorate at the University of Wisconsin at Madison with a specialty in motor development. He was a faculty member at the University of Wisconsin before coming to Michigan State University, where he was named the first director of the Institute for the Study of Youth Sports in 1978, a position he held until retiring in 1995.

Paul Vogel, Ph.D.
Institute for the Study of Youth Sports
Michigan State University

A native of Southeastern Michigan, Paul Vogel participated in high school football, swimming, and track before attending Bowling Green State University, where he was swim team captain. After coaching Bowling Green's freshman swim team, Paul earned his master's degree in 1962. He taught physical education and coached in Wisconsin and Battle Creek, Michigan, where he won coach of the year honors in recognition of his championship swim teams. Paul earned a Ph.D. with emphasis on program design and evaluation and has been at Michigan State University since 1972, except for a two-year stint at the University of Wyoming. Paul's hobbies include skiing, sailing and fishing.

Jennifer J. Waldron, M.Ed.
Institute for the Study of Youth Sports
Michigan State University

Born and raised in Minnesota, Jennifer earned high school varsity letters in cross country, basketball and track and field. After suffering a knee injury, she stayed involved in basketball through volunteer coaching and working sports camps. In 1999, she completed her master's degree in developmental kinesiology from Bowling Green State University. Presently pursuing a Ph.D. in sport psychology, Jennifer is a member of the Institute where she plays an important role in research and out-reach. She enjoys traveling, hiking and playing various sports.

Program for Athletic Coaches' Education

Competency Exam
Edition 3.1

Michigan High School Athletic Association
1616 Ramblewood Drive
East Lansing, MI 48823
Phone: (517) 332-5046
Fax: (517) 332-4071

Section I: Philosophy

1. **Sportsmanship** entails _____
   a) a prerequisite respect for self.
   b) the realization that striving to win is the essence of sport.
   c) a respect for self, opponents, coaches, officials and the sport.
   d) the lack of violence or cheating in competition.
   e) competing aggressively and losing graciously.

2. The **gray area of sportsmanship** occurs when an action _____
   a) is considered good sport conduct.
   b) is completely free of interpretation.
   c) is considered poor sport conduct.
   d) breaks the rules of the game.
   e) is considered good sport conduct by some and poor sport conduct by others.

3. **Sportsmanship is most appropriately taught** _____
   a) in practices and competition throughout the season.
   b) in practices before the competition begins.
   c) in the heat of highly competitive situations.
   d) during reviews of previous competitions.
   e) in post-season reviews of the team's performance.

4. Which statement best defines the **philosophy of interscholastic athletics**?
   a) Interscholastic athletic programs exist for the welfare of the community.
   b) Participation opportunities in sport should be provided for those who possess a high level of skill.
   c) Qualified individuals whose major concern is the procurement of college scholarships for students should be coaching young athletes.
   d) An athletic program should be governed by a philosophy that is appropriate and consistent with the philosophy of the school system.
   e) A favorable win/loss record is evidence of a successful season.

5. You are coaching a team and are limited by staff and budget to only a certain number of athletes. Therefore, you face the task of "**cutting**" athletes following fair tryouts. You should _____
   a) speak with each athlete individually about his/her status.
   b) post a list of players who made the team.
   c) post a list of players who are cut from the team.
   d) post a list of all the players who participated in the tryouts, but put a star next to the players' names who made the team.
   e) post a list of all the players names who participated in the tryouts, but put a star next to the players' names who were cut from the team.

6. Coaches can facilitate **the successful inclusion of disabled athletes** by _____
   a) asking able bodied players to play with less effort.
   b) making no allowances for their disability.
   c) only giving them praise.
   d) modifying sports techniques and equipment.
   e) focusing on their disability and not their ability.

7. A legitimate **benefit of including disabled athletes** into able-bodied sports is _____
   a) less money is spent on disabled sports programs.
   b) able-bodied athletes have more people to compete with.
   c) parents of disabled athletes have more free time.
   d) able-bodied athletes can learn valuable lessons from disabled athletes.
   e) sport teams are not fined for the exclusion of disabled athletes.

Section II: Growth and Development

8. Which of the following statements regarding **development** is true?
   a) The adolescent growth spurt occurs about two years earlier in boys than in girls.
   b) Early maturing individuals have shorter legs compared to their total height than do late maturing individuals.
   c) Typically, females reach their adult height during the last two years of high school.
   d) The bodies of children and youth are basically downsized versions of adult bodies.
   e) The adolescent growth spurt usually lasts for six to eight years.

9. **Young athletes** are more likely than adults to:
   a) use feedback to improve performance.
   b) mentally rehearse game strategies.
   c) process information quickly.
   d) require frequent satisfying experiences.
   e) select appropriate strategies.

10. Which of the following is characteristic of **visual-motor coordination**?
    a) Identifying a target at a distance of 150 feet.
    b) Successfully catching a fly ball in a softball game.
    c) Noticing a teammate entering your field of vision.
    d) Removing only your arrows from a target face in archery.
    e) Selecting an appropriate club on the fairway when playing golf.

11. The **long-range purpose of a training program** is to:
    a) enhance the reputation of the coach.
    b) maximize the overall strength of team members.
    c) increase the health of the participants.
    d) validate the effectiveness of the training equipment.
    e) improve the performance of athletes in a specific sport.

12. **Training programs for prepubescent children** have been most effective in developing:
    a) strength.
    b) flexibility.
    c) balance.
    d) agility.
    e) aerobic fitness.

13. When using the **aerobic energy system**, food is converted into energy in the presence of:
    a) minerals.
    b) fats.
    c) oxygen.
    d) vitamins.
    e) helium.

14. The **anaerobic system**:
    a) produces more energy units per sugar molecule consumed than does the aerobic system.
    b) produces energy from fuel in the presence of oxygen.
    c) uses fats and carbohydrates as fuel.
    d) produces a by-product that can cause temporary fatigue.
    e) removes lactic acid produced by the aerobic system.

15. In **circuit training**, overload can be produced by:
    a) increasing the recovery period between stations.
    b) increasing the number of stations in the circuit.
    c) increasing the time for exercise at each station.
    d) decreasing the number of repetitions per station.
    e) decreasing the number of times the circuit is completed.

16. An athlete with a **well conditioned aerobic system** is:
    a) more susceptible to fatigue toward the end of a contest.
    b) more likely to be able to engage in high quality work throughout a lengthy practice session than a person with an ill conditioned aerobic system.
    c) has an energy production system that tends to use carbohydrates and conserve fats.
    d) can tolerate larger amounts of lactic acid than a person with a well conditioned anaerobic system.
    e) uses protein as a major source of energy during exercise.

17. Which of the following statements is true about well-designed **resistance training programs**?
    a) For the novice trainee, a large number of complex exercises should be prescribed to provide a strong strength base for the upcoming season.
    b) When constructing a resistance training program, it is better to emphasize the physical strengths instead of physical weaknesses. This will enable the athlete to continue to perform well in future strength tests.
    c) If the young athlete is unresponsive or bored with the resistance training program, coaches should intervene immediately and make the necessary changes (i.e. intensity, volume, time) that may initiate positive attitudes towards the program.
    d) In situations where the time allotted for physical training is brief, activities such as running, plyometrics, or flexibility should be completely avoided since they will consume much of the time designated for resistance training.
    e) To ensure athletes are at peak levels of strength for a competition, coaches should have the young athletes participate in a high intensity workout the day before an event.

18. The **competitive season** usually places emphasis on specific sport skills, tactics, and strategy, therefore:
    a) the volume and intensity of resistance training should be increased.
    b) the volume should be increased and the intensity of efforts should be decreased.
    c) the volume of training should decrease, while the intensity of training should stay the same.
    d) all resistance training should completely cease.
    e) only circuit training should be employed for all sports.

19. The formal method of organizing and applying the **overload principle** for a specific segment of time is called:
    a) overtraining.
    b) periodization.
    c) powerlifting.
    d) circuit training.
    e) bodybuilding.

20. Which of the following is true regarding a **precontest meal**?
    a) Protein-rich foods should be consumed during a precontest meal.
    b) Foods high in carbohydrates take longer to leave the stomach and intestine than foods high in fats.
    c) There are no pre-game meals that contain special magical properties that will improve your athletes' performances.
    d) The precontest meal should be consumed immediately (within one hour) prior to competition.
    e) Foods high in fiber and roughage are recommended as part of a precontest meal.

21. Which of the following statements regarding **weight control** is true?
    a) Even when dieting, three balanced meals should be eaten daily.
    b) Gaining weight at a fast rate results in muscle gain rather than fat gain.
    c) Crash diets are not recommended because loss of body protein is only slight.
    d) To gain weight, an underweight athlete should increase caloric intake and reduce physical activity.
    e) Athletes trying to gain weight should eat food high in fats because these foods contain the most calories.

22. The main reason many athletes have **low concentrations of iron** in their blood is because _____
    a) they do not eat enough red meat.
    b) they have high levels of blood plasma.
    c) they use iron as a source of energy.
    d) they do not eat enough leafy green vegetables.
    e) red blood cells are damaged during exercise.

23. According to researchers, young athletes would take **dietary supplements** if _____
    a) they could afford them.
    b) a professional athlete endorsed them.
    c) they thought they were safe and effective.
    d) their friends took them.
    e) they tasted good.

24. Young athletes should be **discouraged from taking creatine** supplements **because** _____
    a) they do not work.
    b) they may lead to heart failure.
    c) they have not been thoroughly tested in children and adolescents.
    d) they promote obesity.
    e) they are linked to diabetes.

25. Products known as **fat-burners often contain** high concentrations of _____
    a) calcium.
    b) ephedrine.
    c) iron.
    d) morphine.
    e) caffeine.

26. **Which** of these groups of **athletes** are most likely to **use dietary supplements**?
    a) Female athletes.
    b) High school football players.
    c) Single sport athletes.
    d) Cheerleaders.
    e) Bench players.

27. **Teenage girls desire** _____
    a) less height and less weight.
    b) more height and more weight.
    c) less height and less girth.
    d) less height and more weight.
    e) more height and less weight.

28. **Chubby children** are typically rated as _____.
   a) friendlier.
   b) funnier.
   c) lazier.
   d) more anxious.
   e) more intelligent.

Section III: Sports Medicine

29. The **Female Athlete Triad** consists of which medical conditions?
   a) disordered eating, amenorrhea and osteoporosis.
   b) disordered eating, anterior cruciate laxity and osteoporosis.
   c) anterior cruciate ligament weakness, joint laxity and osteoporosis.
   d) osteoporosis, joint laxity and imbalances in muscle strength.
   e) amenorrhea, oligomenorrha and osteoporosis.

30. **Osteoporosis** or premature bone loss **or inadequate bone formation** is characteristic of:
   a) early maturing female athletes.
   b) late maturing, underweight female athletes.
   c) females with low blood levels of estrogen.
   d) females with high blood levels of calcium.
   e) females who engage in weight-bearing activities.

31. Which of the following is **a sign of over-training**?
   a) Decreased resting heart rate.
   b) Depression.
   c) Decreased incidence of injury.
   d) Improved performance.
   e) Restful sleep.

32. Which of the following regarding **prevention of injuries** is true?
   a) A fence is an environmental hazard.
   b) Technique has little relationship to the incidence and severity of injuries.
   c) Fatigue is linked to a decreased potential for injury.
   d) Chronic muscle soreness is a sign of over-training.
   e) Contraindicated exercises decrease the chance of sport-related injuries.

33. The **activities before competition** should be conducted in which order?
   a) Stretching, warm-up, skill-oriented drills.
   b) Skill-oriented drills, warm-up, stretching.
   c) Warm-up, skill-oriented drills, stretching.
   d) Stretching, skill-oriented drills, warm-up.
   e) Warm-up, stretching, skill-oriented drills.

34. The acronym **R.I.C.E.** stands for a treatment to be carried out following orthopedic injuries. The four steps of R.I.C.E. are _____
   a) Rehabilitation, Inspection, Cold, Elevation.
   b) Rest, Inflammation, Cold, Elevation.
   c) Rehabilitation, Inspection, Compression, Exercise.
   d) Rest, Ice, Compression, Elevation.
   e) Rest, Ice, Compression, Exercise.

35. Which of the following statements regarding **sports injuries** is true?
    a) If an athlete becomes unconscious, move her or him off the playing field immediately.
    b) A rapid, weak pulse and pale, moist, clammy skin are signs of heat exhaustion.
    c) If a player's tooth is knocked out, clean it off, wrap it in gauze and take it and the athlete to a dentist.
    d) Puncture wounds are usually accompanied by profuse bleeding.
    e) A contusion is a superficial skin wound caused by scraping.

36. Which of the following items do not need to be in the **coach's possession during practices and competitions**?
    a) First-aid kit.
    b) Athlete's Medical Information Form.
    c) Athlete's Medical Treatment Consent.
    d) Summary of Season Injuries Form.
    e) On-Site Injury Report Form.

37. If an injured athlete has been treated by a physician, **written clearance** should be obtained from _____ before the athlete returns to action.
    a) the athlete's parents
    b) the athlete's physician
    c) the athlete's parents and physician
    d) the athlete's parents and the athlete
    e) the athlete's physician and the athlete

38. **Which** of the following **stretches/calisthenics is considered safe** to perform?
    a) sit-ups with straight legs.
    b) sit-ups with hands behind head.
    c) sit-ups with bent knees.
    d) deep knee squats.
    e) hurdler's stretch.

39. Which of the following sequence of events is correct when conducting a **training session**?
    a) Stretching, light aerobic warm-up, main training session, light aerobic cool-down, stretching.
    b) Stretching, light aerobic warm-up, main training session, stretching, light aerobic cool-down.
    c) Light aerobic warm-up, stretching, main training session, stretching, light aerobic cool-down.
    d) Light aerobic warm-up, stretching, main training session, light aerobic cool-down, stretching.
    e) Light aerobic warm-up, stretching, main training session, light aerobic cool-down.

40. **Which** of the following **stretches/calisthenics is contraindicated** because it compresses bony structures, cartilage or nerves?
    a) Deep knee squats.
    b) Neck bridge.
    c) Hurdler's stretch.
    d) Straight leg sit-up.
    e) Shoulder stretch.

41. Which of the following are **essential medical records** to keep?
    a) Medical treatment consent form.
    b) On-site injury report form.
    c) Physician referral form.
    d) Medical information and history form.
    e) All of the above.

42. The **advantages of a station physical examination** over an individual office visit includes greater:
    a) player/physician rapport.
    b) likelihood of follow-up exams if problems are detected.
    c) consistency between exams.
    d) likelihood that sensitive issues will be discussed.
    e) opportunity to counsel youths on other health problems.

43. Athletes **infected with a blood borne pathogen** should _____
    a) be subject to mandatory testing.
    b) be excluded from all sports.
    c) be excluded from contact sports.
    d) be allowed to participate in the majority of sports.
    e) not participate in any forms of physical activity.

44. Athletes who are **actively bleeding** should be _____
    a) allowed to continue participating until there is a suitable stoppage in play.
    b) asked if they require assistance.
    c) treated immediately.
    d) commended for their bravery.
    e) treated following completion of their game/event.

45. During athletic participation, **wounds that are not bleeding** should be _____
    a) covered with Vaseline.
    b) cleaned with water.
    c) remain uncovered to accelerate the healing process.
    d) cleaned and covered.
    e) treated with an analgesic balm.

46. In which sport is the **risk of blood borne pathogen** transmission the **highest**?
    a) Baseball.
    b) Boxing.
    c) Basketball.
    d) Hockey.
    e) Swimming.

47. After observing a lightning flash you count 30 seconds until you hear the sound of the accompanying thunder. Using the **flash-bang method** the lightning flash must have occurred approximately _____
    a) 10 miles away.
    b) 30 miles away.
    c) 15 miles away.
    d) 3 miles away.
    e) 6 miles away.

48. If you are caught **outside when a lighting storm occurs** you should _____
    a) seek shelter under some trees.
    b) stand perfectly still.
    c) crouch down low and cover your ears.
    d) continue playing, lightning strikes are extremely rare.
    e) seek out the highest point of elevation.

49. Which of the following may be the **strongest sign** that an athlete has acquired a problem **associated with chemical involvement?**
    a) Progressive increases in performance levels.
    b) Abrupt changes in friends and relationships.
    c) Sustained efforts in practices and games.
    d) Taking on of additional team responsibilities.
    e) Consistent moods.

50. Which of the following is a **unique pressure among athletes** that may contribute to **chemical involvement?**
    a) Lack of public expectations for improvement.
    b) Peer group pressure.
    c) Development of personal identity.
    d) High public visibility.
    e) Parental pressure.

51. When it is suggested that coaches **recognize boundaries** in dealing with a player who has a problem **related to a chemical involvement,** it means:
    a) coaches should not attempt to surpass their own expertise.
    b) coaches should not intervene in an athlete's personal life.
    c) coaches should define where and when chemical use is appropriate.
    d) coaches need to give guidelines as to how they will handle any case of chemical dependency on their team.
    e) coaches should not attempt to deal with chemical involvement problems.

52. Current problems with chemical abuse in and around athletics demands that **chemical health be promoted:**
    a) as part of pre-season meetings.
    b) as part of school-wide programs,
    c) in a series of meetings through the season.
    d) as part of confronting any suspected chemical abuser.
    e) only to elite athletes.

Section IV: Psychology

53. Young athletes indicate that the most important **reason they participate in sports** is:
    a) to improve skills and learn new ones.
    b) for thrills and excitement.
    c) to please their parents.
    d) to have fun.
    e) to be with friends and make new ones.

54. **Feedback is beneficial to players** when it is:
    a) constructive criticism.
    b) complex and covers all aspects of skill.
    c) simple and focuses on one error at a time.
    d) interesting with a twist of humor.
    e) emphasizing effort and not skill.

55. **Encouragement** as a tool by which **to enhance an individual's self esteem** is best used:
    a) when a skill is being performed well.
    b) when a skill performance is only partially correct.
    c) when very little effort has been shown to do a simple task.
    d) when an individual makes an error he/she rarely makes.
    e) when used as a blanket statement about the whole team.

56. Attempting to enhance **self esteem** by showing acceptance of the individuals on the team involves:
    a) unconditional acceptance of their behaviors.
    b) showing interest only in sport-related matters.
    c) being sensitive to and respecting individual differences.
    d) attending only to the mistakes they make.
    e) ignoring the mistakes they make.

57. When a coach focuses on and **rewards players who display the desired behaviors,** the coach is using a _____ approach.
    a) competitive
    b) negative
    c) cooperative
    d) positive
    e) professional

58. Athletes most **likely to benefit from a positive approach** are likely to have _____
    a) high ability.
    b) low self esteem.
    c) high self esteem.
    d) low ability.
    e) low maturity.

59. In the **initial stages of learning**, coaches should:
    a) intermittently reinforce a desired response.
    b) reinforce every undesired response.
    c) reinforce every other desired response.
    d) reinforce every desired response.
    e) reinforce every fifth desired response.

60. From a positive coaching perspective, **a desired behavior should be reinforced**:
    a) immediately after the practice/game.
    b) during the next break or time-out.
    c) sometime before the practice/game ends.
    d) as soon as it occurs.
    e) at the beginning of the next practice/game.

61. By choosing the **kinds of behaviors that are reinforced,** the coach can:
    a) motivate athletes to perform.
    b) increase a player's intrinsic motivation.
    c) enhance a player's self-esteem.
    d) control the interpersonal relationships on a team.
    e) create a winning team.

62. Coaches can promote a **healthy attitude toward losing** if they attempt to:
    a) schedule opponents of higher ability so that losing is expected.
    b) blame losses on poor officiating.
    c) equate losing with officiating.
    d) view losing as an indication of lack of ability.
    e) view losing as "water under the bridge" and learn from the loss.

63. The terms **arousal, anxiety and stress** _____
    a) all have distinct meanings.
    b) can be used interchangeably, because they define the same behavior.
    c) all represent negative forms of behavior.
    d) all reflect positive forms of behavior.
    e) are too general to be used meaningfully.

64. The **stress response occurs** _____
    a) when the athlete perceives that the demands of the task match their ability.
    b) only during competition.
    c) when the athlete perceives that their ability does not meet the demands of the task.
    d) more often in team sports.
    e) only when others are watching.

65. What is not a **physiological response to stress**?
    a) Shallow breathing.
    b) Increased sweating.
    c) Increased muscle tension.
    d) Increased heart rate.
    e) Increased muscle relaxation.

66. In general, **team goals** should:
    a) take precedence over individual goals.
    b) lead to better individual performances.
    c) lead to greater team cohesion.
    d) improve team performance.
    e) not be made or set.

67. **Correcting athletes' mistakes in a positive manner** should be done by using which of the following sequences?
    a) encourage—correct—compliment.
    b) encourage—compliment—correct.
    c) correct—encourage—compliment.
    d) compliment—encourage—correct.
    e) compliment—correct—encourage.

68. **Athletes should** be encouraged to **compare their skills** to:
    a) their own past performances.
    b) standards set by the coach.
    c) the skill of the best player on the team.
    d) the skill of the worst player on the team.
    e) the skill of the coach.

69. In order **for rewards to be highly effective,** they should be accompanied by:
    a) constructive criticism of the athlete's performance.
    b) a verbal reminder of why the award was given.
    c) an awards banquet.
    d) a "pep talk" to the team.
    e) a congratulatory "pat on the back."

70. When **establishing team rules**, players will follow rules more closely when:
    a) the rules are stricter than they expected.
    b) the rules list every undesirable behavior.
    c) rewards and penalties are included.
    d) the coach also follows the rules.
    e) athletes are involved in establishing the rules.

71. In the coach/athlete relationship, it is important to clearly identify the **coach's responsibility**. This responsibility is:
    a) the athlete's right to make decisions on behalf of others.
    b) the coach's right to make decisions on behalf of others.
    c) behaving in a manner that carries out the role of the coach.
    d) the coach's right to do what he/she wants.
    e) the force that allows the coach to act on his/her decisions.

72. A **dual relationship in coaching** should be avoided because of _____
    a) the imbalance of power between coach and athlete.
    b) the equal authority between coach and athlete.
    c) a coach's responsibility to discipline the athlete.
    d) the athlete's parents have more power than the coach.
    e) the coaches being equipped to deal with many problems.

Section V: Pedagogy

73. Which of the following is the correct **order of events in planning for the season**?
    a) Identify practice objectives, sequence season objectives, identify season goals, identify season objectives.
    b) Identify season goals, identify practice objectives, sequence practice objectives, identify season objectives.
    c) Identify season goals, identify season objectives, sequence season objectives, identify practice objectives.
    d) Identify season objectives, identify practice objectives, sequence practice objectives, identify season goals.
    e) Sequence season goals, identify season objectives, sequence practice objectives, evaluate students.

74. Because **coaches rarely have enough time to cover all of the material** that they would like to, they should:
    a) put less emphasis on planning and be more flexible.
    b) briefly expose the team to all of the material.
    c) increase practice time to four hours.
    d) select high priority objectives and teach them.
    e) omit warm-ups and cool downs.

75. Which of the following statements regarding **effective instruction** is true?
    a) Clearly stated objectives are essential for effective instruction.
    b) Long, detailed explanations are a feature of a good drill.
    c) Feedback is best when it is general and delayed.
    d) Daily practice time must be concentrated on one objective if learning is to occur.
    e) Players tend to achieve in accordance with their peers' expectations.

76. **Performance** of both the athletes and coaching staff **should be evaluated**:
    a) when there is extra time at the end of practice.
    b) to increase the number of athletes on your team.
    c) privately with each athlete.
    d) by parents on a weekly basis.
    e) continuously throughout the season.

77. When athletes are **learning new skills**, it is most effective to:
    a) concentrate on one part of the skill.
    b) give a long, detailed explanation of the skill.
    c) let them try it before you demonstrate it.
    d) ask them to put together all elements of a skilled performance.
    e) introduce the skill at the end of a practice.

78. In order to **keep your athletes motivated**:
    a) use most of your practice time for scrimmaging.
    b) stress winning at all costs.
    c) spend a lot of time explaining skills.
    d) use a variety of drills and activities.
    e) plan practices around a single activity.

79. How can a coach maximize **time on task** for his/her athletes?
    a) Reduce the transition time between drills.
    b) Supervise all instructional stations alone.
    c) Increase practice sessions to four hours.
    d) Reduce equipment present to avoid confusion.
    e) Allow all athletes to arrive before beginning practice.

80. When **rating the improvement** of your players, it is important to remember that:
    a) all players should be expected to improve in all areas.
    b) players with bad attitudes cannot be expected to improve.
    c) at the mastery level, even small improvement can be significant.
    d) you should always use a numerical scale to signify improvement on your evaluation form, never use a simple "Yes" or "No."
    e) an effective coach should see the most improvement in players who began the season with high levels of skill.

81. If all your players make significant gains on 100% of the **season objectives**, it is probably a matter of:
    a) low standards for making the "Yes/No" decisions on your assessment form.
    b) an excellent coaching performance.
    c) a group of players who all had a great deal of room for improvement.
    d) an adequate coaching performance because this is what should be expected.
    e) a "good fit" of coach to players which happens occasionally but can rarely be predicted.

82. The most helpful approach to improve **coaching effectiveness** when results do not meet expectations is to:
    a) assume a lack of talent.
    b) assume a lack of player interest.
    c) assume a weakness in your coaching and attempt to find it.
    d) relax and remember that kids mature differently.
    e) scrap your entire coaching style and try a new one.

83. An **evaluation** should be **based on which** one of the following **questions**?
    a) How can the coach win more games?
    b) Is the coach a good person?
    c) Did the coach work the team hard?
    d) Was the coach effective in achieving his/her purpose(s)?
    e) Did the athletes go on to play sports in college?

84. All of the following are **steps in the evaluation process except** _____
    a) identify the outcomes intended for the athletes.
    b) collect outcome related data.
    c) read numerous books on good coaching.
    d) analyze the data and identify reasons why some coaching actions are ineffective.
    e) implement the needed changes.

85. An example of **collecting data for evaluation** purposes would be:
    a) giving more positive feedback to the athletes.
    b) selecting inappropriate objectives.
    c) seeing how the athletes' perform the skills you taught.
    d) listing the skills you intend to teach.
    e) having an assistant coach complete an evaluation form.

86. All the following are **characteristics of a "good drill" except** _____
    a) it allows mastery of a particular objective.
    b) it follows the principle of "No Pain, No Gain."
    c) it keeps athletes "on task."
    d) it can be used with groups of various sizes.
    e) it provides many opportunities to analyze skills and provide feedback.

87. An example of **a meaningful name for a drill** might be _____
    a) Gut-busters.
    b) Suicides.
    c) Twenty-one.
    d) Mad stork.
    e) Over-the-head.

Section VI: Sports Management

88. All of the following are **administrative responsibilities** of the coach **except** _____
    a) preparing for contests.
    b) overseeing activities of associated personnel.
    c) evaluating various elements of the program.
    d) keeping records.
    e) ordering refreshments for the end of the season party.

89. Examples of **critical records** for the coach to keep include all of the following **except** _____
    a) lists of the sizes and numbers of uniform worn by each athlete.
    b) written communications to or from parents.
    c) notes explaining athletes' absences from activities.
    d) messages to or from administrators.
    e) requests for facility maintenance.

90. Examples of **critical records** for the coach to keep include all of the following **except** _____
    a) equipment inventories.
    b) records of any money collected or spent.
    c) a list of items left in the lost and found.
    d) directions for finding competition sites.
    e) athlete performance ratings.

91. Which of the following duties is the **responsibility of the head coach**?
    a) preparing the athletic budget.
    b) determining the policy for transporting teams.
    c) evaluating the performance of assistant coaches.
    d) arranging transportation to away competitions.
    e) hiring and compensating officials.

92. What **records** are **essential for a head coach** to acquire and file?
   a) Records of each athlete's physical exam and medical history.
   b) Records of all athletes' academic performance.
   c) Records of all athletes daily school attendance'.
   d) Records of who attended the pre-season meeting for parents.
   e) Travel routes to all away sites for the upcoming season.

93. The primary reason for head coaches to **evaluate** their **assistants** is:
   a) to record their deficiencies in case an injury occurs.
   b) to protect one's self in the event of litigation.
   c) to be able to document reasons for dismissing the assistant coach.
   d) to objectively show the assistant coach where improvements can be made.
   e) to assign credit or blame for the win/loss record.

94. When coaches operate under the guidance or supervision of a **school-sponsored sports program**, they are:
   a) immune to lawsuits.
   b) not liable for injuries to players.
   c) nevertheless, responsible for the welfare of players.
   d) subject only to physical injury suits.
   e) prone only to suits against the program itself.

95. In order to establish **liability in a negligence suit**, the plaintiff must demonstrate that there was a breach in a duty to maintain a **standard of care**, which refers to:
   a) medical health standards.
   b) agreements made in a participation waiver.
   c) sport participation laws.
   d) a standard of the coaching profession and/or the court(s).
   e) verbal commitments made by the coach to the players.

96. Which of the following **defenses against negligence apportions damages** according to the degree to which the defendant and the plaintiff were responsible for the accident or injury?
   a) assumption of risk.
   b) contributory negligence.
   c) comparative negligence.
   d) government immunity.
   e) act of God.

97. The best **deterrent** a coach may have **to being sued** is:
   a) a winning record.
   b) a competent attorney.
   c) thorough and comprehensive knowledge.
   d) good communication networks in the league.
   e) state of the art equipment.

98. The coach's responsibilities for **providing care** to injured athletes:
   a) are limited to notifying appropriately trained personnel only.
   b) only include transporting injured players to appropriate facilities.
   c) involve providing or securing appropriate medical assistance.
   d) involve performing CPR only.
   e) require all care necessary to be performed.

99. **Insurance** designed to assist with expenses and judgments **associated with lawsuits** is called _____
    a) life insurance.
    b) health insurance.
    c) medical insurance.
    d) liability insurance.
    e) litigation insurance.

100. Which of the following statements regarding **insurance** is true?
    a) Blisters are usually covered on a group medical insurance policy.
    b) A waiver of liability indicates that a person agrees to sue the administrators, not the coach in case of injury.
    c) Most team medical policies are the same regardless of the sport and/or age group for whom the insurance is provided.
    d) Most courts have determined that public agencies can contract away their liability to those whom they serve.
    e) Officials and administrators are frequently excluded from a team medical insurance plan.

Section I
Philosophy

1
A Philosophy of School Sports

John E. "Jack" Roberts, Executive Director
Michigan High School Athletic Association

INTRODUCTION

A philosophy for interscholastic athletics cannot be considered apart from the objectives of those sponsoring and administering the programs—schools—and the intentions of those institutions when they decided to associate sports with education and began to invest resources into that association.

The current trend in education is toward smaller and more specialized and segregated schools; but throughout most of the 20th century, the first to have sports associating with schools in the United States, the trend was opposite. Public policy supported the consolidation of schools where students could be provided more comprehensive curricular and extracurricular options. Schools were viewed as melting pots for persons of diverse cultural, social, racial, and religious backgrounds and of wide ranging interests in and capabilities for academic and nonacademic activities.

The philosophy of school sports defined here is more consistent with the historical vision of public education than the recent fads. In keeping with this long view of things, we begin with the statement of beliefs and actions presented in 1963 by Clifford B. Fagan, then Executive Secretary of the National Federation of State High School Athletic Associations, to a national conference on values in sports, as reported in the Journal of the American Association for Health, Physical Education and Recreation:

Beliefs

First, we believe that the nature of a nation's sports program reflects, to a large degree, the na-tion's physical well-being and its physical interests. We accept the statement that competition on the fields of Eton made a great contribution to the welfare of the English people over a long, long period of time.

Second, we believe in competition. It is beneficial for the highly skilled to compete, for the less skilled to compete, for the moderately skilled to compete. A desire to win is good, and most benefits occur when extreme effort is made; casual effort does not result in desirable benefits! We believe that there is a difference between recreational sports and competitive sports. And we believe further that competition should be regulated by standards.

Third, we believe that we should win according to the rules and that ethical practices should not be abused or voided in order to win. A program that is properly administered, even though it is competitive, will give the educational benefits we are striving for.

Fourth, we believe that a program with both breadth and depth is needed. There should be a great many sports opportunities for high school students, and students should have a choice of the activity in which they want to participate. We believe that there is need for many teams on various levels. Not all students want to participate in programs that are highly competitive. Some students do not care about this kind of activity; some are not interested in making the sacrifices that are necessary if they are to excel.

Fifth, we believe that sportsmanship is taught and that the objectives we hope to attain can be reached only when sportsmanship is given a consideration. We believe that current approaches to sportsmanship are often 'namby-pamby.' Even with the fear of oversimplifying this important area, we suggest that there are three standards for sportsmanship. You can have acceptable sportsmanship generally if you will play the game according to the rules, both the spirit of the rules and the actual rules. If you win, you do not gloat over it; if you lose, you do not alibi. We believe that some 'window dressing' is insincere in the sportsmanship area, that it is unnecessary. Furthermore, it contributes to a weakness or a fault of our competitive program. We think that it is artificial and we believe that sportsmanship is dependent upon sincerity.

***Finally, we believe that personal and social values can be attained in sports competition but that these objectives are not automatic and, to a great degree, they depend upon leadership.** In addition to those values that are classified as personal and social, there are others which are classified as physical and spiritual. An attitude of sophistication that has developed in the country since World War II is making it more difficult for sports programs to obtain the results which we hope they will. This attitude prevents participants from making sacrifices to accomplish what should be accomplished in sports programs. We believe that this attitude of sophistication has contributed to a weakening of moral fiber.*

Actions

*This we do. **First, we protect in interscholastic programs the individual and the program.** We do this in many ways—limited seasons, eligibility rules, age rules, limited number of games, and so on.*

***Second, we promote.** We believe that the program is worth promoting.*

***Third, we train.** We believe that we teach sports skills effectively. Coaching is one of the best, more efficient programs of teaching in the school. We train officials so that these programs can be conducted according to the rules. And we believe that good and adequate officials reduce the incidence of unsportsmanlike conduct.*

Fourth, we classify, for equal competition.

Fifth, we cooperate with other aspects of the school program.

Finally, we work for the attainment of personal and social values, knowing that these can be attained only when maximum effort is extended and when there are sacrifices for the best possible performance. We regret that there are still many soft spots in this area. We regret that in many places loyalty is ridiculed, that some organizations even penalize people who try to do the best possible job that they can.

ROLE

Both at the time Mr. Fagan articulated the six beliefs and six actions above and in these times, the goals of school sports are twofold: (1) **to help schools reach and educate students; and** (2) **to help students learn skills for life.** Such skills include **hard work** (dedication and discipline), **teamwork** (sacrifice), and **fair play** (ethics and integrity).

It is neither a practical nor legal reality that interscholastic athletics are an integral part of the curriculum of schools or an essential part of a student's education. However, it is proper to characterize voluntary, competitive interscholastic athletics as a tool for helping schools motivate students and to succeed both in the classroom and in later life. While it is not necessarily cause and effect, it is a statistical fact that by most studies it has been found that participants in athletics have higher grade point averages, lower dropout rates, better daily attendance and fewer discipline problems than non-participating students.

Many schools have placed the purpose of interscholastic athletics before their constituents by many different means. Here is a part of what one Michigan school has stated in its **STUDENT ATHLETIC HANDBOOK** that each athlete and his/her parent must verify has been read before the student participates in athletics:

Philosophy of Athletics

V. *American society places a high priority on individual excellence. This excellence has been closely allied with a challenging, competitive environment. Competition has long been considered a measure of excellence in our culture, whether it be in the business world, in scholastic achievement, or in athletics. Educational sports, in their pursuit of excellence, should be cautious not to create a competitive atmosphere so highly charged and intense that it becomes counter-productive for those it is intended to serve. Athletics must always be available to the many, not just the few. Every attempt should be made to encourage as many students as possible to share in the benefits of athletic participation. While participation is to be encouraged, it should be regarded as a privilege to compete for the school and **excessive praise and awards should be discouraged.***

The program shall be so directed that the welfare of the students will be the rule. Every effort should be made to assure broad-based student participation. Continued emphasis shall reinforce the philosophy that the educational sports programs are an integral part of the educational program and are justifiable only to the extent that they are a desirable learning experience. All athletic activities in the school district should be coordinated with the general instructional program and be in complete harmony with all aims and objectives of the total school program.

Objectives of Athletics

VI. An athletic program should have objectives if it is to be meaningful. These objectives should be applicable for all levels. The objectives shouldn't be inconsistent with its philosophy or the educational objectives of our schools.

Our athletic program is dedicated to the following objectives:
1. Provide all athletes with the best teaching and coaching personnel possible.
2. Provide all athletes with the best facilities and equipment possible.
3. Provide the opportunity for all athletes to participate in the best interscholastics possible.
4. Provide the opportunity for all spectators to identify with and support the interscholastic teams of our schools.
5. Provide all athletes an opportunity to grow physically, emotionally, and spiritually through participation in the athletic program.

The Goals of Athletic Participation

VII. The ultimate goal of all athletes is to become a more effective citizen in our democratic society. These can be realized by achieving the goals through athletic participation.
1. *YOU LEARN TEAM WORK*—to work with others in a democratic society a person must develop self-discipline, respect for authority, and the spirit of hard work and sacrifice. You accomplish this by placing the team and its objectives higher than your personal desires.
2. *YOU LEARN TO BE SUCCESSFUL*—our society is very competitive. You will *NOT ALWAYS WIN, but you WILL SUCCEED WHEN YOU CONTINUALLY STRIVE TO DO SO.*
3. *YOU LEARN TO BE A GOOD SPORT*— you must learn to accept success and not let it go to your head. You must also learn to ac-

cept defeat knowing that you've done your best. You must continually strive to treat others as you would have them treat you. Through participation in athletics you must develop positive social traits. Some of these traits worth mentioning are: emotional control, honesty, cooperativeness, and dependability.
4. *YOU LEARN TO ENJOY ATHLETICS*— many athletes are involved in athletics for many reasons, not the least being the enjoyment derived. Hopefully, you will learn to enjoy this period in your life and appreciate your personal rewards.
5. *YOU LEARN DESIRABLE HEALTH HABITS*—to be an active, contributing citizen, it is important to obtain and maintain a high degree of physical fitness through exercise and good health habits. Your participation in athletics should demonstrate to you the importance of good health habits."

DISTINGUISHING CHARACTERISTICS

Interscholastic athletic programs sponsored by schools are distinguished from non-school community athletic programs by four issues to which interscholastic athletics gives special attention. Those issues are **scholarship** (supporting the academic mission of schools), **sportsmanship** (encouraging a civil and respectful environment for competition), **safety** (promoting the physical well-being of participants), and the **scope** of the programs (maintaining limits on awards, travel, seasons and out-of-season activities that are consistent with the primary function of schools, which is education).

These are the issues that have defined school sports throughout the 20th century and more than ever distinguish school sports from programs by all other sponsors on all other levels. They are issues on which the administrators of school sports should not apologize for being different, for it is in these differences that school sports have their place not only in the sports world but also in society as a whole. It is in these differences that schools can justify the role of competitive athletics within schools. Without these differences, boards of education could not justify the time and money spent on these extracurricular programs.

It has been said that the interscholastic athletic program provides a "window to the school." If the school provides special attention to scholarship, sportsmanship, safety and the scope of its athletic program, then the public can be fairly well certain not only that the school's philosophy of athletics is healthy, but also that its philosophy of education is appropriate.

2
Sportsmanship

Jennifer J. Waldron, M.Ed.

QUESTIONS TO CONSIDER

- What is sportsmanship?
- What is the role of the coach in teaching and modeling good sport conduct?
- What is the role of team leaders in promoting good sport conduct?
- How can coaches teach parents about sportsmanship?

At all levels of athletic competition there is growing concern for how athletes, coaches, parents, and fans are behaving and acting. The debate about whether good sport conduct has declined in the last decade has become increasingly heated. Take for example the following stories reported by Hawes (1998):

- In the state of New York a high school ice hockey player punched a referee seven or eight times. As the hockey player was led in handcuffs to a patrol car, the fans cheered for the player.
- In California, a referee was pushed to the ground and kicked repeatedly by the coach of a youth football team. The coach was apparently reacting to the official's decision to penalize one of his players for unsportsmanlike conduct.
- A football game announcer in Alabama used the public address system to say that the officials "need to go back to school" during a high school playoff game. Shortly after this announcement, the two football officials were attacked by a mob of fans.

These are simply a few of the extreme stories of poor sports conduct that are occurring in athletics. However, poor sportsmanship includes other behaviors that are not as severe (e.g., trash talking, swearing, refusing to shake hands with an opponent). This chapter examines the concept of sportsmanship and how to promote good sport conduct in athletics.

DEFINING SPORTSMANSHIP

Sportsmanship for me is when a guy [sic] walks off the court and you really can't tell whether he won or lost, when he carries himself off with pride either way.
Jim Courier, USA tennis player

Two basketball teams are known for a "win-at-all-costs" mentality. These two teams are playing each other in an important conference game. In hopes of good sport conduct, the athletic directors of the schools decided to implement a good sport conduct policy for the game. Any athlete committing violent acts, cheating, or trash talking would be ejected from the game. Because of the possible consequences, no athlete engaged in these behaviors. However, athletes did exchange 'glares' and 'mean looks' with their opponents and the two teams did not shake hands at the end of the game. The athletic directors were pleased with the results. Was sportsmanship actually displayed?

People often define sportsmanship by describing poor sportsmanship. In other words, poor sportsmanship is violence, cheating, and trash talking. Thus, good sportsmanship is characterized by the absence of these behaviors. With this definition, the scenario in the box above is an example of good sport conduct. Yet, good sportsmanship is more than just the lack of violence and cheating. Good sportsmanship is the act of playing sport "respectfully, honestly, and fairly…it is the practice of generosity, amicability, and compassion toward one's opponent" (Rudd and Stoll, 1998). Sportsmanship is having respect for the self, opponents, referees, coaches, and the game. Because the athletes in the scenarios did not display respect for their opponents, they did not truly exhibit good sport conduct.

It is important to understand how athletes identify the concept of sportsmanship. In Canada, 1,600 high school athletes from a variety of sports were asked to define sportsmanship (Vallerand, et al., 1996). From the responses, five major themes were identified; they are listed in Table 2-1. These themes create a holistic profile of sportsmanship. Furthermore, these themes provide evidence that high school athletes understand what sportsmanship entails.

Good sportsmanship can also be described as the Golden Rule: *Treat others, as you would like to be treated.* Using this as a general rule, it becomes easier to determine what behaviors would and would not be deemed sportsmanlike. Table 2-2 is a non-inclusive list of sportsmanlike and unsportsmanlike behaviors.

At the heart of good sportsmanship is showing respect and sensitivity for others, without exception. According to Griffin and Placek (1983), individuals demonstrate sensitivity for others when they:

• Execute drills with different teammates;

• Encourage struggling and less skilled teammates;
• Defend those who are belittled or mocked;
• Sit out to allow teammates to play; and
• Do not use abusive names, stereotypic slurs, and do not mock others.

It is important to highlight that good sport conduct involves not making fun of and not teasing teammates and opponents for any reason, including skill level, gender, and racial or ethnic origin. It is imperative for coaches to intervene when players do not respect or are not sensitive to the needs and feelings of others. By ignoring inappropriate behaviors, coaches are simply giving assent and approval.

Respect and sensitivity are an integral part of sportsmanship. Coaches must be fully committed to this principle of good sportsmanship. As discussed below, coaches need to model, teach, discuss, and encourage their team to respect all individuals and aspects of the sport.

THE ROLE OF THE COACH

Like any sport skill, athletes should be taught to practice sportsmanlike behaviors. The coach is an important force in helping instill the values of sportsmanship in athletes. This responsibility should not be taken lightly. In fact, recent episodes of poor sport conduct involved coaches. If coaches are unable to control their own behaviors, it is highly doubtful that athletes will be able to

Table 2-1. Dimensions of Sportsmanship Identified From Responses of High School Athletes.

DIMENSION	EXAMPLES
A respect and concern for the full commitment to sport participation	Working hard to focus on skill improvement Taking responsibility for success and failure
A respect and concern for the rules and officials	Knowing and understanding rules of the game Accepting and abiding by officials' decisions
A respect and concern for the social conventions	Congratulating opponents in a sincere way Refraining from taunting, trash talking, or making derogatory remarks Winning with humility and losing with grace
A respect and concern for the opponents	Showing concern for others Recognizing and appreciating skilled performance
Avoid the 'win-at-all-costs' mentality	Maintaining self-control even if frustrated Refusing to take advantage of an injured opponent Striving toward excellence

Table 2-2. Sportsmanlike and Unsportsmanlike Behaviors.

Sportsmanlike Behaviors	Unsportsmanlike Behaviors
Applauding the introduction of players, coaches, and officials	Yelling that antagonizes or degrades opponents
Accepting all decisions of the officials	Booing or heckling an official's decision
Engaging in positive school cheers	Engaging in disrespectful or derogatory yells and chants
Shaking hands at the end of the contest, regardless of outcome	Refusing to shake hands at the end of a contest
Treating competition as a game, not a war	Intimidating opponents with rough, dangerous play or trash talking
Sincerely congratulating an opponent for their play	Cheering when an opponent draws a foul or is cited for a violation
Searching out opponents to recognize them for outstanding performance	Blaming losses on others
Applauding at the end of contests for all participants	Laughing at or calling names to distract an opponent
Showing concern for injured players	Ignoring or applauding an opponent's injury
Encouraging others to display good sport conduct	Using profanity

control their behavior. The purpose of this section is to examine how a coach can promote good sport conduct on the athletic team in five steps:

1. Educate yourself in sportsmanship.
2. Establish a personal sportsmanship philosophy.
3. Model your personal philosophy.
4. Create a climate that fosters sportsmanship attitudes.
5. Provide sportsmanship education.

Educate Yourself in Sportsmanship

Reading and thinking about this chapter is a first step in educating yourself about the topic. It is necessary that you have a solid foundation and understanding of sportsmanship before you can adequately teach it to athletes. Discuss incidents you have seen in sport with other coaches and athletic administrators in order to clarify your beliefs. Additionally, seek out other resources to continually educate yourself. For example, coaches can access information concerning sportsmanship at the Michigan High School Athletic Association website < http://mhsaa.com/ >.

Establish a Personal Sportsmanship Philosophy

After becoming educated, it is important to establish your own values regarding sportsmanship. Part of your philosophy could include the behaviors listed in Table 2-2. Additionally, the Institute for the Study of Youth Sports has adopted a code of sportsmanship that can help guide

your philosophy (Seefeldt, et al., 1981). The code of sportsmanship can be found in Table 2-3. Although it is simple to compile a list of sportsmanlike and unsportsmanlike behaviors, it is not always that straightforward. There are interpretations of the rules that need to be considered. A grey area of sportsmanship exists, where certain actions may be judged good sport conduct by some and poor sport conduct by others. For example:

- A player touches the volleyball net. Do you encourage her to admit the error even if the referee misses it?
- In order to win a game, do you hit to the weak or injured player on the opposing team?
- Do you run up the score rather than substituting in players with less experience or less ability?

These are a few dilemmas that occur throughout sport. How would you respond to them? What actions would show respect? These are important issues to think about as you create a sportsmanship philosophy.

One man [sic] practicing good sportsmanship is far better than 50 others preaching it.
Knute K. Rockne, Notre Dame football coach

Model Your Own Personal Philosophy

One of the primary means by which individuals acquire attitudes and values is by observing others whom they respect. Coaches generally are well respected by their team and are a role model to athletes. It is important to follow your own philosophy of sportsmanship in order

Table 2-3. A Code of Sportsmanship.

Areas of Concern	Sportsmanlike Behaviors	Unsportsmanlike Behaviors
Behavior toward officials	when questioning officials, do so in an appropriate manner	arguing with officials swearing at officials
Behavior toward opponents	treat all opponents with respect and dignity at all times	arguing with opponents making sarcastic remarks about opponents making aggressive actions toward opponents swearing at opponents
Behavior toward teammates	give only constructive criticism and positive encouragement	making negative comments or sarcastic remarks swearing or arguing with teammates
Behavior toward spectators	make only positive comments to spectators, ignore negative comments made by spectators	arguing with spectators making negative remarks/swearing at spectators
Rule acceptance and infractions	obey all league rules	intentionally violating league rules taking advantage loopholes in rules
Spectator behavior	make only positive comments to players, coaches, and officials	making negative comments or sarcastic remarks

to facilitate the development of sportsmanship in athletes. In essence, "actions speak louder than words" and coaches must "practice what they preach". Gough (1997) generated the following checklist as a guide that coaches can use to monitor their behaviors:

- Is it right?
- Is it against the rules?
- Is it fair to everyone involved?
- Is it respectful?
- Would my ethical role model do it?

It is also important for athletes to have role models in sport that display good sport conduct. Help athletes find role models that follow your own philosophy of sportsmanship. When unsportsmanlike situations arise, ask the athlete what her or his role model would do in that situation. Through your own behaviors and the behaviors of role models, athletes will learn good sportsmanship.

Create a Sportsmanship Environment

It is important to create an environment that is conducive to good sport conduct during practice and competition. For athletes to learn good sport conduct sportsmanlike behaviors should be reinforced and unsportsmanlike behaviors should be penalized (see Chapter 27, *Maintaining Discipline*). These rules must apply to all individuals in all situations in order for them to be effective. Another aspect of creating a sportsmanship environment is to place winning in perspective by adopting a mastery motivational climate (see Chapter 24, *Motivating Athletes*).

Provide Sportsmanship Education

Part of creating a sportsmanship environment is educating athletes. There are many ways that this can be done. One effective method is the use of team discussions. Coaches can lead weekly discussions on scenarios that involve various aspects of sportsmanship, including examples that have occurred during practice or competition. Coaches are encouraged to look for teachable moments of good or poor sport conduct occurring on the team, other teams, or highlighted in the media. For example, when a soccer player refuses to shake an opponent's hand after the game, the coach can use this moment to teach the team appropriate behavior. The coach had the responsibility of challenging the athletes by asking thought-provoking questions, and teaching athletes "why" behaviors are desirable or undesirable. By engaging in discussions, coaches will help athletes develop their own sportsmanship philosophy. A very useful format to use for discussion is the following:

1. Identify the problem.
2. Identify possible actions (positive and negative).
3. Identify the consequence to each action, including how it will influence all people involved.
4. Choose the best solution.

See how these steps are followed in the sample discussion between coach and players in the box below.

A Sample Discussion Between Coach and Athletes

1. **Identify the problem:**
   I struck out in a softball game

2. **Identify possible actions:**
   a) Yell and scream at the umpire
   b) Throw the helmet and bat
   c) Obsess about striking out
   d) Shake it off and focus on defense

3. **Identify the consequences:**
   a) Thrown out of the game
   b) Get in trouble with the coach and team
   c) Make more mistakes and penalize the team
   d) Refocus and put forth proper effort on defense

4. **Choose the best solution:**
   Shake off the mistake and refocus

The power of teaching sportsmanship and moral concepts to athletes has been shown in research. During physical education classes, 4th, 5th, and 6th grade students received a seven-month curriculum focusing on respect for the rules, opponents, and referees, and maintaining self-control (Gibbons, et al., 1995). Findings indicated that the curriculum resulted in positive changes in the students' moral development. Similar findings have been found in youth sport programs (Bredemeier, et al., 1986). These studies and others provide evidence that moral concepts can be effectively taught to athletes. Thus, it is important for coaches to take the time during practice and competition to teach sportsmanship.

The Role of Team Leaders

Team captains or leaders also play an important role in establishing guidelines of good sport conduct. Team leaders are role models for their team, other teams, and younger athletes. It is vital for team leaders to understand their responsibility, take it seriously, and model good sport conduct. Coaches should discuss this role with the leaders at the beginning of the season.

Besides modeling, there are other things team leaders

can do to promote good sportsmanship. At the beginning of the season, the leaders can send a letter to each player on the team discussing the importance of sportsmanship, a definition of sportsmanship, and experiences the leaders have had with sportsmanship. The letter will set up team expectations about appropriate behavior. The leaders could meet with the team to compile a list of rules that define appropriate conduct. Sample rules could include:

- I will accept responsibility for all my actions.
- I will be a role model for other players.
- I will avoid retaliating against the opponent who makes a flagrant foul.

At this meeting, consequences for breaking these rules should be established (ranging from writing a letter of apology to the team to having to sit out for a competition). In this manner, team leaders become instrumental for ensuring positive sportsmanship behavior.

Teaching Parents

> During a high school basketball game, parents of two players on the same team have to be separated for fighting in the stands. Security is called in as a precautionary measure.

It is unfortunate that more and more situations like this are occurring at the youth, junior high, and high school level. It is apparent that parents are also exhibiting inappropriate behaviors during competition. Therefore, coaches must address and teach parents about sportsmanship. One method is to create a code of conduct that the parents are expected to follow. It is not enough to just send a code of conduct home to the parents. It is imperative that you educate the parents on why behaviors are desirable or undesirable, why the code is important, and your own sportsmanship philosophy. This can be accomplished at a pre-season meeting with parents and athletes (see Chapter 33, *Administrative Responsibilities of Coaches*). The coach must establish consequences for breaking the code of conduct. For example, a "three strikes and the parent is out" system could be imple-

mented. Parents would get two warnings for breaking the code, and the third time the parents are banned from watching competitions.

SUMMARY

Sportsmanship continues to be an important issue facing everyone involved in sport. Each of us plays a role in displaying and teaching sportsmanlike behaviors. If we—coaches, athletes, parents, and fans—cannot behave appropriately, then more rules will be made to control our behavior. For example, some sport organizations have established "Silent Sunday" soccer matches to control the behavior of parents and fans. If we do not want silent days, we must be proactive in teaching and modeling good sports conduct. In the end, we should not "Just Do It", but we should "Do It Justly." (Bredemeier, 1999).

REFERENCES

Bredemeier, B. L. (1999). "Character in Actions: Promoting Moral Behavior in Sport." In R. Lidor and M. Bar-Eli (editors), *Innovations in Sport Psychology: Linking Theory to Practice*. Morgantown, WV: Fitness Information Technology, pp. 247-260.

Bredemeier, B. J., Weiss, M. R., Shields, D. J., and Shewchuk, R. M. (1986). "Promoting Moral Growth in a Summer Sport Camp: The Implementation of Theoretically Grounded Instructional Strategies." *Journal of Moral Education*, 15: 212-220.

Gibbons, S. L., Ebbeck, V., and Weiss, M. R. (1995). "Fair Play for Kids: Effects on the Moral Development of Children in Physical Education." *Research Quarterly for Exercise and Sport*, 66: 247-255.

Gough, R. W. (1997). *Character is Everything: Promoting Ethical Excellence in Sports*. Fort Worth: Harcourt Brace College Publishers.

Griffin, P., and Placek, J. (1983). *Fair Play in the Gym. Race and Sex Equity in Physical Education*. Amherst: MA, University of Massachusetts.

Hawes, K. (1998, June 1). "Sportsmanship: Why Should Anybody Care?" *NCAA News*, pp. 1, 18.

Rudd, A., and Stoll, S. K. (1998). "Learning to Practice Sportsmanship." *Strategies*, pp. 5-7.

Seefeldt, V., Smoll, F. L., Smith, R. E., and Gould, D. (1981). *A Winning Philosophy for Youth Sports Programs*. E. Lansing, MI: Institute for the Study of Youth Sports.

Vallerand, R. J., Deshaies, P., Cuerrier, J., Briere, N. M., and Pelletier, L. G. (1996). "Toward a Multidimensional Definition of Sportsmanship." *Journal of Applied Sport Psychology*, 8: 89-101.

3

The Role of the Coach as Teacher, Mentor, and Role Model

Michael A. Clark, Ph.D.

QUESTIONS TO CONSIDER

- What four groups help define the role of the coach?
- What reasons do athletes give for being involved in athletics?
- What is the role of the coach in educational athletics?
- How does the coach's behavior relate to the role of educator?

INTRODUCTION

People join the coaching profession for a variety of reasons: They played and love the game, or they watch and study it, or they have assisted a "head coach." These experiences can motivate people to get involved as teachers and mentors. However, these experiences often provide little preparation for taking on the diverse responsibilities of a coach.

There are many different versions of what actually is the coach's role. At least these groups—who may have different perceptions of the coach's role—must be considered:

- Sport professionals—the responsible administrators and educators,
- Parents and general community members,
- The athletes themselves, and
- Experienced coaches.

By considering each faction's views, it is possible to begin sketching a picture of the coach's job. But this sketch will be a caricature, for it ends up exaggerating some key elements of the role.

Realizing this and reading what follows, the coach will learn two important things:

- The coach's job is much more complex than it first appears, and

- Everyone concerned looks for the coach to provide educational leadership and to be a "role model."

This knowledge assists each coach in personalizing the job, making it one's own and turning it into a satisfying career.

EXPECTATIONS

Sport professionals—administrators and educators—expect coaches and young athletes to work together to:

- Develop physical skills,
- Become fit,
- Learn appropriate conditioning techniques,
- Create a realistic and positive self-image,
- Develop the habit of being physically active,
- Learn the rules and strategies of sports,
- Come to see rules as the basis of safe and fair competition,
- Enjoy themselves,
- Learn positive personal, social and psychological skills—team work, self-discipline, self-worth, goal-setting, self-control, communication, leadership, and
- Recognize drugs as negative influences. (See Chapter 20, *Chemical Health Education and Coaching*, for a detailed discussion of chemical health).

Parents and community members cite fewer, more specific expectations. According to these people, coaches help players:

- Become better prepared for the world of work,
- Develop socially,
- Learn how to control themselves in social situations, and
- Develop positive habits of fitness and health.

These people also believe sports provide participants with:

- Opportunities in the business world and in entertainment and
- Fun and enjoyment in socially acceptable ways. (Manitoba Parks and Recreation Association, 1988)

By their actions, parents, administrators and teachers reveal that they believe that participation in sports provides young people with a series of positive learning experiences. These adults view the coach as the person responsible for helping players reap the benefits of participation. To them, the coach is the educational leader within the athletic setting.

The athletes themselves are perhaps the most important people to consider when debating the benefits of athletics. A national survey of nearly 26,300 youth revealed the reasons they participate in sport. Considering their responses, one realizes that they feel remarkably like adults, although their thinking is less sophisticated. Some interesting gender differences exist; therefore, it is worth looking at two sets of motives for involvement—one for girls and another for boys (Ewing and Seefeldt, 1989).

Girls cited, in order, the following reasons:
1. Having fun,
2. Staying in shape,
3. Getting exercise,
4. Improving existing skills,
5. Doing something they are good at,
6. Playing as part of a team,
7. Enjoying the excitement of competition,
8. Learning new skills,
9. Being part of a team, and
10. Meeting the challenge of competition.

Boys saw sports as an opportunity for:
1. Improving existing skills,
2. Enjoying the excitement of competition,
3. Doing something they are good at,
4. Having fun,
5. Stay in shape,

6. Playing as part of a team,
7. Winning,
8. Reaching higher levels of competition,
9. Getting exercise, and
10. Meeting the challenge of competition.

It is just as important to consider the most common reasons athletes gave for quitting sports. These include:

- "Not having fun anymore."
- "The coach was a poor teacher."
- "Too much pressure."
- "Not enough time for other things—school work, other activities, friends."
- "Tired of practicing and playing."
- "Coach played favorites."
- "Too much emphasis on winning."

Probably more than their peers, athletes recognize that playing is a mixed blessing; it is possible to have too much of a good thing. They also imply that the coach is the key factor affecting the quality of their experience. Essentially every reason cited for dropping out relates directly to the coach's job.

In short, young athletes expect to be treated fairly, to learn, to play, to enjoy themselves, to be a part of all activities. These expectations have been put into a simple form as a list of rights. More specifically, Table 3-1 presents a Bill of Rights for Young Athletes. Everyone who coaches should study this document carefully. It provides the framework for coaching humanely (Martens and Seefeldt, 1979).

Experienced coaches, when asked to describe their job, provide a number of one- and two-word descriptions.

Table 3-1. Bill of Rights for Young Athletes.

Every young athlete, whether involved in recreational or scholastic sport, has...

1. The right to participate
2. The right to participate at a level appropriate to their ability and maturity
3. The right to qualified adult leadership
4. The right to play as a child and not as an adult
5. The right to share in the leadership and decision-making of their sport participation
6. The right to practice and compete in a safe, healthy environment
7. The right to be properly prepared for participation
8. The right to an equal opportunity to strive for success
9. The right to be treated with dignity
10. The right to have fun

Among the more common ones are: "Teacher," "Mentor," "Role model," "Counselor," "Leader," "Motivator," and "Communicator." But once the idealism dissipates, experienced coaches also say: "Baby sitter," "Chauffeur," "Banker," "Winning," Public relations," "Fund raising," and "Mediator."

Like their athletes, experienced coaches recognize that sports have a dark side, and new coaches must realize that not all their experiences will be enjoyable and satisfying. Whether the players learn and grow through their involvement with sports depends upon the coach. Whether this is done in a positive way depends upon the coach. Whether sportsmanship and integrity are maintained also depends upon the coach.

Research suggests that coaches are the key element in determining the quality of the athletic experience. Further, statistics tell us that practically all youth are involved in organized sport at some point. As a result, coaches have the opportunity to affect the lives of most youth. The role of the coach, therefore, becomes more complex and implies greater importance and responsibility than is generally accorded such a position.

THE ROLE OF THE COACH

- Teaching skills to athletes while helping them deal with competitive pressures and still uphold the principles of sportsmanship.
- Planning ways for athletes to develop and maintain fitness.
- Managing time, evaluating talent, motivating players, communicating with their parents, assisting athletes in developing realistic goals, and aiding in their recovery from injury.
- Promoting the sport, raising funds, interacting with the media, and winning contests.
- Performing all the duties and responsibilities with integrity while maintaining a physically and emotionally safe environment for all team members.

The list of responsibilities involved in the coach's job seems endless. How is a person to proceed? The answer lies in the realization that the really important responsibilities of coaches are essentially educational. This is consistent with the expectations of sport professionals, parents, community members and players—all of whom see the coach as the educational leader within the athletic setting. To enjoy the support of the community while surviving professionally, the coach must function as an educator.

Making the connection between education and athletics must be the coach's primary mission. For if sports are not broadly educational, then there is little reason for school systems to continue sponsoring teams. And if educational institutions cease supporting athletics, then the over-whelming majority of competitive sports would dis-appear. Certainly sports would become even less inclusive. Therefore, maintaining the educational integrity of sport should be part of the coach's job—perhaps even the most crucial element.

Further, the coach is foremost a teacher, albeit one often without the formal credentials associated with a classroom. This translates into the coach's being responsible for planning the instruction of all athletes and seeing that they receive the benefits of sports participation. Far more than teaching new physical skills is involved; important values and skills can be learned through sport—things such as teamwork, respect for others, goal setting, time management, how to deal with disappointment. These qualities underscore the importance of athletics as an educational activity.

Understanding coaching as essentially teaching, the coach's role finally can be summarized: *The coach is the educational leader in the athletic setting. As such, the coach is responsible for reinforcing the connection between sports and academics while planning the instruction of athletes. The goal is for everyone involved with the athletic program to receive the many benefits derived from participation in sports.*

To put this into concrete terms, many program sponsors have prepared codes of ethics for their coaches. These codes describe expected behaviors; another which stresses the educational nature of coaching can be found in Table 3-2. This *Code of Ethics for Coaches* clearly spells out the educational responsibilities of all who serve as coaches.

In this formulation, the coach is an educator whose classroom is a gymnasium, field, pool or rink. The coach formally plans instruction, teaches according to these plans and evaluates the students' performance. Evaluation occurs during practices and competitions. This is the formal portion of the coach's job as an educator, but the coach may be an even more critical element of the athletes' informal education. This occurs when the coach functions as a role model.

THE COACH AS ROLE MODEL

A coach spends many hours helping athletes learn how to make a shot, catch a pass, turn a double play or stick a dismount. A coach worries about the players' strength and conditioning. These elements of athletics seem so important to both coach and athletes during their years of competing together. But later in life, most high school athletes make little use of their physical sports skills and knowledge. Few will have an opportunity to perform at the collegiate level; fewer still will receive athletic scholarships; and essentially none can expect to earn money playing the sports of their youth. For the large majority of scholastic athletes, upon graduation from high school their competitive athletic career is finished.

Table 3-2. Code of Ethics for Coaches.

1. I will treat each player, opposing coach, official, parent and administrator with respect and dignity.
2. I will do my best to learn the basic skills, teaching and evaluation techniques, and strategies of my sport.
3. I will become thoroughly familiar with the rules of my sport.
4. I will become familiar with the objectives of the sports program with which I am affiliated. I will strive to achieve these objectives and communicate them to my players and their parents.
5. I will uphold the authority of officials who are assigned to the contests in which I coach, and I will assist them in every way to conduct fair and impartial competitive contests.
6. I will learn the strengths and weaknesses of my players so that I might place them in situations where they have the maximum opportunity to achieve success.
7. I will conduct my practices and contests so that all players have an opportunity to improve their skill level through participation.
8. I will communicate to my players and their parents the rights and responsibilities of individuals on our team.
9. I will cooperate with the administrators of our program in the enforcement of rules and regulations, and I will report any irregularities that violate sound competitive practices.
10. I will protect the health and safety of my athletes by insisting that all of the activities under my control are conducted for their psychological and physiological welfare, rather than for the vicarious interests of adults.

But a competent coach also has taught them teamwork and expected them to work hard each day. A coach demanded respect—for the game, themselves, opponents, officials and spectators. A coach instructed them in setting goals and making plans. A coach made them realize the value of being prepared for any eventuality. Long after the athletes' competitive careers are over these values, qualities and skills remain. These "life skills" are the truly important attributes that young people realize from their involvement in sport.

How do athletes learn these "life skills?" They learn them from "Coach." This is a person distinctly and uniquely different from the idealized educational leader. This is someone the athletes see every day at practice, in the locker room, on the field. "Coach" begins by knowing skills and strategies and teaching them to athletes. Gradually this person becomes someone the young people look to for more than how to play a zone defense or how to stretch before contests. "Coach" becomes a role model.

Like all young people, athletes model their conduct after that of someone they respect. "Coach" fills that role; consequently, players watch everything about that person:

- Dress,
- Preparation for practices and competitions,
- Attention—or lack of attention—to details,
- Treatment of teammates,
- Response under pressure,
- Respect shown officials,
- Handling wins and losses,
- Whether personal and team goals are set,
- Consistency in enforcing team rules, and
- Compliance with both the letter and spirit of all rules.

The athletes easily associate with the actions of their role models, partly because high school aged players spend so much time with "Coach." Some researchers would say that young people learn best through following examples set by persons whom they respect.

In addition, "Coach" also can influence parents, because at some level they recognize that the coach is supposed to know about sports. Therefore, parents also watch for behavioral clues. The most important thing for parents to learn is sportsmanship, as practically everyone associated with scholastic sports feels that the problem behavior begins in the stands—not on the field or court or ice. "Coach" can influence behavior by showing respect for opponents and officials and by dealing humanely with athletes, especially when they make mistakes. The coach can help everyone maintain a sensible perspective on the importance of sports. Parents can learn from the coach who serves as a positive role model almost as easily as their young athletes do.

SUMMARY

Research suggests that coaches are the key element in determining the quality of the athletic experience. Further, statistics tell us that practically all youth are involved in organized sport at some point. Consequently, coaches have the opportunity to affect the lives of most youth. Coaches can begin to understand their responsibilities by learning what youth, parents and professionals consider important reasons for taking part in sports as well as what experienced coaches say about their profession.

Job descriptions by persons associated with athletics conclude that coaching is essentially an educational activity and that the coach is a teacher. This implies that the coach's work is focused on planning the instruction and measuring the development of athletes. However, the coach also must accept responsibility for preserving sport as a broadly educational enterprise. Scholastic sport has a major role in teaching important "life skills" to the participants and spectators. While players learn some of these lessons through formal instruction, they more often acquire them informally by watching the coach. The coach becomes a role model for the athletes, someone who teaches them without their conscious involvement. The coach may also fulfill this role for parents, who often need to learn better sportsmanship and respect for all elements of sport.

Coaching is complicated and challenging, a position with more subtleties than at first thought. However, every coach must confront these issues in setting about to personalize the job and turning it into a satisfying career.

REFERENCES

Ewing, M., and Seefeldt, V. (1988). *Patterns of Participation and Attrition in American Agency-Sponsored Sports*. West Palm Beach, FL: Sporting Goods' Manufacturers Association.

Manitoba Parks and Recreation Association. (1988). *Fair Play—Let's Get Back to the Game*. The 13th Annual Conference of the Manitoba Parks and Recreation Association; Winnipeg, Manitoba.

Martens, R., and Seefeldt, V. (1979). *Guidelines for Children's Sports*. Washington, D.C.: American Alliance for Health, Physical Education, Recreation and Dance.

Seefeldt, V. (1979). "Code of Ethics for Coaches." *Spotlight on Youth Sports*, 2: 4.

4
Interpersonal Relations

Jim Feldkamp, Ed.S.

QUESTIONS TO CONSIDER

- Who are the key individuals with whom the coach must communicate?
- What basic messages must coaches communicate to principals, athletic directors, parents, teachers, athletes and maintenance workers?
- What are the key elements of effective interpersonal relations?

INTRODUCTION

Why do some coaches who have only mediocre win/loss records have so much support from parents and students, while others who win championships have little or none? How do some coaches get so many students to participate, while others struggle to field a team? Does it appear that the athletic director and principal favor certain coaches? How do some coaches get their facilities maintained spotlessly, while others can't get the custodian to change a light bulb? There are many reasons why these situations exist. There is a good possibility, however, that interpersonal relations play a major role in each scenario.

An extremely important aspect of coaching is the development of positive working relationships with people who support you and your program. These positive relationships generally do not occur by accident; they are components of a coaching style. Some relationships take days to develop; most take months or years. Every coaching situation is unique. However, you control one common element: the amount of effort you are willing to make to create and maintain positive relationships with others.

Interpersonal relationships are part of one's coaching style. Whether or not they are effective depends upon the coach.

While positive results may not appear immediately, the long-term results of effective communication ultimately pay great dividends. The following tips about interacting with specific individuals and groups will serve as a good starting point toward effective communication and the development of positive interpersonal relations that should serve you well throughout your coaching experience.

COMMUNICATION WITH IMPORTANT OTHERS AND GROUPS
The Principal

The principal is the educational leader of the building. He/she is concerned with the total school environment and the well-being of all students and staff. Get to know the principal and make it a point to keep him/her informed of events and experiences relative to your team, both positive and negative. The principal may already be aware of what you are communicating, but it is important to hear it from you.

Coaches should share the principal's concern about the total welfare of the athlete.

Show an interest in and awareness of other school programs. Scan the local newspaper to become familiar with such key issues as standard test scores, a redistricting proposal, the upcoming millage or school board election, the school's recent success in the Science Olympiad, or the recent National Merit Scholarship winners who also happen to be athletes. It is beneficial to be able to discuss topical items that demonstrate your interest, concern, and support for the school and school district.

The Athletic Director

The athletic director leads the athletic program and shares many of the same concerns as the building principal. Dialogue regarding athletics with the principal may be general in nature. However, conversations with the athletic director will most likely be specific. Be sure to communicate with the athletic director about the positive, potentially positive, negative, and potentially negative situations that you face in your sport. He/she may be able to provide sound advice and assist you in alleviating problems and achieving program objectives. Read the school's literature on policies and procedures. Comply with deadlines and end-of-season responsibilities.

Frequent communication with the athletic director will eliminate many problems during the season.

Once the season is over and the athletes have gone on to other things, much remains to be done. The collection and storage of equipment, completion of end-of-season reports, and identification of needs for next season are extremely important to the athletic director. While these duties are not always as enjoyable as working with student athletes, they require your attention. When promptly completed, they will greatly assist you in establishing a positive working relationship with the athletic director.

The Parents

Communication is the key to a good relationship between the coach and parents. Many coaches have encountered problems due to "meddling parents." However, other coaches have discovered how much more meaningful coaching can be by effectively communicating with the parents. Parents want to know who is working with their sons or daughters. They want to know what your philosophy is, and if you really care about kids and their social, emotional, intellectual, and physical development. Parents may want to know how knowledgeable you are about the sport and what your goals are.

The parents' primary concern is the welfare of their child. Coaches who communicate effectively about students' welfare are practicing good interpersonal communication.

Unfortunately, the image of coaches in most movies and comic strips is rarely positive. Coaches are commonly portrayed as self-serving, insensitive, and single-minded. Sports highlights on the evening news aren't much help, as they often feature brawls, ejections, and other unsportsmanlike behavior demonstrated by a few coaches. These displays work against the credibility of coaches and athletics in general. As a result, you should make a conscious effort to meet the parents of your athletes and establish an open line of two-way communication.

If you discipline an athlete or issue a warning regarding future problems, tell the parents. If your actions are interpreted to parents by the athletes, the dinner table version is not always the same one that you would give. If, at a later date, you call these parents for support on an issue, you may find defensive parents who would rather discuss how unfairly their child was treated on that earlier occasion.

Many coaches have found that a pre-season "Meet the Team Night" helps parents get to know them and their programs. A pre-season evening practice during which the coach introduces the team and talks about his/her coaching philosophy, the potential for injury, and team policies in a concise manner, followed by a few drills and an intrasquad scrimmage, serves many purposes. It shows the coach in action (establishes credibility). It allows the coach to say something positive about each athlete (displays an interest). It illustrates to the parents exactly what their sons/daughters will be doing for the next few weeks. Being "on stage" before the season starts may also help relieve first game jitters for the athletes.

The Student Athlete

Sydney Harris, in his poem, *Winners and Losers*, wrote "a winner would rather be admired than liked, although he would prefer both." In Harris' poem the word winner could easily be replaced with coach to emphasize the point of striving to maintain high ideals, a responsible work ethic, and the qualities of good sportsmanship. To the curiously impressionable teenage mind, the coach is a role model who can have a tremendous influence. Coaches may be friends to their players, but must keep in mind that they are not peers. All teams must be governed by rules of conduct. Be firm but fair, and follow the basic rule that we should treat athletes as we would want to be treated. Have as few team rules as possible, and enforce them in a consistent manner. Use positive terminology to replace the time-honored negative ones—"sudden victory" in place of "sudden death" or "pro sprints" in place of "suicide sprints." While many of us used these terms while growing up, times have changed and so have coaching techniques. Remember, not long ago it was considered acceptable for coaches to provide salt tablets and keep athletes away from drinking water to "get them in shape."

Conduct fair team tryouts and have a genuine concern for all who try out. If your team has a limited membership, and reductions are necessary, "cuts" should be the most agonizing experience of the season. There is nothing pleasant about eliminating aspiring members from a team, especially at a time in their lives when acceptance is so important.

Eliminating aspiring athletes during "tryouts" requires great sensitivity on the part of the coaches.

The Number 1 rule of eliminating athletes from teams is *Never Post a List*. Regardless of how many have tried out, take the time to let them know personally that they did not make the team. If you consider that athletes have invested time and money in physical examinations, possibly purchased new equipment such as shoes and practice clothing, had parents fill out emergency and insurance forms, taken the risk of trying out, and cleared other hurdles just to be a member of your team, they deserve to be told by you the reasons why they did not make the squad this season. They should be complimented and thanked for their interest and encouraged to work on those aspects of the sport you identified as weaknesses so they might try again next year. If possible, offer roles as managers, statisticians, or timers to students who do not make the team.

Most will accept that they did not make the team, and your encouragement will be greatly appreciated. However, occasionally an individual may be devastated by the rejection, and additional counseling may be needed. If you sense a problem, contact the parents and explain exactly what has taken place and provide the same encouragement for their child's future development. Do not hesitate to contact the parents about their child's current and future status as a member of the team; the athlete may be concerned about further rejection or embarrassment at home and not tell his/her parents about the team selections. He/she may even decide not to go home after school each day and wander off while the parents think that the child is at practice.

In communicating with your athletes use simple, direct language and be a listener who is objective and concerned. Young people need guidance, direction, consistency, and genuine concern from their coaches. When you fulfill these basic needs, you develop a solid foundation for a successful coaching experience.

The Faculty

At the beginning of the season, consider sending a note to the teachers of your athletes, stating your concern about each athlete's academic progress, citizenship, and attendance. Ask teachers to contact you if the students are not meeting their expectations. Keep in mind that not every member of the faculty is a supporter of the athletic program, but avoid being discouraged by those who consider athletics a necessary evil of the extracurricular school day.

If you are not a teacher in the building where your athletes attend school or you are a non-faculty coach, communication with the faculty will be more difficult, but equally as important. Having a mail box in the school and attending selected school functions will help you to communicate with the faculty.

Coaches who are genuinely concerned about the academic progress of athletes will receive general support for athletic programs from teachers.

A coach who is a strong "teacher" of a sport and who cares about students as total individuals will earn the respect and support of most faculty members. The significance of staff attitudes toward your program should not be underestimated, because they ultimately filter into the student body through classroom communication. A program that has faculty support looks for creative methods to encourage the teaching staff to get involved. Statisticians, ticket takers, scorers, and timers are always needed. Consider a "faculty appreciation night" in conjunction with a game to recognize faculty support.

The Officials

It is important to have a positive mind-set regarding officials. They are hired to enforce the rules of the game. Coaches who choose not to see them as human beings who are hired to enforce rules to the best of their ability make officials a greater part of the game than they were ever intended to be. Throughout the history of athletics, officials have never had a win or a loss; that statistic is always reserved for the athletes and the coaches. Treat officials courteously and fairly. Get to know them by name and never embarrass them. They will make mistakes just as players and coaches do, but the vast majority do a good job. Those who don't will eventually have difficulty being selected as officials. Just as officials develop reputations among coaches, be assured that coaches develop reputations within the community of officials.

The Coaches of Other Sports

Show your colleagues that you care about their programs as well as your own. Inquire about the progress of their teams and, if possible, attend a few of their contests. In general, demonstrate a genuine concern for your fellow coaches. One of the surest ways to alienate yourself from other coaches is to talk down or discourage students from participating in other sports. Another way is to encourage specialization and a total year-round commitment to the sport you are coaching. These actions deprive athletes of well-rounded educational experiences through participation in other sports and should not be tolerated in interscholastic sports.

The Custodians and Maintenance Workers

Regular care of the facilities and locker rooms is extremely important and sometimes taken for granted. Changing lights, mowing grass, lining fields, and setting up pools or gyms usually involve efforts from the maintenance department. Go through the proper channels when making requests for maintenance or custodial service. Whenever possible, submit your requests early. Hot water in the showers, toilet paper in the restrooms, and changed light bulbs generally tend to be maintained better when you have a positive rapport with maintenance people.

The Professional Organizations

Memberships in professional organizations can be extremely beneficial. Information on coaching clinics, books, periodicals, videos, and in some cases, liability insurance are some of the benefits provided by the professional organizations at minimal expense. Organizations welcome coaches from all levels to participate. It's also a way to keep your finger on the pulse of the action in your sport and have the opportunity to bring about change through organized efforts, if you are so inclined.

SUMMARY

Through effective communication and positive interpersonal relations we reinforce the total team concept that coaches often refer to, thereby creating the environment for a successful coaching experience. As a constant reminder of this concept, view the word "TEAM" as an acronym meaning, "Together Everyone Accomplishes More." The coach is the key ingredient in formulating that togetherness as he/she establishes the tone by which the team and the program functions and the way in which they are perceived by others.

SUGGESTED READINGS

Gould, D. (1987). "Your Role as a Youth Sports Coach." In V. Seefeldt (editor), *Handbook for Youth Sport Coaches* (pp. 17-32). Reston, VA: American Alliance for Health, Physical Education, Recreation and Dance.

Malina, R. (Ed.). (1988). *Young Athletes: Biological, Psychological and Educational Perspectives*. Champaign, IL: Human Kinetics.

Small, F., Magill, R., and Ash, M. (editors) (1988). *Children in Sport*. Champaign, IL: Human Kinetics.

5

Including Athletes With Disabilities

Gail M. Dummer, Ph.D.

QUESTIONS TO CONSIDER
- What are the benefits of inclusion for athletes with disabilities and for other members of the sports community?
- How can coaches facilitate the successful inclusion of persons with disabilities?
- What resources are available for coaches who want additional information about including athletes with disabilities in their sports programs?

Approximately 5.25 million children and youth with disabilities, aged 6-21, are educated in the nation's public schools (Office of Special Education Programs, 1998). Like their siblings, neighbors, and friends, many of these children and youth with disabilities enjoy participating in sports. It is inevitable, therefore, that coaches of youth sport programs in school and community settings will be called upon to include athletes with disabilities. This chapter is designed to help coaches meet that challenge.

WHY INCLUDE ATHLETES WITH DISABILITIES?

Inclusion refers to the integration of athletes with disabilities on the same sports teams and at the same competitions as their non-disabled peers. Inclusion is usually a *win-win* situation, with many benefits for athletes with disabilities, non-disabled teammates, coaches and other members of the sports community.

Benefits for Athletes With Disabilities

Persons with disabilities participate in sports for the same reasons that non-disabled people participate (Blinde and McClung, 1997; Brasile, et al., 1991; Castaneda and Sherrill, 1997; Dummer, et al., 1997; Hedrick, 1985; Kozub and Porretta, 1996; Krebs and Block, 1992; Sherrill, 1998; Sherrill, et al., 1990). They participate to have fun, learn new skills, and improve physical fitness, health, and appearance. They enjoy the challenge, excitement, rewards, and travel associated with competition, as

well as being with friends, meeting new friends, and being part of a team atmosphere. Being involved in sports also allows athletes to benefit from improved self-esteem, self-discipline, determination, independence, work ethic, goal-setting, and maturity.

Persons with disabilities may realize additional benefits from sports participation (Blinde and McClung, 1997; Dummer, et al., 1997). In some cases, regular physical activity helps to minimize the characteristics of a disability or to reduce the need for ongoing physical therapy. Athletes learn to cope with their disabilities and develop greater independence, which may facilitate participation and achievement in other activities at school, during work, or in the community. They enjoy the opportunity to participate in the same activities as their non-disabled peers, and they learn from the examples of their non-disabled teammates who must overcome obstacles such as injuries or plateaus in performance. The opportunity to be part of a team is especially important to athletes whose educational experiences may have been routinely individualized, and the opportunity to demonstrate ability and inspire others can be a very satisfying experience for persons who are frequently judged on the basis of what they cannot do.

Inclusion on a *regular* team often results in greater benefits to the athlete than participation on a *special* team (Dummer, et al., 1997). Athletes with disabilities who participate on *regular* teams often benefit from better sport-specific coaching, more rigorous training, more competition in practice, and higher expectations. Many athletes with disabilities belong on *regular* teams because of their skill levels; they keep up and fit in with the able-bodied athletes on the *regular* team. Some athletes with disabilities report higher self-esteem when participating on a *regular* team. Participating on a *regular* team also facilitates socialization with friends and neighbors who attend the same school. Other personal benefits include greater independence in activities of daily living and improved ability to cope with limitations imposed by disabilities. Finally, some athletes with disabilities prefer participating on a *regular* team because of a philosophical belief in inclusion.

Benefits for Other Members of the Sports Community

The entire sports team benefits from inclusion of persons with disabilities. When team members observe the work ethic of athletes with disabilities, teammates have the opportunity to learn about hard work, perseverance, and overcoming obstacles to achieve specific goals. Some coaches report that including athletes with disabilities increases motivation and decreases whining by *able-bodied* athletes during practice. New friendships are another obvious benefit to teammates. Coaches have the opportunity to hone skills with respect to communicating with athletes, teaching sports techniques, and modifying activities and equipment.

Another benefit for coaches who include athletes with disabilities is the possibility of being selected to coach at camps and competitions for athletes with disabilities. In some cases, a sports program may get more publicity because it includes athletes with disabilities. Because the Americans with Disabilities Act (ADA) puts pressure on community agencies to make programs and facilities accessible to persons with disabilities (Block, 1995), sport programs that practice inclusion frequently get more facility time at a lower cost than programs that do not welcome athletes with disabilities. Similarly, external funding such as sponsorship support and small grants may be easier to obtain.

TIPS FOR COACHES

Inclusion in sports does not require a vast repertoire of special coaching skills or extensive knowledge about disability. The most important ingredients for successful inclusion are a demonstrated willingness to accept persons with disabilities and common sense, as indicated by the following advice to coaches from athletes with disabilities who are members of *regular* teams in their communities (Dummer, et al., 1997).

Demonstrate Acceptance

Show athletes that you care by getting to know them and giving individual attention. Show respect by treating athletes with disabilities the same as other athletes and by establishing challenging performance goals.

Focus on Ability, Not Disability

Expect athletes to contribute to your program by learning and performing to the best of their abilities, maintaining a high level of physical fitness, and supporting their teammates. Do not assume that athletes are fragile or incapable because of a disability, and do not focus attention on the disability.

Use Effective Teaching Techniques

Communicate instructions in a variety of ways—demonstrate, provide verbal instructions, and if needed, move the athlete's body through the desired actions. Use accommodations that facilitate learning, such as positioning athletes with low vision where they can see a demonstration, using sign language or simply remembering to face the athlete when communicating directions to athletes who are deaf, and using simple one or two-part directions for athletes with cognitive disabilities.

Modify Sports Techniques and Equipment

Coaches of athletes with disabilities need creativity and problem-solving skills. Use principles of biomechanics to determine the best way for a swimmer with a spinal cord injury to maintain a streamlined body position, the most efficient running gait for a leg amputee, or the most effective position for the wheelchair and the body when hitting a tennis ball. Use and adapt sports equipment to facilitate inclusion (Paciorek and Jones, 2001). For example, a swimmer with a leg amputation might use swim fins to keep up with *able-bodied* swimmers during practice. Athletes with limited hand function often use elastic bandages to help them grip racquets and other sports equipment.

Maintain a Safe Practice Environment

Be sure that athletes possess the skills and fitness needed to perform the activities included in your coaching plan. Know first aid for disability-related health problems such as seizures, diabetic emergencies, and the side effects of medications. Use accommodations that promote safety—examples include the use of gym mats to facilitate safe transfers to and from a wheelchair and alerting blind swimmers that they are approaching the end of the pool by tapping them with a soft-tipped long pole.

Seek Coaching Education

Be an expert in your sport—athletes with disabilities generally value a coach's expertise in sports more than his/her knowledge of the special needs associated with a disability.

WHAT COACHES NEED TO KNOW ABOUT DISABILITIES

How do athletes with disabilities differ from non-disabled athletes? Differences associated with some of the most common disabilities are described in this section; however, the reader should not assume that all persons with disabilities fit a particular pattern or that their abilities match a textbook definition. The effects of a disability depend upon many factors, including age at onset, severity of the disability, and affected body parts (e.g., hemiplegia, paraplegia), as well as personal motivation and prior instruction and training in sports skills.

It is much more important to know the individual than to know the disability!

Health Impairments

An athlete's stamina and vitality may be limited by health impairments such as severe asthma, cardiorespiratory conditions, diabetes, and seizure disorders; however, it is important to note that many athletes (including Olympians) have succeeded in sports despite these challenges. Coaches should learn about indications and contraindications associated with the individual's health problem, and should adjust their expectations for the athlete's performance accordingly (Sherrill, 1998).

Physical Disabilities

Physical disabilities include: (a) amputations and congenital limb deficiencies; (b) neurological conditions such as cerebral palsy, stroke, and head injury; (c) spinal cord conditions such as spinal cord injury, spina bifida, and poliomyelitis; (d) dwarfism; and (e) other disabilities that affect range of joint motion, muscle strength, or skeletal function. Coaches should learn about the athlete's abilities and potential to perform sports skills safely and effectively, and coaches should work with the athlete to develop modifications to sports techniques or equipment that facilitate learning and performance (Goodman, 1995; Lockett and Keyes, 1994; Miller, 1995; Paciorek and Jones, 1994; Sherrill, 1998).

Hearing Loss

This category includes athletes who are deaf (hearing loss of 55 dB or greater) and those who are hard of hearing (lesser degree of hearing loss). Coaches should help athletes to use residual hearing by making sure the athletes are in position to view demonstrations and to hear instructions. If an athlete is deaf, the coach should

consider learning *survival* sign language and should use visual and tactile cues whenever possible. (Goodman, 1995; Sherrill, 1998.)

Vision Loss

Vision loss refers either to a loss of visual acuity (poor near or distance vision) or diminished field of vision (*tunnel* or *doughnut* vision). Coaches may need to modify instruction for athletes with vision loss by orienting the athlete to the sports environment and equipment, providing auditory and tactile cues whenever possible, and coaching the athlete to play a position that is most suited to her/his residual vision. (Goodman, 1995; Paciorek and Jones, 1994; and Sherrill, 1998.)

Cognitive Disabilities

Cognitive disabilities include conditions such as learning disabilities, mental retardation, attention deficit disorder, and pervasive developmental disorders (e.g., Asperger's syndrome and autism). Coaches may need to help these athletes pay attention to relevant cues and exercise good judgment about how to react in a sports situation. Coaches may also need to develop innovative ways to teach abstract concepts such as offense and defense (Goodman, 1995; Sherrill, 1998). It is important to note that the vast majority of cognitive disabilities are mild in nature; thus, in many cases, coaches and teammates will not even be aware that an athlete has a cognitive disability.

Behavior Disorders

Athletes with a behavior disorder behave in ways that are inappropriate to the situation at hand. They may under-react or over-react to stresses and problems in the sports environment. Their reactions may be expressed in unacceptable ways such as verbal or physical abuse. Athletes with behavior disorders may need help from an understanding coach who demonstrates and teaches effective ways to cope with stressful situations, and who provides the athlete with appropriate challenges where success and acceptable behaviors are facilitated (Sherrill, 1998).

Safety is an important concern when coaching any athlete, but especially when coaching an athlete with disabilities (Goodman, 1995; Sherrill, 1998). Coaches should ask the athlete (or parents/guardians) about indicated and contraindicated activities, medications and possible side-effects, health care regimens, and special medical problems such as seizures or atlantoaxial instability (an instability of the cervical spine that affects some people with Down syndrome and dwarfism). In addition, coaches should be proficient in first aid for health problems that the athlete might experience in sports settings.

WHAT COACHES NEED TO KNOW ABOUT SPORT OPPORTUNITIES

Children and youth with disabilities and their families are frequently frustrated in their attempts to locate programs that offer instruction and training in physical activity and sports. Many teachers, coaches, recreation leaders, and physicians simply do not know where to refer the child with disabilities who is interested in sports. *Coaches can help by learning about available programs, both nationally and in your community, and by providing this information to persons with disabilities who could benefit from participation in sports.* In some cases, coaches may need to help the person with disabilities advocate for her/his rights to participate in a sports program.

Skill Development and Training

Opportunities to learn the techniques, rules, strategies, and etiquette associated with specific sports and to develop the physical fitness and skills needed for success in sports are available through a variety of programs. Many athletes with disabilities prefer to practice with *regular* teams where they typically have access to better coaching, training, and facilities, and where they can participate with their friends and neighbors. However, novice athletes with disabilities may prefer *special* sports programs such as the programs offered by disability sport organizations, therapeutic recreation programs, or specially-designed school programs. They may feel more comfortable learning in an environment where their teammates have similar disabilities, where adaptive equipment is available, and where coaches are selected in part because of their knowledge of disability. Often, learn-to-play experiences in *special* sports programs serve as a stepping stone to inclusion in *regular* sports programs.

Most coaches are already familiar with *regular* sports programs such as public school intramural and interscholastic sports programs, community sports and recreation programs, and the network of local clubs associated with national sport governing bodies such as USA Gymnastics, U.S. Figure Skating, USA Swimming, and USA Track and Field. However, few coaches are knowledgeable about the major disability sport organizations (DSOs) in the United States. Each of these organizations offers multiple sport opportunities to eligible persons with disabilities.

- **Disabled Sports USA** (DSUSA) offers a variety of summer, winter, and adventure sports for athletes with amputations, as well as anyone with a permanent physical disability.
- **Dwarf Athletic Association of America** (DAAA) programs provide competitive sports opportunities in several sports for persons with short stature caused by medical conditions such as chondrodystrophy.
- **Special Olympics International** (SOI) is a program of sports training and competition in over 20 sports for individuals with mental retardation and other cognitive disabilities. Located in the United States and over 150 other countries, Special Olympics also conducts programs like Unified Sports (teams must be comprised of an equal number of athletes with cognitive disabilities and athletes who are non-disabled) and the Motor Activities Training Program (for developmental athletes). (See Krebs and Cloutier, 1992).
- **USA Deaf Sports Federation** (USADSF) programs include a variety of summer and winter sports for athletes with a hearing loss of 55 dB or greater.
- **U.S. Association for Blind Athletes** (USABA) programs serve athletes who are blind and visually impaired in both summer and winter sports. Persons with a minimum vision loss of 20/200 or a field of vision 20° or less are eligible to compete in USABA programs.
- **U.S. Cerebral Palsy Athletic Association** (USCPAA) programs provide opportunities for persons with cerebral palsy, stroke, and head injury to participate in a variety of sports.
- **Wheelchair Sports USA** (WSUSA) serves athletes who have limited function of the lower limbs, including those who use wheelchairs, crutches, canes, walkers, braces and other assistive devices for locomotion. A wide variety of sports programs are offered for both junior and adult participants.

Competition

Although many athletes with disabilities prefer learning and training in a *regular* sports program, they may enjoy competing in both *regular* and *special* competitions. *Regular* competitions provide an opportunity for athletes with disabilities to test their skills against *able-bodied* athletes. Other reasons for participating in *regular* competitions include more frequent opportunities to compete, shorter travel distance and lower entry fees than most *special* competitions, opportunity to contribute to the team performance, and hanging out with teammates. In *special* competitions, athletes often are classified according to their functional sport abilities, providing a more level playing field for competition and a better likelihood of recognition, especially for athletes with more severe disabilities. *Special* competitions are offered at the local, regional, and national level by the DSOs. Major international competitions include the Paralympic Games, Deaf World Games, and International Special Olympics Games.

- **Paralympic Games**: The Paralympic Games are the pinnacle of competition for athletes with physical disabilities and vision loss, as well as some athletes with cognitive disabilities. The Paralympic Games are held every four years in the same years as Olympic Games and usually at the same venues as the Olympic Games. Athletes represent their countries and must achieve rigid performance standards to qualify for the Games.

- **Deaf World Games**: Elite athletes who are deaf are eligible to represent their countries in the Deaf World Games. The Deaf World Games are held every four years in the years following the Olympic Games.
- **International Special Olympics Games**: The International Special Olympics Games provide opportunities for athletes with cognitive disabilities to compete and travel. Athletes are selected on the basis of performances in local, regional, or national competitions. The International Special Olympics Games are held every four years in the years preceding the Olympic Games.

LEGAL BASIS FOR INCLUSION IN SPORTS

Most coaches and program administrators practice inclusion because it is the right thing to do for athletes with disabilities. However, to ensure that such opportunities are readily and uniformly available, three federal laws have established a legal structure that promotes inclusion in sports for persons with disabilities.

Americans with Disabilities Act (ADA)

The ADA requires places of exercise such as a gymnasium, health spa, bowling alley, golf course, or swimming pool to make *reasonable accommodations* that facilitate full and equal enjoyment of an activity by *qualified individuals* with disabilities whenever such accommodations are easily accomplished without extraordinary expense (Block, 1995). Activities must be offered in the most integrated setting appropriate to the needs of the person with disabilities. School, university, and community sports programs all must comply with ADA provisions.

- **Qualified individual**. A qualified individual is a person who has the prerequisite skills for participation in the physical activity program. Programs may not impose eligibility criteria that discriminate against persons with disabilities; however, they may impose requirements that protect the safety of participants. Safety requirements must be based on individual assessment and actual risks, not speculation. Some experts advise the use of informed consent statements as a way of educating participants about the activity when there is no adequate way to conduct an individual assessment or when there are no data to substantiate the potential risks to the safety of participants.

- **Reasonable accommodations**. Reasonable accommodations include removing architectural barriers that limit physical accessibility of the facility, adapting instructional methods and equipment, and providing alternate communication methods that facilitate participation. Low-cost, practical solutions usually are possible when athletes, coaches, and program leaders work together.

Olympic and Amateur Sports Act (OASA)

The Amateur Sports Act, as adopted in 1978, requires the United States Olympic Committee (USOC) "to encourage and provide assistance to amateur athletic programs and competition for handicapped individuals, including, where feasible, the expansion of meaningful participation by handicapped individuals in programs of athletic competition for able-bodied individuals." To wit, the USOC has: (a) established a Committee on Sports for the Disabled that considers changes to USOC policies and programs related to disability sports; (b) accepted seven disability sports organizations (DSOs) as members of the USOC; and (c) encouraged national sport governing bodies (NGBs) to facilitate participation in their programs by athletes with disabilities.

Per Amateur Sports Act provisions, each Olympic and Pan American sport has its own national governing body (NGB). The Olympic sports include archery, badminton, baseball, basketball, biathlon, bobsled, boxing, canoe/kayak, curling, cycling, diving, equestrian, fencing, field hockey, figure skating, gymnastics, ice hockey, judo, luge, modern pentathlon, rowing, sailing, shooting, skiing/snowboarding, soccer, softball, speed skating, swimming, synchronized swimming, table tennis, tae kwon do, team handball, tennis, track and field, triathlon, volleyball, water polo, weightlifting, and wrestling. Additional Pan American sports include bowling, karate, racquetball, roller skating, squash, and water skiing.

The Amateur Sports Act was amended in 1998 to become the Olympic Amateur Sports Act. The 1998 amendments strengthen the provisions for services to athletes with disabilities by authorizing the USOC to serve as the National Paralympic Committee and by encouraging NGBs to pursue *vertical integration*, a term that refers to greater NGB responsibility for the development of elite athletes with disabilities.

Individuals with Disabilities Education Act (IDEA)

IDEA is a federal law that governs the education of students with disabilities in the public schools. IDEA specifies physical education as a required educational service, and further defines physical education as "the development of physical and motor fitness; fundamental motor skills and patterns; and skills in aquatics, dance, and individual and group games and sports, including intramural and lifetime sports" (Office of Special Education Programs, 1998. This provision of IDEA facilitates the participation of students with disabilities in public school intramural and interscholastic sports programs.

SUMMARY

The real question is not whether to include athletes with a disability in sports programs, but rather how to help athletes with and without disabilities to benefit optimally from inclusive sports programs. The resources described in this chapter will help coaches who want more information about benefits of inclusion, tips on how to include, disabilities, sport and competition opportunities, and the legal basis for inclusion in sports. However, most coaches already have the tools to succeed—a willingness to try and common sense.

REFERENCES

Blinde, E. M., and McClung, L. R. (1997). "Enhancing the Physical and Social Self Through Recreational Activity: Accounts of Individuals With Physical Disabilities." *Adapted Physical Activity Quarterly*, 14: 327-344.

Block, M. E. (1995). "Americans With Disabilities Act: Its Impact on Youth Sports." *Journal of Physical Education, Recreation and Dance*, 66(1): 28-32.

Brasile, F. M., Kleiber, D. A., and Harnisch, D. (1991). "Analysis of Participation Incentives Among Athletes With and Without Disabilities." *Therapeutic Recreation Journal*, 25: 18-33.

Castaneda, L., and Sherrill, C. (1997). "Challenger Baseball and TOP-Soccer: Sports Success Stories." *Teaching Exceptional Children*, 30(2): 26-29.

Dummer, G. M., Siegel, S. R., Ellis, M. K., Portman, V. A., and Porter, P.A. (1997, November). *What Athletes With Disabilities Say About Inclusion in Physical Activity Programs*. Presented at the Michigan Association for Health, Physical Education, Recreation and Dance, Grand Rapids, MI.

Goodman, S. (1995). *Coaching Athletes With Disabilities: General Principles*. Belconnen, ACT: Australian Sports Commission.

Hedrick, B. N. (1985). "The Effect of Wheelchair Tennis Participation and Mainstreaming Upon the Perceptions of Competence of Physically Disabled Adolescents." *Therapeutic Recreation Journal*, 19: 34-46.

Kozub, F. M., and Porretta, D. (1996). "Including Athletes With Disabilities: Interscholastic Athletic Benefits for All." *Journal of Physical Education, Recreation and Dance*, 67(3): 19-24.

Krebs, P. L., and Block, M. E. (1992). "Transition of Students With Disabilities Into Community Recreation: The Role of the Adapted Physical Educator." *Adapted Physical Activity Quarterly*, 9: 305-315.

Krebs, P. L., and Cloutier, G. (1992). "Unified Sports: I've Seen the Future." *Palaestra*, 8(2): 42-44.

Lockett, K. F., and Keyes, A. M. (1994). *Conditioning With Physical Disabilities*. Champaign, IL: Human Kinetics.

Miller, P. D. (editor). (1995). *Fitness Programming and Physical Disability*. Champaign, IL: Human Kinetics.

Office of Special Education Programs. (1998). *Twentieth Annual Report to Congress on the Implementation of the Individuals With Disabilities Education Act*. Washington, DC: Office of Special Education Programs, Office of Special Education and Rehabilitative Services.

Paciorek, M. J., and Jones, J. A. (2001). *Disability Sport and Recreation Resources, 3rd Ed*. Traverse City, MI: Cooper Publishing Group.

Shifflett, B., Cator, C., and Megginson, N. (1994). "Active Lifestyle Adherence Among Individuals With and Without Disabilities." *Adapted Physical Activity Quarterly*, 11: 359-367.

Sherrill, C. (1998). *Adapted Physical Activity, Recreation, and Sport (5th edition)*. Boston, MA: WCB McGraw-Hill.

Sherrill, C., Hinson, M., Gench, B., Kennedy, S. O., and Low, L. (1990). "Self-Concepts of Disabled Youth Athletes." *Perceptual and Motor Skills*, 70: 1093-1098.

RESOURCES

To Learn More About Disabilities:

- The *Family Village* web site < www.familyvillage. wisc.edu > sponsored by the University of Wisconsin provides a wealth of knowledge about including persons with disabilities in community life, including sports and leisure activities. The *library* feature allows the user to seek information on hundreds of disabilities.

- The publication section of the *National Information Center for Children and Youth with Disabilities* (NICHCY) web site <www.nichcy.org > includes fact sheets on a variety of disabilities

Disability Sport Organization Web Sites:

Disabled Sports USA < www.dsusa.org>
Dwarf Athletic Association of America < www.daaa.org>
Special Olympics International < www.specialolympics.org >
USA Deaf Sports Federation < www.usadsf.org >
U.S. Association for Blind Athletes < www.usaba.org >
U.S. Cerebral Palsy Athletic Association < www.uscpaa.org >
Wheelchair Sports USA < www.wsusa.org >

International Competition Web Sites:

Paralympic Games < www.paralympic.org >
Deaf World Games < www.ciss.org >
International Special Olympics Games < www.specialolympics.org >

For Additional Information About Federal Laws

- The ADA (*Americans with Disabilities Act*) Home Page, located at < www.usdoj.gov/crt/ada/ adahom1.htm > operated by U.S. Department of Justice provides access to technical materials, including the text of the law, technical assistance programs such as standards for accessible facility design, enforcement programs, mediation programs, results of recent ADA lawsuits, and access to a toll-free ADA information line. The *ADA Regulations for Title III* in the section on technical assistance are especially useful to persons who provide leadership to physical activity and sports programs.

- The complete text of the *Olympic and Amateur Sports Act* (OASA) can be accessed on the U.S. Olympic Committee web site at < www.usoc.org >. Click on "About the USOC" then "Olympic and Amateur Sports Act.".

- The IDEA'97 (*Individuals with Disabilities Education Act*) web site is located at < www.ed.gov/offices /OSERS/IDEA/ >. Readers will find both summary and complete versions of the law, as well as materials that are helpful in implementing IDEA in local communities.

Section II
Growth and Development

6
Physical and Cognitive Growth of Children and Youths

John L. Haubenstricker, Ph.D. and Jennifer J. Waldron, M.Ed.

QUESTIONS TO CONSIDER

- Why is knowledge of the physical and cognitive growth of children and adolescents important to the coach?
- What is the normal physical growth pattern for children and adolescents?
- How do boys and girls differ in their physical growth?
- How do boys and girls compare on measures of physical performance?
- How do sport-related cognitive capacities of children and adolescents compare to those of adults?
- What is the role of visual abilities in the motor performance of children and adolescents?

INTRODUCTION

Coaches of middle and high school youths face a unique challenge. Not only must they have a thorough understanding of the skills, rules, and strategies of the sports that they coach, as well as the ability to perform all of the usual coaching responsibilities, they must also adapt these abilities to individuals whose bodies are undergoing physical changes and whose cognitive capacities are not yet mature. Although coaches of mature adults must cope with physical, cognitive, and psychological differences in their athletes, coaches of children and youths have additional responsibilities. They have to contend with growing bones, rapidly changing body tissues and proportions, immature biological systems, delayed strength and coordination, limited cognitive capacity, lack of group experiences, or the extremes that exist for each of these variables among individuals of the same chronological age.

Having an understanding of the physical growth and cognitive development of children and adolescents will enable coaches to be more effective in helping boys and girls become more skilled and better athletes. The awareness that growing children and adolescents are not yet adults should lead to modifications in practice schedules, performance expectations, instructions, drills, activities, and game strategies. The bottom line in coaching must be the welfare of the participating athletes.

When reflecting about the impact of their coaching practices on the growth and development of youths, coaches should ask three questions:

1. Do my coaching practices promote the safety of the participants?
2. Do my coaching practices permit all the participants to learn or achieve according to their abilities?
3. Do my coaching practices result in enjoyable experiences for the participants?

The bottom line in coaching must be the welfare of the athletes.

This chapter provides information about the physical and cognitive growth of boys and girls, as well as the development of their visual abilities. First, the normal physical growth curve will be discussed, including the changing rates of growth in body segments. This will be followed by a consideration of male/female differences in physical dimensions, body composition, and physical performance. Attention will then be devoted to the growth of cognitive function and its relationship to learning sports skills and strategies. Finally, information about the role of visual abilities in performing motor skills will be provided.

THE NORMAL GROWTH CURVE

The general pattern of physical growth for most healthy individuals is quite predictable and applies to a number of physical measures such as standing height, body weight, shoulder width, and hip width. A velocity curve for standing height shown in Figure 6-1 will be used to illustrate this general pattern of growth.

During the first few years following birth, boys and girls grow quite rapidly, but at a declining rate each year as depicted by the deceleration part of the curve. After 5 years of age, the average annual rate of growth in height is about 2.0 to 2.5 inches or 5.1 to 6.4 centimeters (the relatively flat portion of the curve). This period of steady growth continues until the onset of the pubertal growth spurt, commonly known as the adolescent growth spurt. During the childhood years, average annual gains in weight generally range from 5.0 to 7.0 pounds.

Adolescent Growth Spurt

The adolescent growth spurt is characterized by a period of rapidly increasing growth (acceleration) until a peak is reached (peak height velocity), followed by a decline (deceleration) to the pre-spurt rate of growth (Figure 6-1). This growth spurt usually lasts for two to three years in most individuals. During the most intense portion of the spurt, gains in height for some boys may be at the rate of six or more inches per year. The intensity of the growth spurt is less for girls and often of slightly shorter duration than for boys. Annual weight gains of 15 pounds or more are not uncommon during this period.

The adolescent growth spurt in stature generally begins about two years earlier in girls (age 10) than in boys (age 12). Thus, there is a period of time when girls are growing and maturing much more rapidly than boys, with

the result that girls, on the average, are slightly taller and heavier than boys during the middle school years (from approximately age 11 through age 13). Moreover, the timing of this growth spurt can vary greatly from individual to individual, so that in some girls the spurt may begin as early as 9 years of age, and in some boys as late as 17 or 18 years of age.

Variations in Height

The greatest variations in height among boys and among girls occur during the middle school/junior high school years. Table 6-1 contains the maximum, minimum and mean values for the height of males and females across the age range from 5 to 18. An estimate of the variability in growth can be obtained by examining the difference in height between maximum and minimum values for boys and for girls at each age (labeled as "Diff." in Table 6-1). The greatest variability in height for girls occurs at ages 12-14 (over 18 in.), whereas that for boys occurs at ages 13-15 (over 16 in.). Coaches of middle school or junior high school sports where height is important (e.g., basketball, volleyball) should recognize and accommodate extreme height variations among the participants.

Final Phase of Normal Growth

The final phase of the normal growth curve for height involves a gradual decline in the rate of growth until growth ceases. Early maturing females may reach final stature as early as age 14, whereas late maturing

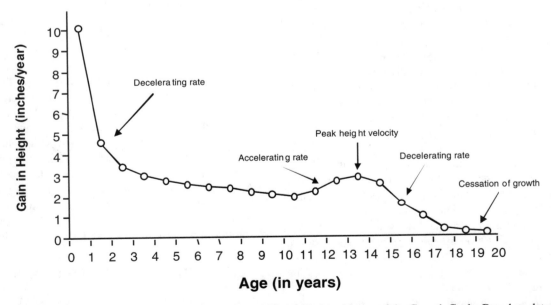

Figure 6-1. Velocity Curve for Height Depicting Rate of Growth During Various Phases of the Growth Cycle. Based on data from the Centers for Disease Control and Prevention (2000) and the Motor Performance Study (Haubenstricker, Seefeldt & Branta, 1999).

males may not do so until their early 20s. More typically, females attain their adult height sometime during the first two years of high school, while most males reach their final stature during the junior or senior year.

Although height and weight follow similar growth patterns, there are essential differences. First, the growth spurt in weight occurs after the spurt in height. Thus, there is a period of time, perhaps up to a year, where the increased size of the skeleton is not accompanied by a comparable amount of muscular tissue growth. The result

may be a momentary decline in balance and coordination, particularly in males with linear skeletons, until muscular growth catches up.

A second difference is that the variations in weight within gender tend to stay relatively large following the adolescent growth spurt, whereas those for height decrease. Examination of the maximum-minimum weight differences in Table 6-2 reveals that greatest difference among females occurs at age 14, whereas that for males occurs at age 17.

Table 6-1. Maximum, Minimum and Mean Values for the Standing Height (Inches) of Males and Females 5-18 Years of Age.

	Females					Males			
Age	Mean	Max.[1]	Min.[2]	Diff.[3]	Age	Mean	Max.	Min.	Diff.
5	43.0	48.0	38.3	9.7	5	43.2	48.1	37.2	10.9
6	45.6	51.5	39.3	12.2	6	46.0	51.2	39.8	11.4
7	47.9	54.4	40.9	13.5	7	48.5	53.9	43.6	10.3
8	50.4	57.0	42.7	14.3	8	50.9	56.1	45.5	10.6
9	52.6	60.0	44.3	15.7	9	53.1	58.5	46.8	11.7
10	54.8	62.8	46.6	16.2	10	55.2	60.9	48.3	12.6
11	57.4	66.2	48.7	17.5	11	57.2	62.9	50.4	12.5
12	60.2	69.1	51.1	18.0	12	59.4	66.3	52.5	13.8
13	62.4	71.0	52.8	18.2	13	62.1	70.6	54.0	16.6
14	63.9	72.8	54.2	18.6	14	65.0	73.0	56.1	16.9
15	64.6	73.0	56.5	16.5	15	67.6	75.8	59.2	16.6
16	65.2	73.6	58.8	14.8	16	69.2	76.3	61.6	14.7
17	65.6	73.5	60.1	13.4	17	70.2	77.4	62.5	14.9
18	66.1	71.2	60.0	11.2	18	70.6	78.1	62.6	15.5

[1]Max. = Maximum value; [2]Min. = Minimum value; [3]Diff. = Difference between maximum and minimum. Data are from the Motor Performance Study, Michigan State University, 1999.

Table 6-2. Maximum, Minimum and Mean Values for the Standing Weight (Pounds) of Males and Females 5-18 Years of Age.

	Females					Males			
Age	Mean	Max.[1]	Min.[2]	Diff.[3]	Age	Mean	Max.	Min.	Diff.
5	40.5	62.0	27.0	35.0	5	41.1	62.0	27.0	35.0
6	45.5	78.0	28.0	50.0	6	46.6	70.0	33.0	37.0
7	51.0	97.0	31.0	66.0	7	52.1	87.0	37.0	50.0
8	57.4	113.0	32.0	81.0	8	59.0	99.0	43.0	56.0
9	64.9	110.0	38.0	72.0	9	66.0	120.0	38.0	82.0
10	72.8	123.0	41.0	82.0	10	73.5	140.0	40.0	100.0
11	82.7	156.0	46.0	110.0	11	80.7	162.0	44.0	118.0
12	93.7	193.0	60.0	122.0	12	90.6	185.0	55.0	130.0
13	105.6	220.0	70.0	150.0	13	102.5	191.0	65.0	126.0
14	114.8	239.0	71.0	168.0	14	116.4	220.0	77.0	143.0
15	119.7	220.0	81.0	139.0	15	130.5	223.0	84.0	129.0
16	122.8	182.0	94.0	88.0	16	142.0	222.0	93.0	129.0
17	125.2	218.0	96.0	122.0	17	149.8	286.0	107.0	179.0
18	127.8	193.0	106.0	87.0	18	154.4	262.0	111.0	151.0

[1]Max. = Maximum value; [2]Min. = Minimum value; [3]Diff. = Difference between maximum and minimum. Data are from the Motor Performance Study, Michigan State University, 1999.

A third difference between height and weight is that growth in height eventually ceases whereas growth in weight can continue into the adult years. It is important for the coach to know whether the weight gains obtained during the growing years represent growth in muscle and bone (e.g., lean body mass) or growth in fatty tissue.

Variations in weight within gender remain large during the senior high school years.

Changing Rates of Growth in Body Segments

An interesting feature of the growth process is that the various body segments do not grow at the same rate. This disproportionate growth of the body segments is required if the body of an infant is to attain adult proportions. For example, the arms and legs of young athletes must grow at a relatively faster rate than the head and trunk. The shoulders of boys must grow faster than their hips, and the hips of girls must grow faster than their shoulders if the body shapes associated with adult males and adult females are to be achieved. Thus, the bodies of children and youth are not just downsized versions of adult bodies.

Growth of the individual body segments also does not occur at a uniform rate across the childhood and adolescent years. During the first year after birth, over half of the growth in body length occurs in the trunk. This coincides with the time the infant gains control over the head and trunk in preparation for upright locomotion. After the first year, nearly two-thirds of the annual gains in height take place in the legs. This trend continues until the individual is well into the secondary growth spurt. Thus, the childhood years are the leg-growing years. This means that early-maturing males or females generally will have shorter legs compared to their total height than their later maturing counterparts who have more time for their legs to grow. During the final years of adolescent growth, most of the gains in height again occur in the trunk as adult stature is attained.

The bodies of children and youth are not just downsized versions of adult bodies.

The rapid growth of the arms and legs, including the hands and feet, contributes to the awkwardness experienced by some individuals during their growth spurts, particularly the late-maturing males and females. Early-maturing males and females generally experience less loss of coordination, and with the benefit of their greater body size and muscle tissue, they may see most of their athletic success during the middle school/junior high and high school years. The late-maturing adolescents may not enjoy similar success until the late high school or college years.

GENDER DIFFERENCES IN PHYSICAL DIMENSIONS AND BODY COMPOSITION

Prior to the onset of puberty, there are few differences in the growth processes and physical dimensions of boys and girls. Examination of Tables 6-1 and 6-2, respectively, reveals that boys are only slightly taller and heavier than girls during the prepubescent years. Measures of other body dimensions including hip and shoulder widths, limb lengths and circumferences, as well as indices of body shape, such as sitting height/standing height ratios (Figure 6-2) and hip/shoulder ratios (Figure 6-3), provide similar results.

These differences are not meaningful from a coaching perspective. In other words, differences in body size and shape alone do not justify separating boys and girls in physical activities prior to puberty. The coach could contribute more to skill development by focusing on and accommodating the physical differences that exist *within* each gender group.

Differences in body size and shape alone do not justify separating boys and girls for physical activity prior to puberty.

There are some differences, however, that may favor boys in some physical activities and girls in others. For example, even at the younger ages boys have a greater proportion of muscle mass and less fatty tissue than girls. This biological difference, coupled with a greater measure of cultural stimulation and aggressiveness, usually results in the superior performance of boys on measures of strength and power including running, jumping, and throwing. On the other hand, girls mature more rapidly than boys, which gives them an advantage over boys, perhaps also through cultural encouragement, on balance and coordination tasks such as rope jumping, hop-scotch, beam stunts, and rhythmic activities.

Changes that occur during puberty, including the secondary growth spurt, the development of primary and secondary sex characteristics, and various hormonal changes, result in marked male/female differences in body size, shape, and composition. For example, the earlier maturation of females provides less time for limb growth and results in a smaller leg length to stature ratio when compared to males (see Figure 6-2). In addition, the reduced growing time produces a typical female adult who is shorter in stature, lighter in weight, and smaller in overall body dimensions than the typical male adult. A more intense growth spurt in the hips than in the shoulders (see Figure 6-3) and a proportionately greater increase in adipose tissue than in muscle tissue place the adolescent female at a disadvantage when competing against adolescent males in power related sport activities.

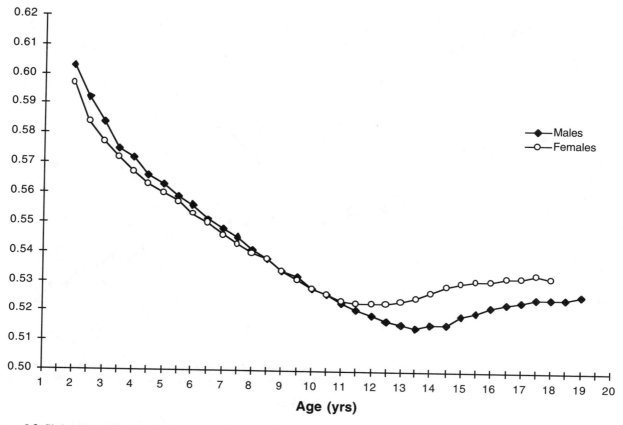

Figure 6-2. Sitting Height/Standing Height Ratio of Boys and Girls. (Longitudinal data from the Motor Performance Study, Michigan State University, 1999).

The changes associated with puberty result in marked male/female differences in body size, shape, and composition.

In contrast to females, males experience a longer growing period. The later timing of puberty permits males to attain greater body size, larger body mass, and longer limbs than females. The rapid growth of the shoulders, the large increase in muscle tissue, and the reduction in body fat during the adolescent growth spurt collectively contribute to male/female differences in body size, shape, and composition during the high school and adult years. The implications of these differences on physical performance are discussed in the following section.

MALE/FEMALE DIFFERENCES IN PHYSICAL PERFORMANCE

There has been considerable interest and controversy over the ability of females to compete with males in various sport activities. Sometimes the issue has focused on the right of a female to compete on a male team in a sport (football or baseball) that was not available to females. On other occasions, the question has centered on the capacity of females to participate or compete successfully with males in instructional or competitive settings. Is there an age or grade level when boys and girls should be separated for competition? The answer is not clear-cut.

If physical size and body shape are the only criteria used for separating males and females for organized competition, then such separation would not need to take place until the high school years, because females match up well with males in height and weight until about age 14 (see Tables 6-1 and 6-2). However, other factors, such as body composition, physiological capacities, strength and motor abilities, skill level, motivation to compete, and aggressiveness also contribute to success in competition. These factors generally favor males because of biological composition and social/cultural opportunities. It is this combination of factors that necessitates the separation of boys and girls for competition during the middle school/junior high school years.

Gender differences in physiological capacities generally occur around age 12 or 13 years (6th or 7th grade), For example, the ability of untrained boys to use oxygen for energy production more effectively than untrained girls becomes significant by age 12. In addition, after this age, males exceed females in the capacity of their blood to carry oxygen, in the volume of air that can be ex-

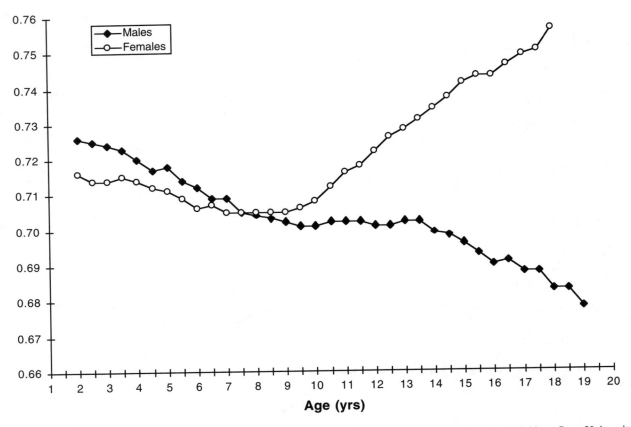

Figure 6-3. Hip/Shoulder Ratio of Boys and Girls. (Longitudinal data from the Motor Performance Study, Michigan State University, 1999).

changed by their lungs, and in the availability of substances to buffer the by-products of exercise, even after gender differences in body size are taken into account. These differences also are present in trained males and females, although they may be somewhat reduced. The implication of these differences is clear. Co-ed competition in endurance activities (e.g., distance runs) during the middle school/junior high school years and thereafter places most females at a distinct disadvantage, even though a small percentage of them may compete quite successfully with males.

Males also show superior performances on tasks that require muscular strength, muscular endurance, and power, particularly those that involve the upper body. Moreover, gender differences on such tasks occur at an earlier age when comparisons are made between high-performing males and high-performing females than when they are made between average or low-performing males and their female counterparts. Because it is the higher skilled individuals who generally seek participation in competitive sports, coaches need to realize that gender differences in performance are likely to be the greatest in competitive settings during the middle school and high school years.

For example, the ability of boys and girls to maintain a flexed-arm hang, which requires upper body muscular strength and endurance, is presented in Figure 6-4. At the 90th percentile, boys already perform better than girls at age 8, whereas similar gender differences do not occur until age 11 and age 14 for children performing at the 50th and 10th percentiles, respectively. During the later high school years, the performance of females at the 90th percentile approximates that of males at the 50th percentile, while that of females it the 50th percentile is similar to the performance of males at the 10th percentile.

A similar pattern of male/female performance occurs on tasks requiring leg power such as the vertical jump or the standing long jump, although gender differences occur later. Figure 6-5 shows the performance of boys and girls on a standing jump-and-reach task. Major performance differences between boys and girls at the 90th percentile do not occur until age 13, whereas gender differences at the 50th and 10th percentiles, respectively, appear about a year later. There may be several reasons for the delay in gender differences on this task when compared to the flexed-arm hang. First, normal daily activities place more stress on the legs than the arms (e.g., supporting body weight while standing, walking, and

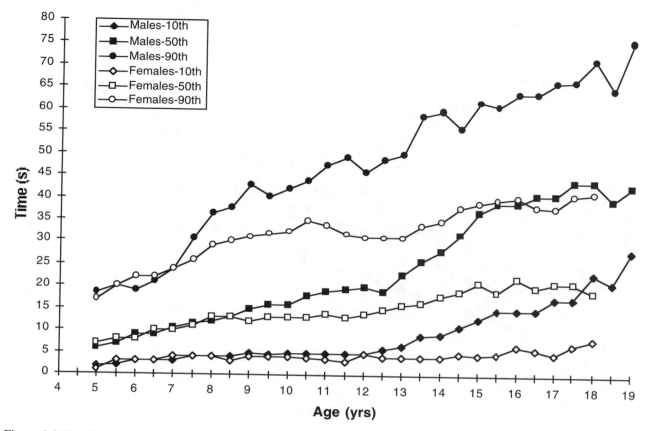

Figure 6-4. Flexed-Arm Hang Performance of Boys and Girls. (Mixed-longitudinal data from the Motor Performance Study, Michigan State University, 1997).

running) for both boys and girls. Second, boys must project slightly more weight than girls during childhood and therefore need more strength to project their bodies the same height or distance as the girls. Third, girls are more mature and have slightly better coordination to offset the modest strength advantage of boys during childhood. The ability to jump vertically plateaus rapidly in girls. By age 15, boys at the 50th percentile can jump as high as girls at the 90th percentile, and boys at the 10th percentile do as well as girls at the 50th percentile.

Figures 6-4 and 6-5 also demonstrate the variability in performance that exists within each gender group. These differences must also be considered by coaches to provide competition that is fair and safe for the participants. Males and females at the extreme ends of their respective performance scales may need to be shifted into higher or lower competitive age groups to prevent injury and/or to provide appropriate challenges.

COGNITIVE GROWTH OF CHILDREN AND YOUTHS

Structurally, the nervous system develops rapidly during infancy and childhood. By the early teen years, the weight of the brain is nearly equal to that of an adult (more than 96%). However, cognitive functioning is not complete until well into adulthood. Coaches of children and youths, therefore, must be aware of the changing cognitive capacities (e.g., to process information, to strategize) and the limited knowledge and experiences of the boys and girls placed in their trust.

The fact that children and youths generally have less knowledge about and experience in sport than do adult athletes should be obvious to coaches. Unfortunately, the obvious is often overlooked. For example, experienced coaches, to whom rules, strategies, skills, and drills have become second nature, often assume that this knowledge is already possessed by the young athlete, only to be reminded during practice or the first contest of the season that this assumption was faulty. On the other hand, beginning coaches may be so involved in establishing their own knowledge of the sport and in organizing for the season that they forget to consider the cognitive abilities and past experiences of their athletes.

Understanding the cognitive capacities of children and youth can have a direct influence on the success or failure of the coaching experience. Such understanding will require modifications in the planning and expecta-

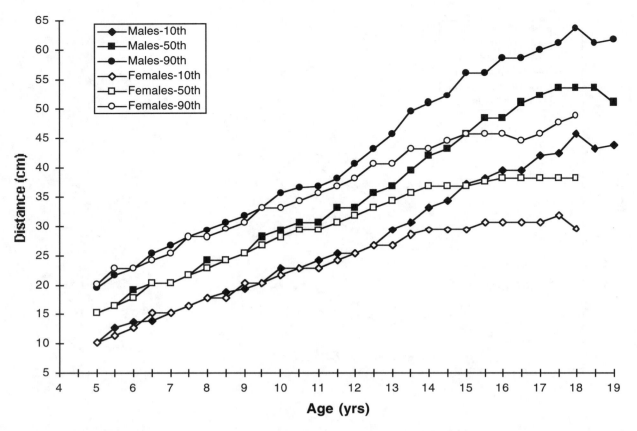

Figure 6-5. Vertical Jump Performance of Boys and Girls. (Mixed-longitudinal data from the Motor Performance Study, Michigan State University, 1997).

tions of coaches. The younger the group of athletes, the greater the modifications needed.

What cognitive capacities or abilities should be of concern to the coach? Because there are many such abilities for the coach to consider, it may be helpful to organize them into groups or components that relate to the processing of information. For example, to acquire knowledge and to learn the skills and strategies of a sport requires motivation, concentration, processing of information, memory, making decisions, and using feedback. This section will examine the extent to which children and adolescents differ from adults on these components.

Understanding the cognitive capacities of children and youth can have a direct influence on the success or failure of the coaching experience.

Motivation

The motivation or desire to learn and participate in a sport can be just as strong in the maturing individual as in the adult. However, the adult has more avenues available to sustain motivation than does the growing athlete. The adult can call upon previous experiences, greater under-

standing, and long-range goals to maintain motivation. Motivation in young athletes often depends on immediate or short-term outcomes. If the immediate experiences are not satisfying, the desire to continue in the activity can be quickly lost. Increasing cognitive capacities with age (e.g., reasoning and abstract thinking) and the support of peers can help young athletes stay motivated. Although important at any age, the coach must provide satisfying experiences, positive reinforcement, and individual attention to the young athlete (see Chapter 22, *Positive Coaching*, and Chapter 24, *Motivating Athletes*).

Concentration

The capacity of young athletes to pay attention is inferior to that of adults. In general, children are more easily distracted and have shorter attention spans than do adults. Moreover, their ability to selectively attend to critical cues in the environment, and to essential components, is not as incisive as that of adults. In fact, young athletes are apt to focus on irrelevant stimuli that may interfere with the task at hand. Because of their lack of skill and experience, younger athletes need to attend to task execution (e.g., dribbling a basketball) and therefore are often oblivious to what is going on around them.

The capacity for attention improves during childhood and approximates that of adults by adolescence. The coach must adjust the length of practice sessions and skill drills to suit the attention spans of children, help them focus on relevant stimuli, provide initial skill learning in noncompetitive settings, and gently redirect the young athletes when distractions occur or concentration wanes.

Processing Information

The sensory receptors that provide information to the central nervous system are nearly mature by the time children enter elementary school. Therefore, the amount of environmental information available to children is similar to the amount that is available to adults. Yet, the amount of information that can be processed and the manner in which it is processed is different for children than it is for adolescents and adults. Even though all individuals, regardless of age, have limited mental resources to process information (Guttentag, 1995), children have the least of such resources. In other words, because children are more limited in their cognitive resources, they are less efficient than adolescents and adults in processing information.

The process by which sensory information is interpreted, coded, and organized into meaningful internal symbols is called perception. The perceptual abilities of children are not equal to those of adults. Primarily, the perceptual judgment skills of elementary school children are slower and less accurate than those of middle school children, whose judgment speed and accuracy in turn are inferior to those of adults. Children do not have the capacity of adults to label, group, and organize information for future use. Because their speed of information processing increases as children develop (Hitch and Towse, 1995), they cannot process the same information as quickly as adults, nor can they process as much information in a given amount of time.

Coaches must be sensitive to the amount of information their athletes can process. Keeping instructions and demonstrations short, simple, and to the point facilitates skill learning in the sport setting. Moreover, the inability of young athletes to make use of available information as rapidly as adults suggests that coaches should expect response times to be slower and that the practice environment should be relatively uncomplicated.

Coaches must be sensitive to the amount of information their athletes can process.

Memory

Memory is closely related to information processing. There are different types of memory; however, "working memory" is of concern here. Working memory is responsible for keeping temporary information in the mind during various mental operations (Hitch and Towse, 1995). For example, working memory helps athletes remember how to correctly perform a new skill when the context demands it. The memory capacity of children is believed to be equal to that of adults. However, because children process information more slowly, and have less knowledge and experience than adults, the working memory of children is limited. Research has found that young children can only hold two to three items in their working memory, while adolescents and adults can store between five and nine items (Dempster, 1981). Thus, it is imperative that coaches limit the amount of information they expect athletes to keep in their working memory.

People often use different strategies to help increase their memory. One skill that can be taught to younger athletes is mental rehearsal. Mental rehearsal is the act of repeating new information in order to remember it. The ability to use this strategy develops at about the age of seven (Kail, 1990). The skill acquisition of children will be enhanced when they learn both a rehearsal strategy and the skill itself (Thomas, Thomas, and Gallagher, 1981). Moreover, children and adolescents have less knowledge and experiences to draw upon than adults to help them in sport situations. For example, children are not as accurate or consistent as adults in predicting and anticipating events. Thus, they have difficulty in selecting appropriate strategies and in planning appropriate responses. Coaches, therefore, must provide specific knowledge, teach appropriate strategies, identify relevant cues, and help younger athletes remember these components through the use of concrete examples and experiences.

The skill acquisition of children can be enhanced if they learn both a rehearsal strategy and the skill itself.

Making Decisions

In addition to processing information more slowly and making fewer appropriate responses than adults, children cannot make decisions as quickly or respond to environmental cues as fast as adults. For example, a child playing goalie in hockey, when reacting to a shot on goal, will take longer than the adult to process relevant cues, such as the speed of the puck, the distance it must travel, its angle of approach, and the position of teammates and opponents in relation to the puck. Because of this complex, dynamic environment, the child may move too slowly or even in the wrong direction to stop the puck. This means that coaches must be patient and avoid unrealistic expectations when young athletes compete in practice and game situations.

Using Feedback

Young athletes also cannot use the feedback resulting from performance as well as adults. Children and youths who do not modify their behavior after an inappropriate response are not using the performance (movement) or outcome (result) information available. Such individuals are not apt to engage in reflective thought or seek ways to improve their next performance. Adults are more likely to be aware of some of the information available to them, especially the results of their responses, and to plan changes, if necessary. The coach must help athletes recognize the feedback available to them, and provide additional cues. Such feedback should be short, simple, positive, and focused on what to do, rather than on what not to do.

VISION AND ATHLETIC PERFORMANCE

No matter what the level of competition, athletes and coaches have continually looked for ways to improve performance, to find that "something special" to give them an advantage over their opponents. The desire for higher performance levels has resulted in athletes attempting to reach their potential on those factors associated with maximum performance such as strength, power, flexibility, nutrition, various mental preparations, and drugs.

A key element often missing from the list of factors associated with maximum performance is visual abilities. To perform many motor tasks effectively, such as catching and striking balls, it is necessary to make precise visual judgments about moving objects in space and the relationships of one's body to other individuals or objects. In all sports and games in which objects or implements are used, accuracy in judging the distance of projected missiles is necessary. Sports such as football, basketball, and volleyball require simultaneous judgments about the location of the ball, teammates, and opponents. The purpose of this section is to: 1) discuss various visual abilities and the development of each; 2) explore how coaches can recognize athletes with potential vision problems; and 3) consider issues of safety and protection.

Visual Abilities

Vision plays an important role in the acquisition and performance of motor skills (Magill, 2001). Visual perceptual abilities are more important early in motor skill learning than in later development because individuals with superior visual skills make the most rapid progress in the early stages of skill acquisition. Important visual abilities in skill acquisition are static acuity, dynamic acuity, depth perception, figure-ground perception, peripheral vision, and visual-motor coordination.

Visual abilities play an important role in the acquisition and performance of motor skills.

Visual acuity is the ability of the visual system to clearly detect or perceive detail. It is another term for sharpness of vision. It can be subdivided into static and dynamic acuity. Gender differences have been found in visual acuity, with males displaying better visual acuity at all ages than females.

Static acuity is the capacity to discriminate detail in an object while both the observer and the object are stationary. Static acuity is what most people automatically think about when they hear the term vision. This aspect of vision is not a primary problem in sport because it usually is easily corrected through eyeglasses or contacts. Sports that rely heavily on static acuity include archery and rifle and pistol shooting.

Dynamic acuity is the ability to discriminate detail in an object when there is relative movement between the observer and the object. Dynamic acuity is primarily a function of the speed of the moving object. For example, dynamic acuity is essential when a speeding baseball comes toward the batter, a basketball player shoots a jump shot while on the run, a fast skating hockey player shoots at the goal, or a volleyball player receives a serve. Dynamic acuity shows great improvement between the ages of 11 and 12, with maturity being reached between the ages of 12 and 13.

Depth Perception

Depth perception is the ability to judge how near or far away one or more objects are from a person's body. It involves the ability to see three-dimensionally. Depth perception begins to develop within the first months of life and matures with experience by about 12 years of age. Object size, color, distance, trajectory, and speed all provide valuable cues for depth perception for an athlete to successfully intercept an object.

Figure-Ground Perception

Figure-ground perception is the ability to extract pertinent detail from the environment while ignoring the irrelevant. For example, a player needs to ignore the crowd in order to concentrate on the basket when shooting a free throw. Lack of figure-ground differentiation makes it difficult for people to detect a white softball against a cloudy, white sky. This ability is quite well developed by the age of 12, but may continue to improve up to 18 years.

Peripheral Vision

Peripheral vision is the ability to see moving objects or people in the outer portions of one's visual field. This ability allows one to see relationships, to have a feel for the whole situation, and to sense the flow of play. Almost all sports demand good peripheral vision. For example, a soccer goalie uses peripheral vision to see offensive players who are not in the vicinity of the ball or a field hockey player uses peripheral vision to detect trailing or cutting teammates.

Visual-Motor Coordination

Visual-motor coordination refers to the ability to move the body or its parts in relation to a stationary or moving target. For example, a diver must complete specified body movements prior to entering the water; a gymnast must coordinate visual information with movements on a beam; and, an outfielder must plan movements based on visual information obtained from the flight of a ball in order to intercept it. The development of the ability to coordinate movements with visual information actually begins in infancy and continues to improve until the early teen years. As dynamic acuity improves, so does the ability to track fast-moving objects.

Symptoms of Potential Vision Problems

Many deficiencies in visual abilities go unrecognized because vision-related sports problems cannot be detected through a routine eye examination. Standard examinations measure static acuity. They do not measure the other aspects of vision, most of which can be improved through practice. Vision screening should take place during preseason physicals; but the screening should be designed specifically for athletes to evaluate the efficiency of visual skills needed for peak performance. In addition to (or in the absence of) such screening, the following is a list of signs that may be symptomatic of a potential vision problem:

- Squinting to focus on distant objects
- Wearing glasses off the field, but not while playing the sport
- Excessive rubbing of the eyes or blinking
- Complaints of blurred vision and headaches
- Misjudging fixed distances to targets
- Misjudging the flight characteristics of objects
- Inability to coordinate body movements to catch, strike, or kick moving object
- Frequent collisions with teammates or opposing players
- Jerky or erratic eye and/or head movements

Safety, Eye Injuries, and Protection

The risk of injury to the eyes is present in nearly all sports, although the risk is greater in some sports than in others. The consequences of severe eye injuries, such as the loss of sight in one eye, can be far-reaching. Not only may a severe eye injury change the entire lifestyle of an individual, it may also impact the economic and social life of the individual, the family, and the society in which the individual lives. Fortunately, most eye injuries in sport can be prevented through adherence to safety rules and game rules, and through the use of protective equipment.

Each year in the United States, over 39,000 individuals suffer sport-related eye injuries serious enough to require emergency room care (Vinger, 2000). The estimate for all sport-related injuries to the eyes is 100,000, and about one-third of these injuries occur to children under the age of 16 (American Academy of Ophthalmology [AAO], 2000). The eye injuries that most commonly occur in sports are abraisons and contusions, detached retinas, corneal lacerations, cataracts, hemorrhages, and the loss of an eye (AAO, 1996).

Most eye and face injuries can be prevented, or the effects minimized, by using protective eye gear. The American Academy of Ophthalmology (1996, 2000) estimates that about 90% of the eye injuries occurring in sports are preventable, and that prevention is the most effective treatment. Balls, equipment, and the body parts of other players can cause injuries to eyes, yet for many years only protection for teeth has been mandatory in some sports such as football, lacrosse, soccer and wrestling. This is puzzling, because teeth replacements are functional, whereas eye replacements can only be cosmetic.

Athletes with only one functional eye are at a particular risk because serious injury to the functional eye would cause a severe visual handicap or possibly permanent blindness. Any athlete whose best-corrected visual acuity is less than 20/40 in the poorest eye is functionally one-eyed. Any athlete who is functionally one-eyed "must wear appropriate eye protection during all sports and recreational activities" (Vinger, 2000). Any athlete testing more than 20/40 when wearing glasses on the screening examination should be evaluated by an optometrist or ophthalmologist to determine if the subnormal vision requires a change in eyeglasses and what eye protection should be worn when participating in sports.

Sport-Specific Risks

The inherent nature of some sports involves a higher risk for injuries to the eyes then that of other sports. High risk sports involve the use of a high speed ball or puck, the use of a bat or stick, close aggressive play with intentional or unintentional collisions, or any combination of these factors. The sports with a high risk of injury to the eyes are basketball, baseball, hockey (ice, field, street, roller), water polo, football, lacrosse, softball, racquet sports, soccer, fencing, paint ball, and downhill skiing (AAO, 1996). The estimates of eye injuries in sports and recreational activities across all ages (as a percentage of the total) for high risk sports are basketball (22.2%), water/pool sports (11.7%), baseball (10.3%), racquet sports (7.0%), hockey (4.1%), football (3.7%), and soccer (3.4%) (Vinger, 2000). The percentage of injuries in sports such as lacrosse and fencing is low because of the limited number of participants in these sports. High risk sports where no adequate eye protection exists or is permitted include boxing and the full contact martial arts (AAO, 1996). Eye injuries in these combative sports comprise about 1.1 percent of the total.

Sports with low risk for eye injuries are those that do not involve a thrown or hit object, or that do not involve close aggressive play with body contact. Examples of such sports include track and field, swimming, gymnastics, rowing, archery, and bowling. Other sports, such as handball, wrestling, slalom skiing, horse racing, and polo involve a moderate risk of eye injury and special eye protection should be worn when participating in these sports (AAO, 1996).

Maturational Differences

Some 12-year old children can throw a baseball 70 mph, while others can hardly swing a bat, let alone avoid a speeding ball. Twelve-year-olds with the physiques of 15 year-olds can be dangerous matches for 12-year-olds with physiques of 9-year-olds. Because of the wide variance in both skill and maturational levels, the frequency of injuries, including eye injuries, is high in young players. The sports in which eye injuries are most common for children under age 15 years are basketball, baseball, water/pool sports, racquet sports, soccer, and football (Vinger, 2000).

Effective Protection

Protective devices have been proven to dramatically reduce eye injuries in sports. Glass lenses, ordinary plastic lenses, and open (lenseless) eye guards do not provide adequate protection for those involved in active sports. Normal "street wear" eyeglass frames with polycarbonate lenses give adequate protection only for those involved in low risk sports. For high risk sports, protective eyewear should be made of polycarbonate frames and lenses (which are 20 times stronger than ordinary lenses), and frames or clear eye-face guards should be attached to helmets (i.e., football, hockey, baseball). These should meet the safety standards of the American Society for Testing and Materials (Vinger, 2000). It is also important that contact wearers use protective sports eyewear because contacts do not provide sufficient protection. Parents or guardians should contact their ophthmologist to determine the recommended eyewear for the specific sport in which their children plan to participate.

Glass lenses, ordinary plastic lenses, and open (lenseless) eye guards do not provide adequate protection for those involved in active sports.

SUMMARY

Knowledge of the physical and cognitive growth of children and youths, and their visual capacities, is important to successful coaching in youth sports and school-sponsored athletic programs. The changes that occur in body dimensions, proportions, and tissue composition, and in the physical and visual capacities of girls and boys as they mature must be accommodated in wholesome sports programs. Coaches also must be cognizant of gender differences in growth and performance so that competition in sports can be made fair and equitable for both boys and girls.

Most cognitive functions discussed in this section continue to develop during childhood and adolescence. By adjusting their expectations, practice sessions, and instructions to meet the cognitive capacities of their athletes, coaches can make sports participation enjoyable for children and youths. Due to the importance of visual abilities in sports, coaches should be cognizant of behavioral symptoms associated with visual problems and promote the use of appropriate safety eyewear and face guards for athletes while participating in sport to prevent and reduce injuries to eyes.

REFERENCES

American Academy of Ophthalmology. (1996). *Sports Eye-Safety Fact Sheet*. [Available on Line] < www.medem.com/search/article_display.cfm?path=n:andmstr=/ZZZEPMUR08C.htmlandsoc=AAOandsrch_typ=NAV_SERCH > Accessed February 23, 2001.

American Academy of Ophthalmology. (2000). *News from AAO: Ninety Percent of Sports Related Eye Injuries are Preventable, Eye MDs Say*. [Available on Line] <www.medem.com/MedLB/ article_detaillb.cfm?article_ID=ZZZVYGPIJ7Candsub-cat > Accessed February 23, 2001.

Centers for Disease Control and Prevention. (2000). *CDC Growth Charts: United States. Advance Data. (No. 314)*. Hyattsville, MD: U.S. Department of Health and Human Services, National Center for Health Statistics.

Dempster, F. N. (1981). "Memory Span: Sources of Individual and Developmental Differences." *Psychological Bulletin*, 89: 63-100.

Guttentag, R. E. (1995). "Mental Efforts and Motivation: Influences on Children's Memory Strategy Use." In F. E. Weinert and W. Schneider (editors), *Memory Performance and Competencies: Issues in Growth and Development*. Mahwah, NJ: Lawrence Erlbaum Associates, pp. 207-224.

Haubenstricker, J. L., Seefeldt, V., and Branta, C. (1997). *Percentile Tables for Selected Motor Tasks*. Unpublished data, Motor Performance Study, Michigan State University, East Lansing, MI.

Haubenstricker, J. L., Seefeldt, V., and Branta, C. (1999). *Means and Standard Deviations for Selected Growth Variables*. Unpublished data, Motor Performance Study, Michigan State University, East Lansing, MI.

Hitch, G. J., and Towse, J. N. (1995). "Working Memory: What Develops?" In F.E. Weinert and W.Schneider (editors), *Memory Perfor-*

mance and Competencies: Issues in Growth and Development. Mahwah, NJ: Lawrence Erlbaum Associates, pp. 3-22.

Kail, R. (1990). *The Development of Memory in Children (3rd edition).* New York: Freeman.

Magill, R. A. (2001). *Motor Learning: Concepts and Applications (6th edition).* Boston: McGraw-Hill.

Thomas, J. R., Thomas, K. T., and Gallagher, J. D. (1981). "Children's Processing of Information in Physical Activity and Sport." *Motor Skills: Theory into Practice Monographs,* 3: 1-8.

Vinger, P. F. (1980). "Sports Related Eye Injury: A Preventable Problem." *Survey of Ophthalmology,* 25: 108-113.

Vinger, P. F. (2000). "A Practical Guide for Sports Eye Protection." *Physician and SportsMedicine,* 28: 49-50, 55-56, 59, 63-66, 69.

SUGGESTED READINGS

Eckert, H. (1987). *Motor Development (3rd edition).* Indianapolis: Benchmark Press.

Ginsburg, H., and Opper, S. (1969). *Piaget's Theory of Intellectual Development: An Introduction.* Englewood Cliffs, NJ; Prentice-Hall, Inc.

Haubenstricker, J. L. (1987). "How Children Grow and Develop." In V. Seefeldt (editor), *Handbook for Youth Sports Coaches.* Reston, VA: American Alliance for Health, Physical Education, Recreation and Dance, pp. 54-69.

Johnson, T. R., Moore, W. M., and Jeffries, J. E. (editors). (1978). *Children are Different. Developmental Physiology (2nd edition).* Columbus, OH: Ross Laboratories.

Thomas, J. R., and Gallagher, J. D. (1986). "Memory Development and Motor Skill Acquisition." In Seefeldt (editor), *Physical Activity and Well-Being.* Reston, VA: American Alliance for Health, Physical Education, Recreation and Dance, pp. 125-139.

7

Trainability of Children and Youth

John L. Haubenstricker, Ph.D. and Rebecca A. Battista, M.S.

QUESTIONS TO CONSIDER

- To what extent can the strength or other attributes of prepubescent children be improved through training?
- What are the effects of resistance training programs on prepubescent boys and girls?
- Are the outcomes of weight training programs the same for prepubescent and post pubescent participants?
- What benefits other than strength gains can result from participation in resistance training programs?
- Does participation in a weight training program result in better performance in sports?

INTRODUCTION

The rapid growth of programs in youth and scholastic sports in the 1960s and early 1970s resulted in the initiation of various training programs to improve individual and team performances. High school coaches sought to gain an edge over opponents by increasing the strength of their players, particularly in football. Subsequently, similar training programs were begun for other sports such as basketball and baseball. Currently, boys and girls in all organized sports programs, including gymnastics and cheerleading, participate in strength training programs as part of their preparation for athletic competition. Data from the recent survey of youth in the United States indicate that 53.5% of the nation's youth engage in strengthening exercises (Youth Risk Behavior Surveillance—United States, 1999). A higher percentage of boys (63.5%) than girls (43.6%) reported participating in such activities. The successful results attained in studies involving pubescent and post-pubescent secondary school athletes triggered interest in the use of training programs with prepubescent children.

PURPOSE OF TRAINING PROGRAMS

The immediate purpose of a training program in sports is to improve the attribute or ability being trained, whether it is strength, power, cardiovascular endurance, agility, or flexibility. A training program usually involves a series of selected exercises, drills or activities that are sequenced in terms of their frequency, intensity and duration to develop a desired attribute or ability. As such, a training program is a means to an end because the ultimate goal of a training program is to enhance the performance of athletes in a specific sport. Unfortunately, improvement of a single attribute or ability does not necessarily guarantee better performance in a sport because success usually depends on numerous attributes and abilities, as well as contextual factors. For example, improving the strength of offensive linemen in football does not mean that they will be better in pass blocking or run blocking if their speed, agility, and blocking skills are inadequate when compared to those of their opponents. On the other hand, if strength is a critical component of a particular sport skill, then increased strength should contribute toward improved performance.

> *A training program is a means to an end because the ultimate goal of a training program is to enhance the performance of athletes in a specific sport.*

EFFECTIVENESS OF TRAINING PROGRAMS

There has been considerable research on the effectiveness of training programs involving children and youth over the past two decades. Various literature reviews and meta-analyses of studies indicate that the primary focus of this research has been on the improvement of muscular strength, power, and endurance (Faigenbaum, 1993; National Strength and Conditioning Association [NSCA], 1996; Payne, Morrow, Johnson, and Dal-

42

ton, 1997) and on aerobic fitness (Payne and Morrow, 1993). No research has been reported on the effectiveness of training programs to improve agility or flexibility in children and youth.

Muscular Strength

Two persistent concerns expressed about strength training programs for children and youth are the effectiveness and the safety of such programs. Most well designed studies have shown that adolescent (post pubescent) males and females can improve their strength significantly through participation in a weight or resistance training program (Payne, et al., 1997; Sale, 1989). However, based on an early study (Hetherington, 1976) in which no strength gains were achieved following a period of training, it was concluded that prepubescent children would not benefit from a weight or resistance training program. This gave rise to the myth that the only gains in strength to be attained by prepubescent children were those associated with normal growth and development (Staver, 1996). The explanation was that circulating hormones associated with puberty, particularly testosterone in males, were needed for significant gains in strength to occur (Blimkie and Bar-Or, 1996).

Subsequent research, however, has demonstrated that both prepubescent boys and girls can achieve significant strength gains through resistance training programs (Faigenbaum, 1993; Faigenbaum, et al., 1996; Payne, et al., 1997; Sale, 1989). Strength gains typically range from 30% to 50%, although some gains have been in excess of 70%. Such gains can occur for both boys and girls, and with little differences in relative (percent) gains between prepubescent and post pubescent participants, although the latter make greater absolute gains in strength (NSCA, 1996). The duration of the training programs generally ranged from 5 to 14 weeks, although a few lasted up to 20 weeks (Faigenbaum, 1993; Sale, 1989). The explanation for gains in strength in prepubescent children is neural adaptation (Sale, 1989; Ozmun, Mikesky, and Surburg, 1994). In other words, the nervous system adjusts to the progressively increasing resistance by becoming better at recruiting the muscle cells and muscle groups needed to move the increased resistance. It is also important to remember that strength gains achieved through resistance training are not permanent. Some of the strength gained through training will be lost if a sufficient maintenance program is not followed (Faigenbaum, et al., 1996). The minimum amount of training needed to maintain the strength gained by prepubescent children is not known at this time.

Both prepubescent boys and girls can achieve significant strength gains through resistance training.

Benefits other than strength gains have been purported for well-designed resistance training programs. These include injury prevention, stronger bones, and improved self-esteem (Faigenbaum, 1993). A well-designed resistance-training program may actually help reduce injuries by developing the major muscle groups of the body and by providing a balance in the relative strength of opposing muscle groups, such as the quadriceps and hamstrings of the thigh or the biceps/brachialis and triceps of the arm. A better balance between opposing muscle groups can help reduce injuries to muscle tissue, ligaments, and joints that might occur if there is too much disparity in strength. Shafer (1991) cited a study by Hejna and his colleagues in which high school athletes who participated in a comprehensive weight-training program experienced fewer injuries (about one-third less) and a 50% reduction in the time required to rehabilitate injuries than athletes not participating in a weight-training program.

The additional stress placed on bones through resistance training, when done appropriately, can stimulate the bones to adapt by becoming thicker and sturdier, thereby strengthening the bones and increasing bone mass (Faigenbaum, 1993; Schafer, 1991). On the other hand, when weight training is done inappropriately, injuries to bones and joints can result.

Positive gains in strength through resistance training can also have psychological benefits. Not only do children and youth know that they can achieve through effort, they know that they did achieve, and this knowledge can have a positive impact on their self-confidence (Faigenbaum, 1993) and their feelings of self-worth (Bryant, 1996). In addition to enhancing strength, well-designed resistance training programs can help prevent injuries, build stronger bones, and improve self-esteem.

A primary concern of physicians and educators about weight training programs for children and adolescents is the potential of injury to the growing musculoskeletal system, particularly injuries to growth (epiphyseal) plates in long bones, tendon insertions on bone, joint cartilage on articulating bone surfaces, and to the lower back (Faigenbaum, 1993; Schafer, 1991). Although injuries to growth plates have been reported, these are rare and they are usually associated with overhead lifts or maximum lifts performed improperly (often unsupervised) in training programs for weight lifting or power lifting, competitive sports that are not recommended for children and youth (American Academy of Pediatrics, 1990; Bryant, 1996; NSCA, 1996; Tanner, 1993). Other injuries to cartilage may occur due to accident, disease or overuse (Schafer, 1991). Studies in the late 1980s and the 1990s have shown that well-planned, supervised resistance training programs that emphasize sub-maximal repetitions rather than single maximum lifts can be both effective and safe for developing strength in prepubescent children (Faigenbaum, 1993; NSCA, 1996).

Anaerobic Power and Muscular Endurance

Anaerobic capacity or power refers to the ability to obtain energy through glycolytic pathways when oxygen cannot be delivered fast enough to meet the energy needs of exercising muscles (Rowland, 1990). Anaerobic energy is needed for explosive, short-duration tasks such as hopping and jumping, and for high energy tasks that take less than 60 seconds to complete (e.g., sprinting 200 meters). Although anerobic power has been assessed physiologically through measures of oxygen debt and levels of post exercise blood and muscle lactate, simpler non-invasive performance tests such as cycle riding and stair climbing have been used with children and adolescents (Inbar, 1996). For example, on the Wingate anaerobic test, the subject performs an all-out 30-second cycle ride. Anaerobic power is measured by the peak power generated during a 2.5 to 5 second interval early in the ride, whereas muscule endurance is determined by the mean power output for the 30-second period (Inbar, 1996).

The anaerobic capacity and local muscle endurance of children and youth increase with age, both in absolute terms and relative to body mass (Inbar, 1996; Rowland, 1990). However, the absolute and relative values of anaerobic capacity for girls peak at around age 15, whereas those for the boys continue to increase to age 18. The absolute and relative leg anaerobic power and endurance is similar for boys and girls until about 11–13 years of age. By age 18, the leg anaerobic power and endurance of girls is only 70-75% that of boys. In contrast, gender differences in the absolute and relative anaerobic power and endurance of the arms already exist by 9 years of age. By age 18, compared to those for the boys, the absolute and relative values for girls are 50% and 25%, respectively (Inbar, 1996).

There is limited information available concerning the trainability of anaerobic power and muscle endurance in children and youth (Blimkie and Bar-Or, 1996). Studies comparing young athletes with non-athletes show that the athletes have greater anaerobic power and muscle endurance than the non-athletes. However, whether these differences are due to training, to preselection, or to a combination of the two is not known. The intervention studies that included control subjects indicated that training effects were dependent on the intensity and duration of the training program as well as the fitness level of the children prior to the start of the training program (Blimkie and Bar-Or, 1996). Although it appears that the anaerobic capacity and muscle endurance of children and adolescents can be improved through training, additional research is needed to determine the net effects of physical training on gains in anaerobic power during the growth period (Inbar, 1996).

The net effects of training on anaerobic power and endurance in children and adolescents need further research.

Aerobic Endurance

Three physiological variables are thought to influence performance in endurance exercise activities such as distance running, cycling, and swimming (Pate and Ward, 1996). These include maximal aerobic power or maximal oxygen consumption (VO_2max), lactate threshold, and economy. Pate and Ward define maximal aerobic power as "the maximal rate at which an individual can use oxygen in the aerobic process". Lactate threshold is the rate of aerobic expenditure at which lactic acid begins to accumulate in the blood due to anaerobic metabolism. Economy is defined as "the rate of oxygen consumption observed at a specified movement pace". Improvement in any of these three variables should result in improved performance involving aerobic demands.

Gains in aerobic power as a result of training are limited in prepubescent boys and girls. In their review of 11 studies that met their criteria (e.g., control group, healthy subjects, specified training regimen), Pate and Ward (1996) found that the net gains in VO_2max ranged from 1% to 16%, with a mean of 9.7%. In contrast, a meta-analysis of 23 training studies by Payne and Morrow (1993) in which pre- and post-test data were available revealed that the average net gain in VO2max was only 2.07 ml/kg/min or about a 4% net gain. Cross-sectional studies that compared groups of athletes to "control" subjects usually reported larger differences in maximal aerobic power than those cited above; however, at least some of the differences may be due to self-selection—the athletes are attracted to the sport because they already possess or have the potential for developing high maximal aerobic power (Rowland, 1990).

In summary, the establishment of intense training programs to improve aerobic capacity in prepubescent children appears to be of limited value. Time may be better spent on developing the skills of the sport (e.g., form in running, stroke mechanics in swimming, posture in cycling).

Gains in aerobic power due to training are limited in prepubescent boys and girls.

Flexibility

There is general agreement among coaches that flexibility is an important attribute for successful participation in most sports, but especially for sports such as cheerleading, gymnastics and diving. Optimizing the flexibility (range of motion) of joints through stretching is one of the objectives of warm-up activities prior to practice and competition for nearly all sports. The ability to move joints through a full range of motion not only has implications for better sports performance, but also for injury prevention because the stretching promotes more efficient contraction and relaxation of the musculature operating on the joints.

How trainable is flexibility in prepubescent children? We do not really know. There is evidence that, as a function of growth and development, the flexibility of the hips and lower back (as measured by the sit-and-reach test) of prepubescent girls is relatively stable across the childhood years, whereas that of boys tends to decrease (Branta, Haubenstricker, and Seefeldt, 1984). However, no studies of training programs specifically designed to increase the flexibility of joints in children were located in the literature. Yet, national organizations, such as the National Strength and Conditioning Association, advocate that a total conditioning program for children should include exercises to enhance flexibility (Pearson, et al., 2000).

A concern about resistance training programs is that such training will result in the participant becoming "muscle bound", with a resulting loss of flexibility in joints. However, the results of resistance training studies with children have shown that there is either no change in flexibility or actual improvement in flexibility (Faigenbaum, 1993; Weltman, et al., 1986). Thus, there is indirect evidence that the flexibility of children can be enhanced through training even though no direct studies of training programs for increasing flexibility in children have been conducted.

There is no evidence that resistance training has resulted in negative effects on the flexibility of children.

Agility

Agility is defined as "the controlled ability to change position and direction rapidly and accurately" (Bosco and Gustafson, 1983). Agility is usually assessed using a shuttle run of a relative short distance (e.g., 10-30 ft.) or some other motor task where the position or direction of the body, or certain body parts, are required to change quickly and often. From a developmental perspective, there is improvement in the agility of children and youth, as measured by a shuttle run, with increasing age (Branta, et al., 1984). However, the effects of training programs specifically designed to develop agility in children and youth has not been reported in the literature. Yet, agility exercises are recommended as part of a comprehensive program of conditioning for children (Pearson, et al., 2000).

Agility has been measured as a potential outcome of training programs that focus on attributes other than agility. For example, participation in weight training programs has resulted in increased arm speed and dexterity in high school males (Calvin, 1959) and in improvement in the agility run time of preadolescent boys (NSCA, 1996). Improvement in agility as a result of strength training might be expected because agility is dependent on strength. In other words, the ability to rapidly change the position or direction of the body or its parts requires muscular strength and power.

WEIGHT TRAINING AND PERFORMANCE IN SPORTS

An underlying assumption of coaches and athletes is that participation in a weight-training program will improve one's performance in sports. From one perspective, this assumption is reasonable because all movements and even postural positions of the body while participating in sports are dependent on some measure of strength. Therefore, the stronger an athlete is the more forcefully and rapidly he or she should be able to move or to resist external forces. Thus, there is intuitive knowledge that strength is important when observing athletes perform in their sport. On the other hand, it is difficult to identify the specific contribution of strength gained through a resistance-training program as it relates to the performance of an individual in a sport setting, for several reasons. First, performance in any sport is dependent upon many factors, of which strength is only one. Second, performance in sports is very complex and difficult to reduce to a single measure. What criterion should be used to measure performance in a sport? In other words, against what measure of performance in a sport should strength gains be compared to determine their effect? This seems almost impossible to do in team sports and dual sports, such as tennis and racquetball, where success also depends not only on personal skills, knowledge, strategies, and experience, but also on those of the opponent.

The effect of gains in strength may be easier to determine in sports where the performance of an athlete is not directly influenced by a teammate or an opponent, such as short sprints and field events in track and field, downhill skiing, swimming, diving, gymnastics, figure skating and golf—assuming that environmental conditions and the other personal characteristics of the athlete have not changed during the training program. If these other variables can be held constant, then the gains in strength might be reflected in improved times or scores.

It is difficult to identify the specific contribution of strength gained through a resistance-training program as it relates to the performance of an individual in a sport setting.

Few studies have examined the value of weight training programs to actual performance in sports in children and youth. Gains in strength have resulted in improved performance in swimmers and in better performance on selected gymnastic events, but not in all studies (NSCA, 1996). Other studies have demonstrated improvement in basic motor skills such as the standing long jump, vertical jump and 30-meter dash following participation in a strength-training program (NSCA, 1996; Sale, 1989). Whether or not improvements in strength and performance occur appears to be dependent in the nature and duration of the training program (Faigenbaum, et al., 1996; Weltman, et al., 1986).

The contributions of participation in strength training programs to performance in sports undoubtedly are related to the demands for strength and power in a given sport. Thus, extra strength should be beneficial to rebounding in basketball, but not necessarily to shooting free throws; and, to the cheerleader in executing leaps and jumps, but not necessarily to the distance runner. This is known as the principle of specificity. Although proficiency, by practicing one task can transfer to performing another task, the greatest gains are made in the specific task that is being performed. For example, Nielson, Nielsen, Behrendt-Hansen and Asmussen (1980) found that the training effects were largest in the tasks for which girls, 7 to 19 years of age, had specifically trained (isometric knee extension, vertical jump, sprinting). There was, however, also some transfer from isometric knee extension to vertical jumping, and vice versa. The available evidence suggests that transfer of the effects of training is more likely to occur to individual sport skills rather than to general performance in a sport; that transfer is greatest when the attribute being trained (e.g., strength) is an important component of the skill; and, that the greatest gains will be made in the specific attribute or skill being trained.

The association between strength training programs and performance in sports depend on the demands for strength and power in a given sport.

SUMMARY

Based on empirical evidence and the research literature, the following statements can be made about the trainability of children and youth, particularly with regard to strength or resistance training.

- Prepubescent boys and girls as well as post-pubescent males and females can benefit from strength training programs.
- The strength gains of prepubescent children through training is largely due to neural adaptation, whereas the strength gains of post-pubescent adolescents are due to both neural adaptation and hypertrophy of muscle. The hypertrophy of muscle is much greater in post-pubescent males than in similar aged females be-

cause of the presence of circulating testosterone in males.
- There are no major differences in the strength of prepubescent boys and girls.
- The relative (percent) gains in strength are similar for prepubescent children and post-pubescent adolescents, although post-pubescent adolescents generally achieve greater absolute gains.
- Strength gained through training can be lost after a training program is discontinued.
- Participation in carefully planned, supervised strength training programs can be as safe as participation in other youth sport activities.
- The effects of training programs to improve anaerobic power and muscular endurance in children and youths are not well documented.
- Gains in aerobic power through training are limited in prepubescent children. Average net gains generally are less than 10%.
- There is little information available concerning the effects of training programs designed to improve flexibility or agility in prepubescent children. Some studies on strength training have shown increased flexibility and agility in prepubescent boys.
- There is no direct evidence that increases in strength through training necessarily results in improvement in sport performance. Improvements are likely to occur in specific motor skills where an increase in strength is related to improved performance, such as running and jumping.
- Other potential benefits of strength training programs are injury prevention, increased bone mass, and increased self-confidence and self-esteem.

This chapter dealt with the response of children and adolescents to training programs. Coaches and other individuals interested in learning how to set up a training program should read Chapter 9, *Principles of Resistance Training.*

REFERENCES

American Academy of Pediatrics. (1990). "Strength Training, Weight and Power Lifting, and Bodybuilding by Children and Adolescents." *Pediatrics*, 86: 801-803.

Blimkie, C. J. R., and Bar-Or, O. (1996). "Trainability of Muscle Strength, Power and Endurance During Childhood." In O. Bar-Or (editor), *The Child and Adolescent Athlete* (pp. 113-129). International Olympic Committee. Oxford, England: Black Science Ltd.

Bosco, J. S., and Gustafson, W. F. (1983). *Measurement and Evaluation in Physical Education, Fitness, and Sports.* Englewood Cliffs, NJ: Prentice-Hall, Inc.

Branta, C., Haubenstricker, J., and Seefeldt, V. (1984). "Age Changes in Motor Skills During Childhood and Adolescence." In R. Terjung (editor), *Exercise and Sport Sciences Reviews* (pp.467-520). Philadelphia: Franklin Press.

Bryant, C. X., and Peterson, J. (1996). "Not for Adults Only." *Fitness Management*, 12: 34-36.

Calvin, S. (1959). "Effects of Progressive Resistive Exercises on the Motor Coordination of Boys." *Research Quarterly*, 30: 387-398.

Faigenbaum, A. D. (1993). "Strength Training: A Guide for Teachers and Coaches." *National Strength and Conditioning Association Journal*, 15: 20-29.

Faigenbaum, A. D., Westcott, W. L., Micheli, L. J., Outerbridge, A. R., Long, C. J., LaRosa-Loud, R., and Zaichkowsky, L. D. (1996). "The Effects of Strength Training and Detraining on Children." *Journal of Strength and Conditioning Research*, 10: 109-114.

Hetherington, M. R. (1976). "Effect of Isometric Training on the Elbow Flexion Force Torque of Grade Five Boys." *Research Quarterly*, 47: 41-47.

Inbar, O. (1996). "Development of Anaerobic Power and Local Muscular Endurance." In O. Bar-Or (editor), *The Child and Adolescent Athlete* (pp. 42-53). International Olympic Committee. Oxford, England: Blackwell Science Ltd.

National Strength and Conditioning Association. (1996). "Youth Resistance Training: Position Statement Paper and Literature Review." *Strength and Conditioning*, 18: 62-75.

Nielson, B., Nielsen, K., Behrendt-Hansen, M., and Asmussen, E. (1980). "Training of "Functional Muscular Strength" in Girls 7-19 Years Old." In K. Berg and B. Eriksson (editors) *Children and Exercise IX* (pp. 69-77). Baltimore, MD: University Park Press.

Ozmun, J. C., Mikesky, A. E., and Surburg, P. R. (1994). "Neuromuscular Adaptations Following Prepubescent Strength Training." *Medicine and Science in Sports and Exercise*, 26: 510-514.

Pate, R. R., and Ward D. S. (1996). "Endurance Trainability of Children and Youths." In O. Bar-Or (editor), *The Child and Adolescent Athlete* (pp. 130-137). Oxford, England: Blackwell Science Ltd.

Payne, V. G., and Morrow, Jr., J. R. (1993). "Exercise and VO$_2$max in Children: A Meta-analysis." *Research Quarterly for Exercise and Sport*, 64: 305-313.

Payne, V.G., Morrow, Jr., J.R., Johnson, L., and Dalton, S.N. (1997). "Resistance Training in Children and Youth: A Meta-analysis." *Research Quarterly for Exercise and Sport*, 68: 80-88.

Pearson, D., Faigenbaum, A., Conley, M., and Kraemer, W. J. (2000). "The National Strength and Conditioning Association's Basic Guidelines for the Resistance Training of Athletes." *Strength and Conditioning Journal*, 22: 14-27.

Rowland, T. W. (1990). *Exercise and Children's Health*. Champaign, IL: Human Kinetics Publishers.

Sale, D. G. (1989). "Strength Training in Children." In C.V. Gisolfi and D.R. Lamb (editors), *Perspectives in Exercise Science and Sports Medicine: Youth, Exercise and Sport* (pp. 165-216). Traverse City, MI: Cooper Publishing Group.

Schafer, J. (1991). "Prepubescent and Adolescent Weight Training: Is It Safe? Is It Beneficial?" *National Strength and Conditioning Association Journal*, 13: 39-46.

Staver, P. (1996). "Dispelling the Myths of Children and Weights." *Fitness Management*, 12: 43-44.

Tanner, S. (1993). "Weighing the Risks: Strength Training for Children and Adolescents." *The Physician and Sportsmedicine*, 21: 105-116.

Weltman, A., Janney, C., Rians, C., Strand, K., Berg, B., Tippit, J., Wide, J., Wide, B., Cahill, B., and Katch, F. (1986). "The Effects of Hydraulic-Resistance Strength Training in Prepubertal Males." *Medicine and Science in Sports and Exercise*, 18: 629-639.

Youth Risk Behavior Surveillance—United States, 1999. [Available on Line] < http://www.cdc.gov/epo/mmwr/preview/mmwrhtml/ss4905a1.htm >

8

Physiological Conditioning of Young Athletes

Joey C. Eisenmann, Ph. D.; Sean P. Cumming, Ph. D. and Eugene Brown, Ph.D.

QUESTIONS TO CONSIDER

- What are the energy production systems, and what role do they play in athletic performance?
- What are muscular strength, power, endurance, and flexibility, and what is their relative importance in sport?
- What are the six principles that should be applied when conditioning young athletes?
- What are plyometrics, sprint training, resistance training, concurrent training, economical training, and how can they be used to enhance athletic performance?
- What is periodization?

INTRODUCTION

Sports conditioning can be defined as the participation in structured physical activity to enhance or maintain physical work capacity (e.g., strength, power, endurance) that may supplement and improve the performance of learned sport skills. Unfortunately, sports conditioning programs are often selected on the basis of individual accomplishments or won-loss records rather than on scientific inquiry. It should be emphasized that an understanding of the general principles of physiological conditioning is fundamental in the design and implementation of safe and effective conditioning programs. This chapter will provide an overview of several aspects of the physiological conditioning of young athletes.

KEY TERMS

Knowledge of key terms is necessary to successfully understand and apply the principles of physiological conditioning. Terms that occur throughout this chapter are as follows:.

Adenosine Triphosphate (ATP): The primary source of energy in muscle cells.
Aerobic: Energy production utilizing oxygen.
Anaerobic: Energy production in the absence of oxygen.
Biomechanics: The application of physical laws to the study of movement.

Endurance: The ability of the muscle to exert a submaximal force for a prolonged period of time and resist fatigue.
Energy: The capacity to do work.
Flexibility: The range of motion that is permitted by a joint.
Force: A push or pull on an object.
Lactic Acid: A byproduct of anaerobic glycolysis.
Metabolism: The sum of chemical and physical changes in the body.
Physiology: The study of the function of the body.
Power: The rate at which a muscle or muscle group does work.
Speed: The time taken to cover a specific distance.
Speed Endurance: The ability of the muscle to resist fatigue at a given speed.
Strength: The ability of a muscle or muscle group to exert force.
Quickness: The rate at which a given speed is reached.

PHYSIOLOGICAL BASIS OF CONDITIONING

The main objective of sport conditioning programs is to cause biological adaptation in various body systems (e.g., cardiovascular, muscular) to enhance physiological work capacity (or the body's ability to work and resist fatigue) and performance. This section will briefly explain the general principles of energy production, and cardiorespiratory and neuromuscular function. The reader is referred elsewhere (Wilmore and Costill, 1998) for a detailed account of the physiology of exercise.

Principles of Energy Production

In order to move, energy must be produced in muscles. Therefore, the conditioning of the energy production systems is central to the conditioning of athletes. Energy production during physical activity occurs along a continuum of two different systems—the anaerobic and aerobic systems (See Table 8-1). To perform any type of work, energy must be released from the energy-rich compound adenosine triphosphate (ATP). The release of energy from ATP takes place whether oxygen is available or not. In humans, only a small amount of ATP is stored within the muscle. Therefore, if exercise is to continue beyond the quick depletion of stored ATP, subsequent energy demands must be met by either anaerobic or aerobic systems.

Anaerobic System

Anaerobic energy production is derived during short-term (0 to 90 seconds), high-intensity (high power outputs) activities such as explosive jumping or sprinting. Besides the immediate availability of stored ATP, the rapid resynthesis of ATP is accomplished by the breakdown of another high-energy phosphate compound called creatine phosphate (CP). In addition to harvesting anaerobic energy via the ATP-CP reaction, carbohydrate metabolism can also contribute to the energy demands of active muscle during short-term, high-intensity work bouts (30 to 90 seconds), or short-term (90 seconds to 3 minutes), moderately high-intensity work bouts by providing additional ATP. Carbohydrate metabolism occurs in a series of chemical reactions. However, it is important to note that during short-term, moderately high to high-intensity exercise, the availability of oxygen is limited. This circumstance poses a problem from the resultant production of waste products in the blood (i.e., lactic acid). Although an effective metabolic strategy during short-term exercise, the anaerobic breakdown of carbohydrate has shortcomings because muscular fatigue is associated with increased levels of lactic acid.

Aerobic System

During prolonged duration (more than 3 minutes) or low to moderate intensity exercise, the supply of oxygen via the cardiorespiratory system can meet the energy demands of working muscle by aerobic metabolism of carbohydrates, fats, and proteins. The aerobic system is often referred to as the "endurance" system due to its function during prolonged duration activities. In contrast to the anaerobic system, the aerobic system is very efficient in converting fuels (carbohydrates, fats, and protein) into energy with relatively little waste (i.e., lactic acid).

It is important to understand that the relative contribution of anaerobic and aerobic energy sources varies depending on the duration and intensity of the activity. At the extremes of the energy spectrum of exercise, almost all of the energy production is supplied by anaerobic and aerobic means. In other cases, a blend of anaerobic and aerobic energy production occurs. For example, an all-out bout of 2 minutes requires about half of the energy from either anaerobic or aerobic systems. An understanding of the energy demands of a particular activity is necessary for the appropriate design of sports conditioning programs.

PRINCIPLES OF CARDIORESPIRATORY PHYSIOLOGY

Cardiorespiratory function is closely related to aerobic energy production because the ability to consume large amounts of oxygen to produce energy at high work rates is necessary during endurance activity. Three measures of cardiorespiratory fitness that contribute to the ability to succeed in prolonged activity are *maximal oxygen consumption, anaerobic threshold and economy of movement*. All three measures are dependent upon the cardiovascular, respiratory, and muscular systems.

Maximal oxygen consumption (VO_2max) is the maximal ability to take up, deliver, and utilize oxygen to produce energy via aerobic metabolism. VO_2max is measured by a progressive exercise test to exhaustion on a motorized treadmill or stationary cycle, and is expressed in either absolute (liters per minute) or relative

Table 8-1. Relative Contribution (% Total Energy Production) of Aerobic and Anaerobic Energy During Near-Maximal or Maximal Activity of Varying Duration.

Energy contribution	Duration of Exercise							
	10 sec	30 sec	60 sec	2 min	4 min	10 min	30 min	60 min
% anaerobic	90	80	70	50	35	15	5	2
% aerobic	10	20	30	50	65	85	95	98

(ml/kg/min) terms. It is advantageous for athletes participating in endurance sports to possess high values for VO_2max. In general, highly-trained adolescent (15-19 yrs) endurance athletes have a VO_2max of 60-75 ml/kg/min. Values for highly-trained pre-adolescent (8-12 yrs) children are slightly lower (55-65 ml/kg/min).

Anaerobic threshold (AT) corresponds to the exercise capacity at which lactic acid, a byproduct of carbohydrate metabolism, begins to accumulate in the blood. Because lactic acid is associated with muscular fatigue, continuous exercise above the AT is limited. The anaerobic threshold is expressed as either the VO_2 at AT (ml/kg/min) or as a percentage of VO_2max (i.e., 85% of VO_2max). It is advantageous for athletes to possess a high AT, which allows the athlete to achieve higher exercise capacities before large amounts of lactic acid accumulate in the blood. Other terms have been used to represent the AT, such as lactate threshold and ventilatory threshold. Although each is assessed differently, the terms are related and generally represent the same concept.

Economy of movement refers to the rate of oxygen consumption or energy expenditure at a given speed of movement. It is advantageous to be more economical (consume less oxygen at a given pace). For example, a cross-country runner who consumes relatively lower amounts of oxygen at a 7 minute per mile pace is more economical than a runner who consumes larger amounts at the same pace.

Principles of Neuromuscular Physiology

A major objective of youth sport programs is to teach correct motor skills. Likewise, a major objective of sport conditioning programs is to enhance neuromuscular strength and power. Central to both of these objectives is the function of the neuromuscular system. To improve neuromuscular strength and power and the learning of a motor skill requires the coordinated integration of both the nervous and muscular systems.

Muscular contraction occurs as a series of complex biochemical and mechanical events within the muscle cell known as excitation-contraction coupling. In order for a muscle to contract (i.e., shorten) and create force, it must receive excitation by nervous tissue. In many ways, the nervous system acts like an electrical device with a central unit (brain and spinal cord), electrical cord (neural pathway), and plug (neuromuscular junction) which interfaces with a power source (muscle). The nerve cell and the specific muscle cells it innervates are called a motor unit. Besides sending information to muscle, the nervous system also receives information from internal and external sources and processes this input to create an understanding of the internal and external environments and to possibly transmit information to muscle.

The determinants of movement and strength are dependent upon both neural and muscular factors. During growth and maturation, muscle mass is a key determinant of force production. However, increases in force production following a period of resistance training in pre-pubertal athletes may occur independent of changes in muscle mass. This observation highlights the neural component of force production, particularly in the early phases of training and in pre-pubertal athletes.

GENERAL PRINCIPLES OF CONDITIONING

The following principles of conditioning should serve as a guideline to design an appropriate and successful conditioning program for youth athletes.

Readiness

Before designing and implementing a conditioning program for youth athletes, it is important to consider the psychological and physiological readiness of the participant(s). In order to make a well informed decision, the coach must compare the demands and benefits of the activity with the capability, responsiveness, and needs of the athlete. Is the child or adolescent sufficiently strong or physically fit to cope with the intensity and duration of the conditioning program? Will the exercise significantly improve his/her performance? Will time spent on conditioning detract from time available for skill development?

General opinion suggests that coaches working with children below approximately 14 years of age should focus more upon the development of motor skills. This period is generally referred to as the 'skill hungry' years, when children are considered to be most receptive to motor instruction. During this period, conditioning is concomitant to motor skill development. Conditioning of functional capacities becomes more important during and after the period of adolescence when sport generally becomes more physically demanding.

Progression of Exercise— Warm Up and Cool Down

It is important to conduct a period of warm up exercises prior to a conditioning session or competition. The goals of the warm up exercises are to gradually increase the heart rate, breathing rate, blood flow, and the temperature and flexibility of the muscles. A successful warm up session will improve the physiological and biomechanical efficiency of the muscles during performance and reduce the likelihood of injury. Warm up exercises should always be performed prior to any stretching exercises.

Appropriate warm up exercises are those that reflect

the patterns of movement required in the specific sport. For example, appropriate warm up exercises for sports, which involve running, might include 5 to 10 minutes of walking, skipping, jogging, or sub-maximal sprints. Similarly, a basketball coach might include skills such as lay ups or jump shots as part of the warm up. The length of time spent on the warm up varies with regard to climate, and the intensity of the subsequent activity. The colder the climate the greater the necessity for warm up exercises. In colder climates, warm up exercises should be conducted indoors because loss of body heat reduces the effectiveness of the warm up session. Because high intensity conditioning sessions place the athlete at greater risk of injury, it is particularly important to warm up prior to the activity. Another important function that the warm up serves is to acquaint or re-acquaint the athlete to the sport setting. This may be helpful in injury prevention.

Following the activity or competition the body should be cooled down. This process should include low intensity aerobic activities such as walking or jogging, which help reduce the pooling of blood and lactic acid in the active muscles, particularly the extremities. The cool down may reduce muscle soreness and increase the recovery process in preparation for the next activity session. The cool down activity should be followed with stretching exercises to help increase and/or maintain flexibility.

Progressive Overload

In order to initiate changes in functional capacity (e.g., strength, aerobic power), a stress (i.e., exercise) must be applied. Repeated exposure to the stress causes a biological system to adapt to a state where it can accommodate the stress more effectively. The term stress is often referred to as an "overload," which means that the system has to work harder than it is accustomed to working. The athlete needs to overload the system in a progressive manner to initiate continual change in functional capacity, hence the term *Progressive Overload*. Progression to an increased workload should be gradual, reducing the chance of injury and allowing adequate recovery time. There are five different factors that can be manipulated to introduce a new "stress" into the conditioning program.

1. Load: Increasing the amount of resistance against which the body has to act.
2. Repetitions: Increasing the number of times a muscular force is applied when moving a load.
3. Duration: Increasing the amount of time that a muscular force is applied when performing a bout of repetitions.
4. Frequency: Increasing the number of training sessions, or increasing the rate of performing exercises.

5. Rest: Reducing the amount of time between bouts of exercise.

Specificity

Conditioning exercises should be specific to the physiological, biomechanical, and psychological demands of the sport or position played by the athlete. What are the physiological and psychological demands of the activity that you coach? Does it require short interrupted periods of intense activity or does it involve longer sustained periods of moderately intense activity? Is the activity predominantly aerobic or anaerobic? Which muscle groups are predominantly used? What are the specific movement patterns? Does the sport require a great degree of flexibility? Does your sport require the psychological ability to tolerate physical discomfort? Answers to these questions should identify which conditioning exercises are most appropriate for a given sport or position.

Individual Differences

The trainability of young children and adolescents is dependent upon a multitude of factors including age, maturational status, gender, prior experiences in physical activity, physical fitness, skill aptitude, social environment, and heredity. This leads to great individual variability in responsiveness to conditioning programs. For example, certain conditioning programs may produce large gains in some athletes but only mediocre or small gains in others. Likewise, some athletes may respond quickly to conditioning programs, while others respond at a slower rate. Such variation may also be due to other factors such as motivation, poor nutrition, poor health, and instruction. Individual differences also influence the initial design and monitoring of conditioning programs. No single conditioning program can fit the needs of every participant.

Reversibility

Simply use or lose it! Once a required level of physical fitness has been attained a maintenance program is necessary to prevent the benefits of conditioning from being lost. Even the fittest of athletes may experience decrements in physical fitness following the cessation of a conditioning program. The intensity of the exercise in the maintenance program is the key variable. It should be noted that in a maintenance program the frequency and duration of exercises can be reduced without a decrease in physical fitness if the intensity of exercise is maintained. This approach is often used during the competitive season to maintain conditioning gains from a pre-season conditioning program.

METHODS OF CONDITIONING

Ask a group of coaches and exercise scientists what are the best training methods for improving performance and you will get several different answers. Although the answers may vary, safe and effective conditioning programs are based on the general principles outlined previously. In this section, training methods for endurance, speed, explosiveness, and strength will be presented. It is recognized that examples are specific to running, however, the general application of these methods to cycling and swimming are generally appropriate.

Training Strategies to Improve Endurance Performance

The major objective of endurance training programs is to enhance the delivery and utilization of oxygen during prolonged activities and to resist fatigue. The following components of endurance training are widely used by coaches and athletes to improve VO_2 max, AT, and economy of movement. It is recognized that the methods described below are for running events. The concepts can be generalized to other forms of movements (i.e., swimming, cycling).

Long duration (30 minutes to 2 hours), moderate intensity (approximately 65-75% maximum heart rate). (Note: Maximum heart rate can be estimated by subtracting age from 220, e.g. 220 - 14 = 216 beats per minute.) Training occurs at a pace slower than competition pace and elicits general changes in the cardiorespiratory and muscular systems. The athlete should be capable of carrying on a conversation with a partner while engaged in the activity. It is also referred to as base or foundation training.

Moderate duration (30 to 60 minutes), high intensity (slightly below AT; approximately 75-85% maximum heart rate). Training occurs at the same pace as competition. It is also referred to as pace or tempo training. This type of training accommodates the athlete to competitive conditions.

Moderate duration (4 to 10 minutes), high intensity (slightly above AT; approximately 75-95% maximum heart rate). This is a form of interval training where the athlete performs a bout of exercise followed by a period of recovery (i.e., slow jog, or rest). For example, the athlete would perform a 30-40 minute training session by running hard for 4-10 minutes and then recovering by jogging slowly for 4 minutes or so. This method of training has also been referred to as "fartlek" training. This type of training, along with training at the pace of competition can be used to specifically increase the AT and the body's ability to tolerate lactic acid.

Short duration (30 seconds to 3 minutes), very high intensity (at maximal capacity; approximately 100%

maximum heart rate). This is also a form of interval training commonly referred to as speed work. An example would be for an athlete to perform repeated bouts of 400-800m sprints followed by a rest between each bout. The rest recovery should be monitored depending on the objective of the training sessions. Full recovery allows for the emphasis of speed, whereas a shorter recovery time between bouts emphasizes speed endurance. The aim of this method of training is to withstand fatigue and increase running velocity.

Speed and Explosiveness

Sprint Training

In most sports, sprint speed is an important determinant of success. Sprint speed is determined by stride frequency, stride length, form/technique, neuromuscular strength, anaerobic energy production, and heredity. Understanding these factors will help develop appropriate speed conditioning programs for young athletes.

Stride Frequency

Improvements in the frequency of movement may be achieved through "speed drills" that enhance a neuromuscular pattern similar to the motor skills required in the sport. Speed drills increase the rate of movement by enhancing the coordination of the active muscle groups involved in the specific skill. Sprint-assisted techniques (downhill running, towing) are often employed by coaches and athletes aiming to improve sprint speed. However, such techniques may promote the development of improper technique as well. Plyometric exercises (a discussion of which follows) may also be used to increase the frequency of movement by reducing the time spent in contact with the surface.

Stride Length

Improving stride length can be accomplished by increasing flexibility and improving technique. A greater range of motion around a joint leads to a greater distance over which force is applied. The key is to focus upon developing flexibility in the areas that are sprint-specific, including the ankles, hip, knees, shoulders and hamstrings.

Although increasing stride length may improve sprint speed, coaches should be cautioned that an optimal stride length exists. Therefore, over-manipulation of stride length (over-striding) can result in diminished sprint speed due to inefficient technique which causes a breakdown of the forward velocity.

Technique

Improving technique allows the athlete to work in an energy efficient manner, thus enhancing performance. Although no two athletes will exhibit exactly the same technique, the basic mechanics of sprinting should remain the same for all athletes. In running, these basics include:

- Driving off the ball of the foot;
- Running erect with a slight forward lean;
- Keeping the head and torso steady;
- Arm swing without the hands crossing the mid-line of the body; and
- Keeping the face, shoulders, arms, and hands relaxed.

Neuromuscular Strength

Resistance training exercises may be used to develop functional strength and power in muscle groups specific to sprinting. Increasing neuromuscular strength allows for a greater application of force throughout the movement. Specifically, resistance exercises should focus upon the lower extremity, hip, and torso. Principles of resistance training are discussed in the following section.

Speed, and in particular speed endurance, may be improved by increasing the energetic capacity of the anaerobic systems. Activities that will improve sprint speed and speed endurance include short duration sprints (e.g., 6-60 seconds) or sprints that cover the distance required in a specific sport (e.g., football, 20-60 yards, basketball, 10-30 yards, baseball, 30-90 yards). To emphasize the development of speed, allow for a full recovery between each sprint. To emphasize speed endurance, reduce the amount of recovery time between bouts.

Plyometrics

Plyometrics, or explosive jump training, is a method of conditioning used to link strength and speed. Plyometric exercises elicit neuromuscular properties that develop proprioception (body awareness) and explosiveness. A key element of plyometric training is to reduce the support phase of jumping.

Several plyometric exercises have been used by coaches and athletes ranging from simple to advanced exercises. Various jumps, hops, and bounds are examples of plyometric exercises. The childhood game of hop-scotch can be considered a simple plyometric activity. Upper body exercises such as medicine ball catch and throws are also considered plyometrics. The reader is referred elsewhere (Baechle, 1994; p. 327-341) for a summary of plyometric exercises. Because plyometric training is a demanding training procedure, establishing safe guidelines is important in the prevention of injury and maximizing performance gains (See Table 8-2).

Resistance Training

Resistance training is defined as a specialized form of conditioning that is used to increase the ability to exert force. Most youth sports demand considerable strength and power; therefore enhancing strength may improve performance. In addition, resistance training has been associated with fewer sports injuries and shorter rehabilitation times.

Despite the increasing number of youth athletes engaging in resistance training, the practice of resistance training in youth athletes remains controversial. The primary concerns are the influence of heavy loading on the growth and maturation of bone, the incidence of musculoskeletal injuries, and the efficacy of resistance training in youth. Each of these concerns lack strong evidence or are a result of inappropriate conditions (e.g., improper nutrition, inadequate supervision, inadequate training programs). Therefore, the National Strength and Conditioning Association (1996), the American Orthopedic Society for Sports Medicine (1988), and the American Academy of Pediatrics (1990) have issued position stands suggesting that youth can benefit from participation in a properly designed and supervised resistance

---

Table 8-2. Guidelines for the Incorporation of Plyometric Training Programs.

- Athlete must possess a sufficient strength base.
- Athlete must be coachable.
- Determine if demands of sport movements are linear, vertical, lateral, or combination.
- Proper footwear must be worn.
- Exercises should be performed on a resilient surface.
- Proper, sturdy equipment should be used.
- Sufficient training area should be available.
- Frequency should not exceed two sessions per week.
- 80-100 foot contacts for beginners, 100-120 foot contacts for intermediate-level athletes, and 120-140 foot contacts for advanced athletes/ Volume may also be expressed as distance (e.g., 300 m).
- Progression from low-intensity, in-place exercises to medium and high-intensity exercises.
- Large athletes should avoid high-volume, high-intensity exercises

training program. A summary of recommendations by the National Strength and Conditioning Association is provided in Table 8-3. (See also Chapter 9, *Principles of Resistance Training*).

Generally, the design of resistance training programs can be divided into four major components:

1. Needs analysis,
2. Acute program variables,
3. Chronic program manipulations, and
4. Administrative concerns.

The needs analysis addresses the biomechanical and physiological requirements of the participant. Movement-specific resistance exercises should meet the biomechanical and physiological requirements of the sport. Certain exercises may also benefit both injury prevention and rehabilitation. The acute program variables determine daily training sessions. In general, one exercise should be performed per major muscle group (legs, chest, back, shoulders, arms, torso/midsection) on 2 to 3 nonconsecutive days per week.

Typically, exercises against resistance are performed from the largest to the smallest muscle groups. The number of sets, repetitions, and load will depend on the age, experience, and goals of the participant. The rest period between sets should be determined by the desired outcome of the resistance training program (i.e., strength or endurance) and the energetic demands of the sport. For example, 2 to 3 minutes is required if strength/power is the desired outcome, whereas only 30 seconds may be warranted if endurance is the aim of the program.

The rest period in resistance training is also influenced by the intensity of the training session as well. The chronic manipulation of the acute program variables is referred to as periodization. Finally, administrative concerns such as time, supervision, number of participants, and facilities need to be considered accordingly. The reader is referred elsewhere (Fleck and Kraemer, 1986; Kraemer and Fleck, 1992) for a complete discussion of the prescription of resistance training and samples of resistance training programs.

Although resistance training improves the strength of children and adolescents, the benefits of activities such as resistance training must be weighed against the potential risks and limitations. Resistance training requires appropriate levels of psychological and behavioral maturity, particularly when adequate supervision cannot always be guaranteed. Furthermore, the coach must ensure that the resistance training equipment and environment are both suitable and safe for the youth athlete. With these issues in mind, a practical approach to incorporating a resistance training program is outlined in Table 8-4. The program progresses from an orientation with resistance

---

Table 8-3. Summary of Recommendations for Designing and Implementing Youth Resistance Training Programs.*

- Require a medical examination prior to participation.
- Each child should be psychologically and physically ready to participate.
- Children should have realistic expectations regarding learning of technique and improvement in physical fitness.
- The facility should be safe.
- The equipment should be in good repair and fit each child.
- Proper warm-up required prior to training session.
- All training sessions should be closely supervised by a trained professional.
- Proper instruction should be provided regarding exercise technique, training guidelines, and spotting procedures. The child should start with a relatively light weight, or even a broomstick, until correct technique is learned.
- Proper weight room etiquette should be provided by the supervisor.
- All major muscle groups should be exercised.
- The resistance should be increased gradually (5-10%).
- Progression may also be achieved by increasing the number of sets, exercises, and training sessions per week. In general, 1-3 sets of 6-15 reps performed on 2 or 3 nonconsecutive days a week is recommended.
- Prohibit 1 repetition maximal lifts.
- Specific multi-joint exercises (bench press, squats, leg press) and advanced multi-joint exercises (Olympic lifts, modified cleans, pulls, and presses) may be introduced into the program depending on individual needs and competencies.
- Competition should be discouraged.
- The child should enjoy resistance training and have fun. Do not force a child to participate in a resistance training program.
- Instructors and parents should be good role models.
- Children should be encouraged to drink plenty of fluids before, during, and after practice.
- Children should be encouraged to participate in a variety of sports and activities.

*Adopted from National Strength and Conditioning Association, "Youth Resistance Training: Position Statement Paper and Literature Review," 1996.

Table 8-4. A Four Step Approach to Resistance Training for Youth.*

Step 1 (2-4 weeks)
- Orientation to resistance training
- Introduction to various resistance exercises including body weight exercises and safety
- Emphasis is on teaching
- One set of 12-15 repetitions (low intensity)
- Duration of 20-30 minutes per session
- 2-3 days per week
- Progression to next step is based on needs and ability of the participant

Step 2 (4-8 weeks)
- Emphasis on safe and effective exercise technique rather than amount of weight lifted
- Fundamentals of resistance training technique (i.e., breathing and body mechanics) should be reviewed throughout this period
- 2 sets of 10-12 repetitions (moderate intensity)
- Duration of 30 minutes per session, 3 days per week
- Careful evaluation of recovery and toleration

Step 3 (8-24 weeks)
- Participant must demonstrate proper technique and physical and emotional readiness to begin more advanced training
- New exercises may be introduced
- 2-3 sets of 8-12 repetitions (moderate to moderately high intensity)
- Periodization model can be incorporated

Step 4 (4-24 weeks)
- Participant must demonstrate mastery of technique
- Advanced multi-joint exercises (e.g., Olympic lifts and modified cleans and pulls) can be introduced; the purpose of teaching advanced lifts should be to develop neuromuscular coordination and technique.
- 3 sets of 6-10 repetitions (high intensity)

*Adapted and modified from Faigenbaum, "Prepubescent Strength Training: A Guide for Teachers and Coaches," 1993 and Kraemer, et al., "Resistance Training and Youth," 1989.

training to the mastery of technique and comprehension of training principles to advanced exercises and program design. It is important to note that individuals may start or progress at varied steps throughout the program.

Concurrent Training

Concurrent exercise training consists of simultaneous training in aerobic and resistance exercise. Concurrent training for cardiorespiratory endurance and neuromuscular strength can be conducted by independent endurance and resistance training sessions or circuit training. Circuit training is a form of concurrent training performed by executing a given number of exercises in a continuous manner. Typically, alternating stations of resistance exercise and aerobic exercise are performed for a given time or number of repetitions.

Economical Training

The relative importance of conditioning for sport must be put into perspective with the importance of meeting the various needs—cognitive, psychosocial, physical and technical. A coach must address these needs, to varying degrees, during practice and games. Given the limited amount of time, coaches should plan activities that simultaneously meet needs in more than one area. This approach is referred to as economical training. For example, the intensity, duration and structure of a passing drill could be organized to enhance components of conditioning and strategy, as well as techniques of passing.

The concept of economical training is important because many coaches erroneously set aside blocks of time within a practice session for conditioning-only activities. Practice time should be spent on learning techniques and strategy of the sport, especially in younger athletes. As athletes develop a higher level of skill mastery, conditioning-only activities could be incorporated into practice sessions.

PERIODIZATION

Periodization is defined as a systematic approach to the prescription of sports training to prevent overtraining and optimize peak performance in which the frequency, intensity, and duration of training is manipulated during the year and competitive season. In general, periodization is an extension of the general principle of progressive overload. By manipulating the acute program variables over a period of time, overtraining can be avoided and continued gains in performance attained.

Various cycles in the training period have been defined. The overall training period is termed a macrocycle. A macrocycle may refer to several months (season), a year, or several years. Within a macrocycle, a few mesocycles of many weeks or months occur. Generally, each mesocycle represents a sequence of the entire macrocycle with various emphasis in each cycle (e.g., base, strength, power, peaking, active rest). A simplified model of periodization for a youth athlete engaged in resistance training is provided in Table 8-5.

OVER-TRAINING

As discussed in the previous section, over-training may result if the total stress (training stress plus other stresses) is too great. Over-training is a general term for any short term or long term condition in which there is an imbalance between training and recovery resulting in severe or prolonged fatigue and possibly injury. During short-term over-training, also referred to as over-reaching, recovery will usually occur within 1 or 2 weeks if training is decreased. Long term over-training culminates in a condition known as over-training syndrome, which can be identified by behavioral, emotional, and physical symptoms (See Table 8-6).

Table 8-5. Periodization Model for a Youth Athlete.*

Training Phase	Sets	Repetitions
Base	3	10-15
Strength	3	6-10
Power	2-3	6-8
Peaking	1-2	6-8
Active rest	Any type of physical activity to maintain physical fitness	

*Adapted from Kramer and Fleck, *Strength Training for Young Athletes*, 1992.

Table 8-6. Signs and symptoms of over-training.

- Apathy
- Lethargy
- Sleep disturbance
- Weight loss
- Elevated resting heart rate
- Muscle pain or soreness
- Mood changes
- Gastrointestinal disturbances
- Retarded recovery from exertion
- Loss of appetite

SUMMARY AND CONCLUSIONS

The safe and effective design and implementation of strength and conditioning programs for young athletes should be based on the scientific principles provided here. However, training is an art based on a science and will never be a purely scientific endeavor. Current knowledge of training practices has been based on scientific investigation, trial-and-error, and intuition. Many questions remain to be examined regarding the efficacy of various training techniques in youth athletes.

Most importantly, coaches need to understand that children are not miniature adults. Thus, conditioning programs designed for adult athletes should not be implemented in youth sport programs without careful consideration. Likewise, the conditioning process should only be supplemental to the overall athletic experience of youth. If a child spends a majority of time and effort on physiological conditioning and neglects the learning and practice of motor skills and understanding of the game, the end result will not reflect an overall improvement in performance. Participants should also be encouraged to engage in a total conditioning program, rather than specializing in one type of conditioning at an early age. Finally, the process of conditioning young athletes should be a positive experience that may assist in developing knowledge and lifetime habits and attitudes towards physical activity.

REFERENCES

American Academy of Pediatrics. (1990). "Strength Training, Weight and Power Lifting and Bodybuilding in Children and Adolescents." *Pediatrics*, 86: 801-803.

American Orthopedic Society for Sports Medicine. (1988). Cahill, B. (editor), *Proceedings of the Conference on Strength Training and the Prepubescent*. Chicago: Author.

Baechle, T. R. (editor). (1994). *Essentials of Strength Training and Conditioning*. Champaign, IL: Human Kinetics.

Dinteman, G., Ward, B., and Tellez, T. (1998). *Sports Speed*. Champaign, IL: Human Kinetics.

Faigenbaum, A. (1993). "Prepubescent Strength Training: A Guide for Teachers and Coaches." *NCSA Journal*, 15(5): 20-29.

Fleck, S. J., and Kraemer, W. J. (1987). *Designing Resistance Exercise Programs*. Champaign, IL: Human Kinetics.

Hawley, J. A., Myburgh, K. H., Noakes, T. D., and Dennis, S. C. (1997). "Training Techniques to Improve Fatigue Resistance and Enhance Endurance Performance." *Journal of Sport Sciences*, 15: 325-333.

Kraemer, W. J., and Fleck, S. J (1993). *Strength Training for Young Athletes*. Champaign, IL: Human Kinetics.

Kraemer, W. J., Fry, A. C., Frykman, P. N., Conroy, B., and Hoffman, J. (1989). "Resistance Training and Youth." *Pediatric Exercise Science*, 1: 336-350.

National Strength and Conditioning Association. (1996). "Youth Resistance Training: Position Statement Paper and Literature Review." *Journal of Strength and Conditioning Research*, 18(6): 62-75.

Noakes, T. D. (1992). *Lore of Running (3rd edition)*. Oxford: Oxford University Press.

Pate, R. R., and Branch, J. D. (1992). "Training for Endurance Sport." *Medicine and Science in Sport and Exercise*, 24: S340-S343.

Wilmore, J., and Costill, D. (1998). *Exercise Physiology*. Champaign, IL: Human Kinetics.

9
Principles of Resistance Training

Anthony Moreno, M.S. and C.S.C.S.

QUESTIONS TO CONSIDER

- Why is resistance training important for youth sport?
- How often and how much resistance should my athletes be lifting?
- What are the differences among bodybuilding, powerlifting and weightlifting?
- How does in-season training differ from pre- and off-season training?

INTRODUCTION

Resistance training has been used for many years at a variety of competitive levels to improve performance and help prevent injury. You, as a youth coach, must have a thorough understanding of why you are using resistance training in your setting. This should include recognizing the benefits and potential risks, evaluating which practices are scientifically sound, and the ability to supervise and administer an effective program in a safe environment.

The term *resistance training*, is often used interchangeably with other terms such as "strength" training or "weight" training. Regardless of which term is used, it is a practice that is designed to enhance "one's ability to exert or resist force" (Bompa, 1993). Implementing a successful resistance training program is dependent on the experience of the teacher or coach, the availability of equipment and space, and the instructional environment. The apparatus commonly found in many facilities may vary from the traditional iron plates, barbells, and dumbells to the use of commercial variable resistance machines, physio-therapy devices, medicine balls, or a combination of all of these products (See Figure 9-1).

Popular resources containing information on resistance training (e.g. the internet, general texts, and popular magazines) often appear to possess sufficient educational material that addresses programming and safety across all populations. However, it should be recognized that pre-pubescent and adolescent youth require special considerations often not discussed or available from these sources. The purpose of this chapter is to provide the youth or volunteer coach basic insight and assistance in

Figure 9-1. Implementing a successful resistance training program is dependent on the experience of the teacher or coach, the availability of equipment and space, and the instructional environment.

establishing a competent, practical, and safe resistance training program for his or her young athletes.

WHY IS RESISTANCE TRAINING IMPORTANT FOR YOUTH SPORTS?

Prevention of Injuries

Resistance training can play an important role in reducing the incidence and severity of injury in youth sport. As with many recreational pastimes, participation in sport carries a potential and risk of injury depending on the type and frequency of the activity. Current evidence suggests that the risk of injury may become compounded because participation numbers for individuals who actively engage in youth sport have increased dramatically during the past few decades (NSCA position statement, 1996).

Resistance training can provide the appropriate biological mechanisms that strengthen the supporting structures (tendons, ligaments, and bones), enhance the ability of tissues to absorb more force prior to failure (tearing) and develop greater muscular balance about specific joints. Research appears to support the vital role that resistance training contributes to the reduction of injury. In a high school study comparing the incidence of injury among male and female adolescent athletes, the injury rate (26.2%) and recovery time (2.02 days) were significantly reduced for those who participated in a supervised strength training program when compared to a control group (72.4% and 4.82 days, respectively) that did not follow a weight training protocol (Henja, Rosenberg, Buturusis, and Krieger, 1982). Cahill and Griffith (1978) reported high school football players were able to reduce the severity and incidence of knee injury by participating in a pre-season weight training regimen. Hewitt, Stroupe, Nance, and Noyes (1996) in a study involving female high school volleyball players, demonstrated that a routine of plyometric and lower extremity strength training was able to minimize landing impact forces. The authors implied that the alleviation of impact forces was instrumental in decreasing the incidence of injury for these athletes.

Although it may be easy to generalize these selected findings to children and adolescent athletes, coaches should remember that the application of resistance training is by itself a physical stress. Factors such as fatigue, aggressiveness, experience, contact in the sport, practice time, and other social or environmental influences play a role in the prevention of injuries. These factors should always be considered in the over-all program of planning practices and physical training sessions.

Performance Enhancement

Many coaches agree that muscular strength, power, and endurance are highly desirable traits for young athletes. The rigid links through which force is produced and transferred throughout the segments of the body consist of muscles, tendons, ligaments, and bone. Concomitant improvements in strength and skill are most evident when athletic performance capacities such as the vertical jump are increased, and sprint and reaction times are noticeably reduced in physical testing.

Youth sport varies on a continuum from non-contact activities such as golf and swimming, to those with a heavy collision component such as hockey and football. Regular strength training induces biochemical adaptations in muscle that lead to mechanical advantages in the muscle-bone-joint leverage systems of the body. As a re-

sult, resistance training can be a useful tool for the sport coach who hopes to improve the athlete's performance characteristics.

Success in sport can be attributed to many factors. However, a structured resistance training program and its influence on the body's structures may well be the cornerstone to a positive outcome in many sport situations.

Psycho-Social Factors

Although direct findings are limited, the available literature and practical observations of many coaches and scientists appear to demonstrate that resistance training has a positive effect on a variety of psycho-social indicators such as self-confidence, self-image, and self-esteem (Faigenbaum, 1995). Enhanced self-confidence may improve the socialization skills needed to bring young athletes together to share bonds that make all participants feel a part of the team (Martinez, 1997). Well constructed programs should be designed with the young participant's best physical and psychological interests in mind. Encouraging self-improvement and persistence may enable athletes to acquire positive psycho-social effects similar to those found in other recreational activities and sports. On the other hand, care must be taken to refrain from excessive levels of training that may be beyond the scope of the athletes' physical and emotional development. Such practices may encourage the athletes to acquire negative psychosocial behaviors (AAP position statement, 2000).

SAFETY ISSUES

Growth, Maturation, and Gender

Although strength training for pre-pubescent children and adolescent youth has been open to controversy for some time, there is sufficient research and literature to support the use of resistance training for these age groups (Faigenbaum, 2001; Payne, Morrow, Johnson & Dalton, 1997; Ozmun, Mikesky, & Sunburg, 1994; Blimkie, 1993; Ramsay et al., 1990). Strength training is an area of prime concern because childhood and adolescence are stages in life where growth and development are especially dynamic. Much of this concern has focused on the occasional incidence of musculoskeletal injury (e.g. epiphyseal fractures, ruptured intervertebral disks, and low back bony disruptions), particularly during performance of the major multi-joint exercises such as the squat or deadlift (Committee on Sports Medicine, 1990).

For the youth coach and parent, confusion often exists as to the appropriate age to begin a weight training program and the associated effects on normal growth and development. Current literature on age appropriateness also appears to be mixed. One study, concerning the effects of resistance training on growth and development, reported no adverse effects as a result of following a weight training program in children as young as six years of age (Blimkie, 1993). The National Strength and Conditioning Association in a paper on youth resistance training (1996), holds the position that properly designed resistance training programs with appropriate supervision can be safe for physiologically and psychologically prepared children and adolescents. However, the position statement does not give a specific age range for males and females (NSCA, 1996). The American Academy of Pediatrics (2000) recommends avoiding the practice of using maximal attempts until adolescents have reached Tanner stage 5 level of developmental maturity (Committee on Sports Medicine, 1990). However, according to several growth studies (Malina, 1991), the Tanner stage 5 level can be quite variable across gender and ethnicity, and this can lead to frustration in determining an acceptable age at which to begin strength training.

Given the general lack of agreement in the literature determining age appropriateness for strength training, coaches should use extreme caution with children and adolescents when designing these programs. For all novice trainees, challenging sub-maximal efforts that require concentration, emphasize technique, address posture and breathing patterns should be utilized. As the athlete matures, increasing the difficulty of the efforts that match the physical maturity of the child is appropriate.

Another area that is commonly misunderstood among coaches is the differences between boys and girls when following a strength training program. Because the risk of anterior cruciate ligament (ACL) and other lower extremity injury in females is generally two to eight times greater than their male counterparts, strength training should become an integral part of the physical conditioning plan (Hewitt et al., 1996). Although there is not as much literature concerning strength training in females as in males, the current evidence indicates that females are able to improve strength from a variety of different weight training protocols (Malina, 1991) (See Figure 9-2).

Facilities

Facilities and structures that house weight training equipment and serve as the focal instructional location for implementing resistance training programs must be user safe to help prevent the injuries. Some important guidelines concerning the safety of the facility are:

- Adhere to local or municipal codes regarding structure, lighting, ventilation, and occupancy.
- Comply with all fire codes and have clearly marked exits.
- Ensure that aisles and walkways are clear of equipment and debris.

Figure 9-2. Excellent resistance training techniques must be emphasized at all stages of physical development. Pre-pubescent youth can utilize lightweight apparatus such as PVC pipe to refine posture, movement and breathing patterns.

- Have a floor covering (e.g., non-slip, carpet, rubber, etc.) appropriate for the type of activities to be conducted.
- Provide clean floor surfaces that are non-slip where needed. Vacuum carpets regularly if they are present.
- Incorporate signage that provides disaster or emergency contingency procedures in obvious, easily accessible locations.

Equipment

Just as important as the appropriate use of equipment is the appropriate maintenance and care of your training "tools". Young athletes deserve a learning environment that uses reliable, safe, and effective equipment. The following requirements are related to equipment safety:

- Plates, barbells, and dumbells should be stored on the appropriate racks or stations when not in use.
- Equipment, racks, audio-visual units or stereos affixed to walls must be securely attached.
- Machines, benches, and platforms should be regularly checked for stability.
- Use a maintenance log to document and coordinate the replacement of broken chains, torn upholstery, and frayed cables.
- The manufacturer's prescribed maintenance and cleaning plan for each piece of equipment must be noted because this schedule may vary from device to device.
- Regularly use sponge disinfectant on the facility equipment upholstery.
- All equipment should be regularly inspected for structural or mechanical problems such as poor welds, metal burring, or loose pins and pulleys that may compromise the safety of those using the equipment.

Supervision and Management

A great facility with state of the art equipment is of little value if the instruction and management of the facility are inadequate. The following are requirements for the proper supervision of a facility:

- The athletic staff should devise and rehearse a disaster/emergency contingency plan.
- All training should be supervised by a qualified staff member.
- There should be an adequate staff/student ratio in the weight room at all times. A common recommendation is one supervisor or instructor per eight to ten athletes.
- Supervisors should be knowledgeable about warm-up and stretching techniques, weight training theory, training progression and first aid.
- An orientation program for athletes should be implemented to ensure that all participants are aware of safety rules and regulations, standards of behavior, warm-up and stretching techniques, and instruction on proper form for the weight training equipment or other apparatus.
- The administration should implement a weekly safety inspection to ensure a safe training facility. This should lead to the removal of defective equipment and the replacement of worn parts.
- Overcrowding of the weight room should be prevented.
- Place signage throughout the facility to ensure that weights, bars, dumbells, or other apparatus are kept clear from aisles and walkways and returned to their proper place for storage after use.

A checklist that can be used to help resistance training supervisors track safety related issues can be found in *Supplement 9-1: Weight Room Safety Checklist* which appears at the end of this chapter.

RESISTANCE TRAINING

Popular Resistance Training Terminology

One of the most important tasks a coach must undertake is the ability to become familiar with the numerous terms used among those in the professions of physical education, health, and recreation. The term *resistance training*, is often used interchangeably with other terms such as "*strength*" training or "*weight*" training. *Resistance training* is a broad term and refers to the use of some implement, device, or simply bodyweight as a resistance to enhance some physical characteristic like strength or muscular endurance. There are many sub-disciplines associated with the practice of resistance training, each with an emphasized adaptation or effect as a result of training regularity.

Although most forms of resistance training will facilitate muscle cell growth (hypertrophy), *bodybuilding* is the practice that utilizes training techniques to enhance body mass and induce hypertrophy without regard to specific strength, muscular endurance, or power gains. *Powerlifting* is a competitive sport that is judged by one's ability to exhibit maximal strength (one repetition maximal) in three exercises: the squat, the bench press, and the deadlift. *Weightlifting* is a competitive olympic and recreational sport that requires complex technique and ample muscular power to perform the two competitive lifts: the snatch and the clean and jerk.

Bodybuilding, powerlifting, and weightlifting each bring positive attributes to a youth resistance training program, provided that the program includes appropriate instruction and supervision. The strengths and weaknesses of each activity must be critically analyzed to ensure that the contributions are in accordance with the training objectives of the athletes, their weight training experience, and the appropriate stage of physical maturation. For these reasons, it is important that the athletic coach become familiar with and understand all the components and definitions needed to construct a basic strength training routine (See Figure 9-3).

Annual/Seasonal Training Models

Creating a seasonal physical training program is an important undertaking for the coach, because this plan will dictate how the athletes physically prepare for the next several weeks, months, or even a year. This task can be difficult because there are many factors that play a role in selecting the exercises, the instructional methods, and determining the amount of time allotted for learning to take place in the weight room. Factors such as academics, sport practices, extracurricular activities, family commitments, and social relationships often compete for time and attention. Involvement in multiple activities requires

Figure 9-3. In situations where equipment and resources are scarce, the use of body weight as a resistance can be effective.

excellent organization in order to be successful in all of them. Not planning accordingly may lead to undue stress, a lack of preparedness and potential injury.

The *overload principle* is the fundamental constant of resistance training. The principle of overload is based on the fact that muscles will adapt and become stronger when exposed to resistances not normally encountered. Over a period of time these same muscles or muscle groups must be subjected to a new "stimulus" that will encourage the body to adapt further or "supercompensate" and thus gain strength (Kuipers, 1998). As the athlete adapts and becomes stronger, greater resistances can be applied. The formal method of organizing the application of the overload principle over a period of time is referred to as *periodization*. Periodization is the organization of training in cycles or phases in order to achieve "peak" levels of athletic performance through the development of greater physical capacities (Bompa, 1993).

Misinformation and poor applications of a training program often lead to the development of *overtraining* syndromes resulting in fatigue, poor performance, and overuse injuries (e.g. tendinitis, bursitis, patello-femoral distress). On the other hand, because the body needs a stress to adapt or supercompensate, too little work will result in an under-trained or poorly prepared athlete, also susceptible to injury. Thus, the coach must monitor progress and make adjustments in the weight training program as necessary. Applying the appropriate amount of stress with the appropriate amount of rest and recovery is one of the key concepts of periodization.

Periodization of an organized weight training program requires a timeline for the training period (e.g. one season, month, 3 months, one year), and the manipulation of three important variables: the *load*, the *volume*, and the *intensity*. *Load* is the weight or resistance to be used for the exercise (e.g. 100 lb. on the bench press). *Volume* is the product of the total number of sets and repetitions (e.g. 3 sets of 10 reps: 3 x 10 = 30 total repetitions). *Intensity* refers to the relative difficulty of the repetitions, often indicated as a percentage (e.g., if someone can press 100 lb. for a one repetition maximum, then 80 lb. would be approximately 80% intensity of what that person can press). The coach should realize that there can be individual variation that affects how athletes perform on any given day.

Appropriate manipulation of the load, volume, and intensity enable one to keep the body from developing a stagnant state of training, from which little progress can be made. This can be done by increasing the load, decreasing the volume, reducing the rest period between sets, changing the order of exercises, or even changing the mode of exercise (such as substituting pushups for the bench press).

The type of training that occurs during the season is called "in-season" conditioning, training prior to the season is "pre-season" conditioning, and training that occurs during the time away from competition is termed, "off-season" conditioning. Because many young athletes participate in a number of sports throughout the year, it is important to understand that the practices and exercises associated with these sports also stress the musculo-skeletal systems of these athletes. For this reason the coach of younger athletes must be careful not to compound any fatigue that might be associated with other activities. This may mean reducing the number of weight training sessions during the week or for several weeks, reducing the training volume, or in extreme cases discontinuing weight training altogether until a transition time between sports occurs.

The bulk of physical changes and intense efforts in the weight room typically occur in the off-season and the pre-season. In the off-season, the intensity of efforts may vary from low to moderately high, with high volume. During the pre-season period, the range of intensity is prescribed as moderate to very high intensity, with a moderate decrease in volume. In the pre-season, athletes begin to emphasize skill components of the specific sport; therefore, the volume of weight training should decrease while the amount of time spent practicing sport skills increases.

The competitive season usually places emphasis on specific sport skills, tactics, and strategy; all of which may be accompanied by emotional and physical stress to the athletes. Therefore, the volume of training is usually decreased to allow for appropriate recovery. However, it is important to maintain the intensity of training even during this period so that strength gained in the off-season and pre-season is maintained. The key to periodization is that it is not a cookbook program that is the same for every athlete year after year. Rather, it is a principle that is subject to change depending on a number of factors. Coaches should continually make adjustments to the rigors of practice, competition, academic requirements, and the individuality of the athletes. Constant monitoring of these changes will optimize the benefits that result in stronger and more powerful athletes.

Selection of Exercise Mode

Proper resistance training begins with the assignment of appropriate exercises and the use of well-maintained equipment. This task can be difficult for the youth or scholastic coach who often is faced with limited resources and facilities. The most commonly available pieces of equipment are typically free weights (barbells and dumbells), variable-resistance machines, and the athlete's bodyweight. Each has particular advantages and disadvantages.

Free weights are typically cheaper when compared to the cost of variable-resistance machines. In general, free weights do not consume as much square footage, and the maintenance of free weight implements is minimal. From a training perspective, one advantage of free weights is that they require more balance and muscular coordination than use of a machine (See Figure 9-4). In addition to the prime movers, the numerous postural and trunk stabilizers (abdominal, spine, and lower back musculature) are included in the exercise, which are often neglected by coaches and athletes alike. However, this same advantage can also be a disadvantage because any activity that requires more control and balance requires more time to master and definitely requires greater supervision.

Variable resistance machines are easy to set up, and they require users to perform simple movements in a restricted environment, thus decreasing the risk of using poor technique. Many machines are not designed for pre-adolescent or adolescent populations so there may be difficulty at times getting users to properly fit into the machines. Although beginners might be better served to use a machine when they are learning technique, postural or breathing patterns, the available research does not suggest that one method of training is better than the other when training exclusively for strength (Haff, 2000). Machines are typically more expensive than their free weight counterparts, and they consume more space. In addition, they generally require more maintenance to ensure that they operate properly and safely. Whether using free weights or machines, quality instruction and supervision are of the utmost importance. This may include alternating between different modes of exercise to keep athletes from becoming bored, stagnant, and unresponsive.

In addition to free weights and machines, other modes of training can include body weight exercises (e.g. pullups, pushups, abdominal crunches), medicine balls, and elastic cords. Body weight exercises can be performed on a field, court, or other open area. For the coach designing a program, the key idea to consider is to select those exercises that will strengthen the muscles, liga-

ments, and tendons susceptible to injury, and to train those muscles which serve as the prime movers and stabilizers of the activity. Coaches who are familiar with injury trends and basic functional anatomy do their athletes a great service by understanding and selecting the appropriate exercises for their specific activity.

For the beginner, simplicity in resistance training is the best approach. This means selecting exercises that are easy to learn and simple to replicate. Demonstrating proper execution of the exercise will help the athlete develop a mental picture of the correct technique, tempo, and breathing patterns. Coaches should not select too many exercises, so that the time spent in the weight room does not compromise other aspects of physical preparation or skill development. Selected exercises may include multiple-joint exercises or single joint exercises, but these exercises should be the most appropriate for the trainee and the current level of physical development (See Figure 9-5).

Order of Exercises

Once the availability and type of equipment to be used has been determined, it becomes necessary to "order" the exercises for the program. The coach must keep in mind that this results in only an outline of a plan. This plan may change during the ensuing weeks or months according to the guiding principle of periodization. Young athletes do not have the musculoskeletal strength and endurance that is usually observed in trained adults. Therefore, a coach should not expect to see young children or adolescents performing with similar loads and volumes. For the absolute beginner, the quantity of exercises selected should be kept to a minimum to establish consistency of training and proper training etiquette (i.e., abiding by weight or recreation room rules and regulations).

Confusion often exists concerning the organizing of

Figure 9-4. The use of free weights (e.g. dumbells and barbells) requires undivided concentration, strict form and postural stabilization.

Figure 9-5. Coaches should be ready to demonstrate the exercises so that an appropriate model is created for young athletes to follow.

exercises by muscle group, and by portion of the body (e.g. the lower body vs. the upper body). For example, when the program calls for strengthening the legs, coaches may be confused about where to place a leg extension (single-joint movement) or squat exercise (multiple-joint movement) in a workout program.

Current research does not provide solid evidence as to whether multi-joint or single joint exercises should be placed first to enhance general strength. However, the efficient use of time is an important consideration for many coaches. In this case it is better to include a majority of the muscle groups in as time-efficient a manner as possible. For this reason, multiple-joint exercises should be placed at the top of the workout chart.

When determining which body parts to include (order) in the routine, it is best to attend to weaknesses first and stronger areas later. If the upper body is extremely weak when compared to the lower body, then multi-joint pressing exercises (e.g. bench press, overhead press, incline press) are the best to initiate the weight training regimen. If the lower extremities are the weakest, then squatting, lunges, and leg presses are the appropriate beginning exercises. After establishing which portion of the body to work with multi-joint movements, single joint exercises (e.g. leg extensions, leg curls, bicep curls) can be placed in a manner of importance to the coach and training philosophy.

Training the various energy systems of the body can be accomplished through resistance training. This is often referred to as *metabolic training*, and it is performed by manipulating exercises, the order of these exercises, and the rest periods involved (Bompa, 1993). Shorter rest periods between sets do not allow for complete replenishment of the metabolic substrates necessary for an optimal, forceful muscle contraction. Training with shorter rest periods may enable the young athletes to develop better muscular endurance, but at the expense of strength. This concept can be reversed by lengthening the rest period between sets. Metabolic training can be designed to imitate game-like levels of intensity and fatigue to help children or adolescents become accustomed to the levels of conditioning necessary for competition.

By manipulating the weight training exercises, one can create "circuits" (also called *circuit weight training*) where alternating upper and lower body exercises (push and pull) with no rest period can create a combination of challenges to enhance both strength and endurance. Exercises can be performed for sets and repetitions, or for a time period at each separate activity station. *Interval training* requires mixes or combinations of strength training, endurance (aerobic) training, and anaerobic conditioning. In this protocol, the different forms of training are conducted over intervals of time. In addition, multi-joint and single joint exercises can be used for both systems of training. Circuit training and interval training are probably best suited for sports like hockey, volleyball, soccer, and basketball that require a mix of both strength and muscular endurance (See Figure 9-6). Sports like football, sprinting, field events, baseball, and softball typically require greater levels of muscular strength and power. Coaches will usually find that the sport for which they are training athletes places disproportionate demands on the elements of the energy systems. The important concept to remember is that these energy systems can be trained directly by manipulating exercises and rest periods.

Constructing the Program

The following provides several sample resistance training routines for specific sports. Coaches must realize these are only samples and may not address the special needs for their team. Variations in the athletes' maturation and experience, the instructional environment, and the availability of equipment may require independent assessments with regard to constructing the training routine that will best serve the goals and objectives of the program. In addition, these examples, like all resistance workouts, must be preceded by appropriate warm-up and stretching.

Athletes will respond positively to the stresses of physical training depending on a variety of influential factors, including intensity, volume, frequency, school, work, and family commitments. Coaches must recognize signs of overtraining (i.e. injury, fatigue, anxiety, loss of appetite, boredom) and implement the necessary changes to the training protocol on an individual basis. These changes may include shortening the duration of the practice sessions, altering the structure of the daily workouts, modifying the amount of resistance training and running volume, and changing the time of day of the workout.

Figure 9-7 represents the first month of an off-season training cycle with a taper in the fourth week that allows for appropriate recovery before beginning the next one-

Figure 9-6. The use of elastic bands and medicine balls are ideal for circuit or interval training.

	SUN	MON	TUE	WED	THURS	FRI	SAT
Week 1	OFF	**Upper**	**Lower**	AGILITY	**Upper**	**Lower**	RUN
Week 2	OFF	**Upper**	**Lower**	AGILITY	**Upper**	**Lower**	RUN
Week 3	OFF	**Upper**	**Lower**	AGILITY	**Upper**	**Lower**	RUN
Week 4	OFF	**Upper**	**Lower**	AGILITY /RUN	OFF	OFF	OFF

Figure 9-7. One-Month Off-Season High School Football Strength Training Cycle—2-Day Split Routine (Summer).

month's cycle. The second month of this cycle is generally smaller in volume, but greater in intensity; therefore, the need for the tapered week. Although in this training scenario the running and agility programs are conducted on non-lifting days, these programs may be conducted before weight training workouts if time is scarce. If this is the case, the running/agility protocol can serve as an adequate warm-up session. Coaches should realize that the primary objectives of an off-season training program are (1) learning proper lifting technique, (2) developing a strength base to prepare for more intense pre-season routines, and (3) maintaining or enhancing muscular body mass. The relative importance of each depends on the sport.

Figure 9-8 is another example of a one-month off-season training cycle for high school football players. This protocol provides three workouts on a weekly basis, with the running and agility programs scheduled between the lifting days. This protocol considers the possibility that athletes may have work or other obligations on the weekends. Notice that the taper period is similar to the end of the fourth week as in Figure 9-7.

Table 9-1 describes a sample upper body routine that can be used with either of the two organization patterns. Similarly, Table 9-2 outlines a possible lower body routine to use with the athletes.

A second example, found in Figure 9-9, focuses on the pre-season for volleyball. This is a demanding time period for both athletes and coaches. It is when athletes need to approach optimal physical condition, while mastering the sport skills and strategies emphasized by the coach. Because of the importance of refining sport techniques and tactics, supervised strength training workouts may be reduced to once per week. This compromises the time allotted for this workout. In this case, the use of a total-body muscle endurance circuit is ideal.

Such circuits enhance physical work capacities with the use of body weight and/or inexpensive resistance training implements (i.e. medicine balls, elastic bands, dumbells). Metabolic capacities are stressed when the athletes are exercising within a range of heart rates that correspond to competition-like conditions (see Chapter 8, *Physiological Conditioning of Young Athletes*).

When constructing a circuit weight training routine, the coach should alternate opposite working muscle groups (quadriceps vs. hamstrings) or body segments (legs vs. chest). If emphasis is placed on a single portion of the body for a period of time, fatigue will occur which increases the likelihood of the athlete's heart rate falling below the desired training range. Circuits can use either a time period (e.g. seconds, minutes) or a set number of

Table 9-1. Sample Upper Body Routine.

Exercise	Muscle Groups	Volume
• Bench Press	• Pectoral muscles, anterior deltoids, triceps	• 3 sets of 8 to 10 repetitions
• Incline Dumbell Press	• Upper pectorals, anterior deltoids, triceps	• 2-3 sets of 10 to 12 repetitions
• Shoulder Press	• Deltoids, upper portion of the pectorals	• 2-3 sets of 10 to 12 repetitions
• Upright Rows	• Deltoids, trapezius, rhomboids, biceps	• 2-3 sets of 10 to 12 repetitions
• Dumbell Shrugs	• Trapezius, rhomboids	• 2-3 sets of 10 to 12 repetitions
• Tricep Extensions	• Triceps	• 2-3 sets of 10 to 12 repetitions
• Pushdown Exercise	• Triceps	• 2-3 sets of 10 to 12 repetitions
• Manual Resistance Neck Exercises	• Upper erectors	• Isometric (for time)
• Supine Medicine Ball Tosses	• Abdominal muscles	• 3-4 sets of 15 to 20 repetitions

	SUN	MON	TUE	WED	THURS	FRI	SAT
Week 1	OFF	**Upper**	RUN	**Lower**	AGILITY	**Upper**	OFF
Week 2	OFF	**Lower**	RUN	**Upper**	AGILITY	**Lower**	OFF
Week 3	OFF	**Upper**	RUN	**Lower**	AGILITY	**Upper**	OFF
Week 4	OFF	**Lower**	RUN/ AGILITY	**Upper**	OFF	OFF	OFF

Figure 9-8. One-Month Off-Season High School Football Strength Training Cycle—3-Day Alternate Routine (Summer).

	SUN	MON	TUE	WED	THURS	FRI	SAT
Week 1	OFF	Practice & **Workout**	Practice	Practice	Practice	OFF	scrimmage
Week 2	OFF	Practice & **Workout**	Practice	Practice	Practice	OFF	scrimmage
Week 3	OFF	Practice & **Workout**	Practice	Practice	Practice	OFF	scrimmage
Week 4	OFF	Practice & **Workout**	Practice	Practice	***1st Game***	Practice	***2nd Game***

Figure 9-9. Pre-season high school girls' volleyball circuit protocol (Oct.–Nov.).

Table 9-2. Sample Lower Body Routine.

Exercise	Muscle Groups	Volume
• Power Cleans	• Lower extremities	• 5 sets of 5 repetitions
• Squat	• Gluteals, quadriceps, and hamstrings	• 3 sets of 8 to 10 repetitions
• Leg Extension	• Quadriceps	• 2-3 sets of 10 to 12 repetitions
• Leg Curl	• Hamstrings	• 2-3 sets of 10 to 12 repetitions
• Heel Raises	• Gastrocnemius and Soleus (Calves)	• 2-3 sets of 10 to 12 repetitions
• Pullups or Pulldowns	• Lattissimus Dorsi	• 2-3 sets of 10 to 12 repetitions
• Seated Rows	• Rhomboids, trapezius, lattissimus dorsi, biceps	• 2-3 sets of 10 to 12 repetitions
• Barbell or Dumbell Curls	• Biceps	• 2-3 sets of 10 to 12 repetitions
• Supine Medicine Ball Tosses	• Abdominal muscles	• 3-4 sets of 15 to 20 repetitions
• Medicine Ball Good Morning Exercises	• Lower erectors	• 3-4 sets of 15 to 20 repetitions

repetitions as the volume to be performed for the session's workout. Table 9-3 provides a sample muscle endurance circuit for athletes who play volleyball. For each person, the coach may select either "10 repetitions" or "30 seconds" for each exercise. It is important that the resistance used be of a sub-maximal value that will allow the athletes to maintain the objective target heart rate (THR). Depending on the fitness status of the participants and the training objectives, complete circuits can be performed from start to finish (one set), or they can be completed several times (several sets).

The purpose of an in-season strength training cycle is to maintain, and in some cases, enhance muscular strength. Maintenance of strength is important over seasons that may last several months. In this case, workouts must be scheduled so that they do not interfere with game performance. Ideally, workouts would be conducted the day after a competition because the next scheduled contest is probably several days or a week away. In situations where games may be scheduled close together or at tournament time, it is best to forego lifting so that the training recovery period does not occur on game-days and thereby cause undue fatigue during competition.

Figure 9-10 outlines an in-season routine that basketball players might follow to maintain their strength. The routines they might follow during training are described in Table 9-4.

Keep in mind that the above samples are hypothetical and do not represent actual training routines. Coaches should assess their training environment and develop a sound program around the abilities of their athletes, and the available equipment and availability of the facility.

Table 9-3. Sample Pre-season Volleyball Muscle Endurance Circuit.

Exercise	Muscle Groups	Volume
• Squats w/ body weight	• Gluteals, quadriceps, and hamstrings	• Repetitions or Time
• Abdominal Crunches	• Abdominals	• Repetitions or Time
• Pushups	• Pectorals, anterior deltoid, triceps	• Repetitions or Time
• Heel Raises	• Gastrocnemius and Soleus (Calves)	• Repetitions or Time
• Medicine Ball Good Mornings	• Lower erectors	• Repetitions or Time
• Modified Pullups	• Lattissimus dorsi, rhomboids, trapezius, biceps	• Repetitions or Time
• Squat Thrusts (Burpees)	• Lower extremities	• Repetitions or Time
• Supine Medicine Ball Tosses or Sit-ups	• Abdominal muscles	• Repetitions or Time
• Dips or Modified Dips	• Pectorals, anterior deltoid, and triceps	• Repetitions or Time
• Medicine Ball "Chops"	• Erectors and obliques	• Repetitions or Time

	SUN	MON	TUE	WED	THURS	FRI	SAT
Week 1	OFF	Practice	*GAME*	Practice	Practice	*GAME*	*Workout*
Week 2	OFF	Practice & *Workout*	Practice	Practice	Practice	Practice	*GAME*
Week 3	OFF	Practice	*GAME*	Practice	Practice	*GAME*	*Workout*
Week 4	OFF	Practice	Practice	*GAME*	Practice	*GAME*	*Workout*

Figure 9-10. In-season high school basketball strength maintenance routine (January).

Table 9-4. Sample In-Season Basketball Strength Maintenance Routine.

Exercise	Muscle Groups	Volume
• Torso circuit 　° sit-ups 　° good mornings 　° Russian twists	• Abdominals, obliques, erectors	• Timed sets
• Squat or Leg Press	• Gluteals, quadriceps, hamstrings	• 2 sets of 6 to 10 repetitions
• Dumbell press or Dumbell shoulder press	• Pectorals, anterior deltoids, triceps	• 2 sets of 6 to 10 repetitions
• Pullups/Pulldowns	• Latissimus dorsi, pectorals, rhomboids	• 2 sets of 8 to 10 repetitions

OTHER FACETS OF CONDITIONING

Testing

Testing in the weight room, on the court, or in the field can provide coaches with information about the current training status of their athletes. In addition, testing sessions and their results can be a powerful motivational tool for the athletes (Bridgeman, 1991). For these reasons testing is a valuable addition to a complete physical training program. The most important factor for coaches who implement strength testing is to provide a safe environment. This includes using exercises and loads that do not jeopardize the muscle-tendon-bone joint complexes of maturing adolescents or pre-adolescent children.

Caution should be utilized to avoid extending athletes beyond their capabilities and risking injury for the sake of exhibiting some personal or team record at the expense of safety and common sense. The performance of athletes on tests should be judged relative to their personal improvement and not the performance of their peers. Coaches that foster a competitive testing environment are in danger of encouraging athletes to conduct exercises with poor technique and overzealous attempts at poundages that may incur serious injury. To avoid these compromising situations, it is suggested that coaches use sub-maximal loads (i.e. 3RM, 5RM, 10RM) and determine estimations of the 1RM lifts using available charts or formulas (Cummings & Finn, 1998; LeSeur, Mc-Cormick, Mayhew, Wasserstein, & Arnold, 1997).

Another important component of testing and weight training is the use of competent supervision and *spotting* techniques. "*Spotting*" is the practice of assisting athletes to complete repetitions at or beyond muscular failure during an exercise, while ensuring that the exercise is completed in a safe manner from start to finish. Coaches and weight room supervisors must ensure that all student-athletes are: (1) aware of proper spotting technique; (2) capable of possessing the strength necessary to assist fellow athletes; and (3) aware of appropriate behavior concerning weight room situations in coeducational settings (see Chapter 27, *Maintaining Discipline*).

Incorporating Running, Agility and Plyometric Exercises With the Weight Training Program

Implementing off-season and pre-season running, agility, and plyometric exercises into a training routine as components of a complete physical conditioning program are commonplace. However, it is important for coaches to realize that these activities place physical stresses upon the body and require their own recovery and recuperative periods. Although not calculated in the total "volume" of weight training, the repetitive stresses placed upon musculoskeletal structures will take their physical toll on athletes if not organized appropriately.

Running, agility, and plyometric exercises require an appropriate warm-up to reduce the ever-present possibility for injury. Warm-up and vigorous use of these activities prior to weight training are optimal when planning for

Figure 9-11. Spotters must be attentive and assume a ready position in event the trainee has difficulty completing the required number of repetitions for the set.

the economical use of time for physical conditioning. Athletes that have completed training sessions in these areas prior to lifting are typically "loose" enough to engage in a weight training session. Nevertheless, coaches must assume responsibility in ensuring that their athletes are appropriately warmed up for any conditioning activities.

The primary concern for coaches and athletes alike is that running, agility, and plyometric training are physical stressors. As such, they present a situation where athletes may be too fatigued to follow the requirements of the day's weight training protocol. If this is the case, volume of training can be decreased, while attempting to maintain intensity as closely as possible to the prescribed workout. If athletes are too fatigued to maintain the intensity requirements, then the coach should make appropriate adjustments to the day's workout to avoid an injurious situation.

If the athletes' and coach's schedules allow, running, agility and plyometric workouts can be scheduled on days or weekends between lifting sessions. The coach must remember these activities can be physically and emotionally stressful for the athlete. Therefore the coach must plan for an appropriate training volume and workout organization that allows the athletes an optimal period of recovery between workout sessions and workout cycles.

SUMMARY

Resistance training is a viable tool for youth and scholastic sports programs. Such training potentially can improve performance and prevent injury. Coaches must realize that there are appropriate procedures and practices that are essential to designing a scientifically sound, practical and safe resistance training program. By recognizing the potential benefits and risks, and by developing an in-house evaluation system, administrators, coaches and parents can play a major role in providing a meaningful experience for their student-athletes and younger aspiring athletes.

GLOSSARY

Bodybuilding—Bodybuilding is a recreational and competitive form of resistance training that places an emphasis on muscle hypertrophy, the symmetry of muscular development, and the display of muscularity.

Circuit weight training—Circuit weight training is a regimen that requires the trainee to utilize several exercises or activities in series to develop muscular endurance, strength or a higher level of metabolic conditioning.

Cycle—The basic unit of periodization that contains the variation and manipulation of the volume, load and intensity variables for a prescribed training model.

Hypertrophy—An increase in the size of a muscle fiber that is initiated by muscular effort or overload.

Intensity—The amount of muscular effort typically represented as a percentage of an individual's 1RM. For example, 80 lb. represents 80% of a 100 lb. maximal effort on a bench press exercise.

Load—The amount of resistance to be used for a given exercise or set. Usually measured in pounds (lb.) or kilograms (kg).

Metabolic training—Metabolic training involves the simultaneous physical conditioning of both the musculo-skeletal and cardio-respiratory systems of the body.

Overtraining—Overtraining is a condition induced by an over-emphasis of volume or intensity without the appropriate recovery time. Injuries, sleeplessness, anxiety, depression, fatigue, and loss of appetite are symptoms often associated with overtraining.

Overload principle—Basic principle of resistance training through which gains in strength and increased hypertrophy are brought about by an "overload" or workload that is beyond the current strength threshold of a muscle or muscle group.

Periodization—Periodization is the organization of physical training in a cyclic structure in order to acquire higher levels of physical fitness

Plyometrics—Plyometrics is a training technique used to enhance muscular power. This methodology utilizes a rapid stretch-shortening contraction of a muscle or muscle group to entice greater rate of force development.

Powerlifting—Powerlifting is a recreational and competitive sport where contestants are judged on their ability to perform maximal single-repetition efforts for the bench press, deadlift and squat exercises. The totals are summed and the winners are granted according to the combined efforts of the three lifts.

Repetition—Repetitions are the unit of quantity concerning the number of times an exercise is repeated within a single set.

Repetition Maximal (RM)—Maximal amount of weight an athlete can lift for one repetition (1 RM) for a given exercise. In performing a "3 RM" lift, an athlete would be lifting a resistance that could be performed for a maximum of 3 repetitions.

Resistance training—The broad practice of enhancing muscular strength and muscular endurance with the use of body weight or weighted implements (i.e. elastic bands, medicine balls, barbells, dumbells).

Set—The set is described as the number of repetitions to be performed for a given exercise.

Strength—The capacity to generate force.

Taper period—The taper period is generally a sequence of days at the end of a training cycle during which either the volume of training, the intensity, or both are significantly reduced. This reduction in training volume and intensity allows for an adequate recovery period prior to beginning the next training cycle.

Volume—Training volume is the product of the total number of sets and the total number of repetitions in a particular workout or training cycle.

Weightlifting—Weightlifting is a competitive sport comprised of two explosive competitive lifts, the clean and jerk and the snatch.

Weight training—Specific method of resistance training using weighted implements (i.e. barbells, dumbells, plates) and variable or accommodating resistance machines or devices.

REFERENCES

Anderson, S. J., Greisemer, B. A., Johnson, M. D., Martin, T. J., McLain, L. G., Rowland, T. W., and Small, E. (2000). "American Academy of Pediatrics Policy Statement: Intensive Training and Sports Specialization in Young Athletes." *Pediatrics*, 106(1): 154-157.

Blimkie, C. J .R. (1993). "Resistance Training During Preadolescence: Issues and

Controversies." *Sports Medicine*, 15(6): 389-407.

Bompa, T. O. (1993). *Periodization of Strength: The New Wave of Strength Training*. Toronto: Veritas Publishing.

Bridgeman, R. (1991). "A Coach's Guide to Testing for Athletic Attributes." *National Strength and Conditioning Association Journal*, 13(3), 34-37.

Cahill, B., and Griffith, E. (1978). "Effect of Preseason Conditioning on the Incidence and Severity of High School Football Knee Injuries." *American Journal of Sports Medicine*, 6: 180-184.

Cummings, B., and Finn, K.J. (1998). "Estimation of a One Repetition Maximum Bench Press for Untrained Women." *Journal of Strength and Conditioning Research*, 12(4): 262-265.

Faigenbaum, A. D. (2001). "Strength Training and Children's Health." *The Journal of Physical Education, Recreation and Dance*, 72(3): 24-30.

Faigenbaum, A. D. (1995). "Psychosocial Benefits of Prepubescent Strength Training." *Strength and Conditioning*, 17(2): 28-32.

Haff, G. G. (2000). "Roundtable Discussion: Machines Versus Free Weights." *Strength and Conditioning Journal*, 22(6): 18-30.

Hewitt, T. E., Stroupe, A. L., Nance, T. A., and Noyes, F. R. (1996). "Plyometric Training in Female Athletes: Decreased Impact Forces and Increased Hamstring Torques." *American Journal of Sport Medicine*, 24: 765-773.

Kuipers, H. (1998). "Training and Overtraining: An Introduction." *Medicine and Science in Sports and Exercise*, 30(7): 1137-1139.

LeSeur, D. A., McCormick, J. H., Mayhew, J. L., Wasserstein, R .L., and Arnold, M. D. (1997). "The Accuracy of Prediction Equations for Estimating 1-RM Performance in the Bench Press, Squat, and Deadlift." *Journal of Strength and Conditioning Research*, 11(4): 211-213.

Malina, R. M., and Bouchard, C. (1991). *Growth, Maturation, and Physical Activity*. Human Kinetics, Champaign, IL.

Martinez, D. M. (1997). "Is Strength and Conditioning Necessary for the Youth Football Athlete?" *Strength and Conditioning*, 19: 13-17.

National Strength and Conditioning Association (1996). "Youth Resistance Training: Position Statement Paper and Literature Review." *Strength and Conditioning*, 18(6): 62-75.

Nelson, M. A., Goldberg, B., Harris, S. S., Landry, G. L., and Risser, W.L. (1990). "Committee on Sports Medicine: Strength Training, Weight and Power Lifting, and Body Building by Children and Adolescents." *Pediatrics*, 86(5): 801-803.

Ozmun, J. C., Mikesky, A. E., and Sunburg, P.R. (1993). "Neuromuscular Adaptations Following Prepubescent Strength Training." *Medicine and Science in Sports and Exercise*, 26(4): 510-514.

Payne, V. G., Morrow, J. R., Johnson, L., and Dalton, S.N. (1997). "Resistance Training in Children and Youth: A Meta-analysis." *Research Quarterly for Exercise and Sport*, 68(1): 80-88.

Pearson, D., Faigenbaum, A., Conley, A., and Kraemer, W.J. (2000). "The National Strength and Conditioning Association's Basic Guidelines for the Resistance Training of Athletes." *Strength and Conditioning Journal*, 22(4), 14-27.

Ramsay, J. A., Blimkie, C. J. R., Smith, K., Garner, S., MacDougal, J. D., and Sale, D. G. (1990). "Strength Training Effects in Prepubescent Boys." *Medicine and Science in Sports and Exercise*, 22(5): 605-614.

SUGGESTED READINGS

Bompa, T. O. (1994). *Theory and Methodology of Training: The Key to Athletic Performance (3rd edition)*. Dubuque, IA: Kendall/Hunt Publishers.

Fahey, T. D. (2000). *Basic Weight Training for Men and Women (4th edition)*. Mountain View, CA: Mayfield Publishing Company.

Fleck, S. J., and Kraemer W.J. (1997). *Designing Resistance Training Programs (2nd edition)*. Champaign, IL: Human Kinetics Publishers.

Malina, R. (1992). "Physical Growth and Biological Maturation of Young Athletes." *Exercise and Sport Science Reviews*, 22: 389-433.

Weight Room Safety Checklist

Facilities

_____ Must adhere to all applicable codes relating to structural, lighting, ventilation and occupancy requirements.

_____ Must comply with all fire codes and have clearly marked exits.

_____ Aisles and walkways should always be clear of equipment and debris.

_____ Floor covering (e.g., non-slip, carpet, rubber, etc.) in each area must be appropriate for the type of activities to be conducted.

_____ Must have clean floor surfaces and use non-slip material where necessary.

_____ Vacuum carpets regularly (if present).

_____ Must post signage that provides disaster or emergency contingency procedures in obvious, easily accessible locations.

Equipment

_____ Plates, barbells, and dumbells should be stored on the appropriate racks or stations when not in use.

_____ Any equipment, racks, audio-visual units, or stereos affixed to walls are secure.

_____ Machines, benches, and platforms are checked regularly for stability.

_____ A maintenance log is used to document and coordinate the replacement of broken chains, torn upholstery, and frayed cables.

_____ All manufacturer's prescribed maintenance and cleaning plans are followed, since the lubrication schedule may vary from device to device.

_____ Sponge disinfectant is used regularly on the facility equipment upholstery.

_____ Checks are conducted regularly for structural or mechanical problems such as poor welds, metal burring, or loose pins and pulleys that may compromise the safety of those using the equipment.

Supervision and Management

_____ Supervisory personnel devise and rehearse a disaster/emergency contingency plan.

_____ All training is supervised by a qualified staff member.

_____ There is an appropriate staff/student ratio in the weight room at all times. One safe ratio commonly in place is one supervisor or instructor per eight to ten athletes.

_____ Supervisors are knowledgeable in warm-up and stretching techniques, weight training theory, training progression, and first aid.

_____ An orientation program for athletes is implemented to ensure that all participants are aware of safety rules and regulations, standards of behavior, warm-up and stretching techniques, and instruction on proper form for the weight training equipment or other apparatus.

_____ The administration implements a weekly safety inspection to ensure a safe training facility, removes defective equipment, and replaces necessary equipment parts.

_____ Overcrowding of the weight room (according to the established local fire code) is prevented.

_____ Signage is placed throughout the facility to ensure that weights, bars, dumbells, or other apparatus are clear from aisles and walkways.

10
Nutrition for Young Athletes

Ronda Bokram, M.S., R.D.

QUESTIONS TO CONSIDER

- Do young athletes and non-athletes have different nutritional requirements?
- Are dietary supplements beneficial for young athletes?
- Are sports drinks a desirable substitute for water?
- What is the best advice to give young athletes on when and what to eat before, during and after competition?

INTRODUCTION

Elementary age through high school is a critical period for physical, social, and emotional growth and development. Energy and nutrient needs are high, especially in the adolescent. Compound these factors with the increased physiological demands of participating in a sport, and the achievement of adequate nutrition to meet all needs can be a challenge. Nutrition is an important factor that has been clearly demonstrated to affect athletic performance. Indeed, studies have shown that appropriate overall eating habits (how the athlete eats during the *entire* week) are of greater benefit than the taking of any type of supplement or even eating the "perfect pregame meal."

Along with the wealth of scientific information supporting the connection between sports performance and nutrition there has emerged a market for products and literature "to give athletes the competitive edge." These popular products and materials are often easier to understand and access than the information found in research journals. Separating facts from fiction can be a challenge to the coach as well as for the athlete and his/her parent or guardian.

This chapter will examine the basics of sports nutrition in order to give you, the coach, guidelines, tools and resources for evaluating the recommendations and information about nutrition pertaining to athletics. This will assure that your athletes receive the most accurate and beneficial information

NUTRITION BASICS

Optimum nutrition is an eating pattern that provides adequate total energy; the right balance (percentage) of protein, fat and carbohydrates; enough of the recommended amounts of vitamin and minerals; and, the amount of water needed for normal bodily functions. These needs are affected by the demands of growth and development, as well as regular daily activities. A variety of foods eaten throughout the day should be sufficient to provide the 40+ nutrients essential for good health. Following the serving recommendations given by the USDA Food Pyramid, found in Table 10-1, should allow for basic needs to be met, especially for the younger athlete. During adolescence, a period of extremely rapid growth, serving amounts will usually need to be significantly increased to meet both the physiological demands of growth and the energy production needed for participation in sports. The age and rate of these increased needs will vary considerably between individuals as they go through growth spurts at different times. Therefore, it is up to the individual athlete to recognize and trust the physiological need to increase intake as needed.

Calories

Calories are the energy content of food. Calories are what fuel our body. If an athlete does not eat enough total energy, even if the balance of nutrients (protein, fat, and carbohydrate) is adequate, performance will be impaired.

Table 10-1. USDA Food Pyramid.

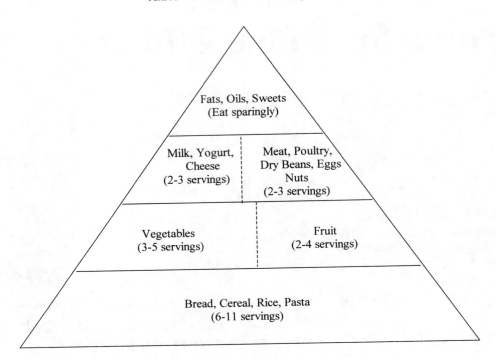

There are guidelines to estimate energy requirements in adults, but limited research has been done on the energy needs of youth, especially in relation to participation in specific activities. Therefore, determination of the energy requirements of young athletes should be done only if required for a specific nutritional goal or concern and then only by a professional trained in the area of sports nutrition.

The total amount of calories that a person needs can vary from day to day and is dependent on several factors: age, gender, rate of growth, and activity level. This is complicated further by the fact that the calorie needs for one's activity level, or the amount of energy required by an individual for use in sports, also is influenced by variables: specifically the intensity and length of the activity as well as the body size of the athlete. For example, during a 45 to 90 minute game or training session, soccer players may burn up to 25% more energy than they do on a day in which they do not practice. Hence, heavy training or twice a day practices may require an additional 400 to 600 or more calories per day to compensate for the calories burned during activity. Given adequate opportunity to eat, young athletes will tend to consume the amounts needed. Adolescents, as they develop concerns with weight and body image, may elect not to eat as much as they require in an attempt to keep a lower weight or smaller body size. Complaints of fatigue and observations of reduced or impaired performance are possible indicators that energy intake may be too low.

The content of protein, fat and carbohydrate (4, 9, and 4 calories per gram, respectively) determines the total caloric value of a particular food or beverage. It is important to recognize the variation in the energy worth of specific foods, especially in relation to meal timing and satiety (sense of fullness). Foods such as fruits and vegetables are low in energy value, but high in nutrient content such as fiber, vitamin C and A. Candy or french fries, on the other hand, have little or no specific nutrient value, but they supply a larger amount of calories. These concentrated sources of calories can make a positive contribution to meeting the high energy demands of a growing adolescent where vitamin and mineral needs are met within Food Pyramid guidelines, while total energy needs are not. It is also important to remember that many of these "empty calorie" foods have social importance in interaction with peers away from practice or competition. A good rule of thumb is that "there are no bad foods, just bad timing." Adults should work with athletes to help them recognize the impact of their choices on both performance and recovery (which will be discussed in more detail later in this chapter).

Carbohydrates

Carbohydrates are the preferred source of fuel for activity. During moderate to high intensity exercise, carbohydrates supply the majority of the energy needed. An athlete can obtain carbohydrates in two ways: diet and body stores (glycogen) from the liver and muscles. The carbohydrate storage capacity of the body is limited, however, and can be greatly decreased by skipping meals, participating in exercise, or restricting the amount of carbohydrates in the diet. The current popularity of high protein, low carbohydrate diets can be quite detrimental to athletes because of the extremely limited carbohydrate intake that is recommended.

Grain products, fruits, vegetables, yogurt and milk are common sources of carbohydrate in American diets. The USDA Food Pyramid was set up with these foods at the base to emphasis the importance of this nutrient in the diet. The majority of caloric intake for non-athletes and athletes alike should consist of carbohydrates. In fact, 55 to 65% of calories should come from carbohydrate foods. A more practical way of communicating this to athletes is having them visualize their plate being 2/3rds full of carbohydrate foods. This proportion of total calories devoted to carbohydrates should allow an athlete to maintain adequate stores in the body.

There has been much controversy and research centered around consumption of carbohydrates in relationship to the possible effect on blood sugar prior to an athletic event. Carbohydrates have been historically classified in two ways: by type (simple versus complex) and by form (liquid versus solid). The use of the glycemic index (the rate at which a food is broken down and enters the bloodstream) of a food has been a recent focus of study. Eating a variety of carbohydrates will ensure that an athlete has consumed low, medium and high glycemic index foods, as well as having received adequate vitamins and minerals.

Protein

Proteins are important as structural components of all body tissues (e.g., muscle, skin, brain) and regulators of metabolism (hormones and enzymes). Protein can also be a contributing energy source during exercise, but to a much lesser degree when compared to carbohydrate or fat utilization. It is the connection between protein and muscle, however, that has frequently put the emphasis on protein in an athlete's diet. It is true that amino acids (breakdown components of all proteins) are necessary for building and maintaining muscle. However, protein is only one of the components required by the body to build muscle. Additional factors include exercising the muscle, adequate fluids, eating enough carbohydrates to have the energy to contract the muscle, and periods of rest to allow the building to occur.

Per kilogram of body weight, the protein needs of children and adolescents have been determined to be higher than those of adults. (See Table 10-2). Limited research has been done on whether the requirements vary

between athletes and non-athletes in these younger age groups. Current recommendations are that approximately 12 to 15% of an athlete's diet should come from protein. Because protein is found in all foods except fruits and fats (see Table 10-3), athletes can usually meet all protein requirements quite easily with a normal diet that provides adequate calories from a variety of food sources.

Parents and coaches can become concerned if young athletes decide to become vegetarian without appropriate

Table 10-2. Recommended Dietary Protein Allowance for Children and Adolescents as compared to Adults.

Gender	Age (years)	Protein Intake (grams/kg)
Male/Female	7 to 10	1.0
Female	11 to 14	1.0
	15 to 18	0.8
Male	11-14	1.0
	15 to 18	0.9
Male/Female	Adult	0.8

SOURCE: *RDA, 10th edition, 1989*

Table 10-3. Protein Content of Common Foods.

2-4 Grams of Protein

Bread—1 slice
Corn—1/2 cup
Baked potato

6-7 Grams of Protein

Special K cereal—1 cup
Rice (cooked)—1 cup
Bagel (1 3 1/2 inch)
Peanuts—1 ounce
Cheddar cheese—1 ounce
Spaghetti (cooked)—1 cup
Refried beans—1/2 cup

8-10 Grams of Protein

Peanut butter—2 tablespoons
Milk—1 cup
Pizza (cheese)—1 slice
Yogurt (fruit flavored)—8 ounces

More Than 10 Grams of Protein

Macaroni and cheese (Kraft)—1 cup
Generic fast food hamburger
Tuna fish (in water)—3 ounces
Chicken breast (w/o skin)— 3 ounces

SOURCE: Bowes and Church Food Values, 17th edition

knowledge or concern in making food choices to meet needs. Vegetarian diets are fairly common, especially in the adolescent age group. There are traditionally 3 types of vegetarians: *lacto-ovo* (who eat eggs and dairy but not meat, fish or poultry), *lacto-vegetarian* (who will eat dairy but no eggs, meat, fish, poultry), and strict vegetarian or *vegan* (who eat no dairy, eggs, or meat/fish/poultry). It is important to determine the type of vegetarian regime being followed and determine what that means for the individual. For example, many people today call themselves "vegetarian" but actually mean that they will eat fish and/or poultry, but not red meat. For vegan athletes, protein sources in the diet will include foods such as dried peas, beans, nuts, cereals, breads and pastas. Individually, vegetable protein foods are "incomplete," lacking in at least 1 of the 9 essential amino acids that have to be supplied by diet. (The body can manufacture the other 11 out of the 20 amino acids required for protein synthesis.) While "food combining" (e. g. eating rice with beans) was formerly recommended to ensure all amino acids were present at the same meal, research now indicates that as long as a variety of foods are eaten throughout the day, all amino acids will be consumed and no supplements will be required. There is a correlation between the decision to become a vegetarian and the development of restricted eating, especially in the adolescent female. The elimination of animal products allows for a socially acceptable way to eliminate specific foods from one's diet without drawing attention to the real reason for doing so.

On the other hand, coaches and athletes should understand that eating more protein than is needed will not translate into increased muscle mass. Rather, excessive protein intake, like the consumption of excessive fats or carbohydrates, will be converted and stored in the body as fat. The kidney will then excrete the waste products from this conversion, extracting significant amounts of water to do so. This places a significant strain on the kidneys. In addition, dehydration can result from the water loss. Dehydration is an extremely, even dangerous impairment to an athlete's health and performance. Therefore, despite the current popularity of high protein diets, protein powders and amino acid supplements, use of such products and diets are to be discouraged.

As previously mentioned, protein needs of young athletes can be and are usually met by the normal diet. In some situations, protein requirements may need to be increased, especially for adolescents starting an exercise program, participating in an endurance activity, taking part in resistance training, and/or participating in a sport where weight classifications cause athletes to restrict caloric intake. (ADA reference)

Fat

Fat is the most concentrated from of energy in the diet. During mild to moderate exercise, fats are an important energy source along with carbohydrates. Fats supply more than twice as many calories per gram of food than is found in similar amounts of protein and carbohydrates. Because of this and the possible relationship of dietary fats to disease, it has become the norm in this country for people to significantly reduce fat in the diet, or even try to totally eliminate this nutrient. It is not uncommon for young athletes to be growing up in a home environment where only fat-free products are available. This "fat phobia" has made it easy for people to forget that fat is an essential nutrient and has many important functions in the body. These functions include carrying vitamins A, D, E and K, building blood vessels and body linings, keeping skin and hair healthy, and providing a concentrated source of calories to influence satiety. Too little fat can actually lead to physiological and psychological problems. Table 10-4 provides a list of some consequences of consuming too little fat.

The current recommendation is that up to 30% of one's daily caloric intake should come from fat sources, with two-thirds of those fats of the unsaturated variety. (These are most commonly found in sources such as liquid oils, fish/seafood, soy and nuts/seeds). This will allow the requirement for essential fatty acids to be met and adequate energy density to be present in the diet.

Foods high in fat content are digested at a slower rate than foods comprised of primarily carbohydrates or protein. Fat takes up to 3 to 5 hours to empty completely from the stomach. Thus if athletes consume a meal high in fat (e. g. french fries, cheeseburger) too close to an event, they may experience significant gastrointestinal discomfort during the competition or practice. This does not mean eliminating fatty foods. Rather, it emphasizes paying attention to when and how much is consumed, especially in relation to timing of participation in physical activity.

Table 10-4. Signs of Too Little Fat in the Diet.

Dry skin and hair
Fatigue
Constantly Hungry
Amenorrhea (loss of menstrual function)
Constantly cold
Poor wound healing

Vitamins and Minerals

Vitamins and minerals are nutrients required by the body in very small amounts for a number of body functions. They do not contain calories and as such do not supply energy. Instead they help the body to use the energy that protein, fat and carbohydrate provide. If an athlete is eating a variety of foods and consuming enough calories, then vitamin and mineral needs (even if increased) can normally be met without the use of a supplement. In fact, amounts consumed in excess of needs will either be stored in the body (with limited capacity) or excreted in the urine. Extra amounts of vitamins and minerals will not enhance performance.

In such sports as wrestling, bodybuilding, gymnastics, and dance, where weight goals may be achieved through restricted eating, food choices and variety will be limited. Therefore, vitamin and mineral supplementation may be advised while working with the athlete to improve and increase their nutrient and energy intake. If vitamin and mineral supplements are used, a single daily multi-vitamin/mineral tablet, providing 100% of the Recommended Dietary Allowance or less for each nutrient is preferable to therapeutic level supplements providing greater amounts. The RDA's of vitamin and minerals are listed in Table 10-5.

One nutrient that deserves special attention, especially in the adolescent age athlete, is calcium. The calcium requirement for 9 to 18 year olds is 1300 mg of calcium per day in order to allow for the significant bone growth and maturation that normally occurs during this period. Individuals often think of meeting calcium needs in terms of how many glasses of milk are consumed per day. The basic requirement (1300 mg) is equivalent to consuming just over four 8-oz glasses of milk. However, there are many other food and beverage sources that can be incorporated into the diet if an athlete is lactose intolerant (some possibilities appear in Table 10-6). Athletes

Table 10-5. Recommended Dietary Allowances (Revised, 1989) Indicating Some Critical Nutrients Necessary for Maintaining Good Nutrition in Most Healthy Children and Youth*.

Category	Weight (lb)	Height (in)	Protein	Fat-Soluble Vitamins			Minerals				Vitamin C (mg)
				Vitamin A (μg)	Vitamin E (mg)	Vitamin K (μg)	Iron (mg)	Zinc (mg)	Iodine (μg)	Selenium (μg)	
Children											
4 to 6	44	44	24	500	7	20	10	10	90	20	45
7 to 10	62	52	28	700	7	30	10	10	120	30	45
Males											
11 to 14	99	62	45	1000	10	45	12	15	150	40	50
15 to 18	145	69	59	1000	10	65	12	15	150	50	60
Females											
11 to 14	101	62	46	800	8	45	15	12	150	45	50
15 to 18	120	64	44	800	8	55	15	12	150	50	60

* Common nutrients not listed generally can be found in revised *Dietary Reference Intake* tables from 1997 and 1998.

Table 10-6. Calcium Content of Common Foods.

Food	Quantity	Calcium Content
Milk, skim to whole	1 cup	300 mg
Yogurt, fruit flavored or plain	8 ounces	300 to 400 mg
Macaroni and cheese	1 cup	362 mg
Calcium fortified orange juice	1 cup	300 mg
Cheddar cheese	1.5 ounces	300 mg
Ice cream, ice milk	1 cup	164 mg
Cottage cheese	1 cup	138 mg
Frozen yogurt, low fat	1 cone	112 mg

SOURCE: *Bowes and Church, Food Values, 17th edition*

who are vegan or who prefer not to drink milk or eat other dairy products may choose to consume foods fortified with calcium; orange juice and dry cereals often fit this description. For athletes who prefer a calcium supplement, there are many to choose from in today's market. Calcium carbonate and calcium citrate are two widely available and well absorbed forms. It is best to select a supplement that provides 600 mgs or less in a tablet, because amounts greater than that are too large for ideal absorption. Calcium supplements with labels indicating that they are from oyster shells, dolomite or bone meal should be avoided as they may contain lead.

Concern about calories and weight can cause an athlete to switch from a nutrient-dense product such as milk to a calorie-free beverage (diet pop, water, tea, coffee), without considering the possible implications for immediate or long term health. In addition, many female athletes, especially runners, will go through a period of amenorrhea. This disappearance of the menstral cycle affects normal estrogen function which is required for adequate bone density. Weight bearing exercise and adequate calcium intake are similarly important influences on bone density. The lack of any of these factors may cause a decrease in bone strength and put the athlete at risk for injury, especially stress fractures. In addition, excess sodium, protein and vitamin A have all been indicated as possible nutrients that can negatively affect bone strength. Excessive protein intake is likely to be the most commonly of these due to the current popularity of high protein diets.

Fluids

Water has a vital role in the nutrition and performance of an athlete. Performance significantly deteriorates after dehydration of more than 2% of body weight. Yet athletes may lose more than 2% of their body weight due to dehydration from prolonged and intense competition or long workouts. Physical exercise increases the amount of heat produced in the body. If sufficient water is not available for perspiration, the body temperature may exceed safe limits. During dehydration, the athlete will tire more rapidly, and in severe cases, heat exhaustion and heat stroke may result. Drinking frequently and in adequate amounts is an absolute necessity, and it should be done before thirst is even felt. In fact, by the time an athlete feels thirsty, he or she may have already suffered a dangerous level of body water depletion. Once dehydration has occurred, it can take several hours to achieve water balance.

Children have a less effective thermo-regulatory system than do adults. Research shows that they tend not to voluntarily drink enough fluids to meet their needs, especially during physical activity and warm weather. Much attention, therefore, has been focused on how coaches

and other adults can get young athletes to drink more often and greater quantities of fluid.

The concern for preventing dehydration has often led coaches to wonder whether to recommend that their athletes consume plain water or a sports drink during practice and/or competitions. Traditionally, plain water has been the recommended fluid of choice during non-endurance activity (e. g. less than 60 to 90 minutes in length). Research in the past few years has suggested there is actually a benefit to consuming a 6 to 8% carbohydrate beverage during some activities of shorter duration (Bar-Or, 2000). Beverages containing a higher concentration of carbohydrates (such as soft drinks and juice) take longer to be digested and absorbed. The carbohydrates will not be available for use during exercise and these drinks will be more likely to cause gastrointestinal distress during activity. This results from their taking longer to digest and absorb. Therefore, an athlete participating in a sport involving intense bursts of energy (such as soccer, hockey, volleyball, basketball) or one considered to be an endurance event (longer than 60 to 90 minutes) can actually benefit from drinking a sports drink. The carbohydrate in such beverages is easily absorbed and readily delivered into the bloodstream to be used for energy. This can avoid or delay depletion of the athlete's muscle stores of glycogen.

In addition, it appears that young people tend to drink more of a beverage that is flavored. Consequently, if flavored beverages are available, young athletes may be more likely to consume adequate fluids without being prompted and so they lessen the risk of dehydration. A recent study determined the fluid intake in 9 to 12 year old boys by offering liquids in a three-group design. Each group was assigned to drink a specific liquid for hydration from unmarked bottles. The bottles contained either plain water, grape-flavored water or grape-flavored water with carbohydrate and sodium. The children consuming the plain water became dehydrated at the rate of 0.2 to 0.3% body weight per hour. The grape-flavored water group remained close to water balance, while the boys drinking the grape-flavored carbohydrate solution actually gained weight (Wilk and Bar-Or 1996).

Keeping enough water or fluids available at sites of practices or competitions may be difficult, especially if there is not a water fountain or similar source at or near the site. While it may be possible to transport a large enough container of water for the athletes, it is recommended that athletes be required to bring their own water bottles with them at all times. This is an essential habit to develop, one that if started early, will enhance athletic performance and become second nature by the time the athletes reach high school.

Specific guidelines for fluid consumption are listed in Table 10-7. In addition, coaches should remember the following points:

Table 10-7. Guidelines for Fluid Consumption to Prevent Dehydration.

Before exercise	0.5 to 1 cup
During Exercise	0.5 cup every 15 minutes
After Exercise	2 cups for every pound lost Or until urine is clear

Source: Adapted from information in *Nutritional Applications in Exercise and Sport*

- Encourage athletes to drink fluids before, during and after exercise.
- Encourage your athletes to drink even before they are thirsty.
- Have athletes drink on a schedule, every 15 to 20 minutes.
- Young athletes drink more if the beverage is flavored rather than plain water.
- Fruit juices and soft drinks are too high in carbohydrates to be absorbed quickly.
- Carbonated beverages can cause upset stomachs, bloating, and a burning sensation in the mouth and should not be used during activity.
- Teach athletes the signs of dehydration: dry lips and tongue, sunken eyes, bright colored or dark urine, infrequent urination, apathy and lethargy.
- Use clear beverage bottles so athletes can see how much they have and have not consumed.
- Salt tablets irritate the stomach and intestines and can increase dehydration by causing diarrhea if taken before a practice or contest.

But, the most important thing for every coach to remember is:

There is no physiological reason for restricting water intake before, during, or after athletic contests or practices.

Meal Timing and Patterning

Preadolescents and adolescents should eat at least 3 to 5 times per day to meet their nutritional needs. Eating at regular intervals throughout the day will allow for a steady supply of energy to maintain stable blood glucose/sugar levels, keep metabolism up, and enhance athletic performance. Many households have several meal and activity schedules to consider. This can make it all too easy for young athletes to miss meals or eat poorly. In addition, especially in adolescents (who often are more responsible for choosing their own foods) concerns over body image and weight can impact the frequency, quality and amount of intake during the day. The coach should reinforce for athletes the importance of regular eating periods with a variety of foods while stressing how eating wisely can positively affect the athlete's ability to perform.

Pre-Event Eating

One of the biggest concerns of athletes and coaches is what should be eaten before competition. Psychologically, players often have "special" foods/beverages that they feel enhance their ability to perform. In reality, there are no foods with any special properties that can improve performances if eaten beforehand. Performance during an event or workout is actually more dependent on food consumed hours, days or even weeks before the event. Therefore, the most important consideration for a coach or athlete is selecting foods that are easily digested, tolerated well by the individual athlete, and likely to help athletes avoid "hitting the wall" during the event. While less likely to be a consideration prior to practices, pre-competition stress can cause an athlete's gastrointestinal system to be less active. Food should be consumed far enough in advance to give sufficient time for digestion and absorption. Guidelines for the consumption of pre-event foods are given in Table 10-8. In addition, the American Dietetic Association (2000) has made the following points:

- Athletes should eat foods that are familiar to them.
- Meals should be eaten 2 to 4 hours prior to game or competition.
- The closer to the activity, the smaller the meal should be.
- Food choices should be primarily composed of carbohydrates and low in fat.
- Eat enough to prevent hunger.
- Athletes should eat what makes them feel good psychologically.

Carbohydrate foods leave the stomach earlier and are digested more readily than either fats or protein. Cereal, bread, spaghetti, pasta, rice, fruits and bagels are examples of such foods. As discussed previously, foods higher in fat content take longer to leave the stomach and intestine, and they may cause discomfort to the athlete if they are eaten too close to competition.

Athletes may prefer a more liquid meal if they have difficulty digesting solid foods before events or who have to eat fairly soon before play. Fluids tend to leave the intestine rapidly, can provide substantial calories, and can be easier to prepare than a meal. Some examples of fluids are broth-based soups, juices and instant breakfast products (made with skim or 1/2% milk).

Table 10-8. Guidelines for Pre-event Food Selection and/or Eating Prior to Exercise.

	Examples of Pre-Exercise Food Selections	
Less than 2 hours prior	**2 to 3 hours prior**	**More than 3 hours prior**
Juice	Juice	Juice
Sports drinks	Sports drinks	Sports drinks
Banana	Fruit	Fruit
	Bread, bagels	Bread, bagels/cream cheese
	Hot or cold cereal	Milk, low fat
	Milk, low fat	Crackers
	Crackers	Yogurt
	Soup, low fat	Spaghetti with meat sauce
	Spaghetti with tomato sauce	Hot or cold cereal
		Peanut butter sandwich

SOURCE: Adapted from *Sports Nutrition: A Guide for the Professional Working With Active People*, American Dietetic Association, 2000.

Eating During Competition

For most events, the goal is not to feed the athlete, but to prevent dehydration. Water is the most important element to replace. However, during intense, prolonged activities such as soccer and distance running, athletes will benefit from both fluid and energy replacement during the event. As discussed in the section on fluids, a 6 to 8% carbohydrate beverage will enhance performance and endurance. Sports beverages are widely available today, but they also can be made at home by diluting juices with plain water.

Post-Event Nutrition

For competitions involving intense prolonged physical activity, it is important to maximize an athlete's energy stores after each bout of activity for them to "recover" and be ready to compete again. Carbohydrates are still the fuel of choice for replenishing muscle glycogen.

If a young athlete is performing more than once in a day, carbohydrate recovery foods will be critical to maximizing the ability to compete without fatigue or impaired performance. The food can be in liquid or solid form. The critical factor is the amount. The addition of a small amount of protein to the carbohydrate has been shown to enhance the uptake of glucose into the muscle and so allow recovery to occur more quickly. Refined or simple sugars such as candy, cookies and syrup not need be avoided, but they should be used in moderation. Such foods will supply carbohydrate and calories but have little nutrient value; and they will not optimize recovery and nutrient uptake into muscle as readily as a carbohydrate that contains other nutrients in addition to carbohydrate.

Weight Concerns

Concerns about gaining and losing weight can be a significant issue for both coaches and athletes. In an era where eating disorders are increasingly common and appearing at younger ages, coaches should be sensitive to the problem of disordered eating by avoiding suggestions or comments about an athlete's body size being either too large or too small. Traditionally, younger athletes (those of elementary age) are less likely to be involved in a sport classifying participants by weight. In the past, young athletes have also been less likely to be as concerned about their weight. However, in middle and high school, young girls and boys are growing and developing at varying rates, and attempts to control one's weight via restricted eating can often take precedence over concern for having sufficient energy for an hour on the soccer field, for example. Simple comments such as "you might run better if you dropped a few pounds" can start an individual on a pattern of reduced eating that will not only impair athletic performance, but can turn into a battle with disordered eating.

Coaches should keep the following in mind when working with athletes:

- There are several variables that influence an individual's weight. These include genetics, age, gender, ethnicity, history of activity, and stage of growth,
- Consider seriously any need to weigh athletes, especially those in the adolescent population. Lower weights do not always enhance performance, especially if restricted eating is required to achieve the lower weight.
- Coaches should recognize their own bias regarding body size/weight and not impose such biases on young athletes.
- Remember the rule: there are no bad foods, just bad

timing. Relate nutrition to performance in a positive way but not in a restrictive way.

- Keep in mind that if a young athlete appears to have gained a significant and inappropriate amount of weight, there often is an underlying emotional issue involved. Addressing the problem as a weight only concern may be unsuccessful. Why the athlete is turning to food to cope with problems is often the real issue.
- Seek professional resources for athletes if there are concerns regarding a possible eating disorder.

Eating on the Road

Young athletes frequently need to travel to compete. As a coach it can be difficult to locate restaurants or fast food establishments that provide the type or quality of food that will enhance the athlete's performance or recovery. There are guidelines that can and should be considered, however, to help athletes make appropriate choices when eating on the road.

The biggest factor for a coach to consider is the timing of the meal in relationship to the event or competition. Are the athletes competing soon after the meal? Do the athlete's need foods to recover from competition? The closer to the athlete's need to perform, the more the meal will need to be smaller in size and comprised primarily of carbohydrates. If the meal is after a contest, consider how soon it will be eaten after the event. Carbohydrates are the recommended fuel for muscle energy replacement, and high carbohydrate foods/beverages should be consumed within the first 30 to 60 minutes after competing and at regular intervals over the next several hours.

The following guidelines should be considered with your athletes when selecting places to eat and/or food to bring along while traveling:

- Breakfast: Breakfast is one of the easiest meals to eat out and get higher carbohydrates, even at fast food restaurants. Choose pancakes, waffles, hot or cold cereal, yogurt, English muffins, bagels or toast. Hot cocoa, milk and juice are full of carbohydrates and not dehydrating, like coffee or tea.
- Lunch/dinner: Chili, spaghetti, thick crust pizzas or broth/bean soups are high carbohydrate menu choices. If ordering a cheeseburger or similar menu item, an athlete can increase the carbohydrate content of the meal by also ordering extra bread, salad, baked potato, milk shake, milk, juice, yogurt or fruit. (Words attached to menu items that indicate fewer carbohydrates and more fat include: fried, crispy, breaded, creamed, buttery, au gratin and gravy.)

Coaches should advise parents to bring or provide carbohydrate dense, lower fat foods and beverages for athletes on the road. Examples of these types of foods include: toaster tarts, boxed juices, bagels, yogurt, fruit, multigrain bars, tortillas, pretzels, cereal, graham crackers, oatmeal, canned fruit, applesauce, bread, animal crackers, carrots, vanilla wafers, granola bars and fig newtons.

SUMMARY

While health is not always a motivating factor for young athletes, they will usually be motivated to improve their performance in order to become more successful in their sport. Coaches can provide athletes with the basic information on how to develop their skills in a particular sport. Providing them with the basics of sound nutritional advice will assist them in obtaining maximum performance through appropriate food choices. Keep in mind the following guidelines when addressing nutritional issues or concerns with young athletes:

- There is no magic from nutrition in terms of achieving optimal performance.
- Carefully review any materials handed out to players or their parents. Eliminate any references to weight control or reducing or eliminating calories/fat.
- Promote positive messages about food/nutrition. Reinforce habits of proper eating, not messages about not eating.
- Most young athletes will not know what to eat to perform better, but they often know what not to eat.
- The nutritional demands that sports place on young athletes are usually minimal in comparison to the demands on nutrition by growth.
- Accurate information will help set their knowledge base for future years, and that includes their attitudes about eating and food.
- Involve parents, especially those of elementary and middle school aged athletes. Be aware of parental bias about food choices. For example, eating "healthy" in our culture today often refers to the practice of eating foods that are low in calories or low or "non fat." These choices are often too restrictive and inadequate in energy and nutrients for a young athlete.
- Recognize that there are many adults who are uninformed/misinformed about nutrition and proper eating habits. Make sure that players are getting scientifically accurate messages about nutrition at practice. Work with parents to ensure that athletes are receiving consistent messages at home.
- Take advantage of professional resources. Numerous books, organizations and sports nutritionists (registered dietitians who specialize in this area) are available. Professional counselors can be a valuable resource in framing information for athletes in ways that will help enhance their sport and their lives.

REFERENCES

American College of Sports Medicine. (1996). "Position Stand on Exercise and Fluid Replacement." *Medical Science in Sports and Exercise*, 28: v-vii.

Bar-Or, O. (2000). "Nutrition for Child and Adolescent Athletes." Sports Science Exchange, 13(2): 1-5.

Clark, N. (1998). "Eating Before Competing." *The Physician and Sports Medicine*. 26(9): 73-74.

Dawson-Hughes, B. (2000). "Calcium and Osteoporosis." *Alternative Therapies in Women's Health*, 2(4): 25-32.

Loosli, A., and J. Ruud. (1998). "Meatless Diets in Female Athletes: A Red Flag." *The Physician and Sports Medicine*, 26(11): 45-55.

Pennington, J. A. T. (editor) (1998) *Bowes and Church's Food Values of Portions Commonly Used (17th edition)*. Philadelphia, PA: Lippencott Press.

National Research Council. (1989). *Recommended Dietary Allowances (10th edition)*. Washington, D.C.: National Academy Press.

Reimers, K, Grandjean, A., and Vanderhoof, J. (1994). "Diet and the Adolescent Athlete." *Pediatric Rounds*, 3(4): 5-7.

Rosenbloom, C. (editor) (2000). *Sports Nutrition: A Guide for the Professional Working with Active People (3rd edition)*. Washington, D.C.: American Dietetic Association.

Wilk, B., and Bar-Or, O. (1996). "Effect of Drink Flavor and NaCl on Voluntary Drinking and Rehydration in Boys Exercising in the Heat." *Journal of Applied Physiology*, 80: 1112-1117.

Wolinsky, I., and Driskell, J. (editors) (2000) *Nutritional Applications in Exercise and Sport*. Boca Raton, FL: CRC Press.

RESOURCES

Organizations:

These are professional organizations that can provide coaches with accurate and current nutritional information and materials to be used with athletes.

SCAN: Sports, Cardiovascular, and Wellness Nutritionists (Practice Group of the American Dietetic Association): < www.NutriFit.org >

American Dietetic Association: < www.eatright.org >

Gatorade Sports Science Institute: < www.gssiweb.com >

International Center for Sports Nutrition: <chn_icsn@unmc.edu >
502 South 44th Street
Omaha, NE 68105
(402) 559-5505

Michigan High School Athletic Association: <www.mhsaa.com >
1661 Ramblewood Drive
East Lansing, MI 48823-7392
(517) 3332-5046

Nutrition on the Move: < www.eatnmove.com >
405 W. Charles Street
Champaign, IL 61820
(217) 355-3815

U. S. Department of Agriculture: < www.nutrition.gov/ >

Books:

Clark, N. (1997). *Sports Nutrition Guidebook, 2nd edition*. Champaign, IL: Human Kinetics Publishers, Inc.

Williams, M. (1998). *The Ergogenics Edge, Pushing the Limits of Sports Performance*. Champaign, IL: Human Kinetics Publishers, Inc.

11
Dietary Supplements and Ergogenic Aids

Sean P. Cumming, Ph.D. and Roderick T. Bartee, Ph.D.

QUESTIONS TO CONSIDER

- What is a dietary supplement?
- What are the most commonly used dietary supplements?
- What are the benefits and risks of using dietary supplements?
- Is it legal to recommend or provide dietary supplements to youth?

Dietary supplements are becoming increasingly popular among youth involved in sports, exercise, weight loss, weight gain, and bodybuilding programs. As a coach, parent or athletic administrators it is important to understand the benefits, risks, ethical and legal issues associated with the use of dietary supplements. Accurate knowledge about dietary supplements is fundamental to successfully developing and implementing policies and educational strategies concerning their use in athletics.

A dietary supplement, as defined by the Dietary Supplement Health and Education Act of 1994, is any …

> product (other then tobacco) that is intended to supplement the diet that bears or contains one or more of the following dietary ingredients: a vitamin, a mineral, an herb or other botanical, an amino acid, a dietary substance for use by man to supplement the diet by increasing the total daily intake, or a concentrate, metabolite, constituent, extract, or combinations of these ingredients, is intended for ingestion in pill, capsule, tablet, or liquid form, and is not represented for use as a conventional food or as the sole item of a meal or diet (Perko, 2000, p.5).

Dietary supplements that are popular among young athletes, exercisers, and body builders include performance drinks, creatine, amino acids, caffeine, ginseng, ephedra, chromium and iron supplements.

Increases in the use of dietary supplements in youth have been attributed to a number of factors including the pressures to succeed and/or conform to gender appropriate body types, competition for college athletic scholarships, increased availability of supplements, and aggressive marketing tactics. Most dietary supplements are widely available to youth and can be purchased in specialist stores, supermarkets or through the Internet. However, many youth are provided with dietary supplements by their coaches or parents. Because the regular use of dietary supplements requires a substantial financial investment, wealth and not just ability is becoming a requirement for athletic success.

The dietary supplement industry has prospered in recent years, with consumers spending more than $6.5 billion on dietary supplements in 1996 alone (FDA, 1998). Adolescents are a population that is a targeted by the manufacturers and marketers of dietary supplements. Adolescents who participate in athletic activities are susceptible to believing the advertising ploys (Jenkins, 1997) and erroneous claims made by dietary supplement manufacturers and merchants regarding the effectiveness of dietary supplements (Grunewald and Bailey, 1993). A study by Barron and VanScoy (1993) found that 42% of the promotional claims they researched were not supported by published scientific evidence and that 32% had some scientific documentation to support promotional claims but were marketed in a misleading manner.

At present the U.S. Food and Drug Administration (FDA) has relatively little control over the regulation and testing of dietary supplements. Because dietary supplements are recognized as foods and not drugs there are no strict guidelines established to test the efficacy or safety of such products before they are placed on the market (Perko, 2000). Like food, dietary supplements only have to satisfy a few conditions. The supplement must not contain any ingredients that are not listed on the product and the product should be judged safe for human consumption.

Unlike drugs, dietary supplements are not subject to pre-marketing safety tests. The FDA serves as a safety watchdog and will only demand safety testing if consumers report adverse effects related to consumption of the product. A lack of stringent testing has resulted in many ingredients with adverse effects or no known use in humans being included in dietary supplements. Research conducted by the International Olympic Committee indicates that many legitimate dietary supplements are cross-contaminated with pro-hormones that the body can use to produce banned substances such as the anabolic steroid nandrolone.

The National Collegiate Athletic Association (NCAA) has increased its education efforts toward dietary supplements due to an increase in positive tests for banned substances. Some athletes were having positive drug tests because there were banned substances in dietary supplements they were taking. These products are available over-the-counter and the banned substances were not listed on the ingredient label. As a result in this shift of positive testing the NCAA states "it is not worth risking eligibility for products that have not been scientifically proven to improve performance and may contain banned substances" (NCAA, 1998, p. 42). The FDA is currently working to classify several dietary supplements that can be bought over the counter as controlled substances, making them harder to obtain and easier to regulate.

Manufacturers of dietary supplements do not have to subject their products to rigorous investigation to prove their efficacy at improving human functioning or fighting specific illness or diseases. The Dietary Supplement Health and Education Act (1994) allows manufacturers to make claims about the effect of products on the structure or function of the body, as long as they do not make claims to diagnose, mitigate, treat, cure, or prevent any specific disease. Manufacturers of dietary supplements often rely upon single case studies or the endorsements of professional athletes, fitness trainers or medical specialists to support their claims regarding the efficacy of their product. Consumer Labs provide independent test results and information to help consumers and healthcare professionals evaluate the effectiveness and safety of dietary supplements. The results of their tests can be viewed online at < http://www.consumerlabs.com > .

In an attempt to control the use of dietary supplements in youth sports lawmakers in Texas and Michigan have authorized legislation making it illegal for public school coaches, teachers, administrators and volunteers to promote or distribute performance-enhancing products to student-athletes. Similarly, over thirty states in the U.S. have taken steps to restrict the availability of products containing ephedrine, pseudoephedrine, and phenylptopanolamine (Popke, 2000). The National Federation of State High School Associations (NFHS) has also taken a stance with regards to the use and promotion of dietary supplements in youth sports. Their position, which is published on the NFHS website <http://www.nfhs.org >, states:

In order to minimize health and safety risks to student athletes, maintain ethical standards and reduce liability risks, school personnel and coaches should never supply, recommend or permit the use of any drug, medication or food supplement solely for performance-enhancing purposes.

As a coach, parent, or athletic administrator it is important to proceed with caution when considering the use or recommendation of dietary supplements. The availability and potential harmfulness of dietary supplements present medical and legal ramifications. A coach or athletic administrator recommending a specific supplement for a physical ailment comes dangerously close to practicing medicine without a license (Perko, 2000). Individuals considering the use of dietary supplements should always consult with a physician before use. Ann Chapman (2000), a dietician for the Watkins Health Center at the University of Kansas and Mike Perko (2000), an assistant professor in the Health, Physical Education and Recreation department at the University of North Carolina in Wilmington, suggest that you ask yourself the following questions before you consider using or recommending a dietary supplement:

- Does the use of this product violate any state laws or organizational policies regarding the use of dietary supplements?
- What are the qualifications of the individuals manufacturing and selling the product?
- Do the claims about the effectiveness of the product seem to good to be true? (If so, they probably are.)
- Is there clinical evidence to support the claims and safety of the product?
- If so, how many studies support these claims, who conducted the research, and on what population was the product tested (e.g. adults, youth, athletes)?
- Have any clinical studies examined the long term effects associated with the use of this product?
- Have these studies been published in scientific journals?
- Has the product been deemed safe for consumption by children and adolescents?
- Do the researchers or individuals promoting the prod-

uct have a financial interest in the product (e.g., sponsorship deals, research grants)?

- Are there any side effects associated with taking this product?
- Does the product produce any adverse reactions when combined with any other substances?
- Are there any contraindications associated with the use of this product? Can everybody use this product safely (e.g., youth, diabetics, individuals taking certain medications, pregnant or lactating mothers)?

According to the American Dietetic Association (ADA; 1994), only certain groups of people, including pregnant women, infants and small children, women of child bearing years, adolescent girls, and young women may need to take dietary supplements. Research suggests that it is unnecessary for youth to take dietary supplements to enhance athletic performance or general health (Williams, 1983). Williams found that iron, zinc, and other deficiencies among female and male adolescents were mostly due to low-calorie intake. A well-balanced diet that meets the energy needs of young athletes would provide all the nutrients necessary (Grisogono, 1991). National Collegiate Athletic Association (NCAA) guidelines provide similar advice to their student-athletes, as stated in the following quote:

A high-carbohydrate diet consisting of complex carbohydrates, five servings of fruits and vegetables a day, low-fat dairy products, adequate protein and whole grains is the optimal diet for peak performance (NCAA, 1998, p. 41).

Researchers in the area of dietary supplements and nutritional ergogenic aids have expressed the need to provide accurate and early education about the use of these substances. Educational programs should take place each year throughout high school, and begin in junior high or middle school (Bartee, 2000). These programs need to address general nutrition knowledge and the limited efficacy, potential harm, and ethical issues of taking dietary supplements or nutritional ergogenic aids, and should attempt to change attitudes among adolescent athletes who may use dietary supplements. Individuals who may facilitate the dissemination of information and education of the athletes should include athletic trainers, coaches, parents, peers, physicians, and former dietary supplement and nutritional ergogenic aid users. Ironically, these individuals must also be educated about nutritional ergogenic aids.

Adults involved in youth sports need to acknowledge the role they play in helping young athletes decide whether or not they should use dietary supplements. The amount of time that coaches, parents, and athletic administrators spend with young athletes and their roles as educators places them in the unique position of confidant and counselor. Many adolescent athletes believe that their parents, coaches, athletic trainers and physicians would support their use of dietary supplements marketed as nutritional ergogenic aids (Perko, Eddy, Bartee, and Dunn, 2000). Similarly, over a half of all adolescent athletes indicate that they would take dietary supplements if their coaches wanted them to (Perko, 2000). Research also indicates that female athletes are more likely to be influenced by significant others than males (Bartee, 2000).

Prevention and intervention strategies should be carefully targeted to specific groups of athletes based upon demographic characteristics such as sex, grade in school, participation in multiple sports, and specific sport of participation. (Bartee, 2000). A general program directed at the entire student athlete population may not be effective for everyone. Athletes in track, baseball, football and wrestling, due to the increased use of dietary supplements in these sports, may need to be addressed separately as well as within an entire group. Parents, coaches, trainers, physicians, and administrators should be informed that youth participating in these sports or multiple sports, and older athletes are more likely to use dietary supplements marketed for sports enhancement (Bartee, 2000). Likewise, educational interventions directed at male and female athletes should be tailored for each sub-population.

The following section reviews some of the most popular dietary supplements that are used to enhance athletic performance. It is designed to educate coaches, parents and athletic administrators on how these supplements are believed to improve performance, the evidence supporting these beliefs, and health risks associated with their use.

Creatine

Creatine is a natural substance that is essential for high intensity muscle contractions (Eichner, 1997). Creatine is produced by the kidneys, liver, and pancreas and can be found in foods such as red meats and fish, in particular herring and mackerel. Those wishing to increase their creatine intake can purchase creatine supplements in either a powder or serum form. The body requires on average 2 grams of creatine per day. The average person in the United States obtains 1 gram of creatine through his/her diet with the deficit being made up by the body. Individuals whose diets are deficient in creatine (e.g., vegetarians) may have a reduced creatine pool and may therefore require dietary supplements.

Creatine, which binds with phosphate to produce creatine phosphate, is used by the phosphagen system to increase the availability of adenosine tri-phosphate (ATP) to the active muscles. The phosphagen system is one of three energy systems (i.e., phosphagen system, aerobic system, and anaerobic system) that the body uses to generate energy for activity and is the first to be used during athletic activities. To generate energy the phosphagen system breaks down adenosine tri-phosphate (ATP) into adenosine di-phosphate (ADP). Because there is a limited supply of ATP stored in the muscles the phosphagen system can only provide energy for high intensity exercises for a short duration, approximately ten seconds. During periods of intense activity the body uses the phosphate from creatine phosphate to convert ADP back into ATP. The increased availability of ATP to the active muscles allows the body to sustain a high level of power output without experiencing fatigue or a decline in performance. The purpose of taking creatine supplements is to increase the availability of creatine phosphate for the regeneration of ADP into ATP.

The American College of Sports Medicine (ACSM, 2000) consensus statement on the use of creatine as an ergogenic aid states that creatine use enhances exercise performance on tasks that involve short periods of extremely powerful anaerobic activity. Creatine supplementation can also enhance strength gains during strength training programs. However, creatine does not enhance aerobic exercise performance or isometric strength. The ACSM panel also stated that, over time, daily doses of 3 grams were as effective as doses of 20 grams at increasing the amount of creatine phosphate stored in the muscles. The panel found no consistent or definitive evidence to support claims that creatine supplementation caused muscle cramping, or gastrointestinal and/or renal complications. Finally, the panel suggested that children or adolescents should not take creatine supplements.

Recent studies of creatine use in youth suggest that it is a popular dietary supplement among high school athletes. One researcher found that children as young as eleven were taking large amounts of creatine to supplement their diet (Popke, 2000). In another study, 44 percent of 1,300 male and female high school senior student-athletes reported taking some form of creatine. A third study, looking at creatine use in over 4,000 Wisconsin high school student athletes, found that 15 percent of all participants reported using creatine. Males and senior athletes were more likely to report the use of creatine. Peer pressure was identified as the most common reason for taking creatine supplements.

Caffeine

Caffeine is an organic substance that is not naturally produced by the body but is found in many foods. Caffeine is a legal (to a urine level of 12 milligrams/mL) and socially acceptable drug that stimulates the central nervous system. It is believed to act as an ergogenic aid in aerobic and anaerobic activities. Athletes seeking to increase their caffeine intake generally rely upon caffeinated beverages (e.g., coffee, tea, and some carbonated soft drinks) or pills containing caffeine. Caffeine is also a common ingredient in many products that are advertised as "fat burners." Products containing caffeine are widely available to youth and are attainable through specialist shops, grocery stores or the Internet.

Research examining the ergogenic effects of caffeine indicates that moderate doses of caffeine may improve performance in aerobic and, to a lesser extent, anaerobic activities (Williams, 1998). Caffeine is believed to improve performance through a number of different mechanisms. Performance gains in aerobic activities (i.e., those lasting longer than 20 minutes) are generally attributed to changes in the metabolic system. Caffeine increases the mobilization of fat stores as energy and decreases the use of glycogen by up to fifty percent of normal, allowing the body to generate energy while conserving valuable glycogen stores. Thus, athletes taking caffeine supplements prior to competition are able to perform for a longer period of time before they have to rely upon their glycogen stores as a source of energy.

Performance gains in aerobic and anaerobic tasks have also been attributed to changes in the central nervous system (CNS) and the muscle cells. Caffeine increases the activity of the CNS causing increases in heart rate, blood pressure, motor-unit recruitment and rate of brain functioning. The effects of caffeine on the brain may reduce perceptions of physical exertion, allowing the athlete to perform at a high intensity for a longer period of time. In the muscle cells caffeine increases the availability and transfer of calcium ions at the calcium-troponin binding sites, allowing the calcium to stimulate muscle contractions more effectively (Williams, 1998). This process may help explain the ergogenic effect of caffeine in short term and high intensity activities (e.g., sprinting, power lifting) where fatty acids are not used as a primary source of energy.

Although caffeine supplementation may enhance performance on aerobic and anaerobic tasks it can also impair human functioning. Caffeine acts as a diuretic and may increase urination, leaving the athlete in a dehydrated state. Consumption of large amounts of caffeine may also cause nausea, muscle tremors, and palpitations. Individuals with heart problems or high blood pressure should consult with a physician before they consider using caffeine as a dietary supplement.

Performance Drinks

Performance drinks are commonly consumed to enhance performance in activities that require endurance. The purpose of these drinks is to maintain normal hydration, electrolyte balance and blood glucose and glycogen levels during and following exercise (Kelly, 1997). Although a wide variety of performance drinks are available on the market, these products generally contain common ingredients at similar concentrations. Performance drinks designed for use during exercise typically contain from 4 to 8 % carbohydrate, in the form glucose, fructose, sucrose or maltodextrins plus small quantities of electrolytes such as sodium, potassium, and chloride (Kelly, 1997). In an attempt to promote general fitness and well being, many performance drink manufacturers now include vitamin supplements and other nutrients.

The majority of research investigating the effectiveness of consuming performance drinks suggests that these products do enhance performance, particularly in endurance activities. The consumption of performance drinks in endurance sports is associated with lower perceptions of exhaustion, greater endurance, and the maintenance of skill quality.

The effectiveness of a performance drink is dependent upon the rate at which it is absorbed in the intestines and the rate at which it provides additional energy. The rate at which fluid can be absorbed is influenced by a number of factors including the carbohydrate concentration of the solution, the intensity of the exercise being performed, and the temperature of the fluid. As the carbohydrate concentration of the fluid increases the absorption rate declines. Research indicates that during exercise fluids containing 8-10% or less of carbohydrates are absorbed as quickly as water. This is why most performance drinks designed for consumption during exercise typically contain a carbohydrate concentration of less than ten percent.

Performance drinks that are designed for consumption after exercise typically contain a greater concentration of carbohydrates, because such products are primarily designed for the restoration of muscle glycogen. Exercise intensity may also influence the absorption rates of fluids. During periods of moderately intense exercise fluids are absorbed at the same rate as they would be at rest. However, when exercising at high levels of intensity fluid absorption is significantly reduced. Finally, to aid absorption performance drinks should be served at a cool (not ice cold) temperature. Research indicates that cold foods or beverages are more readily absorbed in the intestines (Rehre, Beckers, Brouns, Ten Hoor, and Saris, 1989).

The effectiveness of performance drinks is also dependent on when, how frequently and how much fluid is consumed. The American College of Sports Medicine and National Athletic Trainers' Association recommend that athletes should be well hydrated prior to performance. Athletes in a dehydrated state before they perform are at a disadvantage to hydrated athletes. An appropriate level of hydration can be achieved by drinking 400 to 600 ml of water 2 or 3 hours before exercise.

Performance drinks should not be consumed within 15 to 60 minutes prior to performance. An increased level of blood glucose leads to an increase in the production of insulin, which increases the likelihood of hypoglycemia (low levels of blood glucose) occurring during exercise

(Kelly, 1997). Because insulin production is inhibited during exercise the consumption of performance drinks during exercise does not lead to hypoglycemia. Although the amount and frequency of fluid consumption required for optimal performance is dependent upon the nature of the fluid, the intensity of the exercise and the ambient conditions (e.g., humidity, temperature), it is recommended that athletes should try to consume at 150 to 350 ml (6 to 12 oz or approximately 1 to 1½ cups) of fluid at 15 to 20 minute intervals, beginning at the start of exercise (American Dietetic Association, Dietitians of Canada, and the American College of Sports Medicine, 2000). When exercising in hot and humid climates or at high altitude it is advisable to drink slightly larger quantities of water and at a more frequent rate.

During exercise most athletes do not consume either enough fluids or carbohydrates to replace the amount of water and glycogen that they lose. Therefore it is important for coaches to encourage athletes to consume fluids and carbohydrates following exercise. Most experts suggest that to optimally replenish muscle glycogen stores, athletes must consume a drink or food with a high carbohydrate concentration within an hour of exercising. Carbohydrates that are consumed within an hour after exercise are more readily synthesized into glycogen than carbohydrates consumed two to three hours after exercise.

Fluids for consumption after exercise should include, or be consumed with, sodium. Sodium helps the athlete rehydrate by inhibiting urine production (Murray, 1996) and maintaining salt concentration of the blood plasma, thus sustaining the athlete's desire to drink. Because most performance drinks do not include enough sodium for optimal rehydration, it is important to consider alternative sources of sodium. Sources of sodium and carbohydrate that are popular with children and adolescents include potato chips, popcorn, crackers, and pretzels.

Iron Supplements

Iron is a popular dietary supplement among athletes, particularly those involved in endurance sports. This popularity is founded upon the knowledge that iron plays an instrumental role in the cardiovascular system and the belief that participation in endurance activities leads to iron depletion. Iron is required for the production of the proteins hemoglobin and myoglobin, as well as enzymes involved in the metabolic process. Hemoglobin and myoglobin are the oxygen-carrying components of red blood cells that deliver oxygen from the lungs to the muscles.

Athletes participating in endurance sports generally have lower hemoglobin concentrations than the general population. This condition is referred to as *sports anemia*. However, it is not due to iron depletion. Rather, the term sports anemia is in fact a misnomer. The most common cause of low hemoglobin concentrations in endurance athletes is increases in blood plasma and not decreases in the number of red blood cells (Eichner, 1992). This condition is referred to as false anemia and is not associated with health risks or poorer performance on endurance tasks.

True iron deficiency anemia occurs when there is a significant reduction or shortage in the number of red blood cells and is defined by a low level of hemoglobin or hematocrit. Unlike false anemia, true iron deficiency anemia is associated with poorer performance on endurance tasks. Despite concerns, recent investigations demonstrate that the incidence of iron depletion in athletes is not greater than in the general population (Clarkson, 1990).

Regular participation in aerobic exercise typically increases the absolute volume of blood plasma. That increase reduces the concentrations of red blood cells and hemoglobin. Increases in blood plasma may actually enhance aerobic performance because it provides extra fluid for heat loss and thins the blood making it easier for the heart to pump blood (Eichner, 1988).

It is difficult to determine whether a low concentration of hemoglobin or hematocrit is attributable to an increase in blood plasma or a reduction in the number of red blood cells available. One medical expert who has studied anemia in athletes, recommends that physicians who are unsure of whether an athlete has a low concentration of red blood cells due to true or false anemia should prescribe iron supplements (ferrous sulfate, 325 mg thee times a day) for 1 to 2 months. If the concentration of hemoglobin in the blood does not increase then it is unlikely that the athlete is experiencing true anemia and the iron supplements should be stopped (Eichner, 1998).

An inadequate diet and/or menstrual bleeding most likely cause true iron deficiency anemia in athletes. Athletes that are on calorie restricting diets (e.g., wrestlers, gymnasts, and dancers) or are vegetarians are most prone to true iron deficiency anemia. Consuming more red meats, fish or dark poultry meats combined with vegetables, as well as cooking in cast iron pans can alleviate iron deficiency. Eating more breads and cereals and avoiding coffee and tea, particularly after meals, can also increase iron absorption (Eichner, 1992). Athletes should only consider taking iron supplements if they are unable or unwilling to increase their iron consumption through changes in their diet or if they repeatedly develop iron deficiency anemia (Eichner, 1992). When iron supplements are given to individuals with true iron deficiency anemia, exercise and work performance is improved (Haymes, 1987).

Protein Supplements

The development of strength and muscle mass is particularly important for athletes participating in sports (e.g., football, sprinting, wrestling) where increased lean body mass and strength important predictors of success. In an attempt to enhance gains in strength and muscle mass many athletes consume protein supplements. These supplements generally contain amino acids such as arginine, ornithine, histidine, lysine, methionine, and phenylamine. Protein supplements are marketed in the forms of powders, capsules or liquid meals and are easily purchased at specialist stores, gyms, health clubs or grocery stores.

As a nutrient, protein performs a variety of exercise-related functions in the body. Protein is the primary nutrient involved in the growth, development and repair of all body tissues. As an enzyme, protein regulates many of the metabolic processes that provide the body with energy. Protein also serves as an auxiliary source of energy and is metabolized when stores of muscle and liver glycogen are low. Manufacturers of protein supplements claim that amino acid supplementation stimulates muscle growth and repair by increasing the production of human growth hormone and insulin. Increases in the production of human growth hormone and insulin lead to increases in the uptake of amino acids in the muscle cells. The heightened availability of amino acids is believed to promote greater protein synthesis and muscle growth.

Athletes that are involved in strength training or body building programs have significantly higher protein requirements than the normal population. The recommended dietary protein allowances for children aged 11-14 years, and 15-18 years and adults are 1.0 g, 0.9g, and 0.8g per kg of body weight per day, respectively. In contrast the recommended protein intake for an adult maintaining or increasing muscle mass via strength training is 1.5-2.0 g per kg of body weight per day (Williams, 1993). Athletes' can easily meet these additional requirements through the changes in their diet and do not have to rely on protein supplements. Healthy sources of protein include lean meats, fish, milk, nuts, and legumes. Because commercially available amino acid supplements typically contain less than 4 grams per serving, it is unlikely that these products alone will enhance strength development or alter body weight (Clarkson, 1998). Taking amino acid supplements that contain over 4 grams per serving may result in stomach cramps and diarrhea.

The effects of amino acid supplementation on strength development and muscle growth are unclear. A number of studies have reported that amino acid supplementation enhances fat loss, muscle growth, and strength development. However, there is no consistent clinical evidence to suggest that the gains associated with amino acid supplementation are any greater than the gains associated with equivalent changes in the amount of dietary protein (Williams, 1998). Although protein supplements contain less cholesterol or fat than natural sources of protein they lack many other essential nutrients (e.g., iron) that are present in natural sources of protein.

Chromium

Chromium, a trace mineral essential for human functioning, has become a popular dietary supplement among athletes seeking to improve their strength and/or gain muscle mass. As a supplement chromium is most often found in the form of chromium picolinate, but it may also occur as chromium nicotinate, and chromium chloride. Chromium is also found in many natural food sources including whole-grain products, cheese, nuts, brewers yeast, and vegetables such as mushrooms and asparagus (Williams, 1998)

In theory, chromium enhances gains in strength and muscle mass by increasing the production of insulin. As previously discussed, increased insulin production stimulates the uptake of glucose and amino acids by the muscle cells (Clarkson, 1998) leading to greater protein synthesis and growth. Increased production of insulin may also enhance aerobic performance by increasing the amount of glycogen that is stored in the muscles and the liver (Williams, 1998).

Research examining the ergogenic effects of chromium supplementation on the development of strength, muscle mass, and athletic performance has produced mixed results (Clarkson, 1998). A number of early studies reported that short-term chromium supplementation lead to increased gains in strength and muscle mass (Walker, Bemben, Bemben, and Knehans, 1998). However, these studies have been criticized for employing inappropriate analytical methods and research designs (Williams, 1998). More recent studies of chromium supplementation have failed to provide any consistent support for the ergogenic effects of chromium. Although there are no major health risks associated with the short-term use of chromium supplements there is some evidence that long-term use of chromium supplements may adversely affect DNA.

Ephedra

Ephedra, which is sometimes referred to as Ma Huang, is an organic substance derived from plants. It has been used medically to alleviate bronchial constriction, sweating and water retention. The main active constituents of ephedra are the alkaloids ephedrine and pseudoephedrine. Ephedrine and pseudoephedrine perform the same functions as adrenaline and noradrenaline, stimulating the central nervous system while elevating metabolism, blood pressure and heart rate. Both ephedrine and pseudoephedrine are common ingredients in many popular weight loss and fat reduction products. Ephedrine and pseudoephedrine are also common ingredients in many medicines developed for treating asthma, colds and coughs.

Athletes use ephedra to enhance their mental and physical performance. Ephedra stimulates the central nervous system. It is believed to increase arousal, alertness, circulating levels of blood glucose, muscle contractility, oxygen intake and blood flow from the heart. However, the few clinical studies that have attempted to examine the ergogenic effects of ephedra have failed to provide evidence linking ephedra supplementation with enhanced athletic performance. Many athletes, fitness enthusiasts and dieters also use ephedra to reduce body weight (in particular fat mass), through increases in metabolism. There is clinical evidence that ephedra may enhance weight loss in the general population. However, whether or not ephedra enhances weight loss in trained athletes is unclear.

Presently ephedra is banned or restricted in 26 states. Side-effects associated with the use of ephedra include high blood pressure, abnormally high stroke volumes, hyperactivity, diarrhea, dizziness, disorientation, numbness, anxiety, chest pains, breathing difficulties, heart palpitations, irregular heartbeats, hypertension, depression, headaches, insomnia, and death. Further, the FDA has identified Ephedra as causing a number of deaths in the United States. The International Olympic Committee and the governing bodies of many sports prohibit the use of ephedrine and pseudoephedrine as a stimulant. Athletes using products containing ephedrine or pseudoephedrine for medicinal purposes (e.g., asthma) should contact appropriate sponsoring organizations to determine the legal status of these products.

Echinacea

Echinacea is an organic substance derived from plants native to North America, and was used by the early Native Americans to treat a variety of conditions including snakebites and external wounds. More recently, echinacea has been recommended as a supplement for enhancing the immune system and increasing the body's ability to resist viral infections such as colds or the flu. Echinacea is believed to enhance the immune system by increasing the production and activity of white blood cells (in particular those designed to kill infected cells) and interferon (a glycoprotein that prevents or limits spread of viruses between infected and non-infected cells) (Mackinnon, 1999). As intense participation in athletic training can suppress the body's immune system, many professional athletes have begun taking echinacea in the hope of boosting their immune systems. Echinacea is easily purchased in pill form at most pharmacists or nutritional specialty stores.

Research examining the medicinal properties of echinacea is encouraging. The great majority of research has found that echinacea can indeed improve the functioning of the immune system, thereby reducing the frequency and longevity of viral infections. However, the effectiveness of the treatment is dependent upon when it is applied and how frequently. To maintain a healthy immune system echinacea should be used periodically (e.g., week on, week off) or only during flu or cold season. No known side effects associated with the use of echinacea have been reported. However, high doses may cause nausea and dizziness and persons with anemia or vertigo should avoid using echinacea.

HMB (beta hydroxy-beta-methylbutyrate)

Beta hydroxy-beta-methylbutyrate, which is commonly know known as HMB, is a relatively new dietary supplement that is becoming popular among athletes seeking to increase strength and muscle mass or reduce fat mass. HMB is a metabolite of the amino acid leucine, which is produced by the body. It also occurs naturally in foods such a catfish, alfalfa, and citrus fruit. The function of HMB in the body is unclear; however, it is believed to be involved in muscle growth and repair.

A limited amount of clinical research indicates that HMB may enhance the strength development and muscle growth of adults participating in strength training programs. HMB supplementation has also been associated with increased fat reduction and gains in peak VO_2; however, most of this research has not been subjected to peer review. Furthermore, the enhanced gains in strength and muscle mass associated with HMB supplementation have not been remarkable. HMB is presently accepted as a legal supplement in all sports (Williams, 1998) and there are no identified risks or contraindications associated with the short or long term use of HMB. However, a thorough investigation of the short-term or long-term consequences of HMB use has not yet been conducted.

Glutamine

Glutamine is an amino acid produced naturally in the body. It performs a variety of different exercise-related functions. As a dietary supplement glutamine often appears in the form of L-Glutamine; as such it is a common ingredient in many brands of protein powders and drinks. Although these supplements are typically synthesized in laboratories, glutamine can also be found in many foods, particularly those high in protein (e.g., meat, fish, beans, and dairy products).

Glutamine's exercise-related functions are numerous. In the muscle cells, glutamine can be broken down into glucose and provides an additional source of energy. Glutamine also interacts with N-acetyl cysteine to promote the synthesis of glutathione, a naturally occurring antioxidant that helps the body combat free radicals. Advocates of glutamine as a dietary supplement also claim that it plays a central role in muscle growth and repair as well as enhancing the immune system.

Presently there are no known health-related side effects associated with glutamine supplementation; however, it may increase circulating levels of human growth hormone. If glutamine does stimulate the production of human growth hormone then athletes taking glutamine supplements risk testing positive for human growth hormone.

Carnitine/L-carnitine

Carnitine is a non-essential amino acid that is located in the membrane of the mitochondria and is used to metabolize fatty acids into energy. During prolonged exercise, the concentration of fatty acids in the blood plasma is often higher than the energy requirements. This elevation in circulating fatty acids may be due to the inadequate uptake and oxidization of fatty acids by the mitochondria. Those promoting carnitine as an ergogenic aid suggest that the inefficiency of the mitochondria to utilize fatty acids is due to low concentrations of carnitine in the mitochondria. If this is true, then increasing intracellular concentrations of carnitine through supplementation should increase the body's ability to use fats as a source of energy (McArdle, Katch, and Katch, 1996).

Research investigating the ergogenic effects of carnitine supplementation has produced mixed results. There is some indication that carnitine supplementation can enhance physical performance when used to correct a deficiency in carnitine. However, not all research is in agreement that carnitine supplementation enhances athletic performance in trained athletes. A number of studies report that carnitine supplementation leads to gains in aerobic power. However, an equivalent number of studies have failed to report such gains. The general failure to support the ergogenic effects of carnitine may be explained by the lack of studies examining the supposed glycogen-sparing properties of carnitine on prolonged aerobic exercise endurance tasks (Williams, 1998).

As of present carnitine is recognized as a legal supplement. No health risks have been associated with the short-term use of carnitine supplements, providing that appropriate doses are consumed. However, some research indicates that larger doses of carnitine may result in diarrhea (Williams, 1998).

Pyruvate

Pyruvate is a natural substance that is a by-product of the metabolism of carbohydrates. In the presence of oxygen, pyruvate in the form of pyruvic acid is transformed into acetyl coenzyme A (acetyl CoA). Acetyl CoA then enters the Kreb's cycle where it is used to generate more energy. When the availability of oxygen is limited pyruvate is converted to lactic acid. Pyruvate is believed to enhance weight loss, in particular fat free mass, and performance in endurance tasks. Proponents of pyruvate as a dieting aid suggest that pyruvate reduces fat mass by increasing cell metabolism and fat utilization. As an ergogenic aid pyruvate is believed to enhance muscular endurance by increasing the transport of glucose from the blood stream and into the muscle cells. Good sources of pyruvate include red apples, cheese, dark beer and red wine. Pyruvate can also be purchased commercially, generally in the form of capsules, and it is accepted by most sports governing bodies as a legal dietary supplement.

Research examining the ergogenic effects of pyruvate supplements has produced encouraging results. A number of studies have found that pyruvate supplementation is associated with enhanced performance on endurance tasks (Stanko, Robertson, and Spina, 1990; Robertson, Stanko, Goss, et al., 1990) and increased weight and fat reduction (Stanko and Arch, 1996; Stanko, Tiezke, and Arch, 1992a, 1992b). However, the majority of these studies have been conducted with untrained athletes or obese women. Whether or not pyruvate supplementation enhance endurance performances or promotes weight and fat loss in trained athletes is yet unclear. Similarly, few studies have examined the effects of pyruvate supplementation in youth. Although there are no major risks associated with the consumption of pyruvate, high doses can lead to gastrointestinal upset such as gas, bloating and diarrhea.

Coenzyme Q10

Coenzyme Q10, also known as ubiquinone, is an organic substance that is produced naturally in the body and is believed to boost aerobic power. Coenzyme Q10 performs a variety of health related functions. As an antioxidant, coenzyme Q10 helps protect the body against free radicals. As an enzyme, Coenzyme Q10 plays a functional role in the process of mitochondrial energy production.

The functional properties of Coenzyme Q10 have lead many individuals to assume that supplementation with Coenzyme Q10 may enhance athletic performance. However, there is a distinct lack of clinical evidence to back up these claims (Kelly, 1997). Preliminary research suggests that there are no major side effects associated with the consumption of coenzyme Q10. However, it may have a number of positive or negative interactions with certain medications. As of present, most governing bodies recognize Coenzyme Q 10 as a legal dietary supplement.

Panax Ginseng

Panax ginseng is an organic substance that is derived from the plant species Araliaceae. Panax ginseng is often referred to as Chinese or Korean ginseng and is a com-

mon ingredient in many health foods, drinks, and dietary supplements. A number of closely related species of plants are also sold as ginseng. These include American, Himalayan and Japanese ginseng. Ginseng is a popular supplement in Asia where it is used medicinally to treat a variety of ailments and conditions. Ginseng is also believed to increase mental and physical vitality and promote longevity. In light of these claims ginseng has become one of the most popular dietary supplements among athletes, exercisers and others interested in improving their general health and well-being.

Ginseng is believed to exert a number of physiological effects that may lead to enhanced performance in sport. Through stimulation of the hypothalamus, ginseng is believed to promote the production of cortisol, a hormone that is produced in response to physical stress (e.g., strenuous physical exercise). In addition, it has been claimed that ginseng enhances the synthesis of glycogen following exercise and creatine phosphate during exercise. Ginseng has also been associated with lower levels of lactic acid during exercise. Finally, through stimulation of the central nervous system ginseng has also been associated with increased heart rate, blood flow and oxygen carrying capacity in the red blood cells (Williams, 1998).

Although a number of early studies have reported ginseng can lead to enhanced gains in athletic performance they have been criticized for their validity and for not employing appropriate methods or research designs (Williams, 1998). Contemporary clinical research has generally failed to support many of the proposed ergogenic effects associated with ginseng. There are no major side effects associated with the short-term use of ginseng. However, long-term ginseng supplementation has been associated with high blood pressure, anxiety and sleeplessness. Although ginseng is generally considered to be a legal substance, many commercial products containing ginseng also contain ephedrine, which, in many sports, is a banned substance.

SUMMARY

Although there is some evidence to suggest that a few dietary supplements may have an effect upon athletic performance in adults, there is essentially no research focusing upon their use in youth. In addition there is little research examining the long-term consequences of using such supplements. When the legal and ethical issues associated with their use are considered, as well, one can only conclude that most supplements have no place in youth and scholastic sports. However, there may be occasions when an athlete may have to use supplements to address medical or dietary needs.

The use of dietary supplements may be legitimate when a physician has determined that a young athlete has a particular need. This might include with mineral supplements such as iron or calcium, or when a specific medical problem, such as asthma, requires the use of products containing ephedrine. Similarly, sports drinks containing carbohydrates are generally accepted as solutions to dehydration and cramping.

The manufacturing industry is continually developing new products (Nutrition Business Journal, 2001). Therefore it is necessary to keep up with current dietary supplements being marketed to athletes. A sound understanding of the benefits, risks and potential legal and ethical issues associated with the use of dietary supplements and an appreciation for the factors that influence athletes decisions to take dietary supplements will help those involved in youth sports answer questions and/or address issues regarding the use of dietary supplements to enhance athletic performance.

REFERENCES

American College of Sports Medicine. (2000). "The Physiological and Health Effects of Oral Creatine Supplementation." *Medicine and Science in Sports and Exercise*, 32: 706-717.

American Dietetic Association. (1994). "Positions of the American Dietetic Association: Enrichment and Fortification of Foods and Dietary Supplements." *Journal of the American Dietetic Association*, 94: 661-663.

American Dietetic Association, Dietitians of Canada, and the American College of Sports Medicine. (2000). "Nutrition and Athletic Performance: Position of the American Dietetic Association, Dietitians of Canada, and the American College of Sports Medicine." *Journal of the American Dietetic Association*, 100: 1543-1556.

Bartee, R. T., (2000). Predicting the Use of Dietary Supplements Marketed as Nutritional Ergogenic Aids Among High School Athletes. Unpublished doctoral dissertation. The University of Alabama, Tuscaloosa.

Barron, R., and VanScoy, G. (1993). "Natural Products and the Athlete: Facts and Folklore." *Annals of Pharmacotherapy*, 27: 607-615.

Chapman, A., (2000). *The Eating Edge: Ergogenic Aids: Magic Bullets or Double Edged Swords*. [Available on Line] <http://www.coachsedge.com/coaching/eatingedge/ergogenicaids/index.html >

Clarkson, P. M. (1998). "Nutritional Supplements for Weight Gain." *Sports Science Exchange*, 11(1): 1-8.

Clarkson, P. M. (1990). "Tired Blood: Iron Deficiency in Athletes and Effects of Iron Supplementation." *Sports Science Exchange*, 3(28): 1-4.

Eichner, E. R. (1997). "Ergogenic Aids: What Athletes are Using and Why?" *The Physician and Sportsmedicine*, 25(4): 70-83.

Eichner, E. R. (1992). "Sports Anemia, Iron Supplements, and Blood Doping." *Medicine and Science in Sports and Exercise*, 24(9): s315-s318.

Eichner, E. R. (1988). "'Sports Anemia:' Poor Terminology for a Real Phenomenon." *Sports Science Exchange*, 1(6): 1-5.

Grisogono, V. (1991). *Children and Sport: Fitness, Injuries and Diet.* London: John Murray Ltd.

Grunewald K., and Bailey, R. (1993). "Commercially Marketed Supplements for Bodybuilding Athletes." *Sports Medicine*, 15: 90-103.

Haymes, E. M. (1987). "Nutritional Concerns: Need for Iron." *Medicine and Science in Sports and Exercise*, 19: s315-s318.

Jenkins, A. P. (1997). "Herbal Energizers: Speed by Any Other Name." *Journal of Physical Education, Recreation and Dance*, 68: 39-45.

Kelly, G. S. (1997). "Sports Nutrition: A Review of Selected Nutritional Supplements for Endurance Athletes." *Alternative Medicine Review*, 2(4): 282-295.

Mackinnon, L. T. (1999). Advances in Exercise Immunology. Champaign, IL: Human Kinetics.

McArdle, W. D., Katch, F. I., and Katch. V. L. (1996). Exercise Physiology: Energy, Nutrition, and Human Performance. Baltimore, MD: Williams and Wilkins.

Murray, B. (1996). "Fluid Replacement: The American College of Sports Medicine Position Stand." *Sports Science Exchange*, 9 (4): 1-5.

National Collegiate Athletic Association. (1998). *Ergogenic Aids Nutritional Supplements, Guideline Zj.* NCAA Sports Medicine Handbook.

Perko, M. (2000, November/December). "Hey Coach, Does This Stuff Work? What to Know When Discussing Dietary Supplements." *Strategies*, 5-7.

Perko, M. A., Bartee, R. T., Dunn, M. S., Wang, M. Q., and Eddy, J. M. (2000). "Giving New Meaning to the Term 'Taking One For The Team.' Influences on the Use/Non-Use of Dietary Supplements Among Adolescent Athletes." *American Journal of Health Studies*, 16(2): 99-106.

Popke, M. (2000, December). "A Bitter Pill." *Athletic Business*, 75-87.

Rehrer, N. J., Beckers, E., Brouns, F., Ten Hoor, F., and Saris, W. H. M. (1989). "Exercise and Training Effects on Gastric Emptying of Carbohydrate Beverages." *Medicine and Science in Sports and Exercise*, 21(5): 540-549.

Robertson, R. J., Stanko, R. T., Goss, F. L., et al., (1990). "Blood Glucose Extraction as a Mediator of Perceived Exertion During Prolonged Exercise." *European Journal of Applied Physiology*, 61: 100-105.

Sports Nutrition 2000. (2000). *Nutrition Business Journal*, 5(12): 1024.

Stanko, R. T., and Arch, J. E. (1996). "Inhibition of Regain in Body Weight and Fat With Addition of 3-Carbon Compounds to the Diet With Hyperenergetic Refeeding After Weight Reduction." *International Journal of Obesity Related Metabolic Disorders*, 20: 925-930.

Stanko, R. T., Tiezke, D. L., and Arch, J. E. (1992a). "Body Composition, Energy Utilization, and Nitrogen Metabolism With a Severely Restricted Diet Supplemented With Dihydroxyacetone and Pyruvate." *American Journal of Clinical Nutrition*, 55: 771-776.

Stanko, R. T., Tiezke, D. L., and Arch, J. E. (1992b). "Body Composition, Energy Utilization, and Nitrogen Metabolism With a 4.25-MJ/D Low-Energy Diet Supplemented With Pyruvate." *American Journal of Clinical Nutrition*, 56: 630-635.

Stanko, R. T., Robertson, R. J., Spina, R. J., et al., (1990). "Enhancement of Arm Exercise Endurance Capacity With Dihydroxyacetone and Pyruvate." *Journal of Applied Physiology*, 68: 119-124.

Walker, L. S., Bemben, M. G., Bemben, D. A., and Knehans, A. W. (1998). "Chromium Picolinate Effects on Body Composition and Muscular Performance in Wrestlers." *Medicine and Science in Sport and Exercise*, 30(12): 1730-1737.

Williams, M. H. (1983). *Nutrition for fitness and sport (2nd edition)*. Dubuque, IA: Wm. C. Brown.

Williams, M. H. (1993). "Nutritional Supplements for Strength Trained Athletes." *Sports Science Exchange*, 1(6): 1-5.

Williams, M. H., (1998). The Ergogenic Edge: Pushing the Limits of Sports Performance. Champaign, IL: Human Kinetics.

RESOURCES

< http://www.consumerlabs.com >
< http://www.ais.org.au/nutrition/ >

12
Body Image and the Young Athlete

Lonnie Rosen, Ph.D.

QUESTIONS TO CONSIDER

- What is body image and how does it affect performance in sports?
- What is the coach's role in combating negative images about certain body shapes and sizes?
- What is the role of sports governing bodies in the effort to change public perceptions about *appropriate size and shape* of young athletes?

In the culture of certain sports, especially individual sports for girls and women, athletes are judged not only for their physical performance but also for their personal appearance. Slade (1988) described body image as, "...the picture we have in our minds of the size, shape, and form of our bodies." Slade went on to affirm that body image also relates to the feelings we have concerning our size, shape, and form. Emerging adolescents undergo rapid, and often, unsynchronous changes in their physical appearances. This occurs at a time when they are attempting to attain a stable identity and to gain mastery of a wide variety of challenges that are derived from intellectual, physical, psychological, and social domains.

Overall, such challenges are far more congruent and consistent for growing boys than for their female counterparts, in many cultures. For instance, boys work to develop greater strength and desire increased size in terms of height, weight and breadth. Attainment of these qualities tends to be associated with superior social status and an enhanced sense of psychological well-being. On the other hand, the adolescent girl is confronted with contradictory and often confusing demands. Despite the fact that she is growing, often at a rapid rate, she finds herself terrified that her linear growth is accompanied by a corresponding acceleration in weight and girth. The teenage girl, therefore, finds herself confronting what appears to be a frightening paradox; a desire for increasing height and simultaneously, a fear of increasing weight. She believes that she will become a pariah among her peers, if indeed, her increase in girth exceeds, or even matches, her increase in height.

The work of Garfinkel and Garner (1997) makes it clear that over the past 25 years, there has been an increasingly intense glorification of thinness directed solely toward women. Many studies since the early 1970s confirm that women believe slenderness to be the most important single aspect of physical attractiveness.

The discrepancy between males and females regarding idealized body-image perception is illustrated by the work of Fallon and Rozin (1985). A group of students were shown two scales consisting of male and female outlines in gradations from thin to heavy. The students then selected images that most closely resembled their own figure, the figure which they believed to be ideal for their own sex, and the figure they believed to be most attractive to the opposite sex. For males, their perception of their own figure, their perception of the ideal figure, and the figure they believed to be most attractive to the opposite sex were nearly identical. The men, therefore, reconciled their perception of their own shapes with their perceptions of that which would be ideal for themselves and that which women would find most attractive. On the other hand, females perceived themselves as being significantly heavier relative to their ideal and to the shape they believed men would prefer. Furthermore, what females believed to be a figure most attractive to men was far thinner than that which most males would actually prefer.

In a study of age-group swimmers aged 9 to 18 years, Dummer, et al. reported that 60% of average weight girls were dieting, and of even greater concern, 18% of underweight girls were reducing their caloric intake. The main reason given for dieting was to look better (80%), compared with better performance (58%). In this study, girls were far more likely to attempt to lose weight, while the boys were more likely to want to gain weight (Dummer, et al., 1987).

A strong concern regarding physical appearance and subsequent dieting to lose weight, are common in girls as young as 6 or 7 years of age. These attitudes and behaviors escalate significantly through adolescence. For females in this situation, the risk of developing an eating disorder is 8 times higher in dieting than in non-dieting 15 year old girls (Patton, et al., 1987).

In North America, disordered eating patterns appear to be equally common in Caucasian and Hispanic females, less common in African American and Asian females, and most common among Native Americans (Crago, et al., 1996; Rosen, et al., 1988). In Western culture, those exposed to more pressures to diet, such a athletes participating in sports that emphasize leanness for performance or appearance, are at greater risk for the development of eating disorders (Garner and Rosen, 1991).

There is evidence that pressures for the attainment of thinness have intensified over time. Participants in beauty contests, and also fashion models, have become significantly thinner since 1959. However, the actual weights for women in the general population, the same age and height as the beauty contestants and models, have steadily increased over the same time frame. Thus, prevailing shape standards in no way resemble the actual body shape or weight of the average female (Garner, 1997). Unfortunately, social norms for attractiveness which neither resemble the average girl or woman have become interwoven with the notion of "fitness." This has occurred despite the fact that this idealized view of attractiveness more closely resembles that of the classical patient with *anorexia nervosa*.

Prejudice against overweight people, particularly females, is widespread. Jokes and even attacks directed against fat individuals are rarely, if ever, criticized, despite the fact that in today's climate of acceptance of diverse groups, negative comments directed toward specific racial or cultural groups, or toward people with physical defects or handicaps would result in rapid and harsh censure. A thin actress appeared on a late-night television talk show and asserted that fat people pollute the aesthetic environment. This remark received applause from the audience.

Studies have shown that prospective parents rate a picture of a chubby child as less friendly, lazier, more stupid, and dirtier than an average size or thin child. Preschoolers prefer to play with a thin rag doll rather than a fat one. Even overweight children describe the silhouette of a fat child as dirty, lazy, sloppy, ugly, and stupid (Levine, 1987). It takes no great leap in logic then, to appreciate that fat children and adolescents absorb and internalize the culturally acceptable hatred and rejection of fat people. At the same time, it should not be surprising that children and adolescents who are not fat, quickly

learn to fear the prospect and social danger of becoming heavy. The punishments for the "sin" of becoming fat clearly is more severe for females than for males of the same age and degree of obesity. In our culture, the avoidance of becoming fat is far more than simply a medical matter, it has become a moral issue worthy of punishment and humiliation to those who have transgressed. (The association of medical problems and obesity should not go unchallenged; however, that issue is beyond the scope of this chapter)

As hurricanes spawn tornadoes, and famine spawns disease, so is it that the widespread reverence for thinness, and accompanying hatred of obesity, has spawned what is an epidemic of eating disorders along with the associated widespread utilization of pathogenic weight-control behaviors. This epidemic has crossed most cultural and socioeconomic lines in North America. A survey of Native American girls and women revealed that three-quarters of those surveyed were trying to lose weight and that 75% of those who were dieting did so by using potentially hazardous techniques, including, vomiting, prolonged fasting, laxative abuse, and diuretic ingestion (Rosen, et al., 1988).

Athletes have been shown to be particularly at risk for using pathogenic weight control methods in an effort to achieve thinness. The average age for young swimmers to begin using hazardous weight control methods was 14 years. However, within the same population of age-group swimmers, 9 year old girls were taking diet pills, self-induced vomiting began at 11, use of diuretics began at 12, and laxatives were being used by 14 year old competitors (Dummer, et al., 1987). The role that adults, especially coaches play, regarding the developing self-perceptions of these young girls, must not be underrated. In a study involving female gymnasts from a Division I collegiate athletic conference, it was discovered that all of the athletes were dieting. More than 60% of the gymnasts were employing one or more pathogenic weight-control techniques. Most striking however, two-thirds of the gymnasts were told by their coaches, at one time or another, that they were too heavy, and of that group, 75% went on to use pathogenic weight-control methods including self-induced vomiting, laxative and diuretic abuse, prolonged fasting, and heavy use of diet pills. One must appreciate the powerful role the coach plays regarding the female athlete's self-perception, and the lengths to which she will go in order to meet the coach's demands (Rosen and Hough, 1988).

Finally, it is important to comment briefly on the need for reflection regarding the evolving aesthetic ideal for weight and shape in many sports. Regarding sports in which a premium is placed on appearance (diving, figure skating, gymnastics, synchronous swimming, and dance), questions should be raised from within the sports community regarding the potentially destructive standards for shape and weight. When these standards seriously compromise the health and well being of all but the minority who are constitutionally thin, then it should be a matter for concern for all of those involved with the sport. It is a hopeful sign that several national governing boards have begun to develop educational programs regarding eating disorders, guidelines for proper nutrition, and educational materials for coaches and medical personnel. However, unless, on a broader, nationwide level, we learn not to demonize people, particularly females, on the basis of their size, and, at the same time, learn to diminish our tendency to worship at the altar of thinness, we are likely to see increasing numbers of young girls and women develop destructive self-perceptions, and attempt to resolve these perceptions by painful, desperate, and dangerous means.

REFERENCES

Crago, M., Shisslak, C. M., and Estes, L.S. (1996). "Eating Disturbances Among American Minority Groups: A Review." *International Journal of Eating Disorders,* 19: 239-248.

Dummer,G. M., Rosen, L. W., Heusner, W. W., Roberts, P. J., and Counsilman, J. E. (1987). "Pathogenic Weight-Control Behaviors of Young Competitive Swimmers." *The Physician and Sportsmedicine,* 15(May): 75-84.

Fallon, A. E., and Rozin, P. (1985). "Sex Differences in Perceptions of Desirable Body Shape." *Journal of Abnormal Psychology,* 94: 102-105.

Garner, D.M. (1997). "Psychoeducational Principles in Treatment." In D. M.Garner and P. E.Garfinkel (editors), *Handbook of Treatment for Eating Disorders (2nd edition).* New York: Guilford Press.

Garner, D. M., and Rosen, L. W. (1991). "Eating Disorders Among Athletes: Research and Recommendations." *Journal of Applied Sports Sciences and Research,* 5: 100-107.

Levine M. P. (1987). *How Schools Can Help Combat Student Eating Disorders; Anorexia Nervosa and Bulimia.* Washington, D.C.: National Education Association.

Patton, G. C., Johnson-Sabine E., Wood, K., Mann, A. H., and Wakeling, A. (1990). "Abnormal Eating Attitudes in London Schoolgirls—A Prospective Epidemiological Study: Outcome at 12 Month Follow-up." *Psychological Medicine,* 20: 383-394.

Rosen, L. W., Shafer, C. L., Dummer, G. M., Cross, L. K., Deuman, G. W., and Malmaberg, S. R. (1988). "Prevalence of Pathogenic Weight-Control Behaviors Among Native American Women and Girls." *International Journal of Eating Disorders,* 7: 807-811.

Rosen, L. W., and Hough, D. D. (1988). "Pathogenic Weight-Control Behaviors of Female College Gymnasts." *The Physician and Sportsmedicine,* 16: 141-144.

Slade, P. D. (1988). "Body Image in Anorexia Nervosa." *British Journal of Psychiatry,* 153(suppl 2): 20-22.

Section III
Sports Medicine

13
Special Injuries to Girls and Women in Sports

Rebecca Battista, M.S. and Vern Seefeldt, Ph.D.

QUESTIONS TO CONSIDER

- What is the Female Athlete Triad?
- How is the Female Athlete Triad identified?
- Why may females be at a higher risk for stress fractures?
- What may be some concerns with menstrual irregularities?
- What anatomical features may predispose females to knee injuries?
- What influence do training programs have on knee injuries?

INTRODUCTION

The marked increase in sports activity among young athletes during the last three decades has resulted in a concomitant increase in sports-related injuries (Davis, Kuppermann, and Fleisher, 1993). Sports injuries are the most common cause of injuries in the 13 to 19 year age group, resulting in more visits to emergency rooms and admissions to hospitals than any other cause except vehicular injuries (Stevens and Branche-Dorsey, 1996). Records of unintentional injuries to children and youth during the period from 1978 to 1996 reveal that far more boys than girls were victims of serious injuries, including those incurred in sports.

The higher incidence and greater severity of sports-related injuries in boys, as opposed to girls, is misleading for two reasons:

- More boys than girls are involved in sports. Therefore, injuries per unit of exposure rather than incidence of occurrence should be the unit for reporting injuries.
- Boys are more likely to be involved in sports where collisions with opponents are part of the action, such as in football, ice hockey, and rugby.

Passage of the Elementary and Secondary School Education Act in 1972 meant that Title IX began to influence sports for children and youth. This resulted in greater opportunities for girls and women to become involved in sports. Although Title IX was enacted to relieve the disparity of programs between males and females at the interscholastic and intercollegiate levels, its influence extended far beyond the high schools and colleges of the United States. Recreation departments, national governing bodies of the United States Olympic Committee and numerous agencies that had previously sponsored sports exclusively for males began to offer similar programs for females.

The emergence of sports for girls and women raised many questions, especially in the areas of training, conditioning, tolerance for aerobic activities and specific injuries that may be precipitated by lack of athletic experience, over-training and differences in skeletal structure and tissue composition. Many of these questions remain unanswered today, but the science and medicine of sports for girls and women has advanced markedly in the last two decades.

This chapter focuses on several characteristics that distinguish females from males in athletic competition. The first section is devoted to the so-called *female athlete triad*, a combination of conditions that includes disordered eating, amenorrhea, and osteoporosis. Coaches, administrators and parents are provided information that may assist them in detecting the conditions that contribute to the destructive behaviors that accompany the *female athlete triad*. In addition, there are suggested tactics and strategies for coaches to use in conveying appropriate messages to female athletes concerning the management of weight, proper eating habits, and appropriate exercise.

The second section of this chapter compares the gender-related injury patterns of selected sports in which males and females compete under similar conditions. The differences in rates of injuries are discussed in terms of anatomical, biological, and social variables that may be associated with the sport-specific, gender-linked injuries.

THE FEMALE ATHLETE TRIAD

One of the major topics in today's women's athletic arena concerns the Female Athlete Triad. The components of the triad are disordered eating, amenorrhea, and osteoporosis. Disordered eating includes extreme problems such as anorexia nervosa and bulimia nervosa; nonetheless, any kind of ineffective eating behavior may be harmful to an athlete. Amenorrhea is a lack of a menstrual cycle for an extended period of time, such as more than 10 months. While some female athletes may consider being amenorrheic a result of a change to their exercise routine (i.e., change in frequency, intensity or duration) it really is a symptom of an underlying problem and should be taken seriously (Otis, et al., 1997).

The third part of the triad is osteoporosis where the concern is with low bone mass. Low bone mass may lead to more fragile bones and consequently, an increased risk of fractures. The components of the triad are harmful on their own, but together they are a cause of concern. For example, a female athlete who presents with amenorrhea or disordered eating may also exhibit a decreased bone density and an increased risk for osteoporosis (Nichols, Bonnick, and Sanborn, 2000). These factors make it essential for coaches, parents and athletes to be aware of all aspects of the Female Athlete Triad such as the definitions, symptoms, risk factors, as well as possible recommendations for recognition and prevention.

Disordered Eating

Disordered eating includes not only anorexia nervosa and bulimia nervosa but also any harmful eating behavior. Harmful eating behaviors can range from a slight restriction of food intake to an occasional binge and purge and can even include excessive exercise. These practices affect the energy balance of athletes and can ultimately affect their performance (American Academy of Pediatrics, 2000). When considering the population at risk is athletes, any harmful eating behavior may have an impact on performance. Anorexia nervosa involves self-starvation and is usually coupled with extreme exercise (Johnson, 1994). By restricting food intake and over-exercising a serious caloric imbalance occurs. This imbalance can have potentially dangerous outcomes that may affect not only performance but also the athletes' overall health.

Bulimia involves bingeing followed by purging. Often bulimics will perform this binge-purge behavior with varying frequencies. The cycle may begin with a diet or food restriction and result in a binge and purge. The purge is often after large amounts of food have been consumed in brief periods of time. This purging or vomiting involves such health dangers as fluid and electrolyte imbalance as well as other metabolic disturbances (Johnson, 1994). Often, athletes may not fit the exact definition of an eating disordered individual and yet are still at risk for significant weight loss and body image issues. They may not present with the classic definitions of anorexia or bulimia, but do portray some characteristics of an eating disorder that may become a potential problem.

The American Psychiatric Association (1994) provides some criteria concerning disordered eating in addition to the criteria for anorexia and bulimia. Examples include those who manifest all the criteria for anorexia nervosa except that the individual has irregular menses, and the individual's current weight is in the normal range despite a significant weight loss. Examples for bulimia nervosa are those that manifest all the signs for bulimia nervosa except that the binge eating and purging occur less than twice a week for less than three months. In addition, even after small amounts of food are consumed there still remains purging by an individual of normal body weight. There may also be repeated chewing and spitting out but not swallowing of large amounts of food as well as recurrent episodes of binge eating in the absence of the purging.

Disordered eating in the athletic population may include some of the criteria listed above, thus providing a much wider spectrum of harmful and often ineffective eating behaviors that may be used in attempts to lose weight or achieve a lean appearance deemed necessary for performance (Otis, et al., 1997). Unfortunately, disordered eating can create an energy imbalance; calories consumed do not equal calories expended. This can occur by either inadequately replenishing the energy used for the exercise bout or by attempting to lose weight for other reasons.

Eating disorders may affect performance and increase the risk of injury. An energy imbalance can often decrease endurance, strength, reaction time, speed, and the ability to concentrate (American Academy of Pediatrics, 2000). These behaviors may begin as early as adolescence, especially during puberty. For example, during puberty boys often gain muscle mass and are encouraged to gain weight for improved physical performance, whereas girls tend to gain body fat during puberty and are encouraged to lose weight to improve performance and/or appearance (Otis, et al., 1997).

Simply being an athlete may make one more vulnerable for eating disorders because of the often noted increased emphasis to achieve a desired appearance or to maintain an ideal proportion of muscle and fat. Generally speaking, an elite athlete is goal oriented, a perfectionist and is often under the tight control of a strong parent or coach. However, even with such traits common among athletes it is also possible that individuals who are more prone to eating disorders are drawn to sports (Wilmore, 1996). Athletes many times believe that thinner is better, or that they must maintain an ideal weight for their sport. In fact, those beliefs are myths. There is no optimal weight or percent body fat for a sport. There may be a range of weight and percent fat that is acceptable, but often the ideal weight or percent fat is simply individualized. Weighing too much may have a negative impact on performance and weighing too little may affect strength and power and other attributes necessary for performance (Sanborn, et al., 2000). It becomes critical for the coach or parent to discourage beliefs about ideal body weight and percent body fat.

Amenorrhea

Amenorrhea can be defined as less than two menstrual cycles per year (Snow-Carter, 1994). It is a clinical symptom that indicates a disruption of the reproductive cycle (Arendt, 1993). Primary amenorrhea, also called delayed menarche, is defined as an individual who has not started menstruating by age 16 (Lebrun, 2000,). According to the American Academy of Pediatrics (2000) it is not unusual for adolescents who have just had their first menstrual cycle to have irregular cycles for almost a year afterwards, but persistent oligomennorhea (irregular cycle) is considered abnormal. Secondary amenorrhea is the absence of three or more consecutive menstrual cycles after menarche (Lebrun, 2000). Even though only 2-5% of the general population have amenorhea the range is much larger in the athletic population. As many as 3 to over 50% of athletes have been recorded as having amenorrhea (Yeager, et al., 1993). Whether those females involved in athletics are somehow predisposed to amenorrhea is not yet known. Nonetheless, amenorrhea is often the most recognized symptom of the Female Athlete Triad (Otis, et al., 1997).

Athletic amenorrhea has no single cause; however, some believe risk factors may include such factors as low body weight, low percent body fat, rapid weight loss, sudden onset of vigorous exercise, disordered eating, energy imbalance, and psychological stress. These factors may vary from individual to individual. Although high intensity exercise and increased frequency of training are associated with greater incidence of menstrual disorders, there is no scientific evidence of cause and effect (Lebrun, 2000). It has often been thought that low body weight and low percent body fat were the cause of menstrual irregularities, but it is now suspected that energy availability could be the problem.

This lack of available energy is thought to disrupt the gonadotropin releasing hormone (GnRH) pulse generator (Otis, et al., 1997). The GnRH pulse generator controls the release of gonadotropins or sex hormones from the pituitary gland. The frequency of pulses to the GnRH regulate luteinizing hormone (LH) secretion. LH is partly responsible for the growth of the preovular follicles. Pulsatile release of GnRH secretion is important for the maintenance of the normal menstrual cycle (Hadley, 1996) and it is the GnRH pulse generator that is failing to stimulate the pituitary in amenorrheic athletes (Loucks, 1990). How may participating in athletics affect the GnRH pulse generator and LH?

In a study by Loucks, et al., (1998), LH pulsatilty depended on energy availability. This lack of energy was due to the energy expended during exercise that was not replaced with caloric intake. In this study one set of subjects completed four days of intense exercise and yet showed no disruptive effect on LH pulsatility. Loucks et al., (1998) reported the disruption in LH was from the impact of the energy cost (expended) on the energy available; therefore, the energy expended disturbed the LH pulsatility less than the same amount of energy that may have been restricted through dietary practices. Athletes may suffer disruptions of reproductive function despite practicing restrictive type eating behaviors; therefore, energy depleted through exercise may decrease the energy available to the body and may suppress LH pulsatility. The only effect of prolonged aerobic exercise may be the energy cost and its availability (Loucks, Verdun, and Heath, 1998), thus the problem is not just caloric restriction.

Again, the components of the Female Athlete Triad continue to appear conjointly. Disordered eating is associated with amenorrhea because sports that emphasize leanness are more likely to have a high percent of athletes with menstrual disorders (Lebrun, 2000). Disturbances of the menstrual cycle are frequently associated with eating disorders (Hadley, 1996). Those that say exercise training disrupts the menstrual cycle may be correct; yet, this may be true only in some women (Loucks, 1990). In other words, are certain types of females more susceptible to menstrual disorders? Amenorrhea is not caused by inadequate fatness (Loucks, 1990). Although eating disorders and amenorrhea do not represent a cause and effect relationship, they still remain important symptoms or indications of underlying problems and can cause further complications.

Osteoporosis

Osteoporosis is defined as premature bone loss and/or inadequate bone formation that may result in low bone mass microarchitectural deterioration. This deterioration may lead to an increase in skeletal fragility and, therefore, to the possibility of increases in stress fractures (Yeager, et al, 1993). Individual bone density as an adult is a result of peak bone mass achieved during the first 20 years of life, a period which is subjected to a host of factors that can cause bone loss (Nichols, et al., 2000). In addition, bone remodeling will occur throughout the lifespan considering that once peak bone mass is achieved, bone formed equals bone resorbed. Important factors in osteoporosis are the amount of peak bone mass and the rate of bone loss (Nichols, et al., 2000). Yet, why should there be a concern with osteoporosis in young athletes? And why is osteoporosis a part of the Female Athlete Triad?

The problem in amenorrheic athletes is the deficiency of estrogen production (Hadley, 1996). Low bone density in these young athletes is alarming because they are at risk for osteoporosis now and in the future (Nichols, et al., 2000). A low concentration of ovarian hormones common among amenorrheic and oligomenorrheic athletes is associated with decreased bone mass and increased rates of bone loss (Otis, et al., 1997). In spite of this, high intensity exercise in some sports may actually increase bone mineral density in specific skeletal sites despite amenorrhea (American Academy of Pediatrics, 2000). In fact, mechanical loading through physical activity has a positive influence on bone mineral density, and concomitantly, a lack of physical activity has a negative influence on bone mineral density. Not only will physical activity be beneficial for bone mineral density but environmental conditions such as nutritional status of an individual also become important (Dalsky, 1990).

Disordered eating may lead to greater susceptibility to osteoporosis. The occurrence of disordered eating practices often goes hand in hand with low calcium intake. These conditions can combine with menstrual dysfunction and may, in fact, exacerbate bone loss although not all amenorrheic athletes will have low bone mass. Females with a history of amenorrhea have a lower bone mineral density than those with normal cyclic menstrual periods (Otis, et al., 1997). Low bone mass increases the risk of having fractures. Low bone mass may occur in both young and older athletes and is the reason why the Triad is a concern in female athletes.

Clinically, the relationship between exercise and menstrual function is in skeletal demineralization in nonmenstruating athletes, although there is ambiguity regarding the consequences to short term or long term bone health. There remains speculation that females who experience menstrual irregularities secondary to a lack of estrogen may never achieve peak bone mass and may develop later osteoporosis. A primary site to have a decrease in bone mineral density is the spine because it is made mainly of trabecular bone, which has a high rate of remodeling and is therefore more sensitive and responsive to changes in hormones. It still remains important to note that neither menstrual phase nor status alters or limits performance. However, there is a relationship between oligomenorrhea and amenorrhea with decreased bone

mineral density (Arendt, 1993). In other words, it is important to note when menstrual irregularities occur, but regular menstrual cycles have no effect on performance.

Position Stands

The United States Olympic Committee (USOC) and the American College of Sports Medicine (ACSM) position stands list characteristics from certain sports that may make female athletes more susceptible to the Triad. These include:

- Sports that emphasize low body weight, or lean physique as well as those that require tight fitting clothing for competitions
- Sports with a performance score
- Sports that use weight categories for participation
- Sports where success at a young age is important
- Sports that look for an ideal body weight or ideal percent body fat
- Sports that have a sport-athlete mismatch (athlete is not well suited for that particular sport)

Not only will certain sports possess some characteristics that may predispose an athlete to the Triad, but there are some traits or factors of individuals that make them susceptible to the Triad. These include a focus on thinness, life stressors, "win at all costs" attitude, harmful training techniques, a controlling coach or parent, social isolation from teammates, friends, or family, family history, and societal influences.

The recommendations from the USOC and ACSM advise that:

"specific strategies be developed to prevent, recognize and treat this syndrome. Strategies specific to prevention, surveillance, research, health consequences, medical care, public and professional education need to be developed, implemented, and monitored. Target groups for education include coaches, trainers, parents, athletes, peers, athletic administrators, officials of sport governing bodies, and health care providers who work with physically active individuals. Sport administrators and officials of sport governing bodies should develop standards and encourage certification for coaching and training practices and the monitoring of young women to prevent the Female Athlete Triad" (Otis, et al., 1997).

OTHER MENSTRUAL DISORDERS

Other menstrual disorders are dysmenorrhea and oligomenorrhea. Dysmenorrhea is painful or difficult menstruation (i.e. cramps and heavy bleeding). Cramps may occur if ovulation is delayed or missed. The menstrual cycle phase most affected by external factors is the luteal phase. In this phase estrogen levels remain elevated, although not as much as immediately before ovulation, and progesterone increases. Estrogen and progesterone are the hormones responsible for some of the psychological or physiological symptoms (cramping, etc.) (Lebrun, 2000).

Symptoms during dysmenorrhea, also referred to as premenstrual syndrome (PMS), which may suggest ovulation is occurring include breast tenderness, fluid retention, and changes in appetite or mood. These are all normal symptoms but if they last longer than half of the cycle their occurrence may be a reason for concern. However, physical activity may actually help decrease some symptoms of PMS and may be beneficial in decreasing the severity of PMS (Lebrun, 2000).

Oligomenorrhea is three to six menstrual cycles per year with intervals of less than 35 days. Athletic women may have shortened luteal phases (<10 days) or anovulatory cycles (Lebrun, 2000). Another characteristic of oligomenorrhea is having reproductive hormone levels lower than normal. Those who have sporadic periods may end up with lower than normal bone mass because of chronic low progesterone and estrogen (Snow-Carter, 1994) which may be another signal of concern, especially in later life, that osteoporosis is a potential problem.

How Menstrual Function Relates to Injuries

Irregular menstrual functions may have more of an impact than simply affecting performance. Because hormones are important in not only normal menstruation, but also in bone formation, there is a concern when menstruation is disrupted. Estrogen and progesterone are important hormones in bone resorption and bone formation. Estrogen acts to prevent bone resorption and to decrease remodeling, whereas progesterone appears to promote bone formation and accelerates remodeling (Prior, et al., 1990). A lack of estrogen may have an affect on bone mineral loss even with the resumption of normal menses when some of these changes can be irreversible. (Lebrun, 2000). This may be more apparent during adolescence when 60-80% of bone is laid down. If there is not enough estrogen (hypoestrogen), and concurrently, poor nutrition during the adolescent years there is the possibility of further low peak bone mass (Lebrun, 2000).

A study in which the bone mineral density of intensely trained runners was compared to sedentary controls who had regular cycles revealed bone loss over a one year period was associated with an ovulatory disturbance (anovulatory cycles and cycles with short luteal phases) (Prior, et al., 1990). It was concluded that menstrual dysfunction and not intensive endurance training was responsible for bone loss in amenorrheic athletes.

Amenorrhea has been linked to premature loss (Lebrun, 2000). In other words, a decrease in estrogen may ultimately have an effect on bone density. This may be one of the problems in amenorrheic athletes. Low concentrations of ovarian hormones in amenorrheic and oligomenorrheic athletes are associated with reduced bone mass and increased rates of bone loss (Otis, et al., 1997). These low levels of reproductive hormones (estrogen and progesterone) compromise the skeletal health as revealed by low bone mineral density. These low concentrations may yield a higher incidence of stress fractures (Snow-Carter, 1994).

Stress Fractures

Stress fractures are a concern in the athletic population. Bennell, et al. (1996) cited several potential risk factors of stress fractures in females:

- Low fitness level,
- High body fat,
- Lower bone density,
- Endocrine factors, and
- Biomechanical factors.

Stress fractures relate to the individual bone mineralization (Otis, 1994); thus, with a low bone mineral density there may be an increased risk of fractures.

Bone mineral density is positively related to weight and negatively related to menstrual cycle length (Rencken, Chestnut III, and Drinkwater, 1996). This suggests low weight athletes who have been amenorrheic may be at risk for loss in bone density. The authors concluded that body weight and number of months being amenorrheic were predictors of bone mineral density of the lumbar spine in amenorrheic athletes. The duration of the amenorrhea and body weight of amenorrheic athletes predicted bone mineral density. The areas tested were the femoral neck, trochanter, intertrochanteric region and the tibia; areas that may be positively affected by weight bearing activities. The duration of the amenorrhea and the age at which it occurs may affect bone mineral density.

Amenorrheic adolescents may have permanent loss of bone mass (Jonnavithula, et al., 1993). This study asked, "Does estrogen loss from those who were amenorrheic as a young adult have effects later in life?" Results showed that after two years the amenorrheic subjects could increase their bone mass with the resumption of normal menses; however, their values were still lower than normal.

The American Academy of Pediatrics (2000) issued a policy statement corresponding to those of the ACSM and USOC concerning the Female Athlete Triad. The AAP believes that girls of all ages should be encouraged to participate in exercise and sports. For those participating in exercise and sports, all aspects of their training should be reviewed or monitored. Coaches should be aware of and encourage proper dietary practices, use appropriate training properties such as intensity, duration, and frequency of activity. Physicals should include menstrual history as well as any other medical concerns. With regards to aspects of the Female Athlete Triad, menstrual history and menstrual irregularities should not be considered a normal response to exercise. An athlete that reports primary or secondary amenorrhea should complete a medical evaluation. There should also be education as well as counseling provided to athletes, parents and coaches regarding components of the Female Athlete Triad. Coaches and athletes should be given a range of values for percent body fat and/or body weight rather than specific values for their respective sports. Athletes and coaches should be reminded that weight is not an accurate estimate of fitness or fatness, and when weight is lost, muscle and fat are also lost.

SPORTS-RELATED INJURIES AMONG GIRLS AND WOMEN

Basketball

Evidence from numerous studies clearly indicates that the knees (specifically the anterior cruciate ligament—ACL) and ankles of female basketball players are much more susceptible to frequent and severe injuries than those of males (Arndt, 1996; Hosea, et al., 2000; Huston, et al., 2000; Messina, et al., 1999; Moeller, 1997; NATA, 1997; Powell and Barber-Foss, 2000). Reported rates of injuries that are from two to six times greater in girls and women than in boys and men have caused the scientific and medical communities to seek answers to these perplexing problems. Intuitively, the situation regarding injuries to the knee and ankle should be reversed because boys and men jump higher and more often during practices and games; therefore, they land with greater impact forces and more frequently than do girls and women. Basketball as played by boys and men is also regarded as more physical, especially in the vicinity of the basket, where most of the jumping and the player-to-player contact occurs.

Causes of and solutions to knee problems among female basketball players have converged on *intrinsic* and *extrinsic* factors. Intrinsic factors involve the:

- Anatomy of the knee joint,
- Laxity of the knee joint,
- Differences between the genders in quadriceps angles due to the relatively wider hips of females and
- Hormonal differences.

Extrinsic factors include:

- Potentially greater muscle imbalances between the quadriceps and hamstring groups in females,
- Lack of long-term conditioning programs,
- The level of competition, and
- The more frequent use of ankle bracing in females, thus transferring more of the impact and torsion forces to the knee.

Intrinsic (anatomical) factors generally are considered to be unalterable, but they have an important role in the prevention of athletic injuries, because their influence can be modified through the manipulation of extrinsic factors. For example, there is little likelihood that any amount of exercise will change the width and depth of the intercondylar notch of the femur, but by teaching a basketball player to land so that the impact forces are absorbed through greater muscle action, rather than by the ligaments of the knee, the coach may prevent ACL injuries through conditioning and training (Hewett, et al., 1996). Thus, the identification of intrinsic factors that may be associated with specific injuries is an essential first step in designing programs to circumvent or eliminate the influence of conditions that are relatively permanent.

The technique of teaching athletes to recruit their hamstrings rather than to rely upon the ligaments of the knee to absorb the forces of landing is an example of how knowledgeable coaches are able to prevent injuries through proper training programs. As additional information accumulates regarding the interplay between intrinsic and extrinsic factors related to injuries, it will be the informed coach who is able to provide the safest sports environment.

Recent attention to ACL injuries of female basketball players have partially obscured the fact that the most common injury in boys and girls interscholastic basketball is the ankle sprain. Investigators have commonly reported a gender-related difference in the incidence and severity of ankle sprains, but unlike ACL injuries of the knee, no intrinsic causes have been identified. Messina, et al. (1999) reported significantly higher rates of ankle sprains in girls (56%) than in boys (47%). Hosea, et al. (2000) clasified sprains by the degree of severity and reported that girls had significantly higher rates of Grade I (the least severe) sprains; however, the genders did not differ in the rates of Grades II and III sprains. Conversely, Shively, et al. (1981) reported that female high school athletes had a significantly higher incidence and severity of ankle sprains than boys.

If intrinsic factors have an influence on gender-related ankle sprains in youth and scholastic sports, they have not been identified in the literature. Nor is there evidence of effectiveness that links specific training protocols to a reduction in ankle injures sustained by basketball players.

Volleyball

Injury patterns on volleyball are similar to those of basketball, but volleyball lacks the abundant literature that is devoted to injuries in basketball. Because of their dependence on jumping ability, volleyball players sustain a high proportion of their injuries to the ankle and knee. Ankle sprains are the most common injury, with girls and women nearly twice as susceptible as boys and men. Eighty-six percent of ankle sprains occur at the net, either as a result of landing on the foot of an opponent (52%) or on a teammate's foot (24%) (Bahr, et al., 1994).

Injuries to the knee occur so frequently in volleyball that the pattern is commonly referred to as *jumper's knee*. The repetitive overloading of the patellar tendon, resulting in patellar tendinitis, occurs in 30 to 40% of skilled volleyball players and much more frequently in girls and women (Ferretti, 1990). Because girls out number boys by a 2:1 ratio in the 12 to 17 age group of competitive volleyball within the United States, (Sporting Goods Manufacturers' Association, 2000), the injuries also reflect this gender-related pattern.

The occurrence of *jumper's knee* and injuries to the ACL have increased during the last decade because of two evolutionary developments in tactics: (1) Modern attack schemes often have all three front line players jumping, although only one hits the ball. (2) The popularity of the jump serve, which is hit while the server is at maximum height in mid-air, has grown. The extra time required to practice these two maneuvers may be responsible for the increase in knee injuries to young female volleyball players.

Another common injury among 11 to 17 year old volleyball players involves the hand and fingers. Girls are three times more likely than boys to sustain injuries to the hands and fingers, most frequently when the fingers are fully extended while attempting to block the ball (Solgard, et al., 1995). The most common injuries are fractures and sprains to the fifth digit and to the thumb.

The prevalence of knee injuries among female volleyball players prompted the development of a training program designed to decrease landing forces by teaching the athletes neuromuscular control of the legs, and concurrently, to increase the stability of the knee joint by maximizing the strength of the knee musculature (Hewett, et al., 1996). After six weeks of training, Hewett, et al. reported that the eleven female high school volleyball players decreased their landing peak force by 22%, increased maximum knee flexion upon landing by 70%, and increased hamstring power and strength by 33 and 20%, respectively. Most importantly, a follow-up study resulted in a decreased incidence of serious knee injuries to those who were most at risk for having a knee injury. Thus, the jump training program of Hewett, et al. is the only laboratory-tested training regimen that has evidence of its effectiveness.

Soccer

Because of the game's dependence on skills performed by the lower extremity, it is not surprising that the most common type of soccer injury in boys and men and girls and women is the ankle sprain. Powell and Barber-Foss (2000) found a significantly higher rate of injuries (14%) on interscholastic girls teams, when girls and boys played under similar circumstances, including rules, venues and length of season. Girls also had significantly higher rates of knee injuries, reinjuries and injuries that required surgery.

The incidence and rates of soccer-related injuries in females may be influenced greatly by experience and maturity. Elias (2001) reported that the injury rate over a 10-year period in USA Cup Competition decreased by 50%, with the highest rates at the "16 and under" and "14 and under" age groups. The lowest rates of injuries were recorded in the "19 and under" age group. Injuries were related to the heat index, with injuries over four times higher in "hot" years. Girls were also 1.7 times more likely to suffer from heat illness than boys. suggesting that levels of conditioning and acclimateization may have been factors in injuries.

Conclusions

The over-all rate of knee injuries for basketball, soccer and baseball/softball was 44% higher for girls, the knee surgery rate was more than twice as high for girls, and the ACL surgery rate was more than four times higher for girls than for boys. Clearly, when injury rates of comparable sports are analyzed, the knee of female athletes emerges as the anatomical site that sustains the greatest incidence and severity of injuries.

SUMMARY

Coaches, athletes and parents should all become familiar with the possible ramifications that disordered eating, amenorrhea and osteoporosis have on a young female athlete. Other areas in which these components can play a role are in menstrual irregularities and injuries—particularly stress fractures. The position stands and recommendations the ACSM and USOC as well as the AAP provide valuable tools in the recognition and possible prevention of the Female Athlete Triad.

Data from selected sports indicate that injuries are not only sport-specific—they also are gender-specific. Under comparable playing conditions, young female athletes have a greater incidence and severity of knee injuries, a greater number of sprains and fractures to the hands and fingers, and succumb more frequently than males of a similar age to heat illness. Anatomical differences, experience and levels of conditioning have been implicated as possible causes in these identified gender-related sites and types of injuries.

REFERENCES

American Academy of Pediatrics. (2000). "Medical Concerns in the Female Athlete." *Pediatrics*, 106(3): 610-612.

American Psychiatric Association. (1994). *Diagnostic and Statistical Manual of Mental Disorders (DSM-IV-TR), 4th edition.* Washington DC: American Psychiatric Association, pp. 583-595.

Arendt, E. A. (1993). "Osteoporosis in the Athletic Female: Amenorrhea and Amenorrheic Osteoporosis." In A. J. Pearl (editor), *The Athletic Female: American Orthopaedic Society for Sports Medicine.* Champaign, IL: Human Kinetics Publishers, pp. 41-59,

Arendt, E. (1996). "Common Musculoskeletal Injuries in Women." *The Physician and Sportsmedicine*, 24: 39-48.

Bahr, R., Karlsen, R., Lian, Ø., and Øvrebo, R. (1994). "Incidence and Mechanism of Acute Ankle Inversion Injuries in Volleyball." *American Journal of Sports Medicine*, 22: 595-600.

Bennell, K. L., Malcolm, S. A., Thomas, S. A., Wark, J. D., and Brukner, P. D. (1996). "The Incidence and Distribution of Stress Fractures in Competitive Track and Field Athletes." *The American Journal of Sports Medicine*, 24(2): 211-217.

Dalsky, G. P. (1990). "Effect of Exercise on Bone: Permissive Influence of Estrogen and Calcium." *Medicine and Science in Sports and Exercise*, 22(3): 281-285.

Davis, J., Kuppermann, N., and Fleisher, G. (1993). "Serious Sports Injuries Requiring Hospitalization Seen in a Pediatric Emergency Department." *American Journal of Diseases of Children*, 147: 1001-1004.

Elias, S. (2001). "10-Year Trend in USA Cup Soccer Injuries: 1988-1997." *Medicine in Sport and Exercise*, 33: 359-367.

Ferretti, A., Papandrea, P., Conteduca, F., et al. (1992). "Knee Ligament Injuries in Volleyball Players." *The American Journal of Sports Medicine*, 20: 203-207.

Hewett, T., Stroupe, A., Nance, T., and Noyes, F. (1996). "Plyometric Training in Female Athletes." *The American Journal of Sports Medicine*, 24: 765-773.

Hosea, T., Carey, C., and Harrer, M. (2000). "The Gender Issue: Epidemiology of Ankle Injuries in Athletes Who Participate in Basketball." *Clinical Orthopaedics and Related Research*, 372: 45-49.

Huston, L., Greenfield, M., and Wojtys, E. (2000). "Anterior Cruciate Ligament Injuries in the Female Athlete." *Clinical Orthopaedics and Related Research*, 372: 50-63.

Johnson, M. D. (1994). "Disordered Eating in Active and Athletic Women." *Clinics in Sports Medicine*, 13(2): 355-369.

Jonnavithula, S., Warren, M. P., Fox, R. P., and Lazaro, M. I. (1993). "Bone Density is Compromised in Amenorrheic Women Despite Return of Menses: A 2 Year Study." *Obstetrics and Gynecology*, 81(5): 669-674.

Lebrun, C. M. (2000). "Menstrual Cycle Dysfunction." Current Comment from the American College of Sports Medicine.

Loucks, A. B. (1990). "Effects of Exercise Training on the Menstrual Cycle: Existence and Mechanisms." *Medicine and Science in Sports and Exercise*, 22(3): 275-280.

Loucks, A. B., Verdun, M., and Heath, E. M. (1998). "Low Energy Availability, Not Stress of Exercise, Alters LH Pulsatility in Exercising Women." *Journal of Applied Physiology*, 84(1): 37-46.

Messina, D. F., Farney, W. C., and DeLee, J. C. (1999). "The Incidence of Injury in Texas High School Basketball: A Prospective Study Among Male and Female Athletes." *The American Journal of Sports Medicine*, 27: 294-299.

Moeller, J. L., and Lamb, M. M. (1997). "Anterior Cruciate Ligament Injuries in Female Athletes." *The Physician and Sportsmedicine*, 25: 31-54.

NATA. (1997). *1995-1997 Injury Surveillance Study.* [Available on Line] < www.webdude@nata.org >

Nichols, D. L., Bonnick, S. L., and Sanborn, C. F. (2000). "Bone Health and Osteoporosis." *Clinics in Sports Medicine*, 19(2): 233-249.

Otis, C. L. (1994). "Stress Fractures in Athletes." In R. Agostini and S. Titus (editors), *Medical and Orthopedic Issues of Active an Athletic Women.* Philadelphia: Hanley and Belfus, Inc., pp. 325-332.

Otis, C. L., Drinkwater, B., Johnson, M., Loucks, A., and Wilmore, J. (1997). "The ACSM Position Stand on the Female Athlete Triad." *Medicine and Science in Sports and Exercise*, 29(5): i-ix.

Powell, J., and Barber-Foss, K. (2000). "Sex-Related Injury Patterns Among Selected High School Sports." *The American Journal of Sports Medicine*, 28: 385-391.

Prior, J. C., Vigna, Y. M., Schecter, M. T., and Burgess, A. E. (1990). "Spinal Bone Loss and Ovulatory Disturbances." *New England Journal of Medicine*, 323: 1221-1227.

Rencken, M. L., Chestnutt III, C. H., and Drinkwater, B. L. (1996). "Bone Density at Multiple Skeletal Sites in Amenorrheic Athletes." *The Journal of the American Medical Association*, 276: 238-240.

Sanborn, C. F., Horea, M., Siemers, B. J., and Dieringer, K. I. (2000). "Disordered Eating and the Female Athlete Triad." *Clinics in Sports Medicine*, 19(2): 199-213.

Shively, R., Grana, W., and Ellis, D. (1981). "High School Sports Injuries." *The Physician and Sportsmedicine*, 9: 46-50.

Snow-Carter, C. (1994). "Athletic Amenorrhea and Bone Health." In R. Agostini and S. Titus (editors), *Medical and Orthopedic Issues of Active an Athletic Women.* Philadelphia: Hanley and Belfus, Inc., pp. 164-168.

Solgard, L., Nielson, A., Moeller-Madsen, B., and Jacobsen, B. "Volleyball Injuries Presenting in Casualty: A Prospective Study." *British Journal of Sports Medicine*, 29: 200-204.

Sporting Goods Manufacturers' Association. (2000). *U.S. Trends in Team Sports: The SGMA Report 2000.* North Palm Beach, FL: Sporting Goods Manufacturers' Association

Steinbach, P. (2000). "Joint Resolution." *Athletic Business*, 25: 10.

Steven, J., and Branche-Dorsey, C. (1996). *Home and Leisure Injuries in the United States.* Atlanta, GA: National Center for Injury Prevention and Control.

Wilmore, J. (1996). "Eating Disorders in the Young Athlete." In O. Bar-Or (editor), *The Child and Adolescent Athlete.* Oxford: Blackwell Science, pp. 287-303.

Yeager, K. K., Agostini, R., Nattiv, A., and Drinkwater, B. (1993). "The Female Athlete Triad: Disordered Eating, Amenorrhea, Osteoporosis." *Medicine and Science in Sports and Exercise*, 25: 775-777.

14

Prevention of Common Sports Injuries

Rich Kimball, M.A.; Eugene W. Brown, Ph.D.;
Chris McGrew, M.D. and Wade Lillegard, M.D.

QUESTIONS TO CONSIDER

- What constitutes proper equipment and attire for injury prevention?
- How can facilities be made safer for sport?
- What effect can warm-ups, cool downs, and conditioning have on preventing injuries?
- What role does teaching players safety, appropriate sport techniques, and proper drills have in injury prevention?
- What injury prevention techniques can be implemented over the course of a season?

INTRODUCTION

Most sport involves the application of large muscular forces and physical contact at all levels of competition. All of the muscular force and physical contact cannot be eliminated from sport. However, if you follow several steps aimed at preventing injuries, you can make athletics safer. As a coach, you are responsible for doing everything reasonable to allow participants to compete in an environment that is healthy and safe.

INJURY PREVENTION TECHNIQUES

Pre-Participation Exam

The cornerstone for prevention of injuries, the pre-participation physical exam is used to determine if any defects or conditions exist that might place the athlete at an increased risk for injury in a particular sport. it especially is useful for identifying old, inadequately rehabilitated injuries (which easily may be reinjured). See Chapter 17, *Essential Medical Records for Athletes*, and Chapter 18, *The Pre-Participation Physical Examination*, for more details.

Equipment and Apparel

A properly equipped and attired athlete is less likely to be injured. Therefore, it is important that you develop a list of essential equipment for your specific sport and distribute this information to your athletes and their parents. Parents should be informed during a pre-season parents orientation meeting about appropriate equipment and apparel for their children. At the start of the first practice, restate to your athletes what you told the parents about appropriate equipment and apparel.

Determine if:

- All athletes have the essential protective equipment,
- All athletes are properly attired,
- Equipment is in good repair, and
- Equipment properly fits.

This type of inspection should be carried out regularly. Extra essential equipment should be included in the team's equipment bag for athletes who forget their equipment. Note that wearing jewelry is inappropriate during practices and contests. Also, if eyeglasses are essential, they should be safety glasses and worn with safety straps.

Facilities

Inspection of a practice or competition facility for safety hazards is the responsibility of the adults in charge. Prior to and during practices, the coach is responsible for ensuring that the venue is safe. For contests, both the officials and coaches are responsible. Therefore, you or your assistant must inspect the facilities before permitting your athletes to participate in practices and contests. Whoever is responsible should arrive before the athletes to carry out the inspection.

The three categories of safety hazards associated with facilities are:

1. Surface conditions,
2. Structural hazards, and
3. Environmental hazards.

Safety hazards that are not easily corrected must be reported to the athletic director and/or program administrators. If corrections are not made quickly, you should resubmit your concerns in writing. If in your judgment, the venue is unsafe for practices or contests, you are responsible for seeking another venue or canceling the practice of contest.

1. Surface Conditions

The court, field, ice rink, mat, pool and diving board, are examples of surfaces (or media) upon (or within) which sport is contested. The condition of these and other sport surfaces plays an important role in regulating the potential for injuries in sport. Uneven flooring, separations between sections of a wrestling mat, ruts in an ice rink, and rocks protruding from the field are examples of surface conditions that are not safe for competition.

If a safety hazard is present, it must be avoided by relocating, rescheduling, or restricting the activity, or removing the hazard. If the hazardous condition cannot be rectified, it must be reported to the program administrator.

As a coach, you must continually monitor the surfaces upon which your sport is contested and take appropriate action when a surface hazard is noted. Surface conditions may quickly change from safe to unsafe. For example, sweat on the surface of a basketball court may render the court highly hazardous. A broken glass bottle carelessly left on a field can quickly make a safe field hazardous.

2. Structural Hazards

Structural hazards associated with sports are of two types. They may be required by the sport itself (e.g., goals, posts, fences, nets and backboards) or extraneous to the sport (e.g., benches, bleachers, water fountains and vehicles). Structures that are required should be regularly inspected. If it is determined that they do not meet safety standards, these structures should be repaired or replaced. Structures that are extraneous to the sport should be far enough away from the activity area so that they do not create a potential for injury.

3. Environmental Hazards

Environmental hazards are usually associated with sports that are contested outside. Extreme weather conditions such as lightning, high winds, hail, high temperatures, humidity, cold, snow and rain need to be cautiously evaluated as potential safety hazards. Fumes and smog are other potentially hazardous environmental conditions. (See Chapter 19, *Special Conditions in Sports Medicine—Lightning Safety*.)

Activity should not be permitted under the threat of lightning.

Environmental hazards are also possible in an indoor activity area. These hazards include poor lighting, high temperatures and fumes. Whether outdoors or indoors, the environment should be carefully evaluated before athletes are allowed to practice or compete in sport.

Management of Practices and Contests

Every physical activity that occurs during practices and contests has some potential to result in an injury. Fortunately, most activities relating to practices and contests have only a rare chance in resulting in an injury. Injuries that do occur are the result of interactions between the environment in which the activity occurs and the physical status of the athlete. In addition to having an influence over the equipment, apparel and facilities in reducing the risk of injuries, you have a major influence over the physical activities of your athletes during practices and contests. You can take several steps to properly manage the physical activities that occur at practices and contests to reduce the rate and severity of the injuries. These steps include the following:

Teaching Safety to Players

Whenever appropriate, inform your athletes about the potential risks of injury associated with performing certain sports activities and the methods for avoiding injury. By informing your athletes of these dangers and possibly establishing team rules that regulate their performance of high-risk activities, you will reduce the risk of injury to your players.

The key to teaching safety to your athletes is to prudently interject safety tips in your instruction whenever appropriate.

Warming Up

A warm-up at the beginning of your team's practices and before competition provides several important benefits. Specific warm-up suggestions are included in several chapters—Chapter 8, *Physiological Conditioning of*

Young Athletes; Chapter 14, *Prevention of Common Sports Injuries*; and Chapter 16, *Contraindicated Calisthenics, Exercises and Drills.* When warm-ups and stretching are completed, the skill-oriented drills on your practice plan or the formal drills before the game may begin. A warm-up period:

- Increases the breathing rate, heart rate, and muscle temperature to exercise levels,
- Reduces the risks of muscle pulls and strains,
- Increases the shock-absorbing capabilities of the joints, and
- Prepares athletes mentally for practices and competition.

Teaching Appropriate Techniques

The instructions you provide during practices on how to perform specific sport skills have an influence on the risks of injuries to your athletes and their opponents. Teach your athletes the proper ways to perform specific techniques, and *never* teach athletes how to intentionally foul opponents. An improper technique often results in a greater chance of injury to the performer than does the correct technique. Acceptable techniques in sports usually evolve with safety as a concern.

Coaches who promote an atmosphere in which intentional violent fouls are acceptable must be eliminated from athletic programs. You should promote fair and safe participation in practices and contests with strict enforcement of the rules to encourage skill as the primary factor in determining the outcome.

Selecting Proper Drills

Drills that you select or design for your practices and the ways in which they are carried out have an influence on the risks of injuries to your athletes. Drills should be selected and designed with safety as a primary feature. Before implementing a new drill into your practice, several safety questions should be considered:

- Is the drill appropriate for the level of maturation of the athletes?
- Are the athletes sufficiently skilled to comply with the requirements of the drill?
- Are the athletes sufficiently conditioned to handle the stress of participation in the drill?
- Are other, less risky drills available to achieve the same practice results?
- Can the drill be modified to make it less risky and yet achieve the desired training result?

For more detail regarding drills, see Chapter 32, *Drills as Instructional Activities.*

Conditioning

High-intensity work is part of sport. How well your athletes can handle fatigue will often determine how well they perform. Is there, however, any relationship between fatigue and injury? The sequence of events in Figure 14-1 draws an association, linking fatigue with an increased potential for injury. See Chapter 8, *Physiological Conditioning of Young Athletes*, for more details on this topic. In addition to improving performance, every conditioning program should be designed to minimize fatigue and the potential for injury. Being "in shape" can postpone fatigue and its detrimental effects. By progressively intensifying your practices throughout the season, you can produce a conditioning effect that can be an important deterrent to injury. Coaches must also be aware that athletes who engage in intense, frequent practices and contests may need time off as the season wears on. It is possible to over-train and cause, rather than prevent, injuries. Injuries caused by over-training have grown to represent an increased portion of reported sports injuries. Some telltale signs of over-training include:

- Elevated resting heart rate,
- Poor performance,
- Loss of enthusiasm,
- Depression,
- Chronic muscle soreness,
- Disrupted sleeping patterns,
- Higher incidence of injury and
- Longer time to recover from injury.

Antidotes to over-training include time off from practice, shorter practices, alternating in tense practices with lighter workouts, or any combination of these suggestions. Over-training is not usually a problem when athletes are practicing three to five times a week, unless they are also:

- Competing two or more times per week,
- Participating on more than one team and/or,
- Playing on a different sport team during the same season.

(See Chapter 25, *Helping Athletes Cope with Stress*, for additional information on this topic.)

Avoiding Contraindicated Exercises

Over the past several years, researchers and physicians have identified a list of exercises that are commonly used by coaches but potentially harmful to the body. These are called contraindicated exercises. This information has been slow in reaching coaches and athletes. Chapter 16, *Contraindicated Calisthenics, Exercises and Drills*, includes a description of these exercises and ex-

Athlete becomes fatigued

↓

Skilled performance is reduced

↓

Concentration becomes difficult

↓

Reactions slow down

↓

Judgment becomes impaired

↓

Faulty decisions are made

↓

Injuries may result

Figure 14-1. How Fatigue is Linked to an Increased Potential for Injuries

plains how they can be modified to eliminate their undesirable characteristics.

Cooling Down

There are few feelings more uncomfortable than finishing a vigorous workout, sitting down for a while and then trying to walk. Muscles in the body tighten during periods of inactivity following hard work. To minimize the stiffness that usually follows a workout and the soreness the following day, take time to adequately cool down at the end of practice. A gradual reduction of activity (the reverse of the warm-up procedure) facilitates the dissipation of waste products associated with muscular activity. Letting the body cool off gradually may not pre-vent injuries, but the athletes may experience less discomfort and be better able to function at high levels during the next workout.

SUMMARY

This chapter focused on three areas in which you can exert an influence to reduce the potential number and severity of injuries in sport. The first area involves your insistence that your athletes wear appropriate protective equipment and apparel, avoiding safety hazards associated with facilities is the second area. Management of practices and contests is the third area. Proper management includes:

- Teaching your athletes safety, appropriate techniques, and proper drills.
- Running practices with warming-up, conditioning, and cooling down exercises.
- Excluding known contraindicated exercises.

Safety and injury prevention should be a primary factor to consider in whatever plans you make for your team. You will be more than compensated for the extra time and effort required to implement the suggestions found in this chapter by the comfort of knowing that you have done as much as you can to assure that your athletes will have a safe season.

SUGGESTED READINGS

Agre, J. C., and Krotee, M. L. (1981). "Soccer Safety—Prevention and Care." *Journal of Health, Physical Education, Recreation and Dance*, 52(5): 52-54.

Caine, D. J., Caine, C. G., and Lindner, K. J. (editors). (1996). *The Epidemiology of Sports Injuries*. Champaign, IL: Human Kinetics Publishers.

MacDowelll, E. (2000). *First Aid Handbook for Coaches*. Old Greenwich, CT: Parke Publications.

Micheli, L. J. (1985). "Preventing Youth Sports Injuries." *Journal of Health, Physical Education, Recreation and Dance*, 76(6): 52-54.

National Safety Council. (2000). *First Aid and CPR*. Sudbury, MA: Jones and Bartlett, Publishers.

National Safety Council. (1995). *First Responder*. Sudbury, MA: Jones and Bartlett, Publishers.

15
Care of Common Sports Injuries

Rich Kimball, M.A.; Eugene W. Brown, Ph.D.; Wade Lillegard, M.D.; Sally Nogle, Ph.D., A.T.C. and Thomas Mackowiak, A.T.C.

QUESTIONS TO CONSIDER

- Can you identify and provide first-aid for the different medical conditions commonly associated with the sport?
- What items belong in a well-stocked first-aid kit?
- What procedures should you follow when an injury occurs?
- What information should you have about your athletes in case they become injured?

INTRODUCTION

Chris has the soccer ball and only one defensive player protects the area between Chris and the goalkeeper. A feint leaves the fullback out of the play. Only the goalkeeper is left on defense. As Chris sprints toward the goal the goalkeeper leaves the goal area and approaches the ball. Chris momentarily loses control of the dribble, and everyone is uncertain as to who will get to play the ball first. Both Chris and the goalkeeper sprint full speed toward the ball and each other. They arrive simultaneously, neither backing off of the play. There is a collision, and Chris lies motionless on the ground. The referee, sensing the likelihood of injury, immediately signals Chris' coach onto the field to tend to the injured player.

Watching from the bench, the first, and normal, reaction of a coach is to be frightened by the possible outcome of this collision. The sinking feeling in the stomach and the "Oh, no" message sent out by the brain when Chris was injured have been felt by most coaches at some point.

If this, or some similar situation confronted you in your sport, what would you do? Are you prepared to act appropriately? As a coach of young athletes, it is your obligation to be able to deal with such an emergency. Before your first practice, you should: obtain medical information on your athletes, establish emergency procedures, and prepare to provide first-aid.

You must not rely on the likelihood that a serious injury will not occur to your athletes as an excuse for inadequate emergency preparation!

MEDICAL INFORMATION

The completed *Medical Information and Injury History* (Supplement 17-1) and *Medical Treatment Consent* (Supplement 17-3) forms should be in your possession whenever your athletes are under your supervision, Hopefully, the need to use this information will never arise. But, if an injury occurs, the information on these forms will help you and qualified medical personnel respond quickly.

EMERGENCY PROCEDURES

As the coach of an injured athlete, you are responsible for the actions taken until the athlete is placed in the care of competent medical personnel, parents, or guardians. Parents and players expect you to know how to proceed. The *Emergency Plan Form* (Supplement 15-1) has been developed to assist you in properly responding to an emergency.

The *Emergency Plan Form* provides directions for a number of people to carry out responsibilities in an emergency. One completed form is needed for each of the five individuals listed below. The form also contains space for inserting site-specific information about emergency care.

Before the first practice, a number of responsible individuals must be assigned roles to carry out in an emergency. These roles are:

1. Taking charge of the situation (the coach),
2. Attending to an injured athlete,
3. Attending to the uninjured athletes,

4. Calling for emergency medical assistance, and
5. Flagging down the emergency vehicle.

Note that when a medical emergency occurs, all responsibilities must be addressed simultaneously.

1. Taking Charge of the Situation

At most school sponsored sports, a physician or athletic trainer is not present to assist the coach in handling the medical aspects of an emergency. Thus, after taking charge of the situation and directing individuals to their assigned tasks, the coach is likely to be the person to attend to the injured athlete. After the injured player is released to emergency medical personnel, the coach should complete the *On-site Injury Report Form* (Supplement 15-2). Also, if the injured athlete's parents or guardians are unaware of the emergency situation, information on the *Athlete's Medical Information Form* should be used to contact them.

2. Attending to an Injured Athlete

Providing emergency care includes knowledge and skill in cardiopulmonary resuscitation (CPR), controlling bleeding, attending to heat stroke, attending to shock, and knowing how to use an allergic reaction kit. This knowledge and skill are beyond the scope of PACE and should be obtained through Red Cross courses or similar courses under certified instructors offered in most communities. If the coach is not qualified to administer CPR or first-aid, then an unacceptable breach has occurred. Coaches must prepare themselves to deal with emergencies unless these responsibilities have been assigned to qualified individuals who are present at practices and contests. (And even if such personnel are available, the coach still should be prepared to meet these responsibilities.) When emergency medical personnel arrive, responsibility for the injured athlete should be transferred to these professionals. The Athlete's Medical Information and Medical Treatment Consent (Release) forms should be presented to the emergency medical personnel. The person (usually the coach) designated on the *Medical Treatment Consent Form* (Supplement 17-3) must accompany the injured athlete to the medical center.

3. Attending to the Uninjured Athletes

If the coach is attending the injured athlete, the uninjured athletes should be directed to a safe area within voice and vision of the coach. These responsibilities are assigned to the person in charge of the uninjured athletes. An accepted procedure for dismissing the uninjured athletes should also be developed.

4. Calling for Emergency Medical Assistance

The responsibilities of the individual assigned to call for emergency medical assistance are covered in Supplement 15-1-D. This section also includes space for entering site-specific information for the location of the nearest telephone, emergency telephone number, directions to the injured athlete, and the location of the "flag" person. If known, the person calling for assistance should report the nature of the injury to the person answering the call. After completing the call for assistance, this individual should privately report the status of emergency medical assistance to the person attending the injured athlete.

5. Flagging Down the Emergency Vehicle

Whether or not someone is needed to direct the emergency vehicle will depend on the site of the team's activities. If a "flag" person is needed, the procedures to follow are described in Supplement 15-1-E. In rare situations where there is no telephone near the site of the injury, the flag person will be responsible for seeking emergency medical assistance. The solution to this problem is to have a portable telephone available at all times.

Rehearsing emergency care procedures can be invaluable.

Immediate treatment of life-threatening injuries is extremely important. Being certified in basic first-aid and emergency procedures is invaluable and will give you more confidence when dealing with any type of injury.

PROVIDE FIRST-AID

If the athlete is seriously injured, have your assistant coach, a parent, or a responsible athlete take the coins and the list of emergency telephone numbers from the first-aid kit and call an ambulance. (Better yet, have a portable telephone available.) You or your trainer should stay with the injured athlete until help arrives.

Aids for Proper Care

If the injury is less serious and does not require assistance from trained medical personnel, you may be able to move the athlete from the sport setting to an area where care can begin. Two important aids to properly care for an injured athlete include a first-aid kit and ice.

First-Aid Kit

A well-stocked first-aid kit does not have to be large, but it should contain the basic items that may be needed for appropriate care. The checklist in Table 15-1 provides a guide for including commonly used supplies. Your trainer or you may wish to add and subtract from the kit on the basis of your experience and/or local policies or guidelines.

A good rule of thumb for coaches is, "If you can't treat the problems by using the supplies in a well-stocked first-aid kit, then it is too big a problem for you to

Table 15-1. First-Aid Kit Checklist.

- white athletic tape
- sterile gauze pads
- Telfa no-stick pads
- ace bandages
- Band-aids, assorted sizes
- foam rubber/moleskin
- tweezers
- disinfectant
- first-aid cream

- plastic bags for ice
- coins for pay telephone
- emergency care phone numbers
- list of emergency phone numbers
- cotton swabs
- scissors/knife
- safety pins
- soap
- sling

handle." You should be able to attend to bruises, small cuts, strains and sprains. When fractures, dislocations, back or neck injuries occur, call for professional medical assistance.

Ice

Having access to ice is unique to every local setting. Thus, every coach or trainer may have to arrange for its provision in a different way. Ice, however, is very important to proper immediate care of many minor injuries and should, therefore, be readily available.

Care of Minor Injuries

R.I.C.E.

Unless you are also a physician, you should not attempt to care for anything except minor injuries (e.g., bruises, bumps, sprains). Many minor injuries can be cared for by using the R.I.C.E. formula (Table 15-2).

Most minor injuries can benefit from using the R.I.C.E. formula.

When following the R.I.C.E. formula, ice should be kept on the injured area for 20 minutes and taken off for 20 minutes. Repeat this procedure three to four times. Icing should continue three times per day for the first 72 hours following the injury. After three days, extended care is necessary if the injury has not healed. At this time, options for care include:

- Stretching and strengthening exercises,
- Contrast treatments, and
- Visiting a doctor for further diagnosis.

Contrast Treatments

If the injured area is much less swollen after 72 hours, but the pain is not subsiding, contrast treatments will help. Use the following procedure:

1. Place the injured area in an ice bath or cover with an ice bag for one minute.
2. After using the ice, place the injured area in warm water (100 to 110° F.) for three minutes.
3. Continue this rotation for five to seven bouts of ice and four to six bouts of heat.
4. Always end with the ice treatment.

Contrast treatments should be followed for the next three to five days. If swelling or pain still persist after several days of contrast treatments, the athlete should be sent to a physician for further evaluation.

COMMON MEDICAL PROBLEMS IN SPORT

Information about 23 common medical conditions that may occur in sport is presented in this section. The information about each condition includes:

Table 15-2. The R.I.C.E. Formula for Dealing With Minor Injuries.

The **R.I.C.E.** formula for care of minor injuries involves the following steps.	
R = **Rest**	Keep the player out of action.
I = **Ice**	Apply ice to the injured area.
C = **Compression**	Wrap an elastic bandage around the injured area and the ice bag to hold the bag in place. The bandage should not be so tight as to cut off blood flow to the injured area.
E = **Elevation**	Let gravity drain the excess fluid.

- A definition,
- Common symptoms,
- Immediate on-field treatment, and
- Guidelines for returning the athlete to action.

ABRASION

Definition: Superficial skin wound caused by scraping.

Symptoms:
- Minor bleeding
- Redness
- Burning sensation

Care:
- Cleanse the area with soap and water.
- Control the bleeding.
- Cover the area with sterile dressing.
- Monitor over several days for signs of infection.

Return to Action: After providing immediate care.

BACK OR NECK INJURY

Definition: Any injury to the back or neck area that causes the athlete to become immobile or unconscious.

Symptoms:
- Pain and tenderness over the spine
- Numbness
- Weakness or heaviness in limbs; tingling feeling in extremities

Care:
- Do not move the athlete.
- Make sure athlete is breathing.
- Call for medical assistance.
- Do not move neck or back

Return to Action: With physician's permission.

BLISTERS

Definition: Localized collection of fluid in the outer portion of the skin (Figure 15-1).

Symptoms:
- Redness
- Inflammation
- Oozing of fluid
- Discomfort

Care:
- Clean the site with disinfectant.
- Put disinfectant on the area.
- Cut a hole in a stack of several gauze or mole skin pads to be used as a doughnut surrounding the blister.
- Cover the area with a Band-Aid.

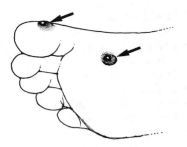

Figure 15-1. Blister.

- Alter the cause of the problem when possible (e.g., proper size and/or shape of the shoes).

Return to Action: Immediately, unless pain is severe.

CONTUSION

Definition: A bruise; an injury in which the skin is not broken (Figure 15-2).

Symptoms:
- Tenderness around the injury
- Swelling
- Localized pain
- Discoloration

Care:
- Apply the R.I.C.E. formula for the first three days.
- Use contrast treatments for days four to eight.
- Restrict activity.
- Provide padding when returning the athlete to activity.

Return to Action: When there is complete absence of pain and full range of motion and strength is restored.

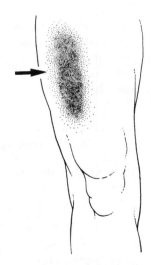

Figure 15-2. Contusion (bruise) in thigh.

CRAMPS

Definition: Involuntary and forceful contraction of a muscle; muscle spasm.

Symptoms:
- Localized pain in contracting muscle

Care:
- Slowly stretch the muscle.
- Massage the muscle.

Return to Action: When pain is gone and full range of motion is restored.

DENTAL INJURY

Definition: Any injury to mouth or teeth.

Symptoms:
- Pain
- Bleeding
- Loss of tooth (partial or total)

Care:
- Clear the airway where necessary.
- Stop the bleeding with direct pressure. Make sure excess blood does not clog the airway.
- Save any teeth that were knocked free; store them in a cup specially designed for this or in the athlete's mouth.
- Transport player to a hospital or dentist.
- Do not rub or clean the tooth. This may kill important cells essential for saving the tooth.

Return to Action: When the pain is gone (usually within two to three days) and with permission of a dentist or physician.

DISLOCATION

Definition: Loss of normal anatomical alignment of a joint (Figure 15-3).

Symptoms:
- Complaints of joint slipping in and out (subluxation)
- Deformity
- Pain at the joint

Care:
- Immobilize before moving,
- Must be treated by a physician.
- Obtain medical care. Do not attempt to put joint back into place.
- R.I.C.E.

Return to Action: With permission of physician.

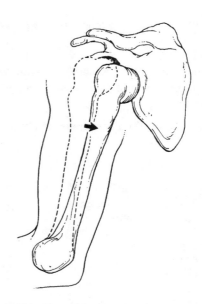

Figure 15-3. Shoulder dislocation—upper arm (humerus) moves totally out of its normal position.

EYE INJURY-CONTUSION

Definition: Direct blow to the eye and region surrounding the eye by a blunt object.

Symptoms:
- Pain
- Redness of eye
- Watery eye

Care:
- Have the athlete lie down with his/her eyes closed.
- Place a folded cloth, soaked in cold water, gently on the eye.
- Seek medical attention if injury is assessed as severe.

Return to Action: For minor injury, athlete may return to action after symptoms clear; for severe injury, with permission of physician.

EYE INJURY-FOREIGN OBJECT

Definition: Object between eyelid and eyeball.

Symptoms:
- Pain
- Redness of eye
- Watery eye
- Inability to keep eye open

Care:
- Do not rub the eye.
- Allow tears to form in eye.

- Carefully try to remove loose object with sterile cotton swab.
- If object is embedded in the eye, have the athlete close both eyes, loosely cover both eyes with sterile dressing, and bring the athlete to an emergency room or ophthalmologist.

Return to Action: With permission of physician.

FAINTING

Definition: Dizziness and loss of consciousness that may be caused by an injury, exhaustion, heat illness, emotional stress, or lack of oxygen.

Symptoms;
- Dizziness
- Cold, clammy skin
- Pale
- Seeing "spots" before one's eyes
- Weak, rapid pulse

Care:
Have the athlete lie down and elevate feet or have the athlete sit with head between knees.

Return to Action: With permission of physician.

FRACTURE

Definition: A crack or complete break in a bone. A simple fracture is a broken bone, but with unbroken skin. An open fracture is a broken bone that also breaks the skin (Figure 15-4).

Symptoms:
- Pain at fracture site
- Tenderness, swelling
- Deformity or unnatural position
- Loss of function in injured area
- Open wound, bleeding (open fracture)

(Note that a simple fracture may not be evident immediately. If localized pain persists, obtain medical assistance.)

Care:
- Stabilize injured bone by using splints, slings, or bandages.
- Do not attempt to straighten an injured part when immobilizing it.
- If skin is broken (open fracture), keep the open wound clean by covering it with the cleanest available cloth. Check for shock and treat if necessary.

Return to Action: With permission of physician.

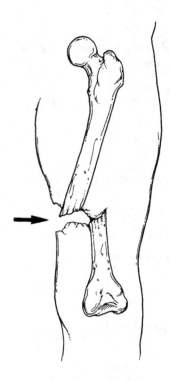

Figure 15-4. Open fracture in thigh.

HEAD INJURY-CONSCIOUS

Definition: Any injury that causes the athlete to be unable to respond in a coherent fashion to known facts (name, date, etc.).

Symptoms:
- Mild: Dizziness, nausea, headache, and confusion
- Severe: Pupils unequal in size and/or non-responsive to light and dark; disorientation

(Note that if the athlete is unconscious, expect an injury to the back or neck and care for the athlete as if it were a back or neck injury.)

Care:
- Mild: If the mild symptoms are present, athlete may be moved carefully when dizziness disappears. Athletes with head injuries should be removed from further practice or competition that day and carefully observed for a minimum of 24 hours. Obtain medical assistance.
- Severe: If severe symptoms are present, do not move the athlete. Call for medical assistance.

Return to Action: With permission of physician.

HEAD INJURY-UNCONSCIOUS

Definition: Any injury in which the athlete is unable to respond to external stimuli by verbal or visual means.

Symptoms:
- Athlete is unconscious
- Cuts or bruises around the head may be evident

Care:
- **ANY TIME AN ATHLETE IS UNCONSCIOUS, ASSUME AN INJURY TO THE SPINAL CORD OR BRAIN.**
- If necessary, clear the airway keeping the player's neck straight. Do not move the athlete.
- Call for medical assistance.

Return to Action: With permission of physician.

HEAT EXHAUSTION

Definition: Heat disorder that may lead to heat stroke.

Symptoms:
- Fatigue
- Profuse sweating
- Chills
- Throbbing pressure in the head
- Nausea
- Normal body temperature
- Pale and clammy skin

Care:
- Remove the athlete from heat and sun.
- Provide plenty of water.
- Rest the athlete in a supine position with feet elevated about 12 inches.
- Loosen or remove the athlete's clothing.
- Reduce the athlete's temperature by applying cold water/ice.

Return to Action: Next day if symptoms are no longer present.

HEATSTROKE

Definition: Life-threatening heat disorder.

Symptoms:
- Extremely high body temperature
- Hot, red, and dry skin
- Rapid and strong pulse
- Disorientation
- Unconsciousness

Care:
- Immediately call for medical assistance.
- Immediately cool body by cold sponging, immersion in cool water, and cold packs.
- Remove clothing.

Return to Action: With permission of physician.

LACERATIONS

Definition: A tearing or cutting of the skin.

Symptoms:
- Bleeding
- Swelling

Care:
- Direct pressure to the wound for four or five minutes usually will stop bleeding.
- Clean the wound with disinfectant.
- If stitches are required, send to a physician within five hours.

Return to Action: As soon as pain is gone, if the wound can be protected from further injury.

LOSS OF WIND

Definition: A forceful blow to mid-abdomen area that causes inability to breathe.

Symptoms:
- Rapid, shallow breathing
- Gasping for breath

Care:
- Check athlete for other injuries.
- Place athlete in a supine position.
- Calm the athlete in order to foster slower breathing.
- Loosen belt and clothing.

Return to Action: After five minutes of rest to regain composure and breathing has returned to normal rate.

NOSE BLEED

Definition: Bleeding from the nose.

Symptoms:
- Bleeding
- Swelling
- Pain
- Deformity of nose

Care:
- Calm the athlete.
- Get the athlete into a sitting position.
- Pinch the nostrils together with fingers while the athlete breathes through the mouth.

- Apply ice.
- If bleeding cannot be controlled, call for medical assistance.
- If the nose is deformed, refer athlete to a physician.

Return to Action: Minor nosebleed—when bleeding has stopped for several minutes. Serious nosebleed—no more competition that day, physician's permission if a fracture has occurred.

PLANTAR FASCIITIS

Definition: Inflammation of the connective tissue (fascia) located between the heel and the toes.

Symptoms:
- Arch and heel pain
- Sharp pain ("stone bruise") near heel
- Gradual onset of pain, which may be tolerated for weeks
- Morning pain may be more severe
- Pain may be noted after sitting
- Pain may decrease throughout day

Care:
- Rest the foot.
- Stretch the Achilles' tendon before exercise.
- Use shoes with firm heel counter, good heel cushion, and arch support
- Use of a heel lift may reduce shock to the foot and decrease the pain.
- Use adhesive strapping to support the arch.

Return to Action: When pain is gone.

PUNCTURE WOUND

Definition: Any hole made by the piercing of a pointed instrument.

Symptoms:
- Breakage of the skin
- Minor bleeding, possibly none
- Tender around wound

Care:
- Cleanse the area with soap and water.
- Control the bleeding.
- Cover the area with sterile dressing.
- Consult physician about the need for a tetanus shot.
- Monitor over several days for signs of infection.

Return to Action: With permission of physician.

SHOCK

Definition: Adverse reaction of the body to physical or psychological trauma.

Symptoms:
- Pale
- Cold, clammy skin
- Dizziness
- Nausea
- Faint feeling

Care:
- Have the athlete lie down.
- Calm the athlete.
- Elevate the feet, unless it is a head injury.
- Send for emergency help.
- Control the player's temperature.
- Loosen tight-fitting clothing.
- Control the pain or bleeding if necessary.

Return to Action: With permission of physician.

SPRAIN

Definition: A stretching or a partial or complete tear of the ligament(s) surrounding a joint (Figure 15-5).

Symptoms:
- Pain at the joint
- Pain aggravated by motion at the joint
- Tenderness and swelling
- Looseness at the joint

Care:
- Immobilize at time of injury if pain is severe; may require a splint.
- Use the R.I.C.E. formula.
- Send the player to a physician.

Return to Action: When pain and swelling are gone, full range of motion is reestablished, and strength and stability are within 95% of the non-injured limb throughout

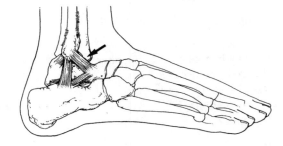

Figure 15-5. Frequently torn ligament in the ankle-anterior talofibular.

range of motion. Also when light formal activity is possible with no favoring of the injury, or moderate to full intensity formal activity can be resumed with no favoring of the injury.

STRAIN

Definition: Stretching or tearing of the muscle or tendons that attach the muscle to the bone—commonly referred to as a "muscle pull." (Figure 15-6).

Symptoms:
- Localized pain brought on by stretching or contracting the muscle in question
- Unequal strength between limbs
- Swelling
- Discolorization after 24 hours if strain is severe

Care:
- Use the R.I.C.E. formula.
- Use contrast treatments for days four through eight.

Return to Action: When the athlete can stretch the injured segment as far as the non-injured segment, when strength is equal to opposite segment, and when the athlete can perform basic skills of the sport without favoring the injury. Depending on the severity of the strain, it may take from one day to more than two weeks to return to action,

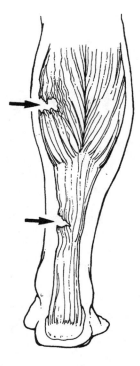

Figure 15-6. Muscle strain in belly of muscle (upper) and in muscle tendon unit (lower).

MAINTAINING APPROPRIATE RECORDS

The immediate care you provide to an injured athlete is important to limit the extent of the injury and to set the stage for appropriate rehabilitation. However, immediate care is not the end of prudent action when an injury occurs. Two additional brief but valuable tasks should be completed. First, complete an *On-Site Injury Report Form* (Supplement 15-2), and record the injury on the *Summary of Season Injuries Form* (Supplement 17-6).

On-Site Injury Report Form

It is important for you or an athletic trainer to maintain a record of the injuries that occur to your athletes. This information may be helpful to guide delayed care or medical treatment and may be very important if any legal problems arise in connection with the injury. Supplement 15-2 includes a standard form that will help guide the recording of pertinent information relative to each injury. These records should be kept for several years following an injury. You should check on legal requirements in your state to determine how long these records should be kept. (See Chapter 33, *Administrative Responsibilities of Coaches*.)

Summary of Season Injuries Form

Supplement 17-6, the *Summary of Season Injuries Form*, lists each of the common medical conditions that occur in sport and also provides a space for you or your trainer to record when each type of injury occurred. At the end of the season, you should total the incidence of each injury type to see if there is any trend to the kind of injuries your team has suffered. If a trend exists, evaluate your training methods in all areas of practices and competition. Try to alter drills or circumstances that may be causing injuries. Review Chapter 14, *Prevention of Common Sports Injuries*, for techniques that may help you prevent injuries. Perhaps your practice routine ignores— or overemphasizes—some area of stretching or conditioning. Decide on a course of action that may be implemented for next season and write your thoughts in the space provided or note the appropriate changes you wish to make on your season or practice plans.

SUMMARY

This chapter acquaints you with various injuries associated with sport and how you and/or your athletic trainer should be prepared to deal with these injuries. If you have prepared your first-aid kit, brought along the medical records, and familiarized yourself with the different types of injuries, you should be able to manage whatever situation arises. Follow the steps that are outlined for you, and remember—you are not a doctor. If you are in doubt about how to proceed, use the coins in your first-aid kit and call for professional medical help. Do not make decisions about treatments if you are not qualified to make them.

Remember, react quickly and with confidence. Most injuries will be minor and the injured athletes will need only a little reassurance before they can be moved to the bench area. Injuries will always occur in sport. Therefore, you must prepare yourself to deal with whatever happens in a calm, responsible manner.

REFERENCES

American Red Cross (2000). *Cardiopulmonary Resuscitation.* Washington, D.C.: American Red Cross.

Ritter, Merrill A. and Albohm, Marjorie J. (2000). *Your Injury: A Common Sense Guide to Sports Injuries, 2nd Ed.* Traverse City, MI: Cooper Publishing Group.

Tanner, S. M., and Harvey, J. S. (1988). "How We Manage Plantar Fasciitis." *The Physician and Sportsmedicine,* 16(8): 39-40, 42, 44, 47.

SUGGESTED READING

National Safety Council. (2000). *First Responder: Your First Response to Emergency Care.* Sudbury, MA: Jones and Bartlett Publishers.Ritter, Merrill A. and Albohm, Marjorie J. (2000). *Your Injury: A Common Sense Guide to Sports Injuries, 2nd Ed.* Traverse City, MI: Cooper Publishing Group.

Ritter, Merrill A. and Albohm, Marjorie J. (2000). *Your Injury: A Common Sense Guide to Sports Injuries, 2nd Ed.* Traverse City, MI: Cooper Publishing Group.

EMERGENCY PLAN FORM*

Essential Items:
1. Well-stocked first aid kit
2. Medical forms for each athlete (Athlete's Medical Information, Athlete's Medical Information Summary, and Medical Release)
3. On-Site Injury Report form

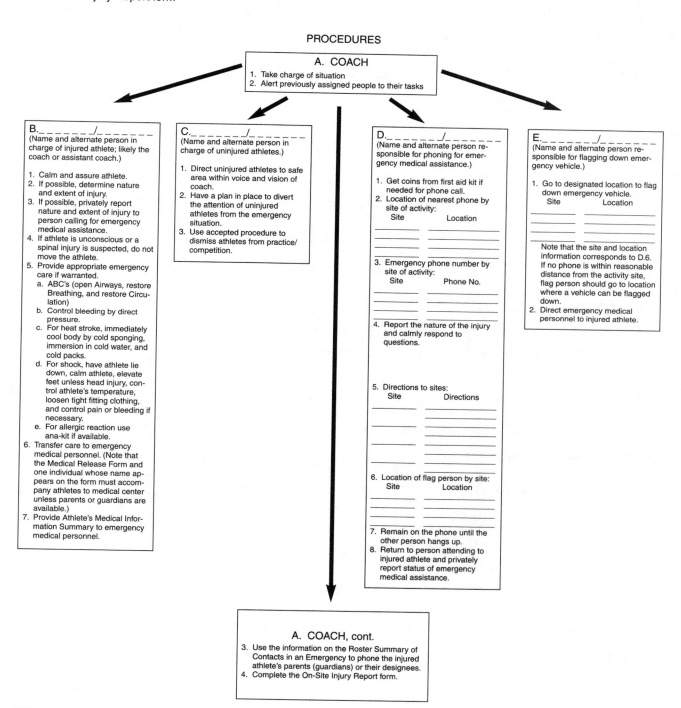

PROCEDURES

A. COACH
1. Take charge of situation
2. Alert previously assigned people to their tasks

B.___/___
(Name and alternate person in charge of injured athlete; likely the coach or assistant coach.)

1. Calm and assure athlete.
2. If possible, determine nature and extent of injury.
3. If possible, privately report nature and extent of injury to person calling for emergency medical assistance.
4. If athlete is unconscious or a spinal injury is suspected, do not move the athlete.
5. Provide appropriate emergency care if warranted.
   a. ABC's (open Airways, restore Breathing, and restore Circulation)
   b. Control bleeding by direct pressure.
   c. For heat stroke, immediately cool body by cold sponging, immersion in cold water, and cold packs.
   d. For shock, have athlete lie down, calm athlete, elevate feet unless head injury, control athlete's temperature, loosen tight fitting clothing, and control pain or bleeding if necessary.
   e. For allergic reaction use ana-kit if available.
6. Transfer care to emergency medical personnel. (Note that the Medical Release Form and one individual whose name appears on the form must accompany athletes to medical center unless parents or guardians are available.)
7. Provide Athlete's Medical Information Summary to emergency medical personnel.

C.___/___
(Name and alternate person in charge of uninjured athletes.)

1. Direct uninjured athletes to safe area within voice and vision of coach.
2. Have a plan in place to divert the attention of uninjured athletes from the emergency situation.
3. Use accepted procedure to dismiss athletes from practice/competition.

D.___/___
(Name and alternate person responsible for phoning for emergency medical assistance.)

1. Get coins from first aid kit if needed for phone call.
2. Location of nearest phone by site of activity:
   Site   Location

3. Emergency phone number by site of activity:
   Site   Phone No.

4. Report the nature of the injury and calmly respond to questions.

5. Directions to sites:
   Site   Directions

6. Location of flag person by site:
   Site   Location

7. Remain on the phone until the other person hangs up.
8. Return to person attending to injured athlete and privately report status of emergency medical assistance.

E.___/___
(Name and alternate person responsible for flagging down emergency vehicle.)

1. Go to designated location to flag down emergency vehicle.
   Site   Location

Note that the site and location information corresponds to D.6. If no phone is within reasonable distance from the activity site, flag person should go to location where a vehicle can be flagged down.
2. Direct emergency medical personnel to injured athlete.

A. COACH, cont.
3. Use the information on the Roster Summary of Contacts in an Emergency to phone the injured athlete's parents (guardians) or their designees.
4. Complete the On-Site Injury Report form.

*A minimum of 4 completed copies of this form is needed; one for each of the individuals with assigned tasks. Make sure that information is included at all practice and competition sites.

On-Site Injury Report Form

Injured Player's Name _____ Date of Injury _____

Address (Street/City/State/Zip) _____

Home Phone _____ Other Phone _____

Nature and extent of injury : _____

_____

How did the injury occur? _____

_____

Describe the first-aid given, including name(s) of attendee(s) : _____

_____

_____

Disposition: _____ To hospital _____ To home _____ To physician

Other: _____

Was protective equipment worn?   Yes   No   (circle one)

Explanation: _____

_____

Names and addresses of witnesses : _____

_____

_____

_____

Other comments: _____

_____

Signed (Date/Title/Position): _____

16
Contraindicated Calisthenics, Exercises and Drills

Eugene W. Brown, Ph.D. and Cathy Lirgg, Ph.D., A. T. C.

QUESTIONS TO CONSIDER

- Why are some physical activities contraindicated?
- How is the structure and function of joints related to their potential for injury from physical activity?
- What are the seven risk factors associated with contraindicated exercises?
- What is the proper way to stretch?
- Why is the hurdler's stretch contraindicated?

INTRODUCTION

The physical activities used to prepare athletes for participation in sport can be generally grouped into the following types: calisthenics, stretching exercises, resistance training, endurance exercise and sport-specific drills and games. Recently, exercise specialists have begun to evaluate and question the safety of many individual physical activities that have been common to preparation for participation in sport. Several activities have been labeled as contraindicated because they are potentially dangerous. Concerns have been raised about the dangers of other activities that are frequently performed incorrectly or that require coaches to state precautions before encouraging athletes to engage in them.

Many common physical activities used to prepare athletes for sport are not only being performed incorrectly but may actually be harmful.

When selecting physical activities to be included in their practice plans, coaches will often draw upon past experiences. They frequently rely upon activities that have been traditional to their sport and ones they have learned from their experiences as athletes. However, there is a disparity between our current knowledge about the biomechanics of physical activities for sport and the assumption that traditional activities have been proven to be safe and effective. Some experts suggest that as many as 90% of the exercise programs used today contain ac-

tivities that are detrimental to the anatomical structure and function of the athlete. Most of these physical activities can be corrected with simple changes in technique, such as adjusting the position of a joint. Other activities should be abandoned.

The science of coaching has progressed from a time when straight leg sit-ups and deep knee bends were a part of most exercise routines; yet, these potentially harmful activities are still being used.

Most coaches place considerable importance on strategy and game plans. However, carefully selecting and properly teaching physical activities for warm-ups, stretching, conditioning, practice drills and games, and cooling down is equally as important. The purpose of this chapter is to provide coaches with an understanding upon which to base the inclusion of physical activities in their training plans and to provide examples of activities that are problematic. A sound, fundamental knowledge of the do's and don'ts of exercise is essential in protecting the well being of young athletes.

REASONS WHY ACTIVITIES ARE CONTRAINDICATED

In general, contraindicated activities are exercises that are inadvisable to perform. Physical activities may be contraindicated for several reasons:

- They are likely to be injurious to bones, joints, ligaments, and muscles.
- They are potentially dangerous when improperly performed, supervised, spotted, or assisted.
- They may aggravate an existing physical problem.
- They do not achieve desired outcomes.
- They are not appropriate for a particular group (e.g., level of maturation, ability, experience, gender, or sport).

This chapter will focus on physical activities that are contraindicated because they pose a risk of injury.

THE ANATOMY OF JOINTS AND THE FUNCTION OF SKELETAL MUSCLES

The risks associated with contraindicated activities are usually related to the structure of joints and how they function. It is important to have some basic understanding of the anatomy of joints and the function of the skeletal muscles that affect a joint.

There are many types of joints and muscles. It is beyond the scope of this chapter to provide the specific characteristics of each. However, Figures 16-1a and b, 16-2 and 16-3 are included to assist you in developing a general understanding of the structure and function of joints and muscles.

A joint is composed of two or more bones and supporting structures that hold these bones together and limit their range of motion. Figures 16-1 and 16-2 are joints that are often implicated with contraindicated exercises.

Several structures should be noted. Figures 16-1 and 16-2 display joint capsules, consisting of strong fibrous sheaths that form a sleeve around the joints and hold the bones of the joints together. Some joints have supportive structures within the space of the surrounding joint capsule. In Figure 16-1b, internal ligaments tie the tibia and femur together and restrict their relative movements. Other joints have external reinforcing ligaments. The external ligaments in Figure 16-1a and 16-1b and the long ligaments in Figure 16-2 are examples of external reinforcing ligaments. Also, fibrous cartilage disks serve as shock absorbers between the bones and stabilize the joints by their contour to the bones of which the joints are comprised.

DEFINITIONS AND FUNCTIONS OF JOINT STRUCTURES

- **Bone**—supportive, rigid element of the skeletal system
- **Cartilage**—comes in three forms: *hyalin cartilage*—covers the surfaces of bones within joints; *fibrous cartilage*—found in disks between bones of some joints, and *elastic cartilage*—found in the external ear and larynx
- **Ligaments**—flexible, tough, fibrous tissue that connects bones of a joint together; sometimes surrounding a joint to form a *joint capsule*

Figure 16-3 displays the components of skeletal muscle. Individual muscles commonly span one or more

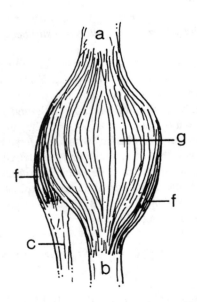

Figure 16-1a. Knee joint superficial tissues. Key: a-femur, b-tibia, c-fibula, f-external ligaments and g-joint capsule.

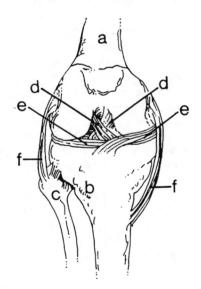

Figure 16-1b. Knee joint deep tissues. Key: a-femur, b-tibia, c-fibula, d-internal ligaments, e-fibrous cartilage disk (meniscus), f-external ligaments (medial and lateral ligaments.)

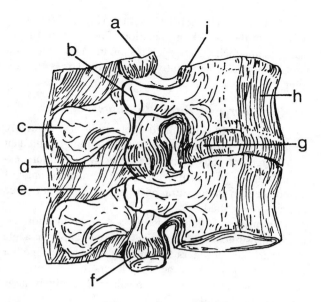

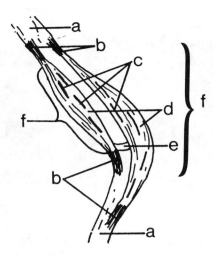

Figure 16-2. Vertebral joints (lateral view of two vertebrae from the left side.) Key: a-superior process, b-transverse process, c-spinous process, d-joint capsule connecting superior and interior processes, e-ligament between the spinous processes, f-inferior process, g-intervertebral disk, h-anterios long ligament, i-posterior long ligament.

Figure 16-3. Schematic drawing of skeletal muscle. Key: a-bone, b-tendons, c-stretch sensitive muscle fibers, d-regular muscle fibers, e-joint, f-belly of the muscle.

joints by attaching to the bones that compose the joint. By contracting (shortening), the attachments are drawn toward the belly of the muscle. This is the mechanism by which muscles move the bones of a joint. Muscles usually exist in pairs on opposite sides of a joint. If one muscle of the pair contracts and the other relaxes, this moves the joint in the direction of the contracting muscle. If the muscles within the pair switch roles, the opposite joint movement occurs.

DEFINITIONS AND FUNCTIONS OF THE COMPONENTS OF SKELETAL MUSCLE

- **Regular muscle fibers**—cells that compose the bulk of a muscle, contract when stimulated
- **Stretch sensitive muscle fibers**—special muscle cells scattered throughout the muscle, sensitive to a stretching of the muscle
- **Tendon**—strong band of fibrous tissue forming the termination of muscle and attaching muscle to bones
- **Belly**—central contractile portion of a muscle

RISK FACTORS OF CONTRAINDICATED EXERCISES

Risk factors explained in the following paragraphs are associated with exercises that may be used in prepara-

tion for sport. An understanding of these concepts will help you determine whether or not specific exercises may be contraindicated.

Forcefully Compressing Bony Structures, Cartilage or Nerves

Explanation—When anatomical structures are forcefully compressed, they may be damaged.

Example—Exercises that hyperextend (overextend) the back and neck may pinch the intervertebral disk, impinge on nerves, and compress the bony spinous processes against each other. The neck bridge is an example of this type of contraindicated exercise (Figure 16-4).

Stretching Ligamentous Structures

Explanation—Stretching exercises are done to lengthen muscles so that they are less likely to be strained or torn by activities in which a joint is moved through its full range of motion. On the other hand, exercises should not stretch the ligaments that hold a joint together. When ligaments are stretched, they loose their ability to maintain the integrity of a joint. The risk of injury to ligaments from an exercise is enhanced when the torque (turning force) on the joint is increased by the weight of the body and/or an external weight.

Example—The use of deep knee bends/squats in resistance training is likely to open the knee joint and stretch the internal knee joint ligaments by compressing

Figure 16-4. Hyperextended neck during wrestler's bridge.

the calf and hamstring muscles (Figure 16-5a and b). The area of contact between these muscles forms a fulcrum resulting in the internal ligaments of the knee joint being stretched apart.

Moving Joints Beyond Normal Range or Twisting Contrary to Normal Direction

Explanation—The bones of which a joint is composed have a natural direction and range of motion that is determined by how the bones fit together and the limits imposed upon the joint by soft tissues (e.g., ligament, joints capsule, and cartilage). Twisting of joints beyond their normal range and contrary to normal direction may result in injury to the bones and supporting structures that make up the joint.

Example—The hurdler's stretch (Figure 16-6a) especially in the back lying position (Figure 16-6b) is an example in which the knee joint is put in an unnatural and twisted position. This activity may also stress the hip joint.

Applying Force or Torque to Joints

Explanation—The rapid application of a relatively large force or torque (twisting force) to a joint is called an acute force or torque. It may lead directly to an injury, especially if the joint is at the limits of its natural range of motion or is in an unnatural position when the acute force or torque is applied.

Example—When assisting a partner in shoulder (pectoral) stretches, it is relatively easy to apply an acute torque to the shoulders by pushing the wrists together (Figure 16-7). The arms are long levers that magnify the force applied at the wrists to result in a relatively large torque at the shoulders.

Repeatedly Applying Force or Torque to Joints

Explanation—Relatively small forces or torques that are chronically applied to a joint may eventually lead to injury. This is especially true if the joint is at the limits of its natural range of motion or in an unnatural position when the force or torque is applied. In other words, repeated microtraumas may predispose the joint to an injury. It should be noted, however, that the activity at the instance an injury occurs is likely to be different than the contraindicated exercise that led to the injury. Therefore,

Figure 16-5a. A deep squat lift.

Figure 16-5b. Stretching the internal ligaments of the knee joint during a squat lift.

under these circumstances, it is difficult to associate the predisposing activity with the occurrence of the injury.

Example—If a distance runner performs the one leg standing hamstring stretch (Figure 16-8) on a daily basis as part of a stretching regimen before and after training, the hyperextension of the knee joints and accompanying stress on the ligaments of the knees, associated with repeated bobbing of the trunk, may eventually result in an injury to one or both knees.

Improperly Displacing Bony Structures

Explanation—Forceful muscular contractions have been known to cause a dislocation of a joint. For example, although unlikely to occur, the freely moving shoulder joint is susceptible to a dislocation from a forceful contraction of the chest (pectoral) muscles. Also, less forceful muscular contractions that are incorrectly applied may result in improper displacement of bony structures.

Example—In the straight leg sit-up, muscles that decrease the angle between the trunk and thigh (hip flexors) are active (Figure 16-9). A pair of these muscles attach to the sides of the vertebrae in the low back. During

each repetition of the straight leg sit-up, these vertebrae are pulled forward. This activity tends to increase the concavity of the low back and pinch the intervertebral disks. These results are not desirable. However, by performing bent knee sit-ups, the hip flexors become lax and less able to contribute to the activity (Figure 16-10), while the trunk flexors become more active. This eliminates the undesirable forward displacement of the vertebrae while increasing the desirable outcome of enhanced abdominal strength. This is an excellent example of how a simple modification can remove the contraindications and thereby enhance the desired outcome.

Forcefully Stretching Muscles

Explanation—From Figure 16-3, it is evident that skeletal muscle is composed of a contractile portion (the muscle fibers at the belly of the muscle) and a noncontractile portion (the tendonous fibers that attach the muscle to the bone). Either of these two portions can be injured if: a) sufficient force is applied to a muscle to stretch it beyond its natural range, or b) the muscle itself forcefully contracts against an external resistance. The resulting injury may be a muscle strain (commonly called

Figure 16-6a. Stretching and twisting the left knee during the hurdler's stretch.

Figure 16-6b. Back lying position during the hurdler's stretch.

Figure 16-7. Shoulder (pectoral) stretch.

Figure 16-8. One leg standing hamstring stretch.

CONTRAINDICATED EXERCISES 125

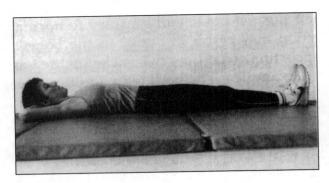

Figure 16-9. Straight leg sit-up (starting position).

Figure 16-10. Bent knee sit-up (starting position).

a muscle pull) from a tearing of some of the muscle fibers or a strained tendon. In severe cases, the entire muscle or tendon may be either completely torn (ruptured) or partially torn, or the tendon may separate from the bone by pulling its bony attachment with it (avulsion fracture).

A proper approach to any training session is to first warm-up the muscles through light aerobic and sport-specific exercises before stretching them. A similar approach should end a training session (light aerobic cool down of the muscles that were active in the training session, followed by stretching). Because it is difficult for a coach to determine whether or not exercises intended to stretch muscles are also stretching the ligamentous structures of a joint, exercise specialists have encouraged the use of the phrase: "Slowly stretch to a point of mild discomfort and hold the stretch." This tends to minimize the potential for a stretching exercise to become contraindicated.

Forceful bouncing or fast ballistic stretching is inadvisable because it activates the stretch-sensitive muscle fibers (see Figure 16-3) that aid in the contraction of the muscle (stretch reflex). These stretch-sensitive muscle fibers act as a protective mechanism against both a rapid stretch or an overstretch of a muscle. Thus, ballistic stretching exercises are contraindicated because of the potential for injury to muscle from forceful extension and because they facilitate muscle contraction when muscle lengthening is desired.

Example—The straight leg toe touch (Figure 16-11), used to stretch the hamstring muscles located at the backs of the thighs, is problematic because of the hyperextension imposed upon the knee joints. This exercise is even more questionable when performed by bobbing the trunk up and down. Ballistic straight leg toe touching increases the strain on the ligaments of the knees and may result in tears of the muscle fibers of the hamstrings. It also invokes the stretch reflex.

SPORTS SKILLS THAT ARE CONTRAINDICATED

Based upon an understanding of the risk factors associated with exercises, the back walkover in gymnastics, the deep squat position assumed by a catcher in baseball or softball, and the wrestler's bridge are only a few of the many sports skills that could be classified as contraindicated. Many other sports also have contraindicated positions or activities. You should evaluate the sports skills that are required for participation in the sport you coach to determine which activities are contraindicated. If some are contraindicated, the following actions should be considered:

Figure 16-11. Straight leg toe touch.

- Alert parents and players about the contraindicated activities so they can make informed judgments about the risks and benefits of participation.
- Plan and implement a conditioning program to protect areas of the body that are exposed to potential injuries from a contraindicated activity.
- Minimize the athletes' exposure to contraindicated activities.
- Seek to modify the rules of competition to enhance safety while maintaining the nature of the sport.
- Develop and/or use safety equipment to protect your athletes from the risks of contraindicated activities.

CONTRAINDICATED EXERCISES AND ALTERNATIVES

The following section contains an outline of information on contraindicated exercises associated with the knee and spine. Safer alternative exercises that achieve the same objectives as the sample contraindicated exercises are provided.

SUMMARY

This chapter has focused on physical activities that are contraindicated because they pose a risk of injury. Information was presented on the anatomy of joints and the function of skeletal muscle to assist the reader's understanding of the risk factors associated with various exercises. Emphasis was given to exercises that are contraindicated for the knee and spine. However, coaches should be able to apply the basic knowledge about the structure and function of joints covered in this chapter to additional physical activities in order to judge whether or not they are contraindicated.

SUGGESTED READINGS

Goodman, C. E. (1987). "Low Back Pain in the Cosmetic Athlete." *The Physician and Sportsmedicine*, 15(8): 97-102.

Levin, M., Lombardo, J., McNeeley, J., and Anderson, T. (1987). "An Analysis of Individual Stretching Programs of Intercollegiate Athletes." *The Physician and Sportsmedicine*, 15(3): 130-136.

Linsay, R., and Corbin, C. (1989). Questionable Exercises—Some Safer Alternatives. *Journal of Physical Education, Recreation and Dance*, 60(8): 26-32.

Lubell, A. (1989). "Potentially Dangerous Exercises: Are They Harmful to All?" *The Physician and Sportsmedicine*, 17(1): 187-192.

Reynolds, C. (1985). "Uses and Abuses of Flexibility Training." *Coaching Review*, 8: 37-41.

Staff. (1982, May). "Stretching and Flexibility." In L. E. Lamb (editor), *The Health Newsletter*, 19(10): 1-4, San Antonio, TX: Communications Inc.

Timmermans, H. M., and Martin, M. (1987). "Top Ten Potentially Dangerous Exercises." *Journal of Physical Education, Recreation and Dance*, 58(6): 29-31.

I. PROBLEM AREA: KNEE JOINT

A. Problem Activity—Hyperflexion (over flexion)

CONTRAINDICATED ACTIVITIES	INTENDED PURPOSES OF ACTIVITIES	SAFER ALTERNATIVES

CONTRAINDICATED ACTIVITIES

1. Hurdler's stretch (Figure 16-12)

INTENDED PURPOSES OF ACTIVITIES

Stretch the hamstrung muscles (back of thigh)

SAFER ALTERNATIVES

Seated straight leg stretch (Figure 16-13)

Standing bent knee thigh pull (Figure 16-14)

Lying hamstring stretch (Figure 16-15)

I. PROBLEM AREA: KNEE JOINT (*continued*)

A. Problem Activity—Hyperflexion (over flexion) (*continued*)

CONTRAINDICATED ACTIVITIES	INTENDED PURPOSES OF ACTIVITIES	SAFER ALTERNATIVES
2. Deep knee bend (Figure 16-16) 	To develop quadriceps (front of thigh), hamstrings, gluteal (buttocks) and back muscles	Half-squat or half knee bend (Figure 16-17) 
3. Lunge (Figure 16-18) 		Wall sit (Figure 16-19) 
4. Landing from jumps (Figure 16-20) 		
5. Deep squat lift (Figure 16-21) 		

I. PROBLEM AREA: KNEE JOINT (*continued*)

A. Problem Activity—Hyperflexion (over flexion) (*continued*)

CONTRAINDICATED ACTIVITIES	INTENDED PURPOSES OF ACTIVITIES	SAFER ALTERNATIVES

6. Squat thrust (Figure 16-22) Stretch quadricep muscles

7. Lying quad stretch (back lying position from hurdler's stretch) (Figure 16-23)

Kneeling thigh stretch (Figure 16-24)

8. Double leg lying quad stretch (Figure 16-25)

9. Standing one leg quad stretch (Figure 16-26)

I. PROBLEM AREA: KNEE JOINT (*continued*)

B. Problem Activity—Hyperextension (over extension)

CONTRAINDICATED ACTIVITIES

INTENDED PURPOSES OF ACTIVITIES

SAFER ALTERNATIVES

10. Standing toe touch (Figure 16-27)

Stretch the hamstrung muscles

Seated straight leg stretch (Figure 16-28)

11. One leg standing hamstring stretch (Figure 16-29)

Standing bent knee thigh pull (Figure 16-30)

Lying hamstring stretch (Figure 16-31)

I. PROBLEM AREA: KNEE JOINT (*continued*)

C. Problem Activity—Twisting or forcing knee joint into unnatural position

CONTRAINDICATED ACTIVITIES	INTENDED PURPOSES OF ACTIVITIES	SAFER ALTERNATIVES

12. Hurdler's stretch—
    see Contraindicated Activity 1

13. Standing one leg quad stretch (Figure 16-32)

Stretch quadricep muscle

Kneeling thigh stretch (Figure 16-33)

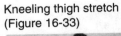

14. Hero (Figure 16-34

I. PROBLEM AREA: KNEE JOINT (*continued*)

C. Problem Activity—Twisting or forcing knee joint into unnatural position (*continued*)

CONTRAINDICATED ACTIVITIES

INTENDED PURPOSES OF ACTIVITIES

SAFER ALTERNATIVES

15. Standing straddle groin stretch (Figure 16-35)

Stretch inner thigh (groin) muscles

Seated straddle groin stretch (Figure 16-36)

Butterfly (Figure 16-37)

Lying groin stretch (Figure 16-38)

Elevated legs straddle groin stretch (Figure 16-39)

II. PROBLEM AREA: SPINE

A. Problem Activity—Forceful hyperflexion of cervical (neck) region

CONTRAINDICATED ACTIVITIES	INTENDED PURPOSES OF ACTIVITIES	SAFER ALTERNATIVES

CONTRAINDICATED ACTIVITIES

16. Yoga plow
(Figure 16-40)

17. Shoulder stand
(Figure 16-42)

INTENDED PURPOSES OF ACTIVITIES

Stretch back and neck muscles

SAFER ALTERNATIVES

Standing bent knee thigh pull
(Figure 16-41)

Alternate yoga plow
(Figure 16-43)
(Note that when lifting legs
from the floor to assume this
position, the knees should
initially be bent.)

Supine tuck (Figure 16-44)

Half neck circle (Figure 16-45)

II. PROBLEM AREA: SPINE (*continued*)

B. Problem Activity—Hyperextension of the spine

CONTRAINDICATED ACTIVITIES	INTENDED PURPOSES OF ACTIVITIES	SAFER ALTERNATIVES

CONTRAINDICATED ACTIVITIES

18. Wrestler's bridge
    (Figure 16-46)

INTENDED PURPOSES OF ACTIVITIES

Stretch neck muscles

SAFER ALTERNATIVES

Half neck circle
(Figure 16-45)

19. Full neck circle
    (Figure 16-47)

20. Partner beck stretch
    (Figure 16-48)

II. PROBLEM AREA: SPINE (*continued*)

B. Problem Activity—Hyperextension of the spine *(continued)*

CONTRAINDICATED ACTIVITIES	INTENDED PURPOSES OF ACTIVITIES	SAFER ALTERNATIVES

21. Donkey kick
(Figure 16-49)

Stretch quadriceps muscles and strengthen gluteal muscles

Kneeling thigh stretch
(Figure 16-50)

22. Full waist circle
(Figure 16-51)

Reduced waist circle
(Figure 16-52)

23. Back bend
(Figure 16-53)

Half squat or half knee bend
(Figure 16-54)

24. Back arching abdominal bend
(Figure 16-55)

II. PROBLEM AREA: SPINE (*continued*)

C. Problem Activity—Excessive lumbar curve or hyperextension of the low back

CONTRAINDICATED ACTIVITIES

INTENDED PURPOSES OF ACTIVITIES

SAFER ALTERNATIVES

25. Straight leg sit-ups
(Figure 16-56)

Strengthen abdominal muscles

Bent knee sit-ups
(Figure 16-57)

26. Double leg lifts
(Figure 16-58)

Reversed sit-up
(Figure 16-59)

17
Essential Medical Records for Athletes

Chris McGrew, M.D.

QUESTIONS TO CONSIDER

- What purposes do medical records for athletes serve?
- What are the essential medical records?
- Who is responsible for keeping the records?
- How should medical records be organized?

INTRODUCTION

Whenever medical care is involved, record keeping is very important. Medical records have been called the "glue" that holds the sports medicine system together. Without them, a comprehensive and cohesive program of care for your athletes' health will be impossible to maintain. Additionally, for reasons of legal liability, complete and understandable medical records are essential.

PURPOSES OF MEDICAL RECORDS

Medical records:
- Document the athlete's pre-season health status and fitness for participation and provide a baseline from which to compare future status if injury or illness occurs,
- Allow for better emergency care of the athlete when parents/guardians are not immediately available,
- Track the progress of an injured athlete during rehabilitation,
- Allow for better communication among those involved—the athlete and his or her family, coaches, nurses and physicians,
- Document injuries and actions taken to care for athletes;
- Protect the coach, athletic director, and school board against claims of liability, and
- Are useful in collecting information about trends in injuries so that decisions can be made about what changes can be made to help prevent or minimize injuries.

WHO IS RESPONSIBLE FOR RECORD KEEPING?

Maintaining medical records is usually the responsibility of the athletic trainer, if one is available. If your school does not have an athletic trainer, the responsibility will probably be delegated to the coach or a coach's assistant. The plan for maintaining medical records should be discussed with the athletic director and the team physician (or a community physician if there is no designated team physician). The school nurse should also be involved, along with any other health care providers associated with the school.

WHAT RECORDS ARE ESSENTIAL?

There are five essential medical records:
1. The Medical Information and Injury History Form (Supplement 17-1),
2. The Pre-Athletic Participation Examination Form (Physical) (Supplement 17-2),
3. The Medical Treatment Consent Form (Supplement 17-3),
4. The On-Site Injury Report Form (Supplement 15-3), and
5. The Physician's Referral Form (Supplement 17-4).

Additionally, if a training room is available, a system for keeping track of injured athletes and their rehabilitation is necessary. Documents for this purpose include:

- Daily Athletic Medical Record (Supplement 17-5) and
- The Summary of Season Injuries Form (Supplement 17-6).

Reviews of these forms are included in following sections of this chapter.

Pre-Season Examination Forms

Three records must be completed before the season begins:
- The Medical Information and Injury History Form,
- The Pre-Athletic Participation (pre-injury) Physical Examination Form, and
- The Medical Treatment Consent Form.

These three records should be completed before the first practice. An ideal time to distribute them is when the pre-participation athletic exam occurs (see Chapter 18, *The Pre-Athletic Participation Physical Examination.*) These forms constitute the baseline of information for the health care of your athletes.

Medical Information and History

This form (Supplement 17-1) should include basic information such as the athlete's name, address, and telephone number; the parents/guardians' work telephone number or the number to be called in an emergency; and the family physician's name and telephone number. It also should include questions about past medical conditions, injury, or surgery as well as illness or injury related to sports. It should have information on allergies, medications, and use of tobacco, alcohol, and other drugs; specific questions about family medical history; and any history of an unexpected sudden death in a close relative. The form should ask specifically if there have been episodes of passing out or fainting while exercising, concussions, and/or heat exhaustion/ stroke. Information pertaining to the athlete's insurance policy name and number should also be included.

The Medical Information and Injury History Form (Supplement 17-1) is written in language that is easy to understand by the general public. The form should be completed by both the athlete and his or her parent/guardian and signed by both. The form should be no more than one page, front and back. **This form is very important.** Fifty to 75% of the problems that will keep a child out of participation will be discovered through the use of this form.

Pre-Athletic Participation Physical Examination

This is the form (Supplement 17-2) on which the health care provider conducting the physical examination will record observations, as well as classify the athlete for participation. These forms usually require only the front of one page. The form should have space for appropriate identifying information (name, student number) and a place for recording height, weight, blood pressure and pulse as well as results of a vision test. The form may include extra space for special testing (body fat, endurance testing) according to individual situations. Finally, it should have an area for classification of the athlete for competition and recommendations of the examiner. The form should be signed and dated by the examiner.

The medical information and injury history, pre-athletic participation physical examination, and medical treatment consent forms for each athlete must accompany the team to all contests and practices.

Four copies of the medical information and injury history form and the pre-athletic participation physical examination form should be made. Copies should be given to the parents/guardians, placed in the school files, and held by the team physician (or physician who did the exam). But most importantly, one copy should be kept in a portable file that accompanies the team to all contests and is available at practice, if necessary. **These records are of no use if they are not available when needed.** One only has to walk into an emergency room in a strange town with an injured, upset 16-year-old to feel the frustration over not having essential information about past illnesses, injuries, allergies, medications, and insurance. Additionally, if a physician is doing a sideline exam, the information can be useful for comparison, for example, in the case of knee ligament laxity.

Medical Treatment Consent Form

This form (Supplement 17-3) requests parents/guardians to give permission for necessary emergency medical treatment if they are not immediately available. It repeats some information from the medical information and injury history form, such as telephone numbers, allergies, and insurance policy name and number. A copy should be kept in the travel file with the medical records.

Injury Report Forms

The On-Site Injury Report Form (See Supplement 15-3) and the Physician's Referral Form (Supplement 17-4) are used if an injury occurs. Copies should be sent to the athlete's parents/guardians, the athlete's school file, and the treating physician. Many schools use pre-printed triplicate self-duplicating forms so that the information can be entered once and the copies separated and sent to the appropriate parties.

On-Site Injury Report Form

In the event of an injury, it is important to provide appropriate first aid (see Chapter 15, *Care of Common*

Sports Injuries) and arrange to have the athlete treated wherever necessary. Afterwards, it is important that what happened and what was done to assist the victim is documented. The On-Site Injury Report Form (Supplement 15-3) includes information that identifies the athlete, the nature of the injury, how it occurred, what first aid was given, the place where the athlete was sent for additional care, information about protective equipment (was it worn, what was its condition), condition of the playing surface, and names of witnesses and their telephone numbers.

Physician's Referral Form

When a player is referred to a physician (or other health care provider) for treatment, a form (Supplement 17-4) on which the physician can record findings and recommendations is useful and necessary. It should include space for the history concerning the injury, findings of the exam, any tests that were ordered and their results, the diagnosis, and the plan for treatment. It should also include the athlete's current status for practice or play and any follow-up appointments, if necessary.

Injury Monitoring Forms

The next category of medical records covers ongoing monitoring of injured athletes and the collection of data concerning injuries during the season. Both are very useful in improving the overall health care of the athlete. An athletic trainer is most helpful in collecting this information.

Daily Medical Reports

All injured athletes should have daily reports (Supplement 17-5) of their status on file in the athletic department. Information about days lost from practice and contests missed should be recorded, along with information about current treatment or rehabilitation. The coach should be aware of which athletes are injured and their current status.

Summary of Season Injuries

A compilation of injuries that have occurred during the season can be quite useful (Supplement 17-6). Knowing what injuries have occurred and when they occurred may make it possible to note trends and related factors and then make appropriate changes to prevent or reduce the amount or severity of future injuries.

Instructional Forms

Although not "officially" a form, an instruction sheet (Supplement 17-7, Instructions to Care Givers) that can be sent home with the athlete, in case of injury, is very useful. This form should have pre-printed information concerning several problems such as injuries to the head, chest, or abdomen along with basic instructions on the first aid regimen of ice, compression, and elevation of sprains and strains. These forms should be provided so the team physician or the athletic trainer may give them to the athletes so that they and their families will have an idea of what to look out for in terms of warning signs of potential problems. These forms should also have appropriate telephone numbers of persons to contact in case of questions.

SUMMARY

A medical records system for athletes is a good idea for many reasons. It helps to upgrade the health care and rehabilitation of young athletes, improves the communication among those concerned with health care, and protects against potential problems of liability. Permission is freely given for copying and using any of the forms in this chapter or in Chapters 15 and 18. They can assist you and your sports medicine personnel in the care of your athletes.

SUGGESTED READINGS

Durant, R., Pendergrast, R., Seymore, C., Gaillard, G., and Donner, J. (1992). "Findings From the Preparticipation Athletic Examination and Athletic Injuries." *American Journal of Diseases in Children*, 146: 85-91.

Glover, D., Maron, B., and Matheson, G. (1999). "The Preparticipation Physical Examination." *The Physician and SportsMedicine*, 27: 29-34.

Magnes, S. Henderson, J., and Hunter, S. (1992). "What Conditions Limit Sports Participation?" *The Physician and SportsMedicine*, 20: 143-158.

Peltz, J., Haskell, W. and Matheson, G. (1999). "A Comprehensive and Cost-Effective Preparticipation Exam Implemented on the World Wide Web." *Medicine and Science in Sports and Exercise*, 31: 1727-1740.

Rich, B. (1999). *Preparticipation Physical Examinations*, American College of Sports Medicine (Current Comments), Indianapolis, IN.

Smith, J., and Laskowski, E. (1998). "Mayo Clinic Researches PPEs." *Mayo Clinic Proceedings*, 73: 419.

Supplement 17-1. Medical Information and Injury History Form.

Medical Health Questionnaire

Sport(s): _____

Date: _____

Name: _____

Last   First   Middle

Student Number: _____ Sex: **F** **M** Date of Birth: _____

Address: _____

Street   City   Zip

Mother's name: _____ Father's name: _____

Mother's Work Phone #: _____ Father's Work Phone #: _____

In Case of Emergency Contact...

_____ _____ _____
Name   Relationship   Phone

No _____ Yes _____ 1. Do you wear glasses or contact lenses?
          If "yes," which? Glasses _____ Contacts _____ Both _____
          If "yes," do you wear them during athletic competition? Yes _____ No _____

No _____ Yes _____ 2. Are the pupils of your eyes unequal in size?
          If "yes," which is larger? R _____ L _____

No _____ Yes _____ 3. Do you wear any dental appliance?   If "yes," which?
          Permanent bridge, permanent crown or jacket, removable partial or full plate.

No _____ Yes _____ 4. Are you on any medications?   If "yes," please list:
_____

No _____ Yes _____ 5. Are you allergic to or have you ever reacted adversely to any medication or anesthetics?
          If "yes," please list: _____

No _____ Yes _____ 6. Has anyone in your family died of heart problems or sudden death before age 50?

                       7. Date of last immunization: Tetanus _____ Measles: _____

                       8. Please check the appropriate box if you have had or presently are having difficulty with the following and explain and boxes marked "Yes."

	Yes	No		Yes	No		Yes	No
Scarlet Fever			Recurrent Headaches			Ruptured Hernia		
Measles			Recurrent Colds			Mononucleosis		
German Measles			Pneumonia			Rheumatic Fever		
Mumps			Eye Trouble			Surgery:		
Diabetes			Ear/Nose/Throat Trouble			Appendectomy		
Epilepsy			Abdominal/Intestinal			Tonsillectomy		
Gum/Tooth Trouble			Chronic Cough			Hernia Repair		
Tumor, Cancer, Cyst			Hay Fever			Other (list)		
Shortness of Breath			Tuberculosis			High/Low Blood Pressure		
Heart Murmur			Asthma			Recent Weight loss/gain		
Heart Palpitations			Allergy:			Paralysis		
Dizziness during exercise			Penicillin			Anemia		
Fainting during exercise			Sulfonamides			Sugar in Urine		
Pain/Pressure in Chest			Serum			Frequent Urination		
Insomnia			Foods (which?)			Skin Conditions		
Frequent Anxiety			Other (list)			Females: Irregular periods		
Frequent Depression			Gallbladder/stone trouble			Excessive Flow		
Worry/Nervousness			Recurrent diarrhea			Severe Cramps		

Supplement 17-1. Medical Information and Injury History Form (*continued*)

1. Have you ever sustained injury or illness to any of the following organs? If "yes," please indicate which organs and what the circumstances were.

No _____ Yes _____ a. Brain   No _____ Yes _____ h. Intestines
No _____ Yes _____ b. Eyes   No _____ Yes _____ i. Bladder
No _____ Yes _____ c. Ears   No _____ Yes _____ j. Spleen
No _____ Yes _____ d. Nose   No _____ Yes _____ k. Kidneys
No _____ Yes _____ e. Heart   No _____ Yes _____ l. Males—testicles
No _____ Yes _____ f. Lungs   No _____ Yes _____ m. Females—ovaries
No _____ Yes _____ g. Stomach   No _____ Yes _____ n. Other

_____

_____

_____

2. Do you have two functioning (working): If "no," please explain.

No _____ Yes _____ a. Eyes
No _____ Yes _____ b. Ears
No _____ Yes _____ c. Kidneys
No _____ Yes _____ d. Females—ovaries
No _____ Yes _____ e. Males—testicles

_____

_____

_____

3. Have you ever sustained a head injury involving any of the symptoms listed? If "yes," please give date of injury and sport.

No _____ Yes _____ a. Loss of memory   No _____ Yes _____ g. Blurry vision
No _____ Yes _____ b. Disorientation   No _____ Yes _____ h. Double vision
No _____ Yes _____ c. Dizziness   No _____ Yes _____ i. Tunnel vision
No _____ Yes _____ d. Mental Confusion   No _____ Yes _____ j. Loss of vision
No _____ Yes _____ e. Headaches   No _____ Yes _____ k. Skull fracture
No _____ Yes _____ f. Unconsciousness

_____

_____

_____

No _____ Yes _____ 4. Have you ever become ill from exercising in the heat? If "yes," indicate how often it happens and date of last episode.

No _____ Yes _____ 5. Do you want to weigh more or less than you do now? If "yes," explain.

No _____ Yes _____ 6. Have you ever taken any supplements or vitamins? If "yes," indicate what and when.

No _____ Yes _____ 7. Have you ever had a neck injury of any kind? If "yes," indicate if chronic or temporary, "pinched nerve," musculo-skeletal, and dates.

No _____ Yes _____   8. Have you ever had any history of back pain? If "yes," indicate chronic or temporary, location and dates.

No _____ Yes _____   9. Have you ever sustained a shoulder injury? If "yes," indicate type of injury: subluxation, separation, muscle or skeletal, and dates (Indicate right or left.)

No _____ Yes _____   10. Have you ever sustained a knee injury? If "yes," indicate which knee, time loss. If surgery was required, diagnosis and dates.

No _____ Yes _____   11. If yes to question 10, does injury still bother you? If "yes," indicate if locking or swelling is present.

No _____ Yes _____   12. Do you have weak ankles or recurrent ankle sprains? If "yes," indicate which ankle, severity, time loss, and dates.

No _____ Yes _____   13. Have you ever had an injury to the elbow, forearm, wrist, hand, or fingers? If "yes," indicate nature of injury, time loss, which body part involved, and dates.

No _____ Yes _____   14. Have you ever worn a special brace, or had modifications made in equipment worn? If "yes," indicate reason, duration worn, and dates.

No _____ Yes _____   15. Have you ever fractured a bone? If "yes," indicate which bone, if surgery was required, and dates.

No _____ Yes _____   16. Have you ever worn a cast for anything besides a fractured bone? If "yes," indicate reason, body part and dates.

No _____ Yes _____   17. Have you ever been treated for a mental condition? If "yes," specify when, where, and give details.

No _____ Yes _____   18. Have you had or have you been advised to have any operations? If "yes," describe and give dates.

No _____ Yes _____   19. Have you ever had shin splints? If "yes," indicate dates.

No _____ Yes _____   20. Have you ever had stress fractures? If "yes," indicate body part and dates

No _____ Yes _____   21. Have you ever passed out during exercise?

No _____ Yes _____   22. Have you ever been dizzy during or after exercise?

No _____ Yes _____   23. Have you ever had chest pain during or after exercise?

No _____ Yes _____   24. Have you ever had racing of your heart or skipped heartbeats?

List any muscle strains: groin, hamstring, quad or other. Indicate right or left. _____

_____

_____

List abnormalities on previous physical exams. _____

_____

_____

List other injuries you have had. _____

_____

_____

Have you ever been medically limited or disqualified from sports activities? If "yes,"
explain. _____

_____

_____

When was your last physical   Where?
exam?   _____   _____

When was your last dental exam? _____   Eye exam? _____

I hereby certify that I have completed this questionnaire completely and correctly to the best of my ability and knowledge. I certify that there are no previous illnesses or injuries that I have incurred, other than those I have listed on the preceding pages.

_____   _____
Mother's Signature   Athlete's Signature

_____   _____
Date   Date

_____   _____
Father's Signature   Athletic Trainer's Signature

_____   _____
Date   Date

Pre-Participation Examination Form (Physical)

Physical examination (to be completed by athletic medicine staff)

Name _____

Height _____ Weight _____ Blood pressure: Resting _____ After exercise _____

Pulse: Resting _____ After exercise _____

Visual acuity: Eyes (R) 20/ _____ **w/o glasses   (L) 20/** _____ **w/o glasses   w/glasses** _____/_____

	NORMAL	ABNORMAL FINDINGS
1. General	1. _____	_____
2. Skin	2. _____	_____
3. HEENT	3. _____	_____
4. Teeth (Dental examination)	4. _____	_____
5. Neck	5. _____	_____
6. Lungs	6. _____	_____
7. Heart	7. _____	_____
8. Breasts	8. _____	_____
9. Abdomen	9. _____	_____
10. Genitalia (hernia)	10. _____	_____
11. Back	11. _____	_____
12. Musculoskeletal	12. _____	_____
13. Peripheral pulses	13. _____	_____
14. Neurological	14. _____	_____
15. Mental status	15. _____	_____

Tanner Stage _____

Assessment

1. Clearance without limitation? _____

Sports _____

2. Clearance deferred? _____

Reason _____

3. Clearance with limitation? _____

Limitation _____

4. Disqualification? _____

Reason _____

Exam Date _____ Physician's signature _____

Supplement 17-3. Medical Treatment Consent Form.

Medical Treatment Consent Form

I hereby give permission for any and all medical attention necessary to be administered to my child in the event of an accident, injury, sickness, etc. under the direction of the persons listed below until such time as I may be contacted. My child's name is _____. This release is effective for the time during which my child is participating in the _____ program for the _____/_____ season, including traveling to or from competition. I also hereby assume the responsibility for payment of any such treatment.

Parents' Name: _____

Home Address (Street/City/State/Zip) _____

Home Phone _____ Work Phone _____ Work Phone _____

Insurance Company _____

Policy Number _____

Family Physician _____

Physician's Address _____ Physician Phone _____

My child's known allergies include _____

Please list any known medical problems your child has _____
_____
_____

In case I cannot be reached, either of the following people is designated:

Coach's Name _____ Phone _____

Assistant Coach's Name _____ Phone _____

Signature of Parent or Guardian _____

Subscribed and sworn before me this day of _____ 20 _____

Signature of Notary Public _____

THE INFORMATION PROVIDED HERE IS STRICTLY CONFIDENTIAL AND WILL BE TREATED AS SUCH. THE PURPOSE OF THIS INFORMATION IS TO BE ABLE TO TREAT THE STUDENT-ATHLETES OF _____ IN A SAFE AND TIMELY MANNER IN THE ABSENCE OF A PARENT.

Physician's Referral Form

Name: _____   Student Number: _____

Injury/Onset Date: _____   Examination Date: _____

Initial Exam: _____   Follow-up Exam: _____

Sport: _____

History: _____

_____

_____

Observation/Palpation: _____

_____

_____

Clinical Testing: _____

_____

Diagnosis: R L B   Ortho: _____   Illness: _____   Local: _____ Systemic: _____

_____

_____

_____

Further Evaluation: Lab Work: _____   X-rays: _____   Hospital Evaluation: _____   Other: _____

_____

Treatment/Management: _____

_____

Status/Comments: _____

_____

Medication, Substance: _____

Potency: _____   Dosage: BID TID QID

Other: _____

Examining Physician: _____

Athletic Trainer: _____

Daily Athletic Medical Record

Name _____ Age _____ Sport/Position _____

Injury _____ Trauma _____ Overuse _____ Reinjury _____

Practice/Game	Date	Activity or Rehabilitation	Treatment	Comments

Totals: Days Injured _____ Practices Missed _____ Modified _____

Physician Referrals _____ Diagnostic Tests _____

SUMMARY OF SEASON INJURIES FORM

Injury Type	First 4 Weeks	Middle Weeks	Last 4 Weeks	Total
1. Abrasion				
2. Back or neck injury				
3. Blisters				
4. Cramps				
5. Contusion				
6. Dental injury				
7. Dislocation				
8. Eye (Foreign object)				
9. Eye (Contusion)				
10. Fainting				
11. Fracture				
12. Head (Conscious)				
13. Head (Unconscious)				
14. Heat exhaustion				
15. Heat stroke				
16. Laceration				
17. Loss of wind				
18. Nose bleed				
19. Plantar fasciitis				
20. Puncture wound				
21. Shock				
22. Sprain				
23. Strain				
24. Other				
25. Other				

Do you see a trend?   YES   NO   **(Circle one)**

Page 1

SUMMARY OF SEASON INJURIES FORM

Steps to take to reduce injuries next season:

1. _____
2. _____
3. _____
4. _____
5. _____
6. _____
7. _____
8. _____
9. _____
10. _____
11. _____
12. _____
13. _____
14. _____
15. _____
16. _____
17. _____
18. _____
19. _____
20. _____
21. _____
22. _____
23. _____
24. _____
25. _____

Page 2

Instructions to Care Givers

CHEST/ABDOMINAL INJURY WARNING INSTRUCTIONS

Name: _____

Date: _____

Diagnosis: _____

You have sustained an injury to your chest/abdomen and must be aware of the following symptoms. If they occur, notify your physician immediately or report to a local hospital emergency room.

1. Nausea
2. Vomiting
3. Inability to eat or drink
4. Progressive abdominal pain
5. Progressive dizziness or fainting
6. Difficulty in urinating
7. Bloody or red urine
8. Progressive chest pain or difficulty breathing

For the first 24 hours, have a family member or friend observe you. Do not stay or sleep alone.

HEAD INJURY WARNING INSTRUCTIONS

Name: _____

Date: _____

Diagnosis: _____

You have sustained an injury to your head and must be aware of the following symptoms. If they occur, notify your physician immediately or report to a local hospital emergency room.

1. Double vision
2. Blurred vision
3. Nausea
4. Vomiting
5. Disorientation
6. Lethargy
7. Severe progressive headaches (mild headaches are to be expected)
8. Colorless fluid or blood coming from ears or nose
9. Slurred speech
10. Seizures or convulsions

For the first 24 hours, have a family member or friend observe you. Do not sleep alone. They should waken you every two hours during the first 12 hours to see if you can communicate normally (be able to answer simple questions: who are you, who are they, where you are).

See the reverse side for additional instructions.

ORTHOPEDIC INJURY INSTRUCTIONS

Name: _____

Date: _____

Diagnosis: _____

You have sustained an orthopedic injury to your _____.
The first aid care for this injury is:

R.I.C.E.—is done for 24 to 48 hours after the injury. This will prevent further injury to the area and will help you recover sooner.

R = REST—The body part injured should not be used after an injury. The length of rest needed depends on the severity of the injury. An injured part may also need to be immobilized during the rest period. After any prolonged length of rest, rehabilitation is necessary before returning to activity.

I = ICE—Place ice on the injured area. Place crushed ice in a plastic bag or towel and place over the injured part. ALWAYS PLACE A TOWEL BETWEEN ICE AND SKIN. Hold ice in place with an elastic bandage. Keep on 20 to 30 minutes. then remove. Repeat every two hours.

C = COMPRESSION—Apply pressure to the area with an elastic bandage. Do not apply bandage so tightly that circulation is impaired.

E = ELEVATION—Prop the body part above the level of the heart if possible.

Person or medical facility to contact in case problem symptoms arise:

Name/Facility _____ Phone Number _____

Attending physician _____

18

The Pre-Athletic Participation Physical Examination

Chris McGrew, M.D.

QUESTIONS TO CONSIDER

- What are the major objectives of the Pre-Athletic Participation Physical Examination?
- What types of examinations are acceptable?
- How often and when should the preparticipation examination occur?
- What is important to include in the preparticipation examination?
- How can the preparticipation examination be implemented?

INTRODUCTION

One of the keys to a successful season for any coach is to start with healthy athletes and to keep them that way. The cornerstone of the athletes' health is the pre-athletic participation physical examination (PPE). The PPE in the past was often a useless, cursory locker room examination done merely to fulfill a school's requirement. Knowledgeable coaches, however, treat the PPE with seriousness and respect so that it fulfills its purpose: to determine the health status of the athlete.

OBJECTIVES

The two primary objectives of the PPE are to:

1. Identify risks of injury or health and
2. Identify and determine necessary rehabiltation or additional evaluations that will lead to a safe return of the athlete to physical activity.

The major question to be asked (and answered) in the PPE is: Will the athlete be at a greater risk of injury or illness in the sport because of a health problem than would normally be expected? Some objectives of the physical exam are to:

- Determine the general health of the athlete,
- Discover problems that may limit participation (e.g., a heart problem),

- Discover conditions that might predispose the athlete to injury (e.g., wearing dental braces),
- Evaluate previous injuries and determine what rehabilitation is necessary,
- Bring attention to areas of weakness or imbalance to be corrected,
- Fulfill requirements of the state high school governing body,
- Assess the size and maturation of the athlete,
- Determine whether an athlete may participate despite a recognized problem,
- Recommend other appropriate activities if certain sports are restricted,
- Fulfill legal and insurance requirements,
- Introduce the athlete to the sports medicine system and/or reintroduce the adolescent to the health care system, and
- Evaluate the nutritional and emotional behaviors of the athlete and assess whether these may place the athlete at risk of injury or ill-health.

The interscholastic athlete's first physical exam uncovers most of the problems that will restrict participation in specific sports. Later on, as the athlete's career progresses, the findings are more likely to concern previous injuries and their rehabilitation. As a coach, you will see this natural progression occur as you become more familiar with your athletes over several seasons.

The PPE is not intended to be a substitute for the routine health care checkups that a child or an adolescent require, but rather, a means to screen for areas of concern, whether for illness or injury.

TYPES OF EXAMS

There are two main types of acceptable physical exams: 1) the individual office physical done by the patient's personal physician, and 2) a well-planned and organized station exam.

Individual Office Physical

The advantages of this type of exam include:

- The attending physician's knowledge of the athlete's past medical/injury history,
- An already established physician-patient relationship that allows sensitive issues to be discussed more easily, and
- Easier and more complete follow-up if problems are detected.

The disadvantages of an individual office physical may include:

- A lack of skill or interest on the part of some family physicians/pediatricians to do a sport-specific exam,
- A lack of consistency among the examinations, as administered by different physicians, for various members of the same team,
- An increased cost per athlete,
- A decreased interaction between the physician and coach,
- The fact that many young people do not have a personal physician, and
- A lack of a thorough understanding of the guidelines for approval of participation in athletics.

Station Exam

The other type of acceptable physical exam is the well-planned and organized station exam. This technique uses multiple personnel in a team approach to evaluate large numbers of athletes in a systematic way. Coaches, trainers, school nurses and physicians are organized in assembly line fashion. At the end, each examination should be reviewed in its entirety by a physician and recommendations should be made. The advantages of a station exam include:

- A probable lower cost per athlete,
- Greater consistency between exams,
- A probable higher detection rate of problems, and

- An increased efficiency.

Disadvantages may include:

- A loss of continuity of care and rapport with a personal physician,
- Missed opportunities to counsel youths on other health problems, and
- Reduced or incomplete knowledge of past medical/injury history.

The type of PPE will depend on several factors (e.g., your school's policy, community resources, and the local medical professionals' approach to the PPE). The key is to remember the basic objectives of the PPE, which should be adapted to your specific situation. In some cases, physicians will prefer to do the PPE in their offices on an individual basis. In this case, you may need to have access to a referral list for those students without personal physicians and investigate options for those students with economic hardship. In other cases, the physicians may prefer to set up mass station-type PPEs at their office, at local health clinics, or at school facilities.

The mass locker room exam, with all the athletes crowded in a small noisy space, with a physician doing an exam, and then moving quickly from athlete to athlete, is totally unacceptable and is *probably worse than no exam at all*. This practice should not occur and is soundly condemned.

For the sake of efficiency in attending to the main objectives of the PPE, all of these concerns cannot be addressed in the station exam. Perhaps, however, some "options or accessories" can be added by 1) having a reference list available for those who don't have a regular physician; 2) having the school nurse available after the exam is completed to discuss individual concerns on such topics as drugs, sex, and emotions; or 3) having information pamphlets on these topics available for the athletes to take home and read.

WHEN TO SCHEDULE THE PHYSICAL EXAM

Ideally, the PPE should be scheduled from four to six weeks prior to the sport season. This allows sufficient time for correction of deficits such as muscle imbalances or rehabilitation of injuries, but it also is sufficiently near the beginning of the season so that new problems may not have occurred. This approach is feasible if individual exams are scheduled with personal physicians or if resources are available for several station-type exams throughout the year.

However, in many instances where station exams are used, only one per year is scheduled, due to limited resources. In this case (and since in most schools the sport with the most athletes will be football), scheduling a station exam at the end of the school year or early into summer vacation will allow about six weeks before pre-season training sessions begin. Many schools may find it easier to assemble the athletes before summer vacation. In this case, athletes who may have missed the scheduled exam still have six weeks in which to arrange exams with their personal physicians.

However, if any injury or health problem occurs after the PPE and before the start of the season, the athlete should report it to the coach so the coach may determine whether a new examination is required. Also, before the start of the season, athletes should complete updated medical and injury history forms to be reviewed by the coach and team physician (Supplement 17-1).

FREQUENCY OF THE PHYSICAL EXAM

Ideally a PPE should be conducted at each level of entry into sports (e,g., junior high, high school, college). In intervening years, each individual should have completed an updated medical history to reveal any new injuries or health problems and an appropriate evaluation by the team physician, if necessary. The American Academy of Pediatrics recommends a health care checkup every two years between 10 and 20 years of age. Conceivably, the PPE could be completed with the athlete's general exam if an office-based physical exam is conducted.

Many state and school districts require a yearly exam and *you may have no choice in the matter.* In this situation, the station-type physical exam becomes a very efficient way to deal with masses of students.

Note that the first physical exam is likely to be the most important. This exam may be the athlete's first contact with a physician since he or she entered school. Subsequent exams tend to reveal less and less new information because of the "funneling" effect of the screening process. All of the PPEs are important, but the first exam upon entering a new level of competition deserves extra attention.

CONTENT OF THE MEDICAL EVALUATION

Medical Information and Injury History

The athlete's medical and injury history is the most important part of the process. Most of the problems will be discovered through the history alone. Impress upon your athletes that they should be very honest and thorough in providing this information. They should be helped by their parents or guardians and should refer to all past medical records. Supplement 17-1 (Medical Information and Injury History Form) is easy to complete, short, and written in easily understood language. Both the athlete and a parent or guardian should sign it.

The history form minimally should include questions concerning:

- Recent and chronic illnesses and hospitalizations,
- Sports-related and non-sports related injuries,
- Allergies,
- Medication—including over the counter substances and supplements,
- Drug use (including tobacco and alcohol),
- Family history—focusing on first degree relatives and others with pertinent cardiac histories,
- Menstrual history (if appropriate),
- Use of appliances (e.g., contacts, glasses, hearing aids, braces, orthodontics and so on),
- Last tetanus vaccination,
- Past problems with exercise (e.g., dizziness, light-headedness, chest pain, fainting), and
- Last visit to personal physician.

The history must be reviewed by the team physician and the trainer (if there is one). The importance of the history cannot be overemphasized—treat it seriously!

Physical Examinations

Emphasis is placed on a sport-specific exam (Supplement 17-2). The Pre-Athletic Participation Physical Examination Form focuses on the heart, muscles, bones, and joints. Minimally the examination should assess the following:

- Blood pressure,
- Pulse,
- Height and weight,
- Vision (use standard eye chart),
- Heart and lungs,
- Abdomen,
- Skin,
- Genitals/hernia,
- Muscles/bones/joints, and
- Physical maturity (stage of sexual development).

Lab Work

There is no need for any routine lab work such as urine testing or blood count during the physical examination. Any lab testing should be based on the physician's evaluation of the individual athlete.

Special Testing

You and the physician may agree to do some further testing as each examination and the demands of each individual sport dictate. Examples include:

- Conducting hearing tests,
- Determining body fat percentage (e.g., for a wrestler),
- Conducting endurance tests (e.g., a timed 1.5 mile run), or
- Conducting agility tests.

Assessment

Every athlete should be classified for sports participation on the basis of the physical exam. Participation should be specific for the athlete's type and level of involvement (e.g., junior high vs. senior high; intramural vs. varsity) and not just a "blanket" approval for any sport. Standard options available for the physician are:

- Clearance, without limitations, for the sport(s) desired.
- Clearance deferred, pending consultation with a specialist (e.g., a cardiologist), pending the use of special equipment or tests, or pending the rehabilitation of a previous injury (This option implies that clearance must be obtained upon completion of the recommendations).
- Clearance, with limitations, accompanied by recommendations for alternative sports (The athlete may not participate in the sport for which he or she was initially examined, but he or she may participate in all sports approved by the physician).
- Disqualification—no athletic participation.

The last option should rarely occur. The goal should always be to determine in what sports the athlete can participate and not to give a blanket disqualification from all sports.

The physician may include recommendations such as how to reach an acceptable body fat range in a wrestler or how to increase hamstring flexibility in a runner. These recommendations then can be incorporated into the athlete's training schedule.

FORMS AND RECORD KEEPING

A thorough discussion of the forms that are essential for an organized and efficient medical care system for athletes is found in Chapter 17—*Essential Medical Records.*

Comprehensive and accurate medical records are essential in establishing a cohesive record system. Identifying athletes at risk and monitoring their progress and clearance to participate is often difficult. Large numbers of participants and the variety of documents necessary to establish proper clearance requires an organized and efficient system. A standard form used for all athletes will help to ensure consistency of the medical evaluation.

Copies of the completed physical examination form should be provided to the athlete, his/her school file, a travel file and the team physician. Additionally, a travel file containing copies of all medical insurance for the athletes, medical treatment consent forms, and all pertinent medical histories should accompany the trainer or coach to all team functions, practices, contests and meetings.

Record keeping is most often the responsibility of the school's athletic trainer. If an athletic trainer is not available, the responsibility is often delegated to the coach or a coach's assistant. Utilizing any and all medical personnel to assist with this process (i.e. team physician, school nurse and so forth) will ease record keeping, improve organization, and maintain medical and school system requirements. School policy should clearly state that all medical records are confidential and designate who has access to the records and how their confidentiality is to be maintained.

SETTING UP A STATION EXAM

If the decision is made to use stations to conduct the physical examinations, preparation is necessary to ensure a smooth operation. Start planning early. Physicians, school nurses, coaches, trainers, athletic directors, principals, parents and athletes should be notified well in advance. Begin planning at least six weeks before the scheduled exam and notify all participants at least one month in advance of the scheduled date. Additionally, arrangements may be needed to reserve an appropriate facility. A school gym, cafeteria, or all-purpose room may be adequate. The facility should be:

- Convenient and accessible (reduces absenteeism),
- Well-lighted,
- Large enough to assemble the athletes for processing, and
- Have some quiet area (e,g., an office or screened-off portion) where the heart, lung, and abdominal exams may take place, and
- Provide tables on which athletes may lie for specific portions of the examination.

If the physicians in charge of the physical examination arrange for the facility (local hospital or clinic) and personnel, much of the work will be taken care of. In that case, your major responsibilities as a coach will be to:

- Make sure the medical and injury history forms are completed in advance,

- Notify the athletes where the exam will take place and make sure they get there on time,
- Make sure the athletes dress appropriately (gym shorts and T-shirts for boys, with girls adding a halter top, top half of a swim suit, or sports bra),
- Help maintain order while the exam is taking place (coaches and assistant coaches should be on hand to ensure an orderly environment),
- Discuss with the physicians any limitations or restrictions on performance, and
- Gather equipment for the exam.

Tables, chairs, clip boards, pens, tape measures, scales, vision chart, blood pressure cuffs, and stethoscopes are the main items of necessary equipment. Discuss with the school nurse and/or team physician exactly what is needed and where to get it. The examining physician in many cases will supply the needed medical equipment.

Format for the Exam Stations

The PPE should be set up with a flow pattern that ensures efficient use of time and space. An example of such a flow pattern includes:

- Check-in area. (As each athlete arrives, his/her name is checked off on a roster, then directed to a waiting area. Make sure athletes have their history forms with them).
- History review. (The history forms are checked for completeness and problem areas are noted. This can be performed by either the school nurse or the physician).
- Measurement of the athlete's blood pressure, pulse, height, and weight. (This can be performed by the nurse, trainer, or other trained person).
- Vision check. (Use a standard eye chart to screen vision. This can be performed by a nurse, a trainer, or other qualified person).
- Orthopedic exam (This should only be a screening exam that lasts approximately two minutes. This exam can be performed by the physician, physician's assistant or physical therapist).
- General medical exam. (This must be performed in a quiet, private area. Depending on the number of physicians available, the work may be divided into segments such as ears/nose/throat/neck and heart/lungs/abdomen/genitals. This is likely to be the slowest step in the exam process).
- Review of the completed form by the team physician. (Assessment for participation and recommendations are made at this time. Plans for follow up on the recommendations should be made and documented).

Other Tips

- Hand out the history form a few days early so that it can be completed by the athlete with the help of a parent/guardian.
- The stations should be clearly marked with signs and numbers. Coaches and teachers can be used to help direct traffic. Arrows taped on the floor or walls can "show the way".
- You may want the athletes to arrive in "waves" (e. g. every half-hour, if space is limited). Dividing athletes alphabetically or by class standing may be useful.
- Keep the process orderly, but not intimidating. The athletes should feel comfortable in asking questions and in sharing information about injuries and illnesses.
- Make attendance mandatory but expect some absentees. Have a back-up plan for those who miss the initial session.

SUMMARY

The medical evaluation of athletes plays an important role in their health and the success of the season. Treat the medical exam with the respect and seriousness that you would give coaching strategy. By remaining flexible and following the basic objectives, the PPE can be a useful and educational tool in your athletic program.

SUGGESTED READINGS

Bar-Or, O., et al. (1988). "The Preparticipation Sports Exam." *Patient Care*, 75-102.

Glover, D., Maron, B., and Matheson, G. (1999). "The Preparticipation Physical Examination." *The Physician and Sportsmedicine*, 27: 29-34.

Hunter, S., McCluskey, G., Blackburn, T., and Cole S. (Undated). *Physical Examination of the High School Athlete*. Columbus, GA: Hughston Sports Medicine Foundation.

Johnson, M. (1992). "Tailoring the Preparticipation Exam to Female Athletes." *The Physician and Sportsmedicine*, 20: 61-72.

McKeag, D.B. (1985). "Preseason Physical Exam for the Prevention of Sports Injuries." *Sports Medicine*, 2: 413 431.

Peltz, J., Haskell, W., and Matheson, G. (1999). "A Comprehensive and Cost-Effective Preparticipation Exam Implemented on the World Wide Web." *Medicine and Science in Sports and Exercise*, 31: 1727-1740.

Rich, B. (1999). *Preparticipation Physical Examinations*. Indianapolis, IN: American College of Sports Medicine (Current Comments).

Wood, R. (1987). "A New Approach to Athletic Physicals." *Journal of School Health*, 57(8): 346-348.

19
Special Conditions in Sports Medicine

Sudden Death Syndrome

Mark D. Carlson, M.D., M.A. and Jeremy Flynn, M.A.

QUESTIONS TO CONSIDER

- How common is sudden death among young athletes?
- What is meant by "sudden death?"
- What two steps are important to minimizing the risk of sudden cardiac death (SCD)?
- What action has the single greatest effect on the likelihood of an athlete surviving a cardiac event?

By participating in sports, athletes assume a number of risks, including that of death. Although it is impossible to prevent all fatalities, a better understanding of sudden cardiac death may assist in decreasing the number of casualties. The purpose of this review is to help coaches, administrators, athletes and medical personnel become more knowledgeable about sudden death in athletics and to use this understanding to design programs that minimize such risks.

OVERVIEW

When a well-conditioned young athlete dies while participating in a sport it impacts tremendously on teammates, coaches, medical staff and the community. The sobering story of the unanticipated death is highlighted in regional headlines. The athlete may have appeared to be in excellent health, having had no prior symptoms and passed physical examinations. When the tragedy of *sudden death* occurs in athletes, numerous legal and ethical questions arise. Most important may be, "What may have been done to prevent such a tragedy?"

Of the nearly 6 million high school and college athletes participating in sports every year, approximately 30 die suddenly (Maron, Shirani, Poliac, et al., 1996). Sudden death is rare and experts predict that only about one

in 100,000 to 300,000 young athletes die while practicing or playing a sport, with a preponderance of such deaths among males (Maron, Shirani, Poliac, et al., 1996). Because it is rare, a dilemma exists regarding what, if any, extra measures should be employed to identify athletes at risk for sudden death.

Sudden death is defined as nontraumatic death that occurs within a short time of the onset of symptoms. The duration of time between the onset of symptoms and death varies in the medical literature between 1 and 24 hours (Basilico, 1999). A commonly used definition in the medical literature is nontraumatic death occurs within 1 hour after the onset of symptoms. Death that occurs after prolonged resuscitative efforts (more than 1 hr) is also considered to be sudden. Death occurring more than 1 hour after the onset of symptoms is considered to be nonsudden. In athletes, sudden death often occurs during or shortly after intense physical exertion. After collapsing, death is almost instantaneous or occurs within a very few minutes (Maron, Shirani, Poliac, et al., 1996).

Mechanisms

During the last 20 years, improvements in equipment and rule changes have improved player safety and so decreased the incidence of traumatic sudden death. As a result, non-traumatic, cardiovascular sudden deaths now outnumber traumatic deaths in high school and college athletes by a ratio of 2 to 1 (Basilico, 1999). In the vast majority of cases, sudden death occurs as the result of a heart rhythm abnormality (arrhythmia). In these cases, sudden death is referred to as cardiac arrest or sudden cardiac death (SCD). Noncardiac sudden death may occur as the result of a stroke (a blood clot or hemorrhage in the brain) or pulmonary embolus (a blood clot in the lung).

Noncardiac sudden death is uncommon in young athletes. A slow heart rhythm (bradyarrythmia) or a fast heart rhythm (tachyarrhythmia) may cause sudden cardiac death. However, ninety per cent of sudden cardiac deaths (and almost all of those in young athletes) occur as a result of abnormally fast heart rhythms: ventricular tachycardia or ventricular fibrillation (tachyarrhythmias originating in the heart's main pumping chambers). Ventricular tachycardia is a fast (greater than 100 beats per minute), but organized, rhythm originating in the ventricles. Ventricular tachycardia can cause such symptoms as a fast heartbeat (palpitation), shortness of breath, and dizziness. When it is very fast, ventricular tachycardia can cause loss of consciousness or degenerate into ventricular fibrillation.

Ventricular fibrillation is a fast, disorganized rhythm that always causes sudden loss of consciousness. Ventricular fibrillation can occur spontaneously or as the result of ventricular tachycardia. Left untreated, ventricular fibrillation causes death within minutes.

Importantly, sudden cardiac death is very unlikely to occur in an athlete with a structurally normal heart. Most athletes who experience sudden cardiac death have an underlying heart abnormality, either structural or electrical, that causes the arrhythmia. Approximately 5 young athletes in 100,000 have a predisposing condition putting them at severe risk for sudden cardiac death (Liberthson, 1996).

Underlying Cardiovascular Disease That May Result in Sudden Cardiac Death (SCD)

The most common cause of sudden death in athletes is the presence of any of a number of cardiovascular abnormalities. The causes differ with regard to age. However, in young athletes, hypertrophic cardiomyopathy is the most common abnormality accounting for about one-third of sudden deaths (Maron, Thompson, Puffer, et al., 1996). Hypertrophic cardiomyopathy affects about one in 500 young athletes, and it is unlikely to be detected during a routine preparticipation physical examination (Basilico, 1999). Most athletes with hypertrophic cardiomyopathy do not exhibit symptoms.

The second most common cause of SCD is a congenital defect of the coronary arteries (the arteries that supply the heart with oxygenated blood). These defects take a number of forms including the absence of a coro-

nary artery or the abnormal origin of a coronary artery. If the malformation significantly limits the delivery of oxygenated blood to the heart, cardiac arrest may occur. Legendary basketball star "Pistol" Pete Maravich died suddenly due to the congenital absence of a coronary artery (Maron, Shirani, Poliac, et al., 1996).

Primary electrical abnormalities (heart rhythm abnormalities) may cause sudden cardiac death in the absence of any apparent structural abnormalities of the heart. The Wolff-Parkinson-White syndrome is caused by a congenital extra electrical connection between the heart's upper chambers (atria) and lower chambers (ventricles). This extra connection predisposes the individual to develop fast heart rhythms that have the potential to cause sudden death. Congenital long QT syndrome is an abnormality of ventricular repolarization (the time during which the ventricles recover after they are electrically activated and contract). When this interval is prolonged, individuals are at risk to develop a type of ventricular tachycardia called Torsades de Pointes which can cause loss of consciousness and sudden death. The Wolf-Parkinson-White syndrome and congenital long QT syndrome can often be detected on an electrocardiogram.

Sudden cardiac death in young persons may also occur in individuals with structurally normal hearts following a blunt blow to the chest (Maron, Poliac, Kaplan, and Mueller, 1995). Cardiac arrest may occur immediately following a blow to the chest wall by a projectile such as a baseball, hockey puck, or an opponent's shoulder, karate kick or football helmet during a tackle (Maron, Poliac, Kaplan, et al., 1995). Often, the blow is not perceived to be particularly forceful. However, such a blow may be lethal in certain individuals when it is delivered at a particular location on the chest during an especially vulnerable period of the cardiac cycle (Maron, Poliac, Kaplan, et al., 1995). Although rare, *commotio cordis* remains the number one cause of death in organized youth baseball (Abrunzo, 1991). During the last 15 years, 34 young athletes have died as a result of being hit in the chest by a baseball or softball (Consumer Product Safety Commission, 1999).

Older athletes (35 years and older), who die suddenly are more likely to do so while running or jogging, perhaps because they are less likely to participate in team sports. In these individuals, coronary artery disease, rather than hypertrophic cardiomyopathy, is the number one cause of sudden death. (Maron, Thompson, Puffer, et al., 1996).

Other cardiac conditions causing sudden death in athletes include, myocarditis, aortic stenosis, right ventricular dysplasia, mitral valve prolapse, and Marfan's syndrome (O'Connor, Kugler, and Driscello, 1998). Cocaine, anabolic steroids, and other drugs may also increase chances for sudden cardiac death (Rund, 1990).

Intense physical exertion and emotional stress may influence structural and electrical abnormalities in a way that predisposes athletes to experience sudden cardiac death during an athletic event. Therefore, sports that require high levels of intensity increase the risk to athletes with these abnormalities to experience sudden cardiac death. The sports of basketball, football, track and soccer have the highest occurrences of sudden cardiac death; baseball, swimming, volleyball and ice hockey follow these (Maron, Shirani, Poliac, et al, 1996).

The risk of male athletes to suffer sudden death is five times that of female athletes (7.47 per million male athletes per year vs 1.33 per million female athletes per year) (Van Camp, Bloor, Mueller, 1995). This difference may be explained by differences in the risk for cardiac disease, higher participation rates among males, different training demands, or cardiac adaptation (Maron, Thompson, Puffer, et al., 1996).

Age may also be a factor in the risk for sudden cardiac death. Older athletes (35 years and older) are more likely to have structural heart disease, which may put them at greater risk for sudden cardiac death. Approximately 1 in 15,000 joggers and 1 of 50,000 marathon runners suffer sudden cardiac death. Thus, the rates of sudden death in joggers and marathon runners are 3 and 8 times higher, respectively, than the national average of sudden death among all athletes (Thompson, Funk, and Carleton, 1982).

It is not certain whether race alters the risk for sudden death in athletes. African-American athletes suffer more frequently from hypertrophic cardiomyopathy (Maron, Thompson, Puffer, et al., 1996). Whether this translates to an increased risk for sudden death is not known.

MINIMIZING THE RISK

Screening and Pre-Participation Physical Examinations

Sudden death in young competitive athletes due to unsuspected cardiovascular causes has heightened interest in preparticipation screening (Pfister, Puffer, and Maron, 2000). There is a prevailing assumption that the standard preparticipation physical examination (PPE) identifies the predisposing factors for SCD in an athlete. The truth is that current screening procedures in American colleges and high schools are very limited in their effectiveness to detect potentially lethal cardiovascular abnormalities (Glover and Maron, 1998; Pfister, et al., 2000). A recent study found that only 25% of high school and colleges used screening procedures recommended by the American Heart Association's (AHA) guidelines for identifying athletes at risk of sudden cardiac death (Lyznicki, Nielsen, and Schneider, 2000; Maron and Strong, 1996; Glover and Maron, 1998).

A number of common pitfalls exist in the current format of many preparticipation physical examinations (PPE). Currently, no uniformly accepted national standards exist for conducting sports PPEs or certifying health professionals who perform these examinations. Decisions regarding PPE content are often made locally by school districts, resulting in a great variation in the way PPEs are conducted (Lyznicki, Nielsen and Schneider, 2000). In addition, often no training or accreditation criteria are required for health workers conducting PPEs. As a result, those athletes at risk for sudden death are less likely to be identified.

The American Heart Association states that a complete and careful personal and family history and a physical examination designed to identify or raise suspicion of cardiovascular abnormalities known to cause sudden death is the most effective means to identify individuals at risk (O'Connor, Kugler and Oriscello, 1998). The AHA recommends that pre-participation cardiovascular screening should be mandatory and conducted every two years for all athletes before participation in organized high school and collegiate sports (O'Connor, Kugler and Oriscello, 1998). Athletes who demonstrate abnormalities on either the history or the physical examination warrant a more detailed examination. This evaluation may include electrocardiography, echocardiography or other tests (O'Connor, Kugler and Oriscello, 1998). Appendix A describes AHA guidelines for identifying athletes at risk of sudden cardiac death. When an athlete is diagnosed as at high risk for sudden cardiac death, the physician should refer to the 26th Bethesda Conference guidelines to determine eligibility status (Mitchell, Maron, and Raven, 1994).

Signs and Symptoms That May Warn of Heart Disease

Athletes at risk for sudden cardiac death may not be identified by the preparticipation examination. Coaches and trainers should be aware of signs and symptoms that may herald the existence of heart disease and an impending cardiac arrest. Symptoms that may occur as the result of heart disease include: dizziness, light headedness, palpitation (the sensation of an irregular, forceful, or fast heart beat), chest pain (which may be described as pressure or tightness), shortness of breath, or inappropriate weakness (Maron, Shirani, Poliac, et al., 1996). Unexplained loss of consciousness (syncope) is a particularly serious symptom that demands immediate medical attention. An athlete who exhibits any of these symptoms should be referred immediately to a physician for further evaluation (Basilico, 1999).

The Role of Medical Tests

Either an electrocardiogram or an echocardiogram can diagnose many of the structural or electrical abnormalities that predispose to sudden death. Currently, the

American Heart Association recommends that an electrocardiogram and echocardiogram be performed if, as a result of the preparticipation examination, an athlete is determined to be at increased risk for sudden death. Some cardiologists have advocated that the preparticipation examination include an electrocardiogram. Whether this will prove to be cost-effective and whether society will bear the cost remains to be seen.

Cardiopulmonary Resuscitation and Automatic External Defibrillators

Athletes who are at significant risk for sudden cardiac death may not be identified by the preparticipation physical examination and also may not exhibit symptoms while participating in sports (Basilico, 1999). The first manifestation of a heart problem may be sudden cardiac death. When an individual experiences cardiac arrest, every second counts. Without oxygenated blood supplied to the brain, a person will die within a few minutes. Of the 220,000 people who experience cardiac arrest each year in the United States, only 3 to 5% (7,000 to 11,000) survive. That number could increase by as much as 50,000 per year if more people knew about and delivered the American Heart Association's "Chain of Survival" (Simons and Berry, 1993). The "chain of survival" is a sequence of actions, which, if properly delivered, improves the chance for survival. The AHA defines the "Chain of Survival" as follows:

1. **Recognition of early warning signs** (i.e. unexplained dizziness, chest pain, dyspnea, pressure, tightness, palpitations, shortness of breath, or weakness);
2. **Activation of the emergency medical system** (call 9-1-1);
3. **Basic cardiopulmonary resuscitation** (CPR);
4. **Defibrillation**;
5. **Intubation**; and
6. **Intravenous administration of medications** (Simons and Berry, 1993).

Trainers, coaches and team physicians should be trained in cardiopulmonary resuscitation (CPR) and in the use of automatic external cardiac defibrillators (Basilico, 1999). Individuals must have competent CPR skills in order to deliver effective therapy to an individual who has experienced cardiac arrest. If executed properly, CPR maximizes the chances of survival by delivering oxygenated blood to the vital organs, but it does not restore the normal heart rhythm. An electrical shock (defibrillation) is usually necessary to accomplish this.

Although all six steps of the "chain" are necessary, defibrillation has the single greatest impact on survival (Simons and Berry, 1993). The less time between collapse and defibrillation, the better. Immediate availability of an automatic external defibrillator (AED) and trained personnel at athletic contests involving high-risk sports decreases response times and improves survival rates.

Automated external defibrillators (AEDs) assess the rhythm of the heart and, when appropriate, deliver an appropriate shock to the victim's chest (Simons and Berry, 1993). AEDs are compact, portable, affordable, and easy to use. After attaching 2 patches to the victim's chest the press of a button causes the AED to analyze the heart rhythm and recommend (by voice command) whether a shock should be delivered. Another press of a button delivers the life-saving shock. Automatic external defibrillators have been proven to be accurate and effective, and they have become the essential link in the "chain of survival" (Simons and Berry, 1993), saving numerous lives in a variety of public facilities. It is recommended that AED's be available in locations where large numbers of people gather, including sports stadiums and arenas.

Before obtaining an AED, the team physician should investigate local and state regulations regarding emergency medical services (Simons and Berry, 1993). Several states have passed legislation that provides legal protection for those operating these devices. Potential first responders to a medical emergency (**including team physicians, trainers, and coaches**) should receive appropriate training (Simons and Berry, 1993). During training, participants learn to identify and respond to cardiac arrest, notify emergency personnel, retrieve and attach the AED, and follow directions for proper AED operation (Simons and Berry, 1993).

SUMMARY

Sudden cardiac death (SCD) is rare but tragic when it takes the life of a young athlete. Causes of SCD differ with regard to age, consisting mostly of, but not limited to, congenital cardiac abnormalities. Although it would be impossible to prevent all sudden deaths, proper preparticipation physical examinations (done in accordance with American Heart Association guidelines) may identify and disqualify athletes at high risk of SCD. Having an automatic external defibrillator on-site at athletic competitions along with adequately trained personnel heightens chances of an athlete's survival in case of a cardiac event. Immediate care and early diagnosis are essential to improving survival rates. With immediate utilization of the "chain of survival" sequence, death may be prevented.

REFERENCES

Abrunzo, T. J. (1991). "Commotio Cordis: The Single, Most Common Cause of Traumatic Death in Youth Baseball." *Sports Medicine*, 145: 1279-1282.

Basilico, F. C. (1999). "Cardiovascular Disease in Athletes." *The American Journal of Sports Medicine*, 27(1): 108-121.

Glover, D. W., and Maron, B. J. (1998). "Profile of Preparticipation Cardiovascular Screening for High School Athletes." *Journal of the American Medical Association*, 279(22), 1817-1819.

Liberthson, R. R. (1996). "Sudden Death From Cardiac Causes in Children and Young Adults." *The New England Journal of Medicine*, 334(16), 1039-1044.

Lyznicki, J. M., Nielsen, N. H., and Schneider, J. F. (2000). "Cardiovascular Screening of Student Athletes." *American Family Physician*, 62(4), 765-774.

Maron, B. J., Poliac, L. C., Kaplan, J. A., and Mueller, F. O. (1995). "Blunt Impact to the Chest Leading to Sudden Death From Cardiac Arrest During Sports Activities." *The New England Journal of Medicine*, 333(6), 337-342.

Maron, B. J., Shirani, J., Poliac, L. C., Mathenge, R., Roberts, W. C., and Mueller, F. O. (1996). "Sudden Death in Young Competitive Athletes: Clinical, Demographic, and Pathological Profiles." *Journal of the American Medical Association*, 276(3), 199-204.

Maron, B. J., and Strong, W. B. (1996). "American Heart Association Issues Nation's First Guidelines for Identifying Athletes at Risk of Sudden Cardiac Death." *NATA News*, 24-25.

Maron, B. J., Thompson, P. D., Puffer, J. C., McGrew, C. A., Strong, W. B., Douglas, P. S., Clark, L. T., Mitten, M. J., Crawford, M. H., Atkins, K. L., Driscoll, D. J., and Epstein, A. E. (1996). "Cardiovascular Preparticipation Screening of Competitive Athletes." *Circulation*, 94, 850-856.

Mitchell, J. H., Maron, B. J., and Raven, P. B. (1994). "26th Bethesda Conference: Recommendations for Determining Eligibility for Competition in Athletes With Cardiovascular Abnormalities." *American College of Cardiology*, 26(10), S223-S283.

O'Connor, F. B., Kugler, J. P., and Oriscello, R. G. (1998). "Sudden Death in Young Athletes: Screening for the Needle in a Haystack." *American Family Physician*, 57(11), 2763-2770.

Pfister, G. C., Puffer, J. C., and Maron, B. J.(2000). "Preparticipation Cardiovascular Screening for U.S. Collegiate Student-Athletes." *Journal of the American Medical Association*, 283(12), 1597-1599.

Rund, D. A. (1990). "Cardiac Arrest." *The Physician and Sportsmedicine*, 18(3), 97-105.

Simons, S. M., and Berry, J. (1993). "Preventing Sudden Death: The Role of Automated Defibrillators." *The Physician and Sportsmedicine*, 21(10), 53-59.

Thompson, P. D., Funk, E. J., Carleton, R. A. (1982). "Incidence of Death During Jogging in Rhode Island From 1975 Through 1980." *Journal of the American Medical Association*, 247, 2535-2538.

U.S. Consumer Product Safety Commission. (1999). "Youth Sports Deaths." *National Youth Sports Safety Foundation*.

Van Camp, S. P., Bloor, C. M., Mueller, F. O., Cantu, R. C., and Olson, H. G. (1995). "Nontraumatic Sports Death in High School and College Athletes." *Medicine and Science in Sports and Exercise*, 27(5), 641-647.

Appendix 19-1. Recommendations of the American Heart Association for Cardiovascular Preparticipation Physical Examinations.

1. A national standard is needed for preparticipation medical evaluations, including cardiovascular screening because of heterogeneity in the design and content of preparticipation screening among states. Some form of cardiovascular preparticipation screening is justifiable and compelling for all high school and college athletes, based on ethical, legal and medical grounds.

2. Cardiovascular preparticipation screening, including a history and physical examination, should be mandatory for all athletes and should be performed before participation in organized high school sports (grades 9 through 12) and college sports.

3. A complete and careful personal and family history and physical examination designed to identify (or raise suspicion of) those cardiovascular lesions known to cause sudden death or disease progression in young athletes is the best available and most practical approach to screening populations of competitive sports participants, regardless of age.

4. The examination is to be performed by a health care worker (preferably a physician) who has the requisite training, medical skills and background to reliably obtain a detailed cardiovascular history, perform a physical examination and recognize heart disease.

5. For high school athletes, screening must occur every two years, with an interim history in intervening years.

Cardiovascular History

Inquire about and seek parental verification of:

- Family history of premature death (sudden or otherwise).
- Family history of heart disease in surviving relatives, or significant disability from cardiovascular disease in close relatives younger than 50 years, or specific knowledge of the occurrence of conditions (i.e. hypertrophic cardiomyopathy, long QT syndrome, Marfan syndrome or clinically important arrhythmias).
- Personal history of heart murmur.
- Personal history of systemic hypertension.
- Personal history of excessive fatigability.
- Personal history of syncope, or excessive shortness of breath (dyspnea), or chest pain/disconfort—particularly if present with exertion.

Physical Examination

- Perform precordial auscultation in supine and standing positions to identify, in particular, heart murmurs consistent with dynamic left ventricular outflow obstruction.
- Assess femoral artery pulses to exclude coarcation of the aorta.
- Recognize physical stigmata of Marfan Syndrome.
- Assess brachial artery blood pressure in the sitting position.

SOURCE: Maron, Thompson, Puffer, et al., 1996; Lyznicki, Nielsen, and Schneider, 2000.

The Transmission of HIV and Other Blood Borne Pathogens in Sports

Sean P. Cumming, Ph.D. and Vern Seefeldt, Ph.D.

QUESTIONS TO CONSIDER

- What are blood-borne pathogens and how are they transmitted?
- What is the prevalence of blood borne pathogen infection in the United States?
- What is the risk of transmitting a blood borne pathogen through sports participation?
- Should athletes infected with blood borne pathogen be allowed to participate in organized sports?
- What precautions can coaches take to reduce the risk of transmitting blood borne pathogens in sport?
- How does participation in physical activity affect the health of athletes infected with blood-borne pathogens?

The occurrence of bleeding in athletic events predisposes athletes, coaches and athletic staff to the risk of becoming infected with blood borne pathogens (American Academy of Pediatrics, 2000). In order to minimize the risk of transmitting blood borne pathogens through sports participation it is important to understand what blood borne pathogens are, and how they are transmitted between individuals. The information in this chapter is designed to help coaches and athletic administrators develop appropriate policies and procedures to minimize the risk of transmitting blood borne pathogens in youth sports programs.

WHAT ARE BLOOD BORNE PATHOGENS?

Blood borne pathogens are viruses that may be spread between individuals through the infusion of body fluids, generally blood or semen. Although these viruses may be present in body fluids such as saliva, vomitus, tears, or urine there is little medical evidence to suggest that they may be transmitted through these substances. Blood borne pathogens are most commonly transmitted through unprotected sex, the sharing of IV needles, the receiving of infected blood products and from infected mothers to their children.

The pathogens that cause the most common concern are the human immunodeficiency virus (HIV), hepatitis B (HBV) and hepatitis C (HCV). The human immunodeficiency virus attacks the individual's immune system, reducing the ability to fight off further infection and may lead to the development of acquired immunodeficiency syndrome (AIDS). Symptoms of the HIV virus include tiredness, fever, diarrhea, night sweats, swollen glands, and loss of appetite. However, because the incubation time of the HIV virus may vary from six months to ten years or more, carriers may feel well and exhibit no symptoms. Hepatitis is an inflammatory process in the liver that and is caused by several viruses, including HBC and HCV. Chronic infection with Hepatitis C and B is associated with liver cirrhosis and liver cancer. Common symptoms of Hepatitis B infection include fever, nausea, loss of appetite, jaundice and abdominal pain. Chronic infection with Hepatitis C is generally mild and asymptomatic.

WHAT IS THE PREVALENCE OF HIV, HBV AND HCV INFECTION IN THE UNITED STATES?

The Centers for Disease Control (CDC; December, 1999) report that 396,239 U.S. citizens, 5,305 of which are below 13 years of age, are currently living with HIV infection or AIDS. Recent estimates, however, suggest that between 650,000 to 900,000 US citizens are now living with HIV, with a least 40,000 new cases occurring each year (CDC, 1998). The prevalence of HBV and HCV in the United States is much greater than that of HIV, however the incidence of both HBV and HCV infections are on the decline. The Centers for Disease Control (2000) estimate that 1 to 1.25 million US citizens are chronically infected with HBV, with approximately 140,000 to 320,000 new infections being diagnosed each year. Estimates suggest that 3.9 million (1.8%) US citizens are currently infected with HCV, of whom 2.7 million are chronically infected. Approximately, 36,000 new cases of HCV are diagnosed each year.

WHAT IS THE RISK OF TRANSMITTING A BLOOD BORN PATHOGEN IN ATHLETIC EVENTS?

The risk of transmitting a blood borne pathogen via skin or mucous membrane exposure to bodily fluids in an athletic event is extremely small (American Academy of Pediatrics, 2000). A recent study of on the field bleeding injuries in professional football concluded that the potential risk of transmitting HIV through player contact was less than 1 per 85 million game contacts (Brown, Drotman, Chu, Brown, and Knowlan, 1995). The reason why the risk of infection is so low is because the viruses associated with HIV, HBV, and HCV are very fragile and cannot survive outside of the body for very long due to exposure to air and differences in temperature.

The risk of transmitting a blood-borne pathogen through athletic participation varies with the nature of the virus, the sport and the population involved. Due to higher concentrations in the blood Hepatitis B is more readily transmitted through blood exposure than HIV. Although less medical knowledge on the Hepatitis C is available, it appears that this virus can also be transmitted efficiently though blood exposure (American Medical Society for Sports Medicine and the American Academy of Sports Medicine, 1995).

According to the US Olympic Committee the greatest risk of transmission of a blood borne pathogen occurs in sports that involve a high degree of physical contact (e.g., football, and rugby) or combat (e.g., tae kwon do, wrestling, and boxing). The increased risk of infection is primarily due to the increased likelihood of bleeding in these sports. However, as of present, no medically documented cases of HIV transmission have been reported in any of the sports identified as high risk. Due to the increased likelihood of infection through sexual contact or drug use, the risk transmission is also greater in adolescent athletes than it is in younger athletes.

Presently, there has been only one medically documented case of possible HIV infection through sport participation (Torre, Sampietro, Ferraro, Zeroli, and Speranza, 1990). This infection was diagnosed in a recreational Italian soccer game when a player collided with an opponent that was HIV infected. Public health officials, however, were unable to establish the collision as the source of infection.

Two cases of HBV transmission through athletic participation have been medically documented. One transmission was diagnosed among a group of Japanese sumo wrestlers, one of whom had tested positive for the Hepatitis B surface antigen and the hepatitis B antigen (Kashiwagi, Hayashi, Ikematsu, Nishigori, Ishihara, and Kaji, 1982). The infected wrestler identified as the source of the transmission was reported to have had numerous scars on his extremities and to have frequently bled from injuries sustained during bouts of wrestling. A second HBV epidemic was reported in Swedish orienteering athletes (Ringertz and Zetterberg, 1967). Although, epidemiologists were unable to identify the source of transmission they concluded that the most likely route of infection was through the shared use of blood-contaminated water to clean wounds caused by branches and thorns.

ETHICAL AND LEGAL ISSUES

The risk of transmitting blood borne pathogens through athletic participation has raised a number of ethical and legal concerns for coaches and athletic administrators. The issues of primary concern are whether or not infected athletes should be allowed to participate in contact sports, and whether or not athletes should be subjected to mandatory testing for blood borne pathogens.

Under the auspices of the Americans with Disabilities Act of 1990 and the Rehabilitation Act of 1973, the United States Supreme Court (1987) ruled that excluding a person with a contagious disease from an activity without medical justification violates federal law (Mitten, 1994). In order to exclude infected athletes an organization must provide medical evidence to indicate that the infection poses a significant risk to other players or that the infected athlete, because of their condition, is not able to cope with the demands of the sport. A number of lower federal courts have ordered the exclusion of HIV infected athletes from participation in school sponsored contact sports. However, as these cases failed to specify any particular sports or cite any medical authorities to justify their reasons for excluding HIV infected athletes, it is unlikely that they would have been upheld if they had been taken to the United States Supreme Court (Mitten, 1994).

Although the risk of becoming infected with a blood borne pathogen through athletic participation is extremely low, the possibility of infection has initiated a debate with regard to whether or not athletes should be subjected to mandatory testing for viruses such as HIV. Proponents of mandatory testing argue that testing provides athletes with the opportunity to begin their treatment earlier and take appropriate actions to reduce the risk of infecting others. Further, it provides non-infected players and training staff with the opportunity to protect themselves from possible infection.

Although mandatory testing might reduce the risks of infection through sports participation its benefits must be weighed against a number of ethical, financial and legal concerns. The financial cost and logistics associated with conducting a mass screening of athletes at all levels would be overwhelming. Opponents of mandatory testing have raised the questions of who will pay for mandatory testing, how frequently should it occur, and at what age will testing will begin.

Opponents of mandatory testing for blood borne pathogens in sport have also voiced concerns with regards to the ramifications associated with positive tests and the issue of medical confidentiality. Critics argue that such procedures violate the athlete's privacy rights as guaranteed by the Fourth Amendment of the U.S. Constitution. The confidentiality of the patient must be maintained and dictated by medical ethics and legal statutes. If an athlete is diagnosed as HIV positive who would have access to the results and to what extent would the athlete be guaranteed protection from public exposure? How would knowledge of a positive test influence the manner in which coaches, staff and athletes treat an infected athlete? As previously indicated under the auspices of the Americans with disabilities act (1990) and the Rehabilitation act (1973) it is illegal to exclude a person with a contagious disease from an activity without medical justification.

Most courts in the United States will only uphold mandatory testing for individuals who present a high risk of transmitting blood borne pathogens. As the risk of transmitting blood borne pathogens through athletic participation is extremely low, the occurrence of mandatory testing in sport is relatively rare. Only in boxing, where the incidence of bleeding occurs relatively frequently, is mandatory testing for blood borne pathogens conducted. At the present time most physicians and the medical authorities (i.e., AMSSM, AASM, and AAP) are against the implementation of mandatory testing for blood borne pathogens in sport.

DEVELOPING APPROPRIATE POLICIES AND PROCEDURES TO MINIMIZE THE RISK OF TRANSMITTING BLOOD BORNE PATHOGENS

There are a number of measures that can be taken on and off the field to reduce the risk of transmitting blood borne pathogens, without excluding those athletes who are infected. The following recommendations are based upon American Academy of Pediatricians position statement on the transmission of blood borne pathogens in sport (2000).

The following measures are designed to reduce the risk of transmission and infection of blood borne pathogens outside the athletic arena.

- Pediatricians or physicians should educate athletes infected with HIV, HBV, or HCV on the nature of their infection and the risk that it poses to themselves and other athletes. Infected athletes should be encouraged to participate in sports that place both themselves and other athletes at no significant risk.

- Athletic programs should educate athletes and their parents on their policies and procedures with regard to the transmission of blood borne pathogens. Athletes and parents should also be educated on the nature of blood born pathogens and the risk of transmission through athletic activity.

- All athletes and staff of athletic programs that are at risk from exposure to blood, as an occupational hazard should be encouraged to receive immunization for HBV. More than 95% of those who receive this immunization will be protected against infection.

- All coaches and athletic trainers should be certified in first aid and emergency care and be trained in the prevention of transmission of blood-borne pathogens in the athletic setting.

- Athletes should be educated about the greater risks of transmission of HIV and other blood-borne pathogens through sexual activity and needle sharing during the illicit use of drugs, including anabolic steroids and the precautions that should be taken to avoid transmission. Athletes should be told not to share personal items, such as razors, toothbrushes, and nail clippers that might be contaminated with blood.

- Schools must comply with Occupational Safety and Health Administration (OSHA) regulations regarding the prevention of the transmission of blood-borne pathogens.

The following precautions should be adopted in sports with direct body contact and other sports in which an athlete's blood or other bodily fluids visibly tinged with blood may contaminate the skin or mucous membranes of other participants or staff members of the athletic program. Even if these precautions are adopted, the risk that a participant or staff member may become infected with a blood-borne pathogen in the athletic setting will not be entirely eliminated.

- Athletes' and caregivers' cuts, abrasions, wounds, or other areas of broken skin should be covered with an occlusive dressing before and during participation.

- Caregivers should wear disposable, water impervious vinyl or latex gloves when treating athletes with bleeding injuries or handling equipment that may have been contaminated with blood. Hands should be cleaned with soap and water or an alcohol based antiseptic handwash as soon as possible after gloves are removed.

- Athletes who are actively bleeding should be removed from competition as soon as possible and the bleeding stopped. Wounds should be cleaned with soap and water. If soap and water are unavailable skin antiseptics can be used. Wounds must be securely covered with an occlusive dressing before the athlete can return to competition.

- Athletes should be encouraged to report any injuries or wounds prior to and during competition. Injuries during competition should be reported immediately.
- Cuts or abrasions that are bleeding should be treated immediately. Any wounds that are not bleeding should be cleaned and covered during scheduled breaks. Any equipment or uniform that is wet with blood, should be immediately replaced or cleaned and disinfected.
- All equipment or playing areas that are contaminated with blood must be cleaned immediately with a germicide solution containing one part bleach in ten parts water. After a minimum contact time of thirty seconds with the germicide solution the equipment or area should be wiped dry with a disposable cloth or be allowed to air dry.
- In the case of serious or life threatening injuries emergency care should not be delayed because gloves or other protective equipment is not available. Equipment such as towels or clothing may be used to cover the wounds until appropriate equipment is available.
- Athletic staff should provide breathing (Ambu) bags and oral airways are available for the purpose of resuscitation. Only when no such equipment is available should caregivers employ mouth-to-mouth resuscitation.
- All those involved in the maintenance of athletic equipment (e.g., equipment handlers, laundry personnel, and janitorial staff) should be educated on the appropriate procedures for handling garments and materials that have been contaminated with blood.

In response to concerns regarding the potential transmission of blood-borne pathogens through athletic activity a number of manufacturers have designed user specific first aid kits for the safe containment and disposal of blood spills. The kits can be purchased from most companies dealing in medical, health or safety supplies and generally contain latex gloves, disposable towels, germicidal contamination cloths, granular fluid absorbers, disinfectant hand wipes, and red bio-hazardous waste disposal bags

WHAT IS THE RISK OF PARTICIPATING IN PHYSICAL ACTIVITY FOR AN ATHLETE INFECTED WITH A BLOOD BORNE PATHOGEN?

As a coach it is important to consider the impact of exercise upon the physical health of athletes infected

with blood borne pathogens. Presently, there is no evidence to suggest that participation in physical activity, as long as it is not exhaustive, does not adversely effect the physical health of athletes infected with HIV. In fact, some research suggests that participation in moderate aerobic exercise may provide a boost to the immune system helping it fight off other viruses. Opinions are mixed with regard to the health benefits of moderate exercise for those infected with hepatitis B and C. The majority of research suggests that light to moderate amounts of exercise may reduce or delay the onset of many of the symptoms associated with infection. However, some sources claim that no amount of aerobic or anaerobic exercise will alter the course of Hepatitis infections.

As the coach or parent of an athlete infected with HIV, HBV or HCV it is important to consider the physical demands of the sport involved and the physical capacity of the athlete. If you are unsure about an athlete's capacity to meet the demands of a specific sport or physical activity it may be of value to consult with a physician and the activity instructor. Elite level competitive sports that demand high levels of physical exertion and conditioning (e.g., swimming, track, cross-country, cycling) may place an athlete infected with HIV, HBV or HCV at some physical risk. Alternative activities that are less competitive or less physically intense may provide more opportunity for infected athletes to participate at their own levels and may be more appropriate from a health perspective.

REFERENCES

American Academy of Pediatrics. (2000). "Human Immunodeficieincy Virus and Other Blood Borne Pathogens in the Athletic Setting." *Pediatrics*, 104(6): 1400-1403.

American Medical Society for Sports Medicine and American Academy of Sports Medicine, (1995). "Human Immunodeficiency Virus and Other Blood-Borne Pathogens in Sports: Joint Position Statement." *Clinical Journal of Sports Medicine*, 5: 199-204.

Brown, L. S. Jnr., Drotman, D. P., Chu, A., Brown, C. L. Jnr., and Knowlan, D. (1995). "Bleeding Injuries in Professional Football: Estimating the Risk for HIV Transmission." *Annals of Internal Medicine*, 122(4): 271-4.

Kashiwagi, S., Hayashi, J., Ikematsu,H., Nishigori, S., Ishihara, and Kaji, M. (1982). "An Outbreak Of Hepatitis B in Members of a High School Sumo Wrestling Club." *Journal of American Medical Association*, 248: 213-4.

Mast, E. E., Goodman, R. A., Bond, W. W., Favero, M. S., and Drotman, D. P. (1995). "Transmission of Blood Borne Pathogens During Sports: Risk and Prevention." *Annals of Internal Medicine*, 122(4): 283-5.

Mitten, M. J., (1994). "Athletic Participation With a Contagious Blood-Borne Disease." *Clinical Journal of Sport Medicine*, 5: 153-154.

Ringertz, O., and Zetterberg, B., (1967). "Serum Hepatitis Among Swedish Track Finders: An Epidemiologic Study." *New England Journal of Medicine*, 276: 540-6.

Torre, D., Sampietro, C., Ferraro, G., Zeroli, C., and Speranza, F. (1990). "Transmission of HIV-1 Infection Via Sports Injury [Letter]." *Lancet*, 335: 1105.

Lightning Safety

Sean P. Cumming, Ph.D. and Vern Seefeldt, Ph.D.

QUESTIONS TO CONSIDER

- How does lightning occur?
- What is the likelihood of being struck by lightning?
- What are the warning signs for lightning?
- What information sources are available to help predict the occurrence of lightning?
- What precautions can I take to reduce the threat of lightning?
- What should I do when somebody for whom I am responsible has been hit by lightning?

The purpose of this chapter is to provide the reader with a basic understanding of how lightning occurs, the dangers it poses, and how to develop an appropriate policy for lightning safety in youth sports. Information from this chapter is drawn from current research and position statements from the National Association of Athletic Trainers (NATA), the National Oceanic and Atmospheric Administration (NOAA) National Weather Service, and the National Lightning Safety Institute (NLSI).

WHAT IS LIGHTNING AND HOW DOES IT OCCUR?

Lightning occurs when rising and descending air within a thunderstorm separates negative and positive charges. As the charges become separated there is a build up and dispersion of electrical energy. Positively charged ice crystals form at the top of the clouds while negatively charged raindrops form at the bottom of the clouds. The ground below becomes positively charged. Lightning occurs when the attraction between the opposite charges becomes strong enough to overcome the air's resistance to electrical flow. The lightning flash originates at the negatively charged base of the cloud and may travel vertically or horizontally. This leads to the formation of different types of lightning, including cloud to air, cloud to cloud, and cloud to ground strikes. Cloud to ground strikes, which pose the most danger to humans, occur when the negative charge at the base of the cloud is attracted to a positive charge on the surface of the earth.

WHAT IS THE LIKELIHOOD OF BEING STRUCK BY LIGHTNING?

The chances of being struck by lightning are considered remote. However, according to the National Sever Storms Laboratory lightning is the second most frequent weather related killer in the United States (Osinski, 2000). Recent summaries of lightning casualties estimate that over 500 people are struck by lightning every year in the United States.

The likelihood of being struck by lightning varies with the seasons, the time of day, and where one is situated, geographically. Lightning is most likely to occur during the spring and summer months and during the afternoon or evening hours. However, lightning may occur year round and any time of the day. Because many youth sports and outdoor activities occur in the spring and summer months and are held in the afternoons and evenings it is important, as a coach or athletic administrator, to recognize the danger of lighting.

In the United States lightning is most likely to occur in the Southern and Central states and is least likely in the West Coast (Osinski, 2000). Data from the National Severe Storms Laboratory indicate that from 1959 to 1994 the States of Florida, Michigan, Pennsylvania, North Carolina, and New York led the nation in lightning deaths and injuries (Walsh, Hanley, Graner, Beam, and Bazluki, 1997). A survey of lightning victims in central Florida indicated that those struck by lightning were most frequently near or in the water, or in the vicinity of trees (Holle, Lopez, and Ortiz, 1993). A similar survey of lightning victims in Colorado found that most victims had been climbing or hiking in the mountains (Lopez, Holle, and Heitkamp, 1995). Because many youth sports and outdoor activities take place in the vicinity of trees, water or at places of high elevation it is important to be aware of these risk factors.

WHAT ARE THE WARNING SIGNS FOR LIGHTNING?

There are a number of environmental clues that may signal the approach of a thunderstorm. Warm, humid conditions are favorable for the development of thunderstorms because strong updrafts feed warm, moist air into thunderstorms. If the air is very unstable, severe thunderstorms with damaging winds, large hail, and sometimes tornadoes may occur. When skies darken or thunderstorms have been forecast sports administrators or coaches should look and listen for increases in wind speed, flashes of lightning, or the sound of thunder. By counting the amount of time between the flash of lightning and the sound of accompanying thunder it is possible to estimate your distance from the storm and the direction in which the storm is travelling. The method used to calculate your distance from the storm is known as the flash-to-bang method. The National Athletic Trainer's Association (2000) offers the following recommendations for using the flash-to-bang method:

To use the flash-to-bang method, begin counting when sighting a lightning flash. Counting is stopped when the associated bang (thunder) is heard. Divide this count by five to determine the distance to the lightning flash (in miles). For example, a flash-to-bang count of thirty seconds equates to a distance of six miles. Lightning has struck from as far away as ten miles from the storm center. *"If you hear it, clear it; if you see it. Flee it."* Postpone or suspend activity if a thunderstorm appears imminent before or during an activity or contest, (irrespective of whether lightning is seen or thunder heard) until the hazard has passed.

Using the flash-to-bang method it is also possible to tell the direction in which the storm is travelling relative to your location (Bennett, 1997). As the thunderstorm approaches your location the amount of time between the flash and the bang will gradually be reduced. When a storm is leaving an area the amount of time between the flash and the bang will gradually increase. This information may be used to help you make the appropriate decisions regarding safety.

Approaching thunderstorms are instantly recognizable by their rapidly towering cumulus clouds that have a black or dark green appearance. Static on your AM radio may also signal the approach of a thunderstorm. Finally, if you feel your hair standing on end and/or hear crackling noises you may be in the lightning's electrical field.

WHAT INFORMATION SOURCES ARE AVAILABLE TO HELP PREDICT THE OCCURRENCE OF LIGHTNING?

One of the differences between reacting to the danger of lightning and reacting to other emergency situations is that with lightning it is possible to gain advanced warning. There are a number or sources from which you can gain information on the presence or likelihood of lightning in your region. It is possible to receive advanced warning of thunderstorms by listening to a NOAA weather radio or tuning a VHF radio to an NOAA weather station. Meteorologists continually assess the weather conditions to determine whether or not they are conducive to the development of thunderstorms. When conditions are favorable for the development of thunderstorms a *thunderstorm watch* is issued. A *severe thunderstorm warning* is only issued when a storm, with winds at or above 58 mph and hail that is three quarters of an inch in diameter (Osinski, 2000) has been observed and is imminent in the immediate area. These warnings are typically issued on most local radio and television stations.

Many swimming pools, both indoor and outdoor, employ lightning detectors to measure electrical field intensity. These detectors allow users to determine the intensity, speed, direction and distance of impending thunderstorms before they pose an immediate threat. Lightning detectors can detect cloud to ground lightning up to half an hour before it is first visible (Osinski, 2000). This information helps users determine when bathers should vacate the swimming pool and when it is safe to return to the water. Lightning detectors are required in some but not all States. If you coach or organize aquatic sports or activities ask your local authorities whether or not the pools you use employ lightning detectors. If lightning detectors are installed in your facility, be sure you are familiar with their functional capacity and mode of activation.

More recently a number of companies have begun producing handheld storm detection devices. These devices can alert the user to oncoming thunderstorms up to sixty miles away and provide detailed readouts of the range, intensity, speed, and estimated time of arrival of the storm. Many of these devices can be found for sale at electrical or outdoor activity stores or on the Internet.

WHAT PRECAUTIONS CAN I TAKE TO REDUCE THE THREAT OF LIGHTNING?

To help protect athletes and staff from the threat of lightning it is important to develop and implement an appropriate policy with regards to lightning safety. An appropriate lightning safety policy should focus upon both education and prevention. Youth, parents, and staff should be educated on the basic physics of lightning, how to recognize and predict impending danger and appropriate safety measures. Prevention must occur prior to the athletic event with specific staff being assigned to monitor the weather for signs of threatening weather. The lighting safety position statement adopted by the National Association for Athletic Training (Walsh, Bennett, Cooper, Holle, Kithil, and Lopez, 2000) provides an appropriate framework from which to develop a lightning policy for your organization.

National Athletic Trainer's Association makes the following recommendations for lightning safety in their position statement.

1. Establish a chain of command that identifies who is to make the call to remove individuals from the field, athletic arena, or venue.
2. Name a designated weather watcher (A person who actively looks for the signs of threatening weather and notifies the chain of command if severe weather becomes dangerous).
3. Have a means of monitoring local weather forecasts and warnings.
4. Designate a safe shelter for each venue.
5. Use the Flash to Bang count to determine when to go to safety. By the time the Flash to Bang count approaches thirty seconds all individuals should be already inside a safe structure.
6. Once activities have been suspended, wait at least thirty minutes following the last sound of thunder or lightning flash prior to resuming an activity or returning outdoors.
7. Avoid being the highest point in an open field, in contact with, or proximity to the highest point, as well as being on the open water. Do not take shelter under or near trees, flagpoles, or light poles.
8. Assume the lightning safe position (crouched on the ground, weight on the balls of the feet, feet together, head lowered, and ears covered) for individuals who feel their hair stand on end, skin tingle, or hear "crackling" noises. Do not lie flat on the ground.
9. Observe the following basic first aid procedures in managing victims of a lightning strike:
    - Survey the scene for safety
    - Activate the local Emergency Medical Services
    - Lightning victims do not 'carry a charge' and are safe to touch.
    - If necessary, move the victim with care to a safer location.
    - Evaluate airway, breathing, and circulation, and begin CPR if necessary.
    - Evaluate and treat for hypothermia, shock, fractures and/or burns.
10. All individuals have the right to leave an athletic site in order to seek a safe structure if the person feels in danger of impending lightning activity, without fear of repercussions or penalty from anyone.

Safe Shelter

1. A safe location is any substantial, frequently inhabited building. The building should have four solid walls (not a dug out), electrical and telephone wiring, as well as plumbing, all of which aid in grounding a structure.
2. The secondary choice for a safer location from the lightning hazard is a fully enclosed vehicle with a metal roof and the windows completely closed. It is important to not touch any part of the metal framework of the vehicle while inside it during ongoing thunderstorms.
3. It is not safe to shower, bathe or talk on landline phones while inside a safe shelter during thunderstorms (cell phones are ok).

REFERENCES

Bennett, B. L. (1997). "A Model Lightning Safety Policy for Athletics." *Journal of Athletic Training*, 32(3): 251-253.

Holle, R. L., Lopez, R. E., and Ortiz, R. (1993). "The Local Meteorological Environment of Lightning Casualties in Central Florida." In *Preprints, 17ᵗʰ Conference of Severe Local Storms and Conference on Atmospheric Electricity*. Boston: American Meteorological Society, pp. 779-84.

Lopez, R. E., Holle, R. L., and Heitkamp, T. A. (1995). "Lightning Casualties and Property Damage in Colorado From 1950 To 1991 Based on Storm Data." *Weather Forecasting*, 9: 114-36.

Osinski, A. (2000, April). "Weathering the Storm." *Aquatics International*, 33-37.

Walsh, K. M., Bennett. B., Cooper, M. A., Holle, R. L., Kithil, R., and Lopez, R. E. (2000). "National Athletic Trainer's Association Position Statement: Lightning Safety for Athletics and Recreation." *Journal of Athletic Training*, 35(4): 471-477.

Walsh, K. M., Hanley, M. J., Graner, S. J., Beam, D., and Bazluki, J. (1997). "A Survey of Lightning Policy in Selected Division I Colleges." *Journal of Athletic Training*, 32: 206-210.

USEFUL WEBSITES

The National Weather Service Homepage
< http://www.nws.noaa.gov/ >
The National Severe Storms Laboratory Homepage
< http://www.nssl.noaa.gov/ >
The National Oceanic and Atmospheric Administration Homepage
< http://www.noaa.gov/ >

20

Chemical Health Education and Coaching (CHEC): Drug Abuse in Sport

James P. Corcoran, M.A.

QUESTIONS TO CONSIDER

- Why should the coach be concerned about drug abuse in sport?
- What are the more commonly abused drugs?
- What are the truths about the effects of abused drugs?
- What are some unique pressures that might lead to drug abuse?
- How can coaches recognize and respond to drug abuse?
- How can coaches educate their athletes to prevent drug abuse?
- What can the athletes do to promote a drug-free environment?

INTRODUCTION

One of the biggest problems facing the athletic arena is drug abuse. Drugs such as alcohol, marijuana, cocaine, nicotine, steroids, and others are believed to enhance performance. Unfortunately, this problem is oftentimes denied or ignored. Why? Because it is a sensitive and complicated issue that many would rather believe exists on other teams or in other communities and schools. However, due to the significant levels of drug abuse experienced by athletes and the amount of problems it causes people, the need for effective action can no longer be denied or ignored.

Many athletes involved in different sports at various levels are regularly exposed for their problems with alcohol and other drugs (AODs). The print and electronic media routinely report an athlete's or coach's AOD-related problem(s). Steps must be taken to educate our young athletes and coaches about the prevention of these problems through the promotion of chemical health, healthy lifestyles, and drug-free environments.

Sports and athletic activities attract a great amount of attention within our society. A survey conducted by USA TODAY reported that 90 percent of high school-aged youths identified sports as their first hobby. Athletes, sports personalities, and coaches serve as influential role

models for youth. Consequently, sport, and its influential participants, is an essential component to establishing a message of chemical health.

While sport may provide numerous opportunities to develop a healthy mind, body, and lifestyle, there also exists a climate of potentially negative mental, physical, and emotional pressures. Young athletes are coached to make decisions regarding their athletic performance and often their choices are plainly visible to teammates, coaches, spectators, parents, and peers. This visibility may contribute to unusual levels of stress in a young athlete's life and can lead to making a choice to abuse drugs to relieve tension or attempt to enhance their athletic performance (Svendsen, Griffin, McIntyre, 1984).

The content of this chapter will address several issues concerning the problem of AOD abuse by athletes. First, information will be provided to improve the coach's awareness of the problem and will include the following: (a) definitions for chemical use, abuse, dependency, and health; (b) chemicals sought by athletes; (c) abuse excuses and the truth about the effects of drugs; and (d) pressures unique to athletics. Second, the coach's role in relation to recognition, response, and prevention will be discussed, followed by methods for getting the team involved in confronting chemical issues. Information on how the coach and athlete can promote healthy, successful, and meaningful athletic and personal experiences will also be provided.

The ultimate goals of this chapter is twofold: 1) to assist coaches and athletes in avoiding problems associated with alcohol and other drugs, and 2) to help coaches and athletes achieve a drug-free athletic experience that contributes to the overall enrichment of their lives. Please remember that coaches are in a position to develop unique relationships with their athletes that can have a lifelong positive effect. Chemical health education and coaching can be an integral part of that lifelong positive effect (Griffin and Hill-Donisch, 1987).

DEFINITIONS

In order to promote chemical health, an understanding of the four different levels (use, abuse, dependence, and health) associated with chemical involvement must be identified and defined. These definitions will help the coach distinguish between problematic and healthy behavior. Those who choose healthy solutions toward the prevention of chemical abuse related problems need to be aware of and understand the differences between these levels and the various ways in which to deal with them.

Note: this text will use the terms of drugs, substances, AODs (alcohol and other drugs), and chemicals interchangeably. Each term is equal/the same. When they are used they refer to, but are not limited to: alcohol, steroids, cocaine, marijuana, barbiturates, nicotine, and caffeine, etc).

Chemical/Drug Use

Alcohol and other drugs (AODs) are not inherently bad or wrong. There are numerous positive, healthy and social needs that they fulfill. However, when they are not used in the manner for which they are intended (abuse), widespread problems arise. Many scenarios exist that exemplify chemical/drug use. The following list provides a few of them:

* The athlete becomes ill or injured and a drug is prescribed for medicinal purposes and recovery,
* A prescribed drug is monitored by a physician,
* The chemical is legal and socially accepted,
* The athlete has control over its consumption,
* The athlete follows the amount and scheduling of the prescribed dosage,
* The athlete stops the use of the chemical when instructed by the physician,
* The athlete refuses to be associated with individuals who are illegally or abusively involved with AODs, and
* The athlete's use of the drug does not interfere with athletic performance or relationships with coaches, teammates, parents, and friends.

Chemical/Drug Abuse

A clear, yet often ignored sign of chemical abuse is the exhibition of dangerous and risky behavior that is (potentially) harmful to the individual or to others. For example, "rowdy weekend parties" oftentimes include abusive binge drinking. The truth of this behavior is that it is alcohol/drug/chemical/substance abuse. Abusive behavior can, and will, cause serious problems in life, problems that may include paralysis and death. Abuse is evident when an athlete becomes involved with a chemical beyond what is legal, controllable, sociable, acceptable, and healthy. The following are examples of alcohol abuse:

* Drunkenness (anytime),
* Binge drinking,
* Passing out (unconsciousness), as a result of drinking,
* Blacking out (loss of memory), as a result of drinking,
* Throwing up (toxic poisoning), as a result of drinking,
* Absenteeism at school, practice and competition, as a result of drinking,
* Performance below one's ability, as a result of drinking,
* Relationship problems with coaches and/or teammates, as a result of drinking,
* The regular and systematic presence (preoccupation) of alcohol, and
* Altercations with the law, as a result of drinking.

Chemical/Drug Dependency

A critical aspect to understanding the levels at which any human being can experience AODs is dependency. Chemical dependency is the repeated abusive consumption of a chemical(s) to a point that causes problems in an individual's emotional, mental, social, spiritual, academic and athletic life. Further, the individual does not, or is unable to, terminate the relationship with or consumption of the chemical(s). Chemical/drug/alcohol dependency is an illness that meets the American Medical Association's criteria for any and all diseases (i.e., Cancer, AIDS, Muscular Sclerosis). These criteria are:

* The illness/dependency can be described,
* The illness/dependency is primary,
* The illness/dependency follows a predictable and progressive course,
* The illness/dependency is permanent or chronic,
* The illness/dependency can be fatal, and
* The illness/dependency is treatable (Michigan State University, 1989b).

Chemical dependency is a disease that meets the above stated criteria and that can only be diagnosed by a trained professional. If an athlete is diagnosed as being chemically dependent, efforts must be made to understand and accept that the athlete is suffering from an illness/disease. Alcoholism and other chemical dependencies are not the result of weaknesses in character, personality or morality. Chemical dependencies are an illness requiring specialized treatment.

Chemical/Drug Health

Chemical health contributes to general health and results in responsible decisions about chemical use and non-use. Chemical health is present when an athlete uses a substance that is legal, socially acceptable, used as directed for its intended purpose, and is safe. The following are some characteristics of chemical health as it relates to alcohol. An individual who has a healthy approach toward alcohol will not only understand the following but will practice them in daily life (Michigan State University, 1989a).

- Obey the drinking laws.
- Obey the drinking and driving laws.
- Recognize that alcohol is an addictive drug.
- Know the physiological impact of alcohol.
- Abstain regularly.
- Understand and respect the family's history (as it relates to AODs).
- Drink moderately for positive reasons.
- Understand what blood alcohol level (BAL) means.

Chemical health education and coaching (CHEC) is an important aspect of the coach's day-to-day responsibilities. Awareness of the various levels of chemical involvement that an athlete can experience will help the coach make more accurate decisions about chemical issues when they arise. Equally beneficial to the coach are:

- An accurate knowledge base of the various substances available to athletes,
- Reasons (justifications, rationalizations, excuses) athletes may employ, and
- The truths about the effects that the substances have upon the body, mind and human performance.

ATHLETES AND CHEMICALS/DRUGS

Why are athletes getting involved with drugs? What drugs might they seek? An introduction into the reasons athletes abuse drugs and listings of the drugs they pursue is provided. While the numerous lists provided in this chapter are detailed, it is beyond the chapter's scope to identify all substances or methodologies that are available. Additionally, the "drug culture" in sport is constantly trying to stay ahead of the "drugs out of sport cul-

ture." Therefore, coaches must remain up-to-date with accurate information. Lastly, each of the lists represent chemicals that are banned, unethical, or illegal.

Justifications/rationalizations/excuses for drug abuse in sport include:

1. Increased energy levels or improving the oxygen carrying capacity of blood.
2. Improved muscle mass, strength, power, and/or attainment of a more muscular physique.
3. Reducing pain and accelerating recovery time.
4. Reducing weight quickly or diluting/eliminating drugs from the body to avoid detection.
5. Alteration of mood, escaping from reality, relieving pressures, feeling better, or feeling nothing at all.

1. Increasing Energy Levels or Improving the Oxygen Carrying Capacity of Blood.

If athletes decide to try an illegal and unethical means to increase their energy level in an attempt to improve performance, they might abuse stimulants. These chemicals act to stimulate the central nervous system and can produce both psychological (aggression) and physical (decreased time to fatigue) effects upon performance. They also create an unfair advantage (cheating) and can place an athlete's health at risk. Information in Tables 20-1, 20-2, and 20-3 is provided by the United States Olympic Committee (Newsom, Waters, and Grice, 1989). It serves as a coaches' guide regarding stimulants, over-the-counter substances containing stimulants, and caffeine-containing products.

More sophisticated (yet, unethical and illegal) athletes may attempt to enhance their performance through the implementation of blood doping, also known as "blood packing" or "blood boosting." Blood doping is the administration of red blood cells, or related blood products, to an athlete for purposes not medically (anemia or acute blood loss) indicated. It involves the intravenous injection of blood into an athlete's body for the purpose of performance enhancement. This may involve the use of blood previously withdrawn from that athlete (autologous) or blood from another person (homologous). Please note that there are other severe health and life risks (rash, fever, jaundice, viral hepatitis, HIV) associated with this unethical and dangerous behavior (Williams, 1981).

As mentioned earlier, there are a variety of reasons (injury, physique, escape, insecurity, peer pressure, etc.), which contribute to an individual's decision to abuse a chemical. However, a primary reason for pursuing AODs is to enhance performance. The sections in the chapter entitled, 'Abuse Excuses and the Truth', provide information regarding thought processes that might be employed by athlete(s) and the truths about the physical, mental, and performance effects of specific substances.

Table 20-1. Stimulants.

Generic Name	Examples
Amfepramone	Apisate. Tenuate, Tepanil
Amfetaminil	Am-1 (Germany)
Amiphenazole	Dapti, Daptizole, Amphisof
Amphetamine	Delcobese, Obetrol, Benzedrine, Dexedrine
Bemegride	Megimide
Benzphotamine	Didrex
Caffeine	12 mcg/ml in the urine = positive (1 cup of coffee 1.5 mog/ml). See also Table 20-3.
Cathine	(Norpseudoephedrine) Adiposetten N (Germany)
Clorphentermine	Pre Sate, Lucofen
Clobenzorex	Dimintel (France)
Clorprenaline	Vortel, Asthone (Japanese)
Cocaine	Surfacine
Cropropamide	(Component of "Micoren")
Crothetamide	(Component of "Micoren")
Diethylpropion	Tenuate, Tepanil
Dimetamfetamfetamine	Amphetamine
Ephedrine Pseudoephedrine*	Tedral, Bronkotabs, Rynatuss, Primatene
Etafedrine	Mercodal, Docapryn, Netamine
Ethamivan	Emivan, Vandid
Etilamfetamine	Apetinil (Netherlands)
Fencamfamine	Envftrol, Aftimine, Phencamine
Fenetylline	Captagon (Germany)
Fenproporex	Antiobes Retard (Spain), Appetizuglar (Germany)
Furfenorex	Frugal (Arg.), Frugalan (Spain)
Isoethadne	Bronkosol. Brokometer, Numotac, Dilabron
Isoproterenol	Isuprel, Norisodrine, Matihaler-iso
Meclofenoxate	Lucidril, Brenal
Mefenorex	Doracil (Argentina), Pondinil (Switzerland), Rondime (Germany)
Metaproterenol	Alupent
Methamphetamine	Desoxyn, Met-Ampi
Mothoxyphenamine	Rkalin, Orthoxicol Cough Syrup
Methylamphetamine	Desoxyn, Met-Ampi
Methylephedrine	Tzbraine, Methop (Germany, England)
Methylphenidate	Ritalin
Morazone	Rosimon-Neu (Germany)
Nikethamide	Coramine
Pemoline	Cylart, Deltamin, Stimul
Pentetrazol	Leptazol
Phendimetrazine	Phonazine, Bontril, Plegine
Phenmetrazine	Preludin
Phentermine	Adipex, Fastin, Ionamin
Phenylpropanolamine*	Sinutab, Contac, Dexatrim, Alka Seltzer Plus
Picrotoxine	Cocculin
Pipradol	Meratran. Constituent of Alertonic
Prolintane	Villescon, Promotil, Katovit
Propylhexedrine*	Benzedrex Inhaler
Pyrovalerone	Centroton, Thymorgex
Strychnine	Movellan (Germany)

*Common ingredients in decongestant cold and sinus medicines. See also Table 24-2.

Table 20-2. Over-the-counter substances containing stimulants.

Generic Name	Examples
Pseudoephedrine	Actifed, Ambenyl, Amamine, Afrinol, Chlorafed, Chlortrimeton-DC, CoTyler*l, Deconamine, Dimacol, Dispheral, Drixoral, Emprazil, Fedahist, Histalet, Isoclor, Lo-Tussin, Nasalspan, Novafed, Nucofed, Ply-Histine, Polaramine Expectorant, Pseudo-Bid, PseudoHist, Rhymosyn, Rondec, Ryna, Sudafed, Triprolidine, Tussend
Phenylephrine	Coricidin, Dristan, NTZ, Neo-Synephrine, Sinex
Phenylpropanolamine	ARM, Allerest, Alka-Seftzer Plus, Contac, Dexatrim, Dietac, 4-Way Formula 44, Naidecon, Novahistine, Amex, Sine-Aid, Sine-Off, Sinutab, Triaminic, Triaminicin, Sucrets Cold Decongestant and related products
Propylhexedrine	Benzedrex inhaler
Ephedrine	Bronkaid, Collyrium with Ephedrine, Pazo Suppository, Wyanoid Supposftory, Vftronol, Spellings Nose Drops, Nyquil Nighttime Cold Medicine, Herbal Teas and Medicines Containing Ma Huang (see below)
Ma Huang	(Herbal Ephedrine) Bishop's Tea, Brigham Tea, Chi Powder, Energy Ris, Ephedra, Excel, Joint Fir, Mexican Tea, Miner's Tea, Mormon Tea, Popotillo, Squaw Tea, Super Charge, Teamster's Tea

Table 20-3. Caffeine-containing products.

Product	Amount/Dose
Decaf. Coffee	2-3 mg.
Coffee (one cup)	100.0 mg
Coca-Cola or Diet Coke (12 oz.)	45.6mg
Tab (12 oz.)	46.8 mg
Dr. Pepper (12 oz.)	39.6 mg
Diet Pepsi (12 oz.)	36.0 mg
Pepsi Light (12 oz.)	36.0 mg
1 No-Doz	100.0 mg
1 Vivarin	200.0 mg
1 APC Empirin or Anacin	32.0 mg
1 Exedrin	65.0 mg
1 Midol	32.4 mg

Stimulants: Abuse Excuses and the Truth

ABUSE EXCUSE: "Stimulants will give me energy, make me braver and more aggressive."

TRUTH: Stimulants cause an increase in heart rate, blood pressure, respiratory rate, and levels of hostility. They have not been shown to increase endurance, improve strength, or enhance performance. Stimulants reduce blood flow to cutaneous (skin) tissue, which could cause hypothermia (below-normal body temperature) during physical activity. This condition could be extremely dangerous in cold weather sports. Stimulants can cause dehydration, cerebral hemorrhage (stroke), heartbeat irregularities, cardiac arrest, disorientation, poor judgment, loss of timing and coordination, confusion, hallucinations, and increased anxiety. Chronic abuse of stimulants can cause addiction and damage to numerous organs in the body. The body "crashes" harder and requires a longer time to recover from training, practice, or competition than it would without the drug.

Signs that may indicate stimulant abuse include: dilated pupils, weight loss, increased perspiration, insomnia, nervousness, rapid heart rate, anxiety, increased blood pressure, paranoia, and hand tremors.

Blood Doping: Abuse Excuses and the Truth

ABUSE EXCUSE: "If I dope my blood I'll increase my oxygen levels, improve my performance, and win."

TRUTH: While blood doping does not involve a

chemical, it requires medical skill and technology. It is unethical and illegal. Whenever blood is involved (transfusions and syringes), the risk for blood-related infections and diseases (i.e., hepatitis, AIDS) is present. However, clotting of blood is the most significant risk factor in blood doping.

2. Improved Muscle Mass, Strength, Power, and/or Attainment of a More Muscular Physique.

Physical training regimens are a part of preparation for competition by athletes. Recently, highly specialized programs have been designed to build muscle and strength for athletes in a variety of sports. Many sports demand a physique that is specific to the requirements of that sport. Consequently, athletes have turned to incorporating (abusing) synthetic substances to facilitate building a body they believe will allow them to succeed. The most commonly abused drugs for this purpose are androgenic-anabolic steroids (A-as). However, other substances that are abused to build a specific body type also include human growth hormone (hGH) and various forms of amino acids. Table 20-4, compiled by the United States Olympic Committee (USOC) lists many of these substances (Newsom, Waters, and Grice, 1989).

A-as are synthetic derivatives of the male hormone testosterone, which affects the growth and development of many tissues. A-as were originally used to treat medical problems such as muscle disease, growth abnormalities, anemia, and burns. Much controversy exists over A-

as abuse by athletes. Many believe that they increase muscle mass, improve strength, and enhance performance. The American College of Sports Medicine (1984) states the following:

"...it can be concluded that the use of steroids, especially with experienced weight trainers, can increase strength gains beyond those seen with training and diet alone. This positive effect on strength is usually small and not exhibited by all individuals—steroids do not increase aerobic power or the capacity for muscular exercise."

The ACSM's paper further claims that the health risks associated with the abuse of these drugs are high. The ACSM stands firmly against the abuse of A-as by athletes.

Androgenic-Anabolic Steroids: Abuse Excuses and the Truth

ABUSE EXCUSE: "Steroids will make me bigger, stronger and faster."

TRUTH: The following six truths are identified by the Michigan State University Sports Medicine Department (1989a):

- Androgenic-anabolic steroids (A-as) abuse is linked to premature fusion of the growth plates of long bones in young athletes resulting in a permanent short stature.
- A-as is linked to abnormal liver function tests and can

Table 20-4. Androgenic Anabolic Steroids compiled by the USOC 9.

Generic Name	Example
Bolasterone, Boldenone	Vebonol, Equipoise
Clostebol	Steranobol
Dehydrochlormethyl-Testosterone	Tumibol
Fluoxymesterone	Android F. Hatotestin, Ora-Testryl, Ultradren
Mesterolone	Androviron, Proviron
Metandienone	Danabol, Dianabol
Metenolone	Primobolan, Primonabol-Depot
Methandrostenolone	Danabol
Methyltestosterone	Andoid, Estratest, Methandren, Oreton, Testred
Nandrolone	Durabolin, Deca-Durabolin, Kabolin, Nandrobolic
Norethandrolone	Nilevar
Oxandrolone	Anavar
Oxymesterone	Oranabol, Theranabol
Oxymetholone	Anadrol, Nilevar, Anapolon 50, Adroyd
Stanozolol	Winstrol, Stromba
Testosterone	Malogen, Malogex, Delatestryl
And related compounds:	
Danazol	Danocrine Zeranol
Human Growth Hormone	
Human Chorionic	
Gonadotrophin	

cause jaundice. Deaths from liver disorders associated with A-as abuse by persons who had no indication of liver malfunction prior to A-as abuse have been reported.

- In women, A-as abuse cause abnormal hair growth, clitoral enlargement, and deepening of the voice; each of which are irreversible. It also causes breast shrinkage and menstrual irregularities.
- Any athlete who abuses A-as through injectables (syringes) is at risk for blood-related diseases (i.e., hepatitis, AIDS).
- The death of an athlete as the result of the AIDS virus contracted from sharing an infected syringe to inject an A-as has been documented.

TRUTH: Haupt and Rovere (1984) and Wright and Stone (1985) provide the following examples of reported negative side effects of using/abusing androgenic-anabolic steroids:

- Gastrointestinal disorders,
- Increased or decreased libido,
- Muscle cramps and spasms,
- Headaches and nosebleeds (hemorrhages),
- Muscle and connective tissue damage,
- Drowsiness or lethargy,
- Dizziness or faintness,
- Insomnia,
- Sore nipples,
- Immune system alteration,
- Genital pain,
- Tumors,
- Mood swings,
- Kidney problems,
- Anger/hostility,
- Testicle shrinkage,
- Acne,
- Cardiovascular system problems,
- Reproductive system malfunctions,
- Alteration of neuron receptors in muscles, and/or
- Skeletal system problems.

3. Reducing Pain and Accelerating Recovery Time.

An athlete who is injured in practice or competition may feel pressured to remain active. This pressure may result from the coach needing the athlete for an upcoming event, or it may result from the athlete thinking that being absent or ineffective due to an injury will obstruct personal or team goals and may jeopardize the athlete's playing time.

Coaches, athletes, administrators, directors, and spectators at times do not exhibit the patience that is required while an athlete recovers from an injury. Therefore, the athlete may seek chemicals as a "quick fix." The

danger of this situation is the belief that chemicals offer the magic remedy to shorten or alleviate the problem. In reality, chemical abuse prolongs the problem and threatens to make it worse.

The implication and danger of the "quick fix" mentality for the coach and athlete alike is the increased possibility that an athlete could return to action before they have fully recovered from an injury. The body needs time to recover naturally. Legal ramifications of such an action could threaten a coach's job and reputation, and an athlete may receive a career ending, permanent, or life-threatening injury.

Various forms of medication are available for rehabilitation from injuries. Antibiotics, muscle relaxants, anti-inflammatories, and painkillers (narcotics) are used/abused by athletes to fight infection and accelerate the healing of an injury.

Narcotic analgesics (Table 20-5) are pain reduction substances (painkillers) that an athlete may decide to abuse to continue practicing or competing. In addition to masking injuries, these substances can lead to dependence. Many medications may be used for specific health-related reasons. Table 20-6 lists examples of medications that are not banned. Some of these chemicals are easily acquired without a prescription. Therefore, an additional concern for the coach is that an athlete may attempt to self-medicate and, consequently, run the risk of toxic poisoning.

Narcotic Analgesics: Abuse Excuses And The Truth

ABUSE EXCUSE: "I just need something to kill the pain. If I don't practice this week, coach will think I'm dogging it. Besides, I'm young and strong. I can take it."

TRUTH: The following are truths about narcotic analgesics:
- Pain reducers mask pain, allowing an athlete to return to action feeling as though the injury is healed.
- Returning to training, practice, or competition prematurely can prolong an injury, cause permanent damage, or end an athletic (or coaching) career.
- Injuries need time to heal, regardless of one's physical health condition or age.
- Medications, when prescribed by an attending physician and used in the manner prescribed, assist in the healing process.

4. Reducing Weight Quickly or Diluting/ Eliminating Drugs to Avoid Detection.

Diuretics are abused by athletes to help eliminate fluids from the tissues (Newsom, Waters, and Grice, 1989). Diuretics also are used to "make weight" or to "mask" traces of banned substances in their urine. (A list of common diuretics appears in Table 20-7; Table 20-8 lists the materials that may be "masked" by diuretic use).

Table 20-5. Narcotic Analgesics.

Generic Name	Example
Alphaprodine	Nisentil
Anileridine	Lerftine, Adodol
Buprenorphine	Buprenex
Codeine	Codicept (Germany), Codiperiussin (Germany)
Dextronioramide	Paffium, Jetrium, Naroolo
Dextropropoxzyphene	Darvon
Diamorphine	Heroin
Dihydrooodeine	Synalogos DC, Paracodin
Dipipanone	Diconal, Wellconal
Ethoheptazine	Panalgin, Equagesic (Italy)
Ethyiniorphine	Diosan comp (Spain), Trachyl (France)
Levorphanol	Levo-Dronioran
Methadone	Dolophine, Amidon
Morphine	Cycliniorph 10, Duromorph, MST-Continus
Nalbuphine	Nubain
Pentazocine	Talvvin
Pethidine	Demerol, Centraigin, Dolantin, Dolosol, Pethold
Penazocine	Narphen
Trimeperidine	Demerol, Mepergan
And related compounds:	
Hydrocodone	Hycodan, Tussionex
Oxocodone	Percodan, Vicodan
Oxomorphine	Narcan
Hydromorphone	Dilaudid
Tincture Opium	Paregoric

Table 20-6. Allowable Medications.

Mild Pain (Analgesics):	Aspirin (plain aspirin), Tylenon (plain acetominophen)
Anti-Inflammatory:	Ibuprofen, Advil, Motrin, Feldene, Naprosyn, Butazolidin, Indocin
Muscle Relaxants:	Flexeril, Soma, Norflex, Parafon
Antihistamines:	Benadryl, Chlor-Trimeton, Seldane
Decongestants:	Oxymetazoline, Afrin Nasal Spray, Sinex Long Acting Nasal Spray
Asthma:	Aminophylline, Theophylline, Cromolyn, Albuterol (aerosol form only), Terbutaline (aerosol form only)
Antibiotics:	All
Eye/Ear Medicines:	Topical use acceptable
Cough Medicines:	Non-narcotic Dextromethorphan
Diarrhea:	Immodium, Kaopectate, Lomotil, Pepto-Bismol
Laxatives:	All laxatives

Table 20-7. Diuretics.

Generic Name	Example
Acetazolamide	Diamox, AK-Zol, Dazamide
Amiloride	Midamor
Bendroflumethiazide	Naturetin
Benzthyiazide	Aquatag, Exna, Hydrex Marazide, Proaqua
Bumetanide	Bumex
Canrenone	Aldactone (Germany), Phanurance, Soldactone (Swtizerland)
Chlormerodrin	Orimercur (Spain)
Chlortalidone	Hygroton, Hylidone, Thalitone
Diclofenamide	Daranide
Ethancrynic Acid	Edecrin
Furosemide	Lasix
Hydrochlorothiazide	Esidrix, Hyro/Diuril, Oretic, Thiuretic
Mersalyl	Mersalyl injection
Spironolactone	Alatone, Aidactone
Triamterene	Dyrenium, Dyazide

Table 20-8. Time needed for body to eliminate traces of various chemicals.

Drug	Approximate Elimination Time
Alcohol	Approximately 48 hours (depending on the quantity consumed)
Stimulants (amphetamines and derivatives)	1 to 7 days
Cocaine (occasional use)	6 to 12 hours
Repeated use within 48 hours	3 to 5 days or longer
Codeine and narcotics in cough medicines	24 to 48 hours
Tranquilizers	4 to 8 days
Marijuana	3 to 5 weeks
Anabolic steroids	
Fat-soluble injectable types	6 to 8 months
Oral or water-soluble types	3 to 6 weeks
Over-the-counter cold medications, decongestants containing ephedrine	48 to 72 hours

ABUSE EXCUSE: "Maybe laxatives, diuretics, or diet pills/speed will control my weight."

TRUTH: Hill-Donisch (1988) proclaimed that diuretics, laxatives, or diet pills/speed have minimal effect upon the weight loss. Abuse of these substances lead to chemical imbalances in the body and may contribute to the development of eating disorders. Eating disorders are as serious a threat to good health as are alcoholism and other drug addictions. Medical, mental, and emotional problems can occur, and the possibility of forming an addiction is as real as with any other addictive chemical. Newsom, Waters, and Grice (1989) noted additional harmful side effects of diuretics including the following:

- Significant fluid loss,
- Loss of electrolytes (i.e., sodium and potassium),
- Leg and stomach muscle cramps,
- Irritation of motor nerves,
- Exhaustion due to irregular body heat, and/or
- Elevated and irregular heartbeat.

5. Alteration of Mood, Escaping From Reality, Relieving Pressures, Feeling Better, or Feeling Nothing at All.

One of the main reasons an individual seeks AODs and one that falls within each of the five categories we are discussing is solving a problem. Whether it is mental, emotional, physical or performance-related, some individuals believe that a drug will take away uncomfortable situations.

Late stage adolescence and early adulthood are trying times for many reasons including one's natural maturation process, need to establish independence, and acceptance by others before personality and character identity have fully matured. Athletes are no different than non-athletes in that they experience feelings of doubt, security, stress, and pressure to perform during these formative and awkward years.

In most communities, sports contribute substantially to the sense of unity and pride among community members. Subsequently, athletes receive much attention and pressure during both seasonal and post-seasonal play. Athletes are also subject to intense mood swings resulting from victory and defeat. These pressures, combined with the problems of development, can create high levels of anxiety in one's life.

Mood swings affect coaches and their staff as well. Just as some athletes turn to abusing drugs to relieve pressures, so do some coaches. AODs are often consumed to temporarily block problems or other uncomfortable feelings.

A common attitude among athletes is, "I train, practice, and compete at 110 percent. Therefore, I am going to party at 110 percent." This thought process can lead to the abuse of any chemical and can have disastrous effects. The coach and athlete alike must confront this attitude. The athlete's personal life, training regimen, and performance will deteriorate if attention, education, and support regarding the prevention of chemical abuse problems are not implemented into the coaching philosophy.

Examples of drugs abused to alter mood, escape, relief, feel better or feel nothing include (but are not limited to) the following:

- Alcohol,
- Barbiturates ("downers"), sleeping aids, sedatives,
- Nicotine (smoke/smokeless), caffeine,
- Amphetamines ("speeders," "uppers"),
- Crystal methamphetamine ("crystal-meth"),
- "Ecstasy,"
- Hallucinogens (LSD),
- Marijuana ("pot," "weed," "smoke"), hashish,
- Cocaine, crack, free-base cocaine, and
- Tranquilizers (valium, zanax).

NOTE: Please be aware that sugar, food, sex, gambling, shopping, the Internet, and computer/video games are other examples of what human beings turn to when they choose the "abuse excuse" rather than the "truth."

ABUSE EXCUSE: "Everybody drinks to, 'get a buzz on' or to get a 'little' drunk. Look at all the drinking that goes on at any sporting event. Anyway, drinking is a part of being an athlete and sports."

TRUTH: Alcohol remains the most prominent chemical/drug problem in society. All other chemicals combined do not present as much of a problem as alcohol, and it is the chemical most abused by teenagers.

- Alcohol causes a decrease in inhibitions and feelings of insecurity.
- Alcohol affects sound judgment and/or reason.
- Alcohol inhibits sensory perception (sight, hearing, smell, touch, and taste).
- Alcohol interferes with muscular coordination (leading to a total loss of control).
- Alcohol affects the involuntary nervous system (cardiovascular, respiratory, etc.).
- Alcohol can lead to coma or death.
- Alcohol-related accidents are the main cause of death for 15-24-year-olds.
- Alcohol problems occur with people (athletes/coaches) of all ages, races, and economic classes.
- Alcohol consumption by minors is illegal.

TRUTH: The American College of Sports Medicine (1982) presents the following evidence of the negative effects that alcohol has upon human physical performances. In sports requiring rapid reactions to changing stimuli, alcohol will have its most adverse effects in the following manner:

- Alcohol impairs information processing.
- Alcohol impairs reaction time, hand-eye and gross motor skill coordination, accuracy, and balance.
- Alcohol impedes the body's energy sources for exercise.
- Alcohol decreases dynamic and isometric strength, power, and muscular output.
- Alcohol does not improve muscular work capacity.
- Alcohol adversely affects performance levels: it does not sharpen one's skills.

ABUSE EXCUSE: "A little weed never hurt anybody. It's not like I'm shooting heroin or smoking crack. Besides, pot isn't addictive."

TRUTH: Marijuana is addictive. Marijuana is illegal. Marijuana is a "gateway drug" to other substances. Marijuana is a very complex substance with psychoactive properties. Marijuana can act as both a central nervous system depressant and stimulant; and it can cause hallucinogenic effects

TRUTH: Effects of marijuana on maximal exercise performance were studied by Renaud and Cormier (1986). They found that marijuana decreased performance by causing the premature achievement of maximal oxygen uptake.

TRUTH: Additional truths about marijuana use include:

- Marijuana is fat soluble and is stored in the body's adipose tissue, where it can remain for-four-to-six-weeks.
- Fifty percent (50%) of the psycho-active chemical (tetrohydrocannabiol or THC) remains in the body for five-to-seven-days.
- Marijuana consumption over long periods of time causes decreased motivation, increased introversion (isolation, withdrawal), problems focusing on tasks at hand and task completion, and frustration.
- Marijuana adversely affects the lungs, running the risk of developing cancer, emphysema, bronchitis, or other chronic pulmonary dysfunction.
- Marijuana impedes judgment, reasoning, and perception.

ABUSE EXCUSE: "Okay, maybe smoking or chewing isn't good for me, but I'm young enough to stop before any problems start. Plus, I don't do it a lot; not as much as some of my friends."

TRUTH: Tobacco (smoked or chewed) contains tars, gasses, and nicotine, each of which cause serious health problems, including addiction. It also has deleterious effects upon physical performance.

- Tobacco is a central nervous system stimulant, therefore, increases blood pressure, heart, and respiratory rates.
- Tobacco causes both heart and lung disease.
- Tobacco causes cancer.
- Smokeless tobacco contains glyceric acid (licorice taste), which has been linked to muscle weakness due to potassium deficiency.
- Smokeless tobacco (chew) is 10 times stronger than one cigarette.

ABUSE EXCUSE: "Cocaine's such a great feeling; it takes all of my problems away. I'll only do it recreationally every now and then."

TRUTH: Truths about cocaine use include:

- Cocaine destroys dreams. Cocaine kills. Cocaine is illegal.
- Cocaine is a foreign substance to the body that acts by penetrating the pleasure centers of the brain.
- Cocaine produces false feelings of excitement, euphoria, grandiosity, and confidence.
- Cocaine mimics a natural chemical in the body (dopamine) which allows us to feel pleasure, power and confidence—naturally.
- Cocaine withdrawal causes depression and confusion.
- Cocaine is physically and mentally addicting.
- Cocaine induces rapid increases and decreases in blood pressure.
- Cocaine changes breathing patterns and body temperature.
- Cocaine causes cardiac dysfunction which may result in death.
- Cocaine causes paranoia, fear, anger, aggressiveness, and malnutrition.

UNIQUE PRESSURES IN THE ATHLETIC DOMAIN

Previous discussions included drug abuse in sport, athletes and chemicals/drugs, and abuse excuses and truths within sports. These alone create a challenge to the coach's ability to recognize and respond to potential drug problems on the team. However, other reasons used by athletes to justify their choosing to be involved with drugs merit discussion as well.

It is important to clarify that while athletes do experience unique pressures that may lead to chemical abuse, this does not imply that their pressures are greater than the pressures of non-athletes. The manner by which problems are identified, confronted, and treated must be consistent in any environment. One such manner is that athletes must stop receiving special treatment. Special treatment including not holding athletes accountable or reducing or eliminating the consequences for their behavior(s) contributes to the AOD abuse problems.

The following examples of unique pressures that athletes experience are presented so the coach and the athlete are able to recognize and discuss issues that might lead to chemical abuse problems. If coaches are going to promote chemical health, they must keep these pressures in mind (Svendsen, Griffin and McIntyre, 1984).

Public visibility and vulnerability to criticism from coaches, spectators, and teammates. An athlete's life, in many respects, is an open book. Spectators, media, classmates, peers, family, girlfriends, and boyfriends are given the opportunity to freely pass judgment upon an athlete's level of skill and performance. "The roar of the crowd" and "the agony of defeat" might create enough pressure in athletes to where they turn to AODs. Entire communities derive a sense of pride from their sports teams. Sometimes this creates pressure that feels insurmountable to athletes.

Many times the athlete is expected to continue the performance, as viewed in the arena by the spectators, outside of the arena as well. Athletes of all ages and levels of ability search for acceptance and peer approval. Younger athletes may be especially vulnerable to the expectations of others who expect them to display behavior necessary in athletics (i.e., aggression) in settings away from the athletic arena. This may lead an athlete to turn to chemicals in an attempt to slip away, isolate, or withdraw.

Athletes are no different from other people in that they need to develop a sense of identity from a variety of experiences, including those away from the sports environment. If an athlete begins to feel that he or she is continuously expected to perform for others, and feels uncomfortable doing so, it may only be a matter of time before chemicals are sought to alleviate the problem. Chemical abuse can, and will, facilitate separation from others.

One of the requirements of sport that athletes learn quickly is the expectation and importance placed upon their continuous improvement. The basic assumption here is that the more skill an athlete exhibits, the better the chance of making the team and/or earning a starting role. Subsequently, personal standards become established and continuous effort is expended to maintain and improve skill, performance, and goals. However, other athletes may challenge those in starting positions, forcing established players into backup roles. How do athletes face these challenges? Does the athlete turn to steroids or amphetamine abuse to bulk up or increase energy levels? Or is alcohol abused as a coping mechanism? Coaches must be sensitive to these issues and need to help their athletes through difficult times.

Many athletes possess an attitude of invincibility and invulnerability. This false and unrealistic attitude creates the perfect mask behind which chemical abuse problems and unacceptable behavior hide. This attitude can stop an athlete from thinking about the negative consequences of their behavior. Athletes may feel "immortal," "untouchable," or "unbeatable." How many times have the following statements been heard? How many times have they gone unchallenged or discussed?

- "Nothing can touch me."
- "I'm going to live forever."
- "Steroids won't hurt me, like they hurt others."
- "I'm young, strong, and in the best shape of my life."
- "What or who could possibly hurt me?"

This attitude presents a formidable challenge to the coach. Bravery, fearlessness, extreme confidence are attitudes that are encouraged, needed and rewarded in competitive sports. Nonetheless, coaches must find a safe and healthy balance for theses issues to co-exist.

It is difficult to detect AOD problems when athletes exhibit these attitudes while performing at expected levels both at practice and in competition. This is not to suggest that the coach should be skeptical of the athlete who exhibits consistent levels of effort and optimal performance. After all, hustle and peak performance are what coaches strive to get from their athletes. The intention of raising this issue is to increase the coach's awareness of the "masking" reality. Allowing an athlete to escape close scrutiny because his or her performance has not been affected will only act to reinforce the athlete's feelings of false invincibility and invulnerability.

There exists a troubling relationship among athlete, sport, and alcohol. The association of commercials that advertise alcoholic beverages with athletics has led many to assume that athletes and alcohol belong together. These are the messages that society receives, believes, and values. Alcohol and nicotine (tobacco products) are often seen in the champion's locker room to celebrate, while the runner-up may be using alcohol to drown the loss. The coach needs to be aware that this societal and marketing influence is highly effective in impressing consumers, especially young athletes. This pressure is a most formidable challenge to the coach.

CHARACTERISTICS/SIGNS OF CHEMICAL ABUSE PROBLEMS

Much has been said thus far concerning the information, facts, and pressures relative to the AOD scene in sport. It is the intention that each point will assist coaches in their attempts to better understand the problems facing their athletes. But what are some of the specific and recognizable attributes an athlete might display that could indicate a problem? Prior to the presentation of recognizable characteristics, it must be understood that these examples of behaviors are inconclusive. Every athlete possesses a unique personality, characteristics, and mannerisms. Again, coaches are challenged to pay attention to their athletes and to watch for signs that may suggest a problem, whether it is AOD-related or not.

One should not assume that chemical problems are present simply because an athlete exhibits uncharacteristic behaviors. Nonetheless, if a reason for concern exists within the coach, action must be taken. One such action that could be used by the coach is to record the day, date, time, incident, and the coach's perception of the behaviors they see. This is suggested so that discrepancies due to the passage of time or mistaken identity can be held to a minimum when the behaviors are confronted and discussed.

Characteristics (signs) associated with chemical/AODs/drug problems:

- Abrupt change in attendance at practice, school, or work,
- A new and questionable group of friends,
- Quality of performance decreases,
- Deterioration of physical appearance,
- Diminished effort in athletics, job, or school,
- Smells of alcohol or marijuana,
- Grades drop,
- Sense of responsibility diminishes,
- Attitude changes,
- Arguments and/or fights with teammates,
- Oversleeping,
- Missed assignments,
- Generally withdraws when alcohol or drugs enter the discussion,
- Slurred speech, bloodshot or glassy eyes, flushed skin,
- Excessive sniffling,
- Decreased muscular coordination,
- Loss of memory,
- Problematic relationships,
- Stealing and unusual borrowing of money,
- Severe mood swings,
- Sudden weight loss or gain,
- Disassociation (withdrawal, isolation) from original peer group,
- Wearing sunglasses at inappropriate times, and
- Inappropriate clothing for current weather conditions.

COACH'S RESPONSE TO CHEMICAL ISSUES

In many ways, the knowledge and identification of chemical problems is the second most complicated component when establishing an attitude of chemical health. A more complicated component presents itself if, and when, the coach chooses to take action (respond). The "if" represents the biggest obstacle to both abolishing denial that a problem may exist and to establishing an *informed attitude* about chemical health.

Coaches have the power to serve as catalysts for a chemical health campaign not only with their teams, but within departments, schools, and communities as well. When coaches believe in and promote chemical health, the likelihood that others will follow improves. Any coach who has earned the respect of athletes, coaches, parents, administrators, and others has also earned the type of visibility that can promote chemical health.

Recognition of a potential problem followed by breaking through the denial to confront an athlete is paramount to the success of the entire process. This is also critical to the personal and athletic success of the athlete. When the coach responds by confronting problematic attitudes or behaviors, there are five keys to consider:

1. Acknowledgement of the problem(s).
2. Genuineness in approach.
3. Use of open communication.
4. Use of effective intervention skills and techniques.
5. Establishment of boundaries.

1. Acknowledgement of the Problem(s)

Chemical use, abuse, and dependency are realities of life. The coach needs to accept this and the responsibilities associated with recognition and confrontation. Any uncomfortable feelings experienced when deciding whether or not to take action will be dramatically outweighed by the true sense of meaningfulness gained from doing what is in the best interest of the athlete and others involved.

2. Genuine Concern

Many people have the ability to discern whether or not someone is "leveling" with them. How can someone who has a history of questionable or unacceptable behaviors confront someone else's questionable or unacceptable behavior and expect them to change? Therefore, it is imperative that coaches assess their own relationships with alcohol, nicotine, caffeine, and other drugs and establish personal guidelines. Double standards are never acceptable and destroy any hope of credibility. Coaches need to be aware of the messages they send to their athletes through their personal behavior and beliefs. Coaches must exhibit attitudes and behaviors that deserve respectful attention. Subsequently, coaches who exhibit personal chemical health are in a position to guide others.

3. Open Communication

Successful relationships are built on trust. Open and honest communication is a means to establishing trust. Once a trusting open communication channel is established, athletes will find it easier to confide in the coach about different issues. Not only will chemical health have a better chance to exist, but the overall cohesiveness of the team will be enhanced. Communication is required to learn about each other's goals, expectations, and needs. Once this is established the likelihood for a more positive and successful experience exists for the athlete(s) and coach(es).

4. Intervention Skills and Techniques

Intervention skills are necessary to assist coaches in identifying, formulating, and implementing measures that will facilitate the establishment of a chemical-free environment. In order for chemical health to exist, coaches need to be aware of how to approach and intervene successfully. Intervention skills are as critical to the establishment of a chemical free environment as strategies and specific physical skills are to coaching a sport. Once the fundamentals of interventions are understood by coaches, it will be easier to implement (practice) them when needed. (See Supplement 20-1 for additional information on intervention skills.)

5. Coach's Boundaries for Chemical Health

Coaches are responsible for teaching and guiding athletes, not only in their respective sport(s), but in other life issues as well. Subsequently, the coach must establish clear-cut boundaries as they relate to what the coach knows, does not know, what actions will be taken, as well as what actions won't be taken. Certainly one of the issues that can interfere with the promotion of an athlete's chemical health is the coaches' fear that their relationship with an athlete will deteriorate if they confront the individual. Most coaches genuinely desire to enhance the athletic and personal development of their athletes. However, the fear that a top performer and/or a close relationship may be lost if action to rectify an AOD-related (or any other) problem is taken may overrule a decision that would protect the best interest of the athlete. Quite frankly, the coach may not want to sacrifice a championship because a member of the team has a personal problem. This may sound shocking to some. Unfortunately, this is a mind-set that does exist. This is a reality that a CHEC attitude will work to diminish.

Lastly, some issues in the lives of athletes are too complex for many, other than a professional (i.e., therapist, psychologist or physician) to address. Coaches are encouraged to seek assistance (from parents, counselor, administrator or others) in determining the best course of action for the athlete (and everyone else) involved.

ATHLETE(S) AND TEAM INVOLVEMENT

One way to get athletes involved in promoting chemical health is to give them opportunities where they can choose chemical health and not an abuse excuse. A key component to the success of the program is the degree to which the athletes become involved and the amount of personal investment and dedication they have toward establishing and maintaining chemical health on the team. Here are some suggestions for initiating team involvement:

- Pre-season meeting with athletes.
- Establishment of chemical health guidelines.
- Creating a chemical-free environment.
- Self and teammate assessment through HALT (Hungry, Angry, Lonely, Tired).
- Alternatives to alcohol and other drugs.

Pre-Season Meeting

Pre-season meetings are not a new idea for most coaches. However, a pre-season meeting with a chemical health component might be something new. The content of the meeting should contain information from this chapter, as well as other accurate information that the coach may obtain from other reliable sources. The delivery should be as personal as the delivery used when presenting a coaching philosophy. Topics such as goals (for the program, team, and individual) or thoughts regarding discipline, effort, and teamwork, are easily interchangeable with chemical health.

Given the current problems with alcohol and other drug abuse in the athletic environment today, the need for the arrangement of a separate pre-season meeting for chemical issues is warranted. Therefore, it is recommended that the coach give considerable thought and preparation to the discussion of chemical issues.

In an attempt to secure a chemical-free team, it may prove beneficial to devote time for periodic meetings to discuss current events in sport as they relate to "life issues." The coach and staff should attempt to eliminate the "one-time-tells-all" shot—not because it will not benefit the athletes but because such a one-time meeting is insufficient to convey information and to reinforce healthy behaviors throughout the season. If learning is to occur and positive habits are to be formulated, the athletes should receive chemical education in a systematic and meaningful manner, similar to the way the coach would present competitive strategy or instruction for the acquisition of a new skill.

Chemical Health Guidelines

The purpose for establishing guidelines is to help the athletes (and coaches) know what behaviors are expected and acceptable and what behaviors are unexpected and unacceptable. Guidelines help to form a stable environment. They should represent the coach's philosophy and goals, but they also should represent the values held by team members. Guidelines can also clarify any discrepancies that may occur between teammates, coaches, or parents. Here are some examples:

- Seasonal curfew,
- In-season and off-season policies,
- Player incentives (rewards),
- Support and recognition for choosing to be chemical-free, and
- Consequences (i.e., Benching, suspension, elimination).

It will also help to keep in mind several fundamental reasons for establishing guidelines. They:

- Assist in decision making,
- Differentiate between behavior and the individual,
- Help to identify and define problems,
- Must include rewards,
- Must include multi-level negative consequences, and
- Must be followed fully and equally by all.

Chemical-Free Environment

Creating a chemically free environment requires the involvement of athletes. Allow them to have meetings of their own to determine what chemical health means to them and how they want to approach the challenge of a chemical-free team (environment). One suggestion might be to organize "straight" parties. Such a party could be planned by the athletes with its implementation (site) provided by the parents or coaches. The only requirement for attendance is an alcohol and other drug-free mind and body.

This can give the athletes, coaches, and parents the opportunity to deal with the feelings associated with winning and losing without the interference of alcohol and other drugs. It encourages the athletes to express their feelings about performances in an informal non-threatening setting that can offer support, acceptance, and constructive feedback from significant people in their lives.

Positive Self-Talk

Another method that can be implemented to help athletes to make healthier decisions is represented by the word **HALT**. More than a word, **HALT** is an acronym representing the keys that can help an athlete to make right choices. **HALT** is also one of the most positive self-talk messages an athlete can give to themselves.

H— stands for hunger. When an athlete is hungry they need to eat. Untreated hunger can lead to a physiologically based weakness that can contribute to a weakened decision making process.

A— stands for anger. When an athlete is angry at a performance, win, or loss, they must learn to express the feeling in a healthy and appropriate manner. Feelings that are not expressed appropriately can lead to a weakened decision making process.

L— stands for lonely. When an athlete feels lonely they must know how to express the feeling and what to do (act) about the feeling. Loneliness can lead to isolation and a desire to withdraw from others. Loneliness can lead to a weakened decision-making process.

T— stands for tired. Being tired following practice or a competition is normal; the athlete must recognize this and take action to rest the body through natural means. Sleep deprivation causes much stress on the mind and body. Tiredness can lead to a weakened decision-making process.

The concept behind this self-talk "tool" is that athletes benefit from being tuned in to what their mind, body and spirit are telling them. Hunger, anger, loneliness and tiredness each can create a weakened consciousness and, therefore, possibly lead to an unhealthy and unsafe decision/action. Likewise, any combination of the above conditions, and especially when all are present, creates a situation ripe for unclear thinking and acting. Encouraging athletes to talk about and use **HALT** will contribute to establishing a healthier, safer, and more enjoyable environment.

Team Involvement

The following list contains suggestions for team involvement in establishing chemical health. Each is a valuable tool for the improvement of athletic performance, personal development, and chemical health.

Legal and acceptable alternatives to chemicals include:

- Positive self-talk,
- Relaxation and imagery techniques,
- Mental toughness and assertiveness,
- Self-confidence and team cohesion,
- Goal setting and sports nutrition,
- Improved concentration,
- Specialized physical training regimens,
- Open and honest communication, and
- Clarification of personal values and self-worth.

SUMMARY

In summary, six steps are suggested for the prevention of drug abuse problems in sport. The following suggested actions to be taken by coaches are designed to lead to a chemical-free athletic environment:

1. Obtain and share accurate information about chemicals and their effects upon health, performance, and life with your athletes.
2. Improve your understanding about the pressures and stresses experienced by your athletes.
3. Teach and guide your athletes toward understanding the positive benefits that sports and chemical health can have on their lives.
4. Promote chemical health by teaching and coaching the athletes about ways to deal with situations where chemicals may be present.
5. Get the parents involved in the promotion of chemical health. Establishing an environment of chemical health requires a commitment and help from others.
6. Team involvement/investment with the establishment of chemical health is required. The athletes will benefit by assisting in the design and implementation of a healthy, positive, and successful attitude that exhibits chemical health.

SOURCES OF INFORMATION FOR CHEMICAL ISSUES

Sports:
Hazelden-Cork Sports Education Program
1400 Park Avenue
South Minneapolis MN 55404-1597
(612) 349-4310 or 1-800 257-7800
Simi Valley High School
1402 Royal Avenue
Simi Valley CA 93065
(805) 527-3232

Target—National Federation of State High School Associations
11724 Plaza Circle
Kansas City MO 64194
(816) 464-5400

United States Sports Academy
P.O. 250
Mobile AL

USOC Drug Education Program
1750 East Boulder Street
Colorado Springs CO 80909

Minnesota Grand Masters Hockey Classic MGM/HC
1720 North Basswood Avenue
Duluth, MN 55811
(218) 727-3647

Other Sources of Information:
American Council for Drug Education (ACDE)
204 Monroe Street, Suite 110
Rockville MD 20850
301.294.0600

Comp Care Publications
2415 Annapolis Lane
Minneapolis MN 55441
1.800.328.3330

Drug Enforcement Administration (DEA)
1405 I Street, NW
Washington D.C. 20537
202.786.4096

Michigan Office of Substance Abuse Services
3423 N. Logan
P.O. Box 30195
Lansing, MI 48909
517.335.8831

National Clearinghouse for Alcohol and Drug Abuse Information (NCADI)
P.O. Box 2345
Rockville MD 20852
301.468.2600

National Council on Alcoholism
12 W. 21st Street
New York NY 10010
212.206.6770 or 1.800.NCA.CALL

National Council on Alcoholism (Michigan Division)
1405 S. Harrison, Suite 308
East Lansing MI 48823
517.337.8417

National Institute on Drug Abuse (NIDA)
U.S. Department of Health and Human Services
5600 Fishers Lane
Rockville MD 20857
301.443.6245 or Hot line 1.800. 662.HELP

Students to Offset Peer Pressure (STOPP)
10 Lindsey Street
Hudson NH 03051
603.889.8163

Toughlove
P.O. Box 1069
Doylestown PA 18901
215.348.7090

Youth Who Care
Box 4074
Grand Junction CO 81502
303.245.4160

REFERENCES

American College of Sports Medicine (1984). "Position Statement on Anabolic-Androgenic Steroids." *Sports Medicine Bulletin*, 19:8-12.
American College of Sports Medicine (1982). *Position Stand on the Use of Alcohol in Sports*. Presented at the Big Ten Athletic Con-

ference Drug Education Seminar. Hyatt Regency O'Hare. Rosemont, IL (1989).

Griffin, T., and Hill-Donisch K. (1987). *Kids, Sports, and Drugs.* A workshop presented by Hazelden-Cork Sports Education Program.

Haupt, H. A., and Rovere, G. D. (1984). "Anabolic Steroids: A Review of the Literature." *The Journal of Sports Medicine*, 12(6):469-484.

Hill-Donisch, K. (1988). "Chemical Use and the Woman Athlete." *National Federation News*, 3(3).

May, J. R., and Asken, M. I. (editors). (1987). *Sport Psychology.* PMA Publishing, pp. 187-211.

Michigan State University Department of Sports Medicine (1989). *Drugs: Effect on Athletic Performance. What Every Player, Coach, and Parent Should Know.* (pp.1-3).

Michigan State University (1989). Department of Student Life Department/Alcohol Education. Information presented in the alcohol education seminar.

Newsom, M. M., Waters, D., and Grice, J. (1989). *Drug Free. United States Olympic Committee Drug Education Handbook.* Colorado Springs, CO.: USOC Drug Education Program.

Renaud, A. M., and Cormier, Y. (1986). "Acute Effects of Marijuana Smoking on Maximal Exercise Performance." *Medicine and Science in Sports and Science*, 18(6): 685-689.

Svendsen, R., Griffin, T., and McIntyre, D. (editors) (1984). *Chemical Health—School Activities and Fine Arts Activities. A Guide for School Officials in Responding to Alcohol and Other Drug Issues.* Center City, MN: Hazelden Foundation.

White House Conference For a Drug Free America. (1988). *Final Report.* Washington, D.C.: Library of Congress (Catalog No. 88-600553).

Williams, M.H. (1981). "Blood Doping: an Update." *The Physician and Sportsmedicine*, 9(7); 59-62.

Wright, J. E., and Stone, M. H. (1985). "The National Strength Coaches' Association (NSCA) Statement on Anabolic Drug Use: A Literature Review." *NSCA Journal*, 7(5): 45- 59.

SUGGESTED READINGS

Eaddy, V. S. (editor) (1986). *Substance Abuse in Athletics: The Realities.* Mobile, AL.: United Medicine. States Sports Academy Publishing Co.

Tricker, R. and Cook, D. (editors) (1990). *Athletes at Risk: Drugs and Sport.* Dubuque, IA.: Brown.

Wadler, G. I., and Hainline, B. (1989). *Drugs and the Athlete.* Philadelphia: Davis.

Chemical Health Education and Coaching (CHEC): Intervention Skills for Coaches

James P. Corcoran, M.A.

The following material is offered to assist coaches in identifying, formulating and implementing intervention skills that will help to facilitate the establishment of a chemical-free environment. If chemical health is to be encouraged and experienced it will be necessary for coaches to be aware of how to intervene successfully when a chemical problem(s) presents itself.

The fundamental components of intervention skills are critical to establishing a chemical-free environment. Just as critical as the teaching of a new skill for a sport is to successful coaching. Once the fundamentals of interventions are understood by coaches, it will be easier to implement (practice) them when needed. Three (3) basic aspects of intervention skills that will be discussed in this supplement include:

1. Identifying and defining negative enabling behavior,
2. Establishing effective communication skills, and
3. Implementing confrontation techniques.

Negative Enabling Behavior

An individual's behavior is related to his/her thoughts and feelings. Consequently, much of what an individual does is based upon enabling him/herself to do what is perceived to be personally beneficial. This "self-enabling behavior" is primarily rooted in experiences, values, needs, and desires that are formed as one develops mentally, physically, and emotionally. Sometimes, however, an individual may engage in certain behaviors that are not in his/her best interest (at-risk), but are not generally seen in this manner by the person. Additionally, and often creating more complexity to an already challenging aspect of life, the at-risk behaviors are rewarding or pleasing in some manner to the individual.

When an individual engages in at-risk behaviors and is unable to see accurately what is going on, or chooses for some reason not to confront and/or stop the adverse behavior, the behaviors and attached attitudes become even more difficult to change. An additional factor that contributes to the difficulty of stopping and/or changing

at-risk behavior(s) is the unwillingness or uneasiness that others experience when faced with having to confront someone about his/her attitude or behavior. This is where the coach must intervene.

Coach have a responsibility to provide a safe environment for their athletes. Subsequently, any concern regarding questionable behaviors or attitudes expressed by the athletes must be addressed by the coach. **If the coach chooses not to take any action, or decides to step forward to protect a troubled athlete from certain consequences (i.e., being benched, suspended, or removed from the team), negative enabling behavior is exhibited. In this particular scenario negative enabling behavior would be defined as, and represented by, the removing of, or the neglect of implementing consequences. Either action, or lack of action, by the coach would therefore act to minimize and reinforce the at-risk behavior.**

The following discussion identifies four key concepts that coaches need to be aware of if they are to reduce or eliminate negative enabling behavior:

1. Almost everyone (i.e., coach, teammate, trainer, parent, sibling or teacher) who is in contact with a troubled athlete enables at least occasionally. However, a chief or primary enabler always exists. This is an individual who has a close relationship with the troubled person. Therefore, it is critical for the coach to be aware that the closeness and uniqueness of a relationship can also cause one not to do what is in the best interest of the athlete/person.

2. Enabling behavior begins slowly and is not easily recognized. The enabler may begin the behavior by making excuses for the athlete or by smoothing over embarrassing incidents—all the while resisting, avoiding or not admitting that a problem exists. Finally, the enabler may commit to hiding the athlete's problem(s) by taking some, if not all of, the responsibility for the athlete's behavior.

3. Negative enabling behavior can act to prevent certain crises or incidents from occurring which often times,

unfortunately, need to occur before a troubled person (and others) will see that help is needed. Intervention can act to keep an athlete from experiencing a crisis. Coaches play a critical role in discouraging the development of alcohol and other drug (AODs) problems by confronting the problems before their level of severity increases.

4. Negative enabling behavior also exists, in large part, because some type of a reward or payoff that the enabler perceives that they are receiving. One such payoff may be a sense of control or power over the individual. The enabler gets caught up in allowing certain behaviors to continue while trying to keep others from occurring

Examples of coaches' negative enabling behavior.

- A coach looks the other way when an athlete comes to practice imparied from alcohol abuse. The coach's reactions may result from feeling that the team can't afford to lose the athlete's talent for an upcoming event.
- Ignoring the smell of alcohol or marijuana or finding syringes, pills or empty bottles of medication and choosing not to confront the team and/or athlete.
- Overhearing conversations in the locker room or in the hallway about dangerous behaviors that included passing-out, blacking-out, or throwing-up from alcohol abuse, and choosing not to confront those involved.
- An athlete comes to practice with a laceration, bruise, sprain or a broken bone that is commonly known to have happened at a "party" and no confrontation takes place.
- Choosing not to discuss a recent AOD-related incident that occurred in the school or community for fear that they may uncover problems on the team which the coach does not want to confront.
- Not enforcing established team chemical health guidelines; or enforcing them differently for different team members.

Examples of statements that contribute to negative enabling behavior(s):

- "Not on my team."
- "That's not a problem in this area."
- "These kids are good, smart kids; they wouldn't do that stuff."
- "If I start to deal with chemical issues with an athlete on my team then I might have to take a closer look at my own use."
- "I'll do something when a sure solution is found and has been proven to be successful. Until then, I don't want to deal with it."

The coach's personal business, the coach's personal involvement with alcohol, nicotine or caffeine may influ-

ence similar behaviors by the athletes. This behavior could possibly send a message to the athletes that tells them, "What I (the coach) do is my business, and what my players do away from the arena is their business."

Every effort possible must be expended if negative enabling behaviors are to be significantly reduced or eliminated. This reduction and elimination will be realized once at-risk attitudes and behaviors are intervened upon and confronted. Effective communication and confrontation techniques are two key elements that coaches will need to employ if they are to reduce and eliminate negative enabling behavior and chemical abuse problems.

Effective Communication

Effective communication is achieved when the message that is intended to be sent by the coach is the message that is received by the athlete. When communication is used effectively it contributes to the development of supportive relationships and unites a team in its efforts to achieve personal and athletic goals. **Coaches must acknowledge its importance and make an effort to remember the following key components of communication** (Tubbs and Moss, 1983).

- Understanding,
- Pleasure,
- Attitude,
- Improved relationships and
- Action.

1. *Understanding*: Poorly sent or inaccurately received messages lead to misunderstandings and are responsible for most failures in communication. Having your message understood is easier to achieve in a one-on-one interaction with an athlete than it is when you try to communicate with the entire team. As the number of receivers of your message increases, so does the difficulty in determining how accurately the message(s) are received. It is common for misunderstandings to exist between a coach and athlete, and some of those misunderstandings will be difficult to resolve. However, if the coach and athlete are a.) willing to try to communicate clearly, and b.) are willing to acknowledge misunderstandings, the likelihood for effective communication will improve.

2. *Pleasure*: Often the coach will just want to communicate a general message of well-being, friendliness, or interest. The amount of pleasure a coach experiences and exhibits when communicating with athletes is representative of the feelings the coach has toward them and the feelings the players have toward their coach. Discovering that communication with a particular athlete is not pleasurable, the coach must be willing to find out why this is so. Initially, the communi-

cation of chemical health may be uncomfortable for both the coach and athlete. However, the feelings that the coach and athlete can experience from their attempt to ensure a healthy and positive personal and athletic experience by being chemically-free will far outweigh any earlier feelings of discomfort that may exist.

3. *Attitude*: Effective communication influences attitudes. Changing unhealthy attitudes about chemicals to healthy attitudes is critical to the CHEC program. If an attitude change does not occur, then the coach will need to reassess the message. Positive attitudes are essential to positive athletic experiences. Positive chemical health attitudes are essential to positive life experiences.

4. *Improved Relationships*: It is commonly accepted that for communication to be effective, a climate of trust must be present. Young athletes want to feel that they can trust their coach. However, if a climate of distrust (possibly from a misunderstanding) exists, it will be easier for the athlete(s) to distort or discredit their coach's message, regardless of how conscientiously it is constructed. Another common reason for breakdowns in communication is the uneasy or strained relationship that may exist between an athlete and the coach. Frustration, anger, or confusion may result from an athlete's or coach's inability to understand a message that is unclear in its meaning. One of the biggest challenges in chemical health education by the coach is attaining trust through consistent messages and behaviors. When this is accomplished, improved relationships may be experienced.

5. *Action*: Communication that requires action on the part of the receiver is a challenge to achieve. This difficulty can be compounded when the action is chemical health behavior. There is less of a challenge to get athletes to agree to change their attitude and/or behavior than it is to get them to take the required action that indicates a change. The coach will experience more success in gaining action or change among athletes when their chemical health message is clearly stated. Effective communication goals for the CHEC program are...
   - Persuading athletes to change unhealthy attitudes and/or behaviors and
   - Encouraging those who are practicing healthy attitudes and behaviors to continue.

Strategies for Effective Communication

What follows are additional suggestions for strategies that can assist coaches in their effort to communicate more effectively with their athletes. Bidol (1986) referred to active listening, purposeful sending, and constructive feedback as key strategies needed for effective communi-cation. These components are discussed in an effort to increase the coach's awareness of issues that are as characteristic and personal as each athlete, and that are consistently present in the communication process in one form or another. If the coach has these components in mind when communicating with the athletes about chemical health, the likelihood of support and success are increased

Active Listening

Taking the time to actively listen to the needs of the athlete(s) is the first critical step that every coach must take in dealing with chemical health. Tubbs and Moss (1983) indicated that most people spend 70% of their waking hours communicating. Rankin (1976) further indicated that 42% of the time is spent listening; 32% talking; 15% reading; and 11% writing. Because we spend most of our communication time listening, one might think it would be the easiest and/or the most developed of our skills. However, listening is the most difficult channel of communication for most individuals. Taking the time to listen actively requires patience. However, patience will be rewarded with improved interpersonal relationships, the ability to make sound decisions, and the capacity to respond appropriately, each of which contributes to an enhanced life and athletic experience.

- *Pleasurable*: The coach might experience pleasure when listening to the athletes express their "awesome feeling" in reference to their coach's leadership during a victory over their cross-town rival. In relation to chemical health, pleasurable listening may be experienced when an athlete who has had a problem with alcohol in the past tells you that he or she decided to hang out with fellow teammates, rather than with his/her normal drinking crowd.
- *Discriminative*: This is most accurately described as serious listening. Discriminative listening is a form of listening in which the individual realizes that what is being said is critical and must be clearly understood and remembered. A coaching example might be when one of the athletes makes a suggestion about a better way to defend a certain opponent. Consequently, the coach listens intently (with discrimination) to what sounds like a useful idea, and asks for clarity or reasoning in the athlete's suggestions. When the coach overhears a chemical abuse discussion by an athlete in which the athlete expressed some behaviors that cause the coach to be concerned the coach needs to listen seriously. Listen with discrimination to understand and remember what was said, knowing that the information he/she is listening to may be useful when confronting the athlete regarding the chemical issue.
- *Critical*: This form of listening helps the coach sort through information that may be biased, unrelated to,

or irrelevant to the current issue at hand. In coaching this might be experienced when one of your athletes is trying to explain to you (make excuses) why he or she missed an assignment or was late to practice. The coach would sort through what is reasonable and believable and disregard what is not.

Critical listening will help the coach in chemical issues as well by focusing on information that is of primary concern, reasonable, believable, and that the coach knows to be true, rather than listening to the athlete provide information that the coach knows is not true. One such example may be evident when an athlete attempts to deny his/her abuse of steroids by providing false information to the coach. Although the false information could prove critical to the overall situation, the coach should be able to determine what is not true and focus upon what is true in an effort to successfully and ethically confront the athlete's behavior.

- *Empathetic*: This helps the coach to be more aware of what the athlete is saying beyond their words. Empathetic listening is the sensitivity, understanding, care, and concern that coaches express through the quality of their listening. For example, an athlete who is upset because you benched him/her for coming to practice late comes to you visibly and verbally angry. The athlete proceeds to tell you (with a shaky voice and watery eyes) that if they didn't have to do what their mom or dad should be doing, then they would not be late coming to practice. As a result of your emphatically listening, you ask the athlete to slow down so you can learn more about what is going on in his/her home. This sensitivity and concern tells the athlete that you care and that you can be trusted. The athlete may be ready to tell someone about his/her parents' drinking problems.

Each of these levels of listening will assist coaches in communicating more effectively with their athletes. Active listening requires time and effort. However, being aware that listening is a skill, similar to complex athletic skills, which require practice and understanding, will enable the coach to be more patient. The following are a few additional suggestions adopted from Bidol (1986) to help a coach become a more successful active listener:

- Listen to your athlete without judgement.
- Listen before responding.
- Paraphrase back to the athlete so they know you listened to them.
- Block out anything that may interfere with your ability to listen.
- Pay attention to the non-verbal messages being sent by the athlete.

- Remember, your rate of thinking is faster than the athlete's rate of talking.
- Accept the athlete's message.
- Respond when asked.
- Remember, acceptance does not mean agreement.

Purposeful Sending

The main idea of purposeful sending is to be aware that what coaches say to their athletes is critical. Subsequently, coaches must think about what they want to convey to the athlete before it is said. Coaches are responsible for sending a clear and meaningful message to their athletes regarding chemical health. If coaches are going to be successful in their purposeful communication they must also be aware of the things that could interfere. Bidol (1986) suggested that individuals should be aware of the following potential barriers to purposeful sending.

- Ego-oriented attention whereby coaches are more interest in their own thoughts and needs rather than the needs of the athletes.
- Hearing only what the coach wants to hear.
- Ignoring the feelings and values expressed in messages sent and/or received.
- Prejudging a message based on the coach's personal frame of reference or past experience.

Confrontation Technique

Confrontation is a critical communication skill that is needed to help the coach define, establish and maintain healthy relationships with the athletes. All coaches use confrontation techniques at one time or another. For example, when it is important to get a new game strategy integrated into a young athlete's mind, and that athlete, due to the newness of the strategy, struggles with its implementation, coaches will confront the athlete about his/her struggle. Similarly, just as there exists a transfer of one motor skill to another similar motor skill in physical activity, there also exists the ability to transfer the confrontation technique to the chemical health education dimension of their coaching.

Confrontation is often misunderstood and mishandled. The word itself is somewhat uncomfortable and can arouse feelings of fear and anxiety in some who are exposed to it. However, confrontation technique is a skill that once learned, practiced, and used appropriately, can act to enhance and deepen relationships between the coach and athlete.

Many view confrontation as "telling someone off" or "getting in someone's face" or that it's a negative, unhappy, and undesirable experience. This is not necessarily true. The manner in which the coach chooses to use this intervention skill can have a positive affect upon the team. Johnson (1972) defined confrontation as a deliberate attempt to help another person examine the consequences of some aspect of his or her behavior. Therefore, a chemical problem on your team presents an opportunity for the coach to encourage an athlete to examine his or her life. This examination could prove to be one of the most important experiences in the athlete's life; one that allows the person to take a serious look at their unhealthy behavior. There are two fundamental approaches to confrontation that Dowd and Joyce (1982) proposed and that can be adopted for the coach's attempt to confront an athlete concerning a chemical-related problem.

Confrontation Content

Informative: This occurs when a coach talks to an athlete about the factual information discovered, and the coach's reaction to the behaviors in question. It is critical that the athlete is not labeled an alcoholic, drug addict, steroid juicer, pot-head, or drug pusher. It is important that the coach does not "name call" the athlete, but only describes what they observed (or have learned from credible and reliable sources) the athlete doing. The main goal is for the coach to clearly and honestly state what is known.

Interpretive: This is as challenging as the informational confrontation, but in a different manner. Here the coach presents to the athlete what he/she thinks or perceives what the behavior means. The coach provides the athlete with their interpretation of the behavior. Interpretive confrontation occurs when the coach brings to the athlete's attention what the coach believes is happening.

Given these two approaches for confronting an athlete with chemical problems there are also some criteria that coaches should be aware of prior to confronting an athlete.

Five Criteria for Confrontation

1. **Get to the point**.
2. **Summarize and integrate** all behaviors that have contributed to the occurrence of the confrontation.
3. **Base the confrontation on accurate information**. The conversation must also attend to the behaviors,

not the personality or character. A confrontation grounded in fact, and that has been well documented, will help the athlete understand more clearly which behaviors have the coach concerned.

4. **Avoid brining up inappropriate or irrelevant past issues** in the "current" confrontation.
5. **Avoid using aggressive tones** that might contribute to the athlete's withdrawal (psychologically or emotionally).

SUMMARY

One must remember that confrontation, when implemented appropriately, can lead to a positive and healthy experience by those involved with the process. For example, as a coach you will occasionally interact with an athlete who struggles with accepting or acknowledging his/her skills, talents, accomplishments, or contributions to the team. In this case confrontation would be used to help give the athlete a clearer and more accurate picture of him/ herself. Confrontation technique can help athletes begin to lose their negative or distorted image of themselves regardless of what the circumstances may entail. This is precisely what the implementation of an appropriate and thoughtfully conceived confrontation technique will achieve for an athlete who may be struggling with a chemical problem.

REFERENCES

Bidol, P. (1986). *Alternative Conflict Management Approaches: A Citizen's Manual*. Environmental Conflict Project, University of Michigan. (pp. 205-208).

Dowd, T. E., and Joyce, M. (editors) (1982). *Level I Human Relations Skills for the Occupational Specialist Working with Groups*. Competency-Based Modular Series. Florida State University, Center for Studies in Vocational Education. (ERIC Document Reproduction Service No. ED 236 435).

Johnson, D. W. (1972). *Reaching Out: Interpersonal Effectiveness and Self-Actualization*. Englewood Cliffs, NJ: Prentice-Hall.

Rankin, P. (1976). *The Measurement of the Ability to Understand Spoken Language*. Unpublished doctoral dissertation, University of Michigan, Ann Arbor.

Tubbs, S. T., and Moss, S. (1983). *Human Communication, (4th edition)*. New York: Random House, Inc., pp. 14-18.

Section IV
Psychology

21
Effective Communication

Jennifer J. Waldron, M.Ed.; Martha E. Ewing, Ph.D. and
Lori Gano-Overway, Ph.D.

QUESTIONS TO CONSIDER

- How can you send clear messages to your athletes?
- What are the characteristics of a good listener?
- How do gender and culture affect communication?
- What are strategies for communicating with parents?

> It is a Friday practice and your baseball team has its first game in a week. At the end of practice, you call the team together and explain to the players that they have to be at practice every day next week in order to play in the game on the following Friday. You observe two of your players talking to each other and you ask if they were paying attention. The players said they were listening. On Thursday, the same two players are not at practice. They come to the game on Friday and cannot believe they will not be playing in the game. They claim that they never heard you say that they had to be at practice to play.

INTRODUCTION

Many of us have had experiences like these when we thought we were communicating with athletes. We believe that we are sending clear messages; however, somewhere along the line a misinterpretation occurs. Why was the message not received? What was ineffective about the communication?

Communication is critical for coaches to effectively carry out the roles of leader, teacher, and motivator. Many of the activities that the coach engages in on a daily basis require communication with others. A coach must effectively communicate with athletes, parents, athletic directors, and others. The focus of this chapter is on communicating with athletes; however, much of the information is also pertinent to other relationships.

Communication consists of sending, receiving, and interpreting messages by verbal or nonverbal means (Yukelson, 1998). Effective communication is a two-way street. The significance of sending messages is fairly obvious. However, being receptive to other people's ideas and concerns is also an important component of communication. Thus, Table 21-1 highlights several types of messages that coaches send to athletes and also several types of messages that coaches receive from athletes.

SENDING MESSAGES

Coaches usually send many messages to athletes. When coaches talk, they convey information through both verbal and nonverbal cues. This section explores different types of verbal messages that coaches send, including organizational information and feedback, as well as nonverbal messages.

> It is the last practice before a softball game. At the beginning of practice, you go over logistical information about the game. Throughout practice and after practice the players keep asking you what time the bus leaves and if they need to bring money. That evening a parent phones asking you if her child needs money for the game.

Organizational Messages

As the example implies, when giving organizational information it is important to get and keep the athlete's

Table 21-1. Types of Messages Coaches Send and Receive.

Messages Sent to Athletes	Messages Received from Athletes
• Instruct	• Ask questions
• Motivate	• Desire clarification
• Encourage and reinforce	• Disclose personal problems
• Discipline	• Provide feedback
• Evaluate	

attention. This can be accomplished by using eye contact and avoiding potential distractions. For example, trying to give instructional information to the junior varsity when the varsity team is waiting for your practice to end will probably ensure that you do not have your athletes' attention. Using direct messages and reducing comments to contain only the important information is also suggested.

Obtain information to determine if the message was interpreted correctly.

Finally, check with the athletes to make sure they understand what you are saying. When you tell your team that the bus leaves at 4:00 p.m. for the competition, ask some of them what time the bus is leaving to make sure that they understand. It is especially important to check with the athletes who you do not think are listening to you. Checking with your athletes is probably the best way that you can make sure your athletes comprehend and interpret the messages correctly.

Feedback

Coaches are constantly giving feedback to athletes, especially in terms of evaluating athletes' skill performances. Evaluative feedback is necessary to help athletes improve their skills and strategies. Furthermore, feedback can also serve to enhance or maintain the athlete's motivation.

Effective evaluative feedback has several important features. It is:

- *Consistent*: It is important to provide effective feedback to each of your players, regardless of their ability.
- *Focused*: When athletes make a mistake in a drill make sure the feedback is simple and focuses on one error at a time. If you tell the athletes everything they did wrong, they may suffer from information overload.
- *Timely*: Give feedback right after the skill is performed so that the athlete remembers exactly what part of the skill you are describing.
- *Specific*: Reduce comments to the specific information that the athlete needs to know.

- *Based on the quality of performance*: Feedback should be based on improvement or the quality of the skill rather than on the outcome (i.e., winning or making the shot). See also Chapter 24, *Motivating Athletes*.
- *Encouraging*: It is important that the athletes know that you support them and believe in them.

One way to give evaluative feedback to athletes is to use the sandwich approach. The key is to "sandwich" the instruction or the technical correction between reinforcement and encouragement. The instruction should indicate what part of the skill is incorrect and how it can be corrected. For example, a basketball player has been working on his free throw shooting. While you are watching, his free throw hits the rim to the left. Using the sandwich approach you could provide him feedback in the following manner:

- *Reinforcement*: "Let's work on that shot. First, your elbow was at a 90-degree angle at the beginning of the shot. That was good."
- *Instruct*: "Next, your arm went across your body as you extended it, causing the ball to travel to the left. So you need to be sure your hand follows through straight to the basket."
- *Encourage*: "Really focus on the follow-through; I know you can do it."

The Sandwich Approach: Reinforce, Instruct, Encourage

It is also helpful to model the correct and incorrect technique to the athlete. This approach not only provides feedback, but it also reinforces what is being done correctly and encourages continued effort. In this manner, you will help to improve the athletes' skills as well as motivate them.

Nonverbal Messages

When communicating with your athletes, your messages will contain verbal as well as nonverbal information. During conversation, about 35% of the message is verbal and 65% of the message is nonverbal (Thomlison,

1999). Thus, nonverbal communication is important. Table 21-2 describes several types of nonverbal cues. People are not always aware when they are sending nonverbal messages, and therefore, they are often difficult to disguise. However, nonverbal messages are often more powerful than verbal messages, and people have a tendency to place more emphasis on nonverbal messages. For example, your shortstop was just hit in the shin by a line drive. You ask him if he needs to sit out for a bit of time. He says no, but his face clearly shows he is in pain and he is not putting any pressure on that leg. You take him out because you recognize his nonverbal messages.

Nonverbal cues are an important aspect to effective communication. Several tips in using nonverbal communication are indicated below:

- Use nonverbal cues in conjunction with the verbal message. It is important to have consistency between the nonverbal cues and the verbal message.
- Monitor the use of your own nonverbal cues. This can be accomplished by having a trusted coach or friend observe you during practice, paying attention to your nonverbal cues.

- Monitor the nonverbal cues of your athletes as you deliver messages. You will gain information from observing their nonverbal cues.
- If you do not understand your athletes' nonverbal cues, obtain feedback from the athletes to ensure that the message was interpreted correctly.

RECEIVING MESSAGES

Being able to listen is also essential to effective communication. Listening makes up half of the communication process. Further, people only interpret and comprehend about 25% of what they hear (Purdy, 1999b). From these statistics, it is obvious that effective listening is very important to communication.

However, listening is not something that is automatic. Hearing is physical and biological, while listening is mental. It is a skill. Thus, people do not reach a certain age and suddenly become good listeners. Listening, like speaking, is a skill that must be developed and practiced. Table 21-3 summarizes seven steps to becoming an effective listener.

When athletes are sending messages, it is important

Table 21-2. Nonverbal Cues.

Categories of Nonverbal Messages

- Posture: how we hold our body and the way we walk
- Facial expressions: especially our eyes and our mouth, time of eye contact
- Gestures: throwing arms up in the air, crossed arms, pointing
- Voice characteristics: not what you say but how you say it
- Body position: distance between ourselves and other people
- Touching: high five, pat on the back

Table 21-3. Steps to Becoming an Effective Listener.

Effective Listening Steps	Here's How
1. Want to listen	Make a conscious choice to listen
2. Give the speaker your attention	Eye contact, acknowledge that you're listening ("hmmmm"), stop making lists or reading
3. Be perceptive and open to the message	Wait for the athlete to complete the message before jumping in
4. Hear the message, not just the words	Athletes may be nervous talking to you—try to put aside these difficulties and understand the message
5. Remember what you heard	Restate what you heard, repeat the message in your head, connect the message to something else
6. Clarify the message by responding	Ask the speaker if your interpretation of the message was correct
7. Care about the speaker	Show compassion, understanding, and support to the listener

Based on Purdy, "Intrapersonal and Interpersonal Listening," 1999b.

to remember the power differential in the coach-athlete relationship. Thus, it is very likely that athletes may be nervous, anxious, or uncomfortable when talking to you, the coach. Therefore, it is essential that as you listen, get past the verbal stumbles of the athletes and listen for the true meaning of the message. By doing so, athletes will be more apt to approach you and talk to you in the future.

There also are behaviors of the listener that may hinder the communication process. Several behaviors that may negatively affect the communication process are summarized in Table 21-4. By engaging in these behaviors, the listener is not being receptive to the message being sent. In other words, you are not being an effective listener. Moreover, these behaviors may also discourage the sender of the message. Therefore, these behaviors can create barriers to effective communication on two levels.

COMMUNICATION BREAKDOWNS

Sender Failures

Contradictory Messages

The scenario described in the box that follows is an example of a coach sending a contradictory message—the coach said one thing at practice and then contradicted the message in competition. Coaches also send contradictory messages when they give different players conflicting information. This can decrease your credibility as a coach because the athletes will simply not believe or trust what you are telling them.

It is the first football game of the season. You told the team that everyone will be playing in the game. There is 5 minutes left in the game. You have the ball on your opponents' 20-yard line, and are down by 3 points. The 2 players who have not played all game are ready to play the last few minutes. You quickly decide that your best players have to be in the game so the team can win; thus, 2 players on the team never got to play

---

Table 21-4. Blocks to Effective Listening.

Ineffective Listening
1. Asking too many questions
2. Giving advice
3. Being judgmental of athletes' opinions, beliefs, values
4. Agreeing or disagreeing
5. Being defensive
6. Using clichés

Based on Purdy, "Intrapersonal and Interpersonal Listening," 1999a.

Verbal Versus Nonverbal Messages

When you send messages to athletes, you may, without thinking, send unintentional nonverbal messages. If the nonverbal message conflicts with the verbal message, confusion often results. For example, when you compliment an athlete on a good job and then let your shoulders slump and heave a heavy sigh, the athlete may be less receptive to your next attempt at praise. Another instance of a mixed message occurs if you tell your athletes that they should never question an official's calls and then you denounce an official's decision. If the need arises to question an official's call, you should ask for clarification in a professional manner.

Receiver Failures

Misinterpreting Messages

Your athlete is trying to tell you that he has to miss practices every Tuesday because he has to care for his little sister. Your interpretation is that he is not serious about soccer and therefore you start treating him differently. However, if you had asked him to clarify the situation and really heard the message, you probably would not have misinterpreted it. By not understanding the situation, you jumped to a conclusion that may not be accurate. Such hasty judgments may have a profound influence on the treatment of athletes. Be certain to accurately understand and interpret the message being sent.

Failure to Listen

There are five minutes left of your open office hours and then you have to rush to a meeting. One of your athletes suddenly walks through the door asking to talk to you. You say "Sure," but are you determined to have her out of the door quickly so you are not late? In this situation, it is likely that you will not give the athlete your full attention and will not be listening to what she is telling you. A better decision would be to explain to the athlete that her thoughts and feelings are important to you, but you have to be somewhere in five minutes and would like to schedule a better time to talk. In this manner, you will be able to properly listen to the athlete when you have the time.

INTERPRETING MESSAGES

The final part of effective communication is being able to correctly interpret the sent message and help others correctly interpret your messages. People send and receive messages based on their personality, experiences, and gender. It is important to become aware of our own communication style and how it may differ from the style of others. In this manner we may be able to more effectively interpret other people's messages and explain our own interpretations. This section explores how prior experiences, gender, and culture can influence communication and the style of interpretation.

Experiences

A coach must realize that athletes will interpret information (e.g., evaluative feedback) differently based on prior experiences, ability level, and personality. Feedback can be given in the form of praise or criticism. One would expect that praise should increase motivation, whereas criticism should decrease motivation. However, this is not always the case because of individual differences in the interpretation of feedback. For example, a low ability athlete receives praise after catching a fly ball, while her teammates always catch a fly ball and do not receive praise. The low ability athlete may think that this is the maximum performance level expected of her. Because each athlete has different experiences and abilities, it is important for coaches to get to know every athlete on an individual basis. Through such interactions coaches begin to understand how each athlete may interpret messages.

Cross-Gender Communication

Cross-gender communication affects a coach, whether it is a male coach of women's teams or a female coach of men's teams. Through different socialization processes, females generally learn to focus on intimacy, whereas males generally learn to focus on independence. Females tend to value connection by having a circle of friends, diminishing differences, and avoiding superiority, while males tend to value status by being able to give orders to others (Tannen, 1990). These value differences also influence the communication styles of men and women.

When communicating, women tend to place importance on feelings and the desire to stay connected. Men, on the other hand, tend to place importance on "facts" and are eager to divulge information. Thus, women may become irritated at men for trying to impress others and men may become annoyed at women for hiding their successes. The following example suggests how gender may influence the process of communication. As coaches, it is important to be sensitive to the responses of individuals and realize that gender may impact the message.

A male gymnastics coach has been very impressed with Stacy's (a freshman) improvement and decides that it is time to move her up to the varsity team. He tells Stacy the news and expects her to be extremely excited and proud because of her increased status. So he is shocked when Stacy simply

---

starts crying. Stacy tries to explain that now she will not get to practice with her friends and she probably will lose them all because they will think she is better than they are. This is an example of a miscommunication based on gender. More effective communication would have occurred if the coach thought about Stacy's reaction to being separated from her friends and having to interact or socialize with juniors and seniors. A possible solution to this problem would be to move another freshman up to the varsity level in order to keep Stacy connected.

Women and men also listen differently. Women tend to use "fillers" when listening, while men tend to be silent listeners. Fillers are sounds such as "uh-huh," "hmmmmm" or "I see" which are used while receiving a message. These fillers inform women that the other person is listening. When a woman is talking to a man and he is listening in silence, the woman may interpret this as a lack of interest or a failure to listen, which could quickly shutdown further communication. On the other hand, when a man is talking to a woman and she continues to use fillers, he may become frustrated that she is constantly agreeing with him.

Today, it is common for men to coach female athletes. Cross-gender coaching may be a more important factor during adolescence as young girls are trying to figure out who they are. Some male coaches have learned strategies to deal with differences in communication styles. Women and girls do not typically respond well to standoffish coaches, or coaches who are constantly yelling orders. Instead, it is beneficial to show female athletes that you care about them and their well being by:

- Acknowledging the feelings behind what they are saying;
- Avoiding sex-stereotyped activities and comments, such as "Don't act like a girl;"
- Avoiding comments about body size and shape;
- Giving praise for their skills and successes, instead of praising them for their appearance (tell them "You did a great job today" not "You looked great today"); and
- Providing sincere, positive encouragement and recognizing effort.

Although it is more common for men to coach girls and women, it is also possible for women to coach boys and men. Males are socialized to understand that they will be yelled at from coaches. Women coaches may not be as likely to scream at and belittle athletes. Thus, communication problems can occur between women coaches and male athletes.

Intercultural Communication

The cultural and ethnic make-up of the United States is changing dramatically, and transcontinental travel is increasingly common. Therefore, it is likely that you may coach athletes that come from a different cultural/ethnic background or country. Thus, it is important to recognize how culture may modify the way people send, receive, and interpret messages.

People from different cultures will experience and perceive life in distinct ways. European American culture generally emphasizes "doing." In other words, clocks and schedules govern lives, work is seen as a separate activity from play, and people try to change the world in order to solve problems. Conversely, cultures that emphasize "being" (such as Asian-Americans and Native Americans) engage in a more relaxed pace of life, do not separate work from play, and accept the world as it is (Lusting and Koester, 1993). Cultures also view the self differently. For example, European Americans tend to value the self as an individual separate from others, while Asian-Americans, African-Americans, and Mexican-Americans tend to value the self in relation to other people.

Cultures also perceive time in a different way. Asian-Americans are past oriented and tend to resist change; Latin-Americans emphasize a present orientation to time; and North Americans are future-oriented. These are only some of the examples of potential cultural differences that can have consequences for efforts to communicate. Thus, it is important that a coach seeks information about the cultural background of athletes, is aware of potential differences, and asks questions in a sensitive manner.

But perhaps more importantly, nonverbal cues vary among different cultures. Cultures often use and interpret the following nonverbal cues differently:

- *Touch*: duration, frequency, and location
- *Space/distance*: responses to personal space
- *Eye contact*: with who and when we make eye contact
- *Silence*

As previously noted, nonverbal messages are usually sent unconsciously. Hence, special importance should be placed on using and interpreting nonverbal cues when cultural variation is involved. Table 21-5 shows how nonverbal greetings and eye contact are used and interpreted by various cultures.

These examples of the verbal and nonverbal communication styles of different cultures show the importance of awareness or cultural sensitivity. It cannot be assumed that we know exactly what the other person meant. When an athlete responds in a way that you do not understand, it is imperative to ask the athlete about the response. It is possible that it is a cultural response and it is necessary to establish this before getting upset and frustrated with the athlete. Beebe, Beebe and Redmond (1996) provided several additional tips for effective intercultural communication:

- Seek information about your athletes' cultural backgrounds.
- Be other-oriented—be aware of the value of your athletes' viewpoint and allow athletes to be who they really are.
- Ask questions in a sensitive manner.
- Be aware of the impact of your comments on the athletes and avoid using stereotypes.
- Tolerate ambiguity or uncertainty.
- Avoid negative judgments—all cultures have their strengths and weaknesses.
- Do not think your culture has all of the answers.

In conclusion, it is important to realize that this section has focused on general patterns that may be found in cross-gender and intercultural communication. Not every man will divulge facts and information when communicating. Nor will all Native Americans avoid eye contact with superiors or will all women use fillers. The purpose of this discussion was to increase awareness that gender and cultural/ethnic background may affect communication. It is important not to make assumptions about athletes but to get to know them and respect them as individuals.

Josie is rolling her eyes at the coach who is explaining how to properly get through a screen in basketball. The coach glares at Josie who arrogantly says, "I already know this stuff". The following conversation occurs:

Coach: "I am tired of your attitude Josie. You need to shape up."

Josie: "Coach, I don't know what you are talking about. I just said I know how to do this."

Coach: "Well that is exactly it. I don't like your attitude."

Josie: "My attitude is fine, coach."

How often has this happened to you? You try to confront athletes about their attitude and they act like they have no idea what is wrong with their attitude. Well, it is likely that they do not know. By simply telling athletes that "I don't like your attitude," you are not telling the athletes' what behaviors you wish would stop or change. Thus, it is important to communicate to athletes what behaviors you have observed that are unacceptable. Let's examine the above scenario in this light:

Coach: "I am tired of your attitude Josie. You need to shape up."

Josie: "Coach, I don't know what you are talking about. I just said I know how to do this."

Table 21-5. Nonverbal Cues and Culture.

Nonverbal Greetings	Eye Contact
North America: Handshake	*European American:* Eye contact while listening
Asia: Bow, sometimes with hands in front of the chest	*African-American:* Eye contact while speaking
Parts of Europe: Hug and kiss on both cheeks	*Native American:* Avoid eye contact when communicating with a superior

CONFRONTATION

It is inevitable that a coach will become emotionally charged at some point during a practice or a competition as a result of athletes' behavior. You may experience anger, frustration, or disappointment with an athlete or the team, and thus, have to confront them with your displeasure. In some situations, such as the ones described in the box above, a confrontation is a relatively simple process that can be resolved by telling an athlete to stop a specific behavior. However, at other times confrontations are more complex. This section suggests guidelines to help coaches learn how to confront athletes.

The first step in confronting an individual is identifying the problem or situation that needs to be changed. For example, the problem was that the coach did not like Josie rolling her eyes during a demonstration of a skill. Once the problem is identified, it is important to stop and think before acting. Doing so allows time to collect thoughts, think calmly, and gain control of the situation. We have all heard of "hot-headed individuals" who let their emotions (i.e., anger, frustration) rule their responses or who act on impulse when they are confronted. Hot-headed reactions are not effective, and people often later regret their actions in such situations. Coaches must think before they act in order to maintain control and remain calm. Suggestions to help a coach "cool-off" include (Guerra, et al., 1995):

- Silently count to 10 or 20.
- Take 5 deep breaths.
- Be proactive.
- Recognize when you are in a bad mood, and try to stay away from potential problems.
- Think of the consequences of your actions.
- Tell the athlete you are too upset to talk right now and confront the athlete when you have sufficiently calmed down.

When confronting others, it is crucial to realize that two people often see the same situation from a different perspective. By correctly understanding the other person's point of view, you will gain additional information about the problem and hopefully will avoid jumping to conclusions. It is only when you stop and think that you will be in the proper mindset to try to recognize the other's perspective in the situation.

Coaches should use an assertive style of confrontation with their athletes. An assertive confrontational style allows coaches to meet their own goals, while keeping the best interests of the athletes in mind. Guidelines to help you adopt an assertive style of confrontation can be summarized as follows:

1. *Own your messages*: It is important to use "I" messages when showing anger or frustration towards your athletes. Instead of saying to an athlete "You played terribly in the game", say "I am disappointed in how you played tonight".
2. *Use supportive messages*: Make sure your athletes realize it is their behavior with which you are angry or disappointed, and not with them as individuals. By using supportive messages, athletes know you respect and care for them as individuals.
3. *State your needs*: Let athletes know what you need from them as a member of a team. For example, if a player is constantly putting down teammates with lesser abilities, tell the player what you need (i.e., not to put down teammates) and why you need it (i.e., it brings down the morale of the team).

Athletes will respond better to confrontation when they know that their coaches care and support them, and when they know it is their behaviors and not them as individuals that is the cause of the coach's anger or disappointment.

In summary, use the following steps when confronting athletes:

1. Identify the problem.
2. Stop and think before taking action.
3. Understand the other person's perspective.
4. Use an assertive style of confrontation.

COMMUNICATION WITH PARENTS

A coach must also communicate with parents during a season. Most parents would like to be "in-the-know." They want to be part of the information loop. Through team meetings, personal discussions or letters, a coach should notify parents about organizational information, expectations, coaching philosophy, and the importance of their support. Parents also want to hear good things about their child from time to time. Thus, let parents know when their son has improved his shot or when their daughter has played excellent defense.

An orientation meeting with parents is an important step in creating a solid foundation for effective communication and in preventing potential problems. The meeting should include your goals for the team and team policies (e.g., missed practice). New or modified rules of the game, potential injuries, and essential practice equipment should be discussed. It is important to explain your expectations for each athlete (e.g., cooperation and effort). This is also the time to explain the responsibilities of parents, which include (Martens, 1978):

- Learning what their child expects from the sport,
- Helping their child understand the meaning of winning and losing,
- Disciplining their child,
- Encouraging their child to meet responsibilities,
- Understanding protocol for approaching the coach, and
- Conducting themselves in an appropriate fashion at competitions.

It is important that you contact parents who were unable to attend the orientation meeting in order to inform them of the discussion. This will ensure that you and all the parents have the same understanding of the policies that will guide your interactions with their child.

For effective communication to occur between the coach and parents, it is important not to place the athlete in the middle of the communication. Placing the athlete in the middle will often ensure a communication breakdown because the message has to go through an extra person. It is important for the coach and parents to work together and not against each other. Let parents know that you would like feedback about their child. Parents also know things about their child that you do not know. For example, parents might know the best way to motivate their child, whereas you may have become frustrated trying one technique after another. Together, the coach and parents need to provide positive support for the athlete and the team.

Nevertheless, there might come a time where you need to confront parents about their child's behavior. Parents can become forceful in demanding information on why their child is not playing or why a certain strategy was used. The section on confrontation can be useful in helping you deal with such a parent. Additional suggestions for intervening with a difficult parent include:

- Confront the parent privately, not in front of the athletes.
- State your observations of the behaviors.
- State the impact of the behaviors on the athlete and the team.
- Ask the parent to refrain from the behaviors.

SUMMARY

Coaches have to communicate with many different people but especially with athletes. The process of communication involves three components: sending, receiving, and interpreting messages. Both organizational information and feedback are important messages that coaches send to athletes. The sandwich approach—reinforce, instruct, and encourage—is an effective method of giving feedback. Like speaking, listening is a skill that has to be developed and practiced. Finally, people interpret messages based on their personality, experiences, gender, and cultural background. It is important to ask yourself which aspect of your communication is the strongest and which is the weakest. Once these are identified, think of ways to improve the weakest part of your communication in order to make yourself a better and more effective communicator.

REFERENCES

Beebe, S. A., Beebe, S. J., and Redmond, M. V. (1996). *Interpersonal Communication: Relating to Others*. Needham Heights, MA: Allyn & Bacon.

Guerra, N. G., Moore, A., and Slaby, R. G. (1995). *A Guide to Conflict Resolution and Decision Making for Adolescents*. Champaign, IL: Research Press.

Lusting, M. W., and Koester, J. (1993). *Intercultural Competence: Interpersonal Communication Across Cultures*. New York: Harper Collins.

Martens, R. (1978). *Coaches Guide to Sport Psychology*. Champaign, IL: Human Kinetics Publishers.

Purdy, M. (1999a). "Intrapersonal and Interpersonal Listening." In D. Borisoff and M. Purdy (editors), *Listening in Everyday Life: A Personal and Professional Approach*. Lanham, MD: University Press of America, pp. 21-58.

Purdy, M. (1999b). "What is Listening?" In D. Borisoff and M. Purdy (editors), *Listening in Everyday Life: A Personal and Professional Approach*. Lanham, MD: University Press of America, pp. 3-20.

Tannen, D. (1990). *You Just Don't Understand: Women and Men in Conversation*. New York: Ballantine Books.

Thomlison, T. D. (1999). "Intercultural Listening." In D. Borisoff and M. Purdy (editors), *Listening in Everyday Life: A Personal and Professional Approach*. Lanham, MD: University Press of America, pp. 87-138.

Yukelson, D. (1998). "Communicating Effectively." In J. M. Williams (editor), *Applied Sport Psychology: Personal Growth to Peak Performance*. Palo Alto, CA: Mayfield, pp. 142-157.

22
Positive Coaching

Martha E. Ewing, Ph.D.; Lori A. Gano-Overway, Ph.D. and Jennifer J. Waldron, M.Ed.

QUESTIONS TO CONSIDER

- What approaches are there to coaching?
- What are the benefits of using the positive approach?
- What problems can occur when using the negative approach?
- How do I develop a positive approach?
- How do I cope with losing when using a positive approach?

INTRODUCTION

When we agree to coach, we seldom give thought to HOW we should coach. Many times we will teach or interact with athletes using the same techniques that our coaches used when we were playing. Or, some of us have vowed that we will NOT treat our athletes as we were treated. The conscious or unconscious decisions we make about our coaching style may be influenced by past experiences and our own personality. Additionally, one's coaching style can depend on the philosophical view of the purpose of sport.

Early research on effective coaching or leadership style focused on how the personality of coaches affected their interactions with athletes. Table 22-1 describes a few of the personalities that were seen among coaches. The study of personality has helped us to understand the differences that we see in coaching behaviors. Because all types of personalities were found to be successful in terms of wins and losses, a critical factor in coaching is how we view our role as coach. Before we embark upon a style of coaching we must consider whether our job is to win games (professional view) or to help people grow into productive adults through the skills and values learned through participation in sport (educational view). Then, we must look at ourselves and determine how we

---

Table 22-1. Descriptions of Various Coaching Personalities.

Characteristics of Coaches with Varying Personalities	
Hard-nosed, Authoritarian Coach:	Highly energetic, uses punitive measures to enforce rules, rigid, very organized, uses threats to motivate, not easy to get "close" to
Nice Person Coach:	Personable, well-liked by others, flexible, deeply concerned with the welfare of his/her players
Intense or Driven Coach:	Emphasizes discipline, strong-willed, aggressive, less punitive and more emotional than authoritarian coach, lacks composure
Easy-going Coach:	Dislikes schedules, does not take things too seriously, completely composed and enjoys pressure, gives impression that everything is under control
Business-like Coach:	Always eager to learn, decisions based on statistics, most important thing is results, not easy to know personally, knows ALL aspects of game, emphasis on out-thinking the opponent, open to new ideas and methods

Taken from Tutko and Richards, *Psychology of Coaching*, 1971.

can best teach young athletes to grow through their involvement on our squad or team. This chapter offers two main approaches to coaching: the positive approach and the negative approach. Evidence of effectiveness for each style will be provided.

THE POSITIVE AND NEGATIVE APPROACHES TO COACHING

The most effective leaders are the ones who satisfy the psychological needs of their followers—David Ogilvy

There are two basic approaches to coaching: the positive approach and the negative approach (Tutko and Richards, 1971). When working with athletes, young or old, it is important to remember that we are dealing with people. The Number 1 rule to keep in mind is that we should treat athletes as we would want to be treated. Most of us respond better to a person who is empathetic with our shortcomings and who is patient with us while we learn. This response from a coach allows athletes to develop confidence as they learn, which is one of the primary ingredients to success as an athlete.

The Positive Approach

The positive approach focuses on positively reinforcing desired behaviors or consequences and asking athletes to behave or perform in a specific manner. This may be similar to our early experiences with athletic participation. All of us spent hours during our youth practicing sport skills and, even though we try to repress the memories, many of our early attempts were failures. However, friends provided us with positive support, plenty of encouragement, and the reassurance that "we'd get it" soon. Our persistence may have been directly related to our friends' support. When friends stopped giving us support and encouragement or ridiculed our attempts, we often withdrew from the activity.

In a similar fashion, the positive approach aims at strengthening the desired behaviors through the use of encouragement, positive reinforcement, and technical instruction. Athletes are generally highly motivated to learn a sport, and the use of positive reinforcement strengthens their enjoyment. For example, if you ask an athlete to take a charge in basketball and the athlete steps in front of the opponent (desired behavior) but is whistled for a block, then you should reward or reinforce the athlete for attempting to execute the desired behavior while, at the same time, providing further technical instruction.

The positive approach also fosters a positive learning environment for youth sport participants. In a positive environment mistakes become "stepping stones to achievement." Athletes learn from their mistakes. They know

that positive coaches will provide them with the technical information to change their performances plus the encouragement and support to try again. Athletes with low self-esteem are likely to benefit most from a positive approach.

Most coaches of sport teams want to be respected and liked by their teams. This mutual respect results in improved communication and fosters a willingness to work together to resolve individual and team problems. This result was reported in a study of Little League coaches (Smith and Smoll, 1995). One group of coaches was taught to be positive and encouraging by increasing the frequency of positive reinforcement by 25%. A second group of "untrained" coaches continued to coach as they normally had. At the end of the season, the athletes who played for the trained coaches reported that:

- They liked the coach more.
- They thought the coach was a better teacher.
- They were more attracted to the team.
- In addition to the positive self-reports of the baseball players, the researchers reported that the athletes coached by the positive coaches had better self-concepts (especially true for athletes who had low self-concepts) and that 75% of the athletes who played for the untrained coaches returned the next season compared to 95% of those who played for the trained coaches.

Coaches who have trouble getting enough athletes out for the team or who coach at small schools will feel the negative effects of this loss the most. A 25% loss of athletes is a significant loss given the time and effort put into teaching and preparing these athletes for the next season. In addition, the participants lose the benefits associated with being involved in athletics.

As demonstrated in the study previously described, participation in sports can enhance the self-esteem of children and youth. Low self-concepts are often the result of being told directly or indirectly how bad we are at a task or how ineffective we are in developing relationships with our peers. If told often enough that they are not very good, athletes begin to believe that they are not very good. Athletes with low self-concepts are particularly vulnerable to failure because they interpret failure as "proof" that they are not very good and, thus, decrease their sense of self. To turn this negative thinking around, coaches must be positive and help these athletes see errors as temporary states that can be corrected with continued positive and appropriate learning experiences. The fact that coaches can be effective in improving self-concepts by increasing their positive reinforcement to athletes by 25 % is powerful evidence of the effectiveness of the positive approach.

In addition to helping athletes feel better about themselves, the positive approach increases the athletes' learning of skills. Part of this learning may be a result of viewing a positive coach as a better teacher. Additionally, the positive approach creates an atmosphere whereby athletes are willing to try new and different skills. In the positive approach, there is no fear of failing. Thus, young athletes will ask more questions and practice more diligently.

People are more easily led than driven—David Fink

The Negative Approach

The negative approach to coaching involves eliminating undesirable behavior through physical and verbal punishment and criticism. This negative approach is based on fear. Although we do not advocate this approach, there is evidence that this approach can eliminate poor performance in certain athletes. There is also evidence that this approach can eliminate athletes as well!

Often we hear coaches tell athletes, "The team that makes the fewest errors will win." Obviously, there is much truth to the saying. Because errors are often easier to see than steady, unspectacular performance, coaches tend to focus on eliminating errors. To eliminate errors, coaches simply punish athletes who make them (i.e., take athletes out of the game, make them run laps, or relegate them to the "dog house"). It is not hard to find examples of coaches who use the negative approach. Many highly successful coaches scream at their athletes for every mistake, grab athletes by their jerseys during timeouts, publicly humiliate them, and may actually hit athletes who are not meeting expectations. These coaches assume that if players are scared enough of making errors, they will be more likely to perform better.

While punishment and verbal abuse may change the behavior of some individuals, there are some undesirable side effects. Perhaps the most serious is the fear of failure that results when athletes are criticized or punished excessively for making mistakes. Fear of failure can be observed in athletes who stop trying to make difficult plays or always "play it safe." For example, a basketball player who has been yelled at numerous times for leaving her player on defense to help another player fails to go for a loose ball for fear of being yelled at again by the coach. A coach may even see the cognitive dilemma that the athlete is experiencing when the player looks at the ball and then at the coach instead of going immediately after the ball. Closely associated with a fear of failure are decreased enjoyment of a task and increased likelihood of more errors. This cycle of fear, leading to more errors and less enjoyment, may cause athletes to become hesitant and uncertain, experience high anxiety about performing in critical situations, or be more vulnerable to injury during competition.

A negative approach often results in an unpleasant teaching situation. Athletes who are exposed to verbal criticism, punishment for errors, or sarcastic comments about their performances will often withdraw socially and emotionally. When this happens, the team becomes very quiet during practices and games. In addition, there is a sense of resentment or hatred by the team members for the coach. With older athletes, these negative emotions may draw the team together and actually strengthen team cohesion, while decreasing their enjoyment of the game. For younger, less experienced athletes, the negative environment may cause them to drop out.

One of the questions frequently asked by coaches is whether they should avoid criticizing or punishing athletes. The answer is no, because these techniques may be useful in maintaining discipline or in motivating athletes, who know the skills, to focus and work harder at improving their skill. However, in order for these techniques to remain effective they must be used sparingly. Unfortunately, we often see coaches who are very successful using the negative approach. This may result because these coaches have very good athletes and/or they are exceptional teachers and strategists. For inexperienced coaches, these successful negative coaches serve as role models. Negative behaviors are imitated, with the naïve coach thinking this abusive behavior causes athletes to perform correctly. These inexperienced coaches do not realize that the negative coaches' success may be due to their effective teaching techniques. Or the negative coach may be able to recruit a specific type of athlete who is unaffected by a negative coaching style.

The technique employed by most coaches is a combination of the positive and negative approaches. There is evidence that a mixture of both positive and negative reinforcement is likely to produce the best results. Athletes know when they have made mistakes, and the coach's credibility rests on being honest in evaluating their performances. However, a coach can be honest and help athletes learn from their experiences or a coach can punish athletes who make errors and create athletes who "fear failure." The effectiveness of a coach's reinforcement may depend on the coach's intention in giving the praise or punishment. There is little doubt that athletes, and most people, respond best to the positive approach.

SUMMARY

The outcomes (i.e., consequences or results) of the positive and negative approaches are summarized in Table 22-2. Each approach will influence the behavior of athletes. Both approaches can result in successful performance. However, the psychological cost (i.e., loss of confidence and self-esteem, loss of joy or enthusiasm for the sport) associated with the negative approach provides strong support for using the positive approach to coach-

Table 22-2. Outcomes Associated With the Positive and Negative Approach to Coaching.

Outcomes Associated with the Positive and Negative Approach to Coaching

Positive Approach
- Errors become learning opportunities
- Athletes are encouraged to learn new and different skills
- Athletes are motivated to improve skills
- Self-esteem is not threatened

Negative Approach
- Increases fear of failure
- Decreases enjoyment
- Increases error frequency
- Increases anxiety and resentment
- Increases number of athletes dropping out of sport
- Increases discipline problems
- Decreases self-esteem and therefore motivation (especially in low self-esteem athletes)

ing. It is through this approach that athletes are empowered to work hard to improve and to feel good about making the improvements. The positive approach results in athletes feeling confident about their abilities to be successful.

DEVELOPING THE POSITIVE APPROACH

Implementing the positive approach begins with the coach's awareness of:

- The value of effort and other desired behaviors,
- Specific behaviors that should be reinforced,
- Effective rewards or reinforcers, and
- How often to use these reinforcers.

Each of these aspects of the positive approach will be discussed in the following section.

Reinforce Effort and Other Desirable Behaviors

Coaches, parents, and even athletes tend to focus most of their attention on outcome—hitting the ball, making the shot, fielding the ball. This focus may be fine for professional athletes who have a great deal of experience and well-developed physical skills. For athletes who are learning or trying to improve their skills, and for most of us who are not consistent in the performance of a skill, coaches should reinforce effort, or the attempt to perform a skill correctly. As mentioned earlier, the negative approach often results in athletes attempting to protect their self-esteem. One way to protect self-esteem is to give only "token" effort. Thus, when they fail, they can save face by acknowledging that they could have gotten a bunt

down if they had tried harder. We do not want to cause athletes to lose the motivation to try because we, as coaches, have challenged their self-esteem. Thus, when we ask a batter to bunt and the batter tries, using good technique, we should acknowledge the effort. The positive reinforcement tells the batter that his or her technique is basically correct and that the effort is appreciated.

The only element of a contest that athletes have control over is the amount of effort they exert. Effort is the key to success in sport, and coaches must be ready to reinforce that effort. A pitcher who pitches a great game but loses on an error by a teammate (as happened to Roger Clemens in the 1986 World Series) should not perceive himself as a loser. His effort and performance were excellent. We must help athletes understand that they control effort; the outcome may be out of their control.

Finally, coaches can effectively change the behavior of athletes toward their teammates and opponents by reinforcing exemplary conduct. Reinforce athletes who help pick up the equipment after practice. Acknowledge instances of good teamwork and athletes encouraging one another. The relationships among the athletes are a direct result of what the coach chooses to reinforce. If athletes are allowed to blame one another for losses, this behavior will escalate to the point that athletes are afraid to try. Athletes quickly will learn to make excuses. To change this environment, or to prevent it from occurring, coaches must state the desired skill and interpersonal behaviors to the athletes and reinforce the occurrences of desired behaviors.

Select and Reinforce Specific Behaviors

In addition to reinforcing effort, coaches must identify the specific behaviors they want to reinforce. In other words, what must the athlete do to earn a reward from the coach? Initially, use your reward power to strengthen skills that a player is learning. The following is an example where rewards and objectives were contradictory: A baseball coach tells his team that the team that plays the best defense will win the upcoming tournament. Therefore, the focus of the day's practice would be on fielding ground balls. Unfortunately, the coach chose to teach fielding by having players field balls hit by their teammates. Although this drill resulted in many ground balls being hit to the infielders, the coach never once commented on how well players fielded nor gave instruction on how to field balls. All his comments were given to the batters. This behavior resulted in a mixed message for the young athletes. Coach says it is important to play good defense but talks only to the hitters during practice. Thus, the athletes conclude that hitting is more important than fielding.

Coaches should break down complex skills into component subskills and concentrate on one subskill at a time. Most sport skills are complex in that many body parts are involved to execute a skill. The coordination of the body parts is critical as is the ability to integrate a moving object (e.g., ball, puck) and other people into the skill. For example, fielding a ball involves "reading" where the ball is going, moving to that spot before the ball arrives, getting into position, catching the ball, and finally, throwing it to another person. Each of these actions could be defined and practiced as a subskill of fielding. This approach provides the athlete a chance to experience success while executing smaller parts of the skill. In addition, the coach has the opportunity to positively reinforce subskills performed correctly while providing pointers on how to improve the next subskill. For example, after you have been working with athletes on fielding a ground ball, the shortstop has a chance to demonstrate the skill in a game. The shortstop "reads" the ball, moves to the spot, fields the ball cleanly, and throws it into the dugout! As a coach, you can choose to:

- Acknowledge and reinforce the three subskills performed very well,
- Reject the entire attempt based on the poor throw,
- Ignore the mistake, and/or
- Provide correction and make a note to review skills during the next practice.

If a coach chooses to reject the entire performance, the athlete is led to believe that nothing was done right, rather than to understand that three-fourths of the skill was performed correctly. By selecting and reinforcing specific behaviors, an athlete gains confidence that she/he will improve with more practice. This outcome alone should result in you feeling successful as a coach.

Choosing Effective Reinforcers

When working with athletes, it is important to know what rewards are effective in changing behavior. In other words, what are the rewards for which athletes are willing to work? Surprisingly, research has shown that the best rewards are free. (See Gould, 1980; Harney and Parker, 1972; Smith, Smoll and Curtis, 1978.) For example, a pat on the back, smile, friendly nod, and verbal praise are all effective reinforcers. In this respect, athletes react to these reinforcers in much the same way as adults do. All of us appreciate this simple acknowledgement of a job well done.

These free rewards are effective with athletes of all ages. Specifically, research was conducted comparing the effectiveness of such rewards as the coaches' attention and giving candy or money to 9 to 15 year-old swimmers for the number of laps swum in practice. The results showed that verbal praise and the coaches' attention are particularly effective with athletes 13 to 15 years of age. (See Smith, Smoll and Curtis, 1978.)

The use of free reinforcers should be combined with instruction or instructional reminders to improve the effectiveness of the rewards (Gould and Weiss, 1980). For example, as you pat the receiver on the back for making a tough catch, you can tell him that he did a good job of watching the ball go into his hands. This instructional reminder provides a cue for the athlete that will help him be successful in the future.

When and How Often Should Reinforcement be Given?

The answer to this question depends on how proficient the athlete is at performing the skill (Gould and Weiss, 1980). When athletes are *learning* a skill, coaches should reinforce every desired response. Until inexperienced athletes have had a lot of practice, they cannot always tell whether they performed the skill correctly. When first learning to kick a soccer ball, all kicks feel the same. Therefore, to determine whether the kick was good or not, athletes look only at the result. If they kick incorrectly and score a goal, they assume the technique was correct. The emphasis in the early stages of learning a sport skill should be on technique and correct decision making, not just outcome.

As athletes become more proficient, coaches should intermittently reinforce the correct behavior. Research has shown that continuous feedback following a learned skill is not as effective as intermittent feedback. As athletes come to know the difference between correct and incorrect technique, the coach's feedback is redundant, and athletes tend to ignore it. However, intermittent feedback either supports or refutes the athlete's own perceptions. Differing perceptions provide the coach with the opportunity to discuss the finer points of the skill—which gives athletes new information to use. Environments must be conducive for athletes to accept and incorporate information that results in performance changes. The positive approach creates this type of environment.

The question of when reinforcement should be given is an easy one to answer. Specifically, coaches should reinforce a desired behavior as soon as it occurs. This is as true during contests as it is during practices. Waiting to tell athletes their faults at the conclusion of a drill often results in athletes not remembering what they did initially. The feedback is neutralized over time.

POSITIVE LOSING: A HEALTHY ATTITUDE

The goal for most athletes and coaches is to be successful. Success has generally been defined as winning. While this is a goal for participants, it should not be the only goal. The fact remains that in every game only 50% of the participants will be winners. If we use winning as the only criterion for success, then we must conclude that the non-winners are losers. There is a problem with this approach to defining success. Specifically, this approach suggests that winning, regardless of how poorly the athletes or team played, is good. Likewise, losing, regardless of how well or poorly the athlete or team played, is bad. This definitional approach to success and failure fosters an unhealthy attitude in athletes.

This attitude promotes the notion that athletes and coaches cannot learn from their mistakes. As most of us have discovered, we can learn more from our mistakes and our losses than we do from our successes. Losing is not fun, but losing should be viewed as "water under the bridge." In fact, the key to viewing losing as positive is to learn from the loss. Even in losing, certain skills or strategies may be executed correctly or better than they had been in the past. Athletes and coaches should understand what aspects of their performance were good. Knowing what was done correctly will prevent coaches and athletes from second-guessing themselves in the next game.

In addition, athletes should learn which of their performances needed improvement. Perhaps the loss was due to the other team's superior size and speed. This is particularly evident in youth sport and high school sports, where athletes must compete with and against older and bigger athletes. While learning and growing, athletes must know that losing is often the result of mismatches in size and experience, and not always the result of them being less skilled at their sport. This latter conclusion can result in athletes dropping out of sport before they fully develop the skills necessary to compete with older athletes. However, if the athletes did misperform skills or strategies, they need to learn what the mistakes were and what they must do to correct them.

The coach is the key in developing a healthy attitude toward losing. Your attitude will be mimicked by the athletes. Even though you may understand that your behavior is the result of disappointment or frustration, the athletes may not. They could view your behavior as the correct way to cope with a loss. Rather than learning from a loss, they associate a negative affect and self-perception with losing.

To foster a healthy attitude toward losing, coaches and athletes should analyze the loss by determining what was done right and what was done wrong. Then forget the loss, and continue to work on improving performance.

The positive view of losing does not lessen the disappointment. However, it does provide insight into one's performance. The value of a positive losing attitude may best be summed up in the following quote from a youth sport participant. "When I was a kid I had a great coach. He taught me how to bounce back when things were tough. I wish I could thank him now, but I can't remember his name" (Rushall and Pettinger, 1969).

REFERENCES

Barnett, N. P., Smoll, F. L., and Smith, R. E. (1992) "Effects of Enhancing Coach-Athlete Relationships on Youth Sport Attrition." *The Sport Psychologist*, 6: 111-127.

Gould, D. (1980). *Motivating Young Athletes*. East Lansing, MI: Institute for the Study of Youth Sports.

Gould, D., and Weiss, M. (1980). *Teaching Sports Skills to Young Athletes*. East Lansing, MI: Institute for the Study of Youth Sports.

Harney, D. M., and Parker, R. (1972). "Effects of Social Reinforcement, Subject Sex, and Experimenter Sex on Children's Motor Performance." *Research Quarterly*, 43: 187-196.

Rushall, B., and Pettinger, J. (1969). "An Evaluation of the Effect of Various Reinforcers Used as Motivators in Swimming." *Research Quarterly*, 40(3): 540-545.

Smith, R. E., Smoll, F. L., and Curtis, B. (1978). "Coaching Behaviors in Little League Baseball." In F. L. Smoll and R. E. Smith (editors), *Psychological Perspectives in Youth Sports*. Washington, D. C.: Hemisphere Press, pp. 173-201.

Tutko, T. A., and Richards, J. W. (1971). *Psychology of Coaching*. Boston, MA: Allyn & Bacon.

23
Goal Setting

Lori Gano-Overway, Ph.D.; Martha E. Ewing, Ph.D. and Jennifer J. Waldron, M. Ed.

QUESTIONS TO CONSIDER

- What is the purpose of goal setting?
- What are the principles of effective goal setting?
- How can you implement a goal setting program?
- How can you help athletes set goals for themselves?

INTRODUCTION

The use of goals in athletics is not new. At the beginning of each season, coaches and athletes often ponder what they hope to accomplish during the season. Many set goals and develop goal setting programs. But, what is the purpose of setting goals? Goals have been found to help one's performance in four main ways (Gould, 1998).

1. To direct attention and action to important aspects of a task,
2. To help increase effort in attempting to achieve a goal,
3. To assist in forming realistic expectations, and
4. To increase persistence at a task.

For goals to be effective they must be applied systematically. For example, when swimmers used several principles of goal setting (including setting realistic, performance based goals), they performed better, were more satisfied, less anxious, concentrated better, and felt more self-confident (Burton, 1983). This chapter focuses on a systematic approach to goal setting. It also addresses how a coach can implement a systematic goal setting program. Although the coach should initiate the goal setting process, over time athletes should be encouraged to become autonomous goal setters. This chapter, therefore, also considers how coaches can help athletes learn effective goal setting strategies.

GOAL SETTING PRINCIPLES

The goal of all athletes is to be successful, but just having a goal will not result in higher achievement. For goal setting to help athletes achieve at higher levels, it should follow certain principles and should be applied systematically, as outlined in Table 23-1 (see Gould, 1998; Weinberg and Gould, 1999; Smith and Smoll, 1996; and Martens, 1987). In general, the individual must set an appropriate goal, choose subgoals and strategies that emphasize the larger goal, commit to the goal, and check progress toward the goal. This process is similar to following a road map. A road map provides the driver with a strategy to get from one location to another. Along the way, the driver will check the map to ensure that he/she is moving in the right direction. Like a road map, goal setting helps us move from a current performance level to some higher level in the future. Without the map, you will not know how to get there. Each of these goal setting principles is subsequently discussed to help develop a systematic approach to goal setting for coaches and athletes.

Table 23-1. Principles of Effective Goal Setting.

- Use performance goals rather than outcome goals
- Set individual goals to emphasize team goals
- Set practice goals
- State goals in positive terms
- Set specific and measurable goals
- Set challenging yet realistic goals
- Set short and long term goals
- Develop a strategy for achieving the goal
- Gain goal commitment
- Evaluate and adapt goals

Use Performance Goals Rather Than Outcome Goals

Performance goals emphasize personal achievement within a competition while outcome goals focus on the outcome of the game (see Table 23-2). Although outcome goals are viable goals, they are not effective in directing the efforts of the athletes because the athletes may have little idea on what they need to focus in order to achieve outcome goals. For example, if an athlete is encouraged to win her race, she may turn her attention to the other athlete (i.e., How can I beat this athlete?). If the athlete would set a performance goal, she would turn her attention to her improvement and effort. Performance goals can provide several strategies upon which to focus in order to help her achieve the goal revolving around her effort.

Goals that emphasize the outcome of competitive events are not only ineffective at directing the effort of an athlete, but also are not under the control of an individual athlete or team. Athletes have little control over how their opponents will perform. It is also difficult to accurately assess how a team will progress through a season. Will your team improve faster than other teams, at the same pace, or develop late? Setting a goal of winning a certain number of contests (e.g., 8 of 10) and losing the first three contests, creates an impossibility of achieving the goal. Such goals seem to cause discouragement among team members and reduce the level of motivation. Over time, athletes may begin to lose their confidence because they are not achieving their outcome goals. For instance, an athlete may perform well in an event but feel unsuccessful because the opponent won the competitive event. Although the athlete should be pleased with the performance, he may be disappointed and frustrated with his performance. Additionally, outcome goals create stress for athletes as they may begin to doubt their ability to beat an opponent (see Chapter 25, *Stress Management for Athletes*).

Performance goals, on the other hand, can be controlled. By emphasizing personal improvement and effort, performance goals both focus attention on strategies to achieve their goals and can also help athletes realize that their effort over time determines their goal achievement and in turn their success. For example, a relay team that does not perform well the first few meets may decide to set goals to improve their times. Over the course of the season, each member can focus on decreasing their time by two-tenths of a second every two weeks. This goal will help direct efforts in practice, an aspect that can be controlled, without reducing the desire to achieve success.

Performance goals also build self-confidence and decrease competitive stress. By focusing on personal effort, athletes can see how they have improved over time, which is a powerful confidence builder. Further, if goals are under the athletes' control, they feel more confident in their abilities to meet the demands of the situation, reducing their competitive stress.

Set Individual Goals to Emphasize Team Goals

In general, team goals are not under anyone's control and are often unrealistic. For example, if a swim coach sets a goal of achieving at least 90 points in each meet, some members of the team may not find the goal meaningful and can become discouraged. Athletes with low ability or less experience may feel that it is their higher ability teammates' responsibility to achieve the goal and, therefore, they may not direct their own efforts toward the goal. Additionally, athletes, who are not scoring for the team, may become discouraged because they are not helping the team achieve the goal. Therefore, goal setting should emphasize individual improvement and let the team's improvement reflect individual improvement. Consequently, coaches should determine what each athlete needs to do individually to achieve team goals. In the example, the coach should sit down with each swimmer and develop individual performance goals that could help achieve the team goal.

Set Practice Goals

When coaches use goal setting, it is often restricted to goals for competitive events. Although it is important to have goals for competition, it is also important to have practice goals. Goals for practice allow athletes to direct their efforts during practice and develop an understanding of the importance of practice to establish the connection between practice goals and competition goals. Practice goals should be more challenging, whereas competition goals should be more realistic. When drills are set up for fielding or throwing, help the players set prac-

---

Table 23-2. A Comparison of Outcome and Performance Goals.

Outcome Goals	Performance Goals
• To get first place in an event • To win the game • To beat your biggest rival	• To improve your time by one second • To increase your free throw percentage to 65% • To limit the number of turnovers to under 10 per game

tice goals that will challenge each of them to exceed a previous performance. For example, when practicing the fielding of hard-hit grounders with a play to first base, the "star" infielder may be asked to make 9 out of 10 successful plays; while another player may be challenged with 7 out of 10. Therefore, each athlete is provided with a personal challenge. However, the coach should not expect the same level of performance in a game because neither the coach nor the players control all of the factors involved. With this approach, motivation at practice can be increased while allowing players, within competition, to have a realistic chance of experiencing enhanced self-esteem.

State Goals in Positive Terms

Positive goals direct the athlete's attention toward what they should do rather than what to avoid. For example, a young gymnast may initially set a goal of not falling off the beam during the meet. This goal can be problematic because it does not identify what the athlete must do to stay on the beam, but focuses the athletes' attention on something less constructive—not falling.

Set Specific and Measurable Goals

When asked to state their goal, many athletes remark that they want to do their best or give 100% effort. Although this is an admirable goal, it is not an effective one. If goals are not specific and measurable, it is difficult for athletes to observe improvement over the course of the season, and more importantly, it is difficult to know where to direct efforts in practice. Therefore, coaches should encourage their athletes to set specific and measurable goals. Examples of specific and measurable goals is highlighted in Table 23-3.

In addition to setting specific and measurable goals, coaches should realize that there are several types of goals including fitness, skills, team interactions, team coordination, and/or sportspersonship. Table 23-4 identifies several different types of goals.

Set Challenging Yet Realistic Goals

When implementing a goal setting program, each athlete must experience some success. In other words, each athlete should perform at a level that demands a best effort for the existing conditions. For example, a distance swimmer, who normally swims a 6:03 in the 500 yard freestyle should not set a goal of 5:30 for the first meet when she has not trained all summer. The coach, therefore, must know the athletes well enough to be aware when they are setting goals that are challenging, realistic, and most importantly, based on what she/he can control—their effort. If a goal is too difficult, the athletes may perceive that it is outside of their capability and may not make a commitment to the goal. Coaches should, therefore, strive to set goals that provide moderate challenges.

Table 23-3. Specific and Measurable Goals.

- Drop one second in the 100 yard freestyle by the end of the season
- To keep the person being guarded from having more than five open shots in tonight's game
- Within three weeks, stick 10 split leaps in a row on the beam
- Increase batting average to .450 by the end of the season.

Table 23-4. Examples of Different Types of Specific and Measurable Goals.

Type of Goal	Example
Skills	• Field 4 of 5 grounders hit to glove side
	• Hit 4 of 6 backhands down the line
Fitness	• Run length of court in 10 seconds
	• Jump rope (continuous without misses) for 2 minutes
Team interactions	• Sincerely compliment a teammate 5 times during a practice
	• Acknowledge the teammate who assisted you on a play
Team coordination	• Hold opponent to under 100 yards rushing
	• Limit the number of turnovers to 4 per game
Sportspersonship	• Compliment the opponent when they make a good play
	• Shake hands with the opponent after the game regardless of the outcome

There may be times, however, when you believe that a goal is realistic and challenging for an athlete; yet, the athlete does not believe that she/he can accomplish the goal. The athlete may not adopt the goal because he/she lacks confidence, fears failure, or may not know his/her capabilities. For example, a freshman volleyball player may not know whether keeping 80% of her serves in bounds during a game by the end of the season is an appropriate goal. In fact, she may doubt your belief in her ability. By developing successful experiences, providing encouragement, and showing her positive role models you can help to build her confidence (see Chapter 24, *Motivating Athletes*) and help her to see that the goal is challenging yet realistic.

Set Short and Long Term Goals

Goal setting is a planning process. Coaches should set short term goals that will help athletes progress toward the long term goal. For instance, a long term or end of season goal may be for an athlete to drop 9 seconds in the 500m freestyle. By using short term or weekly goals athletes should have the motivation to help them attain the long term goal. This method can be visualized as a staircase. The top of the staircase is the long term goal. To get to the top of the staircase, the athlete must climb each step (short term goal) along the way. For the swimmer to reach the long term goal in the 500m freestyle, she may have three short term goals. First, drop 2 seconds from her time by 4 weeks into the season; second, drop 3 additional seconds by 8 weeks into the season; and finally drop 4 more seconds by the end of the season. Just as it is difficult to reach the top of the staircase without walking up each step, it is difficult to visualize achieving a long term goal without taking small steps toward the end goal. By breaking up the long term goal into smaller steps over the course of a season, the athlete becomes more confident as she succeeds in achieving each of the short term goals. Rather than just being motivated toward the end of the season to achieve the long term goal, the inclusion of short term goals also helps the athlete stay motivated throughout the season.

Develop a Strategy for Achieving the Goal

Goals should not only state what the athlete wants to do but also how he/she will accomplish it. The goal to drop 9 seconds in the 500m freestyle can be achieved only if the athlete is clear about what strategies can be used along the way. As Tom Landry, the former Dallas Cowboys coach, stated, "Setting a goal is not the main thing. It is deciding how you will go about achieving it and staying with that plan." Therefore, develop each short-term goal with a set of strategies in mind to help the athlete achieve the long term goal (see Table 23-5).

A coach could create a goal achievement card for each athlete to help in the goal setting process. The card should include goals for each skill or activity on which the athlete will need to focus during the season. Table 23-6 highlights several activities that a basketball coach could use as potential goals along with one complete goal for free throws.

It is also important that strategies for attaining goals be developmentally based on the athlete's ability. For example, as young baseball players are learning to field ground balls, they should practice with balls that are hit softly or rolled directly at them. More advanced players should be encouraged to practice fielding harder hit balls so that they have to move to either side to field them. As players improve, they can move on to more difficult and complex strategies.

Gain Goal Commitment

For goal setting to be effective, athletes must commit to achieving the goal. To help athletes commit to goals, encourage them to post their goals; to share them with their teammates, peers, and parents; or to chart their progress in a journal. You should also support their endeavors throughout the season. Athletes should be rewarded on their progress through verbal feedback and be encouraged to view setbacks as a normal part of the process. Most importantly, coaches must provide athletes with the knowledge and methods of how to set and evaluate their goals. Owning their goals help the athletes stay

---

Table 23-5. Creating Strategies for Short Term Goals.

Specific Short Term Goal	Strategy	Time Line
• Drop 2 seconds (5:25, 1st short term goal)	• Improve flip turn by hitting every flip turn in a set and then progressing to all sets in practice	• 4 weeks into season
• Drop 3 seconds (5:22, 2nd short term goal)	• Work on stroke mechanics (e.g., bending her elbow during the recovery phase for one of the main sets of each practice, then progressing to all sets in practice)	• 8 weeks into season
• Drop 4 seconds (5:18, long term goal time)	• Improve aerobic capacity (e.g., being able to swim a set of 5 x 200 yards in 2:15 with minimal rest)	• End of season

Table 23-6. Goal Achievement Card.*

Skill/Activity	Specific Goal	Strategy	Target Date
Shooting: • Lay-ups • Jump shots • **Free throws** Ball handling Rebounding	**75% from the line**	**Shoot 6 consecutive free throws at the end of practice. Adding 1 additional shot each day.**	**8 weeks into the season**

*Adapted from Gould, "Goal Setting for Peak Performance," 1998.

focused on the goals (This is discussed in more detail later in the chapter.).

Coaches must realize that athletes may have different goals in mind. They may be committed to their own goals, but may show little interest in achieving team goals or specific goals set for them. For instance, a tennis player, with great potential, may be encouraged by the coach to focus her goals on improving her forehand, backhand, and playing aggressively during match play. However, academics are very important for this athlete. She strives to be a NASA engineer and views sport participation as a method of stress relief for her academic schedule. Although she is interested in improvements, her athletic goal is to take a break from studying, learn fundamentals, and enjoy tennis. The coach must also understand the level of commitment that an athlete is willing to give, and make this part of the goal setting process. Goals for improvement can be emphasized and the coach may even help the athlete learn that competition is part of the joy of tennis.

Evaluate and Adapt Goals

Athletes need a way to compare current performance with past performances to determine whether they are successful. Goal setting can help in this process if the athletes evaluate their goals and progress toward the goals. Goals, therefore, should be evaluated frequently, and if necessary, adjusted based on the athlete's success ratio. If an athlete is achieving the set goal, the goal should be raised to provide for greater challenge and motivation. If the goal is too difficult and the athlete is feeling frustrated or fails, the level of the goal should be lowered rather than having the athlete continue to experience failure. But lowering the level of a goal may be frustrating for the athlete. Therefore, it is important to be as accurate as possible when initially setting goals.

Although the idea of monitoring the goals of every member of a team may seem overwhelming, there is a method that can be utilized to help coaches in this process. Coaches can create a chart that lists each athlete

along with his/her corresponding goals. The coach could not only post a goal chart but also the specific skills and strategies that need attention in a practice session. During practice, athletes can review the chart as a reminder of what they need to work on to meet their goal. For example, a basketball coach could have a young player focus on trying to make 5 out of 10 shots from the free throw line. Next to this goal the coach could place key reminders to help the athlete reach the goal (e.g., center body with target and follow through). It is important to remember that publicly recording goal progress may not always be appropriate. Failure to meet goals may lead to higher levels of anxiety, because it is documented publicly. Some athletes may avoid achieving their goal in obvious ways (e.g., by reducing their effort) to avoid appearing unable to achieve their goal in front of others. Overall, coaches should make sure that the goal setting process is clearly defined as a method to help individuals improve their performance, foster a mastery motivational climate (see Chapter 24, *Motivating Athletes*), and provide more private ways to record progress in reaching the goal.

IMPLEMENTING GOAL SETTING

The principles of goal setting are an important starting place for understanding the process. For coaches to effectively use these principles, they must implement a goal setting system within their own program. A system to help coaches in this process includes three phases: planning, meeting, follow-up/evaluation (Gould, 1998; Smith and Smoll, 1996).

Planning Phase

This phase involves defining goals and goal strategies. The coach must first consider what are the best team and individual goals for the season, given the number of athletes, their experience and fitness, and level of commitment. The coach may also need to consider several types of goals such as improving skills, increasing fitness, building sportspersonship, and/or making the experience enjoyable. The coach should then decide how goals might be met by developing goal strategies that can be emphasized in daily practices.

Meeting Phase

After planning individual and team goals, the coach should meet with the team to discuss the goals. The first meeting should include the entire team. The coach introduces the principles of goal setting and asks the athletes to think about what individual and team goals they would like to set for the year. After this meeting, short individual meetings should be set with each athlete to discuss his/her goal setting plan for the year. During this session, the coach and athlete should share thoughts about appropriate goals and together create challenging, yet realistic, goals for the season (beginning players will need more help developing appropriate goals).

Following individual meetings, the coach should determine whether the team goals developed during the planning phase are still feasible, given the individual athlete's goals and levels of commitment. With a revised set of team and individual goals for the season, the coach should develop a season plan. This plan should incorporate the goals and goal strategies into the daily practice schedule. The coach should share this plan with the athletes and inform them how aspects of each practice help them meet the individual and/or team goals.

Follow-up/Evaluation Phase

Evaluation is an important component of the goal setting process. Goals should be evaluated periodically throughout the season to ensure that the athlete and/or team is on track, or to adjust goals accordingly. Given the hectic nature of a competitive season, goal evaluation can often be overlooked. It may be helpful, therefore, to schedule goal evaluation periods at the beginning of a season and mark them clearly on a calendar as a reminder. Coaches should use a systematic method to evaluate goals. The goal achievement card (introduced earlier) can be used as a basis for comparing the athlete's current performance state (based on game statistics, meet times, or practice criteria) with the goal and strategies developed earlier. Systematic evaluation of goals and appropriate feedback on progress towards reaching the goal will give the athletes a better idea about their accomplishments and areas which need attention in the future to help in reaching the long term goal.

HELP ATHLETES IN THE GOAL SETTING PROCESS

Coaches should also provide athletes with the knowledge and methods of how to set and evaluate goals.

When working with younger athletes, coaches need to help them first to set goals and then to monitor the goals. For example, a 14 year old baseball player, who plays first base, could be encouraged to set a goal of accurately throwing to third base. Once given the goal, the coach should provide the athlete with key points about how to achieve an accurate throw (see Chapter 30, *Planning Effective Instruction*). Then as the athlete practices, the coach can remind the athlete of his goal and encourage the player to monitor his own performance to determine how accurately he is throwing the ball. Therefore, the athlete will not only know when he reached the goal, but also will know how to alter his performance to achieve the goal.

Athletes, 13 years and older, should be able to identify and monitor their own goals; but, they should have them checked by the coach to ensure that the goals are realistic, challenging, and compatible with the program. The athletes should be involved in the process. If athletes have been involved in a program that has emphasized goal setting, this will be an easy transitional step. However, if this is a new idea, coaches can use some of the same methods described earlier or ask the athlete to keep track of their own goals by keeping a journal. Periodically, you should also sit down with each athlete and review her/his goals and progress. This will help athletes realize the importance of evaluating goals and understanding the need to be flexible with the goal.

SUMMARY

Many coaches and athletes set goals. For goals to have a positive impact, however, coaches should follow the principles of goal setting. Systematic use of the principles can help a coach to guide her/his athletes to perform at a higher level, motivate them to perform to their potential, and to build their self-confidence.

REFERENCES

Burton, D. (1983). *Evaluation of Goal Setting Training on Selected Cognitions and Performance of Collegiate Swimmers*. Unpublished doctoral dissertation, University of Illinois, Champaign-Urbana, IL.

Gould, D. (1998). "Goal Setting for Peak Performance." In J. Williams (editor), *Applied Sport Psychology: Personal Growth to Peak Performance (3rd edition)*. Mountain View, CA: Mayfield Publishing Company.

Martens, R. (1987). *Coaches Guide to Sport Psychology*. Champaign, IL: Human Kinetics Publishers.

Smith, R. E., and Smoll, F. L. (1996). *Way to Go, Coach: A Scientifically-Proven Approach to Coaching Effectiveness*. Portola Valley, CA: Warde Publishers, Inc.

Weinberg, R. S., and Gould, D. (1999). *Foundations of Sport and Exercise Psychology (2nd edition)*. Champaign, IL: Human Kinetics.

24
Motivating Athletes

Lori Gano-Overway, Ph.D.; Martha E. Ewing, Ph.D. and Jennifer J. Waldron, M. Ed.

QUESTIONS TO CONSIDER

- Why do athletes participate in sports?
- What techniques can you use to minimize the number of "dropouts" from your team?
- What strategies can a coach use to enhance motivation?
- How do the motivational strategies presented effect self-confidence?

INTRODUCTION

Coaches spend a lot of time planning workouts to prepare athletes physically and technically, but a good portion of the time is also spent motivating athletes to perform well, develop a positive view of themselves, and enjoy their sport experiences. As coaches, we wonder, what motivates athletes? There are several factors that influence the motivation of an athlete. These are both within the individual and the environment. This chapter provides strategies that will help you develop a program that encourages your athletes to stay motivated.

WHY ATHLETES PARTICIPATE IN SPORTS

The country is full of good coaches. What it takes to win is a bunch of interested players.
Don Coryell, Former San Diego Chargers Coach

In order to help athletes maintain or improve their motivation in sport, a coach must understand why athletes participate in a sport or discontinue sport participation. If the needs or participation motives of athletes are met by the sport experience, their motivation will be high and they will probably persist in a sport. The coach is important in determining whether the needs of the athletes are fulfilled. So what are these needs? Why do athletes participate in sport?

Surveys from 26,300 ten to eighteen year old athletes, who participated in a variety of sports, indicated several reasons for sport participation (Ewing and Seefeldt, 1996). The top five reasons in order of importance are the following:

1. To have fun,
2. To improve skills and learn new ones,
3. For thrills and excitement of competition,
4. To be with friends or make new friends, and
5. To succeed or win.

Many athletes participate in sport not to win competitions, but to enjoy the process of learning sport skills, testing those skills in a competitive environment, and developing friendships with other athletes. It is this satisfaction and enjoyment that is apparent in the participation motive to have fun. For example, a group of athletes from 8 to 15 years of age were asked to explain what was fun about engaging in tennis and soccer (Harris and Ewing, 1992; Shi and Ewing, 1993). Their definitions of fun are outlined in Table 24-1. Clearly the notions of enhancing personal performance, socializing with others, and experiencing optimal challenges are key characteristics of fun in sport (Wankel and Sefton, 1989).

It is important to note that these definitions of fun and participation motives (noted earlier) are not in opposition to developing a successful program. Success can be achieved by providing enjoyable experiences, focusing on improving skills, developing an appropriate view of success, and helping the athlete develop friendships. By focusing first on these aspects of participation a coach sets up an atmosphere that emphasizes striving toward excellence which can contribute to a successful program. Defining success based on participation motives is partic-

Table 24-1. What is Fun About Sport?

Age of Athlete	What is Considered Fun
• 8 year olds	• Being able to do the skill (i.e., hit the ball)
• 9 year olds	• Learning and improving skills
• 10 year olds	• Playing with friends
• 11 year olds	• Competing with others of about the same ability level
• 12 year olds	• Competing against a challenging opponent
• 13 to 15 year olds	• Winning games

ularly critical for coaches who are working with young athletes or inexperienced teams. At these levels, developing sufficient skills and an understanding of the game is a necessary precursor to a focus on winning. This appears to be the case with 13 to 15 year old soccer players who defined fun as winning competitive events. On average, these athletes had seven years of playing experience, which allowed them to alter their focus from skill development toward winning. Although winning may represent society's view of success, it is important to consider whether it is an appropriate view (this will be elaborated upon in more detail later on in this chapter).

In summary, athletes engage in sport programs that meet their needs. If your program does not allow the athlete to enjoy the experience, learn and improve skills, make friends, enjoy competition, and allow opportunities to strive toward excellence, she or he will be more likely to leave the program.

WHY ATHLETES DROP OUT OF SPORTS

Knowing why some athletes stop participating in a sport can also provide ways to encourage them to continue playing. From a survey of 1,773 ten to eighteen year old athletes who dropped out of various sports, a major reason cited for leaving the sport was because they did not achieve the goals that they set when they initially enrolled to participate (Ewing and Seefeldt, 1996). This is not surprising if you consider that the reasons for getting involved in sport represent goals that can only be achieved through participation. When these goals are not being met, the athlete may drop out. Some reasons often cited for dropping out of sports are as follows:

1. Had other interests,
2. Needed or wanted to work,
3. No longer interested in the sport,
4. Not enough playing time, and
5. Did not like the coach.

Seeking the Perfect Fit

Young people are often very good at assessing their relative ability in various activities. They may "shop around" and participate in several sports and other activities before deciding which ones provide them the greatest enjoyment and chance of being successful. Dropping a sport, such as baseball, to achieve in other activities, such as music, soccer, swimming, dance, and scouting, is understandable. Although these individuals may have enjoyed their sport experiences, other interests may be more important and/or enjoyable.

Youth with interests in other activities should not be forced or pressured by parents, coaches, or peers to continue participation in a specific sport program. Doing so often decreases the athlete's motivation and enjoyment. Parents and coaches should not only give young people, particularly those in elementary or middle school, choices and support in exploring other activities but also should allow them to return to the sport if they so decide. Coaches and parents should also consider the impact of year-round participation in one sport on motivation. Although the athlete may enjoy a sport, being pressured by parents or coaches to become intensely involved in a sport for too long can lead to decreased motivation and burnout (Dale and Weinberg, 1990).

Not Enough Playing Time

Youth sign up for a sport because they anticipate that enjoyment and skill development will result from the involvement. Many athletes who cited "not playing enough" as a reason for dropping out of a sport may have been telling coaches that they needed more playing time in order to achieve these goals.

Young athletes or athletes who are new to a sport want to learn new skills and to see skills improve. However, individual differences in skill levels can be considerable. Therefore, instruction should be designed to show each athlete how he/she can improve in performance abilities and contribute to the team. This is particularly important for low ability athletes who need technical feedback to help them improve. Athletes also need to be taught to define their improvement in realistic terms. Too often, athletes compare their skills to the skills of other athletes rather than to their past performances. It is, therefore, important for coaches to help athletes realize how they have improved in terms of their *personal* performance.

Athletes who cited "not playing enough" for dropping out are not usually asking to be starters or to play the majority of the time. However, not playing during any part of a contest is an indirect way of telling the athlete that she/he is not good at all, which can be devastating to feelings of self-worth. Coaches need to ensure a fair and equitable pattern of play during both practices and contests. Coaches should also inform all athletes about how they can earn more playing time (this is discussed in more detail under clarifying team members' roles and responsibilities).

Did Not Like the Coach

Athletes who did not like their coaches indicated they did not like being yelled at, thought the coaches played only their favorite players, and did not think the coaches were fair. To be effective, coaches must treat athletes with the same respect that they expect from the athletes. It is not necessary or effective to yell at athletes in order to communicate. Sarcastic and degrading comments should be avoided. A positive approach should be used to create an enjoyable and motivating environment for athletes to learn and have fun (See Chapter 22, *Positive Coaching*).

Know Why Your Athletes Are Participating

Although these observations provide insights as to why most youth participate in sports, they only provide a general guide. Athletes differ in personalities, needs, interests, and objectives for participating in sport. The best information, therefore, is obtained from the athletes themselves. Ask your athletes why they participate and what are their personal objectives for the season. This dialogue should occur during practices, special events, or whenever you have a chance to talk one-on-one with an athlete throughout the season. The latter is important because an athlete's motives may change over the course of a competitive season. It may also be helpful to talk with parents to get a better understanding of an athlete's motives to participate.

HOW TO MOTIVATE YOUR ATHLETES

Understanding why athletes participate in sport is the first step to motivating them. Because athletes are most motivated when they obtain what they seek from their participation in sports, motivational techniques should be based upon these reasons. The following strategies may help to improve the motivation of athletes.

Create a Mastery Motivational Climate

The principle is competing against yourself. It's about self-improvement, about being better than you were the day before.

Steve Young,
Quarterback for the San Francisco 49ers

The environment that the coach creates plays a large role in enhancing motivation. Researchers have identified two motivational climates: a mastery climate and a performance climate. The difference between these two climates is the standard of reference that a coach uses to judge success and failure (Ames, 1992; Duda, 1993). In a mastery climate, athletes are encouraged to focus on personal performance by working hard, by improving skills, and by working with others. In a performance climate, emphasis is on outperforming others both on the opposing team and on their own team in order to be successful. Under the performance climate, winning is defined as defeating others. The major contracts of each motivational climate are highlighted in Table 24-2.

The mastery motivational climate tends to benefit athletes. In examining the climate created by a coach from the viewpoint of the athlete, researchers have shown that a mastery motivational climate is associated with several positive motivational outcomes such as increased effort, greater persistence, enhanced self-confidence, and higher levels of enjoyment (Duda, 1993).

Although each climate can contribute to a winning team, from a motivational perspective, two points need to be kept in mind. First, athletes are more motivated to compete when they perceive that they have control over the outcome. Because they cannot control the play or effort of an opponent in a game, athletes will be more motivated when taught to focus on their own effort, which is within their control. Second, the nature of sport tends to emphasize a performance climate because it stresses a competitive relationship in which there is a winner and a loser. Therefore, coaches need to balance potentially negative motivational effects of the performance climate inherent in sport by adopting a mastery climate. Therefore, coaches should remember that "The best inspiration is not to outdo others, but to outdo ourselves" (Author Unknown). Coaches should focus on personal improvement through hard work, planning, and working with others.

The climate created by a coach is the factor that has the greatest influence on athletes' motivation. But what strategies will help you create a mastery climate to positively influence motivation? Several effective strategies are discussed.

Table 24-2. Criteria for Each Climate.*

Environment	Mastery Climate	Performance Climate
Success defined as...	progress, improvement, learning new skills	doing better than others
Emphasis placed on...	process of learning	demonstrating high ability
Important characteristics...	effort, participating	innate ability, talent
Errors are viewed as...	part of the learning process	failure
Reasons for effort are to...	learn new skills or improve skills	outperform others
Reasons for satisfaction, regardless of level of performance are...	Working hard and/or challenging oneself	Doing better than others
Athletes are evaluated by...	The effort put forth and/or making improvements	Comparing them to how others are doing
Athletes' focus of attention...	Learning and mastering skills	Showing that they have high ability or hiding their low ability

*Adapted from Ames, "Achievement Goals, Motivational Climate, and Motivational Processes ," 1992.

Help Athletes Understand the Meaning of Success

Children learn at an early age to equate winning with success and losing with failure. This lesson is often learned from parents, older peers, and/or coaches. Take, for example, the play of Bill and John, members of winning and losing baseball teams respectively, portrayed below.

Bill, who is usually a very good second baseman, commits three throwing errors during the game. You notice that Bill is throwing extremely hard to the first baseman. You also overhear him telling a teammate that the errors were really the first baseman's fault for not catching the ball. The third error by the second baseman results in a go-ahead run for the opponents. John, on the other hand, plays an errorless three innings, gets his first triple of the season, and successfully sacrifices himself to move a teammate into scoring position. Because Bill was a member of the winning team, he was able to "laugh off" the errors that he caused and revel in the success of his team. On the other hand, John felt that his efforts were worthless and joined his teammates in the disappointment of a 6-3 loss.

Although adults easily recognize the inaccuracy of these perceptions, their actions at the end of a contest may tell the athletes that a winning score is what really matters. Equating success or failure with winning or losing sends mixed messages to the athlete. The athlete learns that if they win a game, they should feel good or worthy, while losing should make them feel incompetent or unworthy. This thought process could be very discouraging to athletes.

One of the most important roles of a coach, therefore, is to help athletes keep winning in perspective. Athletes need to know that, although striving to win is an important objective, being successful in a sport also means making personal improvements and doing one's best. This attitude can be developed by:

- Encouraging maximum effort during practices and contests.
- Rewarding effort (refer to Chapter 22, *Positive Coaching*).
- Helping athletes set challenging but realistic goals that emphasize effort based strategies for achievement so that they can see the link between effort and their improvements in ability (see Chapter 23, *Goal Setting*).

Another strategy is to help athletes to understand that winning a game is not always controllable. Take a moment to think about how you and your athletes explain successes and failures. One psychological theory, Attribution Theory, suggests that explanations for successes and failures generally fall into one of four categories—use of effort and strategies, ability concerns, difficulty of the task, or luck (See Martens, 1987.) Table 24-3 summarizes the points.

Of the explanations given in Table 24-3, which ones can be controlled? Clearly, it is effort. Therefore, athletes should be encouraged to focus on aspects of performance that are within their control.

In helping athletes understand the meaning of success, it is also important not to punish them when they fail, particularly if they gave a maximum effort. Losing must also be kept in perspective. Sometimes losing is not

Table 24-3.: Attributional Responses to Success and Failure.

Success Response	Failure Response
We gave 100% out there (effort).	We just did not try hard enough (effort).
We are just good (ability).	We just do not have the talent right now (ability).
We played an easy team—they just are not very good (task difficulty).	It was cold and windy and we do not play well in those conditions (task difficulty).
The officials were on our side (luck).	We did not get any breaks today (luck).

within our control. Athletes must be reminded that some factors, which can determine the outcome of a competition, are not under their control. For example, the other team's pitcher may be throwing the best game of his career. Or, due to injury or illness, a player is forced to play an unfamiliar position. Or, the cold weather is not the most optimal condition in which to play. These examples highlight the need to establish goals for personal improvement consistent with the objective of winning, but not entirely dependent on its achievement, to maintain the motivation of athletes.

Make Practices and Games Enjoyable

One of the main reasons why youth participate in sport is to have fun both from the satisfaction of playing a game well and from just being part of a team. Conversely, if youth do not enjoy being on the team, they are more likely to drop out. Fun, therefore, is an important element in participation. Although fun often occurs spontaneously in sport, a coach should carefully plan to ensure that each

athlete is enjoying the sport experience. Table 24-4 lists several ideas for increasing the likelihood that you and your athletes will enjoy the team experience. The key is to not only allow the athletes a chance to participate but also to engage in practices that are varied, meaningful, challenging, instructive, and that provide positive reinforcement and emphasize fun. Of course, practices and competitions cannot always be fun, but they can emphasize many of the other components of enjoyment. Look at your players' faces. If they regularly smile or laugh, this objective is being met.

Clarify Team Members' Roles and Responsibilities

All athletes want to make a difference for their team by playing in competitive events. Knowledge that they will have a chance to display their skills during the course of a contest is a primary source of motivation. Coaches should make every effort to give each athlete a chance to participate in competitive events.

Table 24-4. Emphasizing Enjoyment.

- Implement well-organized practices; plan practices so all the players have the maximum amount of physical activity possible. Try to eliminate standing in line and waiting for turns as much as possible. If you have a large group, use subgroups in your drills to keep all the players busy.
- Emphasize the reason for doing a set or drill to make it meaningful to their performance.
- Select drills that are suitable for the skill level of the players.
- Create fun ways of learning skills; use innovative drills and games for practicing fundamental skills; ask the players for suggestions.
- Create challenging drills that end only when each person has won or has performed a skill correctly a specific number of times based on their ability level.
- If you use partner drills, make sure athletes change partners frequently.
- Give positive reinforcement related to the effort an athlete puts forth in practice and competitions.
- Take time to make each athlete feel a part of the team, "The team could not function as well as it does without YOU!"
- Encourage athletes to praise, compliment, and encourage each other; do not allow them to criticize each other or use degrading nicknames.
- Allow each athlete to participate as much as possible in competitions.
- Have fun yourself; tolerate some silliness, smile, be enthusiastic, and avoid sarcasm.

Yet, the reality is that it is not always possible to play all team members in a given competition. Under such conditions, coaches need to provide other ways for athletes to be involved, and more importantly, communicate to the athletes how they can achieve playing status. All athletes can be involved in contests even if they are watching from the sidelines. Team members can be watching individuals who are playing similar positions in order to learn from their good techniques and/or their mistakes. They can also watch for strategies used by the opposition to help inform their teammates. Coaches should make clear to all athletes the criteria for achieving playing status. A coach may require that athletes give 100% effort in practice during the week before the competition, or may select competitors based on time trials, or may chose starters on the basis of seniority. Whatever method is used, it is imperative that the criteria are made known to the athletes. When athletes understand how they can achieve playing status, it removes any misconceptions (e.g., the coach only plays her favorites). Athletes can then use these criteria as goals to achieve more playing time during the season and/or off-season. However, the coach must offer strategies to help athletes achieve more playing time.

Create Opportunities for Athletes to Make Decisions

Decision making opportunities can be very motivating because they give the athletes some autonomy in deciding their athletic fate in the sport. Athletes can be involved in choosing a training schedule, training exercises, and game or race strategies. For example, a coach can provide a range of training options during a practice to accomplish sprint training for the day (e.g., an anaerobic quality work, such as a set of 3 x 300 meters with full recovery, or an anaerobic tolerance set of 6 x 300 meters with three minutes of recovery). The athletes can then decide which set would be most helpful and meaningful to them. Team leaders can also be given the opportunity to create the practice for a day. The coach can thus provide the general guidelines for the day and work with athletes to create a workout.

Decision making and providing choice can also be used, with advanced athletes, for choosing strategies for games or races. For example, an athlete can create her choice of strategies for the upcoming cross-country race. Together the athlete and coach discuss the strategies and then reach a consensus for the race. Additionally, team leaders can be involved in developing a line-up for races or deciding what game strategies to use in the upcoming game. Once the athletes have determined their "game plan," they can present their ideas to the coaching staff along with their rationale. Together, the coach and athletes then determine the best game strategy/plan. As an il-lustration, a football coach may ask the quarterback what series of plays he thinks would be useful in the upcoming game. Together they can decide what plays may be the most effective.

Finally, athletes can be taught self-monitoring skills to help them evaluate their own performance or rework team tactics. As an illustration, an athlete who continues to use the wrong stride for hurdling can be videotaped. The coach and athlete then analyze the tape together to examine the problem and come up with appropriate corrections. Through such problem solving procedures the athlete will know what to look for in the future to enhance his performance. In a team sport, coaches can use a freeze play strategy. For instance, a soccer coach can have the athletes freeze in their positions during a practice match, and then question the athletes about:

1. Their offense and if they are in the right location,
2. How the opposing team could respond to this strategy, and
3. How they would respond to the opponent's defense.

Methods that allow athletes to be involved in the decision making process serve two purposes. First and foremost, the athletes gain knowledge about how and why certain training techniques and strategies are used; and they also become better at analyzing their own performances. Secondly, because athletes collaborated in the decision making process they have a vested interest in their training. Providing choices and decision-making opportunities involve athletes in their own development and training, which can be quite motivating and enjoyable.

Encourage Cooperation Among Team Members

Coaches can also enhance motivation by encouraging cooperation among athletes, rather than creating a competitive environment. Teams that emphasize competing against one another in an effort to outdo teammates not only create animosity among players but also create a stressful environment. Under such conditions, it is hard to come together to work as a team. Therefore, coaches must emphasize cooperation among team members not only in competitions but also in practice.

Ask not what your teammates can do for you. Ask what you can do for your teammates.

Magic Johnson

For example, during practices, high ability athletes can work with low ability athletes to help develop fundamental skills. This allows the low ability athlete to gain additional feedback for improvement. Additionally, the low ability athlete may also feel more comfortable seeking answers from a teammate rather than the coach. However, the benefit is not one way. The high ability athletes receive leadership and teaching experience, which can further strengthen their own skills. Teamwork can also occur by having athletes work together in practice to achieve a particular goal or by having junior and senior players serve as mentors to younger players. By using such strategies, a coach can gain a cohesive team and also a team that enjoys being together and that will work hard to achieve for the team.

In summary, a coach can create a mastery motivational climate by emphasizing the following techniques:

1. Help athletes understand the meaning of success,
2. Make practices and games enjoyable,
3. Create opportunities for athletes to make decisions,
4. Clarify team members' roles and responsibilities, and
5. Encourage cooperation among team members.

Allow Athletes to be With Their Friends and Make New Friends

In addition to emphasizing a mastery motivational climate, coaches can also motivate athletes by allowing them to make new friends and interact with old friends within the sport environment. Many athletes view sports participation as a chance to be with friends while doing something they enjoy. Allowing athletes to have fun with friends does not mean practices have to be disrupted. To illustrate, gymnasts can be allowed to work in pairs to perform warm-up exercises, which allow them to get to know one another. The coach can then have the pairs work together to provide peer assessment on gymnastic skills in practice. Peer assessment not only allows athletes to develop friendships but also to build their knowledge of gymnastics techniques. This can encourage an esprit de corps within the team. Social activities, such as a mid-season pasta party, require more time on the coach's or parent's part, but may foster rewarding friendships among athletes, coaches, and perhaps families.

These friendships may provide motivation on another level as well. Within the context of the team, friendships among teammates may provide peer support that can help to motivate athletes. For example, friends can help each other through difficult practices, disappointing losses, and blocks in performance.

Athletes may also have friends on the opposing teams. Encourage athletes to continue these friendships and even develop new friendships with opponents. This will allow the athletes to see their opponents not as the enemy but rather as individuals who will help push them to a higher level by providing a positive challenge within the competitive environment.

This is most eloquently expressed by Mariah Burton Nelson, former Stanford University and professional basketball player, who noted,

An opponent is not an enemy. We challenge each other to do our best. Competition can be a form of love. If I'm a good player, I'm offering my opponent a gift, a way for her to improve, to be inspired to do better.

BUILD YOUR ATHLETES' SELF-CONFIDENCE

You have to expect things of yourself before you can do them.

Michael Jordan

You can try anything. If you feel comfortable within yourself, just believe that you will achieve.

Jollette "Jazzy" Law, Harlem Globetrotter

Believing in yourself is an important precursor to successful execution of skills. The belief that one can successfully accomplish a task is known as *self-confidence*. Successful application of the motivational strategies described throughout this chapter can contribute to enhanced self-confidence.

There are four main sources of self-confidence including, successful past performances, positive verbal persuasion from others, watching a confident role model, and having positive emotional and physiological responses (Feltz, 1992; Weinburg and Gould, 1999). Throughout this chapter, many of the motivational strategies focused on these particular sources. Table 24-5 highlights the sources of confidence along with strategies previously discussed.

Specific to athletics, researchers have also revealed several sources of athlete's confidence (Vealey, et al., 1998). Coaches can also refer to these sources of athlete's confidence to help build or restore confidence (see Table 24-6).

Coaches can also enhance self-confidence by emphasizing preparation and by teaching their athletes to think and act confidently. Coaches spend a great deal of time preparing athletes physically. This preparation can help athletes know that they have done everything possible to prepare themselves for competitions. However, coaches should also prepare athletes mentally. Athletes who have not played competitively or who are competing at a new level can benefit from a coach providing them with a game protocol or telling them what to expect upon their arrival at the competition site, during the warm-ups, and during the game. Coaches should also encourage athletes to think and act confidently by encouraging the use of positive self-talk (e.g., I can make this shot), modeling (e.g., stand tall, keep your head up), and visualization techniques (e.g., imagine yourself making the shot). (See Chapter 22, *Positive Coaching*).

Table 24-5. Building Self-Confidence.

Sources of Confidence	Strategies for Developing Confidence
Successful Past Performances	1) Focus practice sessions on skill development, with regular opportunities for athletes to measure their progress. This can best be accomplished by using the principles of goal setting (discussed in Chapter 23). 2) Emphasize personal improvement rather than making comparisons to other athletes. 3) Set realistic expectations for each athlete so he/she has a chance to experience success.
Verbal Persuasion	1) Give athletes technical feedback to inform them of their progress and future improvement. 2) State your belief in the athlete's ability. 3) Provide encouragement to your athletes.
Modeling	1) Show athletes a confident teammate, opponent , or college/professional athlete that you would like them to emulate. 2) Model a positive attitude or self-confidence.
Positive Emotional Responses	1) Promote and maintain enjoyment in sport. 2) Reduce anxiety (discussed in Chapter 25).

Table 24-6. Athlete's Sources of Self-Confidence.*

Physical and mental preparation—preparing through physical practice or the use of mental skills

Skill mastery—mastering or improving personal skills

Demonstration of ability—show off skills to other individuals

Social support—receiving encouragement or support from coaches, teammates, or parents

Modeling—watching teammates, coaches, or others to gain confidence

Coach's leadership—believing in coach's skill in decision-making and leadership

Physical self-presentation—feeling confident with one's body

Environmental comfort—feeling comfortable in the competitive environment

Situational favorableness—feeling that the breaks of the situation are going in one's favor

*Adapted from Vealey, et. al., "Sources of Sport-Confidence: Conceptualization and Instrument Development," 1998.

SUMMARY

Motivating athletes includes many components. This chapter identified several strategies that may help motivate athletes. The strategies focus on creating a mastery motivational climate by: 1) helping athletes understand the meaning of success, 2) making practices and games enjoyable, 3) clarifying team members' roles and responsibilities, 4) encouraging cooperation among team members, 5) creating opportunities for athletes to make decisions, and 6) encouraging social interactions among teammates. Increased motivation, however, is not the only outcome. Athletes who are involved in a mastery motivational climate are more likely to enjoy their participation in sport and feel more confident as an athlete.

REFERENCES

Ames, C. (1992). "Achievement Goals, Motivational Climate, and Motivational Processes." In G. C. Roberts (editor), *Motivation in Sport and Exercise*. Champaign, IL: Human Kinetics Publishers, pp. 161-176.

Dale, J., and Weinberg, R. (1990). "Burnout in Sport: A Review of Critique." *Journal of Applied Sport Psychology*, 2: 67-83.

Duda, J. L. (1993). "Goals: A Social Cognitive Approach to the Study of Motivation in Sport." In R. Singer, M. Murphey and L. K. Tennant (editors), *Handbook of Research in Sport Psychology*. New York: MacMillan Publishing, pp. 421-436.

Ewing, M. E., and Seefeldt, V. (1996). Participation and Attrition Patterns in American Agency-Sponsored Youth Sports. In F. L. Smoll & R. E. Smith (editors), *Children and Youth in Sport: A Biopsychosocial Perspective*. Dubuque, IA: Brown & Benchmark, pp. 31-46.

Feltz, D.L. (1992). "Understanding Motivation in Sport: A Self-Efficacy Perspective." In G. C. Roberts (editor), *Motivation in Sport and Exercise*. Champaign, IL: Human Kinetics Publishers, pp. 93-106.

Harris, A., and Ewing, M. E. (1992). *Defining the Concept of Fun: A Developmental View of Youth Tennis Players*. Paper presented at the Association for the Advancement of Applied Sport Psychology, Colorado Springs, CO.

Martens, R. (1987). *Coaches Guide to Sport Psychology*. Champaign, IL: Human Kinetics Publishers.

Shi, N., and Ewing, M. E. (1993). *Definitions of Fun for Youth Soccer Players*. Paper presented at the North American Society for the Psychology of Sport and Physical Activity Conference. Brainerd, MN.

Vealey, R. S., Hayashi, S. W., Garner-Homan, M., and Giacobbi, P. (1998). "Sources of Sport-Confidence: Conceptualization and Instrument Development." *Journal of Sport and Exercise Psychology*, 20: 54-80.

Wankel, L. M., and Sefton, J. M. (1989). "A Season-Long Investigation of Fun in Youth Sports." *Journal of Sport and Exercise Psychology*, 11: 355-366.

Weinberg, R. S., and Gould, D. (1999). *Foundations of Sport and Exercise Psychology (2nd edition)*. Champaign, IL: Human Kinetics Publishers.

25

Helping Athletes Cope with Stress: A Vital Aspect of Motivation

Martha E. Ewing, Ph.D.; Jennifer J. Waldron, M.Ed. and Lori A. Gano-Overway, Ph.D.

QUESTIONS TO CONSIDER

- What is stress? How do athletes experience stress? How does it affect performance?
- What are the sources of stress among athletes?
- How can athletes cope with stress?
- What is the coach's role in helping athletes who experience stress?

INTRODUCTION

One of the most challenging aspects of coaching involves working with skilled athletes who are highly motivated to perform but who struggle during critical or pressure situations. If athletes experience this pressure often with the same negative results, they may start to change their behavior in practice. For example, following failure to perform in critical situations, athletes may not work as hard on improving their skills in practice or they may start to complain about injuries that were previously unreported. The use of an injury is a much "safer" explanation for an athlete's poor performance in critical situations than working hard in practice and not being able to produce in a game.

Athletes and coaches will experience pressure, anxiety, or stress at some point during their competition. This chapter will examine how perceived pressure, anxiety or stress affects performance and how coaches can help athletes cope with or overcome the negative motivation and affect often associated with stress.

DEFINING AROUSAL, ANXIETY, AND STRESS

The concepts of arousal, anxiety, and stress are often used interchangeably by coaches, athletes, and researchers. However, these terms have distinct meanings that are important in terms of either their positive or neg-

ative impact on the motivation of athletes. Table 25-1 provides a definition of each term to illustrate their similarity and differences. Throughout the discussion in this chapter, the terms *stress* and *anxiety* will be used to refer to negative influences on performance while *arousal* will be used to refer to the positive influence on performance. Finally, when speaking of anxiety or arousal, athletes will report that they were not "ready" for the game. We will refer to this notion as being *under-aroused*.

Athletes' Response to Stress

When athletes are too anxious, they experience physiological changes, such as increased heart rates, respiration rates, and sweating. Mentally, athletes become over-engaged in a task and may experience the same physiological responses by simply anticipating or dreading the excitement or challenge of an upcoming event.

Anxiety is accompanied by feelings of nervousness and apprehension as well as worry about one's ability to be successful. Responses to anxiety can be seen in different ways among athletes. Some athletes may report being awake all night "worrying" about the game and their performance. This psychological response would be called cognitive anxiety. Other athletes may not worry so much about performance, but rather respond with feelings of nervousness, upset stomach, increased heart rate, and/or feeling out of breath. These physiological responses constitute somatic anxiety.

Table 25-1. Common Terms Used in Discussing Stress.

Arousal
- Occurs on a continuum from deep sleep to extreme excitation. For every task there is an optimal level of arousal that is needed for best performance.
- Athletes may be over-aroused when thinking about playing their chief rival or under-aroused when playing a team with less ability.

Anxiety
- A negative emotional state that results from questioning one's ability to be successful in evaluative situations, such as tryouts or critical games
- Accompanied by feelings of nervousness and apprehension as well as worry about their ability to be successful

Trait Anxiety
- Part of each person's personality which is acquired through learning
- Athletes and coaches may be described as either "laid back" or "Type A" personalities

State Anxiety
- Anxiety that we experience in a specific situation. Weinberg and Gould (1999) suggest that state anxiety refers to our ever-changing moods.
- State anxiety is accompanied by changes in activation or arousal of the nervous system (Spielberger, 1996).

Stress
- "A substantial imbalance between demand and response capability under conditions where failure to meet that demand has important consequences" (McGrath, 1970, p. 20)
- Demands of a task may be either physical (competing in high humidity or altitude without proper training) or psychological (concern with making the team or fear of reinjuring one's self)

The perception that one's abilities may not be sufficient to meet the demands will result in a stress response, i.e., increased physical anxiety or cognitive anxiety. Coaches are seldom aware of athletes' stress levels except through their performance or behavior. In other words, athletes may experience muscle tension or increased heart rate and breathing rate or may worry about what will happen to them if they fail to make the team, thus losing concentration. Coaches will observe that the athlete is not focused but may not be aware of the reason or cause. Athletes who experience stress may start to complain about not feeling well or that their mistakes are not their fault. Their productivity may change or their happiness may suddenly change to dissatisfaction, something coaches can observe.

It is important to know your athletes' level of both trait and state anxiety if you are going to help athletes cope with the anxiety that they are feeling prior to or during competition. Additionally, understand that experience in competitive situations can help mediate the relationship between trait and state anxiety.

Sources of Stress for Athletes

Athletes who compete at either the high school level or more elite levels have reported similar sources of stress (Gould, Horn, and Spreeman, 1983; Gould, Jack-son, and Finch, 1993). Sources of stress for athletes are presented in Table 25-2. These sources can be condensed into two major categories: Situational sources and personal sources.

Situational sources of anxiety include event importance and uncertainty. Personal sources include the ath-

---

Table 25-2. Sources of Stress Among Athletes.

Situational Sources
- Place or not place in tournament or competition
- Event importance
- Uncertainty of outcome (evenly matched teams, critical situations, playing time)
- Time demands on athletes
- Too much media exposure (associated with more elite performers)
- Undesirable training situation
- Financial stress
- Sport politics (usually at more elite levels)

Personal Sources
- Importance to self, coaches, and parents
- Perceived ability
- Confidence or self-doubts
- Pressure to meet high expectations and standards
- Pressure to make it to the top
- Level of trait anxiety

lete's personality (e.g., high trait anxious), level of self-esteem, and self-confidence. In some sports, such as swimming and wrestling, males and females may experience anxiety about their appearance in uniforms that reveal their bodies. Social physique anxiety may be more prevalent during puberty as athletes adjust to the new looks of their maturing bodies. Coaches must be sensitive to comments they make or that peers make to athletes about their bodies.

A comment suggesting that athletes have gained weight to athletes who are sensitive about their bodies can lead athletes to engage in unhealthy eating practices. Athletes may infer that they need to lose weight and, thus, engage in unacceptable weight reduction techniques. (See Chapter 12, *Body Image and the Young Athlete*.)

How Athletes Experience Arousal, Anxiety, and Stress

While the concepts of arousal, anxiety, and stress are distinct, the experience associated with these concepts is subject to individual interpretation. For example, increased nervousness can be a response associated with all three concepts. However, prior to a competition, an athlete may interpret this response as either an indication of readiness to compete (arousal) or as a sign of anxiety or stress. Because we do not know how others are interpreting these responses, we use these terms interchangeably. Indeed, most athletes, and coaches, experience arousal, anxiety or stress in one or more of the following ways: Physiological, cognitive, or behavioral. Each of these response modes will be discussed briefly.

Athletes and coaches vary in the way they experience stress. Table 25-3 illustrates some of the more common responses to stress.

When physiological responses exceed those required to complete the sport task, a decrease in performance will be observed. Likewise, if an athlete is not sufficiently aroused or excited (as often occurs when playing a team that they expect to easily defeat), performance will not be sufficient to perform at one's best. Finding the right level of physiological arousal involves observing when the athlete played very well and having the athlete try to achieve the same level of arousal in subsequent performances.

As performance fails to meet the athletes' standards, they will often experience a loss of confidence and an increase in negative self-talk. In addition, the negative self-talk may also contribute to physiological responses such as increased muscle tension and trying too hard (i.e., rushing movements, doing too much by themselves).

Athletes may experience these responses to stress in either one category or all categories. The following example illustrates the interaction of cognitive and physiological responses to anxiety. Substitutes may be concerned that the coach will pull them out of the game

---

Table 25-3. Signs and Symptoms of Stress.

Physiological Responses
- Increased muscle tension
- Increased heart and respiration rates (feeling out of breath with little activity)
- Increased blood pressure
- "Butterflies" in the stomach
- Increased desire to urinate
- Cold, sweaty palms

Cognitive Responses
- Worry about performance or being good enough
- Worry about NOT meeting coaches', parents', teammates' expectations
- Loss of confidence
- Increased negative self-talk

Behavioral Responses
- Pacing or not being able to sit still
- Abusing drugs and/or alcohol
- Talking when athlete is typically quiet or being quiet when typically very vocal
- Not sleeping the night before the game

---

following their first mistake. Knowing that they will not be allowed the same number of mistakes as starters, they begin to think negatively about the coach and the unfair treatment of team members. This thought causes athletes to keep one eye on the coaches to see how the coaches are responding to the athletes' efforts on the court. This negative self-talk and distraction (lack of concentration) results in a mistake being made, which triggers increased muscle tension and more negative self-talk, and, ultimately, a return to the bench! Some of these responses are quite obvious, while others will require you to talk to the athletes or the parents of the athletes to determine how the athletes experience anxiety.

Many of us are not aware that we are experiencing anxiety. Coaches may see changes in performance in athletes before the changes are detected by the athlete. One effective way to help athletes think about how they respond to anxiety is to ask them to think about situations where they performed very well and situations where they performed poorly. Have the athletes reflect on what they thought, felt, and did during these two situations. Athletes may find that during the good performance they were not aware of thinking about anything, felt relaxed and confident, and slept well the night before the competition. When reflecting on the context in which they performed poorly, they may realize that they slept poorly, could not get stretched out before the contest, and had a lot of self-doubt. Athletes will have their own pattern of responses. Once athletes have identified their responses to stress, the challenge is to develop a strategy for managing the response.

Coping Strategies for Athletes (and Coaches)

Most of us have found ways to cope with our responses to stress through trial and error. However, in sports we cannot leave the ability to manage our anxiety to the chance that we will discover a strategy that is appropriate for the way we experience stress and that will work in the sport environment. Therefore, to be effective in dealing with stress, we must teach athletes several strategies.

Athletes have reported using a variety of strategies for coping with stress in sport. Based on interviews with elite athletes (Gould, Eklund, and Jackson, 1992a, 1992b), the general strategies used are listed in Table 25-4. Coaches must work with their athletes to adapt strategies to meet their athletes' needs. Because athletes experience stress in multiple ways (i.e., cognitive, physiologically, behaviorally), coaches must teach strategies for coping in each of these categories. In some cases, coaches may need to combine strategies to best help the athlete. Likewise, coaches need to listen to strategies that athletes currently use. For example, the use of rituals, prayer, or music may be effective in reducing precompetitive stress for some athletes. A few strategies will be discussed that coaches can teach to their athletes.

Deep Breathing

Proper breathing has often been an effective strategy for decreasing muscle tension and managing anxiety. Athletes will often experience deep and rhythmical breathing when they are performing well and feeling confident and calm. When athletes are under pressure or feeling tense, their breathing may become shallow and irregular. Under pressure, athletes may actually hold their breath which results in an increase in muscle tension. Exhaling deeply decreases muscle tension and, therefore, triggers a relaxation response.

To practice deep breathing, have the athletes fill their lungs completely, holding their breath for several seconds, and slowly exhaling. To help the athletes learn to slow their breathing down, have them inhale to a count of 4 and exhale to a count of 8 (Williams and Harris, 1998). Use this technique when there is a pause in the action during competition (e.g., prior to serving in tennis or volleyball, after getting into the starting blocks, before stepping into the batter's box). Slow and deliberate breathing will help athletes maintain control over their anxiety response.

By focusing on their breathing athletes are less likely to focus on irrelevant cues or distractions, such as crowd noises, the score board, or other competitors. Perhaps the greatest benefit is that deep breathing helps to relax the shoulder and neck muscles that often tighten when athletes experience anxiety. These tight muscles interfere with the execution of many sport skills, such as putting a short golf shot, shooting a free throw, hitting a ball, and throwing a javelin. When breathing properly during a performance, athletes should learn to breathe out during the release. For example, softball pitchers, discus throwers, and shot putters learn to breathe out during the release phase of their performance. With practice, athletes can learn to moderate their breathing with the demands of the skill.

Controlling Self-Talk

When athletes experience stress or increases in anxiety, they frequently engage in self-talk. Self-talk can be both positive and negative. Positive self-talk is an asset that helps athletes focus on specific task-relevant cues. These little reminders that we ask athletes to think about help athletes stay focused (improves concentration) and enhance motivation and performance. Many elite performers have indicated that they use cue words as a reminder to concentrate on certain feelings they want to have as they perform a skill. For example, one football player who ran back kick-offs and punts, used the cue words "Be a monster" prior to the kick to remind himself

---

Table 25-4. Strategies Used by Elite Athletes to Cope with Stress.

- Thought control (blocking distractions, using coping thoughts such as "I can do it")
- Task focus (narrow focus, concentrating on goals)
- Rational thinking and self-talk (taking a rational approach to playing golf in the cold and rain, e.g., "Everyone is playing under the same conditions.")
- Positive focus and orientation (belief in one's ability, changing negative assessments of the situation to positive ones)
- Social support (encouragement from coach, family, and friends)
- Precompetitive mental preparation (mental practice, narrow focus, precompetition routines)
- Anxiety management (mental practice, relaxation strategies, such as deep breathing, Jacobson's Progressive Relaxation)
- Time management (making time for personal growth and daily goals)
- Training hard and smart (work ethic, taking responsibility for one's training)

to be strong and aggressive as he ran the ball back. He believed that he ran harder and was stronger when he used this cue.

Positive self-talk is very beneficial and can be used for a variety of purposes. Self-talk can help athletes in the following ways (Weinberg and Gould, 1999).

- Learning sport skills (cue words focus attention on difficult aspects of the skill)
- Breaking bad habits (cue words are used as reminders of the correction desired)
- Initiating action (cue words may motivate, e.g., explode, stretch, reach)
- Sustaining effort (cue words remind us to keep working hard)

Few athletes are taught how to use positive self-talk. Junior tennis players were observed during games to assess their "self-talk." Both audible comments and gestures were recorded. The findings were clear. More negative self-talk or expression was exhibited than positive self-talk during games and most negative self-talk occurred following mistakes or poor performance (Van Raalte, Brewer, Rivera, and Petipas, 1994). Many learn the power of positive self-talk through trial and error. Positive self-talk (e.g., instructional cues, motivational phrases, self-affirmations) has been shown to enhance performance, particularly when used during practices as well as competition (Ziegler, 1987; Mallett and Hanrahan, 1997; Ming and Martin, 1996). Coaches should teach the use of positive self-talk along with teaching physical skills. Provide positive cue words or phrases as you are teaching skills. Periodically, check with athletes to see what they are saying to themselves after they make a mistake or when they have performed really well.

Negative self-talk is often seen as put downs, e.g., "That was a stupid shot!" These thoughts are distracting and often result in the athlete experiencing more anxiety and attempts to do more (or try harder) rather than focusing on the correct mechanics or feel of a skill. As one fails at a task after trying harder, the athlete begins to question her/his ability to perform the skill or to perform the skill in certain critical situations. Certainly, there is little good that comes from athletes or coaches wrestling with negative self-talk.

One of the most effective strategies for controlling negative self-talk is "thought stopping." (See Table 25-5.) This strategy involves concentrating on the negative or unwanted thought and then using a cue word to stop the thought. The negative thought must then be replaced with a positive or instructional thought to prevent the negative thought from returning. If athletes do not have a replacement thought, the negative thought will return. Athletes must practice this strategy in practice to create confidence in using the skill during competition. Also, coaches should

Table 25-5. Steps to Use in Teaching Thought Stopping.

- Identify negative thoughts and triggers for these thoughts
- Interrupt the thought by yelling "stop" in your head
- Replace the negative thought with a positive thought

encourage athletes to practice the skill in classrooms and in interpersonal situations when negative thoughts creep into the athlete's mind.

Coaches may also find that thought stopping is helpful as a tool when they find themselves becoming frustrated with athletes who continue to make the same mistake or when they think officials are making bad calls. Table 25-6 illustrates some common thoughts for athletes and coaches during games, as well as possible replacement statements. Note that the positive statements should incorporate the use of cue words for focusing attention back on performance or acknowledging mistakes or frustrations but then turning attention to strategies that will help overcome the mistake or let go of thoughts or actions over which one does not have control.

In addition to sports, athletes may experience negative thoughts relative to school assignments or tests. Encourage your athletes to practice the thought stopping technique in these situations, as well.

Imagery

The use of imagery has become a regular part of many elite athletes practice and preparation for competition. Several other terms have been used to describe the phenomenon, e.g., mental rehearsal, mental practice, or visualization. Imagery allows one to recreate an experience in the mind. These video tapes in our head allow us to play through different aspects of the game, changes we might like to make in strategy or personnel, and situations for which we need a plan. Likewise, following a game it is customary to mentally replay the game to analyze the effectiveness of our strategies, plays, or situations that we handled well or that we need to work on in the next practice, and decisions that we made that might have been good or bad.

Imagery is a form of simulation that has many uses. Some of the uses are listed below:

- Acquire and practice sport skills,
- Control emotional responses,
- Improve concentration,
- Build confidence,
- Acquire and practice game strategies, and
- Cope with injury and pain.

Table 25-6. Examples of Negative Thoughts and Replacement Thoughts.

Negative self-talk	Positive self-talk
• "I hate playing in the rain!"	• "We all have to play under the same conditions. Concentrate on hanging onto the ball and you will be fine."
• "You idiot—how could you miss that easy putt?"	• "Everyone makes mistakes. Just relax and trust your stroke."
• "That official has never called a good game. He should retire!"	• "There is nothing I can do about the official. If I play well, I can still win."
• "That was a terrible throw."	• "Slow down, focus on your rhythm and timing.

• "Mental" practice while injured to be prepared and to feel a part of the team, and
• Solve problems.

There are two perspectives that may be used when visualizing. An internal perspective allows athletes to see the activity from their own vantage point. In essence, you see what you would see if you were doing the actual task. This perspective allows athletes to see what is in front of them but not behind them. It also allows the athlete to "feel" the movement and one's emotional response in the moment. An external perspective allows athletes to see themselves as if they are watching themselves on videotape. Using the external perspective, athletes would see what was happening both in front of and behind them. This perspective is excellent for analyzing strategies or for analyzing decisions that athletes made.

Uncertainty and doubt can be eliminated if athletes can see "why" their decision was right or what information in the environment was missed that lead to a poor decision. Knowing why a decision is right or wrong can enhance confidence and reduce anxiety in future performances. Many athletes switch back and forth between internal and external imagery. The perspective is not as important as getting a good, clear, and controllable image that allows the athlete to experience the benefits associated with mental rehearsal.

In teaching athletes to use imagery, it is beneficial to "walk" an athlete through situations that show an athlete how to use imagery effectively. For example, following a practice session have the athletes sit in a comfortable position in the locker room and with their eyes closed lead them through several scenarios that reflect plays you want to use or adjustments you want the team to make. It is helpful to script the scenarios to keep them brief and to the point. You may have athletes practice making free throws in front of a noisy crowd or run their press breaker against a certain kind of press. If the upcoming team is particularly physical, have the athletes practice controlling their emotions after being elbowed or pushed.

Imagery sessions are most effective if athletes can include the senses that accompany the skill or perfor-

mance. One simple but effective way for athletes to practice the idea of using as many senses as possible is to have athletes visualize familiar objects. For example, have the athletes visualize holding an orange in their hand. They should be able to "feel" the bumps on the skin of the orange, "smell" the distinctive aroma of the orange, "see" the color of the orange, and finally, "taste" the orange. If athletes can control their image to experience all of these senses, it is time to move them to their sport.

For example, when visualizing a track event, include the sounds associated with the event, the warmth of the day, the green grass or the color of the lanes of the track, the strength, grace, or speed associated with executing their event. They can hear their teammates encouraging them as they perform, feel the weight of the shot put in their hand, and feel the sweat running down their face. The more senses that are included the more "real" it is for the athlete and the more effective the imagery practice will be.

In general, the focus of imagery should be on successful outcomes. Athletes should see themselves making the play, scoring the game winning point, or performing a perfect gymnastics or cheerleading routine. However, imagery can also be useful for helping athletes recover from mistakes, which are a part of every game or performance. When using imagery with high school athletes and those who are younger, athletes must know what the error or mistake was PLUS what is the correct response. For correcting errors or mistakes, have athletes visualize themselves performing the skill with the correction. With competitive gymnasts, athletes can visualize themselves falling off the beam or bar, taking a moment to calm their nerves and control their negative self-talk, and visualize the remount onto the apparatus and the first part of the routine that they will be doing. This process will help them eliminate the usual wobbles and subsequent errors that often accompany a fall. Likewise, athletes who must perform in weather that is less than ideal can rehearse playing the game under these conditions and performing well.

The use of imagery is only limited by your creativity. Athletes and coaches often use imagery after a game to assess their performance, particularly things they did well. They may also image unsuccessful performances and choose different strategies to use that will lead to success. There are also many stoppages of action in competitions where athletes may use imagery to prepare themselves for the event or to rehearse a skill. Divers use this strategy during the time between dives to mentally prepare for the next dive in as they prepare for their next performance.

For imagery to be effective it must become part of the routine of athletes and coaches. Coaches should build the use of imagery into the practice routine. Seeing themselves perform successfully can build confidence in athletes. This confidence will pay dividends later in contests or in critical situations.

SUMMARY

Helping athletes cope with stress is one of the most challenging aspects of coaching. The first challenge for coaches is to assess "how" athletes respond to stress. Coaches must be able to teach psychological skills and then create situations in practice that allow the athletes to use the skills so that they will be beneficial in more critical situations (e.g., shooting free throws to win the game, throwing a strike with the bases loaded, taking a penalty kick in soccer). To be effective and useful upon demand, coping strategies must be practiced. If you have athletes who engage in maladaptive strategies or suffer continued stress, it may be important to refer the athlete to the school counselor for additional help.

REFERENCES

Gould, D., Ecklund, R., and Jackson, S. (1992a). "Coping Strategies Used by More Versus Less Successful Olympic Wrestlers." *Research Quarterly for Exercise and Sport*, 64: 83-93.

Gould, D., Ecklund, R., and Jackson, S. (1992b). "1988 U. S. Olympic Wrestling Excellence: I. Mental Preparation, Precompetitive Cognition, and Affect." *The Sport Psychologist*, 6: 358-382.

Gould, D., Horn, T., and Spreeman, J. (1983). "Sources of Stress in Junior Elite Wrestlers." *Journal of Sport Psychology*, 5: 159-171.

Gould, D., Jackson, S., and Finch, L. (1993). "Life at the Top: The Experience of U.S. National Champion Figure Skaters." *The Sport Psychologist*, 7: 354-374.

Lazarus, R. S., and Folkman, S. (1984). *Stress, Appraisal and Coping*. New York: Springer-Verlag.

Mallett, C., and Hanrahan, S. (1997). "Race Modeling: An Effective Cognitive Strategy for the 100m Sprinter." *The Sport Psychologist*, 11: 72-85.

McGrath, J. E. (1970). "Major Methodological Issues." In J. E. McGrath (editor), *Social and Psychological Factors in Stress*. New York: Holt, Rinehart, and Winston, pp. 19-49.

Ming, S., and Martin, G. L. (1996). "Single-Subject Evaluation of a Self-Talk Package for Improving Figure Skating Performance." *The Sport Psychologist*, 10: 227-238.

Spielberger, C. D. (1996). "Theory and Research on Anxiety." In C. D. Spielberger (editor), *Anxiety and Behavior*. New York: Academic Press, pp. 3-22.

Van Raalte, J. L., Brewer, B. W., Rivera, P. M., and Petipas, A. J. (1994). "The Relationship Between Self-Talk and Performance of Competitive Junior Tennis Players." (Suppl.) *NASPSPA Conference Abstracts*, 16: S118 (abstract).

Weinberg, R. S. and Gould, D. (1999). *Foundations of Sport and Exercise Psychology, 2nd Edition*. Champaign, IL: Human Kinetics Publishers.

Williams, J. M. and Harris, D. V. (1998). "Relaxation and Energizing Techniques for Regulation of Arousal." In J. M. Williams (editor), *Applied Sport Psychology: Personal Growth to Peak Performance. (3rd edition)*. Mountain View, CA: Mayfield, pp. 158-170.

Ziegler, S. G. (1987). "Effects of Stimulus Cuing on the Acquisition of Ground Strokes by Beginning Tennis Players." *Journal of Applied Behavior Analysis*, 20: 405 - 411.

26
The Effects of Rewards for Athletes

Deborah Feltz, Ph.D.

QUESTIONS TO CONSIDER

- Do awards increase your ability to instruct your athletes?
- How do awards influence intrinsic and extrinsic motivation?
- In which ways can awards control your athletes' behavior?
- What rewards are free, yet effective?

INTRODUCTION

Anyone who has ever attended a postseason team party is aware that presenting trophies and awards is a common practice. Athletes may receive any number of external awards, ranging from small ribbons to large trophies. However, the question of whether it is appropriate to give young athletes these awards is a controversial one.

The advocates of awards such as medals, trophies, ribbons, certificates and jackets indicate that they increase the athletes' desire and motivation to participate. Critics, in contrast, suggest that giving rewards to young athletes for activities in which they are already interested turns play into work and decreases their desire to participate. What is the answer? Awards or no awards?

While the advocates and critics of rewards would have us view the decision as a simple one, researchers have found that no simple answer exists. This chapter provides you with information on how and in what situations external rewards influence young athletes' self-motivation to participate in sports.

UNDERSTANDING REWARDS

An activity is defined as intrinsically motivating if an individual engages in that activity for personal interest and enjoyment, rather than for external reasons, such as receiving a trophy, money, or publicity. In essence, young athletes are intrinsically motivated when they participate in sport for the sake of participation. Until recently, coaches assumed that if external rewards were given for activities that were already intrinsically motivating, the

result would be a further increase in intrinsic motivation. However, research has shown that this is not always the case (Frederick and Ryan, 1995). The presentation of extrinsic rewards for an already self-motivated activity may result in reduced intrinsic motivation. The following adapted (Deci, 1975) story illustrates how rewards can undermine intrinsic motivation.

An old man lived next to an open field that was a perfect location for the neighborhood children's "pickup" baseball games. Every afternoon the children would come to the field, choose sides, and engage in a noisy game. Finally, the noise became too much for the old man so he decided to put an end to the games. However, being a wise old man who did not want to stir up trouble in the neighborhood, he changed the children's behavior in a subtle way.

The old man told the children that he liked to hear them play, but because of his failing hearing, he had trouble doing so. He then told the children that if they would play and create enough noise so he could hear them, he would give each of them a quarter.

The children gladly obliged. After the game, the old man paid the children and asked if they could return the next day. They agreed, and once again they created a great deal of noise during the game. However, this time the old man said he was running short of money and could only pay them 20 cents each. This still satisfied the children. However, when he told them that he would only be able to pay five cents on the third day, the children became angry and indicated that they would not come back. They felt that it was not worth the effort to make so much noise for only five cents apiece.

In this example, giving an external reward (money) for an already intrinsically motivating activity (playing baseball and making noise) resulted in decreased intrinsic motivation in the children. Hence, when the rewards were removed, the amount of participation decreased. It is interestingly suggested that this phenomenon also occurs in organized interscholastic sports. Athletes in many programs are presented with a substantial number of external awards (trophies, jackets, ribbons, etc.) for participating in an already desirable activity. Critics of external awards feel that giving these rewards decreases the athletes' intrinsic motivation and when the rewards are no longer available, they no longer participate. Thus, external rewards may contribute to discontinued participation in sport.

EFFECTS OF EXTRINSIC REWARDS

Two aspects of every reward can influence an athlete's intrinsic motivation. These are the:

- Controlling aspect of the reward, and
- Informational aspect of the reward (Vallerand, et al., 1987).

Controlling Aspects of Rewards

Extrinsic rewards can decrease intrinsic motivation when they cause athletes to perceive that their reasons for participating have shifted from their own internal controls to factors outside (or external to) themselves. This was illustrated clearly in the story of the old man and the children. The children's reasons for playing shifted from internal factors (fun and self-interest) to external factors (money). Then, when the rewards were diminished, they no longer wanted to play. In essence, the children were no longer participating for the fun of it, but were participating solely for the reward. If athletes are made to feel that their primary reason for participating is to receive a trophy or a medal to please their parents, their intrinsic motivation will probably decrease. Therefore, frequently given rewards that attempt to manage performance are not motivational.

Informational Aspect of Rewards

External rewards can also communicate information to individuals about their competence and self-worth. If the reward provides information that causes an increase in an athlete's feelings of personal worth and compe-

tence, it will increase intrinsic motivation. If it provides no information about self-worth or competence or if it reduces these feelings about one's self, it will decrease intrinsic motivation. Thus, rewarding all team members with certificates, regardless of how they perform, provides no information about their competence and is more likely to dampen their interest.

Seek to elevate feelings of self-worth in the awards you give.

A "Most Improved Athlete" award is a good example of how material rewards can enhance motivation. This award usually conveys information to the recipient about competence in the sport and would probably cause an increase in intrinsic motivation. When rewards are given, they should be based upon some known criteria (performance, effort, etc.). This helps ensure that when a reward is earned, it provides the recipient with information to merge feelings of self-worth and competence. This type of reward also contains another important aspect—equal opportunity to receive rewards. Unlike as reward for the highest scorer on the team, which only a few athletes can realistically attain in a season, everyone can achieve rewards based on personal involvement. Therefore, informational rewards can function to enhance motivation across all athletes.

PRACTICAL IMPLICATIONS

Extrinsic rewards have the potential to either increase or decrease intrinsic motivation. There are two key factors in determining which will occur:

1. If athletes perceive their sports involvement as being controlled primarily by the reward (e.g. they're participating only to win the trophy or please Mom or Dad), intrinsic motivation will decrease. In contrast, if athletes feel that they are controlling their own involvement (playing because they want to), intrinsic motivation will increase.
2. If the reward provides information that increases the athletes' feelings of self-worth and competence, intrinsic motivation will increase. If, however, the reward provides no information at all or decreases a person's feelings of competence or self-worth, then intrinsic motivation will decrease.

The results of research pertaining to intrinsic and extrinsic rewards have important implications for you as the coach. Be very careful about using extrinsic rewards! These rewards should be relatively inexpensive and not used to "control" or "coerce" athletes into participation in already desirable activities. The easiest way to accomplish this is to have realistic expectations. Realistic goals can be set for each athlete in terms of improved personal skills. Therefore, athletes can be rewarded for achieving their personal goals. This could be accomplished through the use of "Unsung Hero" and/or "Most Improved Athlete" awards or by offering additional playing time. Moreover, because a coach has such a vital role in determining how athletes perceive rewards, he/she must keep winning in perspective and stress the intangible values of sports participation (fun, personal improvement) in contrast to participating solely for the victory or the reward. Remember, rewards must be given for a reason that has meaning to the athletes. Rewards not given sincerely (not based upon some criteria of success) may decrease intrinsic motivation.

"Official" rewards are not nearly as important, however, as the simple ones that you can regularly give. Remember, some of the most powerful rewards are free (pat on the back, friendly nod, or verbal praise). Use these rewards frequently to acknowledge each athlete's contribution to the team, personal improvement, or achievement of a personal goal. (See Chapter 23, *Goal Setting*.)

> *Some of the most powerful rewards are free-a pat on the back, a friendly nod, or verbal praise. Frequent use of them increases player motivation.*

CULTIVATING INTRINSIC INTEREST

There are some activities, however, that are not naturally motivating for athletes. It may not be enjoyable to do conditioning exercises, practice a weakness, or change a behavior. For example, athletes may find it hard to do conditioning exercises in order to improve flexibility and strength to prevent injuries and to advance in a sport. Athletes are more likely to focus on practicing specific sports skills, which are the source of fun and enjoyment. Under these circumstances, it may be appropriate to offer an award that will motivate athletes to engage in conditioning exercises. However, three essential components must be incorporated into the process:

1. Create personal challenges,
2. Provide information about performance, and
3. Reduce rewards and increase challenges over time.

First, a personal goal that is challenging—yet realistic—should be created for each athlete. Athletes should be informed that as they achieve the goal (e.g., 20 leg lifts) they will receive a reward. Second when the reward is received, the athletes should be reminded how their diligence in completing the conditioning exercises has contributed to improved performance. Encouragement to continue with the exercises should also be provided. As this pattern develops over time, athletes will learn the importance of conditioning exercises, and even though they may not be enjoyable at first, the exercises become self-rewarding in that the athletes continue to see improvements in sports skills—the component they value. Once this link between effort and achievement of goals is established, the rewards should be reduced. However, the personal goals should be increased to provide further challenges for each athlete (e.g., 25 leg lifts) which will continue to enhance motivation. The athletes now have a built-in reward system for their conditioning exercises.

SUMMARY

Extrinsic rewards have the potential to either increase or decrease intrinsic motivation. Extrinsic rewards are most effective when they are inexpensive, kept in perspective, and used to reflect improvements in personal competence. The intangible values of participation in sports should be stressed, as opposed to participating only for winning or for the reward.

REFERENCES

Deci, E. L. (1975). *Intrinsic Motivation*. New York: Plenum.

Frederick, C. M., and Ryan, R. M. (1995). "Self-Determination in Sport. A Review Using Cognitive Evaluation Theory." *International Journal of Sport Psychology*, 26: 5-23.

Gould, D. (1980). *Motivating Youth*. East Lansing, MI: Youth Sports Institute.

Vallerand, R. J., Deci, E. L., and Ryan, R. M. (1987). "Intrinsic Motivation in Sport." In K. Pandolf (editor), *Exercise and Sport Science Reviews*. New York: MacMillan, pp. 389-425.

27
Maintaining Discipline

Deborah Feltz, Ph.D.

QUESTIONS TO CONSIDER

- What is the best way to prevent misbehavior?
- Should athletes be involved in establishing team rules?
- How should team rules be enforced?
- What are the key points of an effective plan for dealing with misconduct?

INTRODUCTION

Coaches often react to their athletes' misbehavior by yelling, lecturing, or using threats. These verbal techniques are used because we often do not know what else to do to regain control. Many discipline problems could be avoided, however, if coaches anticipated the occurrence of misbehavior and developed policies to deal with it.

Harsh comments may prevent misbehavior, but they often create a hostile, negative environment that reduces learning and motivation.

PLAN FOR SOUND DISCIPLINE

Although threats and lectures may prevent misbehavior in the short term, they create a hostile and negative atmosphere. Typically, the effectiveness of verbal threats and ultimatums is short-lived. Moreover, this type of relationship between a coach and team members does not promote a positive environment in which it is fun to learn the sport, nor does it motivate the athletes to accept the coach's instructions. Athletes want clearly defined limits and structure for how they should behave. This can be accomplished without showing anger, lecturing the athletes, or threatening them. As the coach, it is your responsibility to have a systematic plan for maintaining discipline before your season gets underway. Coaches who have taken the time to establish rules of conduct will be in a position to react in a reasonable manner when athletes misbehave. A two-step plan for sound discipline must be in place before misbehavior occurs. The steps are:

- Define team rules, and
- Enforce team rules.

Athletes want clearly defined limits for how they should behave.

Define Team Rules

The first step in developing a plan to maintain discipline is to identify what you consider to be desirable and undesirable conduct by your athletes. This list can then be used to establish relevant team rules. A list of potential behaviors to consider when identifying team rules is included in Table 27-1.

Your athletes should be involved in establishing the rules for the team. Research has shown that athletes are more willing to live by rules when they have had a voice in formulating them. This can be done at a team meeting, early in the season. Smoll and Smith (1979) suggest the use of the following introduction to establish rules with athletes:

I think rules and regulations are an important part of the game because the game happens to be rules and regulations. Our team rules ought to be something we can agree upon. I have a set of rules that I feel are important. But we all have to follow them, so you ought to think about what you want. They should be your rules, too.

Rules of conduct must be defined in clear and specific terms. For instance, a team rule that athletes must

Table 27-1. Examples of Desirable and Undesirable Behaviors to Consider When Making Team Rules.

Desirable Behavior	Undesirable Behavior
Making every effort to attend all practices and contests except when excused for justifiable reasons	Missing practices and contests without legitimate reasons
Being on time for practices and contests	Being late or absent from practices and contests
Listening to instructions	Talking while the coach is giving instructions
Concentrating on drills	Not attending to demonstrations during drills
Treating opponents and teammates with respect	Pushing, fighting, and/or using abusive language with opponents and teammates
Giving positive encouragement to teammates	Making negative comments about teammates
Bringing required equipment to practices and contests	Habitually forgetting to bring required equipment or uniform to contests and practices
Reporting injuries promptly	Waiting until after the team roster is set to report an injury
Helping to pick up equipment after practices	Leaving equipment out for others to pick up

"show good sportsmanship" in their contests is not a very clear and specific rule. What, exactly, is showing good sportsmanship? Does it mean obeying all the rules, calling one's own fouls, or respecting officials' decisions? The Institute for the Study of Youth Sports has adopted a code of sportsmanship that defines sportsmanship in more specific terms (Seefeldt, et al., 1981). This code has been reprinted in Chapter 3, *The Role of the Coach as Teacher, Mentor and Role Model.* You may wish to use some of the items listed as you formulate your team rules.

Athletes are more willing to live by rules they had a voice in formulating.

Remember that you are a part of the team and you should live by the team's rules. You should demonstrate the proper behaviors so the athletes will have a standard to copy. As a coach, you must also emphasize that behaviors of coaches as seen on TV (such as screaming, throwing chairs, and belittling and embarrassing athletes) are also examples of undesirable conduct!

Enforce Team Rules

Not only are rules needed to maintain discipline, but also enforcement of those rules must be carried out so recurrences are less likely. Rules are enforced through rewards and penalties. Players should be rewarded when they abide by the rules and penalized when they break the rules. The next step, therefore, in developing a plan to maintain discipline is to determine the rewards and penalties for each rule. Your players should be asked for suggestions at this point because they will receive the benefits or consequences of the decisions.

The best way to motivate athletes to behave in an acceptable manner is to reward them for good behavior.

When determining rewards and penalties for the behaviors, the most effective approach is to use rewards that are meaningful to your athletes and appropriate to the situation. Withdrawal of rewards should be used for misconduct. Table 27-2 gives a list of potential rewards and penalties.

The best way to motivate athletes to behave in an acceptable manner is to reward them for good behavior. When appropriate behavior is demonstrated, comment accordingly or be ready to use nonverbal interactions such as smiling or applauding. Below are examples of statements coaches could use to reward their athletes for good behavior.

- *"I know you are all very disappointed in losing this game. I was really proud of the way you congratulated and praised the other team after the game."*
- *"Do you realize that for our first five practices everyone was dressed and ready to play at 3:00, our starting time? That helped make the practice go better! Keep it up. Let's see if we can make it a tradition!"*

Penalties are only effective when they are meaningful to the athletes. Examples of ineffective penalties include embarrassing lectures, shouting at an athlete, or assigning physical activity (e.g. running laps, push ups). These penalties are ineffective because they leave no room for positive interactions between you and your athletes. Avoid using physical activity as a form of punishment. The benefits of sport, such as learning skills and gaining strength, are gained through activity. Athletes

Table 27-2. Examples of Rewards and Penalties that Can Be Used.

Rewards	Penalties
Being a starter	Being taken out of a competition
Playing a desired position	Not being allowed to start
Leading an exercise for part of practice	Sitting out during practice until ready to respond properly, for a specific number of minutes, or for the rest of practice (sent home early)
Praise from you in team meetings, to the media, to parents, or directly to the individual	Dismissed from drills for half of a practice, for the next practice, for the next week, or for the rest of the season
Decals, Medals, or Certificates	Informing parents about misbehavior

should not associate this type of physical activity with punishment.

Sometimes it is more effective to ignore inappropriate behavior if the infractions are relatively minor. Continually scolding athletes for minor pranks or "horseplay" can become counterproductive. If team deportment is a constant problem, the coach must ask, "Why?" Misbehavior may be the athletes' way of telling the coach they need attention or they do not have enough to do. Coaches should check to see if the athletes are spending a lot of time standing in lines while waiting a turn to practice. Try to keep your athletes productively involved so they do not have time to misbehave. This is accomplished through well-designed practice plans. (See Chapter 30, *Planning Effective Instruction.*) A lack of meaningful activity in your practices could lead to counterproductive or disruptive behavior.

Misbehavior may be the athletes' way of telling a coach that they need attention or do not have enough to do.

When the rules for proper conduct have been outlined and the rewards and penalties have been determined, they must then be stated clearly so the athletes will understand them. Your athletes must understand the consequences for breaking the rules and the rewards for abiding by the rules. Violators should explain their actions to the coach and apologize to their teammates. You must also follow through, consistently and impartially, with your application of rewards for desirable conduct and penalties for misconduct.

Nothing destroys a plan for discipline more quickly than its inconsistent application. Rules must apply to all athletes equally and in all situations. Thus, if your team is in the championship game and your star athlete violates a rule that requires that he or she not be allowed to start, the rule must still be enforced. If not, you are communicating to your athletes that the rules are not to be taken seriously, especially when the championship is at stake.

It is impossible to predetermine all rules that may ultimately be important during the season. However, by setting up several rules early in the season, standards of expected behavior will be established. Positive and negative behaviors that are not covered by the rules can still be judged relative to these established standard and appropriate rewards or punishments can be given.

KEY POINTS TO AN EFFECTIVE DISCIPLINE PLAN

- Specify desirable and undesirable conduct clearly in terms of rules.
- Involve athletes in establishing the team rules.
- Determine rewards and penalties for rules that are meaningful to athletes and allow for positive interaction between you and your athletes.
- Apply rewards and penalties consistently and impartially.

SUMMARY

Although threats, lectures, and/or yelling may deter misbehavior in the short term, the negative atmosphere that results from such actions reduces long term coaching effectiveness. A more positive approach to handling misbehavior is to prevent it by establishing, with input from your athletes, clear team rules and enforcement policies. Use fair and consistent enforcement of the rules, primarily through rewarding correct behaviors, rather than by penalizing wrong behaviors.

REFERENCES

Seefeldt, V., Smoll, F. L., Smith, R. E., and Gould, D. (1981). *A Winning Philosophy for Youth Sports Programs*. East Lansing, MI: Institute for the Study of Youth Sports.

Smoll, F. L., and Smith, R.E. (1979). *Improving Relationship Skills in Youth Sport Coaches*. East Lansing, MI: Institute for the Study of Youth Sports.

28

Sexual Harassment and Abuse of Power

Jody A. Brylinsky, Ph.D.

QUESTIONS TO CONSIDER

- What are the defining characteristics of the coach-athlete relationship?
- What constitutes sexual harassment?
- What conditions would be considered an abuse of power on the part of the coach?
  —Defamation
  —Battery/corporal punishment
  —Dual relationships
  —Sexual harassment
- What are the steps that can be taken to prevent coach-athlete misconduct?

INTRODUCTION

The goal of this chapter is to help readers understand the special relationship between coach and athlete. This special relationship is based on the understanding of the power and responsibility entrusted to coaches by the school system, parents, and athletes. Knowing how to nurture this relationship without intentionally or unintentionally violating the rights of the athlete is critical to effective and rewarding coaching. The coach must be particularly aware that this unique power relationship carries the potential for sexual harassment or creation of abusive environments.

Historically, teachers and coaches have been permitted the privilege to use intense language and physical contact if it was believed to be reasonably necessary for the student's proper control, training or education. However, there has been an increase in the awareness and occurrence of cases involving sexual harassment and battery brought against coaches, along with an increase in the amount of damages awarded to victims (Breckenridge and Kirby, 1997). Studies suggest that issues of sexual harassment and abuse span the sport scene throughout youth, high school and collegiate athletic programs. While the majority of cases of abuse involve school-age girls, a smaller percentage of school-age boys also experience both verbal and physical harassment

(Hostile Hallways, 1993).The most frequent perpetrator of harassment appears to be an athlete's teammate, followed by a coach, a spectator and even parents and officials (Findlay and Corbet, 1997). There are different degrees of abuse and harassment in the form of physical, sexual, neglectful, and emotionally abusive behaviors. The one common theme is that the attention and sexual attraction is disrupting to the victim no matter how willing the parties involved appear to be.

Recent court action has also established liability for a school official that has knowledge of sexual harassment (similar to child abuse laws) yet fails to respond or is indifferent to the misconduct. Schools must accept responsibility for all actions occurring during the normal course of educational programs. Athletic departments may be faced with five situations involving the potential of harassment (Masteralexis, 1995):

1. Claims against athletic department supervisors by their employees,
2. Claims against coaches and school employees by co-coaches or staff,
3. Claims against non-school coaches by coaches and school staff,
4. Claims against coaches by their student-athletes, and
5. Claims against student-athletes by their peers.

Perhaps society feels that there has been too much violence in the sport environment or perhaps the victims of harassment or abuse have become empowered to no longer be silent. Regardless of its impetus, the way coaches interact with their athletes is analyzed more critically than ever before. Coaches must realize that the relationship between coach and athlete is not one of balances in power; therefore the potential for sexual harassment and abusive conditions exist and steps should be taken to address these issues.

Coach-Athlete Relationship

The coach/athlete relationship can be characterized by clearly identifying the scope of the *coach's authority, responsibility and power*. These concepts can help provide a framework for building a trusting relationship between the athlete and coach.

Authority

This is the coach's right to make decisions on behalf of others. School administrators should accurately describe the authority of the coach through a complete and accurate job description approved by the local board of education. The coach's authority may include the decision on who becomes a member of the team, who remains on the team, who starts, what defense or offense will be run, possibly when practice will be held or even who will be the assistant coach. The school may also give the coach the authority to make decisions in matters that define the scope and safety of the program within the guidelines of their state high school athletic association.

Responsibility

This is the obligation or expectation for behavior in carrying out the role of a coach. Courts and professional associations have been working to establish a legal sense of these responsibilities (duties), many of which are discussed in the chapter on *Legal Issues in Coaching*. It is important to keep in mind that the coach is responsible "**to**" the school, and therefore to the controlling organization to which the school has chosen to belong, as well as to the students and parents, over whom the coach has been given authority. The coach is also responsible "**for**" what a reasonably prudent and prepared coach should know and be able to do. While many of these are included in a list of legal responsibilities, the range of responsibilities may differ in regard to the coaching situation. For example, in some programs the coach has the responsibility for making sure facilities are properly maintained, that transportation of athletes is provided in a safe manner, or to provide sport skill instruction within a religious atmosphere. Clear communication between the school administration, parents and coach can help make this list of responsibilities less ambiguous.

Power

This is the force or actions that allow a coach to use his or her authority. *Official power* includes those actions that are within the specified coaching authority, such as team selection, or granting starting status to certain players. A coach has the "official power" to discipline athletes within the scope of school policy and due process, i.e. suspend from practice, drop from team, request additional practice time and out of season training or withholding athletic letters. A coach has the official power to physically contact a student athlete in order to control that athlete in potentially violent confrontations, i.e. intervening in a fight, removing a weapon or restraining an out-of-control student (Carpenter, 1995).

Most of the time, a coach's ability to be an effective leader does not rely on official power, but rather on *personal power*, the ability to bring about action using social and personal skills. Personal power is appropriately gained when athletes and co-workers are aware of and recognize the coach's experience, knowledge, physical skill, or positive personal characteristics. However, when the demonstration of personal official power creates a hostile or threatening environment, violates an individual's right to due process, or is harassing in regard to gender or expectation of favors in return for a liability interest, it is inappropriate and often illegal.

DEFAMATION OF CHARACTER

Coaches are often asked to provide information about their athletes to other sources in the form of letters of recommendation, progress or recruiting reports and interviews with the press. In fact, Coaches have a *qualified privilege* to discuss the specific characteristics of the athletes with others. However, statements, verbal or written, must be made with a certainty of truth and appropriate cause. If a coach makes a public statement that is false that results in damaging the offended person, it can be considered defamation of character. The following elements are necessary for actions to be considered slanderous (Carpenter, 1995):

- A false statement is made...
- that is published to a third party...
- which holds the subject up to public ridicule...
- thereby causing financial loss.

Comments that are damaging to the core reputation of the offended person may be considered slanderous even if there is no financial loss. This would include comments that reflect on the *moral turpitude* of the individual such as chastity, unprofessional behavior and disease status. Because individuals who place themselves in the public eye are more likely to draw the cynical views from others, they are expected to be more "thick skinned." Comments made about other coaches, officials and in some cases athletes, must be made with malice or reckless disregard for the truth to be considered defamation.

Coaches can feel confident that they are within their bounds if statements are made with no reason to believe they were false. *Truth* is the first and best defense against defamation. Second, be sure that comments to others are within the duties of a coach and serve a purpose other than to hurt the reputation of others or advance the coach's own status. Volunteering information may jeopardize the privileged status between the coach and athlete and therefore place the coach at risk for defamation. If the coach believes something to be true about an athlete or co-worker, but it is negative, there should be a good reason given before sharing it with others.

DISIPLINE USING CORPRAL PUNISHMENT—BATTERY

Our constitution guarantees that individuals will be treated with due process or fair procedures, even in situations where disciplinary actions are being taken. When a coach must act to control a situation that brings harm or unwanted contact to an athlete, the coach may be guilty of battery. *Battery* in civil law refers to any harmful or offensive intentional contact that is unprivileged or not permitted (Carpenter, 1995). The following actions must be met for the act to be considered battery:

1. Intent to contact the student.
2. Contact being made.
3. The contact was harmful or offensive.
4. The contact occurred in an unprivileged or not permitted way.

Notice that there is no requirement that the victim be injured for battery to be claimed. In fact if the above occurs with the intent to harm, then the coach's actions would be considered in a criminal realm. Because most states and schools have prohibitions against corporal punishment, any physical contact in order to punish may be considered suspect of battery.

Sport is built on the notion of physical and mental discipline, which requires the planning and implementation of appropriate training. However, when excessive exercise or cruel and unusual physical demands are requested of the athlete, it may be seen as abusive. While the courts have seen the coach-athlete relationship as one of privilege in which corporal punishment may be acceptable, the courts have also increasingly narrowed what might be considered reasonable in administering such punishment. If reasonableness is exceeded or if the coach violates specific state legislation regarding corporal pun-

ishment, it may be difficult to defend a claim of battery lodged by the student.

IMBLANCE OF POWER— DUAL RELATIONSHIPS

It is both natural and necessary for the coach and athlete to develop strong emotional ties in order to maximize the athletic experience. However, the imbalance of power already existing between the coach and athlete must be recognized as a limitation in creating other social bonds or roles. When the coach attempts to establish the role of friend, counselor, or mentor along with the role of coach, it is considered *a dual relationship* and should be avoided (Hornack and Hornak, 1993). Factors that necessitate holding only the single role of coach are:

- The official authority of the coach creates an imbalance of power,
- Responsibilities attached to the coaching role are not compatible with other social roles and may create a conflict of interest, and
- The fulfillment of additional roles may lead the coach to step over the bounds of appropriate behavior.

The dual role of coach and friend of the athlete may sound beneficial but should be discouraged. The coach's need to be accepted or liked may interfere with the coach's need for objectivity or discipline. Social friendships are based on the expectation of mutual trust and obligations that the coach may not be able to provide to the athlete. If social friendships co-exist in an athlete-coach relationship the athlete stands to not only lose this friendship, but an effective working relationship with his or her coach. The coach may also be misled by what appears to be a genuine friendship on the part of the athlete which may really be a ploy by the athlete for favors and special attention. A personal relationship between athlete and coach is unfair to the athlete and to other members of the team as well as to the coach.

Another source of conflict is the dual role of counselor and coach. While the coach may be able to fill the athlete's need for emotional support within the normal disclosure of feelings inevitable in the sport environment, he or she is not prepared for the emotional intimacies and confidentiality necessary in a mental health professional relationship (Hornack and Hornak, 1993). Because most coaches are not trained to deal with the diagnosis and intervention of emotional disorders, coaches should only try to help the athlete with emotional disorders by referring him/her to professional counseling. It is important that the coach let the athlete know that he or she is not abandoning the athlete, but instead will work "with" the athlete in solving the problem by enlisting the assistance of a trained mental health professional or counselor.

The dual role of coach and mentor can also be abusive if the coach becomes an agent of what is called "positive deviance." Positive deviance is the over-conformity and loyalty of an athlete to his or her coach. Athletes may find themselves doing anything the coach requests without consideration of harmful or extreme consequences. Coaches who use extreme, rigid command styles of control are building dependency relationships similar to those found in abused children and spouses (Coakley, 1993). Athletes in this environment will often make excuses for those who control and abuse them, believing they deserve the inhumane treatment they receive.

In many ways a coach may assume a socially defined role that perpetuates certain myths about pain and suffering in relation to sport achievement. The athlete is led to believe that if playing in pain is noble, then being in agony is even better and is warranted if summoned by the coach. In such violent situations coaches may create environments where athletes are asked to become violent (spear in football), play with chronic injuries, or engage in negative health behaviors (diuretics for weight loss or allowing themselves to be run to exhaustion) for the sake of approval and image.

Attempts to control female athletes' body weight are a frequent part of the domination in male coach-female athlete relationships (Donnelly, 1993). Having athletes demonstrate commitment or "prove" themselves through self-destructive behavior is contrary to the goals of athletic participation. Coaches who attempt to enhance their personal power through such a relationship should be considered abusive.

Clearly coaches need to continually be aware of the impact of the personal ties they build with their athletes and assistant coaches. Athletes report that the unhealthy relationships that led to abuse were not the result of intimidation, but rather a long-standing dependence on the coach for the athlete's success or satisfaction. In many cases the athlete remains silent for years while the coach is oblivious to the situation. Openly communicating about relationship dilemmas can be the first step in dealing with the situation before it becomes harassment.

SEXUAL HARASSMENT

The most sensitive power relationship issues deal with sexual harassment. While no one expects or intends the coach to abuse a relationship with an athlete for the purpose of romantic or sexual interests, it happens. Most of the time, sexual harassment is not founded in romantic or physical attraction between coach and athlete, but rather a display of power and dependence (Goodner and Kolenich, 1993). The hostile environment created by the use of sexual innuendoes or sexist behaviors on the part of the coach, or by other athletes permitted to occur by the coach's action or inaction, is not only unethical but it is illegal.

Sexual harassment is the unwanted imposition of sexual advances, request for sexual favors and other verbal or physical conduct of a sexual nature in the context of a relationship of unequal power. This includes displaying a condescending sex-based attitude toward an individual (Women's Sports Foundation, 1995).

The first type of sexual harassment called *quid pro quo* ("this for that") exists when benefits are granted or withheld (starting status, camp enrollment) as a result of an athlete's willingness or refusal to submit to the sexual demands of a coach. It is not a matter of whether the athlete voluntarily submitted to the act, but whether the conduct she or he submits to is unwanted. Romantic and or sexual behaviors between coach and athletes rarely develop into healthy, long term, mutually beneficial relationships. In the context of athletic programs, it lowers the self-esteem and limits the ability of the athlete to develop his or her full potential. Because of the debilitating effects such relationships have on the athlete and program, it should be clearly identified as unprofessional and unacceptable! It is the coach's responsibility to discourage and stop any romantic advances made by an athlete.

Sexual harassment law has broadened to consider a second form of harassment termed hostile environment. A hostile environment exits when a person's conduct or work environment is permeated with "...conduct [of a sexual nature that] has the purpose or effect of unreasonably interfering with an individuals work performance or creates an intimidating, hostile, or offensive working environment" (Women's Sports Foundation, 1995).

It does not matter whether the harasser's behavior is deliberate and purposeful or simply has the effect of creating an offensive atmosphere. In fact, a team member who witnesses repeated incidents of sexual harassment may also be considered a victim of sexual harassment (Wolohan, 1995). Often sexually hostile behaviors are allowed to continue as a part of the sport environment. The "boys-will-be-boys" attitude allows for hostile behaviors to be considered simple flirting or initiation into a group (Stein, 1995). Regardless how it appears or is rationalized by tradition or customs, sexual harassment interferes with the right to receive an equal education opportunity. Although determining when a situation is considered harassing would be made by reviewing all of the circumstances, the following circumstances are considered suspect (Carpenter, 1995):

1. The sex-related situations are unwelcome by the recipient.
2. A specific or implied connection with an athlete's status is involved.
3. Conduct has the purpose or effect of unreasonably interfering with an individual's school or athletic experi-

ence or creates an intimidating, hostile, or offensive joking environment.
4. The behavior continues after the recipient has made clear that the conduct is unwelcome.

A hostile environment may be determined by examining the unwanted behavior from two perspectives. First, is the unwanted conduct sufficiently severe or pervasive to create an objectively hostile environment that a reasonable person would find hostile or abusive. Second, is the behavior creating a climate that would be considered hostile and abusive. A hostile environment may be created by (Masteralexis, 1995):

1. Unwelcome and unwarranted verbal expressions of a sexual nature (i.e., descriptions of sexual conquests or prowess, talking about the breast size of the opponents, talking about one's clothing such as looking good in a swim suit),
2. Sexually explicit comments and or graphics (i.e., photos or posters that over-emphasize display of anatomy such as beach volleyball or bodybuilding),
3. Actions that cause the recipient discomfort or humiliation of a sexual nature (i.e., referring to the menstrual cycle as a motivational ploy, obscene gestures such as hand gestures or grabbing one's crotch, staring or pointing at a person's body),
4. Unwelcome use of sexually degrading language, jokes, or innuendoes (i.e., referring to the athlete as "babe" or "honey," obscene sounds or gestures, rating of body parts), and
5. Unwelcome and inappropriate touching, patting or pinching (i.e., hugging an athlete for longer than a few seconds, placing of the hand on the athlete's thigh while talking, contact with the face, pats on the buttocks).

The bottom line is that actions which can not be utilized with all athletes, and which are reserved for just a few "special relationships" are probably suspect for review.

RISK MANAGEMENT IN REGARD TO SEXUAL HARASSMENT OR ABUSE OF POWER

It is inevitable that some athletes will come to idolize their coach. Coaches who acknowledge the power they have over their athletes and the multiple roles the coach may play in the athlete's life will be better prepared to act professionally and ethically in carrying out their coaching duties. The following strategy is a proactive approach to dealing with harassment (Women's Sports Foundation, 1995).

1. Each coach should know, understand and appreciate the specific authority, responsibility and official power that accompanies a coaching position.

2. The coach should take a lead role in communicating and setting the boundaries of the coach-athlete relationship and what services or expectations may be requested of the coach or athlete. Your state code of conduct for coaches and athletes should be the basis of this relationship.
3. Coaches should explain to the athlete and athlete's parents the anticipated emotional and or physical contact that coaches will have with the athletes. This should be done in the normal course of explaining season plans and goals as well as implementation of those plans.
4. Early communication may prevent misunderstanding when disciplinary issues arise and demonstrate proper planning and evaluation. Parents and athletes should understand at the beginning of the season how disciplinary action may be taken during the course of the season as well as how due process of the athletes will be protected. It is less likely that a coach will be unaware of his or her abusive nature or a parent will perceive a behavior to be abusive if the behavior is within the scope of pre-established standards.
5. Athletes and parents should be provided with an objective means to evaluate the coach on a regular basis. Through the evaluation the athletes can anonymously report incidents of abuse of power before it escalates and the coach may get a more accurate perspective of how athletes perceive their relationship with the coach.
6. The coach should learn his or her respective school's policy on sexual harassment and procedures to implement that policy. Stopping unfounded or false rumors can save both the coach's and the school's reputation. The coach should know:
   - How a complaint is registered,
   - What happens after a complaint is registered,
   - Who conducts an investigation,
   - How an investigation is conducted, and
   - What disciplinary actions are to be taken.

Because the public's perception of "appropriate" coaching behavior may be biased by the media or disappointment in recent coaching decisions, the coach should be sensitive to how parents and athletes are interpreting his or her conduct. Educating coaches about how to assess their own and other's behaviors can help establish the first line of defense in avoiding claims of abuse. Coaches should also be made aware of how to avoid potentially compromising situations. The following five questions may be useful in guiding decisions regarding questionable behavior (Edwards, 2000):

1. Would I do this if my significant other was here?
2. Would I want someone to do this to my daughter or son?

3. Would I want to be seen on national news saying or doing this?
4. If it were a picture or something visual, would I want it in my house?
5. Is what I am about to do or say likely to make a person feel good or uneasy?

SUMMARY

The sport environment clearly creates a unique opportunity for building healthy, nurturing relationships between coaches and athletes. Coaches should understand the specific boundaries that surround the coach-athlete relationship to ensure that the imbalance of power does not result in physical or emotional harm to the athlete. Sexual harassment and abuse of power can be the subject matter of a number of statutory imperatives such as Title IX, Title VII of the Civil Rights Act of 1964, and the 8th and 14th amendments of the constitution. Whether the coach's abusive behavior is deliberate, purposeful or simply creates an offensive atmosphere does not matter; only the outcome of the behavior is relevant. In addition, an institution and administration may be held liable in hiring a coach with a history of sexual harassment.

Even a well-developed policy on coach-athlete relationships only provides a minimum standard for conduct. Coaches should be proactive by indicating to the athletes, parents, and administrators that they are eager to create a positive and nurturing environment and will be sensitive to the significant interpersonal dynamics that will promote the positive benefits of sports participation. Schools owe it to their constituents to post the laws and policies against sexual harassment and inform employees and students about their rights under the laws and the grievance procedures available.

REFERENCES

Breckenridge, C. H., and Kirby, S. (1997). "Play Safe: Assessing Risk of Sexual Abuse to Elite Child Athletes." *International Review for the Sociology of Sport*, 32: 407-418.

Carpenter, L. J. (1995). *Legal Concepts in Sport: A Primer*. Reston, VA: American Alliance for Health, Physical Education, Recreation and Dance.

Coakley, J. (1993). "Social Dimensions of Intensive Training and Participation in Youth Sports." In B. R. Cahill and A. J. Pearl (editors), *Intensive Participation in Children's Sports*. Champaign, IL: Human Kinetics Publishers, pp. 77-94.

Donnelly, P. (1993). "Problems Associated With Youth Involvement in High Performance Sports." B. R. Cahill and A. J. Pearl (editors), *Intensive Participation in Children's Sports*. Champaign, IL: Human Kinetics Publishers, pp. 95-126.

Edwards, K. (2000, July/August). "Sexual Harassment Prevention Training for Coaches and Athletes: Stay Within the Boundaries." *Strategies*, 13(6): 19-23.

Findlay, H., and Corbet, R. (1997). *What is Harassment: Harassment and Abuse Handbook*. Center for Sport and Law, [Available on Line] hhttp://harassmentinsport.com/Handbook/Sec1ch2.html.

Goodner, E. D., and Kolenich, D. B. (1993). "Sexual Harassment: Perspectives From the Past, Present Practice, Policy and Prevention." *Journal of Continuing Education in Nursing*, 24(2): 57-59.

Hornack, N. J., and Hornak, J. E. (1993). "Coach and Player: Ethics and Dangers of Dual Relationships." *Journal of Physical Education, Recreation and Dance*, (May-June), 84-86.

"Hostile Hallways: The AAUW Survey on Sexual Harassment in America's School." (1993, summer). *WIN(Women's International Network) News*, pp. 74-75.

Masteralexis, L. P. (1995). "Sexual Harassment and Athletics: Legal and Policy Implications for Athletic Departments." *Journal of Sport and Social Issues*, 19(2): 141-156.

Stein, N. (1995). "The Definition of Sexual Harassment Applies to Schools." In D. Bender, et al. (editors) *What is Sexual Harassment?* San Diego, CA: Greenhaven Press, Inc., pp. 19-24.

Wolohan, J. T. (1995). "Title IX and Sexual Harassment of Student Athletes." *Journal of Physical Education, Recreation and Dance*, 66(3): 52-55.

Women's Sports Foundation (1995). *An Educational Resource Kit for Athletic Administrators: Prevention of Sexual Harassment in Athletic Settings*. East Meadow, NY: Author.

SUGGESTED READINGS AND RESOURCES

Child Abuse and Youth Sports: A Comprehensive Risk Management Plan (1998). National Alliance for Youth Sports [available on line] < www.nays.org >.

"Don't Stand for Sexual Harassment." (1995). *Aussie Sport Action*, 6(4) [Available on line] < www.ausport.gov.au/act646.html >.

Findlay, H., and Corbett, R. (1997). *What Is Harassment: Harassment and Abuse Handbook*. Center for Sport and Law, [Available on Line] < http://harassmentinsport.com/Handbook/Sec1ch2.html >.

Nelson, M. B. (1994). *The Stronger Women Get, the More Men Love Football: Sexism and the American culture*. New York: Harcourt Brace & Company.

Sport Safe. (1998). *Coach's Game Plan: Guidelines to Creating a Safer Environment*. Victoria, B.C.: Province of British Columbia.

Section V
Pedagogy

29
Planning for the Season

Ray Allen, Ph.D.

QUESTIONS TO CONSIDER

- Why should planning the season be a priority for the coach?
- What steps should the coach follow in planning the season?
- What four kinds of objectives are involved in planning the season?
- What role does a season calendar have in this process?

INTRODUCTION: WHY PLAN?

Perhaps no aspect of coaching is more influential to success than the coaches' ability to plan. Every team's performance level depends upon the degree to which it is prepared, and preparedness in turn is dependent upon judicious use of limited time and resources. Poor season planning is analogous to a hungry person who shops for groceries without a list. Most everything in every aisle is attractive and has some value. Decisions are made according to personal whims and what appears valuable at the time. Returning home, the shopper finds that some essentials for the week are forgotten and a good deal of resources were spent on frilly items. Time and money are lost on return trips to the store, or some essential items are lacking because resources are expended.

A careful planner will consider what he/she currently has, what will be needed over the next period of time, and what resources are available. The result will be a list of items to be purchased that will include all the essentials. It will also include non-essentials, but the non-essentials will complement and not come at the expense of the essential items.

So it is with practice planning. Disorganized practices often result in the failure of athletes to obtain those skills, capacities and attitudes that coaches deem most essential for success, due in part to poor allocation of resources. Ineffective practices can also contribute to injuries or the acquisition of outcomes that may be incorrect or inappropriate. Organized practices contribute to maximizing the benefits of participation while mini-mizing potentially negative effects. Efficient season and practice planning prior to the start of the first practice can result in the following benefits:

- Efficient use of limited practice time,
- Emphasis of season objectives that are most important,
- Focus on the right objectives at the time, through the year, to maximize performance,
- Direction for the selection of practice activities that maximizes long and short term goals and objectives,
- Reduction of the total time required for planning,
- Enhanced preparation of the team for competition,
- Improved ability to make day-to-day adjustments in practice objectives, and
- Records that may rebut lawsuits contending negligence.

HOW TO PLAN FOR THE SEASON

Effective season planning consists of four sequential steps (Cristina and Corcos, 1988).

1. Identification of performance objectives for the year,
2. Division of the season into stages,
3. Identification of benchmarks to be achieved in each stage of the season, and
4. Specification of objectives to address in each practice.

The remainder of the chapter will explain each step and explain how to accomplish each.

Identification of Performance Objectives for the Year

Performance objectives define what specifically needs to be performed by team members, and how well it must be performed in measurable terms (Mager, 1975). This may be the most critical stage in the planning process. Identifying performance objectives will provide the coach and athletes with clear targets to work towards, and focus their energy on areas that will make the greatest impact on their success. If a coach focuses on the wrong objectives or fails to allocate appropriate amounts of energy to teaching the objectives, it does not matter how well he/she coaches.

A team's (or individual's) level of performance depends upon how well they meet a combination of objectives from the following categories (Fuoss and Troppmann, 1981):

- Ability to perform activity-related skills,
- Technical knowledge related to performing the activity,
- Physical conditioning, and
- Personality and character traits related to attitude and team chemistry.

While the coach must address objectives from each area, the specific objectives that must be addressed and the performer's level of proficiency will vary by sport and level of competition. For example, a freshman football team will require less technical knowledge of the passing game than a varsity team.

Selection of Skill Objectives

A coach should begin by identifying the categories of skills that must be addressed for the team to perform competitively within the specified sport. As an example, a list of skill categories in the sports of baseball and softball appear in Table 29-1. The coach must then identify those specific skills within each category that must be performed well. Table 29-2 lists a set of candidates that might be addressed with regard to baserunning. The coach would select those objectives that are most appropriate for the level of play and most important to the team's success. A freshman baseball or softball coach may choose to focus on teaching a single sliding technique, knowing that sliding skills may be lacking and that teaching proper techniques will require a significant amount of instruction. On the other hand, a varsity coach with a veteran team may be convinced that coaching multiple methods may be to the team's advantage and worth the time required to teach each technique.

Once specific skills are identified, the coach must address how well a player must perform each skill for the team to be successful (again, higher levels of competition

Table 29-1. Categories of Performance Objectives for Baseball.

- Baserunning
- Hitting
- Fundamental Throwing/Fielding
- Fielding Combinations
- Pitching
- Position Play
- Rules/Safety/Etiquette
- Defensive Strategies
- Offensive Strategies

Table 29-2. Skills Specific to Baserunning in Baseball/Softball.

- Running to first base
- Leading off first base
- Leading off second base
- Leading off third base
- Rounding bases
- Tagging on fly balls
- Stealing bases
- Double steals
- Pop-up slide
- Bent-leg slide
- Head-first slide
- Offensive Strategies

may require higher performance levels). Because safe, effective, consistent performance is directly related to proper form, the objective should also include key elements of form. For example, a varsity basketball coach may determine that the team should make at least 70 percent of their free throws in games. An example of a performance objective for free throws appears in Table 29-3.

Time taken to identify performance objectives gives the coach and players clear pictures of how well they must be able to perform to be successful. It helps the coach decide what should be the focus in practice, and it helps the athlete discern what she/he does well and what elements require additional attention in practices.

Selection of Knowledge Objectives

Cognitive objectives (e.g., knowledge of rules, safety procedures, strategies and information related to physical conditioning) are critical to success. Knowing what to do in specific situations and how to do it can make a significant contribution to individual and team performance. As with skill objectives, coaches are well advised to define what their athletes should know and how well they should know it as part of their planning process. Doing so helps coaches focus on what needs to be taught and how much time must be spent in teaching it. It also provides

Table 29-3. Season Performance Objective for Free Throw Shooting.

SEASON OBJECTIVE: Free Throw Shooting

Standard

Shoot free throws with correct form and make an average of at least 70 percent of them in interscholastic competition over the course of the season.

Criteria:

Stance
- Fingers of the shooting hand spread, with middle finger bisecting the ball.
- Non shooting hand on the side of the ball with fingers spread.
- Feet spread at near shoulder width, with the shooting-side foot forward.
- Knees slightly flexed.

Preparation
- Raise the ball while flexing the wrist and elbow, so the ball, elbow, knee and toes on the shooting-hand side are aligned when viewed from the front.
- Flex the knees while raising the ball.

Action
- Extend the knees and ankles with the weight distributed evenly.
- Push the ball upward by extending the elbow.
- Extend the wrist as the elbow nears full extension so the ball rolls off from the fingers with a backward rotation.

Completion
- Fully extend the knees and shooting arm.
- Point the palm of the shooting hand to the floor, with fingers pointing at the basket.
- Distribute the weight evenly on the balls of both feet.

---

the information coaches need to make sure that the athletes know prior to competition (For example, football coaches often test their lineman on blocking assignments prior to playing games, to make sure assignments are correct.) Identifying and articulating knowledge objectives increases the likelihood that they will be taught at appropriate times during the season and at an appropriate level of understanding. Table 29-4 provides examples of cognitive objectives for baseball.

Selection of Fitness Objectives

How does a coach determine if the amount of time spent on conditioning is inadequate, sufficient or too much? The only way to answer this question is to identify appropriate fitness objectives and assess the fitness levels of athletes relative to those standards. Clearly, more time must be spent on becoming fit than in maintaining a given fitness level. Assume then, a football defensive back can squat 300 pounds. Should the defensive back spend more time in the weight room to increase the squat to 350 pounds, or should the athlete spend less time to maintain his current level and use the time saved on developing more speed and agility? Often times, a significant amount of conditioning can occur through participation in intense practices. For example, basketball or volleyball practices can be extremely intense, and therefore, they may provide all or most of the needed aerobic conditioning. In this case, less time can be spent on formal conditioning drills and re-allocated to skill develop-

ment. On the other hand, practices may not provide sufficient stress to increase or maintain sufficient fitness levels; for example, baseball players may not maintain a sufficient aerobic base simply playing baseball. Table 29-5 includes examples of fitness objectives to consider for inclusion in a season plan.

Selection of Personal and Social Skill Objectives

Personal/social character traits include skills such as persistence, self-control, tolerance, respect for authority, encouragement of teammates, concentration on the task, how to handle winning and losing, commitment to best efforts, and cooperation. Coaches should not underestimate the importance of appropriate personal and social character traits to the success of their teams. The way one athlete responds to adverse conditions (in games, practice situations, and/or with coaches) can impact the outcome of a game or the attitude and eventual performance of other athletes. How team members interact with each other from moment-to-moment has implications on how well they play and how much they learn.

Athletes need guidance (modeling, encouragement, gentle rebuking and, in some cases, firm discipline) to develop such attributes. When achieved, these personal and social skills can contribute to improved performance. A coach can make an important and lasting contribution to athletes by helping them improve their feelings of self-worth and other socially desirable qualities of character. Teaching athletes to focus on qualities under their control

Table 29-4. Potential Cognitive Objectives for Baseball.

POSITION PLAY:
1. Catching position (C)
2. First base (1B)
3. Second base (2B)
4. Shortstop (SS)
5. Third base (313)
6. Pitcher (P)
7. Left field (LF)
8. Center field (CF)
9. Right field (RF)

RULES/SAFETY/ETIQUETTE:
1. Rules of play
2. Safety
3. Team
4. Etiquette

DEFENSIVE STRATEGIES:
1. Rundowns
2. Double steal
3. Bunt defenses
4. Hit and run defenses
5. Steal coverages

OFFENSIVE STRATEGIES:
1. Bunting
2. Hit and run
3. Bunt and run
4. Stealing

STRATEGIES OF PLAY:
1. Ground ball hit to infield (no runners on base)
2. Ground ball hit to infield (with base runners)
3. Ground ball hit to outfield (no runners on base)
4. Ground ball hit to outfield (with base runners)
5. Fly ball to outfield

Table 29-5. Sport-Related Fitness Objectives.

POTENTIAL SEASON OBJECTIVES

Energy Production
1. aerobic capacity
2. anaerobic capacity
3. aerobic /anaerobic capacity

Muscular Fitness (strength, endurance, power)
1. neck
2. shoulder
3. upper arm
4. lower arm
5. wrist
6. abdominal
7. hip/spine
8. low back
9. groin
10. upper leg
11. lower leg
12. ankle

Muscular Flexibility
1. neck
2. shoulder
3. trunk
4. hip
5. ankle

Other Sport Specific Fitness Objectives
1.
2.
3.

(such as effort) rather than variables beyond their control (such as winning awards) can contribute significantly to their personal character.

The development of personal and social traits should not be limited to incidental learning. Development of personal and social traits should be planned and implemented proactively. In an extensive review of research on sport and character, Shields and Bredemeier (1995) concluded that sport does not automatically build character or "characters." They concluded that the influence sport has on participants depends on a complex set of factors tied to the specific sport and the social interactions present. A coach is in a good position to positively influence what is learned by clearly defining outcomes and expectations in terms of performance objectives. A sample performance objective for a personal/social skill appears in Table 29-6.

Division of the Season into Stages

After performance objectives have been defined, the coach must decide how to best address them through the season. With good coaching, teams can be expected to improve in all four areas (skill, knowledge, fitness, personal/social) as their season progresses. However, it may not be possible—or in a team's best interest—to progress in all areas at the same rate across the year. For example, a cross-country team may not want to be too fit at the first part of their season. They may use the first contests as opportunities to condition, with the intent of maximizing fitness levels near the end of the season. "Peaking" too soon can be detrimental to achieving season goals. In contrast, a football team may require relatively high levels of fitness for their first contest then make gradual gains as the season progresses. The coach decides what to

Table 29-6. Season Performance Objective for Competing Appropriately.

SEASON OBJECTIVE: Competitive Behavior

Demonstrate competitive behavior appropriate for the situation nearly all the time prior to, during, and after games and practices.

Criteria:

   a. Works hard to achieve an outcome regardless of the circumstances.
   b. Encourages teammates when winning or losing.
   c. Interprets the context in which specific physical activity is occurring and adjusts personal behavior accordingly.
   d. Evaluates outcomes to determine necessary actions to improve the performance of self and others without placing blame.
   e. Acknowledges outstanding performances by teammates and opponents regardless of outcome.
   f. Refrains from taunting, bragging, or gloating.

---

focus on and how much practice time to devote to these objectives at various times in the season. This process can significantly affect the team's success.

A critical step in planning for the season is to determine how well team members need to perform specific objectives at specific times of the season. Doing this will help the coach decide how to delegate limited time and resources to the various objectives. This should be done so that time is spent on what will pay the greatest dividends as the season progresses. This can be accomplished systematically in three steps: First, the coach divides the season into significant periods, or stages. Then expected performance levels for the chosen objectives are established as benchmarks for each stage of the season. Finally, the coach plans practices in ways that will focus on those objectives most likely to contribute significantly to the team's success during each phase of the season.

Most sport seasons can be sub-divided into four stages:

- *Preseason* (the period of time prior to the first official practice),
- *Early season* (extending from the first day of practice to the first contest),
- *Mid-season* (the time during which the bulk of the contests are played), and
- *Late season* (when championships are determined and when tournaments occur).

Each stage will consist of a specified number of days, practice sessions and contests.

Identification of Benchmarks to be Achieved by Stage of the Season

Once season stages are identified, the coach can decide which objectives to focus on most heavily during each stage and what would be ideal levels of performance for each. Players' current (or anticipated) status and the amount of practice time available will heavily influence

these decisions. For example, a basketball coach may want the team to install two zone defenses, a one-on-one defense, one player offense out of two formations, two zone offenses, one full court zone press, one half-court zone press, press breaks for half and full-court presses, two out-of bounds plays and one jump ball play—all in the early season. Unfortunately, the team may have only fifteen official practices before their first game. Installing the entire package before the first game may compromise how well the team executes each and greatly restrict the practice time available to work on fundamental skills and conditioning. Prioritizing objectives and establishing performance levels for each stage assist the coach in making decisions that contribute most to the team's over-all success. An example of possible early season benchmarks for basketball appear in Table 29-7.

It is imperative that measurable performance benchmarks be identified for each stage of the season. The benchmarks guide the coach in determining how much time must be devoted to the instruction and practice of each objective in order for athletes to attain the performance level on each objective. **Merely exposing teams to the objectives without spending sufficient time for them to be learned results in frustration for the coach and athletes.** Athletes must receive sufficient instruction, practice and feedback to make significant improvements on their ability to perform. Accordingly, the coach must select, teach and practice only the objectives that are essential to the sport and level of play. Objectives can always be added if the team progresses faster than anticipated, but time wasted on too many objectives cannot be recovered.

Specification of Objectives to Address in Each Practice

Create a Practice Calendar

Once content is selected for each phase of the season and desired performance benchmarks are defined, a

Table 29-7. Samples of Early Season Performance Benchmarks for Basketball.

Individual Skills

Control Dribble
Execute a control dribble well enough to limit turnovers to no more than two per ten possessions.

Jump Shot
Shoot jump shots with good form, making at least 40 percent of attempts in practice scrimmages.

Rebounding
Execute an appropriate box out at least 75 percent of the time when participating in practice scrimmages.

Free Throw Shooting
Shoot free throws with good form, making an average of at least 60 percent of attempts in practice scrimmages.

Moves Facing the Basket
Execute a proper jab step and read, resulting in a good decision (pass, shot, or offensive reset) on at least 75 percent of one-on-one situations.

Moves Back to the Basket
Execute a proper read, resulting in a good decision (pass, shot, or offensive reset) on at least 75 percent of one-on-one situations.

Defense on the Ball
Execute a proper stance and position at least 75 percent of the time when confronting the ball when participating in practice scrimmages.

Defense off the Ball
Maintain a correct position when defending offensive players most of the time (75 percent) without the ball in the context of practice scrimmages.

Offensive Strategies
Executes a single offensive play against player-to-player and zone defenses well enough to result in a high percentage shot on at least three of five possessions in practice scrimmages.

Defensive Strategies
Assumes proper positions and stances when running man and zone defense so that at least 75 percent of field goals taken are contested in practice scrimmages.

Press Offense
Recognizes the kind of press being applied and gets in correct positions to break the press almost all the time in practice scrimmages.

Fitness Capacities
Executes eight consecutive suicides (line drill) in under 30 seconds, and without varying more than five seconds per attempt, at the conclusion of an average early-season practice.

---

coach can construct a season calendar that specifies the objectives to be addressed during each practice. This season calendar will provide a guide from which daily practice plans can be developed. An example appears in Figure 29-1. The following list includes examples of entries that should be included on the season calendar.

- Eligibility dates and deadlines,
- Date of first team meeting,
- Dates and times for coaches' education meetings and/or coaching clinics,
- Equipment distribution date and times,
- Date and time for parents' orientation meeting,
- Dates and times for league meetings,
- Sequential numbers designating practices (e.g., #1 designates first practice),
- Practice objectives and time allocation,

- Game days and times,
- Tournament dates,
- Dates and times for other special events, and
- Date and time for awards banquet.

The most important part of developing a season calendar is deciding what objectives to include in which practices and how much practice time to devote to each objective during each practice. Clearly, a significant amount of time is required to introduce any objective, and athletes need enough time to practice objectives to meet the intended benchmark. As objectives are mastered, less time is needed to maintain performance.

Supplement 29-1 provides a blank reproducible worksheet that can be used to develop a master calendar of practices.

Season Calendar

Coach: Sims   **Team:** 7th Grade Basketball   **Season:** 1998-99

Mon	Tue	Wed	Thu	Fri	Sat	Sun
		Sign-ups 6-8 PM Woods Cafeteria				
		Organizing Meeting Woods Multi-Use 4:00				
1st Practice Skills Test Rules Test Vocab Test Condition		2nd Practice Lay-ups Jumpers Def stance Def shuffle		3rd Practice Passing lanes Dribbling 2-on-2 Off		
4th Practice 2-on-2 Off 3-on-3 Off Help Defense Free Throws		Parents Meeting 7:30 PM Woods Multi-Use		5th Practice Team Off/Defense Pre-Game Line-ups and Subs	1st Game	
6th Practice Review		7th Practice		8th Practice	2nd Game	

Figure 29-1. An Example of a Season Calendar.

Using the season plan worksheet, objectives that are selected to include in the first practice are entered in the space labeled Practice #1. This process should be repeated for the second, third, and subsequent practices through the early, mid-, and late season division. Time estimates are made for each objective within each practice, ensuring that the amount of time needed matches the time available for each practice.

This integral procedure will take less time for planning the season and practices than if planning is done on a practice-by-practice basis. In addition, as each stage of the season comes to an end the coach will have substantive information to guide planning decisions for the subsequent stage. Finally, a completed plan that has been implemented and refined is an invaluable resource for subsequent seasons, or it can be a guide for new coaches coming into the program who may have only vague perceptions of how to organize for the season. Integrating the results of decisions about which objectives to emphasize during the four stages of the season into a calendar (Figure 29-2) will result in a master plan of practices. Supplement 29-2 is a blank, reproducible form that can be used to select and order objectives for the season.

SUMMARY

The coach's role can best be filled through the leadership and instruction provided in practice and competition. Clearly, those coaches who are most effective in helping their athletes acquire the necessary physical skills, knowledge, fitness, and personal and social skills are those who have clear objectives and who plan their season to achieve them. Organization of the season by selecting and teaching high priority objectives in their proper order and for an appropriate amount of time is a major step toward helping athletes acquire the benefits available through participation in athletics. Further, this effort increases the likelihood of success.

BIBLIOGRAPHY

Cristina, R. W., and Corcos, D. M. (1988). "Post Season: Evaluate Athletes' Outgoing Competencies, Evaluate Entire Program and Coaching Staff." *Coaches Guide to Teaching Sport Skills*. Champaign, IL: Human Kinetics Publishers.

Fuoss, D. E., and Troppmann, R. J. (1981). *Effective Coaching: A Psychological Approach*. New York: Wiley and Sons.

Mager, R. F. (1975). *Preparing Instructional Objectives*. Belmont: Pitman Learning, (pp. 2).

Shields, D. L., and Bredemeier, B. J. (1995). *Character Development and Physical Activity*. Champaign, IL.: Human Kinetics Publishers.

Season Planning Form

Coach: Sims
Team: 7th Grade Basketball   Season: 1998-99

Physical Skills	Pre	Early	Middle	Late
Defensive stance and shuffle		√	√	
Help and Recover Team Defense		√	√	
Lay-ups: strong hand		√		
off-hand		√	√	
Jump shots		√	√	
Passing/Catching passes		√	√	√
Dribbling		√	√	√
Rebounding		√	√	√
Defensive double-team				√

Rules and Strategies	Pre	Early	Middle	Late
Team offense		√	√	
Team defense		√	√	√
When/how to double team				√
Fast break			√	√
In-bounds under the basket			√	√
Time rules: 3 sec., 5 sec., 10 sec.	√	√		

Fitness	Pre	Early	Middle	Late
Aerobic capacity		√		
Anaerobic capacity		√	√	
Lateral shuffle		√	√	√

Personal and Social Skills	Pre	Early	Middle	Late
Team		√	√	√
Sportsmanship		√	√	√
Leadership			√	√
Respect for officials and opponents			√	√
Self-esteem		√	√	√

Figure 29-2. An Example of How Objectives Can be Placed in the Appropriate Stages of a Season.

Supplement 29-1. A Blank Season Calendar.

Season Calendar

Coach: Team: Season:

Mon	Tue	Wed	Thu	Fri	Sat	Sun

Supplement 29-2. A Blank Form to Use in Choosing Objectives and Placing Them in Appropriate Stages of a Season.

Season Planning Form

Coach:

Team:

Season:

Physical Skills	Pre	Early	Middle	Late
_____				
_____				
_____				
_____				
_____				
_____				
_____				
_____				
_____				

Rules and Strategies	Pre	Early	Middle	Late
_____				
_____				
_____				
_____				
_____				
_____				

Fitness	Pre	Early	Middle	Late
_____				
_____				
_____				

Personal and Social Skills	Pre	Early	Middle	Late
_____				
_____				
_____				

30
Planning Effective Instruction

Ray Allen, Ph.D.

QUESTIONS TO CONSIDER

- What four steps can coaches follow to systematically instruct their athletes?
- What guidelines for instruction should be applied to ensure effective instruction?
- What are the features of an effective practice plan?
- What are the characteristics of a good drill?

INTRODUCTION

Effective instruction is the foundation of quality coaching. In fact, perhaps the best indicator of quality coaching is the degree to which players improve while under the coach's tutelage. Win/loss records may not be good indicators of success, in that the number of wins in a season depends in part on a number of factors outside a coach's control (e.g., who chooses to participate, the caliber of the opposition, key injuries, factors at home). Coaching success then has to be determined according to how effective the coach is in positively influencing those factors that are within his/her control, and the coach can have his/her greatest influence through practice sessions. Regardless of the outside influences and genetic pools, a coach's responsibility is to help players play better. How players perform in contests is heavily influenced by what occurs in practice.

Success in competition is directly related to what players obtain through practice sessions; therefore, it behooves the coach to conduct practices in ways that maximize what participants learn and how well they learn it. The professional literature has much to say about effective teaching and learning. Unfortunately, according to McCallister, Blinde and Weiss (2000), coaches are not adequately prepared to structure experiences into functional learning environments. They also contend that external pressures make it difficult for coaches to fully implement practices that reflected their personal philosophies. In any case, coaches will insure they are doing all they can to maximize what their athletes learn from practice by becoming aware if these concepts, and assessing their practices relative to them. Even the most knowledgeable coaches are more effective when they organize and plan instruction prior to meeting with players.

PHASES OF PLANNING TO FACILITATE IMPROVED PERFORMANCE

What participants learn and how fast they learn in practice sessions depends on what occurs within three phases of practice planning. The rest of this chapter will be dedicated to presenting these phases and identifying the critical principles and concepts in conducting each phase effectively.

Phase 1. Systematic planning for the season. A thorough season practice plan specifies what participants need to know and how well they need to know it across the season. An effective season's plan sets performance benchmarks in measurable terms at critical times in the season. This enables coaches to plan individual practices that are most likely to meet performance benchmarks at those critical times. It will enable athletes to improve performance on a daily basis. The process of creating an effective season plan is addressed in detail in Chapter 29, *Planning the Season*. It should be noted that this is a critical first step that must be done well. The season plan articulates what must be accomplished in each practice. It really doesn't matter how well something is taught if what is taught doesn't match the athletes' timely needs.

Phase 2. Planning effective practices. How a practice is organized can facilitate or interfere with the participant's progress towards achievement in all four domains (skill, knowledge, fitness capacities, and personal/social character traits). An organized practice prepares an athlete to respond optimally at critical points in practices, thus maximizing the benefits that are obtained from practice sessions. It prepares the athlete's body for the stressful components of a practice. It helps the athlete focus on the key points to be learned, maximizes the use of time, and provides them with optimal opportunities to master the content and use it in appropriate situations. In contrast, poorly organized practices can waste precious time, create distractions for athletes, and can actually interfere with the athletes' ability to learn a skill or fully reap the benefits of conditioning exercises. The coach and athlete will benefit by adopting a practice plan format that adheres to effective learning principles.

Phase 3. Principles of effective instruction. Once an individual practice is organized to maximize what a participant learns, the coach must consider how to present what is to be practiced in the most effective, efficient manner. Some of the benefits of using effective instructional principles include:

- Ensuring the athlete's attention is focused on what they need to know,
- Providing information and activities in ways that maximize learning,
- Maximizing meaningful repetitions while minimizing incorrect repetitions,
- Enabling the athlete to monitor their own progress,
- Maximizing the athletes' motivation, and
- Recognizing what has been accomplished, thus enhancing feelings of gratification and self-efficacy.

PLANNING EFFECTIVE PRACTICES

Practices should be designed to maximize learning on a day-to-day basis. How much is learned in a practice setting can be enhanced by two basic factors. First, every practice should follow a regular and consistent pattern. This allows the coach and athletes to become familiar with routines. These routines benefit the athletes in that they know what occurs when in a practice, and what the coach's expectations are during each part of the practice. This reduces the amount of time wasted in transitions, organizing groups, and down time due to the lack of an activity's clear purposes. Problems in systematic organization may result in a practice where athletes are actively engaged as little as 50 percent of the available practice time (Karweit, 1989; McGarity and Butts, 1984). Regular routines can also help the coach improve the ability to instruct. This is because the familiarity with the practice procedure allows the coach to focus more on what occurs in each segment, rather than focusing energy on management issues during each segment.

The second factor that can enhance how much is learned is the inclusion of elements of a practice that have been shown to facilitate learning. Numerous authors (e.g., Hunter, 1982; Moore, 1998; Saffici, 1998; Rink, 1998, etc.) have presented elements that should be part of an effective instruction, and numerous studies have confirmed their impact on learning (Graham, 1983; Kwak, 1993; Masser, 1990). Each part is described below, with its rationale. A sample of a practice plan format is illustrated in Figure 30-1. A sample practice plan is provided in Supplement 30-1, and a full-sized copy of the practice plan that can be reproduced is included in Supplement 30-2.

Date and practice number. Each practice plan should be numbered and dated, according to the day it was implemented. This is important as an organizational tool. Coaches can use information obtained through implementing specific practices when planning practices in subsequent years. It also can be an important piece of information if issues of negligence ever occur (see Chapter 34, *Legal Issues in Coaching*).

Equipment needs and set-up. Practices should designate what equipment should be used, how much of each kind of equipment is needed, and where the equipment should be positioned prior to practice. Too little equipment may reduce the number of meaningful repetitions in which athletes engage, and too much equipment may result it lack of sufficient supervision. Either case can impede the rate at which athletes progress. Often, valuable practice time is lost because the equipment is not immediately accessible or not located where it should be, there is insufficient (or too much) equipment, and/or multiple coaches need the same equipment. The little time expended to make these decisions prior to engaging in practice can provide significant returns in time spent on meaningful activity.

Practice objectives. Every practice should be based on specific objectives that must be obtained for the team's continued improvement. Prior to any practice, the coach (or coaching staff) needs to assess the team's current status and identify current strengths and weaknesses relative to performance objectives. Those areas needing the greatest amount of work must be identified as practice objectives.

Practice objectives serve as a guide to planning and implementing the entire practice. They guide the coach in planning a practice that sufficiently addresses these key points, they help communicate the practice intent to athletes in meaningful terms, and they help the coach assess the practice's effectiveness in achieving those outcomes. Taking the time to identify practice objectives according to what needs to be accomplished is the only way a coach can plan practices that effectively aid teams in making systematic progress through the season. Samples of possible early and mid-season practice objectives appear in Figure 30-2.

Practice overview and anticipatory set. Every practice should begin by meeting with the team to

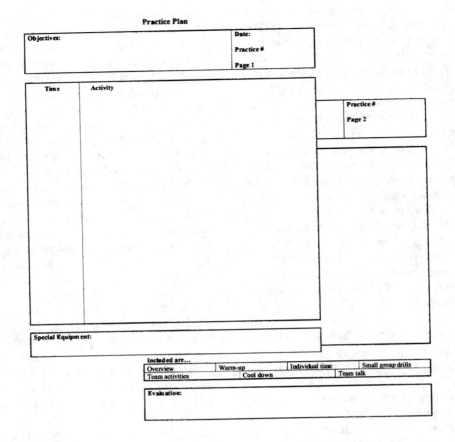

Figure 30-1. Practice Plan Format.

Sample Early Season Practice Objectives:

Motor skill:

Control Dribble:	Execute in half-court offense without losing control in 90 percent of possessions.
Passing:	Successful completion of at least 90 percent of passes in half-court game.
Jump Shot:	Make at least 40 percent of shots with good footwork in drills.
Free throws:	Make at least 60 percent of all taken during practice.

Knowledge:

Player Offense:	Execute the primary options of motion without mental errors against live defense.
Full court zone press:	Execute the press without mental errors.
Man and zone defense:	Execute both without mental errors.

Fitness:
Complete five line drills, each under 28 seconds at the conclusion of practice.

Personal/Social:
Positive work ethic
Encourage teammates

Figure 30-2a. Sample of Early Season Objectives for Basketball.

Sample Mid Season Practice Objectives:

Motor skill:

Jump Shot:	Make at least 40 percent of shots when executing 2-on-2 offensive combinations.
Free throws:	Make at least 75 percent of all taken during practice.

Knowledge:

Player Offense:	Run well enough to get a high percentage shot at least 75% of the time.
Full court press break:	Recognize the kind of press and execute the appropriate break successfully at least 80% of the time.
Man and zone defense:	Alternate defenses by possession without mental errors or giving up uncontested shots.

Fitness:
Complete five line drills, each under 25 seconds at the conclusion of practice.

Personal/Social:
Maintain composure under pressure.
Demonstrate sportsmanship when winning and losing.

Figure 30-2b. Sample of Mid-Season Objectives for Basketball.

overview the day's practice. An effective practice overview will accomplish the following:

- Explain what will be accomplished in the day's practice (practice objectives),
- Share the coach's expectations with regard to behavior and performance,
- Share what the practice will look like, and
- Tell why the athletes ought to stay on task and achieve the practice objectives.

A successful practice overview will help the athletes' know what to do, how well they have to do it, and why it is worth their concerted effort. It will help the athletes' focus on the practice's intended purposes, and the result will be a more productive practice.

Warm-up. Athletes must be prepared physically and mentally for the intense parts of practice. Physically, athletes should start exercising at a light to moderate level, and gradually increase intensity until they obtain the desired practice intensity. Athletes need to be prepared mentally in the same way. It is unreasonable to expect athletes to shift from a completely unfocused mental state to become totally focused on practice objectives in an instant.

An efficient warm-up period ought to be skill specific. A traditional, general warm-up might consist of three to five minutes (the time necessary to sufficiently increase the core temperature) to jog or "shoot around." A skill-specific warm-up can begin with a walk-through of important skills or team concepts, progress to practicing specific skills at a moderate speed, and finally conclude with athletes performing at a relatively high intensity. While the skill-specific warm-up results in the same physical condition (noticeable perspiration and increased respiration rate), it also uses the time to practice important movement patterns and helps the athlete focus on practicing.

Practice activities and key points. After an appropriate practice overview and warm-up, athletes should engage in practice activities specifically designed to meet practice objectives, and those objectives should focus on specific elements that need to be improved. The degree to which a performer improves on a motor skill is directly related to the quality of a practice (i.e., the degree to which the practice focuses on intended learning) than practice quantity (Ashy, Lee and Landin, 1988; Goldberger and Gerney, 1990). In fact, practicing skills that are already mastered under constant conditions may not be beneficial to learning (Magill, 2001). Athletes may lose their motivation to perform correctly or at a high intensity, resulting in patterns and trials that fail to meet desired standards. An athlete needs to enter each practice activity with clear learning objectives and a procedure to monitor their own improvement. Accordingly, the key

points that the coach desires his/her athletes to obtain as a result of each practice activity should be identified and used to monitor practice trials.

The selection and implementation of instructional activities, drills or contests should account for most of the time in each practice session. Because a large amount of instruction occurs within the context of drills, drills should be selected or developed to include several important features:

- Require a relatively short explanation,
- Provide an excellent context for mastering an objective,
- Match skill, knowledge or fitness objectives,
- Accommodate small, medium or small groups,
- Are easily modified to accommodate skilled and unskilled performers, and
- Accommodate skill analysis and feedback to athletes.

Drills that are selected or developed can be written on independent cards or sheets. A more detailed discussion of drills can be found in Chapter 32, *Drills as Instructional Activities*. In addition to a look at what goes into a "good" drill, a format for collecting drill information is explained. A reproduction *Drill Information Card* is included as Supplement 32-1.

Practice sessions should progress from simple application of the practice objectives to game-like application. In general, athletes should begin with practice of skills on an individual basis, then apply the skills in small group drills with limited combinations of variables, then apply the skill objective in game-like situations. For example, a basketball coach's practice objective may be to work on good footwork and an economic release when shooting from the field. Coaches would be wise to have their athletes practice their footwork and release during shooting drills early in the practice. This allows the athletes to focus solely on the movement patterns without interruption. Then coaches should embed the shooting skill in a combination drill, such as shooting field goals when engaged in two-on-two offensive drills. This facilitates a high number of shooting repetitions in a controlled setting, but includes the application of good footwork and a quick release. Finally, the skill would be embedded in five-on-five scrimmages near the end of practice.

Time allocation for each part of the practice. How much time is allocated to each part of a practice (and practice time spent on each lesson objective) is a difficult but important decision. Clearly, what participants learn is directly related to the amount of time that they have to practice. (Graham, 1983). Assigning too little practice time to specific lesson objectives, and/or practicing the objective in conditions that are too complex too soon may result in exposing athletes to the objective, but with little or no permanent change in behavior. On the other hand, allocating too much time to any single objective or part of a lesson may be demotivating or result in insufficient time spent on other objectives.

Designating times in practice plans serves two purposes. First, it helps the coach or coaches stay on task through practice. Coaches can easily become so engrossed with a specific part of practice that they lose track of time. The result can be elimination or neglect of another important part of practice. The second purpose is to assess and refine time allocations in the future. Coaches can compare how much time is spent on individual components of practice to the degree to which players meet intended objectives. This information can help assess the appropriateness of time spent in past practices, making future practices more efficient and effective.

Cool-down. A cool-down is a period of moderate to moderately-light activity near the conclusion of practice. As with other components of an effective practice, a cool down serves multiple purposes. Physically, a cool-down helps the body eliminate accumulated waste products in the muscles, reduces the pooling of the blood in the extremities, reduces the potential for muscle soreness, and prevents the loss of flexibility that may accompany intense muscular exercise. Mentally, it gives athletes the opportunity to separate themselves from the complexities of full-team activities and refocus on specific objectives that were the primary purpose of practice.

Review. Every practice should culminate in a team talk. This is an opportunity for the coach to remind athletes what needed to be accomplished during the practice session, tell them what they did well, and what they need to accomplish in the next practice. It is an opportunity to motivate athletes by pointing out what was achieved during practice, how their effort during practice affected the outcomes, and reinforce the benefits of good practice habits. Finally, it is a time during which the coach can share expectations of players from the end of practice until the next practice or game.

Practice overviews and reviews are extremely important factors to facilitate learning. Review sessions, however, may be the most neglected component by most coaches. Often, coaches become so focused in the team practice session that insufficient time is left at the end of practice for conditioning and/or reviewing the day's activities. Coaches would be well advised to terminate practice sessions sufficiently early to always include a review of the practice.

Practice Evaluation. Space should be reserved on every practice plan to record reflections on the day's practice. Coaches should take a few minutes after practice to record notes on their perceptions of the practice. Some of the most important information might include how accurate the time allocations were, what lesson objectives were not met, what parts of practice were neglected and/or inserted, and what parts of practice simply did not go well. This kind of information can be used to plan or revise practice plans in subsequent days or seasons. In both cases, the information makes practices and coaching behaviors more effective and efficient.

PRINCIPLES OF EFFECTIVE INSTRUCTION

It is the coach's responsibility to provide his/her athletes with the best opportunity to learn in every practice. Whereas the effective planning of practice addresses how a practice should be structured to facilitate learning, principles of effective instruction address how a practice should be implemented to maximize outcomes. The following guidelines summarize the current research findings concerning teaching and learning. Coaches sincerely concerned with helping athletes improve should become familiar with these guidelines and implement them as much as possible. The guidelines are listed below, then explained in detail in subsequent sections.

1. Communicate intended outcomes clearly,
2. Establish an orderly environment,
3. Communicate high learning expectations,
4. Plan appropriate levels of practice,
5. Monitor progress and provide feedback,
6. Promote a sense of control,
7. Group athletes according to the objective, and
8. Maximize time on task.

Communicate Intended Outcomes Clearly

The first step in creating an optimal atmosphere for learning is to specifically identify what constitutes an ideal performance, then compare each participant's status relative to the learning objective. This enables the coach to focus the learner's attention to one aspect of a skill at a time, which facilitates learning.

It is then the responsibility of the coach to communicate what needs to be learned in ways that best prepares the participants to engage in appropriate practice. This communication should include five elements. First, the coach must have the athletes' full attention. Presentations of information should be made under conditions where the players are still and silent, and the coach can make eye contact with each participant. Distractions must be minimal. Second, the coach should share what is to be learned in as few words as possible. Sharing only essential information helps ensure that the performers will focus on the essentials. Third, performance standards should be communicated in measurable terms, enabling the athletes to determine how close their performance matches the ideal. If appropriate, the performers should be provided with examples of correct and incorrect performances, to ensure that they know the difference.

Fourth, the coach must communicate why athletes need to master this component so they will stay on task and maintain a high level of motivation. Finally, the coach should check for understanding, ensuring that the athletes know what to practice and why. Investing a few minutes on these elements of communication prior to practicing specific content will pay substantial dividends in terms of what and how much athletes improve.

Establish an Orderly Environment

High achievement is directly related to:

- Safe, orderly, business-like environments with clear expectations,
- Holding learners accountable for effort and achievement, and
- Relating rewards to achievement of expectations (Fisher, et al., 1980).

Implementing orderly, disciplined practices, and establishing clear reasonable rules that are fairly and consistently enforced will minimize behavioral problems that interfere with learning, while enhancing pride and responsibility within team members (Wubbels and Levy, 1993).

Coaches must understand, however, that establishing and maintaining an orderly environment is not equivalent to strict authoritarianism. Orderly environments require cooperation between coaches and athletes (Doyle, 1986; Clark, 1989), and athletes are more likely to be cooperative when athletes find policies to be reasonable and meaningful. Research indicates that learners have more positive feelings towards instructors that provide leadership and order in combination with friendly, understanding behavior (Brekelmans, Wubbels and Creton, 1990). The best of circumstances is a relaxed, enjoyable but business-like environment. The ability to balance these two forces (business-like atmosphere and enjoyment) may be one of a coach's most difficult tasks.

Rewards must also be used appropriately. Clearly, effective coaches will provide performers with rewards for desirable accomplishments. Misuse of rewards however can be contraindicated. Weinstein's (1996) recommends using verbal rewards to increase intrinsic motivation for achievement, and save tangible rewards for behaviors that performers find unattractive. (See Chapter 26, *The Effects of Rewards on Athletes*.)

Communicate High Learning Expectations

The expectations a coach communicates to performers can create a positive climate and influence learning (Rutter, et al., 1979). According to Brophy (1982) effective teachers see students as capable of learning and perceive themselves as capable of teaching them effectively.

Coaches appear to interact differently with athletes for whom they hold different expectations. Athletes perceived to be low performers are (Fisher, et al., 1978):

- More often positioned farther away from the coach,
- Addressed in groups rather than individually,
- Smiled at less,
- Less likely to receive eye contact,
- Called on less to answer questions,
- Praised more often for marginal and inadequate performances, and
- Praised less frequently for successful participation and interrupted more often.

Clearly, these kinds of behaviors can influence motivation and achievement. Because a team's success depends on the continuous progress of all players—not to mention that it is a coach's ethical responsibility to coach athletes under his/her tutelage—the coach must communicate the expectation that all athletes will improve. Adherence to two guidelines can assist the coach in communicating high expectations for learning:

- Expect to make significant changes in the skills, fitness capacities, knowledge and behaviors of all athletes through the course of the season.
- Set realistic goals for each athlete, and make a commitment to help each athlete achieve them.

Plan Appropriate Levels of Practice

The rate at which performers learn and their motivation to learn is directly related to the difficulty of the task. Social cognitive theory suggests that the degree to which a performer is motivated is directly related to the learner's expectation for success and the value placed upon achieving it (Feather, 1982). If tasks are too easy, the learner may lose focus and become demotivated. On the other hand, tasks that are too difficult may frustrate the performer and be demotivating, as well.

What guidelines should a coach adhere to that will result in optimal progress? A coach will serve his/her athletes by providing practices that require the performer to exert a concerted effort to achieve, but can make significant improvement on a regular basis. Generally speaking, practice tasks are too difficult if the performer is successful in less than 50 percent of the trials. It is probably not challenging enough if the performer is successful in more than 80 percent of the trials. This necessitates the planning of practice trials in ways that the player can monitor his/her own performance in measurable terms.

Monitor Progress and Provide Feedback

It is fair to assume that sharing information on performance is a critical component of sport skill acquisition. Feedback can be used to motivate performers, maintain on-task behavior, and reinforce correct performance patterns (Rickard, 1991).

When coaches are actively moving about, monitoring progress and providing individual and small groups instructional feedback, athletes will make greater gains (Fisher, et al., 1980). Within this context, the coach will be able to provide corrective feedback, contingent praise and emotionally-neutral criticism (constructive in nature, devoid of personal attacks and sarcasm) for inappropriate behavior. These actions have a positive influence on behavior, achievement, and attitude.

Promote a Sense of Control

Athletes should feel they have some control over their own destinies if they are to reach their potential in sports. Athletes who are allowed to overcome challenging tasks through persistence tend to acquire a strong sense of self-efficacy (Weiner, 1980), and performers with high perceptions of competence tend to expect performance gains and improve performance (Rudisill, 1989).

A sense of control can be promoted by:

- Encouraging athletes to set personal (realistic) performance goals,
- Organizing practice sessions that allow athletes to assess themselves and monitor their own progress,
- Organizing instruction to result in many successful experiences (i.e., opportunities for athletes to receive positive feedback),
- Reinforcing the positive relationship between effort and achievement, and
- Demonstrating appreciation for achievement by all performers.

Group According to the Objective

Decisions about size and composition of groups for various learning tasks are complex, but have been shown to be related to achievement. With regard to facilitating skill acquisition, heterogeneous grouping is seldom the most advantageous (Webb, 1980). Typically, with groups of mixed ability, the performer with average ability suffers a loss in achievement while the athlete with low ability does slightly better. A critical condition for grouping to be effective is to have athletes practice at skill levels needed to advance their playing ability. This typically involves groups of similar ability, so they can be appropriately challenged.

In most sports a team will have many different levels of ability. This situation presents a difficult grouping task. There are however, several potential solutions.

When a skill, rule, or strategy is being taught that all athletes need to know, use a single group for instruction.

As differences among athletes' abilities are identified on specific tasks, divisions can be made by similar abilities in small groups when working on those tasks.

When a skill, rule, or strategy is being practiced where individual athletes are at several levels of ability (initial, intermediate, or later learning levels), establish learning stations that focus on specific outcomes to meet each groups' needs.

The placement of athletes into smaller groups for learning various skills, rules and strategies must be independently decided for each skill, rule and strategy. An athlete who is placed in a high level group for practicing one skill should not necessarily be place in a high level group for practicing another.

Maximize Time on Task

The amount of practice time that athletes are actually engaged on learning tasks can range from 30 to 50 percent of the total practice time. Clearly, the greater the amount of time athletes practice, the more they learn. Consequently, coaches should be very concerned with maximizing the amount of practice time athletes spend on task. Several actions can be taken to maximize use of available time.

- Reduce the number of athletes waiting in line by using more subgroups in drills.
- Secure sufficient supplies and equipment so athletes do not wait.
- Reduce the transition time between drills by planning practices to minimize reformulation of groups and equipment set-up time.
- Use instructional grouping practices that have athletes practicing skills at appropriate performance levels.
- Clearly outline and/or diagram each portion of a practice and communicate as much of this information as possible before entering the practice facilities.
- Complete as many pre-and post- warm-up/cool down activities outside the scheduled practice time as possible and
- Recruit assistants to help with instructional stations under your supervision.

While maximizing the amount of time athletes spend engaged in practicing the day's objectives is a high priority, it is not the only contributor to learning. Accordingly, there are some situations that occur in practice that should take priority over getting as many athletes active as possible:

- Taking the time to set up a meaningful experience,
- Limiting the number of simultaneous performances when unique and/or important learning is initiated, so practice occurs under the coach's direct observation,

- Using extra time to explain and demonstrate a skill or drill to enhance the degree to which it is performed, and
- Safety is an issue and maximum activity would not be advantageous.

SUMMARY

Effective instruction is the foundation of successful coaching. It requires practices that include clear communication of what is to be learned, a practice format that facilitates a safe, effective environment for learning, and application of principles of instruction that maximizes learning.

In general, coaches are not adequately prepared to structure experiences into functional learning environments. External pressures make it difficult for coaches to fully implement practices that reflected their personal philosophies. Coaches will have a greater impact on what athletes learn, and work from a framework that will enable them to improve their instruction each year, by planning individual practices that include the components described in this chapter. They will also improve their ability to coach effectively if they plan their instruction according to this chapter's instructional guidelines. Even the most knowledgeable coaches are more effective when they organize and plan instruction prior to meeting with players.

REFERENCES

Ashy, M., Lee, A., and Landin, D. (1988). "Relationship of Practice Using Correct Technique to Achievement in a Motor Skill." *Journal of Teaching Physical Education*, 7(2): 115-120.

Brekelmans, M., Wubbels, T., and Creton, H. (1990). "A Study of Student Perceptions of Physics Teachers Behavior." *Journal of Research in Science Teaching*. 27(4): 335-350.

Brophy, J. (1982). "Successful Teaching Strategies for the Inner-city Child." *Phi Delta Kappan*. 63: 527-530.

Clark, C. (1989). *The Good Teacher*. Plenary lecture, the Norwegian Research Council for Science and the Humanities Conference, Trondheim, Norway.

Doyle, W. (1986). "Classroom Organization and Management." In M.C. Wittrock (editor), *Handbook of Research on Teaching*. New York: Macmillan.

Feather, N. (1982). *Expectations and Actions*. Hillsdale, NJ: Lawrence Erlbaum Associates.

Fisher, C. W., Berliner, D. C., Filby, N. N., Marliave, R. S., Caher, L. S., and Dishaw, M. M. (1980). "Teaching Behaviors, Academic Learning Time and Student Achievement: An overview." In C. Denham and A. Lieberman (editors), *Time to Learn*. Washington, D.C.: U.S. Department of Education, National Institute of Education.

Fisher, C. W., Filby, N. N., Marliave, R. S., Caher, L. S., Dishaw, M. M,

Moore, J. E. and Berliner, D. C. (1978). *Teaching Behaviors, Academic Learning Time and Student Achievement*. San Francisco, CA: Far West Laboratory for Educational Research and Development.

Goldberger, M., and Gerney, P. (1990). "Effects of Learner Use of Practice Time on Skill Acquisition." *Journal of Teaching Physical Education*, 10: 84-95.

Graham, G. (1983). "Review and Implications of Physical Education Experimental Teaching Unit Research." In T.J. Templin and J.K. Olson (editors), *Teaching in Physical Education*. Champaign, IL: Human Kinetics Publishers.

Graham, G., Holt-Hale, S., and Pouku, M. (1998). *Children Moving. A Reflective approach to Teaching Physical Education (4th edition)*. Mountain View, CA: Mayfield Publishers

Hunter, M. (1982). *Mastery Teaching*. El Segundo, Ca: TIP.

Karweit, N. (1989). "Time and Learning: A Review." In R. E. Slavin (editor), *School and Classroom Organization*. Hillsdale, NJ: Lawrence Erlbaum Associates.

Kwak, E. C., (1993). *The Initial Effects of Various Task Presentation Conditions on Students' Performance of the Lacrosse Throw*. Unpublished doctoral dissertation. The University of South Carolina.

Magill, R. A. (2001). *Motor Learning: Concepts and Applications*. Boston: McGraw-Hill.

Masser, L. S. (1990). "Teaching for Affective Learning in Elementary Physical Education." *Journal of Health, Physical Education, Recreation and Dance*, 62: 18-19.

McCallister, S. G., Blinde, E. M., and Weiss, W. M. (2000). "Teaching Values and Implementing Philosophies: Dilemmas of the Youth Sport Coach." *The Physical Educator*, 57 (1): 35-45

McGarity, J. R., and Butts, D. P. (1984). "The Relationship Among Teacher Classroom Management Behavior, Student Engagement, and Student Achievement of Middle And High School Science Students of Varying Aptitude." *Journal of Research in Science Teaching*, 21 (1): 55-61.

Moore, K. (1998). *Classroom Teaching Skills*. Boston: McGraw-Hill.

Rickard, L. (1991). "The Short Term Relationship of Teacher Feedback and Student Practice." *Journal of Teaching Physical Education*, 10: 275-285.

Rink, J. E. (1998). *Teaching Physical Education for Teaching, 3rd edition*. Boston: McGraw-Hill

Rink, J. E. (D. 1991). *Developing Teaching Skills in Physical Education, 3rd edition*. Palo Alto, CA: Mayfield Publishing.

Rudisill, M. (1989). "Influence of Perceived Competence and Casual Dimension Orientation on Expectations, Persistence, and Performance During Perceived Failure." *Research Quarterly for Exercise and Sport*, 60: 166-175.

Rutter, M., Maugham, B., Mortmore, P., and Ousten, J. (1979). *Fifteen Thousand Hours*. Cambridge, MA: Harvard Press.

Saffici, C. L. (1998). "Conducting a Coaching Session." *Journal of Health, Physical Education, Recreation and Dance*, 68(8): 44-46.

Webb, N. M. (1980). "A Process-Outcome Analysis of Learning in Group and Individual Settings" *Educational Psychologist*, 15: 69-83.

Weiner, B. (1980). *Human Motivation*. Chicago: Holt, Rinehart and Winston

Weinstein, C. S. (1996). *Secondary Classroom Management: Lessons from Research and Practice*. Boston: McGraw-Hill.

Wubbels, T., and Levy, J. (editors). (1993). "Do You Know What You Look Like?" *Interpersonal relationships in education*. Washington, DC: Falmer Press.

Supplement 30-1. Sample Practice Plan.

Objectives: Fielding skills—Ground balls and fly balls. Conditioning. Base running. Beginning sliding instruction.	**Date:** 3-22
	Practice # 1
	Page 1

Time	Activity
3:15	Overview of practice
3:20	Warm-up jog followed by stretches. Review basic stretches. Go over solo vs. partner stretches. Discuss purpose of stretching. Stress proper technique.
3:30	Pitchers/Catchers
	Willis: Warm-up. Then 10 mins—5 mins rest—15 mins. Half speed.
	Ricks: Warm-up. Form pitching. Long toss (50 ft. at half speed). Then 25 pitches (full speed), 5 mins rest, 35 pitches full speed.
	Infielders
	Ground ball repetition: Emphasize charging the ball and fielding the ball in position to throw.
	Outfielders
	Fly balls: Review judging fly balls. Emphasize two hands. Get in lots of repetitions.
	"Relay" relay
4:15	Infielders
	Range drill (in pairs)
	Outfielders
	Backing up: Infielders. Outfield partner in the gap.
4:45	Base running
	Running through first. Hit front, outside corner of the bag. Runner's box and the rule.
	Turning the corner for second. "S" turn, arc. Hitting the inside corner of first with right foot. "Skating" toward second.

Special Equipment:
Throw down bases (plates for pitchers; bases for running drills); Mini-cones (range drill)

Supplement 30-1. Sample Practice Plan (*continued*).

Practice Plan

Objectives:	**Practice # 1, (3-22)**
	Page 2

Time	Activity
5:00	Finding the sliding leg
5:10	Cool down and review
	Review why to do cool downs. Don't let anybody go until they have finished.
	Go over major points—especially base running and finding the sliding leg. (Remind them that they can practice sliding leg at home.) Remind infielders to practice fielding position at home.

Included are...

Overview	X	Warm-up	X	Individual time	X	Small group drills	X
Team activities		Cool down	X		Team talk	X	

Evaluation:

Pitchers looked pretty good for early in the season. Infielders were inconsistent about charging the ball. Outfielders did relays well but need to work more on judging flies. Team speed looked so-so, but they seemed aggressive about base running. Finding the sliding leg went over big!
We need more work on basic fielding/throwing.

Supplement 30-2. Reproducible Practice Planning Form.

Practice Plan

Objectives:	Date:
	Practice #
	Page 1

Time	Activity

Special Equipment:

Supplement 30-2. Reproducible Practice Planning Form (*continued*).

Practice Plan

Objectives:	Practice #
	Page 2

Time	Activity

Included are...

Overview	Warm-up	Individual time	Small group drills
Team activities	Cool down		Team talk

Evaluation:

31
Evaluating Coaching Effectiveness

Ray Allen, Ph.D.

QUESTIONS TO CONSIDER

- Why evaluate coaching effectiveness?
- What should be evaluated?
- Who should evaluate coaching effectiveness?
- What steps can be used to conduct an evaluation?

INTRODUCTION

Evaluating coaching effectiveness is essential to providing a quality athletic program. Participation in athletics clearly results in both positive and negative experiences by athletes. It is the coach's responsibility to provide a program where the positive affects of participation outweigh the negative effects, especially with regard to his/her immediate interactions with athletes.

All coaches miss the mark of coaching perfection in many of the potential outcome areas for one or more of their athletes. Coaches have a responsibility to themselves and their players to evaluate their coaching performances and constantly improve. Although beginning coaches may benefit most from conducting evaluations, even experienced professional can significantly improve their coaching abilities by conducting evaluations and acting on the findings.

Coaches are also accountable to stakeholders, such as parents and administrators (Fuoss and Troppmann, 1981; McKenzie and Smeltzer, 1997). They must be able to communicate the program's intended outcomes and those outcomes must have a broad base of support (Behrens, 1983; Fuoss and Troppmann, 1981; Wolfe, Slack and Rose-Hearn, 1993). They also must be able to demonstrate that what they do in their program is having a positive impact.

Evaluation (making a judgment of program merit) is useful to identify which benefits occurred or did not occur, why they occurred, and what changes can be made to improve coaching actions. Whether they realize it or not, coaches are constantly evaluating their effectiveness.

Many coaches use wins and losses, game statistics, reactions of players and fans, and casual and formal conversations to obtain information. Unfortunately, these kinds of informal assessments may not provide the coach with reliable, valid information that is helpful in improving their coaching performances. The coaching evaluation steps in this chapter provide a systematic, but relatively simple approach to evaluating the effects of coaching efforts. It will also lead to the identification of ways in which a coach can improve effectiveness.

Evaluation efforts should address at least two basic questions: 1) Was the coaching effective in achieving its purposes; and 2) What changes can be made to improve the quality of coaching? Answers to these questions can provide important information that can be used to systematically improve coaching effectiveness and consequently, the sport experiences of athletes.

WHAT SHOULD BE EVALUATED?

The most important indicator of coaching effectiveness can be obtained by determining the degree to which participants achieve the objectives established for the season. Objectives are precise, measurable judgements that, in the judgement of the program designer, define what must be accomplished to achieve the broader goal (Green and Kreuter, 1991). Unless these objectives are clearly identified, it will be difficult to complete a meaningful evaluation (see Chapter 29, *Planning for the Season*).

It should be noted that there is a difference between evaluating program effectiveness and coaching effectiveness. Coaches can be very effective in teaching whatever they teach, but what they teach may not significantly contribute to achieving program goals. On the other hand, if coaches are ineffective teachers, what they attempt to teach becomes a moot point. That said, the coach's initial concern has to be coaching effectiveness. If the coaching is less than effective, the coaching practices can be improved. If the coaching practices are effective in achieving intended objectives, only then can the objectives' appropriateness be evaluated. For example, a baseball/softball coach's objective may be to limit strikeouts to three per game. If the objective is not achieved, coaching procedures may be altered. If the objective is achieved, the coach can assess the degree to which it contributes to winning games.

The worksheet in Figure 31-1 provides a means of identifying and recording program objectives that are identified in the season planning stage, so they can be evaluated. A reproducible form of the worksheet can be found as Supplement 31-1. Note that the evaluation form contains space for evaluating each athlete's outcome in the skill, knowledge, fitness, and personal-social areas. Within each of these outcome areas there is space to enter season objectives that you have identified as important for the athletes to obtain. The evaluation form provides a way to collect and analyze information regarding the achievement of the objectives included in the season plan. The procedure for using this form is described later in the chapter.

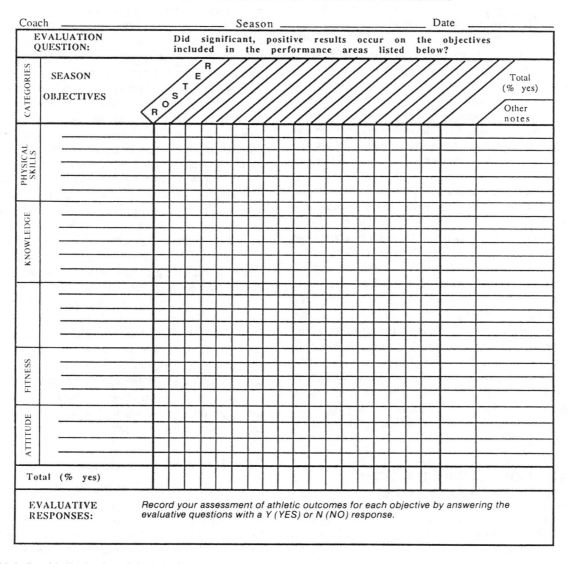

Figure 31-1. Coach's Evaluation of Athletic Outcomes.

WHO SHOULD EVALUATE?

The coach should be primarily responsible for evaluating their own effectiveness in facilitating desired outcomes. Self-evaluation is often the most important source of information for improving coaching practices. However, there are some changes that are apparent to others that can be missed in a self-evaluation. Accordingly, coaches may be well advised to obtain additional insight from others. For example, by using the coach's evaluation form, the coach may rate athletes as achieving one or more objectives pertaining to physical, knowledge, fitness, or personal-social skills included in the season plans. However, a review by another unbiased observer may reveal that what the coach thought was an appropriate objective turned out to be an inappropriate technique, incorrect rule, contraindicated exercise, or inappropriate attitude. Input from others either serves to confirm the coach's observations or identifies and corrects errors in evaluation.

It takes a considerable amount of security, humility and courage on the coach's part to procure this kind of input from others, but the information is invaluable.

Individuals used to collect this kind of information should be familiar with the coach's practices and the athletes' progress. They also should be individuals whose judgement the coach respects. These persons could be assistant coaches, parents, officials, league supervisors, other coaches, locally available experts or one or more of the athletes.

A variation of the evaluation form appears in Figure 31-2. This form provides a way to obtain information relative to coaching effectiveness as perceived by others. The form can be used to estimate a coach's effectiveness with an individual athlete or with the team as a whole. Inspection of the evaluation form reveals that the form is similar to the form in Figure 31-1, but less specific in terms of season objectives. As a result, it requires less time to complete and is easier to use. The purpose of the form is to reveal areas (low ratings) that need follow-up. Follow-up can be completed in a debriefing session with the rater to determine the reasons for low ratings and to identify what can be done to strengthen them. Debriefing sessions with this type of focus have proven to be highly effective in identifying ways to improve programs and procedures. A blank, reproducible version of this evaluation form appears in Supplement 31-2.

WHAT STEPS CAN BE USED TO CONDUCT AN EVALUATION?

A complete evaluation of coaching effectiveness must include at least the following four steps (McKenzie and Smeltzer, 1997).

1. Identify the outcomes intended for the athletes,
2. Collect outcome related data,
3. Analyze the data and identify reasons why some coaching actions are ineffective, and
4. Implement the needed changes.

Step 1: Identify the Intended Outcomes.

The best information a coach can use to evaluate his/her coaching effectiveness is a measure of the extent to which they influence their athletes' achievement. Accordingly, the outcomes selected as objectives for athletes to obtain must be clearly defined. The Coach's Evaluation of Athletic Outcomes form (Figure 31-1) can be used for this task. Completing this step clearly identifies what the coach believes is most important for the athletes to master or make significant progress toward mastering. It also provides a clear indication of the outcomes upon which athletes should be evaluated.

This procedure for identifying season objectives provides the basis for the remaining evaluation steps. It also provides a good opportunity for the coach to have his/her decisions concerning season objectives validated by persons whose opinion he/she respects. Outside reviewers can judge the appropriateness of the season objectives and helpful suggestions regarding additions, deletions, or alterations in objectives. In contrast, the decision not to identify intended outcomes of coaching in terms of coaching objectives makes it difficult to assess coaching effectiveness or determine how to improve coaching practices. Coaches who fail to define what they intend to achieve make it difficult to determine if and when they arrive, or if they have used the most efficient way to achieve it. Without a clear objective, it is impossible for the coach, local expert, or other person to provide helpful feedback regarding the appropriateness of intents, accomplishments of athletes, or coaching effectiveness.

Clearly specifying season objectives has two other important benefits. First, it clarifies what the outcomes should be in the coach's mind, which helps them organize the season and plan its practices. Second, to the degree that season objectives are effectively communicated to athletes, it will help them learn what the coach is trying to teach. Research on effective instruction reveals that clear specification of intended outcomes is strongly related to higher achievement.

Step 2: Collect the Evaluation Data.

The primary source of evaluative data should come from self-evaluation of the results of all or various parts of the season. However, assessments by selected others, in combination with self-assessment, are more valuable for identifying important athletic outcomes and potential

Evaluator _____ Athlete/Team _____ Season _____

EVALUATION QUESTION:	In comparison with other players in this league, how does the player (or team) listed above perform in the areas listed below?						
PERFORMANCE AREAS	**PLAYER OR TEAM PERFORMANCE LEVELS**						
	SEASON START			SEASON END			COMMENTS
	TOP 25%	MID 50%	BOTTOM 25%	TOP 25%	MID 50%	BOTTOM 25%	
Individual Techniques — OFFENSIVE							
DEFENSIVE							
Knowledge — RULES							
INJURY PREVENTION							
CONDITIONING							
NUTRITION							
TERMINOLOGY							
OTHER							
Tactics — OFFENSIVE							
DEFENSIVE							
Fitness — STRENGTH							
ENDURANCE							
FLEXIBILITY							
Attitude — PERSONAL							
SOCIAL							

INDIVIDUAL EVALUATION:
For each performance area indicate, by placing a check in the top, mid, or bottom column, the start and end of the season performance level of the player.

TEAM EVALUATION:
For each performance area estimate the number of players (% or actual numbers) in the top, mid, or bottom performance levels at the start and end of the season.

Figure 31-2. Evaluation of Athletic Performance as Perceived by Individuals Other Than the Coach.

coaching improvements. For this reason, both approaches are recommended.

Completing the Coach's Assessment of Athletic Performance

After outcomes have been identified and entered into the first column of the evaluation form, the athlete's names are entered into the spaces across the top of the form. The coach then chooses one of two courses of action to record athletes' achievement. The first course is to consider the following question with regard to each objective for each athlete: "Did significant improvements occur?" The coach can record their response with a "Yes" or "No", depending upon their response. The alternative question can be, "Did the athlete achieve the bench-

mark?" This question shifts the evaluation from determining if *significant progress* was made, to determining if the *program was effective*.

In the first case, deciding what score to record in each space on the form requires that some standards be defined. For example, all the athletes may have improved in one of the season's objectives but the coach may feel that several of those athletes did not achieve enough to receive a "Yes." A "No" however, may also seem inappropriate. The coach can resolve this difficulty by defining the level of performance they are willing to accept as evidence of a meaningful gain. There is no exact method of determining how much gain is enough. Therefore, the coach must rely on his/her own estimates of these standards.

Coaches should not be too concerned about this

issue, however. The procedures suggested in this chapter allow for correction of erroneous judgments in this area. One way to avoid the initial problem of entering a "Yes" or "No" is to use a scale that further divides the response options. For example, you could use a scale like: 0 = none, I = very little, 2 = little, 3 = some, 4 = large, and 5 = very large. Given ratings of this type you could at a later time establish 4 and/or 5 ratings as large enough to be categorized as a "Yes" and ratings of 3 or less as "No" responses.

It is important to remember that athletes who begin the season at low levels of skill have the potential for more improvement than those who are near mastery, have mastered an objective, or are seeking to refine an ability that is essentially mastered. At the mastery level, even small gains may deserve a "Yes" or "No."

In the second case, given that performance objectives are clearly defined in the season-planning stage, assessment decisions are clearer. The evaluation decision is simply a matter of determining if performers meet or exceed the objective.

Detrimental effects of participation should be viewed as a zero or negative change. Injury, decreases or lack of increases in fitness capacities, or development of inappropriate physical skills, knowledge, or personal-social skills are detrimental effects that can occur and should be identified. In this situation, the appropriate entry is a "No" that is enhanced by circling it to distinguish it from small or slight gains.

The completed evaluation form will reveal the coach's perception of the degree to which athletes achieved important objectives. Patterns of achievement can be observed by studying the data by objective (e.g., coaching behaviors may facilitate improvements in fitness capacities and knowledge objectives, but fail to alter skill performance) or by athlete.

Obtaining Information from Selected Other Persons

The form illustrated in Figure 31-2 is used to obtain information on coaching effectiveness from others. This form can be used to assess individual athletes or an entire team. Note that estimates of performance should be relative to other athletes at similar levels of competition. When rating individual athletes, the user of the form places a check in the appropriate column (top 25%, mid 50%, or bottom 25%) for each performance area. When rating the entire team, the rater estimates the percentage or number of athletes judged to be in each column.

Ratings of performance objectives should occur at each critical period of the season (pre, early, mid and late season) to effectively guide instructional practices. Ratings at the end of the season (or other evaluation periods) are not very useful without knowing performance levels at the beginning of the season. It is the changes in performance levels of the athletes that provide insights into coaching effectiveness. While the ideal would be to obtain ratings on each objective at regular intervals, the time it takes external evaluators may make multiple ratings difficult to obtain. An alternative is to have the evaluators record observations at the onset and completion of the season.

For example, if three athletes were perceived to be in the top 25% of their peers at the beginning of the season and seven were deemed in that performance level at the end of the season, the net gain in this performance category would be four.

While the coach desires that all athletes move into the top category through the course of the season, those expectations may be unrealistic. A more realistic outcome may be to observe 50 percent of the athletes move from the bottom to the middle group, or from the middle to the top performance levels. Evaluations that result in all athletes achieving the objective either indicates that the coaching was entirely effective or the standards of assessment were extremely relaxed.

Evaluations with no variation in ratings would not be helpful for improving coaching effectiveness. All coaches vary in their ability to change behavior across the stated objectives and across various individual athletes on the team. It is the objectives and individual athletes who do not attain the high ratings that are most useful in revealing the principles coaching effectiveness that are being violated.

Accordingly, it is important to use standards for the coach's self-ratings (or for the ratings of others) that result in variation in performance ratings. As a rule, no more than 80 percent of the responses for any single category should be "Yes" (on the coach's form), or appear in the top, middle or bottom categories of performance when rated by others. As it will be noted in Step 3: Analyze the Data, ratings that are well distributed among the response options are the most helpful for determining areas where coaching effectiveness may be improved.

The form "Evaluation of Athlete/Team Performance Relative to Others" provides the coach with an estimate of change in athletic performance as viewed by persons whose judgment the coach respects. The relatively broad performance areas upon which the evaluation is based do not, however, provide enough detailed information to fully interpret the data. Simply stated, more information is needed. A debriefing session can provide an opportunity to obtain additional information and discuss potential changes in coaching techniques called for by the evaluation findings. The following process would facilitate receiving helpful information:

- Thank the evaluator for taking the time to complete the evaluation form and for agreeing to meet and discuss the implications.
- Indicate that the purpose of the debriefing session is to

identify both strengths and weaknesses in coaching techniques, but that emphasis needs to be focused on weaknesses, and how they may be improved.

- Proceed through the outcome areas and their corresponding ratings, seeking to understand *why* each area was rated high or low. For example, if a disproportionate number of athletes were rated low relative to their peers on offensive skills and there were very small gains from the beginning to the end of the evaluation period, you need more information. Attempt to determine what offensive skills were weak and what could be changed to help strengthen them in the coming season.

- Probe for the things that can be done (or avoided) that may produce better results. Make a special attempt to identify the reasons why a suggested alternative may produce better results.

- Take careful notes during the discussion. Record the alternative ideas that have good supporting rationales and how they might be implemented.

Information collected in this way identifies good ideas for increasing the coach's ability to help athletes achieve future objectives.

Step 3: Analyze the Data.

The data collected on the coach's self-evaluation form are analyzed by:

- Totaling the number of "Yes" responses entered for each athlete across all objectives,
- Dividing the number of "Yes" responses by the total number of objectives, and
- Entering the percent of "Yes" responses in the row labeled "Total" for each athlete.

In the same way, total the number of "Yes" responses across athletes for each objective and enter the percent of "Yes" responses in the column labeled "Total" for each season objective.

Insights as to what kinds of changes in coaching procedures would have positive affects on specific kinds of participants can be obtained by comparing characteristics of those athletes achieving the highest ratings to those who receive the lowest. This same type of comparison provides insight into how to be more effective in teaching specific performance objectives included in the season plan.

The real benefits of evaluating athletic achievement on season objectives are obtained by evaluating why none or few athletes received "Yes" responses (i.e., areas in which coaching was ineffective). It is the answers to these "Why?" questions that reveal changes coaches can make to improve their effectiveness.

A checklist of effective coaching actions was devel-

oped to help coaches determine why they were (or were not) sufficiently successful in addressing specific objectives. The checklist (Supplement 31-3) provides a number of ratable items that may help the coach identify ways they can increase their coaching effectiveness. For example, if five athletes made insufficient progress in the physical skill of shooting, the coach could review the items included on the check list to identify coaching actions that were used (or not used) that could account for the pattern of outcomes that emerge.

Interpreting Unmet Expectations

Completion of the three evaluation steps provides a systematic way for a coach to assess and improve their coaching ability. Failure for athletes to meet expectations should be attributed to one of three factors. First, coaching practices were less effective than they can be. Second, the performance expectations were unrealistic. Third, the coach is trying to accomplish too much in too little time. Lack of achievement may be attributed to characteristics other than coaching behaviors, such as lack of talent or motivation. These kinds of conclusions however fail to maximize a coach's contribution to the performance of his/her athletes.

Effective coaches can improve their athletes' performance levels consistently throughout the season. Rarely, even with below-average talent, will teams who make continuous progress though the season perform poorly in league competition, particularly in the latter portion of the season. The most helpful approach to improving coaching effectiveness is to assume that when results do not meet expectations, the solutions to the problems will be found in coaching practices. While this may at times prove to be incorrect, it insures that the coach does all in their power to positively affect performance.

It is possible that expectations that a coach holds for his/her athletes are unrealistic. This should be entertained only after the coach honestly considers and determines that lack of achievement cannot be attributed to ineffective coaching actions. Because motivation is enhanced when athletes perceive that they are improving, unreasonably high expectations can have a negative effect on motivation and improvement. High expectations that are divided into achievable, sequential, performance steps are the effective way to establish appropriate standards of performance.

Failure to allocate sufficient time to the practice of each objective can also result in poor athletic achievement, even when performance expectations and other coaching actions are appropriate. Athletes must have sufficient time to attempt a task, make errors, obtain feedback, refine their attempts, and habituate the intended abilities before it is reasonable to expect them to be used within a competitive context. Attempting to cover too many objectives within a limited amount of practice time is a major cause of insufficient achievement. Even when the quality of coaching is excellent, athletic performance expectation may not be met, simply because the amount of coaching and practice time was too short.

Step 4: Act on the Needed Changes.

The primary reason for evaluating coaching effectiveness is to learn what can be done to improve the achievement levels. Most coaches would like to see their athletes rate in the highest categories across all objectives. While some coaches warrant high ratings in most categories, no one attains coaching perfection. Every coach can find ways to improve. Improvements can occur in season or practice planning, implementation of plans, knowledge of the sport, or even in our ability to evaluate ourselves. Regardless of our level of expertise, by systematically evaluating our coaching actions, we can find ways to become more effective and more efficient. Identifying the changes that will lead to improvements, however, is a waste of time if those changes are not implemented,

SUMMARY

Systematic evaluation of athletic performance on the intended season outcomes can provide coaches with an ongoing means of monitoring and improving coaching practices. Limited achievement by athletes in some performance areas can signal a need to change some of your coaching actions. Use of the forms and procedures outlined in this chapter can reveal changes that will improve your coaching effectiveness. By taking action on the changes that are identified, you can take a significant step toward becoming a more effective and efficient coach.

REFERENCES

Behrens, R. (1983). *Work-site Health Promotion: Some Questions and Answers to Help You Get Started*. Washington, DC: Office of Disease Prevention and Health Promotion.

Fuoss, D.E., Troppmann, R.J. 1981). *Effective Coaching: A Psychological Approach*. Wiley and Sons: New York pp. 22.

Green, L.W., Kreuter, M.W. (1991). *Health Promotion Planning: An Educational and Environmental Approach (2nd edition)*. Mountain View, CA: Mayfield.

McKenzie, J.F.; Smeltzer, J.L. (1997). *Planning, Implementing and Evaluating Health Promotion Programs*. Needham Heights, MA: Allyn and Bacon.

Wolfe, R.; Slack, T., Rose-Hearn, T. (1993). Factors influencing the adoption and maintenance of Canadian, facility-based worksite health promotion programs. *The American Journal of Health Promotion*, 7(3): 189-198.

SUGGESTED READINGS

Baungarten, S. (1984). "It Can Be Done! A Model Youth Sports Program." *Journal of Physical Education, Recreation and Dance*, 55(7): 55-58.

Bunker, L.K. (1981). "Elementary Physical Education and Youth Sport." *Journal of Physical Education, Recreation and Dance*, 52(2): 26-28.

Fink, A., and Kosecoff, J. (1978). *An Evaluation Primer*. Beverly Hills, CA: Sage.

Lord, R.H., and Kozar, B. (1982). "A Test for Volunteer Youth Sport Coaches." *Journal of Sport Behavior*, 5(2): 77-82.

Rarick, G. L. (1969). "Competitive Sports for Young Boys: Controversial Issues." *Medicine and Science in Sports*, 1: 181-184.

Smith, R. E., Smoll, F. L., and Curtis, B. (1979). "Coach Effectiveness Training: A Cognitive-Behavioral Approach to Enhancing Relationship Skills in Youth Sport Coaches." *Journal of Sport Psychology*, 1: 59-75.

Smith, R. E., Smoll, F. L., and Hunt, E. (1977). "A System for the Behavioral Assessment of Athletic Coaches." *Research Quarterly*, 48: 401-407.

Wandzilak, T., Potter, G., and Ansorge, C. (1985). "Re-evaluating a Youth Sports Basketball Program." *Journal of Physical Education, Recreation and Dance*, 56(8): 21-23.

Supplement 31-1. Coach's Evaluation of Athletic Outcomes.

COACH'S EVALUATION OF PLAYERS OUTCOMES

Coach_____ Season _____ Date _____

EVALUATION QUESTION:	Did significant results occur on the objectives included in the performance areas listed below?		

CATEGORIES	SEASON OBJECTIVES	ROSTER	TOTAL %YES	OTHER NOTES

TOTAL (% YES)

EVALUATIVE RESPONSES:	Record your assessment of player outcomes for each objective by answering the evaluative questions with a Y (YES) or N (NO) response.

Supplement 31-2: Evaluation of Athletic Performance as Perceived by Individuals Other Than the Coach.

EVALUATION OF PLAYER/TEAM PERFORMANCE RELATIVE TO OTHERS

Evaluator:_____ Player/Team _____ Season _____

EVALUATION QUESTION: In comparison with other players in the league, how does the player (or team) listed above perform in the areas listed below?

PERFORMANCE AREAS	PLAYER OR TEAM PERFORMANCE LEVELS						COMMENTS
	SEASON START			SEASON END			
	TOP 25%	MID 50%	BOTTOM 25%	TOP 25%	MID 50%	BOTTOM 25%	

INDIVIDUAL EVALUATION:

For each performance area indicate, by placing a check in the top, mid, or bottom column, the start and end performance level of the player.

TEAM EVALUATION:

For each performance area estimate the number of players (% or actual numbers) in the top, mid, or bottom performance levels at the start and end of the season.

Supplement 31-3. Checklist of Effective Coaching Actions*

INTRODUCTION

This check list can be used to identify coaching actions that may be related to athletic achievement (or lack of achievement) of desired outcomes. It, therefore, serves as an aid to identify the reason(s) why your athlete(s) did not achieve one or more of your expected outcomes.

To use the check list in this way, read the items in each content category (i.e., coaching role, organization, effective instruction) and ask yourself: Could the coaching actions (or inactions) implied by this item have contributed to the unmet expectation? Answer the question by responding with a Y or N. If you wish to rate the degree to which your actions (inactions) were consistent with the guidelines implied by the items, use the five-point rating scale that follows. Items that result in No or low ratings suggest that you are not following effective coaching practices. The process of seeking answers to specific concerns identified by your reaction to check list items is an excellent way to obtain information most likely to help you become more effective as a coach.

DIRECTIONS

Rate the degree to which you incorporate each of the following items into your coaching activities. Check Y or N or use the following five-point scale where: 1 = Strongly Disagree, 2 = Disagree, 3 = Neutral, 4 = Agree, and 5 Strongly Agree.

1. My primary purpose for coaching was to maximize the benefits of participation for all of the athletes. (No) 1 2 3 4 5 (Yes)
2. The beneficial (individual techniques. knowledge, tactics, fitness, attitudes) and detrimental (time, money, injury, etc.) effects of participation were constantly in mind during planning and coaching times. (No) 1 2 3 4 5 (Yes)
3. I communicated through actions and words that I expected each athlete to succeed in improving his/her level of performance. (No) 1 2 3 4 5 (Yes)

Organization

4. I completed a plan for the season to guide the conduct of my practices. (No) 1 2 3 4 5 (Yes)
5. Performance expectations set for the athletes were realistic and attainable. (No) 1 2 3 4 5 (Yes)
6. I conscientiously decided which objectives must be emphasized in the pre-, early, mid-, and late season. (No) 1 2 3 4 5 (Yes)
7. Objectives for developing my practices were drawn from those identified and sequenced from pre- to late season (No) 1 2 3 4 5 (Yes)
8. The amount of total practice time allocated to each season objective was sufficient. (No) 1 2 3 4 5 (Yes)
9. Others would characterize my practices as orderly, safe, businesslike, and enjoyable. (No) 1 2 3 4 5 (Yes)
10. Objectives were broken down as necessary to allow athletes to achieve them in several small steps. (No) 1 2 3 4 5 (Yes)

Knowledge of the Sport

11. I am familiar with each season objective selected and clearly communicated to my athletes its purpose and described how it is performed. (No) 1 2 3 4 5 (Yes)
12. I was able to identify the key elements of performance necessary for achievement of each season objective. (No) 1 2 3 4 5 (Yes)

Effective Instruction

13. I clearly communicated (by word and/or example) the key elements to be learned for each objective included in a practice. (No) 1 2 3 4 5 (Yes)
14. Practice on an objective was initiated with a rationale for why the objective is important. (No) 1 2 3 4 5 (Yes)
15. Instruction did not continue without the attention of the athletes. (No) 1 2 3 4 5 (Yes)
16. Practice on an objective provided each athlete with many practice trials and with specific, immediate, and positive feedback on many trials. (No) 1 2 3 4 5 (Yes)
17. During practice, I regularly grouped the athletes in accordance with their different practice needs on the season's objectives. (No) 1 2 3 4 5 (Yes)
18. I used questions to determine if the athletes understood the objectives and instruction. (No) 1 2 3 4 5 (Yes)
19. The athletes sensed a fooling of control over their own learning, which resulted from my emphasis of clearly identifying what they needed to learn and then encouraging maximum effort. (No) 1 2 3 4 5 (Yes)

*Modified from Vogel, P. G. (1987). "Post season Evaluation: What Did We Accomplish?" In V. D. Seefeldt (editor) *Handbook for Youth Sport Coaches.* Reston, VA: American Alliance for Health, Physical Education, Recreation and Dance.

20. My practices were planned and clearly associated the use of learning activities, drills, and games with the season objectives.	(No)	1	2	3	4	5	(Yes)
21. I evaluated my practices and incorporated appropriate changes for subsequent practices.	(No)	1	2	3	4	5	(Yes)

Motivation

22. Practices and competition resulted in the athletes achieving many of their goals for participation.	(No)	1	2	3	4	5	(Yes)
23. I taught the athletes how to realistically define success in terms of effort and self-improvement.	(No)	1	2	3	4	5	(Yes)
24. An expert would agree, upon observing my practices, that I use a positive, rather than a negative, coaching approach.	(No)	1	2	3	4	5	(Yes)
25. The athletes would agree that practice, games; and overall season was an enjoyable experience.	(No)	1	2	3	4	5	(Yes)

Communication

26. There was no conflict between the verbal and non- verbal messages I communicated to my athletes.	(No)	1	2	3	4	5	(Yes)
27. I facilitated communication with the athletes by being a good listener.	(No)	1	2	3	4	5	(Yes)
28. Accepted behaviors (and consequences of misbehavior) were communicated to athletes at the beginning of the season.	(No)	1	2	3	4	5	(Yes)
29. Athletes were involved in developing or confirming team rules.	(No)	1	2	3	4	5	(Yes)
30. Enforcement of team rules was consistent for all athletes throughout the season.	(No)	1	2	3	4	5	(Yes)

Involvement with Parents

31. Parents of the athletes were a positive, rather than a negative, influence on athletes' achievement of the season objectives.	(No)	1	2	3	4	5	(Yes)
32. I communicated to the parents my responsibilities and the responsibilities of parents and athletes to the team.	(No)	1	2	3	4	5	(Yes)

Conditioning

33. The intensity, duration, and frequency of the physical conditioning I used were appropriate for the age of the athletes.	(No)	1	2	3	4	5	(Yes)
34. I routinely used a systematic warm-up and cool down before and after practices and contests.	(No)	1	2	3	4	5	(Yes)
35. When skilled performance began to erode, conditioning load was reduced or rest intervals were increased.	(No)	1	2	3	4	5	(Yes)
36. The physical conditioning aspects of my practices appropriately simulated the requirements of the sport.	(No)	1	2	3	4	5	(Yes)

Injury Prevention

37. I followed all recommended safety procedures for the use of equipment and facilities.	(No)	1	2	3	4	5	(Yes)
38. I did not use any contraindicated exercises in my practices.	(No)	1	2	3	4	5	(Yes)

Care of Common Injuries

39. I established and followed appropriate emergency procedures and simple first aid as needed.	(No)	1	2	3	4	5	(Yes)
40. I had a well-stocked first aid kit at each practice and contest, including the athletes' medical history information and medical release forms.	(No)	1	2	3	4	5	(Yes)

Rehabilitation of Injuries

41. None of the athletes experienced a recurrence of an injury that could be attributed to inappropriate rehabilitation.	(No)	1	2	3	4	5	(Yes)
42. Before returning any athlete to full physical activity after an injury, he/she had no pain, full range of motion, normal strength and size, normal speed and agility, and normal level of fitness.	(No)	1	2	3	4	5	(Yes)

Evaluation

43. I completed an evaluation of athletic improvement on the season objectives.	(No)	1	2	3	4	5	(Yes)
44. I identified the coaching actions (or in-actions) that appeared most closely related to unmet expectations of my athletes.	(No)	1	2	3	4	5	(Yes)
45. I made the changes in coaching action needed to improve my coaching effectiveness.	(No)	1	2	3	4	5	(Yes)

32
Drills as Instructional Activities

Paul Vogel, Ph.D.; Eugene W. Brown, Ph.D. and Michael A. Clark, Ph.D.

QUESTIONS TO CONSIDER

- What are the characteristics of a good drill?
- How can the coach keep track of effective drills?
- What are some reasons for limiting time spent scrimmaging?
- When is it a good idea to regularly include scrimmages?

INTRODUCTION

Coaches use a variety of instructional activities. However, even as reviewing video has become common at all levels of competition and computer-based instruction is appearing, the oldest coaching technique still prevails. Drills, activities intended "to teach and train by repeated exercise or repetition of acts," dominate practices.

Every sport includes in its literature any number of books devoted exclusively to drills; titles like *The Treasury of Baseball Drills* and *101 Drills for Winning Basketball* are typical. Coaches attend clinics and watch other coaches at work. They search coaching sites on the Internet. They modify drills or create new ones to suit their athletes. The difficulty lies not in finding drills to use at practice. Rather, the problem for coaches is deciding whether the drills are "good" ones.

CHARACTERISTICS OF A GOOD DRILL

As in so many situations, a "good" drill reflects the needs of the coach and athletes. Drills are an efficient, yet effective means of teaching an important outcome. Therefore, a good drill:

- Has a meaningful name,
- Needs only a short explanation,
- Allows mastery of a particular objective,
- Fits the skill, knowledge or fitness requirements of the sport,
- Keeps athletes "on task",
- Can be used with groups of various sizes,
- Can be modified for use with both skilled and unskilled athletes, and
- Provides many opportunities to analyze skills and provide feedback.

A meaningful name communicates something important about the drill. The coach may have learned a drill by watching the Pittsburgh Pirates warm-up and thus calls it the "Pirate drill." This name does not mean anything to the players. However, because they will try to catch a ball thrown over their head, the coach might refer to the activity as "Over-the-head." This gives everybody an idea of what happens in the drill. The name also helps the athletes remember the drill the next time the coach calls for "Over-the-head." It may also save time in that no additional explanation may be needed to get the athletes ready for the drill.

Another consideration for the coach is the unintended meaning communicated by a choice of name. For example, a coach might call a particular activity "Gutbusters," "Suicides" or the like. Aside from the fact that these names are essentially meaningless, they have a negative impact. The very name can cause problems for the coach. For example, consider the consequences if someone is injured while involved in a drill called "Suicides."

A short explanation should be all that is required to set up a drill for the athletes. Coach and athletes have little enough time together; therefore, it has to be used wisely. This implies that the majority of time should be spent in teaching and learning. Long explanations take time away from instruction and may cause problems in holding the players' attention. Setting up the drill and explaining its execution should move quickly. If this is not the case, the activity may be too complicated, and the coach should reduce the drill into a series of simpler elements. The coach should also plan the explanation when introducing a drill. This will reduce the time required and minimize confusion that might arise.

Mastering a particular objective is important. The coach should not expect to accomplish too much with a single drill. Just as they should require a minimum of explanation, drills should be simple to perform. Players should attend to a single skill while the coach watches how they execute it. This is not to suggest that a drill cannot serve multiple functions, especially if conditioning is one of the elements. However, trying to use one drill to achieve two or three functions may overload the athletes and challenge the coach's observational skills. It usually is better to replace a complex activity with several simpler ones that may require less time and concentration.

A fit between the skill, knowledge and fitness requirements of the sport and the drill is important. For example, baseball and softball players have to move quickly to either side on defense. However, they seldom need to run at top speed for more than 120 to 180 feet. As a result, activities in these sports should emphasize anaerobic rather than aerobic conditioning. Drills involving sprinting from home plate to second base are good drills for baseball and softball players. On the other hand, basketball players need aerobic conditioning, and soccer players need still greater aerobic capacity. Their drills should involve running longer distances at various speeds. Conversely, the same drills would not be suited to hockey goalies and soccer goalkeepers. Nor would contemporary baseball players necessarily need to learn how to slap bunt, although those in softball must develop this skill early on.

Athletes must be kept "on task" during drills. Instructional time is wasted and discipline problems develop when young athletes are not actually involved in practice. The coach should choose drills that allow the maximum number of repetitions while providing every person with chances to perform and learn. Groups should be small. This can be accomplished by choosing activities that fit into "stations" or "circuit training" arrangements. If drills focus on a single task and require little explanation, keeping athletes on-task is more easily achieved. If the activities require little special set-up time, less "down time" occurs for the athletes.

Groups of various sizes should be accommodated. The coach should choose drills that do not require the entire team to be present nor should a specific number of athletes be needed. Rather, drills should have sufficient flexibility to accommodate a few more—or a few less—than the normal complement. Similarly, the coach should choose drills that meet a variety of needs. Not every person has to do the same thing at the same time. Not only does this flexibility increase the effectiveness of practice time, it also relates directly to the following characteristic of a good drill.

Both skilled and unskilled athletes should have their needs served by the drill. A good drill provides time for skilled athletes to review their progress, and for the less capable players the same activity provides time for instruction. Talented players sharpen technique; others may spend time on individual elements of a skill. One person practices the complete form; another attends to the smaller elements of a skill. Both groups of athletes can work together on the skill in the same drill if the drill is designed to accommodate a variety of skill levels.

Many opportunities for the coach to analyze skills and provide feedback to athletes arise within the context of effective drills. Drills are not time fillers; they have an instructional purpose. The coach uses the time to observe and evaluate performances. The coach sees who can perform the skill and who needs additional practice. Skilled athletes receive positive feedback or get assistance with the finer points of execution. Less skilled players have time for additional instruction. In either case, the coach is actively teaching as the drill continues.

KEEPING TRACK OF EFFECTIVE DRILLS

As the seasons progress, the coach discovers a variety of drills that seem to work well with a typical group of athletes. These teaching activities become the focal point of instruction. Drills often are given the most time, but they may receive the least consideration. Thus, the coach may forget drills that work well or modifications that make an activity more useful. To avoid these pitfalls, the coach should develop the habit of taking notes. Some means of evaluating drills and keeping track of those that are effective should become a daily task for the coach. Figure 32-1 provides an example of how this might be done. Note that there is space for both drawn and written descriptions of the drill, an evaluation, and a reminder about equipment needed. A blank, reproducible version of the form appears in Supplement 32-1.

DRILLS AS OPPOSED TO SCRIMMAGE

The majority of practice time should be spent on drills, as suggested previously. A thoughtful coach can find—or create—drills that provide more opportunities for the athletes to practice a skill than they might get within many more minutes of scrimmage time. The greater number of repetitions and the fewer potential distractions in drills creates a better learning environment. Drills isolate elements that the coach has decided are essential to the team. In addition, drills typically involve every athlete at some level, while scrimmages seldom in-

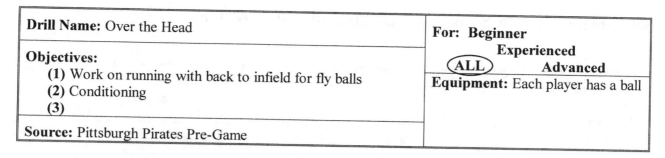

Drill Name: Over the Head	For: Beginner
Objectives: (1) Work on running with back to infield for fly balls (2) Conditioning (3)	Experienced (ALL) Advanced
	Equipment: Each player has a ball
Source: Pittsburgh Pirates Pre-Game	

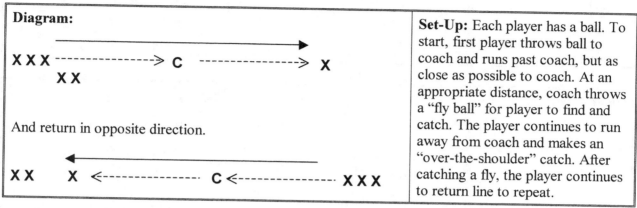

Diagram:

And return in opposite direction.

Set-Up: Each player has a ball. To start, first player throws ball to coach and runs past coach, but as close as possible to coach. At an appropriate distance, coach throws a "fly ball" for player to find and catch. The player continues to run away from coach and makes an "over-the-shoulder" catch. After catching a fly, the player continues to return line to repeat.

Comments/Evaluation: A great conditioning drill as well as an excellent way to get the players thinking about turning their backs to run for fly balls hit over their head. Works with any level. Athletes will be challenged and eventually get to the point of wanting to do the drill longer than planned.

Figure 32-1: Sample of a completed drill evaluation form.

clude the full team. Athletes that are not actively involved probably will not be learning and may become discipline problems.

This does not imply that scrimmages should never be part of practices. Rather, scrimmages must be focused and limited. The term "controlled scrimmage" is often used to describe this situation. In a "controlled scrimmage" the coach creates specific situations and the athletes are free to perform as they feel appropriate. Such controlled scrimmages provide a natural transition from drills to competition.

Further, a "controlled scrimmage" makes certain situations easier to manage. A coach who is instructing younger athletes—those of junior high age or younger—may find that athletes do not feel that they have practiced the sport unless they have scrimmaged. It may well be that this situation calls for the coach to plan for scrimmages more often than might otherwise be desirable. This makes it possible for the players to go home and explain that they "played" when the question of what they did is raised. This can be an effective motivational activity for younger athletes, because they typically want to have "fun" even more than they desire to learn.

However, as athletes become more skilled and experienced, the coach may find it desirable to limit scrimmages. Controlled scrimmages allow the coach to arrange particular conditions that test certain skills, and many repetitions can occur in a limited time. Older, more experienced athletes also are motivated differently. Thus, while "fun" remains an important factor, athletes come to recognize that developing skills and winning may be more important. As a result, they more readily accept drills and controlled play as a bigger part of practice.

SUMMARY

Even as modern instructional technologies are beginning to influence the way coaches teach, drills are an essential part of every practice. Drills allow coaches and players to attend to a single aspect of the sport. There may be no more effective means of developing skill than through carefully organized drills. Every coach should learn the characteristics of a good drill and develop a file of such activities. Using these quality learning activities makes practices more efficient, enhances the athletes learning, and generates enthusiasm for the sport.

Supplement 32-1. A blank, reproducible drill evaluation form.

Drill Name:	For: Beginner
	Experienced
Objectives:	ALL Advanced
(1)	Equipment:
(2)	
(3)	
Source:	

Diagram:	Set-Up:

Comments/Evaluation:

Section VI
Sports Management

33
Administrative Responsibilities of Coaches

Michael A. Clark, Ph.D.

QUESTIONS TO CONSIDER

- What are the administrative responsibilities of coaches?
- What three types of evaluations do coaches need to make?
- What records should coaches keep?
- What responsibilities do coaches have besides those related to what happens during practices and competitions?

INTRODUCTION

Coaches by their nature are "doers." They think in terms of teaching, determining starting line-ups, and choosing the strategy for the next contest. They do not see themselves as administrators. Coaching is like running any enterprise. It involves goals, long- and short-term plans, record keeping, personnel evaluations and strategies for improving performances—among others. In these respects, coaches have a variety of administrative responsibilities.

Establishing goals and making plans are considered in Chapter 23, *Goal Setting*. Both are keys to successful coaching. Goals give direction to efforts at every level of play. Similarly, over-all season and individual practice plans provide the framework for good teaching.

Coaches also perform numerous functions to meet their administrative responsibilities, and several of these impact practices and competitions:

- Preparing themselves and their athletes for contests,
- Overseeing activities of associated personnel,
- Scouting opponents,
- Evaluating various elements of the program, and
- Keeping records.

Coaches also have responsibilities with less obvious connections to what happens "between the lines." These can be described as connecting the sport to the broader community and include:

- Working with booster groups,
- Raising funds,
- Promoting the sport and their team, and
- Interacting with the media.

CONTEST PREPARATION

For many coaches, preparing for a contest means preparing a "game plan." This is true at every level of competition, from junior high through varsity level sports. However, a game plan is only part of successful preparation. Several other activities are part of the coach's preparing for competition.

Settling on Points to Emphasize

This requires both long- and short-term thinking. While the particular sport may influence specific points, there are some general things that must be considered: How important is sportsmanship? How can the needs of the "team" be balanced with those of individual players? Is the point of playing sports learning to survive, to do one's best, to win, to compete fairly, or to beat the opponent? How are athletes expected to behave before, during and after contests? What will influence the decisions regarding personnel and strategy the coach has to make? How does any given contest fit into the season? How will short-term gains be balanced against long-term goals?

These questions are pertinent to every coach, and

others will arise as the coach goes about answering these. Even an experienced coach should reconsider these questions before each new season. Evidence suggests that athletes learn what the coach stresses. Therefore, whether in practice or contests, the coach must send consistent messages. This is accomplished by planning what is taught.

Deciding How Best to Utilize Athletes

Each sport involves unique strategies, but the principle remains the same: Who is to compete in which events? Alternatively, who is in the starting line-up? What role does each athlete play? When and in what order will substitutions be made? What reason should the coach have for substituting for an athlete? Who replaces an athlete in case of injury or illness? What is to be done to mentally prepare athletes for competition? These issues are too important to be left to chance or "spur-of-the-moment" thinking. Once decisions are made, they should be put in written form. Being able to consult lists and notes makes dealing with competitive pressures easier once competition begins.

The preceding does not exclude a willingness to make changes. It is equally important for the coach to be flexible: Who has performed well in practice? Which athlete has a particular skill that the contest requires? Does the coach have confidence in a player—or group of players—being able to perform at the moment? These also are important questions to consider. Nevertheless, personnel utilization must be thought through well in advance of competition.

Determining Strategy

The strategy to be followed during play should be thought through ahead of time. Although sports differ, typical issues might include: What elements go into a high-scoring gymnastics routine, and can the athlete perform them well enough to risk using them? Who swims the anchor leg for a relay team? When should a singles player become part of a doubles team in tennis? Will a basketball team be able to press the opponents? How should the coach handle a contest when the team is well ahead or when the team is losing badly? How will substitutions and time-outs be used? As with personnel decisions, the coach must weigh these matters prior to the contest. Further, by writing down the answers, the coach will be more likely to follow through with these decisions.

Contest preparation involves these three elements no matter the level of play:

• Settling on what to emphasize each time out,
• Deciding how best to utilize athletes, and
• Determining strategy.

However, the relative importance of each varies with the age of the athletes, their skill level and the level of competition. For example, every junior high volleyball player should have the experience of "starting" a match, and they all deserve to try various positions—setter, blocker, front-row and so on. However, junior varsity team members likely have well-defined roles. Some may only play the back row; others may block and spike; still others may only serve. Similarly, in most sports, younger players often find complicated strategies difficult to follow, whereas older athletes are capable of handling complex situations. And while varsity volleyball players can be expected to "back set," a back set by a junior high player probably is an accident.

Competitive pressure often forces the coach into making quick decisions, but quick decisions need not be hasty or thoughtless. Rather, a well-prepared coach has anticipated many of the situations that might arise and considered what to do in each case. By considering the options ahead of time and weighing the advantages of each, the coach is better prepared to make good choices during the contest.

Coaches learn what to do and what to expect in various ways. Watching athletes in practice is important; so is seeing what the opponents do. Talking with experienced coaches and consulting reference books are valuable sources of information. However, much about preparing for competition can only be learned by doing it. Deciding what to emphasize, developing the athletes' roles and choosing a strategy should be thought through ahead of time. However, actual performance can be evaluated only after the competition.

ORGANIZING THE WORK OF ASSOCIATED PERSONNEL

At even the lowest level of youth and scholastic sport, the demands on coaches are beyond the ability of a single person. Therefore, paid or volunteer assistants are often necessary. Once other coaches appear on the scene, someone must be designated the "head coach." This person speaks in a leadership capacity—to athletes, parents and administrators. While other duties such as planning, teaching, directing competitions, evaluating performances and over-seeing the athlete's safety may be shared, the "head" coach has the responsibility to direct and evaluate the work of assistants.

Ideally, the head coach plans what assistants do and integrates them into the coaching program. Knowledgeable and informed assistants can make practices more effective. An assistant might teach a single skill to the team or work on re-teaching a skill to a small group of athletes. An assistant might be allowed to focus on a single aspect of competition—how "match-ups" are going, when to call time outs or a particular strategy to use. An assistant might be assigned certain record keeping tasks or be asked to take charge of over-seeing the academic progress of players. The list of possible assignments for assistant coaches is as long as that for head coaches. By preparing assistants to take on certain roles, the head coach can involve them in improving every aspect of the athletes' performance and experience.

Consequently, the head coach must consider the preparation of assistant coaches. This not only involves their formal credentials but also how they fit into the program. The head coach should assign responsibilities based on each assistant's ability and background. In addition, the head coach should encourage and promote the professional growth of assistants. This includes expecting them to gradually take on more duties. The head coach also must help assistants by expecting them to attend clinics, take formal courses and attain appropriate certifications.

SCOUTING

Next in importance might well be checking on opponents—their strengths and weaknesses, what strategies they employ, and what "match ups" are most likely to be successful. These activities are commonly referred to as scouting.

While scouting may not be terribly important at some levels of competition, it is always worthwhile to know something about one's opponents. This information can assist the coach in making appropriate decisions about personnel and strategy. It also may be of use in preparing athletes for other challenges, such as difficult playing conditions or poor sportsmanship on the part of opponents. Assistants often are given scouting duties; sometimes video is used. In any case, the coach of competitive athletes can benefit from advance knowledge about the opposition.

Once the coach and assistant have developed their scouting skills, they can use them with their own team. By looking at the athletes, their performances and the coaching as an opponent might, the staff can better evaluate both themselves and their players. The athletes' abilities come into better focus, as do their shortcomings. Similarly, any particular coaching tendencies become apparent. Both can then become part of a program to improve the over-all performance of the team.

MAKING EVALUATIONS

At various points during the season, the coach should formally evaluate the progress of everyone involved. Most coaches regularly assess the performance of the athletes and, by extension, the team. Likewise, at some point most coaches consider their own performance. A head coach also has broader responsibilities, which include rating the work of assistants and the progress of the entire program.

Evaluating Athletes

This subject is dealt with at length in Chapter 30 (*Planning Effective Instruction*) and Chapter 31 (*Evaluating Coaching Effectiveness*). Here it simply is important to note that this is one of the coach's major administrative responsibilities. Moreover, the coach's ability to manage this process can influence long-term coaching success.

Making sound assessments of each player's ability is essential to good coaching. However, communicating the results of such judgments to the athlete and parents may be more critical. The coach must help the player develop a realistic sense of his/her current ability while outlining what needs to be done for continued development. The same information must be given to parents in a meaningful way. The goal is to give both athletes and parents a realistic picture of the young person's existing and potential skill level. Accomplishing this is a fundamental element in creating the trust among coach, athletes, and parents that is so essential to successful coaching.

Evaluating Coaching Performance

Chapter 31, *Evaluating Coaching Effectiveness*, goes into great detail describing how to evaluate coaching. Several approaches are suggested, including one that focuses on the athletes' learning. If problems are identified, they often relate to how the coach functions as a teacher. Typical areas that need improvement include...

- Season and practice planning,
- Putting plans into action,
- Knowledge of the sport's skills and strategies,
- Preparing regular evaluations of coaching performance,
- Motivating players,
- Communicating with athletes,
- Working with parents,
- Principles and techniques of conditioning,
- Preventing injuries, and
- Caring for injuries.

The challenge is recognizing the need to change. The coach may have trouble admitting that things can be done better. However, once this hurdle is taken, the coach will find many resources for improving coaching behavior. Clinics and workshops, books, talking with other coaches and web sites are all legitimate ways to learn. However, the key is for the coach to develop the habit of evaluating coaching performance and trying to improve all facets of the program.

Evaluating Assistant Coaches

A head coach has to evaluate assistants; this is a critical part of the over-all assessment. The primary goal should be to determine how each assistant contributes to the success of the team. Quite probably the simplest approach is to use the form entitled How Does Your Coaching Rate? (This appears in Chapter 31 as Supplement 31-3.) By simply change the "I" into "we," the head coach can assess how the team and coaches interacted. This reveals much about the quality of coaching; it also identifies potential problem areas.

If any difficulties are noted, the head coach can look closer at how assistant coaches are interacting with athletes. (Assistants generally do not have reason to deal with parents, teachers, administrators, the media or other non-team members.) The process of evaluating assistant coaches actually is similar to evaluating players: write down what should be known and done, watch performances, "coach" for improved performance, and provide a written assessment. If change is necessary, prepare individualized, written action plans for the assistants to follow to improving their coaching.

KEEPING RECORDS

Maintaining and retaining records is an essential administrative function, especially because so much paper crosses the desk of even a junior high school coach. Four questions must be considered:

1. What records should be kept?
2. Where should the coach keep records?
3. How long must records be kept?
4. How should records be used?

What Records Should be Kept?

Many written communications touch upon the athletic program. The following is a suggestive but not inclusive list of essential information:

- Written communications to or from parents,
- Notes explaining athletes' absences from activities,
- Messages to or from administrators,
- Requests for facility maintenance,
- Equipment inventories,
- Scheduling information,
- Contracts for officials and ratings of officials,
- Records of any money collected or spent,
- Transportation requests,
- Directions for finding competition sites,
- Player performance ratings,
- Job descriptions for assistant coaches, and
- Evaluations of assistant coaches.

Some of these records actually may be the responsibility of other personnel associated with the athletic program. Trainers, athletic directors, area supervisors and principals may be accountable for them. Nevertheless, coaches should know whether records are being properly maintained, especially those that relate to their team. To assist coaches in sorting through this process, Supplement 33-1 is a *Checklist of Essential Records*. Individual coaches can use the list to determine whether critical records are being retained.

The coach's record-keeping responsibilities involve more than knowing who is tracking which records. There are some essential pieces of information that every coach should have readily to hand. Among these are those dealing with the health and safety of athletes:

- Agreements to Participate (see Supplement 34-1),
- Medical Information and Injury History Forms (see Supplement 17-1),
- Medical Treatment Consent Forms (see Supplement 17-3),
- Attendance records (Supplement 33-3),
- Season plans (see Chapter 29),
- Practice plans (see Chapter 30), and
- Injury assessments (see Chapters 15 and 17).

Supplement 33-2, *Key Records for Every Athlete*, provides a form for tracking the first three pieces of information for each athlete. These bits of information must be obtained from each athlete and kept on file. More importantly, the Medical Information and Agreement to Participate forms should be in the coach's possession whenever athletes are being supervised. Equally important is taking *Attendance*. Supplement 33-3 provides a form that can be used to track whether athletes are at practices and contests. This is important, because it can be combined with practice plans to assess the need to re-teach various aspects of the game.

These various checklists are a good start on deciding what records to maintain. However, there is an even simpler guideline the coach can follow: Whenever the coach writes something down or receives a written communication, the paper should be kept. Supplement 33-4 describes some *Additional Records and Communications* that may come to a coach's attention. Note that it includes a column headed "Maintained By" and another titled "File Location." It is important for the coach to know who is responsible for tracking information and where it can be found.

Where Should the Coach Keep Records?

Quite simply, records should be maintained where they will not be accidentally destroyed. The old-fashioned way probably would still serve the coach well in most situations—file folders, properly labeled, stored in a drawer where they can be found quickly. In this modern era, computers, personal electronic assistants, e-mail, fax machines and cell phones are playing an ever-larger role in coaching. This new technology will require the coach to become competent in storing and maintaining electronic records. In either case, the coach should avoid having records stack up. Filing/record keeping must be done regularly, possibly even daily. Additionally, it is important to note where information is located. Note again that several of the appendices outlining which records to hold also expect the user to indicate where they can be found.

How Long Must Records be Kept?

Most records can be disposed of at the start of the ensuing season. However, some should be held a bit longer. Among these are:

- Season and daily practice plans,
- Samples of written communications to parents,
- Requests for facility maintenance,
- Equipment inventories,
- Player performance ratings (especially those for returning athletes),
- Directions for finding competition sites,
- Job descriptions for assistant coaches, and
- Evaluations of assistant coaches.

Records relating to injuries merit special consideration. Injuries may lead to litigation, which may require long-term possession of records. Laws differ from one jurisdiction to the next. Therefore, it is difficult to determine the length of time that specific records should be maintained. The professional advice of an attorney should be sought regarding this matter. (Since practice plans often are at issue in litigation, they should be held for an extended period as well.)

How Should Records be Used?

Records should be consulted as the need arises. Generally, this occurs when the coach needs to review what has been done previously. Most obviously, any previous season and practice plans should be reviewed regularly. These reveal the order in which the objectives and competencies were taught. They also include evaluations of the strategies and actions that were successful and those that were not. These plans also call to mind forgotten drills and suggest potential trouble spots.

Other uses for records include:

- Parent meeting agenda and notes to parents that remind the coach of things to discuss.

- Repair requests suggesting what the coach should inspect before the season starts.
- Equipment inventories that reveal repairs and needs.
- Player records that provide the coach with an idea of what to expect from returning athletes. The evaluations also identify potential individual and team strengths.
- Job descriptions for assistant coaches that outline each person's responsibilities.
- Evaluations of assistants designed to enhance their professional development. The systematic maintenance and filing of these records also allow the head coach to use assistants more effectively.

Finally, by reviewing injury information the coach can discover any patterns. (See Chapter 17, *Essential Medical Records for Athletes*.) Reviewing this information with a medical professional can help the coach understand what conditions might cause injuries. This, in turn, can assist the coach in developing an injury prevention program.

ADMINISTRATIVE RESPONSIBILITIES OUTSIDE THE LINES

Generally, the activities discussed to this point have some relationship, albeit remote, to what happens in practice and competition. However, the remaining responsibilities involve the coach in events far removed from the field, court, rink or pool. Some scholastic coaches fail to recognize the need to perform these tasks. Nevertheless, they have become increasingly important at even the beginning levels of sport, and how the coach manages them can greatly affect the team, the program and the coach's career.

Working With Booster Groups and Raising Funds

Practically all schools and athletic programs have booster groups. These usually coalesce from the interests of parents and community members. In most instances, individuals who support the athletic program perceive "needs" within the programs and conclude that only additional financial resources will meet them. Often this may be the case. However, such situations require the attention of the coach, who should be aware that booster programs can become quite time-consuming. Not only must the coach deal with boosters and assist in fund raising, the coach also has an obligation (at least ethical, if not legal) to see that these activities are carried out in accordance with established procedures. If no procedures are in place, then coaches must work with boosters and school administrators to establish guidelines.

Keeping things in perspective and maintaining the

program's integrity are two prerequisites for a coach involved with a booster club. It is easy for everyone to focus on raising money, but this harmony often ends in disagreements about its handling and distribution. A firm stand may have to be taken; the coach should work with the athletic director to take control of all income and expenditures related to booster activities. Top level (varsity) coaches can reasonably be expected to take on this task. However, in these times, even coaches working with the youngest athletes likely will have to work with boosters and raise funds.

As noted earlier, most coaches will have to learn how to manage these issues "on the job." The most essential achievement is to learn the rules that apply to boosters and outside funding. Governing bodies (such as the state athletic association) and school systems often prescribe allowable activities. Each head coach should learn these rules and communicate them to all assistants. Further, all coaches should be prepared to explain the rules and the need to follow them to boosters and other people outside the program. Coaches have a responsibility to maintain control, or they risk allowing decisions to be made that will undermine the nature of educational athletics. The activities of booster clubs that function for the benefit of interscholastic programs may have more restrictive guidelines than those that govern agency sponsored sports; but scholastic sports are designed to be educational in nature. However, when bringing in money becomes a major concern, decisions may be made for financial rather than educational reasons. This serves neither the athletes nor their schools.

Promoting the Sport and the Team and Interacting With the Media

No longer is it enough for coaches to throw open the doors and expect athletes and spectators to throng to the sport. A wide variety of activities compete for the time and interest of people, including those who might be athletes. Consequently, coaches must sell their sport and their team. To do this, they must be involved with the media at some level—even if it is only a school paper, a Web site or a public access cable channel.

Coaches should prepare for their roles in public relations just as they ready themselves for other aspects of the job. They should be able to explain why athletes should play and why spectators should come to the contests. This is especially true for coaches promoting a new program or activity; they may even need to explain the rules and strategies to people. But all coaches should seek out opportunities to promote their sport, its benefits to athletes and the joy of playing it. Failure to promote a sport may well result in shrinking numbers and support.

Similarly, coaches should stand ready to explain how involvement with athletics can benefit young people and the community in general. There are many short- and long-term benefits, but if athletes drop out or never begin to play, these will not be fully realized. Coaches must constantly remind young and old alike of why athletics are an essential part of the educational experience. Further, coaches' decisions should reflect this attitude. What they expect of athletes, how players are treated, and how coach and athletes fit into the community are important items for coaches to communicate to their supporters.

Coaches should enumerate the potential benefits of athletics and incorporate these benefits in a "game plan" for promoting their sport and its play. Clearly, the media have a role to play in this. Coaches must understand the needs of the media and maintain a working relationship with them. This does not mean that coaches curry favor with media representatives. Rather, coaches should respond cordially to reasonable requests for information. Coaches also ought to keep the media informed about important developments affecting the sport and team. It is far easier to maintain a good relationship than to rebuild one that has been damaged.

The skills required to maintain good public relations often do not come naturally to coaches. These skills need to be developed and practiced, just as athletes improve their skills. The long-term success of programs may depend on how well coaches perform these functions.

SUMMARY

Coaches generally do not think of themselves as administrators. However, there are many essential coaching duties that can only be described as "administrative." At a minimum, these include:

- Preparing for contests,
- Organizing associated personnel,
- Scouting,
- Evaluating personnel,
- Keeping records,
- Working with booster groups,
- Raising funds,
- Promoting the sport and the team, and
- Dealing with the media.

These aspects of coaching lack the excitement of teaching and "bench coaching." These administrative tasks are often learned by doing them. But they must be learned, for they affect a coach's career in many ways. A successful coach who has enjoyed a long career is also a good administrator.

Supplement 33-1. Checklist of Essential Records.

Type of Record	On File?		
	Yes	No	Don't Know
Pre-participation physical for each athlete			
Medical information form for each athlete			
Medical treatment consent (Release) form for each athlete			
Emergency plans for each practice and competition site			
On-site injury reports for all injuries			
Summary of season injuries			
Copies of injury assessments if professional assistance is required			
Copies of rehabilitation plans for injured athletes			
Safety checklist for practice and competition sites			
Agreements to participate for each athlete			
Agendas for pre-season meeting with parents			
Season plans			
Daily practice plans			
Attendance records for all athletes			
Excuses for absences from team activities			
Copies of communication to and from parents			
Copies of communication between coaches and administrators			
Copies of requests for facility maintenance			
Copies of equipment inventories: Pre-season			
Post-season			
Requests for equipment repair/replacement			
Budgets and budget requests			
Records of money collected and spent			
Copies of communications with booster groups			

Scheduling information and schedules			
Copies of communications with league officials			
Copies of communications with sanctioning organizations			
Copies of contracts with opponents for competition			
Copies of communications with opponents			
Copies of contracts with officials			
Ratings of officials			
Copies of communications with officials			
Transportation requests			
Directions to all contest sites—home and away			
Evaluations of all athletes			
Copies of off-season plans for all athletes			
Job descriptions for head coaches			
Copies of evaluations by administrators			
Copies of self-evaluations by coaches			
Job descriptions for assistant coaches			
Evaluations of assistant coaches			
Job descriptions for other team personnel			
Evaluations of additional personnel			

Supplement 33-2. Key Records for Every Athlete.

Athlete	Agreement to Participate	Date Received
1.		
2.		
3.		
4.		
5.		
6.		
7.		
8.		
9.		
10.		
11.		
12.		
13.		
14.		
15.		
16.		
17.		
18.		
19.		
20.		
21.		
22.		
23.		
24.		
25.		

Records are filed (location):

Supplement 33-2. Key Records for Every Athlete (*continued*)

Athlete	Medical Information	Date Received
1.		
2.		
3.		
4.		
5.		
6.		
7.		
8.		
9.		
10.		
11.		
12.		
13.		
14.		
15.		
16.		
17.		
18.		
19.		
20.		
21.		
22.		
23.		
24.		
25.		

Records are filed (location):

Athlete	Medical Releases	Date Received
1.		
2.		
3.		
4.		
5.		
6.		
7.		
8.		
9.		
10.		
11.		
12.		
13.		
14.		
15.		
16.		
17.		
18.		
19.		
20.		
21.		
22.		
23.		
24.		
25.		

Records are filed (location):

Supplement 33-3. Attendance.*

Athlete	Date	Date	Date	Date	Date
1.					
2.					
3.					
4.					
5.					
6.					
7.					
8.					
9.					
10.					
11.					
12.					
13.					
14.					
15.					
16.					
17.					
18.					
19.					
20.					

Records are filed (location):

* Note whether any athletes arrive late or leave early. You may want to record reasons for missing part of practice. Make additional copies of this form as needed.

Supplement 33-4. Additional Records and Communications.

Record	Maintained by	File Location
1. Season and daily practice plans		
2. Excuses for athletes' absences from activities		
3. Emergency plans for each practice and competition site		
4. Copies of injury reports		
5. Injury assessments		
6. Copies of rehabilitation plans for athletes		
7. Summary of season injuries		
8. Agendas for pre-season parents' meetings		
9. Written communications to and from parents		
10. Messages to and from administrators		
11. Requests for facility maintenance		
12. Equipment inventories		
13. Requests for equipment repair/replacement		
14. Annual budget information		
15. Scouting reports		
16. Schedules and scheduling information		
17. Ratings of officials		
18. Records of money collected and spent		
19. Communications with boosters		
20. Transportation requests		
21. Directions for finding competition sites		
22. Player performance ratings		
23. Off-season plans for players		
24. Self-evaluations		
25. Evaluations by administrators		
26. Job descriptions for assistant coaches		
27. Evaluations of assistant coaches		
28. Job descriptions for additional team personnel (mangers and so forth)		
29. Evaluations of additional personnel		
30.		

34

Legal Issues in Coaching

Thomas H. Sawyer, Ed.D.

QUESTIONS TO CONSIDER

- What is negligence?
- What are the defenses against negligence?
- What basic obligations do all coaches have to athletes?
- What are the most common occurrences that lead to lawsuits filed against coaches?
- What should interscholastic athletic coaches do to protect themselves against lawsuits?
- What should the coach and athletic administrator know about risk management?

INTRODUCTION

Less than 20 years ago, coaches seldom gave a second thought to the possibility of becoming involved in lawsuits related to their coaching efforts. Yet, today, the fear of becoming involved in litigation is as common as the fear of losing the big game. The coaching profession at all levels is vulnerable in our present litigious society.

A landmark lawsuit in 1982 (Thompson V. Seattle Public School District) opened a new and interesting era in sport litigation with far-reaching implications for sport at all levels. In that case, after a lower court award of $6.3 million to a young man against the Seattle school district and coach for a football injury that left him a quadriplegic in 1975, the case was appealed and settled out of court for $3.78 million. The player sued the coach for *failure to warn* of the dangers inherent in football and for *improper instruction* in coaching.

The Thompson lawsuit marked a shift from product liability to responsibility of coaches and school districts for the injuries incurred in youth sports. Many suits prior to 1980 in sport were based on equipment, or what is termed *products liability*. The lower court suit also found the school administrators were negligent in not providing a sport-specific teaching curriculum and safety manual and for not providing a formal evaluation procedure for coaches.

Appenzeller and Lewis (1985) and van der Smissen (1990) indicated that schools and their agents need to be cognizant of the factors that influence liable conditions which give rise to liability. These factors include:

- Failure to instruct,
- Failure to warn, and
- Failure to supervise.

Do not assume you are immune from litigation merely because you participate in an agency-sponsored, non-profit program of athletic competition for children. Whether you are paid for coaching services or volunteer your time, you are responsible for the welfare of the athletes. This chapter discusses various legal issues and what is meant by being a reasonable, prudent person during the conduct of one's duties as a youth sports coach. By following the suggestions in this chapter, you may deter a lawsuit from being filed, or if sued, you will aid your defense.

NEGLIGENCE

The vast majority of litigation dealing with coaches involves *negligence*. Negligence is the failure to exercise *reasonable* or *ordinary* care in a situation that causes harm to someone or something. Further, negligence is any conduct which falls below the *standard of care* established by the court(s) and based on professional practices /standards for the protection of others against unreasonable risk of harm.

The predominate test used to determine negligence is *foreseeability*, that is, whether or not the coach should have been able to foresee the danger of harm to a player, that the player was in a situation of an unreasonable risk of injury.

Negligence occurs when the coach either carelessly performs a duty(ies) or carelessly fails to perform a duty(ies).

Liability in negligence has four elements and requires affirmative answers to four questions:

1. Does the law recognize responsibility in this kind of situation?

   The law must recognize that a *duty* to conform to the requisite *standard of care* established by the court(s) and/or the coaching profession existed to protect another against the kind of harm in question. Duty is determined by relationship, and there seldom is a question in a coach-athlete relationship—duty is owed to protect against unreasonable risks of injury.

2. Was the coach *careless*; i.e., did his or her conduct fall short of the requisite *standard of care*? Did the coach *breach his/her duty*?

   The breach can either be due to *careless* performance or *careless* absence of performance.

3. Did the coach's *carelessness* in fact cause the damage or injury?

   The court must determine whether or not there is a reasonable *proximate causal* link between the *breach of duty* (carelessness), the coach's action or lack of action and the actual harm or injury.

4. To what extent is the coach at fault?

   Damage the fourth element, is essential in negligence; however, there seldom is any dispute, except for the amount. The question is to what extent is the coach *at fault*. Most states apply comparative negligence (see Defenses), for which coach's fault is an integral part.

The vast majority of litigation against coaches is based on the negligence or careless performance or lack of performance of the coach's legal obligation or duty.

Defenses Against Negligence

Carelessness is a fact of life. We all make mistakes in our professional capacities, and sometimes those careless errors cause injury to others. It is helpful to understand the appropriate defenses for negligence in case you are sued. There are five common defenses for negligence:

- Failing to prove all elements of negligence,
- Assumption of risk,
- Contributory negligence,
- Act of God, and
- Governmental immunity.

Comparative negligence, often referred to as a defense, is a method of apportioning damages and utilizes both assumption of risk and contributory negligence in determination.

The plaintiff must prove all elements of negligence in order to win a case against the defendant. If one of the four elements is not proved, the plaintiff will lose the case. Therefore it is necessary for the defendant's attorney to prove that one or more of the elements of negligence is absent.

Assumption of risk is based on the theory that people who know, understand and appreciate the danger involved in an activity and voluntarily engage in it willingly expose themselves to certain predictable inherent risks. The defense of assumption of risk is in fact quite narrowly confined and restricted by two requirements:

- It applies only to risks inherent in the sport and
- The plaintiff must know, understand and appreciate the risk being voluntarily incurred.

The plaintiff (athlete) does not assume any risks due to negligence on the part of the defendant (coach).

In order for a person to assume an inherent risk, he or she must know, understand and appreciate the danger and freely volunteer to incur it.

Contributory negligence is conduct on the part of the plaintiff that contributes as a legal cause to the harm suffered. It is conduct which falls below the standard to which the plaintiff is required to conform for his/her own protection. Unlike assumption of risk, the defense does not rest upon the idea that the defendant is relieved of responsibility toward the plaintiff. Rather, the plaintiff is denied recovery because his/her own conduct disentitles him/her to maintain the action even though the defendant has breached his/her duty, has been negligent, and would otherwise be liable. In the eyes of the law, both parties in contributory negligence are at fault; and the defense in this situation contends that negligence by the plaintiff rather then the defendant's innocence should be a bar to recovering any money for damages. Only a few states still use contributory negligence as a total bar to recovery. Most have gone to comparative negligence.

If the plaintiff contributes in any way to his or her injury, it is considered contributory negligence.

Comparative negligence, unlike contributory negligence, does not place upon one party the entire burden of a loss for which two are responsible. The negligence of the defendant has played no less a part in causing the damage; the plaintiff's deviation from the community standard of conduct may even be relatively slight, and the defendant's more extreme. In comparative negligence, the fault of the parties is compared on a percentage basis. Although most of the states adhere to comparative negligence, the states vary in application. In a majority of states, a player cannot recover if his or her fault contributes 50 percent or more to the accident, while in some other states the player can recover any percentage of fault by the defendant.

Generally, plaintiffs can only recover, under comparative negligence, if they are found to be less negligent than the defendant.

Government immunity is a common law theory that holds that because the state and its agencies are sovereign, they cannot be sued without their consent and should not be held liable for the negligence of their employees. However, this doctrine has been modified in nearly all states by enactment of Tort Claims Statutes. The statutes vary state to state in their limiting of liability. Generally, where discretionary decision-making has taken place, there is no liability. Where there may otherwise be immunity, the purchase of liability insurance may constitute a waiver of such immunity. In most jurisdictions there is liability for defective facilities and dangerous conditions. Some Tort Claim Acts protect employees from liability, unless there has been willful and wanton misconduct.

Government immunity is a defense used to protect government entities, but it is quite limited today.

Act of God is a defense made when the cause of the injury is attributed to natural force. For example, if a sudden burst of lightening exploded a transformer, which fell on a player who suffered severe burns and a broken leg, the defense might allege that the injury occurred because of an act of God. This defense is only applicable when the accident would have occurred even if prudent action had been taken.

Act of God is a defense used when the forces beyond the control of man cause an injury.

THE LEGAL RESPONSIBILITIES OF COACHES

For over a decade courts, lawyers, and professional associations have been establishing a coach's legal responsibilities. These responsibilities include providing adequate supervision, a safe environment, proper instruction, adequate and proper planning, adequate evaluation for injury or incapacity, appropriate emergency procedures and first aid training, adequate and proper equipment, appropriate warnings, and adequate matching of competitors. These duties are to be met by the coach while he/she is involved in any supervisory situation related to his/her coaching responsibilities.

Supervision

Supervision means you are in charge of others as they perform some activity(ies). As a coach, it means you are in charge of your athletes and assistant coaches.

The more dangerous the activity, the more specific the supervision required.

There are two levels of supervision: general and specific. The basic requirement for *general supervision* is that the supervisor maintains visual and auditory contact with the area and individuals under supervision and be able to respond quickly. Locker, shower, and equipment rooms; bleachers; hallways; and stages adjacent to a gymnasium are all examples of areas where general supervision is required. The coach, in order to meet this supervisory responsibility, should be:

- Immediately accessible to the activity,
- Able to observe the entire program,
- Alert to conditions that may be dangerous to athletes and take necessary action to modify the conditions, and
- Able to react quickly and appropriately to emergencies.

The basic requirement for general supervision is that the supervisor be in a position where he/she has visual and auditory contact with the area and those to be supervised, and is able to respond quickly.

Specific supervision is instructional in nature and directed toward the actual teaching or coaching of the activity. Someone who coaches a team on the court is primarily engaged in specific supervision. At the same time, he/she usually has general responsibility for adjacent areas.

Specific supervision is the actual teaching of an activity or the coaching of a team.

A qualified supervisor is a person who has adequate education and certification to perform the specific task(s) assigned. For example, a person assigned to coach should be:

- Able to perform CPR and basic first aid,
- Knowledgeable about the specific sport,

- Able to perform the sport skills of the specific sport,
- Knowledgeable in the area of sport philosophy, sport psychology, motivation, communication, sport management, sports injuries and rehabilitation,
- Able to measure athletic potential,
- Able to teach sport skills, and
- Knowledgeable of sport physiology and counseling.

Further, the qualified supervisor knows how to complete the following supervisory tasks:

- Plan appropriately for activities,
- Teach the appropriate skills according to accepted practices and rules,
- Present clear warning of inherent risk(s) within the activity,
- Evaluate participants for injury and incapacity,
- Match and equate participants properly for the activity, and
- Administer first aid and CPR, and activate the emergency medical system.

Supervision is a learned skill, and the school administration should provide for appropriate in-service sessions for all supervisors. School administrators should have written policies and procedures about supervision for all personnel. The in-service training and supervisory plan must take into consideration these questions.

- What should the supervisor look for?
- What should the supervisor listen for?
- Where should the supervisor stand in specific situations?
- How should the supervisor move?
- What should the supervisor do if a problem arises?
- How should the supervisor identify all potential dangerous activities?
- How close should the supervisor be to the activity?
- How can the supervisor understand the warning signs of impending trouble during an activity?
- What is a stop signal that can be used when the supervisor must immediately suspend activity?

Finally, for both general and specific supervision, the questions below should be answered by school administrators and their agents.

- Who can be a supervisor?
- What is the scope of the supervisor's duties?
- What does instruction involve?
- How many supervisors are needed?
- Where should supervisors be located?
- To what should supervisors attend?

Maintaining a Safe Environment

Coaches are frequently involved in litigation that involves a facility, piece of apparatus or equipment that was considered unsafe at the time of injury. The common causes for litigation involving facilities, apparatus or equipment are faulty design, improper maintenance, defective products associated with the facility, and faulty protective equipment.

Any time the coach detects a problem with a facility or item of equipment, the coach should immediately correct the problem if he or she has the authority. If not, the coach should notify, in writing, the person who has the authority to correct the situation. This detection or direct knowledge is called *actual notice*.

The term "notice" is defined as the knowledge of a fact or state of affairs that would naturally lead a reasonable and prudent person to make inquiry. A person has notice of a fact if he or she knows the fact, has reason to know it, should know it, or has been given notification of it.

Actual notice should be transmitted to the next level in written form with a copy placed in your file, and a verbal follow-up to confirm receipt of the written notice.

A second type of notice is *constructive notice*. It is defined as possession of information or knowledge that a person could have discovered by proper diligence. Or put another way, the coach is responsible for all knowledge that encompasses that specialty area.

The reasonable and prudent coach has the responsibility to perform the following responsibilities in relation to providing a safe facility and equipment.

- Conduct regular and thorough inspections of facilities and equipment, record the results in written form, and file for future reference.
- Maintain current standards for the appropriateness of facility and equipment for the activities being implemented.
- Develop a regular preventative maintenance schedule for the facility and equipment.
- Advise all personnel of the "shared responsibility doctrine" which states that all parties share in the responsibility for conducting programs safely by fulfilling their shared responsibilities in a manner that is consistent with preventative maintenance.
- Purchase the best equipment affordable for the activity.
- Be aware of changes in equipment and standards of safety relating to equipment.
- Take care when adjusting, fitting or repairing equipment.
- Be wary of new untested equipment.

- Avoid illegal equipment.
- Present necessary warnings relating to equipment as specified by the manufacturer.
- Avoid home-made equipment.
- Teach proper techniques for using the equipment.
- Avoid hand-me-downs.
- Be sure insurance reflects the current status of equipment.
- If equipment is not used, make it inaccessible.

Proper Instruction Defined

A coach is responsible for the players' safety during practices and games. Responsibility for the players' safety may be shared among coaches, officials, administrators, and other players; but specific portions of the players' involvement in practices and games are the direct responsibility of the coach.

The coach must recognize and understand the hazards of all activities and facilities; remove unnecessary hazards from facilities, equipment and programs; and modify facilities, equipment and programs to lessen hazards that cannot be removed.

The coach is responsible for teaching the physical skills of the sport in a manner that will reduce the likelihood of injury. This implies that a coach must first know the proper mechanics, sport strategies, and progressions in skill development and conditioning, and then know how to implement them, based on the readiness of athletes to coordinate new levels of proficiency. Coaches, generally with the eager compliance of athletes, have a tendency to exceed the body's readiness to accept new levels of stress. Athletes are particularly vulnerable to overexertion early in the season.

The burden of proper training and conditioning rests with the coach.

Rules and regulations govern the conduct of all sports. All participants must know and agree to abide by the rules and regulations. Rules and regulations exist to help participants evaluate goal-directed behavior, promote fair play, and conduct the activity safely. If the coach fails to teach players the rules and a player violates a rule that is directly responsible for an injury, then the coach may be liable. The coach is responsible for reviewing the old rules and regulations and teaching new rules and regulations to the players.

All participants must know and agree to abide by the rules and regulations.

Planning

Planning must precede everything a coach does with a student-athlete. Plans must be reasonable, well thought out, and based on past experiences and readiness of the athlete. All plans should be reviewed continuously and kept for the record. Finally the plan should contain properly written performance objectives, and document a logical sequence and progression for learning the skills.

No plan is complete without written performance objectives.

Coaches should state their desired outcomes as performance objectives (Nygaard and Boone, 1989). The objectives should describe what the participants will be doing during a session, rather than focusing on what the instructor will be doing. The performance objectives are a critical component of any adequate plan.

The writing of performance objectives should not be taken lightly. The objectives should have three parts to them:

- The task to be performed,
- The conditions under which the performance will occur, and
- The minimal level of acceptable performance.

Further, the objectives should be reviewed and modified regularly.

The following are examples of statements used as performance objectives. The first statement is not a performance objective, the second meets the minimum requirements of an objective, and the third statement is an example of how to write an objective so that all three parts flow together and read smoothly.

- "I will teach the goalie how to dropkick a soccer ball."
- "During this session, each goalie will dropkick 10 soccer balls, five of which will go beyond midfield in the air."
- "During this session:
  1. Each goalie will dropkick 10 soccer balls.
  2. These soccer balls should be dropkicked from the penalty box at the south end of the field toward midfield and from a position in the center of the box.
  3. In order to be successful each goalie must kick at least five soccer balls in the air, and cause the soccer ball to land beyond the midfield line on the right side, inside the touch line."

In the latter example, the players have a much better idea of what they are to accomplish. Further, they are more likely to ask questions and express concerns about their impending tasks when they know precisely what is to be accomplished. This type of planning effort will promote safer play.

An adequate plan must have an appropriate sequence and progression. The coach should consider and understand the Law of Readiness. This law basically says a plan is not ready for implementation until it affirmatively answers the following queries:.

- Is (are) the participant(s) able to safely perform this activity?
- What lead-up activities are necessary in order for the athletes to learn this skill?
- Who can perform safely under what conditions?
- What about new participants—those students who come out late to practice? Are they able to participate safely in these drills/activities?

Teaching skills to athletes in the proper progression reduces the chances of personal injury from improper techniques and/or inappropriate levels of competition.

The following recommendations are for the sequence and progression that should be considered when developing the practice plan.

- Determine the typical, usual, or recommended sequence and progression of an activity.
- Review pertinent literature concerning the specific activity.
- Consult existing plans.
- Have the plan sequence and progression approved by your supervisor.

Maintaining Proper Records

The proof that is often needed in court to defend against alleged negligence exists in written records of action(s) taken. Many coaches despise record keeping, but it is essential for maintaining and retrieving data about injuries. The coach is well advised to keep records of all instructional plans.

All records should be kept in a safe place.

The records that should be kept include:

- Injury(ies) reports,
- Instructional plans,
- Records of facility inspection and maintenance,
- Records of equipment purchasing and inventory,
- Warnings given to athletes and their parents,
- Waiver forms,

- Reports of equipment reconditioning,
- Copies of attendance records for in-service programs, and
- Copies of all certifications held by coaches.

Evaluating Injuries and Incapacity

The coach should consider temperature, humidity, wind, or other environmental factors when scheduling practice sessions. Further, the coach should be aware of each student- athletes physical condition. Each student-athlete should be required to take a physical examination administered by a registered physician prior to participating in vigorous physical activity. Any special medical conditions must be noted and understood by the coach.

In the case of an injured athlete, the coach's duty becomes one of preventing further injury or harm to that injured party. No athlete should be allowed to participate after a major injury until a doctor's release is obtained.

A coach must use due care to prevent an unreasonable risk of injury to athletes.

Coaches, regardless of whether athletic trainers are available, should know how to perform CPR, basic first aid, and emergency procedures. Coaches have been found liable for their failure to know and use adequate first aid for heat stroke and for not knowing how to move players with suspected neck or back injuries.

Coaches must be able to provide or secure reasonable medical assistance for the injured party as soon as possible. Coaches should never take it upon themselves to transport an injured athlete. Instead they should perform immediate and temporary first aid and send for emergency medical personnel.

The coach should develop a good working relationship with local physicians who have an interest in sports medicine; be prepared for injuries; develop and follow reasonable procedures to deal with injuries; and above all, document injuries that occur and how they have been treated.

Emergency Procedures

It is the coach's responsibility to provide or secure appropriate medical assistance for injured athletes. If appropriate medical assistance is not immediately available, the coach has the duty to provide immediate and temporary care. Therefore, it is imperative that coaches be provided in-service programs annually relating to first aid and CPR. These programs should be taught by either certified emergency medical personnel and/or an athletic trainer certified by the National Athletic Trainers Association.

All coaches should be certified in CPR and first aid.

School administrators, in cooperation with the coaches, athletic trainers, and local emergency medical personnel should develop a written Emergency Medical Assistance Plan (EMAP). The EMAP should be approved by the board of education. Further, the EMAP should become a regular component of the emergency medical assistance in-service plan for all coaches and related personnel. The EMAP should include statements that explain what needs to be done in a variety of life threatening situations (heart attack, stroke, heat stroke, diabetic coma, etc.); who should contact emergency personnel; appropriate telephone numbers; appropriate contact people; how to transport an injured athlete; who contacts the parents and appropriate school officials; how to complete an injury report; where to file a copy(ies) of the report; a description of the conditions of the contest area; and what to do with evidence that might explain why the injury occurred. (See Chapter 15, *Care of Common Sports Injuries*, and Chapter 17, *Essential Medical Records for Athletes*, for more information.)

It is very important, whenever possible, that the coach transfer the risk associated with emergencies to more qualified people. All home games involving a contact sport should have a physician on site who understands sport injuries.

Adequate and Proper Equipment

The coach is responsible for providing athletes with the best equipment in order to provide the greatest degree of safety. Courts have indicated that coaches must be diligent in the manner in which equipment is selected, distributed, used, and repaired. If equipment is used improperly, the coach can be and has been held liable for any resulting injuries to the student-athlete.

The two sports that cause the greatest concern in the area of adequate and appropriate equipment are football and gymnastics. The piece of equipment that has caused the greatest problem in sports is the football helmet. The National Operating Committee for Standards in Athletic Equipment (NOCSAE) has published recommendations for football helmets and the reconditioning of football helmets. If coaches do not follow these recommendations and an athlete is hurt, coaches can be found negligent for their failure to follow the recommendations.

In 1990, Riddel, the largest manufacturer of football helmets, informed all users of Riddel helmets that Riddel could not and would not guarantee their helmets beyond 10 years, and if a user decided to continue use after 10 years, the user would absorb the liability for helmet failure. Riddel based this decision on a durability study that found after eight years there was a slight decrease in

structural integrity of the helmet and a significant decrease after 10 years. This evidence suggests that coaches who are considered reasonable and prudent would properly dispose of all helmets, not just those manufactured by Riddel, older than 10 years.

All equipment must meet any existing codes or standards, and it must be maintained and repaired on a regular basis. If equipment is not used, it should be inaccessible.

Exculpatory Agreements (Waivers and Releases)

An exculpatory agreement is an agreement signed by an activity participant (and parent(s) if the participant is a minor) in which the participant (parents) agree not to hold the people in charge of the activity responsible for an injury(ies) that might result from participation in the activity. The common type of exculpatory agreements are embodied in *waivers* and *releases*. However, since such agreement is a contract, it is not valid for minors and parents cannot sign away the rights of their children. Notwithstanding, often waivers are recommended for other values, such as warning of inherent risk. Perhaps more appropriate would be an Agreement to Participate document. (See Supplement 34-1.)

Before a waiver is valid the participant must be warned of inherent risk in the activity.

Warning of Inherent Risk

A warning is any device that informs one in advance of impending or possible harm or risk. An inherent risk is the possibility that the participant may be harmed while performing in a particular activity. Before a person can assume a risk, he or she must be aware of the inherent risk(s) involved in the activity to be performed. The person must also be aware that improper, dangerous techniques increase the risk of injury.

There are three levels of comprehension that must be reached when designing a warning: *Knowing* and *Understanding* the sport and *Appreciating* the risk(s) involved. This is also known as KUA. A one-time brief explanation or summary of the inherent risk(s) within an activity is not sufficient warning for participants. The younger the participants, the greater the need for explanation. The warning must be thorough, clear, and repeated.

The perception of risk is skill-related. A beginner does not have the same comprehension or appreciation as an intermediate or advanced participant.

Inherent risk(s) can, and often do, change depending on improvement in equipment and facilities, rule(s) modification, and personnel changes. The coach must remember that athletes can assume only those risks that are an inherent part of the activities. Coaches must do whatever can be done to assure the athletes know, understand, and appreciate those risks.

A warning should:

- Specify the risks presented by the activity; be consistent with the activity,
- Provide a reason(s) for the warning,
- Attempt to reach foreseeable participants; be specific and clear so that it creates knowledge, understanding, and appreciation in the participants' minds, and
- Be written, and explained orally if possible.

An adequate warning is:

- Conspicuous, so it attracts the user's eye,
- Specific, so it is understood by the user, and
- Forceful, so it convinces the user of the range and magnitude of the potential harm.

When developing a warning, the coach or school administrator should consider the following points:

- Estimate physiological demands,
- Request medical certification,
- Encourage safe performance,
- Emphasize any major standard warning(s), if present,
- Emphasize other common risk(s) ranging from major to minor, and frequent to rare,
- Explain any inherent safety rule(s) /protocol(s),
- Emphasize any major, unique, inherent risk(s),
- Explain equipment recommendations and use,
- Explain necessary etiquette,
- Solicit and encourage questions,
- Summarize the know, understand, and appreciate (kua) statement,
- Request that the warning statement be signed and dated (do not require that the form be signed), and
- File the warning statement.

Waiver

A waiver is a form of an exculpatory or fault-free agreement or contract between parties of majority age. The purpose of the exculpatory clause is to relieve one party of all or a part of its responsibility to another. A number of factors make the value of an exculpatory clause questionable or even nonexistent. They are as follows:

- A strong public policy that prohibits such a clause,
- One party being in a clearly dominant position, such as a coach-player relationship,
- The presence of any fraud or misrepresentation in the clause,

- The agreement which is signed under duress,
- The clause or the conditions it creates are unreasonable,
- The agreement is ambiguous,
- The signature for such an agreement does not immediately follow the agreement, and
- Presence of wanton, intentional, or reckless misconduct.

For all these reasons, exculpatory agreements, waivers, and releases of liability must be used with great care. In the event of negligence, do not rely on them as a defense.

Matching of Competitors

The coach is responsible for matching athletes. Numerous lawsuits allege that athletes have been mismatched when participating in sports. The sports most commonly involved in this type of litigation have been field hockey, football, lacrosse, ice hockey, soccer, and wrestling. Coaches need to be particularly careful in these sports when matching athletes for competition. Matching of opponents should not be done arbitrarily; rather coaches should be taking into consideration the following parameters:

- Skill level,
- Experience,
- Chronological age,
- Height,
- Weight,
- Maturity,
- Gender in coeducational activities, and
- Fitness level.

The skill levels of athletes vary from one activity to another.

Mismatches can occur when athletes return to competition after serious injury(ies). Coaches must use good judgment in returning athletes to practice and competition. The athlete should be reintroduced gradually to full intensity activities. Further, the coach should request medical advice on proper rehabilitation of an injured athlete. Coaches should also provide proper consideration to any athlete with a disability.

RISK MANAGEMENT

Risk, unfortunately, is inherent in everything that is done in the sporting world. Risk management is the planned and thoughtful practice of eliminating or minimizing risk in order to maximize the desired outcome. In doing this, the potential for litigation is minimized. Just as importantly, risk management is a way of telling the people involved that they are important and the organization is concerned about their safety. Further, it is an active way of attempting to avoid potentially dangerous situations.

Courts look favorably upon organizations that attempt to provide a safe environment.

Risk management concerns itself with areas of potential loss that include personnel contracts, facilities, and equipment. Risk management does not merely attend to potentials for personal injury through involvement in a sport.

The role of the risk management plan is to identify problem areas and recommend corrective action to the proper school administrators. The five phases to a sound risk management plan are listed below:

- **Identification:** This phase identifies all potential risks involved with a particular activity.
- **Assessment:** After the risks have been identified, they are assessed, predicting the frequency of occurrence and the magnitude of the danger.
- **Classification:** This phase uses the data collected and assessments from the first two phases and determines the probability that a loss will occur. The frequency and magnitude of the risk have a distinct bearing on the final classification of the risk. Each identified risk will be prioritized in order of greatest risk to participants.
- **Risk treatment:** After each risk has been classified, a decision is made about how to reduce the overall risk of the activity for the participants. Four commonly used treatments for risk include avoidance, acceptance, transfer, and reduction. Any one or combination of treatments can be used to treat the risk(s). Avoidance simply means you avoid the risk, and acceptance means the risk is understood and accepted, but nothing is done to reduce the participant's exposure because of the low frequency and magnitude of the risk. Transfer means the risk is assigned to another party either through warnings and waivers or insurance coverage. Reduction is a process designed to lessen risk by modifying the activity.
- **Evaluation:** This is the final phase in the plan of action. The risk management plan must be reviewed on a regular basis to see if any of the risks have changed, whether the classification is different, or the treatment needs to be changed. The plan should be evaluated at least annually.

Risk Management Considerations

The following is a list of risk management suggestions that all coaches and administrators should take into consideration when planning a safe interscholastic athletic program.

- Parents and students should sign an Agreement to Participate form.
- Parents should sign a Consent and Release form.
- School administrators should adopt written guidelines or policies concerning the following:
  a. Minimum qualifications for coaches,
  b. General safety guidelines and procedures,
  c. Continuing education for coaches,
  d. Payment for coaches' continuing education,
  e. Instructional guides and materials for each sport,
  f. Sports library and audiovisual materials related to sports safety,
  g. Coaches' maintenance of current CPR and first aid, and
  h. Maintenance of standardized injury reports.
- Parents and students should be provided written information regarding the potential catastrophic injuries that can occur in each sport.
- Coaches should be provided with current informational, instructional, and illustrative materials dealing with physical conditioning, sports skills, and sports safety.
- Coaches must be closely screened and evaluated by qualified personnel regarding their qualifications and performance.
- The instructional and safety programs at each school should be audited by a qualified person on an ongoing basis.
- The responsibility and authority of building administrators, activity coordinators, and athletic office staff should be clearly defined in terms of:
  a. Selection, orientation, and supervision of coaches,
  b. Auditing and enforcement of district policies and procedures, and
  c. Evaluation of coaches and athletic activity coordinators.
- School administrators should be involved in the continuous evaluation of policies, procedures, coaches' performance, and all segments of the athletic program.
- Coaches and administrators who are considered "reasonable and prudent" by the courts provide a safe environment, proper instruction, adequate supervision, warnings of inherent risk, proper planning, proper matching of athletes, and proper preparation and conditioning of athletes.
- Require all athletes to participate fully in conditioning drills that are designed to strengthen muscles, tendons, and ligaments that are vulnerable to the stresses of physical contact.
- Athletes should wear required, properly fitted, protective equipment. Those articles that are worn or inadequate should be replaced.

- After an injury occurs the following should be considered (again also see Chapters 15 and 17):
  a. Record all facts surrounding the injury in writing,
  b. Preserve any evidence that might explain why the injury occurred,
  c. Obtain statements, identities, and addresses of witnesses and photographs or films that may have recorded the event,
  d. Complete a full report of the accident, the persons present, who attended the victim on the scene, and what provisions were made for his/her medical care after the injury,
  e. Call the parents or guardians and inform them of the injury, what arrangements were made for the injured player, and the disposition of the athlete,
  f. Make a record of conditions in the contest area, and
  g. Avoid speculation about why the injury occurred or who caused it. Do not suggest fault or wrongdoing on the part of anyone.
- Coaches should never assume duty(ies) beyond their levels of competence.
- Coaches must realize and recognize that the standard of care may change in the same activity, within the same time frame, as the risk increases.
- Coaches and administrators should learn to recognize the following situations:
  a. Behavior which could be negligent,
  b. An act not properly done,
  c. Appropriate care not provided, or
  d. Circumstance under which an action occurs that could create risk or create situations that are unreasonably dangerous to others.
- Athletic directors and principals, in conjunction with the coaches, should develop very detailed plans for the general and specific supervision of athletes to be utilized by all personnel involved in athletics.
- School administrators should secure legal consultants to assist in the development of sport warnings and waivers.
- Athletic administrators should maintain a master list of all equipment with a record of risk classification, latest inspection report, and a record of all repairs completed.
- All instructions and warnings from equipment manufacturers should be posted in a conspicuous place so all participants and coaches can see them.
- Equipment should be maintained according to the manufacturer's specifications. The athletic administrator should develop regular inspection procedures and schedules for all athletic facilities and equipment.

SUMMARY

The legal responsibilities that coaches have for the welfare of their athletes include the teaching of skills, values, and knowledge that will allow young athletes to safely participate in practices and games. Coaches are also accountable for the supervision of their athletes during pre-game, intermission and post-game activities that are commonly associated with athletic competition. Specific information about skill progressions, conditioning and first aid is essential; however, the judgment required in the application of this information to the sport program is a much more important prerequisite to successful coaching than certificates or diplomas.

The responsibilities of the coach have been divided into 11 categories:

1. The need for adequate supervision,
2. A safe environment,
3. Proper instruction,
4. Proper planning,
5. Proper records,
6. Evaluating injuries and incapacity,
7. Adequate emergency procedures and first aid,
8. Adequate and proper equipment,
9. Appropriate warnings and waivers,
10. Adequate matching, and
11. Risk management.

Liability insurance is an essential form of protection for coaches. Due to the unpredictable nature of sport injuries, coaches should also be financially protected by some form of liability insurance. Conditions of coverage and restrictions are specific to each policy; therefore, coaches should be informed about their current protection and the duration of its coverage. (See also Chapter 35, Insurance for Athletes and Coaches.)

Knowledge of a coach's legal responsibilities can serve two useful purposes. The most important of these is that such information provides a potent stimulus to discharge one's duties in a diligent manner, ever mindful that carelessness provokes situations that could induce injuries. The second purpose is that if coaches have used every possible precaution to prevent injuries, they are in a good position to defend themselves against litigation.

REFERENCES

Adam, S., and Bayless, M. (1982). "How the Seattle Decision Affects Liability and You." *Athletic Purchasing and Facilities*, 6: 12-14.

Appenzeller, H., and Lewis, G. (Eds.) (1985). *Successful Sport Management*. Charlottesville, VA: Michie Co.

van der Smissen, B. (1990). *Legal Liability and Risk Management for Public and Private Entities*. Cincinnati: Anderson Publishing Co.

SUGGESTED READINGS

Appenzeller, H. (editor) (1985). *Sports & Law: Contemporary Issues*. Charlottesville, VA: Michie Co.

Appenzeller, H. and Appenzeller, T. (1980). *Sports and the Courts*. Charlottesville, VA: Michie Co.

Ball, R. (1983). "Legal Liability." In, *Tips on Training*, Athletic Training Council, National Association for Girls and Women in Sport, pp. 33-49.

Bayless, M. and Adams, S. (1985). "A Liability Checklist." *Journal of Physical Education, Recreation and Dance*, 57: 49.

Blue Line Club, Inc. (1982). *Hockey Coaches and Administrators Liability Protection Program*. Madison, Wisconsin. (To order copies, write to Fenton Kelsey, Publisher, Athletic Business, P.O. Box 7006, Madison, WI, 53707.)

Borkowski, R. (1984). "A Mini-course for the Youth Sport Coach on Legal Responsibilities." *Spotlight on Youth Sports*, 7: 1-2.

Clement, A. (1988). *Law in Sport and Physical Activity*. Indianapolis: Benchmark Press.

Drowatzky, J. N. (1987). "Legal Liabilities of the Coach." In Seefeldt, V. (editor) *Handbook for Youth Sports Coaches*. Reston, VA: National Association of Sport and Physical Education and American Alliance for Health, Physical Education, Recreation and Dance, pp. 297-309.

Kaiser, R. (1984). "Program Liability Waivers: Do They Protect the Agency and Staff?" *Journal of Physical Education, Recreation and Dance*, 55: 54-56.

Maloy, B. P. (1988). *Law in Sport: Liability Cases in Management and Administration*. Indianapolis: Benchmark Press.

Moss, G. (1978). "Legal Responsibilities in Athletic Injuries." In K. Scriber and E. Burke, (editors) Relevant Topics in Athletic Training. Ithaca, NY: Movement Publications, pp. 126-127).

Nygaard, G. & Boone, T. H. (1989). *Law for Physical Educators and Coaches*. Columbus, OH: Horizon Publications.

Rutherford, G., Miles, R., Brown, V., and MacDonald, B. (1981). *Overview of Sports Related Injuries to Persons 5-14 Years of Age*. Washington, D.C.: US Consumer Product Safety Commission.

Stotlar, D. and Stewart, S. (1984). "Liability in Recreation: Sound Risk Management Can Prevent Litigation." *Athletic Business*, 8: 48-50.

Wong, G. M. (1988). *Essentials of Amateur Sports Law*. Dover, MA: Auburn House Publishing Co.

Supplement 34-1. Agreement to Participate.

Player's Agreement to Participate in Youth or Scholastic (Specific Sport) and Parental Consent Form

Young athletes get hours of enjoyment from (sport). The rules of the game stress safe, fair competition. Through play, athletes learn many things related to both sport and life. They also improve their fitness and health. But to enjoy these benefits, they must become responsible for their actions.

Most important is learning how to avoid injuries—to self, teammates, and opponents. (Sport) rules are written to prevent injuries. And required equipment protects vulnerable body parts. All in all, (sport) is not a hazardous sport. But players **do** risk injury.

Minor injuries happen. (Bruises and blisters. Cramps and bloody nose. Sprains and strains.) More serious events occur. (Broken bones and concussions. Injuries to eyes and teeth.) And very rarely, we see catastrophic injuries. Paralysis, even death. Every one involved with youth and scholastic (sport) works to make play safe. Such grave injuries are not at all common. However, they can only be minimized, not eliminated.

(sport) players must help coaches reduce the chance of injury. They do so by learning and following the rules, following the instructions of coaches, and being properly conditioned.

1. Following the rules involves:
   • Obeying the letter and spirit of the rules,
   • Using your body and equipment only as allowed by the rules,
   • Discouraging rule violations by your teammates and opponents,
   • Avoiding aggressive acts, and
   • Controlling your emotions at all times.
   By doing otherwise, you may harm others. Such "reckless disregard" for their safety is wrong. And it makes you legally responsible for injuries.

2. Paying attention to the coaches' instruction and direction means:
   • Giving undivided attention to instruction on the skills and techniques of the sport, and
   • Trying your best to perform according to instructions.
   If you have trouble doing what is asked, get help from the coach. Coaches and other adult leaders are there for your safety. Follow their directions—whether at practice, traveling to and from contests or practices, or waiting for games. Obey their instructions about how to behave.

3. Players must...
   • Wear appropriate clothing for games and practices,
   • Have and wear protective equipment, and
   • Inspect equipment before every practice and contest.
   Tell the coach of problems with clothing or equipment. Ask to have torn or defective equipment repaired or replaced. Report gear that is too large or too small or items that fit incorrectly.

4. Being in condition to play is part of avoiding injury. Therefore, you must...
   - Participate in all conditioning and training drills.
     Such drills are designed to...
     - Strengthen your muscles, tendons, and ligaments,
     - Improve your flexibility for (sport); and
     - Build your cardiovascular fitness.
   - Report your physical problems and injuries to coaches and parents.
   - Get medical help if pain continues.
   - Get back to playing after an injury only when...
     — You have completed the rehabilitation prescribed by a physician/trainer.
     — You have no more pain.
     — You can move the injured part through its full range of motion.
     — The injury is as strong as ever, and any swelling has disappeared.
     — You can turn, pivot and move as usual.
     — And if you needed medical treatment, the physician approves your return.

5. You must play with a clear mind. Avoid any chemical substance that may affect vision or intelligence.

By signing this form, I acknowledge that I have read and agree to accept my responsibility as a player. I also understand and appreciate the fact that playing may result in injury, as indicated. I do voluntarily assume the inherent risks in participation in the sport of (sport).

Signature of athlete _____Date_____

Consent of Parent or Guardian

Having read the description of a player's responsibilities and possibility of injury, I (we) hereby give my (our) consent for_____

to participate in the (sport) program sponsored by _____

for the period of _____to_____

Signature of parent or guardian _____Date_____

35

Insurance for Athletes and Coaches

Vern Seefeldt, Ph.D. and B. Patrick Maloy, J.D., M.S.A.

QUESTIONS TO CONSIDER

- Who is covered by the insurance policies of the school or league?
- What is covered by the insurance policies that apply to coaches?
- When does the insurance take effect?
- When does the insurance expire?
- What is not covered by this policy?
- Is activity outside of regularly scheduled practices and contests included in the coverage?
- Is transportation to and from practices and contests included in the coverage?

INTRODUCTION

The purpose of this chapter is to create an awareness of the issues surrounding medical and liability insurance among coaches of interscholastic programs. Questions concerning specific insurance programs should be addressed to athletic directors and legal advisors.

There are many kinds of insurance, but they all have one common purpose: to provide benefits for individuals who have sustained losses. Whether the loss represents compensation for injury or for an assessment of damages levied by a judge or jury, the insured person hopes that the coverage is sufficient to offset the sustained loss or adjudicated assessment.

Athletes are most likely to require insurance for losses incurred as a result of injuries, while coaches may require insurance for other purposes: 1) as compensation for injuries received in their role as coaches, and 2) to offset judgments that have been awarded to plaintiffs who challenged the way coaches discharged their duties. These reasons underscore the axiom: "The time to acquire insurance is before the accident occurs or the lawsuit is filed."

Two types of insurance are discussed in this chapter: *medical*, for injuries and accidents that have occurred as a result of participation in physical activities and sports, and *liability*, which is designed to assist individuals with expenses and judgments associated with lawsuits filed against them.

MEDICAL INSURANCE

Medical insurance is designed to protect athletes, coaches, officials, and administrators from financial losses due to injuries arising from participation in legitimate athletic and associated activities. The conditions under which medical coverage is extended to participants are specifically defined in most policies. Coaches, officials, and parents should read the policies carefully to ensure that the conditions contained therein are compatible with the needs of the organization, team, and individuals. Policies vary, depending upon the sport and age group for whom the insurance is provided. The following questions should be asked before a contract for insurance is signed.

Who is Covered?

Many group policies stipulate that all members of a team must subscribe to the plan, regardless of whether they are already covered by another plan. Coaches are often included in a team plan, whereas officials and administrators (who may also be coaches) are frequently excluded.

What is Covered?

Accidental injuries that occur in regularly scheduled contests and practices are usually covered, but they are commonly included on a predetermined maximum dollar amount per incidence. In addition, travel to and from contests via public transportation is usually included in the protection.

What is Not Covered?

Exclusions to coverage are often numerous. The following conditions are frequently listed:

- Suicide or attempt thereof,
- Any intentional, self-inflicted wound,
- Blisters,
- Hernias,
- Expenses involving eyeglasses or contact lenses,
- Eye examinations and prescriptions, air travel in a private plane,
- Mental or nervous disorders,
- Pre-existing or congenital conditions that were aggravated by this sport,
- Manipulation or massage, and
- Drugs.

When Does the Insurance Apply?

Some policies will pay for expenses only after all other benefits from existing plans have been exhausted. If all coaches and athletes already have adequate coverage with another carrier, this type of insurance may not be desirable for you. However, the provision of primary coverage is generally a decision that is left to the head of the household. Therefore, coaches often do not know if their athletes have primary insurance coverage. Frequently the primary insurance ends when employment is terminated. In such situations, athletes may have insurance one day and be without it the next day because their guardian's employment was terminated.

Group insurance contracts for the purpose of protecting athletes and/or coaches from financial loss are likely to list numerous conditions for which the policy does not provide coverage. These restrictions are not unusual because a policy is generally designed for one sport, rather than the general coverage of a comprehensive family policy. Other restrictions may include:

- The number of days following the injury after which any claim is invalid,
- The number of claims that may be filed or body parts included in a claim as the result of the same accident (usually one),
- The limits of coverage, per incident, in dollar amounts,
- Any property owner's liability,
- Actual coverage of the accident, if it is secondary to any other valid and collectible insurance carried by the insured,

- Treatment by other than a legally qualified physician or nurse, and
- Treatment by other than a legally constituted hospital.

Administrators of athletic programs may have direct experience with the insurance carriers in the area and their policy provisions. If assistance is needed in determining whether the terms of a policy meet your requirements and those of team members, consult an attorney for an opinion.

It is essential to know the extent of your insurance coverage before an accident occurs.

LIABILITY INSURANCE

Coaches should be aware that they will be held to a high standard of supervision and control over their athletes. Because sports are not injury-free, and coaches are commonly providing instruction or supervision when injuries occur, they are more likely to be sued than other teachers or supervisors. Each coach should be covered by liability insurance because of the unpredictable nature of many athletic injuries. Being on the premises and in charge of athletes may be all the association a coach has with an injury; yet, if a lawsuit is filed, the coach may be named as a defendant.

Adequate Coverage

Coaches, officials, and administrators should inquire if their schools and/or associations provide liability insurance. You should determine the extent of the coverage and the conditions under which it is in effect. You should ask the same questions about liability insurance that were posed in the previous section under medical insurance. The peace of mind that you obtain by knowing the conditions of your liability protection is a bargain for the small amount of time it takes to obtain that information.

Waiver and Release of Liability

By definition, a waiver of liability indicates that a person voluntarily agrees to forego a right or claim for damages sustained in a specific activity or series of events. Waivers of liability have recently acquired extensive use in interscholastic sports programs, but they may be of limited value, depending on the circumstances under which they are enacted. (See Chapter 34, *Legal Issues in Coaching*, for a more thorough discussion of this topic.)

The fundamental principle of negligence law is that one should be held responsible for negligent acts that cause injury to others.

Waivers and release of liability typically purport to release the principal, superintendent, school board members, coach, or any other party from any or all liability resulting from any loss that may occur by a named participant during the course of an athletic practice or contest. These two conflicting circumstances are the basis for interpretations involving waivers of liability.

Waiver of liability agreements are subject to different interpretations, depending on whether the school system is publicly or privately controlled. These interpretations occur because public agencies (in this situation—public school systems) are charged to uphold the *public policy of the state*. Most courts have determined that agencies that provide public services may not contract away their liability to those for whom they provide services. However, a private agency may enter into agreements that transfer the burden for risk of harm to their clients.

Certain obligations for the safety of their clients apply to both public and private agencies (or school systems). When a standard of care or type of conduct has been established or described by a legislative body, both public and private agencies (in this context—school systems) are obligated to uphold it. In other words, when public policy has been established for the private sector, agencies may not use a waiver to transfer the risk of an activity to their clients. Waivers of liability do not give permission to agencies (school systems) or their representatives (coaches, officials and administrators) to act in negligent ways.

Waivers of liability may also have limited value in several other circumstances, including cases where ambiguous language is used and when minors are involved. By definition, the waiver must contain a full disclosure of the facts pertaining to the event. It must then be read, understood, and signed by the client (athlete). In addition, it must not be so one-sided or restive that it represents a take-it or leave-it choice for participation in the event. Any waiver of liability that is viewed by the court as coercive is not likely to be enforced.

Waivers of liability signed by minors are also difficult to enforce. Courts have ruled that minors may invalidate waivers so long as the signing of the waiver is done during the age of minority or shortly thereafter. Parents or guardians may forfeit their own rights to claims, but they may not surrender the independent claims of a minor child.

Are Waivers of Any Use?

Despite the fact that courts have been reluctant to enforce waivers of liability against recipients of public services, a carefully worded waiver of liability serves two useful purposes:

1. It enumerates the hazards, risks, and dangers of the activity, thereby nullifying the claim of athletes and their parents that they were not warned of the potential injuries or losses that could occur, and
2. It may serve as evidence that the athletes participated under the "assumption of risk."

Evidence that the school system had fulfilled its responsibility about the potential for injuries through information provided in a waiver of liability may invalidate claims that the school system "failed to warn." It can also provide evidence that athletes participated under full knowledge of the "assumption of risk." Administrators and coaches who wish to use waivers of liability should consult legal advice about contents and applicability to their local situations.

SUMMARY

Medical insurance is an essential form of protection for players, coaches, and administrators. Due to the unpredictable nature of athletic injuries, adults who conduct youth sports programs should also be protected by some form of liability insurance. Conditions of coverage and restrictions are specific to each policy; therefore, insurees, whether coaches or athletes, should be knowledgeable about their current protection and the duration of its coverage.

Knowledge of ones legal responsibilities can serve two useful purposes. The most important of these is that such information provides a potent stimulus to discharge one's duties in a diligent manner, ever mindful that carelessness provokes situations that could induce injuries. The second purpose is that if adults who conduct the programs have used every possible precaution to prevent injuries, they are in a good position to defend themselves against litigation.

SUGGESTED READINGS

Cotton, D., and Cotton, M. (1997). *Legal Aspects of Waivers in Sport, Recreation and Fitness Activities.* Canton, OH: PRC Publishing.

Herbert, D. (1994). *Legal Aspects of Preventative, Rehabilitative and Recreational Exercise Programs (3rd edition).* Canton, OH: PRC Publishing.

Kaiser, R. (1986). "Liability Insurance." In R. Kaiser (editor), *Liability and Law in Recreation, Parks and Sports.* Englewood Cliffs, NJ: Prentice Hall, pp. 234-238.

Riffer, J. (1987). An Overview of Law on Releases in Recreational Program Settings. *The Sports, Parks and Recreation Law Reporter,* 37: 40.

Tremper, C., and Kostin, G. (1993). *No Surprises: Controlling Risks in Volunteer Programs.* Washington, D.C.: Non-Profit Risk Management Center.

Wong, G. (1998). "The Sports Law Decade." *Athletic Business,* 22: 33-37.